Prefaces to Shakespeare

Prefaces to
SHAKESPEARE

By Harley Granville-Barker, 1877–
1946

VOLUME I

Hamlet · King Lear
The Merchant of Venice
Antony and Cleopatra
Cymbeline

PRINCETON, NEW JERSEY

PRINCETON UNIVERSITY PRESS, 1952

Author's Preface

I BEGAN writing these "Prefaces" some twenty-five years ago. They were commissioned as contributions to an edition called *The Players' Shakespeare* (a beautiful piece of bookmaking, one play to a volume, published in London by Ernest Benn, Limited). It was never completed; and when it became clear that it would not be, I was free to go ahead independently with my own share of the work. This, with the years, quite outgrew the dimensions originally allotted it, the purpose too. But it did not seem worth while to change the title.

For various reasons the publication of an American edition has been delayed until now. In preparing it I have made only a few changes (there are some of comparative importance in *King Lear*, and one in *Julius Cæsar*). Not but that I could—as I hope—have improved upon the earlier work. But I should have been tempted to rewrite it altogether; and this would not have been practical. Also I have now omitted the usual acknowledgments for the use of texts, and my thanks to various authorities, and to my fellow-students for their help. This is not from any lessening of gratitude. But the Prefaces have now all been rearranged, and it would have caused confusion. Anyone needing to know about such things will find them recorded in the still obtainable English edition.

H. G.-B.

New York.
May 1945.

Contents

Contents

Introduction

WE have still much to learn about Shakespeare the playwright. Strange that it should be so, after three centuries of commentary and performance, but explicable. For the Procrustean methods of a changed theater deformed the plays, and put the art of them to confusion; and scholars, with this much excuse, have been apt to divorce their Shakespeare from the theater altogether, to think him a poet whose use of the stage was quite incidental, whose glory had small relation to it, for whose lapses it was to blame.

The Study and the Stage

THIS much is to be said for Garrick and his predecessors and successors in the practice of reshaping Shakespeare's work to the theater of their time. The essence of it was living drama to them, and they meant to keep it alive for their public. They wanted to avoid whatever would provoke question and so check that spontaneity of response upon which acted drama depends. Garrick saw the plays, with their lack of "art," through the spectacles of contemporary culture; and the bare Elizabethan stage, if it met his mind's eye at all, doubtless as a barbarous makeshift. Shakespeare was for him a problem; he tackled it, from our point of view, misguidedly and with an overplus of enthusiasm. His was a positive world; too near in time, moreover, as well as too opposed in taste to Shakespeare's to treat it perspectively. The romantic movement might have brought a more concordant outlook. But by then the scholars were off their own way; while the theater began to think of its Shakespeare from the point of view

of the picturesque, and, later, in terms of upholstery. Nineteenth
century drama developed along the lines of realistic illusion, and
the staging of Shakespeare was further subdued to this, with
inevitably disastrous effect on the speaking of his verse; there was
less perversion of text perhaps, but actually more wrenching of
the construction of the plays for the convenience of the stage car-
penter. The public appetite for this sort of thing having been
gorged, producers then turned to newer—and older—contrivances,
leaving "realism" (so called) to the modern comedy that had fath-
ered it. Amid much vaporous theorizing—but let us humbly own
how hard it is not to write nonsense about art, which seems ever
pleading to be enjoyed and not written about at all—the surprising discovery had been made that varieties of stagecraft and stage
were not historical accidents but artistic obligations, that Greek
drama belonged in a Greek theater, that Elizabethan plays, therefore, would, presumably, do best upon an Elizabethan stage, that
there was nothing sacrosanct about scenery, footlights, drop-
curtain or any of their belongings. This brings us to the present
situation.

There are few enough Greek theaters in which Greek tragedy
can be played; few enough people want to see it, and they will
applaud it encouragingly however it is done. Some acknowledg-
ment is due to the altruism of the doers! Shakespeare is another
matter. The English theater, doubtful of its destiny, of necessity
venal, opening its doors to all comers, seems yet, as by some instinct, to seek renewal of strength in him. An actor, unless success
has made him cynical, or his talent be merely trivial, may take
some pride in the hall mark of Shakespearean achievement. So
may a manager if he thinks he can afford it. The public (or their
spokesmen) seem to consider Shakespeare and his genius a sort
of national property, which, truly, they do nothing to conserve,
but in which they have moral rights not lightly to be flouted. The
production of the plays is thus still apt to be marked by a timid
respect for "the usual thing"; their acting is crippled by pseudo-
traditions, which are inert because they are not Shakespearean at
all. They are the accumulation of two centuries of progressive mis-
conception and distortion of his playwright's art. On the other
hand, England has been spared production of Shakespeare according to this or that even more irrelevant theory of presentationalism,

symbolism, constructivism or what not. There is the breach in the wall of "realism," but we have not yet made up our minds to pass through, taking our Shakespeare with us.

Incidentally, we owe the beginning of the breach to Mr. William Poel, who, with fanatical courage, when "realism" was at the tottering height of its triumph in the later revivals of Sir Henry Irving, and the yet more richly upholstered revelations of Sir Herbert Tree, thrust the Elizabethan stage in all its apparent eccentricity upon our unwilling notice.[1] Mr. Poel shook complacency. He could not expect to do much more; for he was a logical reformer. He showed us the Elizabethan stage, with Antony and Cleopatra, Troilus and Cressida, in their ruffs and farthingales as for Shakespeare's audiences they lived. Q.E.D. There, however, as far as the popular theater was concerned, the matter seemed to rest for twenty years or so. But it was just such a demonstration that was needed; anything less drastic and provocative might have been passed over with mild approval.

To get the balance true, let us admit that while Shakespeare was an Elizabethan playwright he was—and now is to us—predominantly something much more. Therefore we had better not too unquestioningly thrust him back within the confines his genius has escaped, nor presume him to have felt the pettier circumstances of his theater sacrosanct. Nor can we turn Elizabethans as we watch the plays; and every mental effort to do so will subtract from our enjoyment of them. This is the case against the circumstantial reproduction of Shakespeare's staging. But Mr. Poel's achievement remains; he cleared for us from Shakespeare's stagecraft the scenic rubbish by which it had been so long encumbered and disguised. And we could now, if we would, make a promising fresh start. For the scholars, on their side, have lately— the scholarly among them—cut clear of the transcendental fog (scenic illusion of another sort) in which their nineteenth century peers loved to lose themselves, and they too are beginning again at the beginning. A text acquires virtue now by its claim to be a prompt book, and the most comprehensive work of our time upon the Elizabethan stage is an elaborate sorting-out of plays, com-

---

[1] But it should not be forgotten that Sir Herbert Tree, happy in the orthodoxy of public favor, welcomed the heretic Mr. Poel more than once to a share in his Shakespeare Festivals.

panies and theaters. On Dr. Pollard's treatment of the texts and
on the foundations of fact laid by Sir Edmund Chambers a new
scholarship is rising, aiming first to see Shakespeare in the theater
for which he wrote. It is a scholarship, therefore, by which the
theater of today can profit, to which, by its acting of Shakespeare,
it could contribute, one would hope. Nor should the scholars disdain the help; for criticism cannot live upon criticism, it needs
refreshment from the living art. Besides, what is all the criticism
and scholarship finally for if not to keep Shakespeare alive? And
he must always be most alive—even if roughly and rudely alive—
in the theater. Let the scholars force a way in there, if need be. Its
fervid atmosphere will do them good; the benefit will be mutual.

These Prefaces are an attempt to profit by this new scholarship
and to contribute to it some research into Shakespeare's stagecraft,
by examining the plays, one after another, in the light of the interpretation he designed for them, so far as this can be deduced; to
discover, if possible, the production he would have desired for
them, all merely incidental circumstances apart. They might profit
more written a generation hence, for the ground they build upon
is still far from clear. And this Introduction is by no means a
conspectus of the subject; that can only come as a sequel. There
has been, in this branch of Shakespearean study, too much gen-
eralization and far too little analysis of material.[2]

Shakespeare's Stagecraft

SHAKESPEARE's own career was not a long one. The whole history
of the theater he wrote for does not cover a century. Between
Marlowe and Massinger, from the first blaze to the glowing of
the embers, it is but fifty years. Yet even while Shakespeare was
at work, the stage to which he fitted his plays underwent constant
and perhaps radical change. From Burbage's first theater to the
Globe, then to Blackfriars, not to mention excursions to Court and
into the great halls—change of audiences and their behavior, of
their taste, development of the art of acting, change of the stage
itself and its resources were all involved in the progress, and are
all, we may be sure, reflected to some degree in the plays them-

---

[2] I do not deal in general therefore with certain vexed questions, such as act-
division, which still need to be looked at, I think, in the light of the particular play.

selves. We guess at the conditions of each sort of stage and theater, but there is often the teasing question to which of them had a play, as we have it now, been adapted. And of the "private" theater, most in vogue for the ten years preceding the printing of the First Folio, so far we know least. The dating of texts and their ascription to the usages of a particular theater may often be a searchlight upon their stagecraft. Here is much work for the new scholarship.

Conversely, the watchful working-out of the plays in action upon this stage or that would be of use to the scholars, who otherwise must reconstruct their theaters and gloss their texts as in a vacuum. The play was once fitted to the stage; it is by no means impossible to rebuild that stage now, with its doors, balconies, curtains and machines, by measuring the needs of the play. It is idle, for instance, to imagine scenes upon inner or upper stage without evidence that they will be audible or visible there; and editing is still vitiated by lack of this simple knowledge. Here, if nowhere else, this present research must fall short, for its method should rightly be experimental; more than one mind should be at work on it, moreover.

The text of a play is a score waiting performance, and the performance and its preparation are, almost from the beginning, a work of collaboration. A producer may direct the preparation, certainly. But if he only knows how to give orders, he has mistaken his vocation; he had better be a drill-sergeant. He might talk to his company when they all met together for the first time to study *Love's Labour's Lost*, *Julius Cæsar* or *King Lear*, on some such lines as these Prefaces pursue, giving a considered opinion of the play, drawing a picture of it in action, providing, in fact, a hypothesis which mutual study would prove—and might partly disprove. No sort of study of a play can better the preparation of its performance if this is rightly done. The matured art of the playwright lies in giving life to characters in action, and the secret of it in giving each character a due chance in the battle, the action of a play becoming literally the fighting of a battle of character. So the greater the playwright, the wider and deeper his sympathies, the more genuine this opposition will be and the less easily will a single mind grasp it, as it must be grasped, in the fullness of its emotion. The dialogue of a play runs—and often intricately—

upon lines of reason, but it is charged besides with an emotion which speech releases, yet only releases fully when the speaker is —as an actor is—identified with the character. There is further the incidental action, implicit in the dialogue, which springs to life only when a scene is in being. A play, in fact, as we find it written, is a magic spell; and even the magician cannot always foresee the full effect of it.

Not every play, it must be owned, will respond to such intensive study. Many, ambitiously conceived, would collapse under the strain. Many are mere occasions for display of their actors' wit or eloquence, good looks or nice behavior, and meant to be no more; and if they are skillfully contrived the parts fit together and the whole machine should go like clockwork. Nor, in fact, are even the greatest plays often so studied. There is hardly a theater in the world where masterpiece and trumpery alike are not rushed through rehearsals to an arbitrarily effective performance, little more learned of them than the words, gaps in the understanding of them filled up with "business"—effect without cause, the demand for this being the curse of the theater as of other arts, as of other things than art. Not to such treatment will the greater plays of Shakespeare yield their secrets. But working upon a stage which reproduced the essential conditions of his, working as students, not as showmen merely, a company of actors might well find many of the riddles of the library answering themselves unasked. And these Prefaces could best be a record of such work, if such work were to be done.

We cannot, on the other hand, begin our research by postulating the principles of the Elizabethan stage. One is tempted to say it had none, was too much a child of nature to bother about such things. Principles were doubtless imposed upon it when it reached respectability, and heads would be bowed to the yoke. Shakespeare's among them? He had served a most practical apprenticeship to his trade. If he did not hold horses at the door, he sat behind the curtains, we may be sure, and held the prompt book on occasion. He acted, he cobbled other men's plays, he could write his own to order. Such a one may stay a journeyman if he is not a genius, but he will not become a doctrinaire. Shakespeare's work shows such principles as the growth of a tree shows. It is not haphazard merely because it is not formal; it is shaped by inner strength. The theater, as he found it, allowed him and encouraged him to great freedom of development. Because the material resources of a stage are simple, it does not follow that the technique of its playwriting will stay so. Crude work may show up more crudely, when there are none of the fal-lals of illusion to disguise it that the modern theater provides. But, if he has it in him, a dramatist can, so unfettered, develop the essentials of his art more boldly and more subtly too. The Elizabethan drama made an amazingly quick advance from crudity to an excellence which was often technically most elaborate. The advance and the not less amazing gulf which divides its best from its worst may be ascribed to the simplicity of the machinery it employed. That its decadence was precipitated by the influence of the Masque and the shifting of its center of interest from the barer public stage to the candle-lit private theater, where the machinery of the Masque became effective, it would be rash to assert; but the occurrences are suspiciously related. Man and machine (here at any rate is a postulate, if a platitude!) are false allies in the theater, secretly at odds; and when man gets the worst of it, drama is impoverished; and the struggle, we may add, is perennial. No great drama depends upon pageantry. All great drama tends to concentrate upon character; and, even so, not upon picturing men as they show themselves to the world like figures on a stage—though that is how it must ostensibly show them—but on the hidden man. And the progress of Shakespeare's art from *Love's Labour's Lost* to *Hamlet*, and thereafter with a difference, lies in the simplifying of this paradox and the solving of the problem it presents; and the process involves the developing of a very subtle sort of stagecraft indeed.

For one result we have what we may call a very self-contained drama. Its chief values, as we know, have not changed with the fashions of the theater. It relies much on the music of the spoken word, and a company of schoolchildren with pleasant voices, and an ear for rhythm, may vociferate through a play to some effect. It is as much to be enjoyed in the reading, if we hear it in imagination as we read, as drama meant to be acted can be. As with its simplicities then, so it should be, we presume, with its complexities. The subtly emotional use of verse and the interplay of motive and character, can these not be appreciated apart from the bare boards

of their original setting? It does not follow. It neither follows that
the advantages of the Elizabethan stage were wholly negative
nor that, with our present knowledge, we can imagine the full
effect of a play in action upon it. The imagining of a play in
action is, under no circumstances, an easy thing.[3] What would
one not give to go backward through the centuries to see the first
performance of *Hamlet*, played as Shakespeare had it played![4] In
default, if we could but make ourselves read it as if it were a
manuscript fresh from its author's hands! There is much to be
said for turning one's back on the editors, even, when possible,
upon the First Folio with its demarcation of acts and scenes, in
favor of the Quartos—Dr. Pollard's "good" Quartos—in their yet
greater simplicity.

The Convention of Place

It is, for instance, hard to discount the impression made merely
by reading: *Scene i—Elsinore. A platform before the Castle*; and
most of us have, to boot, early memories of painted battlements
and tenth century castles (of aging Hamlets and their portly
mothers for that matter) very difficult to dismiss. No great harm,
one protests; it was a help, perhaps, to the unimaginative. But it
is a first step to the certain misunderstanding of Shakespeare's
stagecraft. The "if, how and when" of the presenting of localities
on the Elizabethan stage is, of course, a complex question. Shakespeare himself seems to have followed, consciously, no principles
in the matter, nor was his practice very logical, nor at all consistent. It may vary with the play he is writing and the particular
stage he is writing for; it will best be studied in relation to each
play. We can, however, free ourselves from one general miscon-
ception which belongs to our own overlogical standpoint. When
we learn with a shock of surprise—having begun in the school-

---

[3] I remember a most intelligent reader of a modern play missing the whole point
of a scene through which the chief character was to sit conspicuously and eloquently
silent. He counted only with the written dialogue. I remember, when I thought I
knew *King Lear* well enough, being amazed at the effect, all dialogue apart, of the
mere meeting, when I saw it, of blind Gloucester and mad Lear.

[4] Though, in a sense, there was no first performance of *Hamlet*. And doubtless
many of the audience for Shakespeare's new version of the old play only thought
he had spoiled a good story of murder and revenge by adding too much talk to it.

room upon the Shakespeare of the editors, it comes as belated news to us—that neither battlements, throne rooms nor picturesque churchyards were to be seen at the Globe, and that *Elsinore. A platform before the Castle* is not Shakespeare at all, we yet imagine ourselves among the audience there busily conjuring these things up before the eye of faith. The Elizabethan audience was at no such pains. Nor was this their alternative to seeing the actors undisguisedly concerned with the doors, curtains and balconies which, by the play's requirements, should have been anything but what they were. As we, when a play has no hold on us, may fall to thinking about the scenery, so to a Globe audience, unmoved, the stage might be an obvious bare stage. But are we conscious of the scenery behind the actor when the play really moves us? If we are, there is something very wrong with the scenery, which should know its place as a background. The audience was not conscious of curtain and balcony when Burbage played Hamlet to them. They were conscious of Hamlet. That conventional background faded as does our painted illusion, and they certainly did not deliberately conjure up in its place mental pictures of Elsinore. The genus audience is passive, if expectant, imaginatively lazy till roused, never, one may be sure, at pains to make any effort that is generally *un*necessary to enjoyment.

With Shakespeare the locality of a scene has dramatic importance, or it has none; and this is as true of his early plays as his late ones. Both in *Richard II* and *Antony and Cleopatra*, scene after scene passes with no exact indication of where we may be. With Cleopatra we are surely in Egypt, with Cæsar in Rome. Pompey appears, and the talk tells us that both Egypt and Rome are elsewhere; but positively where Pompey is at the moment we never learn.[5] Indoors or outdoors? The action of the scene or the clothing of the characters will tell us this if we need to know. But, suddenly transported to the Parthian war, our whereabouts is made amply plain. It is, however, made plain by allusion. The information peeps out through talk of kindred things; we are hardly aware we are being told, and, again, we learn no more than we need to learn. This, truly, is a striking development from the plump and plain

---

[5] Unless it may be said that we learn in the scene after whereabouts he *was*.

Barkloughly Castle call they this at hand?

of *Richard II*, even from the more descriptive

> I am a stranger here in Gloucestershire:
> These high wild hills and rough, uneven ways
> Draw out our miles. . . .

by which Shakespeare pictures and localizes the maneuvers of Richard and Bolingbroke when he wants to. But the purpose is the same, and the method essentially the same.[6] Towards the end of the later play come scene after scene of the marching and countermarching of armies, of fighting, of truce, all the happenings of a three days' battle. Acts III and IV contain twenty-eight scenes long and short; some of them are very short; three of them have but four lines apiece. The editors conscientiously ticket them *A plain near Actium, Another part of the plain, Another part of the plain* and so on, and conclude that Shakespeare is really going too far and too fast, is indeed (I quote Sir Edmund Chambers) "in some danger of outrunning the apprehensions of his auditory." Indeed he might be if this cinematographic view of his intentions were the right one! But it utterly falsifies them. Show an audience such a succession of painted scenes—if you could at the pace required—and they would give attention to nothing else whatever; the drama would pass unnoticed. Had Shakespeare tried to define the whereabouts of every scene in any but the baldest phrases—the protesting editors seem not to see that he makes no attempt to; only *they* do!—he would have had to lengthen and complicate them; had he written only a labeling line or two he would still have distracted his audience from the essential drama. Ignoring whereabouts, letting it at most transpire when it naturally will, the characters capture all attention. This is the true gain of the bare stage; unless to some dramatic end no precious words need be spent, in complying with the undramatic demands of space and time; incarnation of character can be all in all. Given such a crisis as this the gain is yet greater. We are carried through the phases of the three days' battle; and what other stage convention would allow us so varied a view of it, could so

---

[6] And in *Coriolanus*, which probably postdates *Antony and Cleopatra*, with Marcius' "A goodly city is this Antium," we are back to the barely informative. It serves Shakespeare's purpose; he asks no more.

isolate the true drama of it? For do we not pass through such a crisis in reality with just that indifference to time and place? These scenes, in their kind, show Shakespeare's stagecraft, not at its most reckless, but at its very best, and exemplify perfectly the freedom he enjoyed that the stage of visual illusion has inevitably lost. His drama is attached solely to its actors and their acting; that, perhaps, puts it in a phrase. They carry place and time with them as they move. The modern theater still accepts the convention that measures time more or less by a play's convenience; a half-hour stands for an hour or more, and we never question the vagary. It was no more strange to an Elizabethan audience to see a street in Rome turned, in the use made of it, to the Senate House by the drawing of a curtain and the disclosure of Cæsar's state, to find Cleopatra's Monument now on the upper stage because Antony had to be drawn up to it, later on the lower because Cleopatra's death-scene could best be played there; it would seem that they were not too astonished even when Juliet, having taken leave of Romeo on the balcony of her bedroom and watched him descend to the lower stage, the scene continuing, came down, a few lines later, to the lower stage herself, bringing, so to speak, her bedroom with her—since this apparently is what she must have done.[7] For neither Senate House, Monument nor balcony had rights and reality of their own. They existed for the convenience of the actors, whose touch gave them life, a shadowy life at most; neglected, they existed no longer.[8]

Shakespeare's stagecraft concentrates, and inevitably, upon opportunity for the actor. We think now of the plays themselves; their first public knew them by their acting; and the development of the actor's art from the agilities and funniments of the clown, and from round-mouthed rhetoric to imaginative interpreting of character by such standards as Hamlet set up for his players, was a factor in the drama's triumph that we now too often ignore. Shakespeare himself, intent more and more upon plucking out

[7] I fancy, though, that the later Shakespeare would have thought this a clumsy device.

[8] How far this is true of other dramatists than Shakespeare I do not pretend to say; nor how far, with him, the influence of the private theater, making undoubtedly towards the scenic stage and (much later) for illusion, did not modify his practice, when he had that stage to consider. A question, again, for the bibliographers and historians.

the heart of the human mystery, stimulated his actors to a poignancy and intimacy of emotional expression—still can stimulate them to it—as no other playwright has quite learned to do.

The Speaking of the Verse

His verse was, of course, his chief means to this emotional expression; and when it comes to staging the plays, the speaking of the verse must be the foundation of all study. The changes of three hundred years have of themselves put difficulties in our way here; though there are some besides—as one imagines—of Shakespeare's own making. Surely his syntax must now and then have puzzled even his contemporaries. Could they have made much more than we can of Leontes'

> Affection! thy intention stabs the centre;
> Thou dost make possible things not so held,
> Communicat'st with dreams;—How can this be?
> With what's unreal thou coactive art,
> And fellow'st nothing; then, 'tis very credent
> Thou may'st co-join with something; and thou dost;
> And that beyond commission; and I find it,
> And that to the infection of my brains,
> And hardening of my brows.

The confusion of thought and intricacy of language is dramatically justified. Shakespeare is picturing a genuinely jealous man (the sort of man that Othello was *not*) in the grip of a mental epilepsy. We parse the passage and dispute its sense; spoken, as it was meant to be, in a choking torrent of passion, probably a modicum of sense slipped through, and its first hearers did not find it a mere rigmarole. But we are apt to miss even that much. Other passages, of early and late writing, may always have had as much sound as sense to them; but now, to the casual hearer, they will convey more sound than sense by far. Nor do puns mean to us what they meant to the Elizabethans, delighting in their language for its own sake. Juliet's tragic fantasia upon "Aye" and "I" sounds all but ridiculous, and one sympathizes with an actress hesitating to venture on it. How far, apart from the shifting of accents and the recoloring of vowels, has not the whole habit of English speech changed in these three hundred years? In the theater it was slowing down, one fancies, throughout the eighteenth century; and in the nineteenth, as far as Shakespeare was concerned, it grew slower and slower, till on occasions one thought—even hoped—that shortly the actor would stop altogether. There may have been more than one cause; imitation of the French Augustans, the effort to make antiquated phrases understood, the increasing size of the theaters themselves would all contribute to it. The result, in any case, is disastrous. Elizabethan drama was built upon vigor and beauty of speech. The groundlings may often have deserved Shakespeare's strictures, but they would stand in discomfort for an hour or so to be stirred by the sound of verse. Some of the actors no doubt were robustious periwig-pated fellows, but, equally, it was no empty ideal of acting he put into Hamlet's mouth—and Burbage's. We may suppose that at its best the mere speaking of the plays was a very brilliant thing, comparable to *bel canto*, or to a pianist's virtuosity. The emotional appeal of our modern music was in it, and it could be tested by ears trained to the rich and delicate fretwork of the music of that day. Most Hamlets—not being playwrights—make a mild joke of telling us they'd as lief the town-crier spoke their lines, but we may hear in it the echo of some of Shakespeare's sorest trials.

The speaking of his verse must be studied, of course, in relation to the verse's own development. The actor must not attack its supple complexities in *Antony and Cleopatra* and *Cymbeline*, the mysterious dynamics of *Macbeth*, the nobilities of *Othello*, its final pastoral simplicities in *A Winter's Tale* and *The Tempest* without preliminary training in the lyricism, the swift brilliance and the masculine clarity of the earlier plays. A modern actor, alas, thinks it simple enough to make his way, splayfooted, through

> The cloud-capped towers, the gorgeous palaces . . .

though Berowne's

> I, forsooth, in love . . .

or one of Oberon's apostrophes will defeat him utterly. And, without an ear trained to the delicacy of the earlier work, his hearers, for their part, will never know how shamefully he is betraying the superb ease of the later. If we are to make Shakespeare our own again we must all be put to a little trouble about it. We must recapture as far as may be his lost meanings; and the sense of a phrase we *can* recapture, though instinctive emotional response to it may be a loss forever. The tunes that he writes to, the whole great art of his music-making, we can master. Actors can train their ears and tongues and can train our ears to it. We talk of lost arts. No art is ever lost while the means to it survive. Our faculties rust by disuse and by misuse are coarsened, but they quickly recover delight in a beautiful thing. Here, at any rate, is the touchstone by which all interpreting of Shakespeare the playwright must first—and last—be tried.

The Boy-Actress

MORE than one of the conditions of his theater made this medium of accomplished speech of such worth to him. Boys played the women parts; and what could a boy bring to Juliet, Rosalind or Cleopatra beyond grace of manner and charm of speech? We have been used to women on the stage for two hundred and fifty years or more, and a boy Juliet—if the name on the program revealed one, for nothing else might—would seem an odd fish to us; no one would risk a squeaking Cleopatra; though, as for Rosalind, through three-parts of the play a boy would have the best of it. But the parts were written for boys; not, therefore, without consideration of how boys could act them most convincingly. Hence, of course, the popularity of the heroine so disguised. The disguise was perfect; the make-believe one degree more complex, certainly, than it needs to be with us; but once you start make-believe it matters little how far you go with it; there is, indeed, some enjoyment in the make-believe itself. But, further, it is Shakespeare's constant care to demand nothing of a boy-actress that might turn to unseemliness or ridicule. He had not much taste for what is called "domestic drama," nor does he dose us very heavily with Doll Tearsheet, Mistress Overdone and their like. Constance mourns Arthur's loss, Lady Macduff has her little son, but no mother croons over the child in her arms. Paulina brings Hermione's baby to Leontes, it is true; but see with what tact, from this point of view, the episode is managed. And love-scenes are most carefully contrived. Romeo and Juliet are seldom alone together; never for long, but in the balcony-scene; and in this, the most famous of love-scenes, they are kept from all contact with each other. Consider *Antony and Cleopatra*. Here is a tragedy of sex without one single scene of sexual appeal. That aspect of Cleopatra is reflected for us in talk about her; mainly by Enobarbus, who is not mealymouthed; but his famed description of her voluptuousness is given us when she has been out of our sight for several scenes. The play opens with her parting from Antony, and in their two short encounters we see her swaying him by wit, malice and with the moods of her mind. Not till the story takes its tragic plunge and sex is drowned in deeper passion are they ever intimately together; till he is brought to her dying there has been occasion for but one embrace. Contrast this with a possible Cleopatra planned to the advantage of the actress of today.

Shakespeare, artist that he was, turned this limitation to account, made loss into a gain.[9] Feminine charm—of which the modern stage makes such capital—was a medium denied him. So his men and women encounter upon a plane where their relation is made rarer and intenser by poetry, or enfranchised in a humor which surpasses more primitive love-making. And thus, perhaps, he was helped to discover that the true stuff of tragedy and of the liveliest comedy lies beyond sensual bounds. His studies of women seem often to be begun from some spiritual paces beyond the point at which a modern dramatist leaves off. Curious that not a little of the praise lavished upon the beauty and truth of them—mainly by women—may be due to their having been written to be played by boys!

Much could be said for the restoring of the celibate stage; but the argument, one fears, would be academic. Here, though, is practical counsel. Let the usurping actress remember that her sex is a liability, not an asset. The dramatist of today may refuse to exploit its allurements, but may legitimately allow for the sympathetic effect of it; though the less he does so, perhaps, the better for his play and the more gratitude the better sort of actress will show him. But Shakespeare makes no such demands, has left no

---

[9] There is no evidence, of course, that he felt it a loss, no such reference to the insufficiency of the boy-actress as there is to the overself-sufficiency of the clown. Women did appear in the Masques, if only to dance, so the gulf to be bridged was not a broad one. But the Elizabethan was as shocked by the notion of women appearing upon the public stage as the Chinese playgoer is today.

blank spaces for her to fill with her charm. He asks instead for self-forgetful clarity of perception, and for a sensitive, spirited, athletic beauty of speech and conduct, which will leave prettiness and its lures at a loss, and the crudities of more Circean appeal looking very crude indeed.

The Soliloquy

THIS convention of the boy-actress may be said to give a certain remoteness to a play's acting. The soliloquy brings a compensating intimacy, and its use was an important part of Shakespeare's stagecraft. Its recognized usefulness was for the disclosing of the plot, but he soon improved upon this. Soliloquy becomes the means by which he brings us not only to a knowledge of the more secret thoughts of his characters, but into the closest emotional touch with them too. Here the platform stage helped him, as the stage of scenic illusion now defeats his purpose. But it is not altogether a question of "realism" and the supposed obligation this lays upon a real man in a real-looking room to do nothing he would not do if the whole affair were real.

There is no escape from convention in the theater, and all conventions can be made acceptable, though they cannot all be used indiscriminately, for they are founded in the physical conditions of the stage of their origin and are often interdependent one with another. Together they form a code, and they are as a treaty made with the audience. No article of it is to be abrogated unless we can be persuaded to consent, and upon its basis we surrender our imaginations to the playwright.

With the soliloquy upon the platform stage it is a case—as so often where convention is concerned—of extremes meeting. There is no illusion, so there is every illusion. Nothing very strange about this man, not even the dress he wears, leaning forward a little we could touch him; we are as intimate and familiar with him as it is possible to be. We agree to call him "Hamlet," to suppose that he is where he says he is, we admit that he thinks aloud and in blank verse too. It is possible that the more we are asked to imagine the easier we find it to do. It is certain that, once our imagination is working, visual illusion will count for little in the stimulating of emotion beside this intimacy that allows the magnetism of personality full play.

There is no more important task for the producer of Shakespeare than to restore to the soliloquy its rightful place in a play's economy, and in particular to regain for it full emotional effect. We now accept the convention frigidly, the actor maneuvers with it timidly. Banished behind footlights into that other world of illusion, the solitary self-communing figure rouses our curiosity at best. Yet further adapted to the self-contained methods of modern acting, the soliloquy has quite inevitably become a slack link in the play's action, when it should be a recurring reinforcement to its strength. Shakespeare never pinned so many dramatic fortunes to a merely utilitarian device. Time and again he may be feeling his way through a scene for a grip on his audience, and it is the soliloquy ending it that will give him—and his actor—the stranglehold. When he wishes to quicken the pulse of the action, to screw up its tension in a second or so, the soliloquy serves him well. For a parallel to its full effectiveness on Shakespeare's stage we should really look to the modern music-hall comedian getting on terms with his audience. We may measure the response to Burbage's

O, that this too too solid flesh would melt . . .

by recalling—those of us that happily can—Dan Leno as a washerwoman, confiding domestic troubles to a theater full of friends, and taken unhindered to their hearts. The problem is not really a difficult one. If we solve the physical side of it by restoring, in essentials, the relation between actor and audience that the intimacy of the platform stage provided, the rest should soon solve itself.

Costume

THE problem of costume, when it arises, is a subtler one; nor probably is it capable of any logical solution. Half the plays can be quite appropriately dressed in the costume of Shakespeare's own time. It is a false logic which suggests that to match their first staging we should dress them in the costume of ours. For with costume goes custom and manners—or the lack of them. It may be both a purge and a tonic to the sluggish-fancied spectator to be shown a Prince of Denmark in coat and trousers and a Grave-digger in a bowler hat, for reminder that here is a play, not a collection of ritualized quotations. But physic is for the sick; also, there may be less drastic cures. When archaeology took hold upon the nineteenth century mind it became a matter of moment to lodge Hamlet in historic surroundings; and withers were wrung by the anachronisms of ducats and a murder of Gonzago, French rapiers and the rest. A needlessly teasing difficulty; why reproduce it in terms of a young man in a dinner jacket searching for a sword—a thing not likely to be lying about in his modern moth-er's sitting room—with which to kill Polonius, who certainly has window curtains to hide behind instead of arras? This gain of intimacy—with a Hamlet we might find sitting opposite at a dinner party—may well be a gain in sympathy. It was originally a great gain, a gift to Shakespeare's audience. But we pay too high a price for it.

What was the actual Elizabethan practice in this matter of cos-tuming is not comprehensively known. We can only say safely that, as with other matters, it was neither constant, consistent, nor, from our present point of view, rational. It was based upon the use of the clothes of the time; but these might be freely and fan-tastically adapted to suit a particular play or advantage some char-acter in it. Dramatic effect was probably the first consideration and the last. There were such fancy dresses as Oberon or Puck or Caliban might wear; there was always the symbolizing of royalty, and a king would wear a crown whenever he could; there was the utility of knowing Romans from Britons by sight in *Cymbe-line*, the martial Roman from the effete Egyptian in *Antony and Cleopatra*, and a Scottish lord when you saw him in *Macbeth*, if we may judge by Malcolm's comment upon Rosse's appearance:

> My countryman; and yet I know him not.

Our difficulty, of course, arises mainly over the historical plays. Not over the English Histories, even so; we can dress Richard III or Henry V by the light of our own superior knowledge of what they wore, and never find it clash violently with anything Shake-speare has put on their backs or in their mouths. But when we come to Julius Cæsar plucking open his doublet, to the conspirators against him with their hats about their ears, and to Cleopatra's

Cut my lace, Charmian.

not to mention British Imogen in her doublet and hose, we must stop and consider.

The common practice is, in these instances, to ignore the details of Shakespeare's text altogether; to dress Cæsar in his toga, Cleopatra in her habit as she lived, with never a stay-lace about her (though, truly, the costumier, let alone, will tend to get his fashion a few thousand years wrong and turn her out more like the wife of Tutankhamen); and as to Imogen and her surroundings, we do our best to compromise with skins and woad. This may be a lesser evil than presenting a Cæsar recalling Sir Walter Raleigh and a Cleopatra who would make us think of Mary Queen of Scots, but it is no solution of the problem. For the actors have to speak these lines, and if action and appearance contradict them, credibility is destroyed. And the constant credibility of the actor must be a producer's first care. Nor is this all, nor is it, perhaps, the most important thing to consider. The plays are full of reference, direct and indirect, to Elizabethan custom. They are, further, impregnated with what we call "Renaissance feeling," some more, some less, but all to a degree. Now of this last we have a sense which is likelier to be a better help to their appreciation than any newfangled knowledge of the correct cut of Cleopatra's clothes will be! We know Iago for a Machiavellian figure (so called), and miss none of Shakespeare's intention. But if ever two men breathed the air of a sixteenth century Court, Hamlet and Claudius of Denmark do, and to relate them in habit and behavior to the twilight figures of Saxo Grammaticus is as much a misinterpretation as any mauling of the text can be. They exist essentially doubtless—as do all the major characters of the plays—in their perennial humanity. But never let us forget the means by which this deeper truth of them is made vivid and actual. There have been better intellects than Shakespeare's, and poetry as good as his. He holds his supreme place by his dramatist's necessary power of bringing thought and vague emotion to the terms of action and convincing speech; further, and far more than is often allowed, by his peculiar gift of bringing into contribution the commonplace traffic of life. However wide the spoken word may range, there must be the actor, anchored to the stage. However high, then, with Shakespeare, the thought or emotion may soar, we shall always find the transcendental set in the familiar. He keeps this balance constantly adjusted; and, at his play's greatest moments, when he must make most sure of our response, he will employ the simplest means. The higher arguments of the plays are thus kept always within range, and their rooted humanity blossoms in a fertile upspringing of expressive little things. Neglect or misinterpret these, the inner wealth of Shakespeare will remain, no doubt, and we may mine for it, but we shall have leveled his landscape bare.

Shakespeare's own attitude in this matter of costume and customs was as inconsistent as his practice was casual. He knew what *his* Cæsar or Cleopatra would be wearing and would casually drop in a reference to it. Yet the great Romans themselves were aliens to him. The great idea of Rome fired his imagination. Brutus, Cassius and Antony do not turn typical Elizabethan gentlemen; and to the end of that play he is striving to translate Plutarch. Whenever, on the other hand, even for a moment he has made a character all his own, he cannot but clothe it in lively familiar detail. Cleopatra's are the coquetries of a great lady of his own time, in their phrasing, in their savor. When the heights of the tragedy have to be scaled, manners will not so much matter. But if we make her, at the play's beginning, a pseudo-classic, languishing Oriental, we must do it in spite of Shakespeare, not by his help. What then is the solution of this problem, if the sight of the serpent of old Nile in a farthingale will too dreadfully offend us? We can compromise. Look at Tintoretto's and Paolo Veronese's paintings of "classic" subjects. We accept them readily enough.

Sometimes, within the boundaries of a play, the centuries seem all at odds. *Cymbeline* need not trouble us, its Roman Britain is pure "once upon a time." But in *King Lear*, for instance, Shakespeare is at unwonted pains to throw us back into some heathen past. Yet Edmund is another Iago, Edgar might have been at Wittenberg with Hamlet, and Oswald steps straight from the seventeenth century London streets. Here, though, the dominant barbarism is the important thing; the setting for Goneril and

Regan, Lear's tyranny and madness, and Gloucester's blinding. To a seventeenth century audience Oswald was so identifiable a figure that it would not matter greatly how he dressed; the modern designer of costume must show him up as best he may. Each play, in fine, if it presents a problem at all, presents its own.

The Integrity of the Text

THE text, one says at first blush, can present no problem at all. The plays should be acted as Shakespeare wrote them—how dispute it? They should be; and it is as well, before we discuss hard cases, to have the principle freely admitted. Lip service enough is done it nowadays, and Colley Cibber's *Richard III*, Tate's *Lear* and Garrick's improvements are at the back of our bookshelves, but we still find Messrs. John Doe and Richard Roe slicing out lines by the dozen and even a scene or so, or chopping and changing them to suit their scenery. This will not do. Shakespeare was not a perfect playwright; there can be no such thing. Nor did he aim at a mechanical perfection, but at vitality, and this he achieved. At best then, we cut and carve the body of a play to its peril. It may be robustly, but it may be very delicately organized. And we still know little enough of the laws of its existence, and some of us, perhaps, are not such very skillful surgeons; nor is any surgeon to be recommended who operates for his own convenience.

This good rule laid down, what are the exceptions that go to prove it? There is the pornographic difficulty. This is not such a stumbling block to us as it was to Bowdler, to some bright young eyes nowadays it is quite imperceptible, in fact. Yet, saving their presence, it exists; for it exists aesthetically. Shakespeare's characters often make obscene jokes. The manners of his time permitted it. The public manners of ours still do not. Now the dramatic value of a joke is to be measured by its effect upon an audience, and each is meant to make its own sort of effect. If then, instead of giving them a passing moment's amusement, it makes a thousand people uncomfortable and for the next five minutes very self-conscious, it fails of its true effect. This argument must not be stretched to cover the silliness of turning "God" into "Heaven" and of making Othello call Desdemona a "wanton" (the practice,

as I recollect, of the eighteen-nineties), nor to such deodorizing
of *Measure for Measure* that it becomes hard to discover what all
the fuss is about. If an audience cannot think of Angelo and the
Duke, Pompey and Lucio, Isabella and Mistress Overdone, and
themselves to boot, as fellow-creatures all, the play is not for them.
Othello must call Desdemona a "whore," and let those that do
not like it leave the theater; what have such queasy minds to do
with the pity and terror of her murder and his death? Again, to
make Beatrice so mealymouthed that she may not tell us how the
devil is to meet her at the gates of hell, "like an old cuckold with
horns on his head," is to dress her in a crinoline, not a farthingale.
But suppression of a few of the more scabrous jokes will not leave
a play much the poorer; nor, one may add, will the average playgoer be much the wiser or merrier for hearing them, since they
are often quite hard to understand.

Topical passages are a similar difficulty. With their savor, if not
their very meaning lost, they show like dead wood in the living
tree of the dialogue and are better, one would suppose, cut away.
But no hard and fast rule will apply. Macbeth's porter's farmer
and equivocator will never win spontaneous laughter again. But
we cannot away with them, or nothing is left of the porter. Still
the baffled low comedian must not, as his wont is, obscure the
lines with bibulous antics. There will be that little dead spot in
the play, and nothing can be done about it. Rosencrantz' reference
to the "eyrie of children" is meaningless except to the student. Is
the play the poorer for the loss of it? But the logic that will take
this out had better not rob us of

> Dead shepherd, now I find thy saw of might;
> Who ever loved that loved not at first sight?

And there is the strange case of

> The lady of the Strachy married the yeoman of the wardrobe.

Nobody knows what it means, but everybody finds it funny when
it is spoken in its place. And this has its parallels.

In general, however, better play the plays as we find them. The
blue pencil is a dangerous weapon; and its use grows on a man,
for it solves too many little difficulties far too easily.

Lastly, for a golden rule, whether staging or costuming or cutting is in question, and a comprehensive creed, a producer might

well pin this on his wall: Gain Shakespeare's effects by Shakespeare's means when you can; for, plainly, this will be the better way. But gain Shakespeare's effects; and it is your business to discern them.

1927

Hamlet

The Nature of the Play

THE GENIUS OF THE WORKSHOP

FEW things throw more light on the nature of Shakespeare's art than does the fact that his masterpiece—not his greatest piece of work, perhaps, but the one in which he attains to a freedom and fullness of dramatic impression unknown before—should be the recasting, in all probability, of a ready-made play. Hamlet himself, it may be said, the most lifelike and "original" of his creations, was a ready-made character too; the conventional Elizabethan "melancholy man." His achievement was in the reconciling of these seeming contradictions.

But he "wanted art," said Jonson; and Milton implied it; and Dryden, despite his admiration for him, felt bound to confess it And if we mean, as Jonson and Dryden will have meant, a scheme of consistent principles and a studied method of expressing them, the Shakespeare of the greater plays lacks that most decidedly. There is an aspect of him which turns towards pure beauty of form, and the discipline and the limitations involved. It shows in the poems and in the earlier plays—in the exceptional homogeneity of *Richard II* and the graces of *A Midsummer Night's Dream*— and we may divine it in his instructed love for the music of his time. Had he begun by writing plays to please himself, it is possible that the lyric poet in him would have prevailed. We can imagine him in Lyly's place, with schoolboys for his actors, delicate, docile instruments, to be taught their parts line by line; the result an etherealized semiclassic drama, of which Jonson could have approved without cavil. But he found himself instead learning his playwright's trade amid the comradely give-and-take of the common theater workshop; and the result was very different. Let us cheerfully admit that he "wanted art"; he was the genius of the workshop.

What he learned there was to think directly in terms of the medium in which he worked; in the movement of the scene, in the humanity of the actors and their acting. Heroic acting, as Shakespeare found it, left the actor's identity with the character still not quite complete. It was comparable to those Japanese puppet-shows, in which the puppet, life-size and gorgeous, is handled by its black-suited showman in full view of the audience, who take pleasure in the patent skill of the handling. Tamburlaine was very much such a puppet. Alleyne himself wore the finery and went through the motions; but Marlowe had made the character something rather to be exhibited than acted. The trick of speech by which Tamburlaine and Zenocrate—Barabas, Hieronimo, Alphonsus and the rest—so often address themselves by name has its significance.

But the instinct of the actor is to identify himself with the character he plays, and this instinct Shakespeare the actor would naturally encourage Shakespeare the dramatist to gratify. The progress here is rapid. Richard III is still somewhat the magnificent puppet, yet the effect already will be less that of Burbage exhibiting the character than of Richard himself "showing off." The gain is great. With the actors forgetting themselves in their characters the spectators the more easily forget their own world for the world of the play. The illusion so created, we should note, is lodged in the actors and characters alone. Shakespeare's theater does not lend itself to the visual illusion, which, by the aid of realistic scenery and lighting, seems physically to isolate them in that other world. But he can, helped by the ubiquity of his platform stage, preserve the intimacy which this sacrifices. His aim is to keep the actor, now identified with the character, in as close a relation to the spectators—as that by which the clown, in his own right, exercises sway over them. It is not merely or mainly by being funny that the clown captures and holds his audience, but by personal appeal, the intimacy set up, the persuading them that what he has to say is his own concern—and theirs. It is with the comic and semicomic

characters—from Angelica and Shylock to Falstaff—that we are
first brought into this fellowship; and whatever conventions
Shakespeare may discard, it will not be the revealing soliloquy
and aside. A large part of the technical achievement of Hamlet
lies in the bringing home his intimate griefs so directly to us. In
whatever actor's guise we see him he is Hamlet, yet the appeal is
as genuine as if the man before us were making it in his own
person. But the actor does not lose himself in the character he
plays. On the contrary, He not only presents it under his own
aspect, he lends it his own emotions too, and he must repass the
thought of which it is built through the sieve of his own mind. He
dissects it and then reconstructs it in terms of his own personality.
He realizes himself in Hamlet. And if he did not his performance
would be lifeless. The thing is as true of a Falstaff. If the humor is
no more a part of the actor than the padding is, our laughter will
be empty.

Shakespeare learned the secret of this intimate and fruitful
collaboration in the workshop of the theater. And it is the dramatist's master-secret. He has to learn, for his part, just what sort
of material to give to the actors of his characters; the nature, the
quality, also the effective quantity of it, neither more nor less. If
it is dialogue of little more substance than have the skeleton scenes
of the *Commedia dell' Arte*—for a dramatist may have his characters fully imagined, and still leave them as inexpressive as they
might be in real life—that will allow the actor too much initiative.
Actors who are in themselves interesting, lively and resourceful
can make a passingly brilliant effect with such material. But, like
other fairy gold, it will be dead leaves in the morning. The records
of the theater are choked with such empty, perished plays. The
dramatist must not, on the other hand, try to do for the actor
what the actor can do as well, and better, for himself. It is waste
of time—and nothing in the theater is more precious—to construct
a character complete in every detail, to dictate personal appearance
(unless, as with Falstaff, there is dramatic capital in this), to
elaborate habits and tricks and minor traits. A hint or so will
suffice. The actor takes these things in his stride. It is even better
to leave him to devise the incidentals of a character for himself.
They will fit his personal presentment of it the more closely; there
will be a gain in spontaneity and increase of illusion. Nor must

the actor be burdened with matter, however fine, which does not give the character life, which he cannot convert to its self-expression. It was here that the University poets, with their contempt for the actor, were blind; and here "literary dramatists," in their ignorance of his art, are still likeliest to fail. The actor, to them, is a mouthpiece—the written word made more eloquent—for their poetry, their ideas. That they must put consideration of the character itself and the actor of it before this, that the character acquires a certain freedom, and the actor even a certain property in it, is a thing they find hard to understand, harder still to profit by. Yet actually to profit by this self-abnegation is what the dramatist must cunningly learn to do. To provide raw material for acting; is there something undignified about it? Shakespeare, in the theater workshop, and an actor himself, will soon have been cured of that notion if ever he had it. The play as it leaves his hands is not a finished product, only its performance makes it that. Nor is it finished even then. Good actors never stereotype the playing of their parts, they keep them alive by continual little changes and developments. Shakespeare, in the same spirit, would retouch and recast his plays. Had he not retouched and recast other men's? That was the custom of the workshop. It could hardly result in perfection of form. But it made, both with dramatist and actor, for resourcefulness and flexibility, those needs of a crescent art. And the give-and-take of this continuing collaboration, the united force and the never-checked flow of it, did give free play to that sheer vitality, which, when all else is done, is the making of the drama, without which nothing avails.

Shakespeare learns to work in the living medium of the actors and their acting, the thing that is peculiar to the theater; if the dramatist cannot work in it, clearly he is no dramatist at all. He soon sees, moreover, that it is the essential thing, which no pageantry must be let overshadow, nor mechanical tricks degrade. His progress is marked by a discarding of the artifices—presenters, dumb shows, Latin tags, elaborate formulas of speech—which constrict its humanity; and, positively, by an ever-increasing enrichment of the human character it is to paint for him. But there is no drastic change of method. The economy of the workshop forbids this. Also the human medium is not a passive one; actors will only do well what they know how to do and like to do. Shake-

speare may add what he can to the dramatic commonwealth; he must
see that he loses nothing of account, nor leaves any of his fellows
in it impoverished. When he has provided the clown with a
Touchstone or a Feste, then—but only then—can he insist on his
speaking no more than is set down for him. I doubt if the
exiguous Peter of *Romeo and Juliet* could be so controlled; nor, it
would seem, was it to the advantage of the entertainment that he
should be. *Romeo and Juliet* abounds in artifices which are quite
soon to be discarded; antiphonies, Euphuisms, volleys of puns.
They stand incongruous now beside its vital dramatic poetry and
forthright prose. But if the actors can make these inherited, still
recognized conventions effective, and his own invention has momentarily failed him, the dramatist does well to furnish them. For
the sustained effect upon the audience; that is the thing. And very
certainly, here or elsewhere, he must sacrifice none of the power
of the magnificent rhetoric, by which it is that Marlowe and those
others have recreated this theater he works for, by which the actors
can so stir their audience, until he has found some means to that
same end of even greater power.

He comes to need this. There comes a time when the life in
his poetry flags; when, beside Falstaff's humor, King Henry's
rhetoric sounds hollow, when he turns to prose for Benedick and
Beatrice, Rosalind and Orlando, and, with a tributary sigh for the
"dead shepherd," can allow Jaques his gibe of

Nay, God be wi' you, and you talk in blank verse. . . .

What has happened? He is now a masterly creator of character.
But the old rhetoric robs these creatures of flesh and blood of their
reality. Yet while prose may suffice for comedy, for pathos and the
poignancy of tragedy it will not. Nor can he think of impoverishing the theater and its actors by depriving them altogether of the
enhancing magic of poetic speech. Moreover he is a poet, predominantly that; and poetry will out. What he needs is a poetic
method by which to realize character.

The development to come is, in some kind, inevitable. It follows
from the identifying of actor and character, from the dramatist's
sense that he is collaborating with the actor, and from the fact
that the dramatist, in this case, was a poet who had learned to
think in terms of drama. He will keep the rhetoric for rhetorical

purposes; his captains and kings will always have occasion for it. But, once the actor is realizing the character, eloquent self-description becomes superfluous. With what, then, can his collaborator the dramatist best provide him, apart from what is called for by the sheer action of the play?—and this will be little; for the thing to be done in drama is better done than talked of, if the talk has no other end. With what can he best provide him for self-expression? It follows, if the actor can fulfill in himself the greater part of what we may call the "physics" of the character, that the dramatist will devote himself more and more to its "metaphysics." And when the dramatist is such a poet as was Shakespeare, these "metaphysics" will be of the kind with which poetry is most concerned, the world of the imagination and the things of the spirit; they will, it is not too fantastic to say, begin to give the character something very like an immortal soul. This is the development which leads him to Hamlet.

It involves no fresh departure. He has realized character in poetry before now; in old Angelica, in Hotspur very notably. But there was little of the metaphysical in either of them; abounding unself-consciously in a perfect conceit of themselves, as boldly self-expressive as two children. It involves no drastic changes of poetic form. He is too skilled a craftsman now to be fettered by rule. When his verse is alive it is such a natural language to him that it seems spontaneously to fall into form. Much enrichment of its substance, that there will be; a fresh vocabulary needed, a dramatic syntax, a dynamic use both of the sense and sound of words. And there will be a devising of action and situations which carry their poetry in them, with, at most, an illuminating touch or so to replace the direct description of the earlier plays. For dramatic poetry is not primarily a matter of words, but of the poetic conception of character and action. Where, before *Hamlet*, can we find such a "setting" contrived as that for the first scene on the battlements? Compare it, for method and effect, with the tomb-scene in *Romeo and Juliet*, or the storm in *Julius Cæsar*, and this again with the storm-scenes in *King Lear*.

The development may not affect the whole play. We do not need to know minor characters intimately. Some are simply the functionaries of the story. Shakespeare will not be calling upon the minor actors to do more than they know how to do, nor anything very different from what they have done so far. He must, on the other hand, see that these "metaphysics" do not so rarefy a dominant character as to rob it of the reality it has gained; he must not exchange the rhetorical for the merely abstract. His task now, in fact, is to give—the actor aiding him—to these creatures of his imagination, by a single means, both actuality and the larger and profounder life with which poetry can endow them. His plays never lack the actualities of action; and the practice of his theater provides for its continuous flow. But the sublimer the poetry, the more intimate now, we shall find, may be its images; and he will salt the greatest dramatic occasions with familiar little touches. There is the balance secured. Why is *King Lear* so full of them? Because he must take particular care to make that primitive colossus humanly real to us.

THE DEVELOPMENT OF HAMLET

There is more than one tentative at Hamlet in earlier work. Facets of him show already in Romeo and Richard II; Jaques is the "melancholy man" derided; and in Brutus, the sensitive philosopher misgivingly impelled to action, the likeness is distinct. Shakespeare could not have his way with Brutus. He had too much respect for Plutarch, and those stoic Romans are spiritual strangers to him. But here, clearly seen, if not yet fully felt, is the man whose tragedy is within him—and where else, if it can but be shown, does true tragedy lie? What he now needs is suppler material to work upon; and this he finds in the story and play of *Hamlet.* We can only guess at the changes he made, and how much of the Hamlet we have he found there. But, with the character already half-ripe in his mind, we can, I think, detect him developing it further out of the very obligations of the borrowed story. And a very remarkable process this is; a masterpiece in workshop economy, did nothing more masterly come out of it.

In the older play there was apparently much ado about Hamlet's shamming madness. This was his protection while he plotted against the King; and it may have furnished incidents enough to fill up the time between the Ghost's first crying "Revenge" and the final catastrophe, if there were "whole . . . handfulls of tragical speeches" to be delivered besides. Shakespeare takes over this device. He could hardly have done otherwise. Hamlet without his madness would not have been Hamlet at all. But though it allows for an amusing passage or so with Polonius, some oracular talk with Rosencrantz and Guildenstern, and remains an effective ambush against the King, beyond this—if it is to be simple shamming—it must prove more hindrance than help. For how can he develop Hamlet's character if the man is to be continually behind a mask? There can be revealing soliloquies, of course; and the candor of the friendship with Horatio will be useful. But with the Queen, and with Ophelia; here also a Hamlet feelingly himself is needed. Nor can an artificially antic disposition support scenes of crisis, nor carry a tragedy of character to its consummation. So Shakespeare's Hamlet is impelled beyond simple shamming. Yet it cannot be into sheer inconsequent lunacy, for there is no making that dominate a play either. Is not this the origin of the alloy of sanity and insanity, pretense and reality, which we vainly try to resolve into its elements again?

Shakespeare does marvels with this Hamlet who is neither mad nor sane, both "mad in craft" and "punished with sore distraction"; the victim—as we all at some time feel we are—of the world's "sane" view of his "insane" perplexities; the man—as which of us has not been?—at war within himself; and a traveler, with that passport, into strange twilight regions of the soul. But he cannot, for all his skill, so assimilate character and story that no incongruities appear. For the two are of a different dramatic nature. To do this he would have had to recast the play's whole scheme. He will not let his Hamlet suffer; but the other characters and their share in the action inevitably must.

He never, I think, made this mistake again. In *Measure for Measure* he rather takes the opposite course; the characters, one and all, are constricted to the borrowed story. But since the Moor of Cinthio's excellent tale (a far likelier tale than Shakespeare's version of it) has none of the nobility with which he means to dower Othello, since in Leir and the old chronicle behind him there is none of the catastrophic grandeur which is to be the making of Lear, in each case the story is first remolded to the man, and the other characters are fitted to his support or opposing. This effective opposition of character to character is the strength of drama. It composes the structure in which Shakespeare's sense of form came, in the maturity of his art, chiefly to lie; for his theater's freedom in space and time encourages him to maneuver the mere action as he will, to be an opportunist in that. This opposition and structure and strength is certainly lacking in *Hamlet*.

But the character of Hamlet suffers too. Is it not odd, when we are studying it, how many of its details will, without the keenest watchfulness, escape us, and that students should still dispute the significance of some of the most salient things about it? Ought we to be able to ask so many—quite intelligent—questions? It is partly, of course, that Hamlet himself is struggling amid obscurities and contradictions; and here is our genius of the workshop, as usual, not only adapting means to end, but end to means, and making capital out of shortcomings. And the result stands the test of performance, which was all he had to care about. But put the play—as the student has a right to—on the dissecting table, and the flaw, and I think the cause of it, are apparent. Shakespeare has not—paradox though this may seem—finally *dramatized* Hamlet. Here is the character, at which he has had more than one immature and fragmentary try, fully and vividly imagined at last—what character was ever more so? But he does not submit it to the final discipline which would make it an integral part of the play. He could do so by reducing it to an equality with the rest. Such limitation would bring clarity. But this is just what he now will not do. The play, when he has finished with it, may be a masterpiece of the workshop, but with Hamlet himself he is pioneering a new world of drama. Later he will learn how to shape and economize that to his theater's needs. Meanwhile—and we may be thankful for it—no lesser considerations turn him back.

The Nature of the Action

THE FIVE ACTS OF THE EDITORS

THE long-accepted division of the play into five acts is not, of course, authentic. Here, as with other plays, the editors of the Folio were bent upon giving their author this classic dignity; and it may be, besides, that by 1623 theatrical practice had itself imposed this division upon such of his plays as were still being acted. In the private theaters it had commonly been the custom to divide plays into acts and to provide music for intervals. The practice of the public theaters is a matter of dispute. If they did observe act divisions—four of them—they are hardly likely to have done so more than formally unless or until they also had some entertaining means of filling the gaps.[1] It is possible that their practice changed, and this during Shakespeare's own lifetime. He certainly did not (except for one instance) think out his plays in five-act form; whatever the exigencies of its performance are to be, the play itself is an indivisible whole. It was the telling of a story; its shape would be dictated by the nature of the story and the need to make this dramatically effective. And that meant, among other things, that if there were to be breaks in its progress, one generally did better to minimize than to accentuate them; for the attention of an audience, once captured, must be held.

In the dividing-up of *Hamlet* the Folio editors for some reason get no further than *Actus Secundus*[2]; and not till the "Players' Quarto" of 1676, do we find an end made of their Act II, and a III, IV and V. That almost certainly represents the theatrical practice of the Restoration; but quite possibly it has an earlier origin in the performance of the play in private theaters about the date of the printing of the Folio. Rowe (who, for text, picks and chooses between Q2 and F1) adopts it, and later editors follow him.[3]

But, whatever its origin, it illustrates no consistent dramatic purpose on Shakespeare's part. It cannot but to some extent thwart his technique; and at one point—in the contriving of the

[1] Or unless the strain upon the audience became too great. That might entail a definite pause or so for recovery; but hardly four pauses. The Elizabethans, moreover, could apparently support sieges from which their modern descendants shrink. Their sermons ran notably to length. While the plays could be acted through in two hours or a little longer, there would be no physical need for a pause.

[2] To be quite accurate, they mark it *Scaena Secunda* and stop there. But scene-division is another matter. This is implicit in the text; for it depends, customarily, upon the incidence of a cleared stage.

[3] It the more certainly represents Restoration theatrical practice that this Quarto (of Davenant's editing, presumably) marks passages "to be omitted in representation," which are not included in the Folio's abbreviation of Q2. It will still be a homage to classical tradition; but there is no doubt, I think, that, whatever had been done earlier, the Restoration theater did observe the five-act division, either by formal or appreciable pauses in the performance.

end of a third act and a beginning for a fourth—the offense is patent and the cobbling of the clumsiest.[4]

A unit of dramatic action for a first act—if there had to be one —was not hard to find; for the story, as Shakespeare tells it, carries us at a sustained stretch and upon a plainly indicated time-scheme to the Ghost's revelation and Hamlet's heartsick acceptance of his task. So definite an "act" is this, on both counts, that an editor is tempted to set down as definitely at the end of it: *Some weeks pass.*[5] Now Shakespeare certainly suggests in the next scene that time has been passing; a remark of Ophelia's several scenes later makes it, in fact, a calculable two months. But, to realize this, we should need, as the line is spoken, to connect it mentally with another line spoken by Hamlet almost as long before, and do a small sum in subtraction—which we certainly shall not do at that moment. No such exact impression, therefore, is meant to be made on us.

The divider ends his second act upon Hamlet's resolution to put Claudius to the test of the play. This is an important milestone in the story; the scene is sure to gain applause; and in the following scene, if we are listening carefully, we shall gather that between the two a night has passed. So here, for the act-divider, are excuses enough for a few minutes' halt. Hamlet will have wrought us to share in his excitement; we shall relieve our feelings by applauding; we shall be given time to adjust our recollection of what has passed and prepare for what is promised. It may well be that Shakespeare's own actors found they had to give their audience an occasional rest from the strain of attention to such a play as *Hamlet;* it would be a greater mental-plus-emotional strain than any earlier play had exacted. It may even be that, Shakespeare consenting, they picked on this juncture as the likeliest for the purpose hereabouts; he might even pick on it himself. Never-

---

[4] Dr. Johnson comments severely on it, and other editors may note its ineptitude. But Dowden (for instance) only says in the introduction to the *Hamlet* volume of the Arden Shakespeare that "the received division between III. and IV. is unfortunate," taking for granted, apparently, that for some sort of five-act form Shakespeare himself was responsible. And while he records the pertinent variants in his *apparatus criticus,* he leaves them without comment. Of so little importance did this aspect of Shakespeare's stagecraft seem even to him.

[5] Dover Wilson does so in the new Cambridge Shakespeare. In *What Happens in Hamlet* (p. 94, note), however, he modifies the statement; and I find myself in agreement with him.

theless, since he did not so plan the play, the halt and the pause betray his stagecraft. He is not apt to check the impulse of his action at an emotional crisis which only anticipates a sharper crisis still, but rather to find means to relax the tension, yet without so loosening it as to lose hold on his audience. And his dramatic intention here is plain. It is to carry us straight from the deadly intent of Hamlet's

> The play 's the thing
> Wherein I'll catch the conscience of the King.

to the sight of the puzzled King and Queen questioning the still equally puzzled Rosencrantz and Guildenstern, but learning with relief—that the harmless pastime of a play is in hand!

> it doth much content me
> To hear him so inclin'd.
> Good gentlemen, give him a further edge,
> And drive his purpose on to these delights.

says the unsuspecting Claudius. With the loss of the quick sequence of the scenes, the irony of this will be largely lost.

Further, not five minutes should elapse (there are fifty-five lines to speak) between that passionate soliloquy with its ringing and resolute end (the sound of it will be still in our ears) and the pessimism of

> To be or not to be . . .

This is one of a series of such contrasts, a capital feature in the presenting of the character. Here, too, the full effect will be lost if the continuity of the action is broken.

As to the passing of a night between the scenes; at a guess, Shakespeare did not think about the matter at all till he came to write the sentence in the second scene indicating that a night has passed. (Nor, even so, is this a certain sign that it has; the performance may have been impatiently hurried forward.) It was natural in the earlier scene for Hamlet to set the play for "to-morrow night," since he had to write the "speech of some dozen or sixteen lines" to be inserted in it. But after the passionate

> O, what a rogue and peasant slave am I! . . .

what concerns Shakespeare is to see that the unavoidable anticlimax is at least given some antidote. Rosencrantz's reply to the Queen, the

> certain players
> . . . have already order
> *This night* to play before him.

provides this. It restimulates our interest. The exciting event we are expecting is already nearer. That is the dramatic worth of the statement; the chronology is incidental to it.

For a halt and a pause at the end of what is known as the closet-scene there can, as we said, be no excuse whatever. By a very usual turn of Elizabethan technique one scene simply evolves into another when the characters pass from the inner stage (the closet) to the outer (some antechamber or lobby).[6] And a change in the Folio—made by whatever hand—does but better Shakespeare's main intention, which plainly is to carry forward the action here with as little slackening as possible. It is the King who is driving it ahead; for his purpose is to rid himself of his enemy without delay. And the pulse of the play has never been more feverish, nor Hamlet more beside himself; and he knows he "must to England." If somehow or other hereabouts this now lengthy third act **must** be brought to an end, the act-divider has but to let pass another hundred and fifty lines. Hamlet by then will be gone, and Claudius gain a breathing-space, and we can be allowed one too.

To complete the customary tale one has now only to find an end for the fourth and as likely a beginning for a fifth act. Our act-divider could hardly have done much better than he does. We hear of Ophelia's death; there is finality in that. The ensnaring of Hamlet has been prepared against his promised return, so that the pause intervening will be an expectant one. And—since the last act is to begin with the Gravediggers—it will give the stage carpenters a good chance to open the grave-trap and make all ready.

---

6   Hamlet in madness hath Polonius slain,
　　　　And from his mother's closet hath he dragged him. . . .

—the King tells Rosencrantz and Guildenstern; *i.e.* from some place other than this in which he now stands speaking. The Elizabethan imagination will have responded the more readily to this changing of place by passing from inner stage to outer since it answered to the disposition of the Elizabethan house, in which one passed, as a rule, directly from room to room, not by a corridor.

The various alternatives offered at this point by Q2 and the Folio are more fully discussed in the footnote to p. 108.

But, once again, Shakespeare's intentions (though here they may
not be grossly thwarted) are falsified. The suspense between the
news of Hamlet's return (brought first to Horatio, then to the
King) and his actual appearance is fully provided for by the scenes
which intervene. And a break in the action here can only weaken
the effect of the apposition of the tragic fantasy of Ophelia's madness, the warped cunning of the King's plotting with Laertes, the
lyric beauty of the tale of the girl's death on the one hand, and on
the other the wholesome prose humor of the Clowns. Hamlet,
when he arrives, is, by that colloquy in the graveyard, to point
this contrast for us. The simple and the clever, the innocent and
the guilty alike all come to the grave—to the plain prose of the
grave. But how much more effective the pointing will be if we
have also let Shakespeare realize the contrast for us, as he has
planned to!

For our own convenience we may make pauses in the performance of the plays. Shakespeare himself had doubtless sometimes to
show his audiences that consideration. If he did not at first, the
growing length of his maturer work will surely have compelled
him to. It would be both a sturdy and a spellbound crowd, indeed,
that could—literally, as to about half of them—stand up to an
uninterrupted performance of *Hamlet, King Lear* or *Antony and
Cleopatra.* But he never ceased to conceive a play as a single
organic whole, nor its action as a continuous progress—which a
never-halted performance of the shorter *Comedy of Errors, Love's
Labour's Lost* or *The Merchant of Venice* could quite well show
it to be.⁷ And to learn how to minimize our dramatic loss, if we

⁷ I believe this to be essentially true, but subject—as with so much else to be
said about his work—to qualification and exception. Among the earlier plays, the
exceptional length of *Richard III* is puzzling; among the later, one seems to detect
a positive effort to keep *Measure for Measure* and *Othello* within bounds. *Henry V*
is definitely divided into acts. *Romeo and Juliet* shows some rudiments of a
division by choruses. *A Winter's Tale* is dramatically divided into two parts. It
may be hazarded, perhaps, that Shakespeare was indifferent to external form,
though as willing to experiment in it—as he was to take a popular subject for the
making of a play, or to pay a passing compliment to Elizabeth or James. But he
did most eagerly experiment in the expression of the dramatic *ideas* which
possessed him.

Another point. In estimating the acting-time of a play one must always consider
the nature of the subject and the method of the writing; mere line measurement
can be deceptive. *A Comedy of Errors* and *Love's Labour's Lost* will move far
more swiftly than *As You Like It* or *Twelfth Night. Hamlet* moves at very varying

must interrupt a performance here and there, the Procrustean editors should first be forgotten; then the play's natural structure will appear, and divisions can at least be made to conform, as far as possible, to that.[8]

PLACE-STRUCTURE AND TIME-STRUCTURE

There is both a place-structure and a time-structure in *Hamlet*. The place-structure depends upon no exact localization of scenes. The time-structure answers to no scheme of act-division. But each has its dramatic import.

The action of *Hamlet* is concentrated at Elsinore; and this though there is much external interest, and the story abounds in journeys. As a rule in such a case, unless they are mere messengers, we travel with the travelers. But we do not see Laertes in Paris, nor, more surprisingly, Hamlet among the pirates; and the Norwegian affair is dealt with by hearsay till the play is two-thirds over. This is not done to economize time, or to leave space for more capital events. Scenes in Norway or Paris or aboard ship need be no longer than the talk of them, and Hamlet's discovery of the King's plot against him is a capital event. Shakespeare is deliberately concentrating his action at Elsinore. When he does at last introduce Fortinbras he stretches probability to bring him and his army seemingly to its very suburbs; and, sooner than that Hamlet should carry the action abroad with him, Horatio is left

speeds; averaged out, the pace both of *Measure for Measure* and *Coriolanus* will probably be slower. It is likely, again, that any play would then have been acted at a quicker pace than it commonly is today. The verse, and even the prose, would be spoken quicker; first, because the art of speaking was the actor's primary achievement; secondly, because in that age of little reading and much public discourse audiences would be better listeners too.

Yet another. The quickest shifting of the simplest scenes will add, say, half an hour to a quite straightforward "platform" performance of *Antony and Cleopatra*.

[8] It is hard to wipe the five-act division clean from one's consciousness. Most modern editions insist on retaining it, with a bare reference, if that, to its unauthenticity. Dover Wilson, in the new Cambridge Shakespeare, relegates it to the margin. That is a gain; and it is no doubt hard to go further, since some system of reference from text to notes and from one edition to another is needed, and this is on all counts the most convenient. The thing is to remember, when one is considering the play aesthetically, that these acts—and sometimes the scenes—have no true existence. The student must constantly have this in mind, or he will find himself still thinking of the play in acts and scenes—and thinking wrong. And it is for this reason that I have—with some difficulty for myself; I hope less for my readers—avoided all reference to acts and numbered scenes in this Preface.

behind there to keep him in our minds. On the other hand he still, by allusion, makes the most of this movement abroad which he does not represent; he even adds to our sense of it by such seemingly superfluous touches as tell us that Horatio has journeyed from Wittenberg, that Rosencrantz and Guildenstern have been "sent for"—and even the Players are traveling.

The double dramatic purpose is plain. Here is a tragedy of inaction; the center of it is Hamlet, who is physically inactive too, has "foregone all custom of exercises," will not "walk out of the air," but only, book in hand, for "four hours together, here in the lobby." The concentration at Elsinore of all that happens enhances the impression of this inactivity, which is enhanced again by the sense also given us of the constant coming and going around Hamlet of the busier world without. The place itself, moreover, thus acquires a personality, and even develops a sort of sinister power; so that when at last Hamlet does depart from it (his duty still unfulfilled) and we are left with the conscience-sick Gertrude and the guilty King, the mad Ophelia, a Laertes set on his own revenge, among a

> people muddied,
> Thick and unwholesome in their thoughts and whispers . . .

we almost seem to feel it, and the unpurged sin of it, summoning him back to his duty and his doom. Shakespeare has, in fact, here adopted something very like unity of place; upon no principle, but to gain a specific dramatic end.

He turns time to dramatic use also, ignores or remarks its passing, and uses clock or calendar or falsifies or neglects them just as it suits him.

The play opens upon the stroke of midnight, an ominous and "dramatic" hour. The first scene is measured out to dawn and gains importance by that. In the second Hamlet's "not two months dead" and "within a month . . ." give past events convincing definition, and his "tonight . . . tonight . . . upon the platform 'twixt eleven and twelve" a specific imminence to what is to come. The second scene upon the platform is also definitely measured out from midnight to near dawn. This framing of the exordium to the tragedy within a precise two nights and a day gives a convincing lifelikeness to the action, and sets its pulse beating rhythmically and arrestingly.[9]

But now the conduct of the action changes, and with this the treatment of time. Hamlet's resolution—we shall soon gather—has paled, his purpose has slackened. He passes hour upon hour pacing the lobbies, reading or lost in thought, oblivious apparently to time's passing, lapsed—he himself supplies the phrase later—"lapsed in time." So Shakespeare also for a while tacitly ignores the calendar. When Polonius dispatches Reynaldo we are not told whether Laertes has already reached Paris. Presumably he has, but the point is left vague. The Ambassadors return from their mission to Norway. They must, one would suppose, have been absent for some weeks; but again, we are not told. Why not insist at once that Hamlet has let a solid two months pass and made no move, instead of letting us learn it quite incidentally later? There is more than one reason for not doing so. If the fact is explicitly stated that two months separate this scene from the last, that breaks our sense of a continuity in the action; a thing not to be done if it can be avoided, for this sense of continuity helps to sustain illusion, and so to hold us attentive. An alternative would be to insert a scene or more dealing with occurrences during these two months, and thus bridge the gap in time. But a surplusage of incidental matter is also and always to be avoided. Polonius' talk to Reynaldo, Shakespeare feels, is relaxation and distraction enough; for with that scene only halfway through he returns to his main theme.

He could, however, circumvent such difficulties if he would. His capital reason for ignoring time hereabouts is that Hamlet is ignoring it, and he wants to attune the whole action—and us—to

---

[9] It is perhaps worth remarking that, while the first scene upon the platform closes with Horatio's cheerfully beautiful

> But look, the morn, in russet mantle clad,
> Walks o'er the dew of yon high eastern hill. . . .

in the second, when the Ghost scents the morning air, we have:

> The glow-worm shows the matin to be near,
> And 'gins to pale his uneffectual fire. . . .

—and then no more, nothing of hopeful dawn or cheerful day at all. An audience may not consciously observe the difference. Shakespeare evidently did not attach much importance to it, and he had, of course, no means of giving it scenic effect. But the producer of today, with light at his command, may do well to indicate it.

Hamlet's mood. He takes advantage of this passivity; we learn to know our man, as it were, at leisure. Facet after facet of him is turned to us. Polonius and Rosencrantz and Guildenstern are mirrors surrounding and reflecting him. His silence as he sits listening to the Players—and we, as we listen, watch him—admits us to closer touch with him. And when, lest the tension of the action slacken too much in this atmosphere of timelessness, the clock must be restarted, a simple, incidental, phrase or two is made to serve.

It is not until later that Shakespeare, by a cunning little stroke, puts himself right—so to speak—with the past. *The Murder of Gonzago* is about to begin when Hamlet says to Ophelia:

> look you, how cheerfully my mother looks, and my father
> died within's two hours.

—to be answered

> Nay, 'tis twice two months, my lord.

There is the calendar reestablished; unostentatiously, and therefore with no forfeiting of illusion. Yet at that moment we are expectantly attentive, so every word will tell. And it is a stroke of character too. For here is Hamlet, himself so lately roused from his obliviousness, gibing at his mother for hers.

But the use of time for current effect has begun again, and very appropriately, with Hamlet's fresh impulse to action, and his decision, reached while he listens abstractedly to the Player's speech, to test the King's guilt:

> we'll hear a play to-morrow. Dost thou hear me, old friend;
> can you play the Murder of Gonzago? ... We'll ha't to-mor-
> row night.

We do not yet know what is in his mind. But from this moment the pressure and pace of the play's action are to increase; and the brisk "tomorrow" and "tomorrow night" help give the initial impulse. The increase is progressive. In the next scene the play is no longer to be "tomorrow" but "tonight." The King, a little later, adds to the pressure. When he has overheard Hamlet with Ophelia:

> I have in quick determination
> Thus set it down; he shall with speed to England. . . .

And this—still progressively—becomes, after the play-scene and the killing of Polonius:

> The sun no sooner shall the mountains touch
> But we will ship him hence. . . .

After the spell of timelessness, then, we have an exciting stretch of the action carried through in a demonstrated day and a night. But the time-measure is not in itself the important thing. It is only used to validate the dramatic speed, even as was timelessness to help slow the action down.

After this comes more ignoring of the calendar, though the dramatic purpose in doing so is somewhat different. The scene which follows Hamlet's departure opens with the news of Ophelia's madness. We are not told how much time has elapsed. For the moment the incidental signs are against any pronounced gap. Polonius has already been buried, but "in hugger-mugger"; and Ophelia, whom we last saw smiling and suffering under Hamlet's torture, might well have lost her wits at the very news that her father had been killed, and that the man she loved had killed him. But suddenly Laertes appears in full-blown rebellion. With this it is clear why the calendar has been ignored. Shakespeare has had to face the same sort of difficulty as before. Let him admit a definite gap in time, realistically required for the return of Laertes and the raising of the rebellion, and he must either break the seeming continuity of the action, or build a bridge of superfluous matter and slacken a tension already sufficiently slackened by the passing of the Fortinbras army and Hamlet's "How all occasions . . ." soliloquy. So he takes a similar way out, ignoring incongruities, merely putting in the King's mouth the passing excuse that Laertes

> is *in secret* come from France . . .
> And wants not buzzers to infect his ear
> With pestilent speeches of his father's death . . .

—an excuse which would hardly bear consideration if we were allowed to consider it; but it is at this very instant that the tumult begins. And once again the technical maneuvering is turned to dramatic account. The surprise of Laertes' appearance, the very inadequacy and confusion of its explanation, and his prompt success, are in pertinent contrast to Hamlet's elaborate preparations —and his failure.[10]

Only with news of Hamlet do we revert to the calendar, and then with good reason. By setting a certain time for his return, the tension of the action is automatically increased. First, in the letter to Horatio, the past is built up:

> Ere we were *two days* old at sea, a pirate of very warlike appointment gave us chase.

Then, in a letter to the King:

> *To-morrow* shall I beg leave to see your kingly eyes. . . .[11]

[10] Does this contriving, however, stand the test of performance? Personally I have always felt so far that it did not, that Laertes' appearance was a little too surprising, that the King's excuse only made the matter worse, that Shakespeare has, for once, been too slapdash, in fact that the flawed illusion of the action is not restored till Ophelia reappears, and in the pathos of the sight of her the rebellion is forgotten both by us and by Laertes. But this is perhaps to be overnice of apprehension; and such a performance as Shakespeare would stage might cover the weakness.

[11] There is another but not very noticeable piece of upbuilding of the past in the King's line to Laertes:

> Two months since
> Here was a gentleman of Normandy. . . .

This with what follows implies that Laertes has been absent from Denmark for an appreciably longer time—and incidentally it falsifies the play's calculable calendar. But that is, of course—since, as listeners, we go by impressions, not calculation—no great matter; and the dramatic intention clearly is to give, by this passing touch, an added sense of solidity to the time-structure.

There is yet another to come, a more subtle and a far more effective one, in Hamlet's talk to the Gravediggers, in the passage about Yorick. Why does Shakespeare take the trouble, thus late in the day, to establish Hamlet's age so exactly? To counteract the impression of the youthful prince, which circumstances—his studentship at Wittenberg, Gertrude still in the heyday of her blood, and, as played by a boy, her youthful appearance—will have made on us; and thus late in the day, because, with the great central mass of the play's thought and passion behind him, Hamlet is inevitably a maturer figure than was the morbid young rebel of its beginning.

But the immediate effect, though we probably receive it unconsciously, is more dramatically valuable even than this. The play is nearing its end, and it must be, we feel, a tragic end; we know of the plot against Hamlet, which he can hardly escape. And the casting-back of his thoughts to his birth, to his childhood, gives us the sense of a life approaching its term. He stands with the skull in his hands; it is thirty years since he was born, three and twenty since the dead jester used to carry him laughing on his back. To this complexion must he also come—how soon? The picture, and the tale of the years, will set flowing some such undercurrent of imagination in us; nothing more explicit, for we travel with Hamlet, not ahead of him. But this is typical of the true use that Shakespeare makes of time.

—the resumption of the war between them is made imminent. The scene in the graveyard thus takes place on the morrow; and this is verified for us as it ends, by the King's whisper to Laertes:

> Strengthen your patience in our *last night's* speech. . . .

The general effect produced—not, and it need not be, a very marked one—is of events moving steadily now, unhurriedly, according to plan; the deliberation of Hamlet's returning talk to the Gravediggers suggests this, and it accords with the King's cold-blooded plot and Laertes' resolution.

The calendar must again be ignored after the angry parting of Hamlet and Laertes over Ophelia's grave. If it were not, Shakespeare would either have to bring in superfluous matter and most probably slacken tension (which he will certainly not want to do so near the end of his play) or explain and excuse an indecently swift passing from a funeral to a fencing match. He inserts instead a solid wedge of the history of the King's treachery and the trick played on the wretched Rosencrantz and Guildenstern. This sufficiently absorbs our attention, and dramatically separates the two incongruous events. It incidentally builds up the past still more solidly; and there is again a falsifying hint of time elapsed in Horatio's comment that

> It must be shortly known to him [Claudius] from England
> What is the issue of the business there.

—which is to be justified when all is over by the actual arrival of the English ambassadors to announce that the

> commandment is fulfilled,
> That Rosencrantz and Guildenstern are dead.

But this will simply be to give a sense of completeness to the action. Nothing is said or done to check its steady progress from the graveyard scene to the end; for that is the capital consideration involved.

It comes to this, I think. Shakespeare's true concern is with *tempo*, not time. He uses time as an auxiliary, and makes free with it, and with the calendar to make his use of it convincing.[12]

---

[12] Exceptionally the story itself (as with *The Merchant of Venice*) or a part of it (as in *Romeo and Juliet*) may depend upon a question of time. He must then give it attention for its own sake; but he will manage to keep it fairly malleable, and to make something of his habitual use of it, even so.

When he came to playwriting, time, it is true enough to say, was commonly being put to no dramatic use at all. A few passing references to "tonight," "tomorrow" or "the other day" there might be; for the rest, a play's end would leave a vague impression that so many events must have asked a fair amount of time for their enacting. This was not freedom—though it might seem to be —but anarchy; and he soon saw that some scheme of time would strengthen a play's action and add to the illusion.[13] For the unlikeliest story can be made more convincing by supplying it with a date or so.

An accurately realistic time-scheme, with the clock of the action going tick by tick with the watches in our pockets—that the theater can hardly be brought to accommodate. Few good stories can be made to pass in the two or three hours allowed for the acting of a play, still fewer if they must include striking and varied events. There are three main ways of dealing with the matter. Each belongs to a different sort of theater and a different type of drama. There is the so-called "classic" way. This may involve rather the ignoring than any plain falsifying of time. The drama accommodating it is apt to concentrate upon one capital event, the approaches to it elaborately prepared; and—with a master dramatist at work—motive after motive, trait after trait of character, will be unfolded like petals, till the heart of the matter is disclosed and the inevitable conclusion reached. There is the normal modern method of a suggested realism in "time," appropriate to a scenic theater's realism of place.[14] This commonly goes with a selecting of various events to be presented, one (or it may be more) to an act, the gaps in time between them accounted for by the act-divisions, the rest of the story relegated to hearsay and a sort of no man's land between the acts. Each act then becomes something of a play in itself as well as a part of one, the resulting whole a solid multiple structure, the economy of its technique akin to that of sound building, as thrifty and precise.

Lastly there is Shakespeare's freedom in time, which is the natural product of his stage's freedom in space, and which—

---

[13] Which is not to say that he was the only dramatist who saw this.

[14] The ratio will not be exact; but, generally speaking, the less realism in scenic place the less sense of realism shall we expect in time.

coupled with this—permits him a panoramic display of his entire story if need be, and uninterrupted action. And, having brought time out of anarchy, he is not concerned to regulate his use of it very strictly. He adds it to his other freedoms. Moreover he may take the greater liberties with it, because, for his audience, in their own actual world, the sense of time is so uncertain.

In nothing are we more open to illusion and suggestion than in our sense of time. We live imaginative lives of our own to quite another measure than the calendar's; a year ago might be yesterday; tomorrow will be days in coming, and gone in an hour. The Elizabethan convention of freedom in space, which depended upon the planning of the theater, shrank with each restrictive change in this and at last disappeared; but the dramatist may still exercise—in the most realistic surroundings—a discreet freedom in time. We readily welcome that fiction.[15]

Study of Shakespeare's stagecraft has shown us how we wrong it by depriving the plays when we present them of their freedom in space, by obstructing those swift, frictionless passages from here to there, or by defining whereabouts when he knew better than to define it. This freedom in time is also a part of his imaginative privilege. He makes his play a thing of movement, even as music is, and obedient to much the same laws; and the clock and the calendar are merely among the means by which this movement is made expressive.

For our convenience in performing the play, one or two stopping places can be found; there are two, at least, where the check and the pause will do little harm. For the purpose of this study, then, and as a hint to producers, I divide the play into three parts. But, as a reminder, "movements" will perhaps be the better word to use for them. The first will carry us from the beginning to Hamlet's acceptance of his mission (it coincides with the first act of the editors); the second from Reynaldo's dispatch to Hamlet's departure for England; the third from the news of Ophelia's madness to the end.

---

[15] Shakespeare's treatment of time is most notable in *Othello*. There is the undisguised freedom of the scene of the landing at Cyprus, when three separate vessels come into sight, ride out the storm, make harbor and disembark their passengers within the undivided speaking-space of 180 lines. There is the complex latent use of time throughout the rest of the play.

A First Movement

In the play's first four scenes[1] (which by the compactness of their time-scheme and the synthesis of their events lend themselves besides to definition as an "act") its action is fully set in train; the main current of it which Hamlet is to dominate, and the auxiliary action which Laertes will vitalize when, the play three parts through and Hamlet absent for a while, he returns from France —that also is prepared for now.

Horatio is brought to encounter the Ghost and we hear of the dangers that threaten Denmark.

The first scene of the four gives us the appearance and reappearance of the Ghost, the talk in the interval between Horatio, Marcellus and Bernardo about the already troubled times, and their final resolve to tell young Hamlet of the matter. For an opening and purely preparatory scene it is lengthy; but its contents are of unusual import. It lasts in imagined time, as we are definitely reminded, from midnight to dawn; and the sense of this adds to its importance. The passing of these hours is suggested when, after the quick give-and-take of the dialogue about the Ghost, Marcellus says:

> Good now, sit down and tell me, he that knows . . .

and they, all three, do sit down and relax; and there follows the smooth flow of Horatio's long narrative. But note how the danger (attendant upon all narrative in drama) of too great a slackening of the tension is avoided. Nothing is said to show that the three men expect the Ghost's return, but *we* inevitably do. So while we listen we are also alert for this, and rather the more alert because the characters in the scene seem not to be. Incidentally, the narrative adds stature to the Ghost. It is the spirit not only of a King but of a renowned King that we have seen:

> our valiant Hamlet—
> For so this side of our known world esteem'd him . . .

Note besides that the Ghost's obstinate silence is a dramatic promise of speech later; and Horatio's last important line—that we may be left expectant of the scene to come—so interprets it:

[1] Four scenes, not five. See p. 57.

This spirit, dumb to us, will speak to him.

—to Hamlet. Also that Horatio and Bernardo are on a wrong scent in their explanations of the portent and are meant to set us on one too; so that when in the next scene Hamlet immediately fastens on the right one—not danger from abroad but some foul deed done here—that will be a surprise, a thing of some dramatic value always, and of double value in this case since the swift prevision will enhance him in our eyes.[2] Also that the tale of preparation for war, the sight of

> this same strict and most observant watch . . .

while the spirit of the warrior king passes among the sentries, and even "honest" Francisco, who has seen nothing, is "sick at heart" —all this, so emphatically pictured, gives us a grim first impression of a Denmark demoralized and in danger, its tried leader gone. Shakespeare cannot allow much space to the political background of his story; the more reason, then, that he should impress it upon us while our attention is fresh, and in its sternest reality. This picture will be quickly succeeded by its contrast and complement, a sight of the Court under King Claudius, the man of words, the diplomatist, the voluptuary, surrounded by acquiescent councilors; in which setting the greater part of the action is to pass.[3] But the play begins martially, and so ends, with

> The soldiers' music and the rites of war . . .

and there is the half-removed passing of Fortinbras and his army rather more than halfway through it; another setoff to the continuing picture of the brilliant and debased Court.

---

[2] An effect now lost by too great familiarity with the play.

[3] The train of the play's "foreign policy," though we have but occasional glimpses of it, is very consistently developed. Claudius' diplomacy diverts Fortinbras and his "lawless resolutes" towards Poland for the time being. But having done well there, the young conqueror calls, all uninvited, at Elsinore on his way back. Hamlet, he says,

> was likely, had he been put on,
> To have proved most royally.

But as to King Claudius, though he did not lack personal courage, the inference throughout the play is that he was nothing of a fighter. And it looks—and the actor can make it look—as if, had Fortinbras found him alive, the

> I have some rights of memory in this kingdom,
> Which now to claim my vantage doth invite me.

might still have been spoken, but to more truculent purpose.

Finally, the scene's lengthiness is counteracted by the simple fact that

> 'Tis bitter cold.

—for thus it must be briskly played.

Claudius, the new King, and Queen Gertrude hold their first Council. Laertes is granted leave to return to France, Hamlet refused it for his return to Wittenberg. We learn of the shame and grief with which his mother's remarriage fills him; he learns of the appearance of the Ghost.

THE second scene is launched upon a veritable shock of contrast. A flourish of trumpets; and the King and Queen come in state to preside at Council.[4] The King makes a brilliant figure—the "very, very peacock" of Hamlet's later gibe—and the courtiers, happily released from their recent mourning, would respectfully ape his fashion. In every aspect he is a contrast to that gaunt apparition of armored royalty which we have just seen stalking the night.

There is but one blot on the splendor; Hamlet himself in his "nighted colour." But we do not yet know who this is that so jars upon the general contentment. We are to listen to the King, addressing his Council, dispatching one piece of business after another; and only by degrees will the significance of the incongruous, recalcitrant figure be made clear. The business flows smoothly on; and there could surely be no better judged conclusion to the mourning for our dear brother's death than appears in that "wisest sorrow," in discretion's victory over nature, nor seal more tactfully set upon the ambiguous business of his marriage (an

---

[4] Q2's stage direction definitely gives us "Counsaile," and the proceedings are like those of a Privy Council meeting; and there should be no need to argue the matter except that the Folio stage direction adds Ophelia, and that theatrical practice has long falsified both the surroundings and dramatic purpose of the scene, has made vague and ineffective what Shakespeare made definite and significant. It is true that the Queen is there; but she is—and as if in explanation—referred to within the first ten lines as

> The imperial jointress of this warlike state. . .

This may not precisely mean that she is the Queen Mary to Claudius' King William, but the impression conveyed is certainly that she has a right to be present. Dover Wilson strongly insists on this reading of the matter, and puts the case, I think, quite unanswerably.

affair of state, however, after all) than the avowal that he has
contracted it

> as 'twere with a defeated joy,
> With one auspicious and one dropping eye,
> With mirth in funeral and with dirge in marriage,
> In equal scale weighing delight and dole . . .

—unless perhaps it may all sound a little too elaborate, smack too
much of an apology. He becomes succinct enough about Fortinbras and with the Ambassadors, and then quite affectionately
gracious upon

> And now, Laertes, what's the news with you?
> You told us of some suit; what is't, Laertes?
> You cannot speak of reason to the Dane,
> And lose your voice. What would'st thou beg, Laertes,
> That shall not be my offer, not thy asking? . . .

—the repeated name is almost a caress.[5]

Finally—our curiosity having been well aroused by the delay—
Claudius provides an answer to the question we have been asking,
and joins the play's great issue by turning to that cryptic figure
with a quiet

> But now, my cousin Hamlet, and my son.

From the first—and the actor of Claudius can easily show it—he
will have resentfully noted this defiant mourning brought to a
Council called for the attesting of his marriage: it is little short
of an insult. The Prince's fellow-councilors will note it too, and
be awaiting the inevitable royal rebuke. The subtle Claudius,
however, first belittles the matter by ignoring it. And even now—
though there is added provocation in the muttered

> A little more than kin, and less than kind.

(it is not mannerly when your sovereign addresses you at the
council table to indulge in obscure comment)—he contents himself with a mild, if slightly ironic

> How is it that the clouds still hang on you?

He is repaid by the tart

---

[5] A point made by Mr. Harold Child.

There is no stage direction to tell us that Laertes retires after his suit has been
granted. But he is not a member of the Council, so he probably should.

> Not so, my lord; I am too much i' the sun.

—King, Queen and Court, the whole gaudy gathering lashed alike by the bitter jest. It is time for Gertrude to intervene:

> Good Hamlet, cast thy nighted colour off,
> And let thine eye look like a friend on Denmark. . . .

But the best she can do is to drive her son into a defensive argument—which serves, incidentally, to give us our first glimpse of his metaphysical mind. And it is ironically significant that he who is so soon to be ravaged by doubt should begin with that scornfully positive

> Seems, madam? Nay, it is. I know not 'seems.'

Claudius, expert himself at an argument, and still admirably calm and kindly, then delivers a veritable sermon, which both sets us questioning what sort of nature can be hidden beneath such banal piety, and shows—this is at once plain—that, clever as he may be, he quite misconstrues Hamlet, or he would not, surely, treat him in his sorrow to such frigidities as

> For what we know must be, and is as common
> As any the most vulgar thing to sense,
> Why should we, in our peevish opposition,
> Take it to heart? Fie, 'tis a fault to heaven,
> A fault against the dead, a fault to nature,
> To reason most absurd; whose common theme
> Is death of fathers. . . .

or, very certainly, ask him for consolation to

> think of us
> As of a father; for let the world take note,
> You are the most immediate to our throne. . . .

Hamlet indeed, the sermon ended, makes no response at all, stays obstinately silent. Gertrude intervenes again, to beg him at the least to

> stay with us; go not to Wittenberg.

She wins only a cold

> I shall in all my best obey you, madam.

Claudius promptly and diplomatically seizes upon this as

> a loving and a fair reply . . .

(which obviously it is not), declares that

> This gentle and unforced accord of Hamlet . . .

(it is as obviously neither: he is a prisoner)

> Sits smiling to my heart . . .

(his own so ready smile a trifle forced as he says it), and, with a little jovial bombast, breaks up the Council lest worse befall.

This accounts for only 128 lines of the scene—and I have written as many more about them. But it is important to note how categorically, for a start, Shakespeare establishes the triangle of false relations, within which the action is framed. Claudius, presented to us at the height of his good fortune, married to his mistress (that scandalous specter laid unrevealed) and confirmed in this as in his assumption of the crown by a complaisant Council, is naturally content that Hamlet should be his heir, genuinely ready, no doubt, to play the loving father to him. But his tactless tact, the mellifluous excess of speech, the smiling kindness overdone—such falseness shows that he feels his position to be false. By his concluding emphasis on the question of the succession, he implies— he will prefer it to be thought—that there is the secret, the "is" as against the "seems" of Hamlet's recalcitrance. Gertrude, as we learn later, knows better. It is, besides his father's death, her "o'er-hasty marriage" that is the trouble; not that Claudius is on the throne, but that she sits there beside him; and the constraint of her intervention tells us that, with her son, she too feels her position to be false. The pair still have their secret—the adultery— to guard from Hamlet and the rest, and Claudius keeps a deadlier one from her. As to Hamlet; that incongruous sequence of the long silence, the curt phrases, and the lucid and elaborate apology will leave us wondering what can be to come from him.[6]

---

[6] Why—since relations are inevitably so strained between them—did Claudius not let Hamlet go back to Wittenberg? I think no modern audience asks the question (if only they *would* ask questions about this play they think they know so well, how much more they would enjoy it!), but we, as students, may; since here perhaps is one of those points which, as Dover Wilson says, Shakespeare left unstressed because he knew that his own audience would instinctively grasp them. No one, of course, could leave England to travel abroad without permission; and in Shakespeare's Denmark the same laws apply. Laertes, having his father's leave, may return to Paris, for he is a person of no political importance (though in that, as it turns out, Claudius is to prove wrong). But one does not let a discontented

We have not long to wait. The Council over and the Court gone, the ash-grey surface of his calm breaks and seethes, on the instant, into the convulsive

> O, that this too too solid flesh would melt,
> Thaw, and resolve itself into a dew!...[7]

This is the first of the seven soliloquies by which we are brought into unimpeded contact with Hamlet's mind; an exceptional number, but Shakespeare has need of them all if he is to keep the secret instabilities of that mind an effective center of the action.[8] This one is turned to manifold use. It explains that oddly ambiguous attitude each toward other of King, Queen and Prince. It dates for us this marriage, made not a month since and within a month of the brother's, husband's, father's death.[9] It gives us, in its explosive mixture of anger and disgust, Hamlet's true mood of the moment. But beneath this shows something of the pith of his character too; a sensitive reverence for the beautiful and good (so, to him, was his father's marriage, and even as much as he yet

~~~~~~

heir to the throne go abroad and out of reach; and the Elizabethan audience would well appreciate that behind the King's smiling

> And we beseech you, bend you to remain
> Here in the cheer and comfort of our eye....

there lay a grave consideration.

[7] Dover Wilson is all for "sullied," and he finds a more extended dramatic value in it than I fear I can. But the tripled emphasis of

> ... melt,
> Thaw, and resolve itself into a dew!

does turn "solid" flesh into almost too explicit an image, whereas it both clarifies and enriches "sullied." On that ground (for one) the innovation may be counted dramatically preferable.

[8]
> My father's spirit in arms ...

would make eight; but this is no more than a flourish for the finishing of an important scene. On the other hand, while he is not alone on the stage for

> Now might I do it pat ...

that is a true soliloquy.

[9] It can be assumed that the marriage has only just taken place; "within a month," that is to say, of the funeral, which was itself delayed a little less than a month. But I think the intention is clearly otherwise. "Within a month ... she married": the past definite tense does not properly apply to yesterday or the day before. The importance of the point is that Hamlet is not here presented as a man suffering under a quite recent shock (we shall see the immediate effect upon him of a severer one later). He has been brooding over the miserable business for the best part of a month.

knows of his mother's treason to it is treason to an ideal); his consciousness of his own weakness, in the casual

> no more like my father
> Than I to Hercules.

and in that final declension to

> But break, my heart, for I must hold my tongue.

And in the trick of iteration of thought and phrase there is already something of that flogging of the will which is to be so manifest later.

The dramatist's business is with action and character in action; and it is not easy to indicate other traits of character than those which the action immediately quickens without resorting to reminiscence and description and similar enfeebling and dilatory devices. Yet it is important to do this; we need to know something of what a man would be under other circumstances if we are to appreciate his conduct under present ones. It is the more important with Hamlet, swayed as he is to be this way and that, to make what is constant in his disposition clear; and to do this too before the shock comes which will set him, in mind and emotions both, violently swaying, so that we may not lay even more to its account than should be laid.[10]

By contrast with the orderly business of the Council and the King's silky urbanities, this uprush of self-devouring, self-exhausting, purposeless passion is the more eloquent of Hamlet's helplessness and loneliness. And he has come, he feels, to the end of things. Claudius is on the throne; the Council has "freely" set a seal both on this and on the horrible business of his mother's marriage; affairs of state are going their wonted way again.

> It is not nor it cannot come to good. . . .

—yet what can he do? At which zero point it is (we guessing already that here is not an end of things but the beginning) that he looks up to find those three sober figures standing waiting his pleasure.[11]

---

[10] But Shakespeare finds later some other less direct means of doing this: cf. pp. 244 *et seq.*

[11] Dover Wilson says that he does not recognize Horatio for the moment through the mist of his tears, and I feel sure this is right. Shakespeare's men fairly frequently break into passionate tears, "unmanly drops" though they may be called.

The march of the action is resumed. From here to its finish the pulse of the scene will beat quicker and quicker and ever more strongly. But it is to finish only upon suspense of purpose, expectation still, the incline of the climax not mounted very far; so the first steps must be restrained.

Shakespeare manages this by letting Hamlet draw Horatio from the others (who stay respectfully by the door) to stroll or stand with him, friendly arm through arm, while he questions and confides; and Horatio must await an opening to say what he has come to say.[12] But there is no undue slackening of tension or loss of tone; for Hamlet has gladdened at the sight of his friend, and the pulse of our own expectancy will be beating quickly enough while we wait for Horatio to begin. When, at last—with that deft

> My lord, I think I saw him yesternight.
> Saw! Who?
> My lord, the King your father.

—he does, there follows a stretch of verse dialogue, swift, vivid, simple, and close-knit, combining the actuality of prose with all that is needed of poetic power, done with a superlative ease, the finest thing, indeed, of its sort in the play, and perhaps in all Shakespeare. A four-voiced interchange; Horatio's exact and calm, Hamlet's ever tenser and keener, Marcellus' and Bernardo's ballast to the mounting excitement. This is let mount no higher than to

> I will watch to-night;
> Perchance 'twill walk again.
> I warrant it will.
> If it assume my noble father's person
> I'll speak to it, though hell itself should gape
> And bid me hold my peace. . . .[13]

Then the three are dismissed, and the scene is wound up with

So did the Elizabethans in real life. So do Frenchmen still, without being ashamed of it. I am not sure about Italians and Spaniards. And I do not know when it first became "the thing" for Englishmen not to cry.

[12] It is unthinkable that Hamlet would speak as he does of his mother's wedding in the hearing of Marcellus and Bernardo. But the conventional distances of the platform stage leave the two friends, if they are at the front of it, in perfect privacy. The two others do not approach till Horatio turns to them with

> Upon the witness of these gentlemen. . .

[13] This piece of dialogue is more minutely analyzed on pp. 191 et seq.

four swift lines, which will suffice to keep the enkindled Hamlet vividly in our minds, and which give us (if we do not—as we should not—already know the play's story) the first hint of the truth:

> I doubt some foul play. . . .

He is quick at a surmise; we shall find him later preternaturally so. And in the iterated "foul deeds . . ." there is even a touch of gratifying anticipation.

Laertes departs after warning his sister against Hamlet, and Polonius orders her to see no more of him.

BETWEEN the resolve to confront the Ghost and the encounter itself comes a scene for Laertes, Ophelia and Polonius. Some scene interposed there must be, if the interval of time is to be bridged while the sense of continuity of action is sustained. But this is of capital use also. Laertes is to be long absent from the action, and his loving care for his sister should keep memory of him alive for us till his return. Nor could our first sight of her come at a more significant—a more ironically significant—juncture.

> For Hamlet and the trifling of his favour,
> Hold it a fashion and a toy in blood,
> A violet in the youth of primy nature,
> Forward, not permanent, sweet, not lasting. . . .
> 　　　　Perhaps he loves you now;
> And now no soil nor cautel doth besmirch
> The virtue of his will; but you must fear,
> His greatness weigh'd, his will is not his own. . . .
> Then weigh what loss your honour may sustain
> If with too credent ear you list his songs,
> Or lose your heart, or your chaste treasure open
> To his unmastered importunity.
> Fear it, Ophelia, fear it, my dear sister. . . .

This is how Laertes sees the danger; Polonius too. Ophelia herself, wistfully protesting, only knows of the Hamlet—melancholy of late, it is true, since his father died—who is courtier, scholar, soldier, and has importuned her "with love in honourable fashion." But *we* have just seen into a man's mind, poisoned already by brooding on his mother's shame, and have left him prepared to learn worse things still. What will such as he have to do with love-making, honorable or other? He is to wreck her life indeed, but in far other fashion than father and brother fear. Here is the dramatic value of the scene; of its sententious talk, of the cheerful picture of the three, so secure in fortune as they seem—only a little worldly wisdom needed to carry them still prosperously ahead. They lavish good advice on each other; but the dark machine is already moving, in which they are, all three, to be caught and broken.

Hamlet himself encounters the Ghost, learns of his mother's adultery with his uncle, and of how his father died.

Now follows the discovery of the murder.

We have here, of course, one scene, not two. The Folio (though its scene- and act-division extend to beyond this point) marks no division after Horatio and Marcellus have followed Hamlet and the Ghost, even though there is the technical excuse of a cleared stage; nor does the Players' Quarto, nor did Rowe.[14]

What is involved? At such a critical juncture Shakespeare will not want the impetus of the action to be checked, as it will be if the integrity of the scene is broken even by a moment's clearing of the stage. But he must have Hamlet and the Ghost alone together; and Horatio and Marcellus can hardly be ordered off—like children told to leave the room. The ghostly mystery will be heightened by that silently repeated beckoning, the terror increased by the disappearance of the Ghost, and Hamlet's disappearance after it. The conventional vagueness of place allows them to pass out, through (say) the doorway on the main stage to the right. This leaves Horatio and Marcellus to sustain the ten-

---

[14] It filters in with Pope, Theobald and Warburton. But Pope is dividing his scenes "classically," not by location. Dover Wilson thinks that to this point the scene was meant to be played upon the upper stage (and that the first ghost-scene should be played there too), the Ghost and Hamlet re-entering upon the lower stage as Horatio and Marcellus disappear above. I see several objections to this. The scenes are long and the space is cramped. The Ghost—unless he was to be hidden from the groundlings—would have to be "on the top of" his interlocutors. In the first scene, moreover, Horatio and the others would themselves not be very visible when they sit down to talk politics unless they were to sit close to the balustrade; and from that position, though it is possible, it would not be effectively easy to see the Ghost. Generally speaking, I think the first scene is both too long and too important for the upper stage. Play this upon the lower, and it would be inappropriate to begin the second scene above.

sion by their five swift lines; then, as they follow into the imagined darkness, the Ghost will re-enter (I think) upon the inner
stage, Hamlet still following. And so both the integrity and intensity of the scene will be preserved. The technique of the matter
is no more complex than that.

The scene is begun (as was the first scene) by a brisk, picturesque exchange, which sets us again (this time the more easily)
in the midnight darkness and cold. Then Shakespeare unexpectedly changes the subject. We have in Q2

A florish of trumpets and 2. peeces goes of.

and, for explanation, the verbal picture of the oblivious King,
keeping wassail, drinking deep, reeling the "swaggering upspring" in comfortable warmth and light; a contrast heightening
the effect of the cloaked, close-standing, nervously expectant three.
But Q2 gives us, besides this, twenty-four lines from Hamlet
about drunkenness in Denmark (or England) and the one inborn
defect—

some vicious mole of nature . . .

or

the o'ergrowth of some complexion
Oft breaking down the pales and forts of reason . . .

—which may damn a man's whole reputation.

One might think this superfluous stuff, and the Folio cuts it
out.[15] But it has a definite dramatic purpose. Once again we are
given a glimpse of the intrinsic Hamlet. Of whom is he thinking
when he speaks of "the o'ergrowth of some complexion" which
can even break down "the pales and forts of reason," and of the
one defect—

Being nature's livery, or fortune's star . . .

—which may vitiate all other qualities in a man? Not of Claudius,
certainly. Of whom but himself?—and the actor can show this
well enough. As significant is the complex of parenthetical dialectic itself. Here already is the Hamlet who will think, not so
"precisely" as dispersedly, upon whatever event. Here he is also,
at this expectant moment, taking refuge, so to say, from its emo-

---

[15] Possibly, however, only because it would have offended Anne of Denmark,
and because James's Court was none too sober a place.

tions in the labyrinth of his mind. What is to come will shake his sanity to its base; but already (we are thus shown) the fine nature is perilously overwrought.

There is, besides, the effect gained by the abstracting, with this detached talk, of all immediate emotion from the scene. Upon the dry vacuum thus created the Ghost's advent tells profoundly; and the impression made on Hamlet by the simple sight of his dead father, can, in the sudden silence that falls, be felt.

His mind's immediate response is one of self-defensive doubt:

> Angels and ministers of grace defend us!
> Be thou a spirit of health, or goblin damned,
> Bring with thee airs from heaven, or blasts from hell,
> Be thy intents wicked or charitable. . . .

—for long not to be wholly cleared away. But in the increasingly poignant music of the lines that follow sounds the response of Hamlet's heart; devoted surrender. Here also is something of the intrinsic man.

Throughout the play Shakespeare makes much use of suspense. The story is, it might be said, one long essay in it; the single deed to be done, and to the last minute the doubt that it ever will be. And its incidental use is continual and various. We have had the suspense between the Ghost's first two appearances, the delay between the telling of the tale of them and this midnight; and now that the moment has come, we have this still obstinate silence. And when it is not suspense incidental to the action and imposed on him, there will be the checks, the delays, the zigzags of thought and intention in Hamlet himself to hold us in suspense.

Here it culminates in the deadlock of a physical struggle:

> It waves me still.
> Go on; I'll follow thee.
> You shall not go, my lord.
>   Hold off your hands!
> Be ruled; you shall not go.
>   My fate cries out,
> And makes each petty artery in this body
> As hardy as the Nemean lion's nerve.
> Still am I called! Unhand me, gentlemen;
> By heaven, I'll make a ghost of him that lets me!

And (for a piece of technical skill) note how the coming short interval of absence has a bridge built for it in the continuity between the

> Go on, I'll follow thee.

with which Hamlet and the Ghost disappear, and the

> Whither wilt thou lead me? Speak, I'll go no farther.

of their reappearance. Hamlet thus still "holds" the scene; until, after an empty moment, responding to the effortless

> Mark me.

he surrenders it and himself, with that simple

> I will.

The disclosure follows. There is remoteness in the level melody of the verse, and something of hypnosis too; but, to balance that, its clear syllabic articulation stimulates attention:

> But that I am forbid
> To tell the secrets of my prison-house,
> I could a tale unfold whose lightest word
> Would harrow up thy soul, freeze thy young blood,
> Make thy two eyes, like stars, start from their spheres,
> Thy knotted and combined locks to part
> And each particular hair to stand on end,
> Like quills upon the fretful porcupine. . . .

—while, punctuating such passages, we have the hammer blows of

> So art thou to revenge, when thou shalt hear. . . .

> Revenge his foul and most unnatural murder. . . .

>   but know, thou noble youth,
> The serpent that did sting thy father's life
> Now wears his crown.

To the rest of the truth the approach is more devious; the tone is more rueful:

> Ay, that incestuous, that adulterate beast,
> With witchcraft of his wit, with traitorous gifts—
> O wicked wit and gifts, that have the power
> So to seduce!—won to his shameful lust
> The will of my most seeming virtuous queen. . . .[16]

---

[16] At which point Devrient the actor used to veil his face in his cloak. It is possible also for a Hamlet, taking his cue from "adulterate," to show that he has half expected and dreaded this, and the shame of it.

The infamy of the adultery is stressed, and the physical foulness of the poison made vivid to us—so elaborately vivid that when, much later, there is talk of poisoning Hamlet himself, and when the Queen is dying from its effects, the picture should come before our eyes again. After which, but for the vehement backwash of that

> O, horrible! O, horrible! most horrible!
> If thou hast nature in thee, bear it not. . . .

which itself subsides into the compassion of

> Taint not thy mind, nor let thy soul contrive
> Against thy mother aught . . . .

the occult passion of the speech fades; till, with the

> Adieu, adieu, adieu! remember me.

the Ghost itself fades from our sight.[17]

Hamlet is left as in some limbo, from which to struggle back to the certitudes of the world. He has not spoken since that

> O my prophetic soul! my uncle!

was wrung out of him; he listened in silence to the tale of his mother's shame. Now, with an

> O all you host of heaven! O earth! What else?
> And shall I couple hell? O, fie! . . .

he emerges; "recovers his senses" we cannot say—for that, it will appear, is just what he does not completely do. From this moment indeed until (after that critical night of the adventure of the play,

---

[17] "Fades" is, I fear, an euphemism if one is thinking of Shakespeare's stage. At the Globe it is probable—though not certain—that the Ghost descended by a trap. But note that it did not so disappear in the first scene, when first it stalked away, or later when it

> started like a guilty thing
> Upon a fearful summons.

and passed swiftly out, while the three men were hesitating whether to strike at it or no.

Shakespeare's object would partly be to provide differently for two superficially similar scenes. In the first the sudden crowing of the cock is the signal for a quick disappearance. Here

> The glow-worm shows the matin to be near,
> And 'gins to pale his uneffectual fire . . . .

And, while there was nothing better to be done than lower the Ghost slowly out of sight, the lines would at least give some sense of a slow fading away.

the killing of Polonius and the grim hide-and-seek through the palace) it begins to seem, as he sets out on his journey in the morning, that the ill is purged, from now till then Hamlet is "mad." How mad, whether by a modern alienist's standard certifiably so—Shakespeare does not think in those terms. He uses the word as unprecisely as we still commonly do. Says Polonius,

> to define true madness,
> What is't but to be nothing else but mad?

Hamlet speaks of himself as mad; half ironically, while he is under the spell; when he is free of it, as having been

> punished
> With sore distraction.

He is not ironical there. But he speaks in riddles. And this we may fairly accept as Shakespeare's conclusion too; that the thing in itself is a riddle. He attempts no answer. Nor need he, since he is writing a play, not a pamphlet. All he has to do is to show us what madness amounts to in this particular case. Hamlet will also pretend to be mad, and the pretense and the reality will not easily be distinguished. That there is reality mixed with the pretense—so much is plain. The reality, and the riddle of it, is Shakespeare's addition to the old story and its pretense, and is the leaven which, lifting the character above the story's needs, gives the play its enduring significance. For while few of us have murdered fathers to avenge, and not so many adulterous mothers to shame us, there will be hardly a man in any audience to whom that word "madness," in some one of its meanings, has not at one time or another come dreadfully home.[18]

The lifting of the supernatural spell releases Hamlet to violent physical excitement. His first clear thought:

> And shall I couple hell? O, fie!

is a remorseful rejection of his doubts of the Ghost. It is "a spirit of health" and not a "goblin damned"; and, as if in atonement, he will, from the table of his memory

> wipe away all trivial fond records,
> All saws of books . . .

---

[18] Madness, it is just worth remarking, is one of the minor issues in the close-neighboring *Twelfth Night*. And the Clown asks Malvolio:

> But tell me true, are you not mad indeed? or do you but counterfeit?

all student scepticism, in fact, so-called philosophy, and such like "baser matter." He swears it.

It is significant that his next thought is not of Claudius' guilt, but his mother's:

> O most pernicious woman!

For there has been his wound, and it is widened now and deepened. And the more fully, vilely filled-in picture of the pair of them, of her and the "smiling"—the seductively smiling—"damned villain," so convulses and shakes him that he tries the seemingly ridiculous remedy of setting down upon the actual tables taken from his pocket

> That one may smile and smile and be a villain.

But the simple steadying of the hand to write the words does steady his mind.[19]

There are all the signs of incipient madness in his greeting to Horatio and Marcellus; in the inconsequent cunning, the crookedly flashing suspicion even of his friend, the as quick sensitiveness to reproach, the taking refuge in a web of words. Here, half involuntary, is already the "antic disposition," a spontaneous lesson given to the still self-observant Hamlet in its putting-on. The two feed suspicion in him, certainly, by their reluctance—natural though it is—to be sworn to silence under these unhallowed auspices. Then comes the yet more equivocal voice from the cellarage; to which he anticly answers rather as to a "goblin damned" than any "spirit of health," as if in surrender to whatever the power may be, will it but serve him!—at the moment, to scare this oath from them. He secures it, if only in silence, and seals it with the regained reverence of

> Rest, rest, perturbed spirit!

And in the simplicity and courtesy of

> So, gentlemen,
> With all my love I do command me to you:
> And what so poor a man as Hamlet is
> May do, to express his love and friending to you,
> God willing, shall not lack.

---

[19] A corrective very much, one may suppose, within Shakespeare's own experience, the reduction of "wild and whirling" thoughts to words on paper.

the Hamlet they know speaks again; in the gentle appeal, too, of

> Let us go in together,
> And still your fingers on your lips, I pray.

But with the sudden cry:

> The time is out of joint! O cursed spite,
> That ever I was born to set it right!

he faces the dawning day opening its new account for him, in which his own now dedicate spirit will find, he knows, no rest.

Note finally that Shakespeare does not end the scene upon this resonant rhymed couplet, but with a repeated, quiet,

> Nay, come, let's go together.

—upon a Hamlet exhausted, in need almost of physical aid, in need of friendship; and this burden promises but to make him a lonelier man than ever.

Note.—Upon the question of the Ghost and upon the implication of this "cellarage" business, what Professor Dover Wilson has to say should be carefully studied. Briefly it comes to this or something like it: These four men that encounter the Ghost might well—as representative Elizabethans—take very different views of it; and so would men like them in the audience. Marcellus and Bernardo seem simply to assume that it is, without doubt, the spirit of the King back from purgatory. That would be, incidentally, the old Catholic view. To the "scholar" and "philosopher" Horatio, it is—till he has seen it—a "fantasy," and, even after, may still be only an "illusion." But when it would lure Hamlet away, his scepticism is resolved into fear that it may be some demon in the King's guise. And this is the orthodox contemporary Protestant view of the matter. Hamlet is something of a "philosopher" himself and is a student at Protestant Wittenberg. But he is more imaginative than the others, and, under the circumstances, more ready to believe. He does not, for a moment, think the Ghost a mere illusion. But he is torn between the two beliefs. When the Ghost is there he feels sure—despite his questionings—that it is the spirit of his father; when the experience is only a memory he thinks that it may have been a "devil." The point is that to Shakespeare's audience these doubts would seem quite natural. The whole matter would be a living—even a burning—question; and, as Dover Wilson insists, it is, until the play-scene provides proof enough, as much the Ghost that is on trial (for its credibility) as Claudius.

As to the "cellarage" business; profiting by what Dover Wilson says, I yet venture to differ a little from his conclusions. This, roughly, is my reading of what happens. Horatio and Marcellus find Hamlet half off his head. For their desire to know what is between him and the Ghost they must overmaster it as they may; and they are never to make known what they have seen. Has this spirit bewitched him? That would be their first question. The voice from the cellarage would increase their suspicions of this, for it obviously belongs rather to a "goblin damned" than a "spirit of health"; and his own conduct and response to it—the "Art thou there, true-penny?" the "*Hic et ubique?*" the "Well said, old mole!"—is the reverse of reassuring. Hamlet does not, I think (and as I say above), do all this quite deliberately. He is in such a state of nervous excitement that he instinctively plays up—as an actor would put it—to the fresh manifestation, and mischievously gives it an extra diabolic twist; it may scare them into keeping silence! For Horatio and Marcellus are very naturally unwilling to take the oath that he demands of them. Would it not be sacrilegious, even spiritually dangerous, to swear a solemn oath under such circumstances? They give their word they will divulge nothing. He asks them to swear it, and they promise further that "in faith" they will not. Horatio procrastinatingly yields to the extent of a "Propose the oath, my lord." But they never do take the oath in words, though Hamlet may choose to assume—and, his frenzy passing, this may content him— that they do so silently.

But the scene is a picture set before us, not a proposition argued. This is, roughly speaking, I suggest, the effect meant to be made. We are not asked to draw more exact conclusions.

I should perhaps here note my personal preference for two Q2 readings, which editors, for some reason, do not commonly adopt.

HAMLET. Come hither, gentlemen,
And lay your hands again upon my sword.
Swear by my sword
Never to speak of this that you have heard.
GHOST. Swear by his sword.

This last—which stands in the place of the Folio's repetition for the third time of the simple "Swear"—clearly will give, and surely is meant to, an increased importance to the mysterious voice.

Q2 also, at the third proposing of the oath, makes the Ghost take the word out of Hamlet's mouth altogether. Here again is a far more arresting effect than lies in the Folio's mere echo by the Ghost of Hamlet's own "Swear."

A Second Movement

Polonius sends Reynaldo to Paris with money for Laertes, and to spy upon his conduct there. Ophelia, much affrighted, relates how Hamlet has suddenly appeared in her closet—"mad for thy love," says Polonius, and goes, taking her with him, to tell the King.

THE slightly relaxed tension of the last scene's ending is at once further and very sensibly relaxed by Polonius' prolix injunctions to Reynaldo, with which this scene begins; by such verbiage as

Look you, sir,
Inquire me first what Danskers are in Paris;
And how, and who, what means, and where they keep,
What company, at what expense; and finding,
By this encompassment and drift of question,

> That they do know my son, come you more nearer
> Than your particular demands will touch it:
> Take you, as 'twere, some distant knowledge of him;
> As thus . . .

—and so on, for seventy lines and more.[1] The circumlocution and hairsplitting, and the flaccidity of the verse give us besides—and vividly—Polonius himself, the tedious old wiseacre who meddles his way to his doom, a figure manifestly modified from that of the earlier scene,[2] with its terse dispensing of sound worldly wisdom. And the matter of the talk suggests to us that time must have passed, since Laertes is in Paris and needs money.

But the key of the whole action is to be changed, transposed from the mystery and terror of those haunted battlements, the poignancy of Hamlet's grief and shame, to the rippling movement of a Court life now restored to its normal round. In this deceptive climate the tragedy will be becalmed for a while. It is upon such waters that Polonius confidently steers, with his

> See you now:
> Your bait of falsehood takes this carp of truth;
> And thus do we of wisdom and of reach,
> With windlasses and with assays of bias,
> By indirections find directions out.

Such will shortly be the sense of the King's bidding to Rosencrantz and Guildenstern, and something such the method of Hamlet's counterminings. Duplicity, maneuvering, ambush and trap, no one knowing how much the other knows; that is the new phase. And it appropriately falls to Polonius to initiate it with the sending of his mean little embassy to spy upon his son. For he is to make himself the center of its wiles, and to suffer, a type of its futility, at last.

Note one technical detail. Reynaldo is just off on his journey. These last-minute injunctions, heaped hastily one on another, give the scene an impetus, which will compensate somewhat for its slackness of fiber.

~~~~~~~~~~

[1] Nor, to Elizabethan understanding, would the Danskers be at all surprised to find Polonius' agent spying amongst them. A very close watch was kept upon the doings of students abroad—and is, one may remark, by certain European states, not too happy in their home politics and fearful of conspiracies hatched elsewhere, at this day.

[2] Cf. p. 204.

As Reynaldo departs, Ophelia enters, dumbfounded with alarm. When she can speak we learn that

> as I was sewing in my closet,
> Lord Hamlet, with his doublet all unbraced,
> No hat upon his head, his stockings fouled,
> Ungartered, and down-gyved to his ancle,
> Pale as his shirt, his knees knocking together,
> And with a look so piteous in purport
> As if he had been loosed out of hell
> To speak of horrors—he comes before me—

Polonius finishes the sentence for her:

> Mad—for thy love!

and she fears it may be so.

Hamlet's conduct, here described, has been subject to various explanations, and much abstruse argument. But what is the impression the tale of it makes on us; now as we listen, and by the aid of what we remember, with a little allowance to be made also for what is to come, and to be seen or heard by the aid of what we shall then remember of this? Behind that complex of impressions we are not called upon to peer. And if by chance there is fuller explanation, the clue to it lodged and now lost in some earlier, discarded, version of the play, it has no dramatic validity. If Shakespeare leaves the listener searching after this, there he blunders. But I do not think he does.

We shall remember, as we listen, that Hamlet had been courting Ophelia "in honourable fashion," but that Polonius, mistrusting this, bade her avoid him—as it happened, at the moment when the Ghost's shattering revelation was pending. And our yet more recent sight of him, after the Ghost's disappearance, looking then indeed

> As if he had been loosed out of hell
> To speak of horrors . . .

will be vivid.

"Mad—for thy love." We may accept the "mad," but not the explanation: Polonius is plainly on the wrong track. And even the "mad" will be qualified by recollection of that pointed

> How strange or odd soe'er I bear myself,

> As I perchance hereafter shall think meet
> To put an antic disposition on . . .

But this will be qualified again by the descriptive

> Long stayed he so;
> At last, a little shaking of mine arm,
> And thrice his head thus waving up and down,
> He raised a sigh so piteous and profound
> That it did seem to shatter all his bulk
> And end his being. . . .

—for here is surely something more than "antic"; and, "affrighted" though the girl has been, she is evidently telling the truth. As to Hamlet, then, we shall be left puzzled. Is he still as frenzied as we have ourselves seen him to be, or only pretending to be so, or partly pretending to be so and partly—? But what Shakespeare wants is just to this extent to puzzle us, to make us curious to see Hamlet for ourselves again, and to prepare us to put the same questions when we do see him; when, however, we shall still be left almost as puzzled.

He could hardly do better, surely, than use Ophelia for this purpose. Hearsay is necessary; if we saw the scene for ourselves, Hamlet's conduct could not be left quite inexplicable. The tragic distortion of the relation between the two is initiated, their second meeting (which we shall see) is prepared for. And this interim sight of him through her loving and troubled eyes keeps our compassion for him alive. For there is much in madness that is repellent and grotesque, and that side of Hamlet's is soon to be apparent. To Ophelia, moreover, he will very markedly reveal it; and his own undoubted suffering, here pictured to us, is something of a setoff to that, and to his later treatment of her.[3]

Rosencrantz and Guildenstern are set to work. The Ambassadors return from Norway. Polonius plans to prove that Hamlet is mad for the love of Ophelia. The Players arrive. Hamlet awakes from his lethargy and, for his part, plans to prove the King's guilt by showing him its reflection in THE MURDER OF GONZAGO.

---

[3] The modern playing of Hamlet is, as a rule, and by much, both too sane and too sentimental; and the indecency of some of his talk to Ophelia is lost on modern audiences. But I fancy that Burbage shirked neither the grotesque nor the brutal.

THE scene which follows is the play's longest, and it advances the action not a jot. But its dramatic significance lies just in this; in the casual (or so seeming) encounters and the evasively irrelevant talk, diluted at last into topical gossip of theatrical affairs—the smallest of small beer!—silenced only to hear a strolling actor declaim an old-fashioned speech about the burning of Troy. It is a sustained preparation for that outburst of self-reproach:

> O, what a rogue and peasant slave am I! . . .

which, when it comes, is by how much the more effective for the delay! Not that Shakespeare lets the main threads of the action drop or neglects to weave in circumstance as well as character as he goes. There are no real irrelevances, little that is not somehow allusive, nothing quite empty of dramatic purpose.[4]

Rosencrantz and Guildenstern have been sent for, and in haste:

> The need we have to use you did provoke
> Our hasty sending. Something have you heard
> Of Hamlet's transformation. . . .

That "hasty" suggests that some sudden misgiving had seized the King, it arrests our attention and gives the scene an initial impetus; the second sentence tells us that it must be some little while since the "transformation" began, and reinforces the impression of passing time already made on us in the scene before. For the rest, Claudius is as mellifluously charming as at our first sight of him. The young men are "dear Rosencrantz and Guildenstern"; and though he is in effect charging them to spy on their friend, it is with the best intent. There is a pleasant informality about the business, and he does not make too much of it.[5] On the other hand, if his talk of fatherly affection is to ring true, he must show himself sufficiently anxious—as he does a moment later with Polonius—to arrive at the "head and source" of the trouble. But indeed he is so, if only to make quite sure that it comes nowhere near the one fatal source.

---

[4] Even the topical talk of the "eyrie of children" is not. There, we are inclined to say, the illusion is broken altogether—though it is doubtful if for an Elizabethan audience the division between real and mimic world was so precisely drawn as that. But its dramatic effect is plain; the lowering of the emotional tension to as near zero point as may be.

[5] The customary presenting of the King and Queen on their thrones with the two kneeling before them is quite out of keeping.

But first the returned Ambassadors must be received. This play of hidden struggle is never left for long without the counterpoise —by reference if no more—of the overt march of events; and against inaction here are set tidings of action elsewhere. This is the third reference made to Fortinbras and his affairs. Next we shall see him, but Hamlet and he will pass each other by. At last they will meet, the one living and the other dead.

This is an item, too, in the scene's cumulative suggestion of delay. And, the Ambassadors dismissed, there is the additional delay of Polonius' chatter, which is stressed for us by the Queen's impatience of it. And it is she—careless of the plotting to "loose" Ophelia to him—who suddenly arrests it by her

> But look, where sadly the poor wretch comes reading.

—for Hamlet has appeared. The madman, whom we last saw wrought to distraction, have heard of but a while since piteously suffering, comes quietly in

> *reading on a Booke.*

A surprising and fittingly enigmatic first sight of the Hamlet whose tragedy has now sunk, we are to find, so deep in him, beyond even his own ken.

Polonius' unceremonious ejection of the King and Queen contrasts pleasantly with the obeisances of the Ambassadors. Then he cooingly encounters the madman:

> How does my good Lord Hamlet?

And Hamlet answers:

> Well, God-a-mercy.

There could not be a more unaffected beginning.

Since drama is the presentation of character in action, the concentrating of a play's interest upon a man's inaction must give rise to difficulties. Action of some sort there must be; something must continually be happening, and the chief character must have a chief share in it. It must not be too passive a share, lest we lose interest in him. Then, to be illustrative of him, it must be futile or frustrate action. It must pertain to the play's main theme, lest we lose interest in that. Yet it must not trench on it to the point—in this case—of too plainly endangering Hamlet's secret. For once that is out he must act, and the play will either end, or his and its character must be changed. Why does Hamlet delay? Because if he did not, there would be no play. It is a true but an empty answer. For it blinds us to the achievement involved in making the very delay dramatic. To picture inaction in terms of action, and make it as interesting, asks skillful stagecraft.

Hamlet is now—so he says of himself later—sunk into apathy. Shock and strain have dulled his feelings and weakened the will they prompted; and in the background, excusing the weak will, is doubt.

> The spirit that I have seen
> May be the devil. . . .[6]

But such apathy of will only leaves the mind more active, nakedly sensitive, preternaturally clear. Moral restraint will be lacking, since that part of the man is sick. And from the disequilibrium comes this "madness"; the mind falls sick, too, of a fever. So it is that, dull and muddy-mettled as he *feels*, Hamlet is startlingly quick to suspect Polonius and his schemes, his schoolfellows' duplicity, Ophelia's innocent guile; quick, yet uncertain, for the unbalanced mind takes no bearings. He is as quick to retaliate, though his weapon is but the will-less man's "Words, words, words"—which he despises, and himself for using it, and for being masterly in its use. And so at each encounter, after a little watchful fence, we find him taking the initiative and turning the talk to his own account; to some distraction from his misery, screening of his secret, or whetting of his almost blunted purpose; or he may let it lead him no matter whither, as long as it be away from this unmanageable world of facts and consequences. And thus Shakespeare manages to keep him—even upon the defensive—the moving spirit of a scene.

Polonius treats him as a harmless lunatic. He obligingly plays the part, mischievously salting his jargon with a few nuggets of

---

[6] This comes, we notice, towards the end of the "O, what a rogue and peasant slave . . ." soliloquy, as a comparatively calm sequel to its passion. The implication is, I think, that, when he considers the matter coolly, he is genuinely uncertain, but that this is not the chief trouble. It is will that is lacking; he has lost for a while the will to believe.

the old wiseacre's own brand of wisdom, riddling sardonic approval of the worldly-wise paternal care which has kept Ophelia safe from his gallantries.

He greets Rosencrantz and Guildenstern as cordially as he greeted Horatio. But on the very instant he is chilled, his

> Good lads, how do ye both?

being answered by the self-conscious artifice of Rosencrantz'

> As the indifferent children of the earth.

by Guildenstern's

> Happy in that we are not over-happy;
> On fortune's cap we are not the very button.

So he responds in kind:

> Nor the soles of her shoe? . . .
> Then you live about her waist, or in the middle of her favours?

—and the three chop logic and wit for a while as clever young men will. But the sensitive mind is quickly at work. Why have they so unexpectedly appeared, these "excellent good friends"?

They walk—they the snarers—into the simple snare which he sets:

> what have you, my good friends, deserved at the hands of fortune that she sends you to prison hither?
> Prison, my lord?
> Denmark's a prison.

Upon his repetition of the word, Rosencrantz casts his own bait:

> Why, then your ambition makes it one . . . .

and Guildenstern harps on that "ambition," and Rosencrantz yet again. Claudius did not need to tell two supple young courtiers whereabouts to seek for the disinherited Hamlet's secret.

He knows well enough now why they are here. Let them but confess it, that will be some mitigation. But they shift and shuffle beneath his gaze; and even his appeal—

> by the rights of our fellowship, by the consonancy of our youth, by the obligation of our ever-preserved love, and by what more dear a better proposer could charge you withal, be even and direct with me, whether you were sent for or no.

—barely wrings it out of them. But his means of defense are clear.

He has only to speak the truth, though not all of it. Denmark is but such a prison as the world is. A minute since Polonius was asking him:

> Will you walk out of the air, my lord?
> Into my grave?

He wishes he could; there is all the liberty he longs for. He has only to paint them the world as he sees it:—

> this goodly frame, the earth . . . a sterile promontory; this most excellent canopy the air, look you, this brave o'erhanging firmament, this majestical roof fretted with golden fire—why, it appears no other thing to me than a foul and pestilent congregation of vapours . . . .

—and man as a worthless quintessence of dust, and they will report him merely mad. For so he must seem to their servile wisdom; and so perhaps he is, to see the world so, this merry, sensual, practical world, in which his uncle-father and aunt-mother carry it so triumphantly. But even in that world he is but mad north-north-west. When the wind is southerly, he knows a hawk from a handsaw—and spies from friends.

Through all he says there is threaded the longing to be free from the corrupt realities of life; and he jumps to the subject of the Players—incarnation of the unreal—with a kind of ironic delight.[7] Gossip about their momentous affairs eases the strain; here, with nothing more disquieting than this between them, are the three boyhood friends again. And in a moment the pedant Polonius presents himself, the perfect butt. The Players follow.

We note not the courtesy only, but the friendly warmth of his greeting:

> You are welcome, masters; welcome, all. I am glad to see thee well. Welcome, good friends. O, my old friend!—why, thy face is valanced since I saw thee last; comest thou to beard me in Denmark? What, my young lady and mistress! . . . Masters, you are all welcome . . . .

—and he loses himself forthwith in their mimic world.

This passage with the Players crowns and completes the main

---

[7] It is worth noting how, in the scene-sequence of Q1, this note of longing to escape is sounded hereabouts far more intensely but also far more obviously by the "To be or not to be" soliloquy. Cf. pp. 162 *et seq.*

dramatic purpose of the scene. An idle prince, indeed, who not only walks reading and musing by the hour together in the lobby, but will sit fastidiously exchanging with a player the recital of Æneas' tale to Dido! And a weakling, who can seek refuge from his own "cue for passion" in facile pity for Hecuba! We shall learn in a moment that, even as he sat there listening, this stultifying self-picture was forming in his own mind. But Shakespeare has first painted it thus elaborately for us, and stressed the febrile talk with his friends, the mocking of Polonius, the keen interest in the petty politics of the theater, the call for "a passionate speech," the contented surrender to its music, so that we may first begin to wonder when, if ever, the revulsion will come. Then, when it comes, we welcome it the more.

There is the seed of remorse in that demand for "a passionate speech." He is asking the actor—how far consciously?—to simulate for his amusement what he is incapable of feeling himself. And the woes of Troy bring reminder of his own. The chord in him is quick to vibrate:

> But who, O, who had seen the mobled queen . . .

Is it only the unusual epithet that makes him exclaim? Does he not see, in his mind's eye, as he repeats it, his mother, muffled in her widow's weeds—yet how unlike Hecuba in her mourning? For the rest of the speech his passive silence should become (so to say) an active one, which will set us asking what fresh train of thought can be firing in his mind. There is a resolved calm, flickering with humor, in his parting with the Players and Polonius; and in the

> Follow him, friends; we'll hear a play to-morrow.

an intent, made more vivid in the oracular sequel:

> Dost thou hear me, old friend? Can you play *The Murder of Gonzago?*

—for we have not heard that fatal word since father and son thrice exchanged it upon the battlements. He continues:

> You could, for a need, study a speech of some dozen or sixteen lines, which I would set down and insert in't . . . .

—and has forgotten Rosencrantz and Guildenstern, whose ears are pricked to hear what is passing apart there with the Player.

He dismisses them impatiently, his mind now pregnant with its purpose. Then comes the

> Now I am alone.

Only a prince, constantly attended, can appreciate to the full the relief in that; Hamlet, moreover, knows that he is attended by spies. But, being alone, instead of pursuing his purpose, he abruptly plunges, we remark, into the self-reproach of

> O, what a rogue and peasant slave am I! . . .

Nor, till he has purged himself of all this disabling poison, can he come back upon his course again, set it with an

> About, my brain! Hum, I have heard
> That guilty creatures, sitting at a play . . .

The soliloquy recharges the action to the full with the emotion which has been so long lacking, and restores to us the Hamlet bent on his revenge. He sums up in it, besides, all the flaws and failings in him that have let him reach this point, time lapsed, and nothing done. It is a most inconclusive summing-up, however; questions asked, and not answered; later to be asked again, and never plainly answered. And even were he heartless and a coward —which he certainly is not—and in yet deeper doubt, the cause of this strange impotence, we feel, would not be there. But what we ourselves have seen and heard of him (since that unexpected

> The time is out of joint! O cursed spite,
> That ever I was born to set it right!

warned us of coming change) leaves us, in sum, with about this impression: of a nature whose spiritual integrity that supernatural mandate—like an electric current splitting a substance into its elements—has for the while quite wrecked, completing thus what misery and disillusion had begun. The faculties are dislocated and at war. Feeling, faith, intellect and will; each one is still alert, and only the more alert unfettered by the others, but too aware of the others for concord, and each is too critical of the others for the lending of mutual aid. Hamlet is now at odds, not merely with the ills of this world, but within himself, and cannot but be impotent so.

Finally, we should remark the means by which, despite the scene's distractions, the main theme of the action has been pur-

sued and our interest in it kept alive. When Claudius confides
their delicate mission to Rosencrantz and Guildenstern there
begins what one may call the countermovement of the play, the
King's against Hamlet; defensive at first, to turn offensive later.
Polonius joins in it unbidden; and, from then on, he, or the two
young men, or all three of them together are there to keep a keen
eye on their quarry, to note every gesture, with a keen ear for
every phrase. Even while they listen to the Player it is Hamlet
they watch. His movement against the King may be at a standstill,
but the King's against him is active if only in the eloquent presence of these three; and thus the necessary dramatic tension is
sustained. Then, upon their dismissal, we are given the one
arresting hint of ". . . *The Murder of Gonzago* . . . a speech of
some dozen or sixteen lines. . . ." That is enough to hold us expectant through the self-reproachings of the soliloquy; until, towards
its end, the hint is given substance, the plan revealed, our roused
curiosity satisfied, and the offensive against the King is started
again.

*Rosencrantz and Guildenstern report that Hamlet is about to dis-
tract himself—and amuse the Court—with the performance of
a play. Ophelia is set in his way while the King and Polonius
hide and watch. Hamlet discovers this, and suspects Ophelia
of being a willing decoy. The King is satisfied that it is not
love which has driven him mad, that indeed he is not mad
at all.*

THE next scene opens at a sensibly lower pitch. But fresh impetus
is given to the King's countermovement by his appearance with
the Queen, accompanied by all four instruments of its policy:
Rosencrantz and Guildenstern, already apter for their task and
talking of "crafty madness"; Polonius, who now yields initiative
to the King; and Ophelia, docile, silent. The tension is keyed up
a little too; first by the advancing of the prospect of the play to
"this night," then by the imminence of Hamlet's approach. But
Shakespeare delays this for an instant; to show us Ophelia and
the Queen together, and to point the contrast between them, between the sensitive, innocent girl and the pretty, kindly, smirched,
bedizened woman; also to let Polonius "sugar o'er" his slight
misgiving over this ambush they are setting, and the baiting of

it, with an accustomed platitude (is he a little less ready since that "Let her not walk i' the sun . . ." to "loose" his daughter to the madman?), which, in turn, provokes a revealing aside from the King. From now on, we need have no doubt of his guilt.[8] The two "bestow" themselves behind the arras. Ophelia obediently walks apart, and Hamlet appears.

Before his last quiet entrance, reading on a book, we had heard of him distractedly intruding upon Ophelia. But a few moments since we have seen him equally torn with emotion; and here he is, outwardly calm and self-contained as never before. It is a similar effect of contrast and surprise. But while that

> The play's the thing
> Wherein I'll catch the conscience of the King.

was wrought with passion, it was set in concentrated purpose too; and this succeeding calm is far from passionless, it is passion at a still, white heat, fused into thought.

> To be or not to be, that is the question. . . .

These unmodulated changes from storm to calm smack a little —and are meant to—of "madness." But how the man's moral quality shows in the fact that he can thus escape from his suffering to this stoically detached contemplation of greater issues! Only towards the soliloquy's end, with the

> And thus the native hue of resolution
> Is sicklied o'er with the pale cast of thought;
> And enterprises of great pitch and moment
> With this regard their currents turn awry
> And lose the name of action.

does its thought turn a point or so inward—to regain touch with the main trend of the action. Note besides the technical skill which, lodging this parenthesis of calm and seeming irrelevance before the nervous outbreak to come, has first made us conscious of Ophelia there in the background, thus keeping us expectant, and the tension sustained.[9]

---

[8] For some discussion of this, see p. 218.

[9] I think it most likely that Ophelia is meant to enter upon the inner stage and kneel at her faldstool (but she rises again at once at the sound of Hamlet's voice) at about the cue ". . . lose the name of action." It is just possible that she is kneeling there the whole time. But Polonius' "Walk you here" is against this, and more

The meeting, for its first few moments, passes as any such meeting may between two sensitive creatures sundered by no quarrel of their own; in reserve, in reproachful sorrow that they have let themselves be sundered, and a provoking of more misunderstanding by which to justify reproach. He may choose to think her

> Good my lord,
> How does your honour for this many a day?

a little uncandid, ignoring the fact that if she shut herself away from him it was by her father's orders. She will hear princely irony in his

> I humbly thank you; well, well, well.

She has brought back his gifts, and that will wound him. He roughly denies them; she can then tax him with unkindness. She knows that they are being watched; and though it is all done for his good, she supposes, this will add to her constraint.

In his sardonic

> are you honest? . . . Are you fair?

sounds an unspoken "so my mother seemed"; and at her first close approach to him with the gifts he cannot but have gained—supersensitive as he now is, she unskilled in deceit—a sense of her discomfort. But in a little his abiding sense of his own profounder guilt draws from him the

> I did love you once. . . . You should not have believed me. . . .
> I loved you not.

—that also being a paradox to which the time has given proof. And he passes to the pitiful conclusion:

> Get thee to a nunnery; why wouldst thou be a breeder of sinners? I am myself indifferent honest, but yet I could accuse me of such things that it were better my mother had not borne me. . . . What should such fellows as I do crawling between earth and heaven? We are arrant knaves all; believe none of us. Go thy ways to a nunnery.

—conclusion likewise to the train of thought begun upon "To be or not to be . . ," and answer to that question.

He suddenly becomes aware that they are being watched; and

so the fact that her presence, even so aloof, would distract our attention from the soliloquy.

can he resist the conclusion that she is in league with the watchers? It is one more spy and decoy set in his way, that is all. By stage tradition his inconsequent:

> Where's your father?

is prompted by a movement of the arras and an actual glimpse of Polonius, or the King, or both. Something of the sort, no doubt, is intended. But it should not be too obvious, for that will discount the peculiar sensitiveness to things and thoughts hidden around him, the quick, uncertain clairvoyance of the "mad" mind.

Her clumsy, fearful lie:

> At home, my lord.

(but there is danger in his look; what if he did find her father lurking?—the question has its tragic answer later) shatters her credit with him. It is the second such wound. The first ranked his mother an adultress; and the poison of it infected all womanhood for him. But he has let himself still believe in this seeming innocence; and now it proves in its own fashion as false. And just such a brainstorm sweeps him as followed the Ghost's disappearance, and as will sweep him again when the King's guilt is proved; but it is an angrier, and therefore harsher, outbreak than these. The mind's lack of mastery is betrayed in the rash threat to the King:

> those that are married already, all but one, shall live. . . .

And here is the vengeful iconoclast, distorting the image he once worshiped to the shape of his new loathing of it, that he may the better break and forget it:

> I have heard of your paintings too, well enough; God has given you one face, and you make yourselves another; you jig, you amble, and you lisp, and nickname God's creatures, and make your wantonness your ignorance. Go to, I'll no more on't; it hath made me mad. . . .

That is Ophelia in the guise of his mother the harlot; Ophelia made symbol and scapegoat of her kind.[10]

Her bewildered, heart-broken outcry when he leaves her:

---

[10] Note the significant change from the "thou" and the "get thee to a nunnery" to the "your . . . you . . . yourselves."

> O, what a noble mind is here o'erthrown!
> The courtier's, soldier's, scholar's eye, tongue, sword,
> The expectancy and rose of the fair state . . .

completes by likeness (in the return to verse) and contrast (between his calm thought and her agony) this section of the scene, soliloquy and duologue.[11]

Next the King and Polonius reappear. Their minds are upon Hamlet, and they all but ignore the miserably sobbing girl, now that she has served her turn.[12] The King's disquiet is visibly increased; his misgivings are turning like a compass needle towards the truth:

> There's something in his soul
> O'er which his melancholy sits on brood;
> And I do doubt the hatch and the disclose
> Will be some danger . . .

and the countermovement (and the lagging action of the play) is promptly advanced a step:

> which for to prevent,
> I have in quick determination
> Thus set it down: he shall with speed to England. . . .

Another valuable stroke of contrast; his "quick determination" is set against Hamlet's interminable talk and delay.

Ophelia may well overhear the

> he shall with speed to England,
> For the demand of our neglected tribute . . . .

since, as we are to learn a few scenes later, the matter is not kept secret; also her father's more sinister:

> or confine him where
> Your wisdom best shall think.

----

[11] It is more minutely studied on pp. 213; 241 *et seq.*

[12] They do, that is to say, according to F1, and most editors follow it. Q2 gives her an *exit* at the end of her speech and implies a—quite arbitrary—re-entrance later. From every point of view, I think, F1 does better. The continuity of the action will then not be broken by a cleared stage (and applause for Ophelia); and the oblivious concern of the two men with the growing menace of Hamlet's conduct is emphasized. Shakespeare stresses, what is more, this neglect of Ophelia in the text itself by giving Polonius that offhand

> How now, Ophelia;
> You need not tell us what Lord Hamlet said;
> We heard it all.

She has been caught in the toil of matters too high and too hard for her. She stands apart; shaken, silent, ignored. Then she escapes.[13]

Hamlet prepares the play, and it is acted and answers its purpose. He is excitedly triumphant, for the King's guilt is now manifest. But when he seems to be at last about to "swoop" to his revenge, he is summoned to his mother's closet, and the thought of her guilt takes first place again in his mind.

BUT no sooner has the King departed with his

> Madness in great ones must not unwatched go.

than Hamlet returns. His wild invective is still fresh in our ears; and he is here again, and at his sanest. Nor at his sanest merely, but with his mind wholly occupied by his opinions upon the art of acting.

It is the third use of this trick of surprise and contrast. We heard of him rushing wildly into Ophelia's presence, and next saw him quietly absorbed in a book. He rushed away, excited to full pitch by his plot to trap the King, and returned calmly deliberating upon death—but his own death!—and the hereafter. Now we have just seen him crazed with anger at discovering the trap laid for him, and baited—she consenting—with Ophelia; yet, but a few minutes later[14]:

> Speak the speech, I pray you, as I pronounced it to you, trippingly on the tongue; but if you mouth it, as many of your players do, I had as lief the town-crier spoke my lines. Nor do not saw the air too much with your hand, thus. . . .

and so on for fifty lines more, in an elaborate and delicately ironical conspectus of dramatic criticism!

But it is not a mere dramatic trick, and only the extremes of contrast smack of madness. And these do but exaggerate a normal quality in him, the ability to range swiftly and clearly from one

[13] I do not think that this is to impose too much alien imagination upon the text. Ophelia is not dismissed; and, having employed her so far, I do not think they trouble to speak so that she cannot overhear. On the other hand they have done with her—and show it. She would not follow them, then, when they depart, but simply "make herself scarce."

[14] "But a few minutes": this is the actual time involved; and as Shakespeare interposes no other, no *dramatic* time indication, this is the impression sustained.

mood to another. There is a touch of genius in it. We saw it operate in his first greeting of Horatio, and while he awaited the Ghost on the platform; we shall see it again when he returns from his adventurous voyage purged of his madness, and can pass obliviously from Ophelia's grave and its emotions to the tale of the plot against him, to amusing himself with Osric, from that to preparing his mind for death.

Nor, in his seeming absorption here in these superfluously fine means to his end has he forgotten the end itself. This concern as to how that fateful speech shall be spoken is both safety valve and disguise for his secret anxiety. And the clarity and concentration of his talk (though he lets it run away with him; the unreal world always more satisfying than the real) are but a measure of the keen mind alert again and ready to face the imminent issue.[15] We feel the controlled excitement beneath; and this dramatically validates the long digression at such a stage of climax.

There follows a notable little piece of Shakespearean stagecraft; of minor importance, but a good example of what can be done in the freedom of the platform stage.

> *Exeunt Players. Enter Polonius, Rosencrantz and Guildenstern.*
>
> HAMLET.   How now, my lord; will the King hear this piece
>   of work?
> POLONIUS.   And the Queen too, and that presently.
> HAMLET.   Bid the players make haste.
>   *Exit Polonius.*
>   Will you two help to hasten them?
> Ros.
> GUILD.   } We will, my lord.
>   *Exeunt.*
> HAMLET.   What ho, Horatio!
>   *Enter Horatio.*
> HORATIO.   Here, sweet lord; at your service.

Those fifty-five lines of digression are offset by this brisk return to the action and its speeding forward; a moment or so of diversion separating the long speech to the Players and another long one to Horatio. And see how the slight occasion is enriched. A messenger to say that the King would hear the play would have

---

15 Compare this speech to those careless, detached, references to the "eyrie of children."

sufficed. But Polonius adds the importance of his own self-impor-
tance to the matter, while Hamlet finds mischievous satisfaction
in dispatching him—this high state dignitary and lately detected
eavesdropper—like a lackey, to

> Bid the players make haste.

Here are Rosencrantz and Guildenstern too. Their pretextless
arrival suggests the hovering spies, Hamlet's prompt dismissal of
them his growing distrust; and there is mockery in the very
superfluity of their errand:

> Will you two help to hasten them?

Then, for contrast, the false friends are replaced by the true one;
Hamlet turns contemptuously from them to find him.[16] And
how eloquent is the change:

> Horatio, thou art e'en as just a man
> As e'er my conversation coped withal.

A kaleidoscopic two minutes, barely that; if the actors are alive
to their work, how illuminating! But only against the anonymous
background of the platform stage can the effect be gained so
economically and easily.

The thirty-line speech to Horatio, thus begun, serves a manifold
purpose. It ballasts and steadies the action by providing a space of
controlled quiet, of smooth-flowing and harmonious verse, between Hamlet's glancing cerebrations and the deeper disturbance
which the play-scene begins. And it does this in showing us the
most equably minded Hamlet we have seen yet. While he waited
with Horatio on the platform for the Ghost to appear he spoke of

> particular men,
> That for some vicious mole of nature in them . . .
> Carrying, I say, the stamp of one defect,
> Being nature's livery, or fortune's star . . .
> Shall in the general censure take corruption
> From that particular fault . . . .

and had, surely, his own tendency to "weakness and melancholy"
in mind—which we have since seen so obsessing him. Now he is

---

[16] By the Folio's stage direction he does find him already standing there; by
Q2's he calls him in. The Folio's may well be the better effect, the contrast being
easier to point, if Hamlet has only to turn from false friends to true and exclaim:
"Horatio, *thou* [a very slight stress will serve] are e'en as just a man . . ."

for the first time alone with Horatio, and they are together for the
first time since then.[17] And he forgets himself and his troubles,
not in such self-delighting talk as he lavished on the Players, but
in loving praise of his friend, whose virtues, he knows, are the very
ones he himself lacks; and he seeks, upon the verge of this ordeal,
to strengthen himself in their strength. And one might suppose,
by this measured calm, that the Hamlet who is passion's slave, the
victim of that "vicious mole of nature," was now well in hand. He
admits that Horatio's original scepticism may be justified after all.
For if the King's

> occulted guilt
> Do not itself unkennel in one speech,
> It is a damned ghost that we have seen,
> And my imaginations are as foul
> As Vulcan's stithy. . . .

No more trade, then, with the supernatural; no more imaginings,
be they good or ill; but "grounds more relative":

> Give him heedful note;
> For I mine eyes will rivet to his face,
> And after we will both our judgments join
> In censure of his seeming.

The Murder of Gonzago, that is to say, is to be acted peaceably to
its end, the two are to compare notes after and determine—or not
—upon a sound plan for a righteous vengeance. That is what
Horatio would do; and it is what Hamlet, taking color from him,
intends himself to do. So the speech and his demeanor here are
meant—ironically by the sequel—to tell us.

Now for the second time we see King, Queen and Court in
ceremonial state; and to enhance upon the first occasion, the
music of the *kettledrums and trumpets*, the *Danish march* and the
guard with their torches are added. Before our eyes Hamlet puts
on, as he might a mask, his "antic disposition"; it disguises his
excitement, is an ambush from which to shoot his mockeries—
arrows, plucked from his own flesh, poisoned by his own misery,
which is assuaged when he can see them rankling elsewhere.

A tartness in the King's tone, as they passingly encounter,

---

[17] All this in terms of the action. With what may be supposed to go on behind
the scenes, unless Shakespeare indicates it, we have of course no concern. It is
inexistent.

might warn him that his enemy was on guard. Polonius is a ridiculously easy prey to a jest. But the sight of his mother, gay and bedecked for the occasion, and her prettily affectionate

> Come hither, my dear Hamlet, sit by me.

sting him. He does not retaliate upon her; he cannot, of course, sit by her, for then he could not watch the King. So at whom should he strike but Ophelia?[18] The short exchange that follows is covertly poignant. They parted but a while ago; he savagely enraged, yet suffering too; she heartbroken, yet blaming only his madness. The tragic end, it seemed, to a once-beautiful, an always honorable love. Now, before all the Court, he marks her out for his attentions—with an indecent joke. There was freedom of speech enough in Renaissance Courts. But Ophelia is very young and not light-tongued herself, and the thing is an insult. Yet she cannot as publicly resent it, for Hamlet is a prince. Gossip has given him to her as a lover; in what sense a lover, in what esteem he holds her, must not such joking show? Her answers:

> No, my lord. . . . Ay, my lord. . . . I think nothing, my lord.
> . . . You are merry, my lord.

(the last as reproachful as she dare make it) show her miserably shamed, but turning the dignity of a gentle deference to her defense; until, recovering, and remembering his "madness," she rallies to the smile and the response which courtliness demands. But this will be worse torture to her than his rage, by far. He sees her now as the demure decoy, the hypocrite, the wanton at heart; and on her, at least, he can be swiftly and cruelly revenged. It is the first outcropping of his cruelty; that flaw in a nature sensitive even to weakness, ever tempted to shirk its battle against the strong to triumph over one weaker still.

The Murder of Gonzago, compared to *Hamlet* itself, is a slightly old-fashioned affair, with its dumb show and its lengths of sententious verse. But, for a play within a play to be effective, some such difference, some distinction between the immediate

---

[18] Hamlet and the Queen have not met (always in terms of the play's action) since the scene at the Council table, when she entreated him so lovingly and he so coldly responded. The same thing happens here; he even repeats that ironical "Good mother." We must remember, too, the sort of woman that Gertrude is; the aging beauty, attractive still, but having to make the most of what charms are left her, and not above coquetting in public, even playfully with her son.

illusion and the illusion at second hand, must be made. Its verse is not of the strength or quality of Æneas' tale to Dido. But that had to stir Hamlet from his lethargy. This is to provide a quiet and—till the moment of the poisoning—a negative background to the drama which must command our chief attention, the tense, silent and complex drama played by Hamlet, Horatio and the King, another facet of it by Hamlet and Ophelia, yet another by Hamlet, the Queen and the courtiers around.

One scene, we have just been told, is to "come near the circumstance" of the old King's murder, and we shall more vaguely remember that Hamlet meant to write "a speech of some dozen or sixteen lines"—presumably to point the likeness. We are prepared for such a climax to the business. But before the play proper can begin:

> *Hoboyes play. The dumbe shewe enters.*
> *Enter a King and Queene, very lovingly; the Queene embracing him. She kneeles, and makes shew of Protestation unto him. He takes her up, and declines his head upon her neck. Layes him downe upon a Banke of Flowers. She seeing him a-sleepe, leaves him. Anon comes in a Fellow, takes off his Crowne, kisses it, and powres poyson in the King's eares, and Exits. The Queene returnes, findes the King dead, and makes passionate Action. The Poysoner, with some two or three Mutes, comes in againe, seeming to lament with her. The dead body is carried away: The Poysoner Wooes the Queene with Gifts, she seemes loath and unwilling awhile, but in the end accepts his love.*
> *Exeunt.*[19]

Does not this fatally anticipate the promised critical scene? Will Claudius not "blench" at so close a picturing—though a picturing only—of his crime? Let him do so, and is not Hamlet's purpose at once served, but Shakespeare's (so to say) aborted, the rest of the scene being then superfluous? Or, if Claudius manages to control himself, will he not, since "this show imports the argument of the play," stop the proceedings then and there? These questions have fomented controversy enough about the Dumb Show. Editors have answered them variously, producers in the main by omitting it. One editorial answer is that the King is at

---

[19] Thus F1, which does not vary substantially from Q2, though it is worth noting that "a Fellow" replaces "another man."

the moment talking to the Queen or Polonius, and does not see
it. That can hardly be. Shakespeare does not leave such crucial
matters in the air. Failing plain indication to the contrary, we
must assume, I think, that whatever there is to be seen the King
sees. Another answer is that while he sees the Show he does not
suppose it to "import the argument," and is content to let it pass
for an unlucky coincidence which no one can remark but he; for
dumb shows are apt to be, as Hamlet says, "inexplicable," and the
likeness may not be striking. This is more tenable; the Folio's
labeling of the murderer as *a Fellow* does, in fact, suggest no
such figure as the King's. And it is likely, I think, that the
method of acting a dumb show differed greatly from that developed by this time for the acting of a play. It must inevitably
have had more of the formal mime in it, which we commonly
associate with ballet and the *Commedia dell'Arte*.[20] But the right
answer will emerge from the text and the situation involved in it;
we have only straightforwardly to work this out, instead of
dodging or shirking the issue.

When the King sees the Dumb Show he is at once alert.
Though here may be a coincidence and no more, whatever Hamlet has a hand in will now be matter for suspicion. But what
should he do? If the thing is mere coincidence, nothing. If it is a
trap laid, he is not the man to walk straight into it—as he would
by stopping the play for no reason he could give before it had
well begun. He must wait and be wary. Ophelia (the acting of
the Dumb Show has let her recover herself a little) voices the
question for him:

> What means this, my lord? . . . Belike this show imports the
> argument of the play?

And Hamlet's answer:

> Marry, this is miching mallecho; it means mischief.

and his comment on the Prologue:

> the players cannot keep counsel: they'll tell all.

point disquietingly away from coincidence. "Miching mallecho
. . . mischief . . . tell all"; Claudius must be wary indeed.

---

[20] In the 1932 revival by the *Comédie Française*, the Dumb Show was acted in
this fashion, fantastically and swiftly, and the King's ignoring it did not seem very
strange.

Here, then, is the battle joined at once, between the watcher and the watched. On the defensive is the King, whose best tactics, without doubt, are to brave the business out, calmly, smilingly, giving no slightest sign that he sees anything extraordinary in it; for the attack, Horatio, whose steady eye—he has assured us—nothing will escape, and Hamlet, a-quiver with suppressed excitement, who after a while will try—still vainly—by mocking look and word, to pierce that admirable composure. But for a long first round, from the entry of the player King and Queen, it is a still and silent battle. Its background is the line after line of their smoothly flowing verse, which we hear but need not greatly heed. Our attention is for the three: for Claudius, conscious that he is being watched, and Hamlet and Horatio, their eyes riveted to his face.

The Dumb Show falls quite pertinently into Hamlet's—and Shakespeare's—scheme. The mimic play as a whole is a calculated insult both to King and Queen. The "one scene" which "comes near the circumstance" of the old King's death, and into which Hamlet has inserted his "dozen or sixteen lines," is to be the finishing stroke merely. Were it a single one, Claudius might outface it. It is the prolonged preliminary ordeal which is to wear him down. Upon the point of dramatic technique, too, if the test of his guilt is to be limited to the one scrambled and excited moment of the

> Thoughts black, hands apt, drugs fit . . .

—when our eyes and ears are everywhere at once, upon Hamlet, Lucianus and the King, upon the Queen and the courtiers, too—the play's most vital crisis must be half lost in confusion. What Shakespeare means, surely, is to make this simply the culmination of a long, tense, deliberate struggle to break down the King's composure, on his part to maintain it. Treat it thus and the confusion, when at last it comes, makes its true effect. And the eighty lines of the spineless verse of *The Murder of Gonzago* are all they should be as a placid accompaniment to a silent and enthralling struggle. If the struggle is not the salient thing, if the ambling of the verse is made so instead, it must lower the tension of the scene disastrously.[21] And we may, I think, acquit Shakespeare of meaning to do that.

But there is a minor theme for them to accompany, besides. After twenty-five lines the intention of the dialogue sharpens—in the Player Queen's

> In second husband let me be accurst!
> None wed the second but who killed the first . . . .
> The instances that second marriage move
> Are base respects of thrift, but none of love;
> A second time I kill my husband dead,
> When second husband kisses me in bed.

—to a glancing attack upon the Queen herself as she sits there. She, unlike Claudius, winces at once; and Hamlet, with his

> That's wormwood, wormwood!

rashly endorsing this petty, superfluous triumph, encourages thereby the King's growing certitude that here *is* a trap laid for him, no mere coincidence.

This baiting of Gertrude will also set the whole Court agog, will, on the other hand, prevent both her and them from remarking the sterner struggle proceeding. She outfaces the mockery as best she may. They glance aside at her from their watching of the play, scandalized, suppressing their smiles. They glance, apprehensively, at the King; what has he to say to the outrage? He is caught between the obligation to resent it and the need to keep calm under the deadlier and secret accusation. To this enrichment of the foreground picture the background of the mimic play will prove none too ample.

Upon the Player Queen's oath:

> Nor earth to me give food, nor Heaven light!
> Sport and repose lock from me day and night! . . .
> Both here and hence pursue me lasting strife,
> If, once a widow, ever I be wife!

Hamlet seals his complicity by the satiric, audibly muttered:

> If she should break it now!

[21] As producers of the play discover. They cut the Dumb Show and with it the cue for the silent struggle with the King. Then there is nothing much left to do but listen to those rather dreary lines and wait for Lucianus. Quite justifiably, that being so, as many of the lines as possible are cut. But Shakespeare did not put them in for nothing.

It is like him that he cannot even now, when his purpose is at least well afoot, pursue it single-mindedly, must endanger it by these sinister diversions. For endanger it he plainly does. Horatio we see sticking to the task set him, steadily watching the King. But here is Hamlet, yielded to the old obsession of his mother's guilt, veritably provoking interference—and upon another count— before the critical scene, the finally revealing moment, is reached. To taunt the Queen to her face; and before Claudius, before the Court, to challenge her with that

> Madam, how like you this play?

is to jeopardize his whole plan. The plan does still succeed; but here also is the seed of his own subsequent failure to exploit its success. Did not the Ghost warn him:

> Taint not thy mind, nor let thy soul contrive
> Against thy mother aught . . . .

But this chance of wounding and publicly shaming her he cannot bear to miss. And later, when she sends for him, the thought of scourging her with reproaches will dominate all else; and he will spare the King at his prayers, because of his unlikeness to a lustful, guilty lover; and, lost in the sating of his wrath against her, he will kill Polonius, and so deliver himself into his enemy's hands.

But, for the time, the tide is with him. The Queen does not appeal to Claudius to stop the play; she puts up no better defense than the wryly merry:

> The lady doth protest too much, methinks.

And Claudius dare not stop it, lest that should prove him guilty upon the graver count. He is reduced to demanding, lamely:

> Have you heard the argument? is there no offence in't?

No offense!—when already his Queen and his marriage have been publicly insulted by these hired and abetted players. Hamlet, seeing that the courage is out of him, lashes him, stingingly, pointedly, casting, for the first time, the one fatal word full in his face:

> No, no, they do but jest, *poison* in jest; no offence i' the world!

—mockingly dares him to unmask, knowing he dare not; and, upon the still supiner

> What do you call the play?

himself unmasks, scornfully sure now of victory. His savagely
comic impromptu title labels his enemy mere vermin:

> The Mouse-trap. Marry, how? Tropically. This play is the
> image of a murder done in Vienna: Gonzago is the duke's name;
> his wife, Baptista. You shall see anon; 'tis a knavish piece of work:
> but what of that? your majesty, and we that have free souls, it
> touches us not: let the galled jade wince, our withers are unwrung.
>
> *Enter Lucianus. . . .*

The critical scene has come. Again, how like Hamlet to have
forestalled it and discounted its value by giving Claudius such
open warning of what was coming! But a sense of triumph possesses him. By the outflung

> This is one Lucianus, nephew to the king.

(to the king, to King Hamlet, not Duke Gonzago) he avows
himself master of these puppets. It is with a sort of insolent confidence that he momentarily turns for another bout of bawdry
with Ophelia, and then back for his firing of the mine:

> Begin, murderer; pox, leave thy damnable faces, and begin. . . .

He seems indeed to have Claudius beaten. And with the

> He poisons him i' the garden for 's estate. His name's Gonzago;
> the story is extant, and written in very choice Italian. You shall see
> anon how the murderer gets the love of Gonzago's wife.

he scourges him from the field.

But it is a barren victory, lacking its conclusive stroke, and to be
turned against the victor. Hamlet—all forgetful of the promised
joining of judgments with Horatio—was, it would seem, about to
bridge fiction to fact, tax Claudius with the murder to his face
and before the world, and take his revenge, if it might be, then
and there. But, failing to do this, it is a fatal error to unmask. For
Claudius, in the safe retreat he gains, will turn that now useless
"madness" to his own protection and profit, leaving his enemy
meanwhile to vaunt his triumph in sounding words.[22]

[22] Since I owe so much to Dr. Dover Wilson's latest editing of the play, it is
perhaps only right to record my total disagreement with his interpretation of the
play-scene.

He thinks the King does not see the Dumb Show. I have already given my
reasons against that. But the Dumb Show is also, he holds, a deliberate betrayal
by the Players of Hamlet's plan; the fact that the King does not see it is a

King, Queen, Court, attendants and Players all vanish clamorously. At this point, and with this help, the actor of Hamlet is accustomed to lift his part in the scene to such a high pitch of emotion that descent from it is most difficult, and transition into the key of what follows must seem forced. Hamlet is, of course, intensely excited; but it is an intellectual excitement and one not beyond his control. Hence Shakespeare's use of the light and inconsequent lyric:

> Why, let the stricken deer go weep,
>   The hart ungalled play;
> For some must watch, while some must sleep:
>   So runs the world away . . . .

and the ironically fanciful:

> Would not this, sir, and a forest of feathers, if the rest of my fortunes turn Turk with me, with two Provincial roses on my razed shoes, get me a fellowship in a cry of players, sir?

instead of such verse—into which emotion more naturally flows— as follows the Ghost's disappearance, or as we shall find in the scene to come with his mother, or of such hammering phrases as those he leveled at Ophelia when she denied that her father was spying on them. And the fantasy and banter serve to relieve the strain of what has gone before.

---

providential stroke of luck; Hamlet's "miching mallecho" is an expression of anger at the mishap, his "the players cannot keep counsel . . ." an apprehension of more trouble to come. The "posy-prologue" is another offense and Lucianus' "damnable faces" and his speaking of "thoughts black . . ." yet another, a willful disregard of the advice to speak the speech "trippingly," not to "strut and bellow." The scene, by this reading of it, faces, so to speak, two ways. There is the effect of the play upon the King and Queen (duplicate already in itself) and there will be the effect upon Hamlet of the jeopardy of his plan.

I might argue that with the material Dr. Dover Wilson selects no actor of Hamlet could convey to an audience all this extra and very different kind of anxiety. Nor do I see how the actors of *The Murder of Gonzago* could help him much. But the proof of that pudding, it might be answered, is in the eating; who is to decide that the thing cannot be done? I prefer to plead that it is, in itself, a thing which Shakespeare would never try to do. He would never dissipate the force of such a scene by so dividing its interest, or handicap Hamlet at this juncture with a quite extraneous difficulty. Besides, there is literally nothing in the play which is not, in some way or another, germane to its story or illustrative of Hamlet's character, or a consequence, direct or indirect, of what he does or leaves undone. Such an irrelevancy as this betrayal of his plan by the Players, springing from nothing, leading nowhere, would be a rift in the fabric, and dramatically meaningless.

Then follows:

> O good Horatio! I'll take the ghost's word for a thousand
> pound. Didst perceive?
> Very well, my lord.
> Upon the talk of the poisoning?
> I did very well note him.

—and we are back into the main current of the action again.

Rosencrantz and Guildenstern return.[23] At a glance he reads
something of their mission in their faces; and, for a mischievous
impediment to it, calls after the Players to bring back their music,[24]
coolly observing, as he waits, and keeps them waiting there,
chafing and ignored:

> For if the king like not the comedy,
> Why, then, belike, he likes it not, perdy.
> Come, some music!

[23] Here, I think, F1's directions are certainly preferable to Q2's, which bring the
two on only after music and the recorders have been called for. F1 makes them
enter upon Horatio's

> I did verie well note him.

and Hamlet to exclaim, surely at the sight of them:

> Oh, ha! Come some Musick. Come ye Recorders. . . .

—makes him, that is to say, since he guesses that they come from the King,
promptly provide himself with a distraction and a screen against their unwelcome
attentions. Even the difference between Q2's "Ah ha!" and F1's "Oh ha!" is an
effective one, as a direction to the actor.

[24] The Dumb Show had been accompanied by music. Q2 merely says, *The
Trumpets sound. Dumbe show followes*; F1 has *Hoboyes play. The dumbe shewe
enters.* Music was customary at private theaters and Court performances before
the play began, and between the acts if the play was so divided. The public
theaters had music when the play needed it, and it would be a great addition to
a dumb show. For *The Murder of Gonzago* played at the Court of Elsinore
Shakespeare's company would make the most appropriate provision they could
afford. The later stage direction in Q2

> *Enter the Players with Recorders.*

may well imply that this had been the accompaniment of the Dumb Show. F1
has only:

> *Enter one with a Recorder.*

and the subsequent text is altered accordingly. But then the Dumb Show here has
been accompanied by "Hoboyes," and a hoboye cannot be used in the business of
the scene. All that matters in a modern production is that there should have been
suitable music, if possible visibly played. What is absurd is for Hamlet to exclaim:

> Come, some music. Come, the recorders . . . .

as if it were an entirely new idea; and, later, for the Player to bring one on, as if
it had been produced from nowhere.

—or, in other words: This entertainment, my good friends, is not over yet.

The severe tone his good friends take with him reflects the temper in which the King has sent them, though they filter this through a sort of sorrowful reproach. Hamlet is a little hard on these young men. They are courtiers, and timeservers, no doubt, and moral nonentities; but their behavior, the circumstances considered, is surely unexceptionable. All ease of comradeship between the three has, however, now vanished. Guildenstern broaches their errand—to Hamlet's still oblivious back, it would seem:

> Good my lord, vouchsafe me a word with you.

He is turned on with a menacingly bland

> Sir, a whole history.

and a veritable duel begins; "Sirs" and "my lord" on one side and the other; Hamlet bitingly ironic, Guildenstern helpless to pass his guard. He does touch him, however, with the unexpected

> The Queen, your mother, in most great affliction of spirit, hath sent me to you.

That canker spot is set throbbing again; and there could be no better way—we may imagine or not the King thinking so—tc distract Hamlet's mind from its deadly purpose. He responds, on the instant, blandly still:

> You are welcome.

But a second, too familiar "your mother . . ." foments such a dangerously teeming

> Sir, I cannot. . . . Make you a wholesome answer; my wit's diseased; but, sir, such answer as I can make, you shall command; or rather, as you say, my mother: therefore no more, but to the matter: my mother, you say,—

that Guildenstern gives way and Rosencrantz comes fresh to the rescue. The Queen also is amazed at his conduct. The infection works on; this "mother . . . mother . . . mother . . ." beating like a pulse:

> O wonderful son, that can so astonish a mother! But is there no sequel at the heels of this mother's admiration? Impart.

He is to speak with her in her closet ere he goes to bed.

> We shall obey, were she ten times our mother.

—and obeying, and slaking his stored bitterness upon her, he will avenge, not a father's murder, but a husband's shame, hers too and his own, and gratify and exhaust and betray himself in doing so. While Claudius is assuring his own safety, this will absorb him.

The diplomat Rosencrantz, to his royally harsh

> Have you any further trade with us?

offers a pathetic

> My lord, you once did love me.

But the frank, confiding Hamlet is no more. He does not trouble to put a term to such friendship, derides it instead:

> So I do still, by these pickers and stealers.

And in place of the secret they would pick and steal from him (yet how should they even now imagine what this "grief" is that he denies them?) he pays them once more with the false coin of

> Sir, I lack advancement.

and mischievously turns—the dilettante prince again!—to give impressive greeting to the recorders.

He then turns back to the now somewhat sulky Guildenstern; first with a warning question:

> why do you go about to recover the wind of me, as if you would drive me into a toil?

and, since that draws a canting answer, to deriding him also, with the

> Will you play upon this pipe? . . .

and the rest. And he ends with a sharper warning still:

> 'Sblood, do you think I am easier to be played on than a pipe? Call me what instrument you will, though you can fret me, you cannot play upon me.

They had better have taken it in time, those two. At which point Polonius appears.

Here is in some sort a repetition of the earlier picture of Hamlet, Polonius, the two friends, and the Players in attendance, when he sat trifling his time away, they smilingly subservient to his mood, and the notion of *The Murder of Gonzago* was about to dawn on him. All four are harshly astrain now, and Polonius is peremptory and—though precariously—much upon his dignity:

> My lord, the Queen would speak with you, and presently.[25]

But an extra and outrageous turn of the antic disposition effectively deflates him:

> Do you see yonder cloud that's almost in shape of a camel?
> By the mass and 'tis like a camel, indeed.
> Methinks it is like a weasel.
> It is backed like a weasel.
> Or like a whale?
> Very like a whale.
> Then will I come to my mother by and by.

(Fool a madman to the top of his bent; if, less mad than you think, he fools you in return, that is but fair.) Then, with a single gesture, and a

> Leave me, friends.

he rids himself of them all.[26]

Does that repeated "by and by," which he opposes to Polonius' sharp "presently," speak of a suddenly stinging thought that he might best go to his mother after—only after!—he had done his deadly business with the King?[27] I think so; and the actor can convey it well enough by look and intonation, and by now letting the swift, irritable sequence ignite and flame out in

> 'Tis now the very witching time of night,
> When churchyards yawn and hell itself breathes out

---

[25] The word, so continually used by Shakespeare for "at once," has unluckily lost that meaning to us; though, to Scottish audiences, it has not.

[26] Another instance of the frictionless technique of the Elizabethan stage. Here are five or six characters dismissed from the scene at a word, yet the effect will not be one of rabbits scurrying mutely into their holes, as it would be upon a realistically scenic stage. For when Rosencrantz and Guildenstern appeared, Horatio lapsed into onlooking; so did they when Polonius came; and the Players with the recorders are impersonal figures. Therefore all of them but Polonius, when the moment comes for their dismissal, have, against the negative background, lost individuality a little, have been brought, in comparison with the solid and vital figure of Hamlet, to something the dramatic value of a bas-relief; and they can— this is the point—disappear without distracting our attention from Hamlet, or checking the impetus of the scene. And this is a very important point, since the end of the scene is now so near.

[27] "By and by" can also mean "at once," but I think that in this instance it does not. The O.E.D. gives earlier examples of both senses.

Contagion to this world: now could I drink hot blood,
And do such bitter business as the day
Would quake to look on.

But with that the little blaze of excitement—for it is no more, it does not resolve into purpose—dies down. The more deeply rankling injury in him stirs again:

Soft! now to my mother. . . .

But he pauses before he goes, in a sort of dread, in something very like prayer:

O heart! lose not thy nature; let not ever
The soul of Nero enter this firm bosom;
Let me be cruel, not unnatural;
I will speak daggers to her, but use none. . . .

For it comes to him that he has changed and hardened since his task was laid on him, and he learned with what he had to do; with treachery, and adultery, and murder at its foulest. And self-thwarting and self-contempt have helped to make him cruel of heart. But he needs to be cruel, to be callous and ruthless too. Of what use are finer qualities, with everything around him—comradeship, love, even his mother's love for him—turned by his enemy to instruments of evil? He must strike, and spare no one. Yet along what paths, and towards what spiritual abysses may not this temper lead him? We have seen him vengefully torturing Ophelia. His love for his mother lies deeper than that love lay, its ruin in him may be the more destructive.

The King, momentarily secure, decides to expedite Hamlet's departure for England. The sight of the mimic murder has roused his sleeping, stubborn conscience, and, left alone, he struggles with it. And—Hamlet being by now, he must suppose, safe in his mother's closet—he even kneels and tries to pray. But Hamlet, as it happens, is still only on his way there; and passing by, he has the unknowing King at his mercy. Yet he spares him, lest, killed at prayer, his enemy should escape everlasting damnation.

SHAKESPEARE, at this juncture, must make sure that, despite the excitement, the threads of his story hold taut, and that none of its various interests is forgotten. So while the King has been out of our sight his messengers have kept us in mind of him, and the coming scene with the Queen has been prepared. Here is more preparation for it and for what is to happen after it. Hamlet shall be sent "forthwith" to England. Claudius looks ahead; his adversary only tangles himself in each new snare set in his path. Then comes Polonius with the news that Hamlet is on his way to the Queen. The old gentleman moves like a rapidly connecting shuttle between these three scenes—the present, the last and the next, very usefully links them together, they themselves being the link between the crisis of the play-scene and the strenuous closet-scene —and helps speed them along.

But this scene at the outset has been rather oddly held up by Rosencrantz and Guildenstern. The King tells them that such outbreaks of lunacy begin to make him fear for his life—which is both the truth and a politic reason for what he means to do. It behooves them to express their concern; but Guildenstern's

> Most holy and religious fear it is
> To keep those many many bodies safe
> That live and feed upon your majesty.

and Rosencrantz' heavily charged homily which follows, upon the transcendent value of a kingly life, come strangely from these two. The whole passage has an artificial air. "Topical allusion," one exclaims; and the assassination of kings was, indeed, in Shakespeare's day a perennially topical subject. But there is explanation enough within the play's own bounds.

Claudius will not send the heir to the throne overseas without consulting his Council. A scene or so later we have his

> Come, Gertrude, we'll call up our wisest friends
> And let them know both what we mean to do,
> And what's untimely done . . . .

—the case against Hamlet being by then an even better one, since he has killed Polonius. And when, soon after that, he appears to pass judgment on the culprit, he does so attended by his Councilors—though Q2 must put it thriftily: *Enter King and two or three* —his authority sustained by theirs. Shakespeare's first idea, I fancy, was to bring this Council into the present scene; and these speeches, inappropriately given now to Rosencrantz and Guildenstern, are the remnant of it. The change—if there was one—is certainly an improvement. The action flows more swiftly here without the Councilors; and they are more dramatically useful later when they confront, hands on swords, the then convictedly dangerous Hamlet.

Rosencrantz and Guildenstern departed to arm them for their "speedy voyage," Polonius to warn the Queen of Hamlet's coming and "convey" himself behind the arras before he can arrive, Claudius is left alone. It is the first time that we see him so. And the adulterer, the murderer and usurper, so cool and collected till now—but for that one moment during the mimic play[28]—now incontinently bends and writhes under the dreadful burden of his remorse. We have been prepared for some such revulsion by the earlier lines, spoken aside, about the harlot's cheek beautied with plastering art being not more ugly than is his deed to his painted word, and by the "O heavy burden!" with which they end. But I strongly suspect that these were inserted as an afterthought (lest the turn here should prove *too* unexpected to be convincing, or seem a mere superficial consequence of the shock of the play-scene,)[29] and that the original effect was meant to be one of arresting surprise. For here, not in the revelation during the play-scene, is the action's true turning point. That was a flash in the pan. But upon what happens now—or, rather, does *not* happen —the rest of the play depends; from this moment the tragedy and its holocaust are precipitated. Incidentally, it is always referred to as "the prayer-scene." But this is a misnomer more than usually misleading; since the whole point is that though Claudius strives to pray he cannot, that Hamlet spares him because he thinks he is praying, while, if he knew what was in his mind, he would presumably dispatch him then and there, and all, but for Gertrude's grief and the scandal, would be well over. It is upon this

---

[28] And the breakdown there is commonly much exaggerated by actors. Claudius should, even at that moment, keep some measure of self-control and depart as much apparently in anger as in fear. We hear of him immediately after "in his retirement marvellous distempered . . . with choler"—for which he has the excellent excuse of the insult offered to the Queen, the scandalous tenor of the play from that point of view. It is in this that he would wish the Court to see Hamlet's particular offense, and in his madness generally the danger to be dealt with.

[29] They have just that manufactured air about them. The actor may give to the speaking of them all the conviction he can, they remain "dead." For further discussion of this point, see p. 218.

master stroke of irony that everything turns; upon a Claudius battling within himself for his salvation and losing, and a Hamlet refusing to kill him lest he should *not* be damned.

The technical make-up of the scene; Claudius' soliloquy lapsing into the silence of the attempted prayer, the surprise of Hamlet's appearance (we imagine him, as Claudius must, already with his mother, Polonius having outsped him there), *his* surprise at the chance offered him, his soliloquy imposed, so to speak, upon the other—all that is unique in the play. Nor are we anywhere given harder or closer-knit argument. Each competes with the other in this; and we have a solid intellectual knot tied, a steadying inter-lude between the excitements of the play-scene and the emotions of the coming encounter with the Queen. Each antagonist is unaware of the other, Claudius of Hamlet's presence, Hamlet of what is in Claudius' mind. Each reaches a characteristic conclu-sion; Hamlet, with his revenge to his hand, is dissatisfied with its quality and refuses it; Claudius faces the truth about himself as he rises from his knees—

> My words fly up, my thoughts remain below;
> Words without thoughts never to heaven go.

—and, his own life spared, goes, single-minded again, to write the letter which is to compass Hamlet's death. And all Hamlet has gained is a fresh reminder of him

> in the incestuous pleasure of his bed. . .

—more fuel, that is to say, for the already dangerous mood in which he now takes his interrupted way to his mother.

Hamlet comes to reproach his mother for her sin. Discovering that for the second time he is being spied on, he "whips out his rapier" and kills the unseen Polonius. Despite his father's bidding, he is upon the point, in his rage, of telling his mother that her lover and husband was her husband's murderer, when the Ghost's reappearance prevents this. It is a gentler "visitation," and softens him for a while. But he departs savage and embittered still. Claudius comes for news of what has passed, learns of Polonius' death, and sends Rosencrantz and Guildenstern with guards to arrest this now provedly dan-gerous madman.

THE encounter with the Queen, as acted, too often becomes a moral lecture delivered by a grieved young man to a conscience-stricken matron. It is not meant, of course, to be anything of the sort. For one thing, Shakespeare would never bring this most passionate theme to a sententious crisis. For another, he habitually treats age in his characters as freely as he treats time in a play's action, conventionally, or (within the bounds of likelihood) for dramatic effect alone—and so he does here. Hamlet is "young." It looks as if Shakespeare first thought of him as about twenty, as the student returning to Wittenberg; late in the play he takes the trouble to make him a definite thirty, evidently to justify the developed maturity of his mind. But he remains conventionally "young." Gertrude—if we argue the matter out, but we do not—might then be approaching fifty by the calendar, and in real life have come to look matronly and middle-aged enough. But, played by a boy upon Shakespeare's stage, this is just what she could not plausibly be made to look. There she must be either conventionally "old" or conventionally "young." And since she must be shown sensually in love with Claudius, and seductive enough to make him commit murder for her sake, she clearly— the sole choice lying between the two—must be "young." And the force of Hamlet's reproach that at her age

> The heyday in the blood is tame, it's humble,
> And waits upon the judgment . . . .

is that, while to intolerant youth (never so intolerant as upon this issue) this should be so with her, it all too patently is not. From this, in fact, springs the tragedy; poor Gertrude's blood was not tame. In this the story of the play is rooted, and much of its meaning will be missed if the point is not from first to last kept clear.

The "movement" or "make-up" of this scene is also a little unusual. First come five lines of bustling prelude from Polonius, which link it to the two scenes just past. Then we hear Hamlet coming, vociferating as he comes; once more it is that obsessive

> Mother, mother, mother![30]

---

[30] Only the Folio gives it (though Q1 indicates something of the sort), and it has been held to be an interpolation by Burbage. It has, in any case, dramatic value. It helps bind these scenes together, strengthens a little the fresh resurgence of Hamlet's wrath against the Queen, and warns her to brace herself for his coming.

Begging Gertrude to be "round with him," Polonius slips behind
the arras; and the—somewhat tremulous—bravado of her

> I'll warrant you,
> Fear me not.

prepares us for the imminent clash.

They are alone together for the first time; and their estrangement till now—her gentle efforts to mend it countered by his
constrained courtesy or insolent sarcasm—has been but a longer
preparation for the moment. She has amply enough now to
incense her in the insult of *The Murder of Gonzago*; and her own
anger, as we noted, will blind her to any further reason for the
King's. Without prelude, then (and with an almost childish lack
of dignity), they join battle:

> Now, mother, what's the matter?
> Hamlet, thou hast thy father much offended.
> Mother, you have my father much offended.
> Come, come, you answer with an idle tongue.
> Go, go, you question with a wicked tongue.
> Why, how now, Hamlet!
> What's the matter now?
> Have you forgot me?
> No, by the rood, not so:
> You are the queen, your husband's brother's wife;
> And—would it were not so!—you are my mother.

—to which last savage stroke she has no answer. And upon her
impotent and most imprudent

> Nay then, I'll set those to you that can speak.

she finds herself in his hard grasp and flung back in her chair
again (where she had enthroned herself to receive him), and next
so menaced by the fierceness of his

> you shall not budge;
> You go not till I set you up a glass
> Where you may see the inmost part of you.

that she cries aloud for help. It is not that threat which frights
her, but plainer danger. For despite him, and as he feared, the
"soul of Nero" is astir in Hamlet. And did not Polonius from his
hiding echo her cry and draw the frenzied rage upon himself, the

sword thrust that despatches him might truly, in a moment more, have been for her.

For there is a mad, Neronic gaiety in the

> How now, a rat? Dead, for a ducat, dead!

the sanguine

> is it the King?

and the jingle of

> A bloody deed! almost as bad, good mother,
> As kill a king and marry with his brother.

In her bewildered horror she can only echo vaguely

> As kill a king!

and he is himself again in the ominously stern

> Ay, lady, 'twas my word.

They face each other, anger purged by calamity. And she is spared the imminent revelation; for Hamlet turns to the slain:

> Thou wretched, rash, intruding fool, farewell!
> I took thee for thy better; take thy fortune;
> Thou find'st to be too busy is some danger.

But this, in cold blood, from the sensitive and chivalrous Hamlet for elegy upon an old man—Ophelia's father too—whom he has recklessly killed![81] It is proof of the dire change worked in him; and for Gertrude, as he turns back to her, some warning of what —be he mad or sane—she may now expect. The deed itself, too, futile as it proves to be, its mere doing (for him, the *doing* of anything after the long thwarting and inaction), gives him, for the moment, a terrible authority, under which she shrinks cowed.

This unusual initial crisis over—but we may call Polonius' fate the catastrophe of his busybodying through the two preceding

---

[81] Is Hamlet meant to think that the eavesdropper is the King, and the actor to show this? I believe not; for we are aware that he has just come swiftly from the King's closet where he has left him on his knees. And this unlikelihood can be pointed if Polonius hides on the opposite side of the stage. He is not, surely, meant to *think* at all. He reacts, as if by instinct, to the cry from behind the arras; he is so excited as to be "beyond himself." The connection of ideas, if any, will be with the former eavesdropping, and his murderous impulse then. His "Is it the King?" is the unreasoningly hopeful question of the imaginative man, who always expects good luck to do better for him than he can for himself.

scenes, and the uninterrupted action makes this view of it effective—the encounter, as Hamlet has meant it to be, begins; with his

> Peace! sit you down,
> And let me wring your heart. . . .

But he talks a language she does not understand, less of ill deeds
themselves than the hidden springs of them, and of the infection
their evil may spread till the whole world be "thought-sick"
with it.

So he begins again, and speaks as to a child—

> Look here, upon this picture, and on this;
> The counterfeit presentment of two brothers. . . .[82]

—to try to make her understand. But that does not move her
either. He reasons, he scolds, he bullies; until, battering her with
ever grosser and grosser words, he at last has her morally down,
and pitifully crying:

> O Hamlet! speak no more;
> Thou turn'st mine eyes into my very soul. . . .

And then he treads her in the mire:

> Nay, but to live
> In the rank sweat of an enseamed bed,
> Stew'd in corruption, honeying and making love
> Over the nasty sty—

Such sparks of the dreaded "soul of Nero" as there were in him
flamed and died with the killing of Polonius. But here is cruelty
enough, in the loosing upon the wretched woman of this long-
pent store of resentful rage. And so transported is he as to come
again to the very point of dealing her the deadlier blow, which
will turn these mad hints of murder to plain fact—when, providentially, the Ghost appears.

~~~~~~~~~~~

[82] Does Hamlet point to two pictures on the wall, compare two miniatures, the
one of his father which he wears, the other of Claudius worn by Gertrude, or see—
and try to make her see—the two in his mind's eye? Personally, I pronounce
without hesitation for the miniatures. The pictures on the wall seem hardly in
place, either in Gertrude's closet or the Globe Theatre. That they appear in an
illustration to Rowe's edition is no recommendation at all. And the pictures seen
in the mind's eye will not point the dramatic contrast between the tremendous and
obscure metaphors in the surrounding speeches and the clear simplicity of this
imagery, while the miniatures in the actor's hands help to do so.

A very different "visitation" this from the imposing vision of the battlements; no armed imperious figure, but

> My father, in his habit as he liv'd![33]

—lived even here in unsuspicious happiness with wife and son; no sternly renewed mandate, nor the condemnation Hamlet looks for of his lapse in time and passion. But a gently reproachful

> Do not forget . . . .

—a pale, inverted, echo of that parting, commanding "Remember me," and the pitiful

> But, look! amazement on thy mother sits;
> O, step between her and her fighting soul . . . .

—for he divines a grace in her, as Hamlet does not, as she herself, it may be, does not yet. Then, after a little, a silent stealing-away. It is as if, with the passing of time, the spirit had lost material power, was nearer to its rest, and to oblivion.

These thirty-five lines make a center of calm in storm. It is a strange reunion for the three; and its pathos is epitomized in the question and answer between mother and son:

> To whom do you speak this?
> > Do you see nothing there?
> Nothing at all; yet all that is I see.
> Nor did you nothing hear?
> > No, nothing but ourselves.

"Nothing at all; *yet all that is I see*." So speak the spiritually blind.

Hamlet rages at her no more. But the compassion stirred in him soon hardens to irony. He has, she tells him, cleft her heart in twain. His

> O, throw away the worser part of it,
> And live the purer with the other half. . . .

only preludes the

> Good-night; but go not to mine uncle's bed;
> Assume a virtue if you have it not . . . .

and praise of "that monster custom." Trust not to change of

---

[33] *Enter the Ghost in his night-gowne* (*i.e.* the long robe which the King would have worn at night in the ease of his private apartments) says the occasionally most useful Q1.

heart. Put on the "frock and livery" of repentance, and you may come to be what you pretend to be. The unheroic way is best. For him, he must be Heaven's "scourge and minister" and "cruel to be kind." Yet these so "stern effects" in him are, it would seem, something of a frock and livery too. For, his passion spent, his cruelty sated, he now himself melts into repentant tears over old Polonius' body. But worse than this ill deed "remains behind"; the work prescribed him is still to do.

At which point, upon the rhymed couplet, it looks as if he had once been meant to depart and the scene between the two to conclude. But there were various technical reasons against that. For one, our interest must be guided out of this seething eddy—as the purposeless, forbidden attack upon Gertrude has been—back to the main stream of action again, the struggle between Hamlet and Claudius. Shakespeare provides a short cut to it by making Hamlet already aware of his so-called mission to England (we may suppose, if we question the matter, that the project had not been kept secret: it was spoken of before Ophelia), and even leaps ahead in allowing him prevision of its treachery— of which we have still to learn. For another reason; the action— Claudius in command—is now sweeping forward to his departure, and such a "full close" would badly check its flow.[34] Nor (upon the point of character) will Hamlet finish with his mother in such a gentle mood. He "must be cruel"; and he turns back to whet his cruelty once more on her. No passionate indignation here, nor compassionate appeal to her to repent; but for answer to her miserable

What shall I do?

the cold sarcasm of

> Not this, by no means, that I bid you do:
> Let the bloat king tempt you again to bed;
> Pinch wanton on your cheek, call you his mouse . . . .

He even taunts her with being ready, no doubt, to sell her son— at such a price!—to her paramour:

> And let him, for a pair of reechy kisses,
> Or paddling in your neck with his damn'd fingers,

---

[34] Shakespeare, as we have already noted (p. 36), does even more to avoid this by not "ending" the scene at all, but "transposing" it into the next.

Make you to ravel all this matter out,
That I essentially am not in madness,
But mad in craft.[35]

He has recovered his cruelty, too, when he turns once more to the dead Polonius; that

> For this same lord,
> I do repent . . . .

giving place to

> I'll lug the guts into the neighbour room.

---

[35] The scene has not been swept clear of all tokens of the disclosure of the murder—explicit in Q1. Hamlet has given her no particular evidence—as the text now stands—of being only "mad in craft"; rather the contrary. And her protest that she has "no life to breathe" what he has said to her is not what seems called for merely by his ravings against her union with Claudius, or even by his general reckless abuse of him—in which, certainly, the phrase "a murderer and a villain" did occur, but it was of a piece with the rest.

Dover Wilson has it that an important part of Hamlet's problem must be whether or no to justify his killing of the King by telling the world the truth. Will they believe it if he does? Is he thus to blacken his mother's name? Will she not inevitably be accounted an accomplice in the murder? On the other hand, if he does not, or if he only tells the Queen, will he not be accounted a mere murderer himself, striking to recover the crown? But the problem is surely insoluble; and for that excellent reason Shakespeare does not direct our attention to it. At some stage of the play's development Hamlet did explicitly tell the Queen, of that there can be little doubt. Why the change? Because the Queen could not carry the knowledge through the rest of the play without her relations to Claudius being gravely affected by it, and Shakespeare does not want to add this complication to the story. I am disposed to think that at no time did he let himself in for it, but that the postulated "assembler" of Q1 (in which, as it happens, this scene's text is more than usually corrupt) could not resist the temptation to make the more obvious effect, either upon his own account or by borrowing it from the earlier play; the consequences were of small concern to him.

Whether or no the scene was once meant to end upon the "cruel to be kind" couplet, there is a difference of text between F1 and Q2 in its immediate continuation which involves a slight dramatic difference and is worth noting. In F1, Hamlet is brought back by Gertrude's cry—of a woman left lonely and helpless, she can make it:

> What shall I do?

This carries the scene smoothly on. In Q2, Hamlet, of his own motion, returns with a

> One word more, good lady.

That marks his deliberate intention not to leave her in any gentle mood. The change was probably made in order to eliminate the "dead moment" occasioned by Hamlet's "false exit" (to use the technical phrase) and his return, the Queen left at a dramatic loss the while.

And in the final

Good night, mother!

is summed up all his past play of mockery on the word.

Hamlet gone, Claudius arrives.[36] He has been too apprehensive

---

[36] I have dealt on p. 36 with the question of the false act-division here. There is also that of the difference in the text itself between Q2 and F1. Which version should we follow? Q2 gives us:

> *Exit.*
> *Enter King, and Queene, with Rosencraus and Guyldensterne.*
> KING.　There's matter in these sighes, these profound heaves,
> 　　　　You must translate, tis fit we understand them,
> 　　　　Where is your sonne?
> GER.　Bestow this place on us a little while.
> 　　　　Ah mine owne Lord, what I have seene to-night?

—which can be made to imply either that Hamlet goes out on the inner stage and that the Queen goes out simultaneously in the opposite direction, to re-enter immediately on the outer stage with the King, Rosencrantz and Guildenstern, or that she emerges from the inner stage to encounter them there, or that the King and the two courtiers enter to her on the inner stage—though "this place" is a likelier reference to the no-man's-land of the outer stage than to the closet—and that she and the King emerge upon the outer stage later, possibly upon the King's:

> O Gertrude! come away. . . .

Upon the outer stage they certainly must be six lines later, for Rosencrantz and Guildenstern are told that

> Hamlet in madness hath Polonius slain,
> And from his mother's closet hath he dragg'd him. . . .

i.e. from some place other than this.

The Folio has:

> *Exit Hamlet tugging in Polonius.*
> *Enter King.*

—and the dialogue follows practically as in Q2, except that, Rosencrantz and Guildenstern being absent, the line dismissing them is naturally omitted. The King can, again, either enter on the outer stage, Gertrude emerging to greet him; or on the inner, and they can both emerge later—between which alternatives there is little dramatically to choose. But the Folio text, in omitting Rosencrantz and Guildenstern's first appearance altogether, and sparing us the slight delay of their dismissal, carries the action forward without check to its impulse; and, as there are other signs that this hereabouts is in general Shakespeare's aim, I think it may well represent his own second thoughts, and I recommend it to producers.

There remains the question of the King's opening lines. They fit—though a little clumsily—an entrance *with* Gertrude, as given in Q2; and they would about fill in the time it must take him to advance with her to the center of the outer stage talking the while. They do not fit the Folio's entrance for him, whether it to wait for Polonius' promised return with news; and we note that his first thought when he hears of the "good old man's" slaying—after a somewhat perfunctory "O heavy deed!"—is that

> It had been so with us had we been there.

For though, as we shall see later when he fronts Laertes, he is no poltroon, his nerve is shaken now. Yet the supple brain works but the quicker and better under the pressure of fear; casting about and ahead, anticipating arguments, devising answers and excuses, planning new moves, and keenly alert—diplomatist that he is—to the ever-shifting pattern of events. But he is anxious above all at the moment to be out of the neighborhood of the lurking Hamlet, surrounded by his guards again, and his "wisest friends." And the scene's concluding rhymed couplet rings with his anxiety.

> *Rosencrantz and Guildenstern, with what help they have mustered, find Hamlet and—speaking fair, as they have been bidden to—summon him to go with them to the King. He pretends to comply, but suddenly turns and runs, an obvious lunatic; and they all have to chase after him.*

It is a macabre business, this torchlight hue and cry through the darkened castle after a lunatic homicide, and the search for the body—which he has ignominiously bundled beneath a staircase. The Folio gives us, for the short scene's opening:

> *Enter Hamlet.*
> HAM. Safely stowed.
> GENTLEMEN WITHIN. *Hamlet,* Lord *Hamlet.*
> HAM. What noise? Who calls on *Hamlet?*
> Oh heere they come.
> *Enter Ros. and Guildensterne.*

Take Q2's more cursory

> *Enter Hamlet, Rosencraus, and others.*

be directly to her on the inner stage, or on the outer to be joined there by her. The obvious beginning here is with his

> Where is your son?

or with her

> Ah! my good lord, what have I seen to-night!

Does not then "There's matter . . . understand them" remain in the Folio text by oversight, and will not the producer—if he follows the Folio; and I think he should —be right to omit it?

into consideration also, and we have Hamlet stealing in, possibly
from between the now-closed curtains of the inner stage,[37] the distant voices of men seeking him, his sight of their torches as they
come. It proves to be Rosencrantz and Guildenstern, securely
joined now "with some further aid"; and, though they "speak
fair," turned peremptory too:

> What have you done, my lord, with the dead body?

Twenty-five lines of combative dialogue follow; Hamlet, masterly in madness, hitting hard, Rosencrantz driven back upon
futile dignity for self-defense. Before fellow-courtiers and servants,
to have his princely companion call him a "sponge"!

> Ay, sir; that soaks up the King's countenance, his rewards, his
> authorities. But such officers do the King best service in the end:
> he keeps them, like an ape, in the corner of his jaw; first mouthed,
> to be last swallowed: when he needs what you have gleaned, it is
> but squeezing you, and, sponge, you shall be dry again.

—a change, indeed, from that first welcome to "my excellent good
friends," and most unpleasantly near the mark. But, homicide and
madman though he be, Hamlet is still a prince. He must go with
them to the King, but they treat him with consideration still. And
despite his wild talk he seems about to go quietly:

> The body is with the King, but the King is not with the body.
> The King is a thing. . . . Of nothing: bring me to him.

—when suddenly, with a

> Hide fox, and all after.[38]

he bolts away from them down the dark corridors, madder than
ever. And the hue and cry goes on.

*The King, having hastily called up his "wisest friends," i.e. gath-
ered a few members of his Council round him (and being
certainly now attended by his guards), has Hamlet brought
before him, to be dispatched at once to England. Against
force and authority there is no appeal, and Hamlet makes
none. When he is gone we learn that on reaching England he
is to be put to death.*

---

[37] They must be closed, if only for the removing of the furniture of the closet-
scene.

[38] F1 only; and our only indication of the running-away—which may, therefore,
be a late addition. But it is a valuable one.

ANOTHER short scene; and this succession of them, by contrast with the long ones gone before, helps to give us a sense of events now speeding on.

Q2's economical stage direction

Enter King, and two or three.

we may, I think, legitimately translate into his appearance attended by such of his Council—of his "wisest friends"—as could be hastily "called up" to approve of what he means to do.[39] He has regained some outward equanimity at least:

> How dangerous is it that this man goes loose!
> Yet must not we put the strong law on him:
> He's loved of the distracted multitude,
> Who like not in their judgment, but their eyes;
> And where 'tis so, the offender's scourge is weigh'd,
> But never the offence. To bear all smooth and even,
> This sudden sending him away must seem
> Deliberate pause. . . .

It is the first we hear of the distracted multitude and their love—soon, moreover, to be fastened on Laertes. We may even suspect that the idea has only now struck Claudius—and Shakespeare! It is none the worse a one for that. Did the murder of their colleague not move them, fear of the mob is ever wakeful in the Conciliar mind.

Then, with

Enter Rosencrantz and all the rest.

[39] F1's *Enter King*, which turns the following speech into a soliloquy, is, of course, inadmissible. Claudius' private thoughts and plans we are to know later; these are the reasons of state he gives to his Councilors. Modern editions are apt to have *Enter King, attended*—which is a little too vague. Dover Wilson gives us *The King seated at a table on the dais with "two or three" councillors of state*. If this implies a setting upon the inner stage at the Globe, there would hardly be time (between the closet-scene and now) to arrange it. But a more important objection is that while such "a discovery of the King in Council"—or something very like it—will lend importance to the scene itself, it destroys the fluidity of movement which gives us a Claudius, at this juncture, coming to no halt till he has rid himself of his enemy. There are the checks of the "prayer-" and the "closet-" scenes; but, these apart, and to compensate for them, the action from the crisis of the play-scene to Hamlet's departure is—metaphorically and literally—"on foot." The sense of this will be appreciably lessened by even a short passage for Claudius "seated at a table." The mere physical aspect of a play's action can sometimes be as significant as the dialogue itself.

the King finds himself surrounded and supported by courtiers and guards besides, panoplied in authority and power. And Hamlet has been securely caught this time:

> But where is he?
> Without, my lord; guarded, to know your pleasure.
> Bring him before us.
> Ho, Guildenstern! bring in my lord.

It is the haling of a prisoner before his judge.[40]

From their last encounter, from the sight of the mimic poisoning, it was Claudius who fled, leaving Hamlet ecstatically triumphant. And we have had fine verbal displays from him since; in the rating of Rosencrantz and Guildenstern, the refusal to kill the King at prayer, in his moral victory over his mother. But the quieter "counteraction" has proved by so much the more efficient that here he is, captive and disarmed, the sword suspended such a short while since above his unconscious enemy in Guildenstern's safekeeping, a dozen others ready to be drawn against him, and branded as a dangerous maniac before the world.

We are halfway through the story. And not by words, but in this single picture, the situation and its irony (the harvest to date) is summed up and made eloquent. Here is Claudius, the grieved father and merciful king, sympathy and approval surrounding him, and before him stands the culprit, the homicide, Hamlet. And while we listen, with the Councilors and courtiers, to the King's curt questions and Hamlet's oracular replies (he has his "madness" for defense still; it is gladly allowed him), we know, as

---

[40] Once again, stage directions are in question. Most modern editions follow the Folio with a simple *Enter Rosecnrantz*; some add *. . . and others*, and, of their own accord, commit themselves later to a few nondescript "attendants." But the hint to the producer in Q2's *Enter Rosencraus and all the rest* was to bring on the full strength of the company, surround the King with every safeguard and give to Hamlet's banishment all possible importance. A significant and striking dramatic effect. Dover Wilson gives us

> *Rosencrantz, Guildenstern and others enter.*

and prefers Q2's

> Ho [actually "How"], bring in the Lord.

to F1's

> Hoa, Guildensterne? Bring in my Lord.

This last may not be the logical sequel to *and all the rest* (though even that "all" still excludes Hamlet's guards), but it gives us Guildenstern in personal charge, as he would be, of the distinguished prisoner, and carrying the surrendered sword.

they do not, that all this is beside the point. For Claudius cares no more about the dead Polonius at this juncture than Hamlet does; and it is in the latent thoughts of the two as they face each other that the drama lies. At the crisis of the play-scene it seemed as if the struggle would surge into the open, but here each is back in his ambush again. We shall guess at Hamlet's thought, when we hear that so innocently astonished

> For England?

—since behind it, and the blithely reiterated

> But, come; for England! . . . Come, for England!

with which he beckons after him the schoolfellows turned jailers, will echo for us his recent grim forebodings of treachery in the "letters sealed," and the mandate marshaling him to knavery. The remembrance should sharpen too our questioning of Claudius' gentle

> Hamlet, this deed, for thine especial safety,
> Which we do tender, as we dearly grieve
> For that which thou hast done, must send thee hence
> With fiery quickness . . . .

and his so suspiciously kindly air.

To Claudius' inmost mind we have till now been sparingly and, as it were, but grudgingly admitted; fitly so, for he does not love exploring it himself. Shakespeare has let him keep up appearances. Except for a solitary (and it may be a subsequently added) aside, not till *The Murder of Gonzago* shook him to the depths was there any avowal of guilt. This apart, we have seen him as Gertrude and his Court see him, with Hamlet's jealous hatred to be discounted, with only the Ghost's word for it that he is other than he seems. He is, moreover, one of those most clever scoundrels; he never lies when he need not and lets the straight road carry him just as far as it will. This dispatch to England; patently, for Hamlet's sake, it is the right thing to do. And the game seems so certainly in his hands that he cannot deny himself a little fun with his victim:

> For England?
>   Ay, Hamlet.
>   Good.
> So is it, if thou knew'st our purposes.

Hamlet, as we know, suspects something of them, and is an adept himself at equivoque:

> I see a cherub that sees them.

So, for a moment, the two stand there, as if mutually enjoying some secret joke to the confounding of the lookers-on.

They part. Claudius is left alone; the mask comes off, his mind is revealed; Hamlet's intuition is verified:

> And England, if my love thou hold'st at aught,
>   . . . thou mayst not coldly set
> Our sovereign process, which imports at full,
> By letters conjuring to that effect,
> The present death of Hamlet. Do it, England;
> For like the hectic in my blood he rages,
> And thou must cure me. Till I know 'tis done,
> Howe'er my haps, my joys were ne'er begun.

With which conventional full-close this chapter of the story and the struggle ends; and another is foreshadowed, with the "counter-action" definitely in the ascendant and Hamlet on the defensive.

While this is passing at Elsinore, Fortinbras and his army are traversing Danish territory nearby. On his way to the harbor, Hamlet encounters one of its officers. He reflects upon the contrast between Fortinbras' confident march towards victory and glory, and his own present defeat.

> *Enter Fortinbras and his army over the stage.*

—it is again one of Shakespeare's well-tried effects of contrast. Against the treacherous King and his Court are set the frank young soldier and his "lawless resolutes"; he is on his way with them to prove his "unimproved mettle." We have heard enough of him already for the contrast to make its effect. Incidentally the courtesy of his speech belies his and his army's earlier reputation:

> Go, captain, from me greet the Danish King;
> Tell him that, by his licence, Fortinbras
> Craves the conveyance of a promis'd march
> Over his kingdom. You know the rendezvous.
> If that his majesty would aught with us,
> We shall express our duty in his eye,
> And let him know so.

Here then, we are meant to feel, is a leader who is disciplining both himself and his men.

But the contrast is to be intensified. For hardly has the martial little pageant passed than

> *Enter Hamlet, Rosencraus, etc . . .*

—Hamlet the doomed exile, disarmed and under guard.[41]

By just so much he misses an encounter with his spiritual rival. They are not to meet till Fortinbras, "with conquest come from Poland," will pass this way again to find him a conqueror, too, and dead. He detains instead the returning captain, who does not know this prisoner for what he is—they politely "Sir" each other as equals[42]—and, in answer to his questions, tells him that

> We go to gain a little patch of ground
> That hath in it no profit but the name.
> To pay five ducats, five, I would not farm it;
> Nor will it yield to Norway or the Pole
> A ranker rate, should it be sold in fee.

Yet it appears that two armies are to "debate the question of this straw" to the death. The captain goes his way; and the stage is cleared for Hamlet's commentary:

> How all occasions do inform against me,
> And spur my dull revenge! . . .[43]

---

[41] This does not, I think, stretch Q2's summary, etc., too far. He is treated with the respect due to a prince. He is under arrest nevertheless.

[42] The intention is stressed in their farewell

> I humbly thank you, sir.
> God be wi' you, sir.

with Rosencrantz'

> Will 't please you go, my lord?

coming immediately after.

[43] "The stage is cleared"—quite undisguisedly.

> ROSENCRANTZ. Will 't please you go, my lord?
> HAMLET. I'll be with you straight. Go a little before.

—and leave me to soliloquize!

Shakespeare was not interested, it would seem, in nice stagecraft for its own sake. Still, he seldom, in his maturity, takes refuge in such simplicities as this. Its verisimilitude will pass, *just* pass. Is his mind so occupied with the *matter* of the scene, that his sense of the theater is in momentary abeyance?

The Folio omits the soliloquy and the rest of Hamlet's share in the scene. If the play had to be shortened, here, at a stroke, were several minutes saved; and, though the character suffers, the story hardly does.

With scenery's scene-division destroying continuity of action, it soon became

He is to pass out of the action for a while. That would be reason enough for overlaying our most recent sight of him, masked in his madness, with a juster one. But we are to be given, besides, a view of Hamlet which we have hardly had before, a judgment at parting. And in the light of it we shall look on him a little differently when he returns.

He has intimately revealed himself to us more than once. But till now he has only once measured himself against any standard but his own; when, upon the brink of the ordeal of the play-scene, he made Horatio's calm strength the text of some wistful self-reproach. That adventure is over. He has thrown away the fruits of it; and he now stands contemplating Fortinbras of the "strong hand and terms compulsatory," seeing himself in that light as nakedly as men do upon the morrow of a failure.

His self-indictment is the bitterer for its cold detachment:

> What is a man,
> If his chief good and market of his time
> Be but to sleep and feed? a beast, no more.
> Sure he that made us with such large discourse,
> Looking before and after, gave us not
> That capability and god-like reason
> To fust in us unus'd. . . .

He has not left it unused. Yet to what use has he put it? To fostering

> some craven scruple
> Of thinking too precisely on the event;
> A thought which, quartered, hath but one part wisdom
> And ever three parts coward. . . .

customary in the theater to omit Fortinbras and his army too; the entire scene disappears. But upon Shakespeare's stage this would not do. There some bridge was wanted, which would both separate and link the two scenes, one dealing with the death of Polonius and the banishing of Hamlet, the other with Ophelia's madness, Polonius by then in his grave and Hamlet far away. Besides which Shakespeare wants, I think, to keep Hamlet's "madness" and Ophelia's madness apart.

Dover Wilson (in *The Manuscript of Shakespeare's Hamlet*, p. 31), arguing that the soliloquy cannot be, as some critics have held, a late addition to the play, says, "The Fortinbras scene was patently written in order to give occasion to the soliloquy." This, I venture to think, goes too far. Hamlet's appearance can certainly be called the most important thing in the scene. But, apart from the technical need for some bridge scene here, the dramatic effect made by Fortinbras and his army as a contrast to Claudius and his Court is important in itself.

—but even in the misery of defeat he knows he is no coward. The merciless truth suddenly rings out in the baffled

> I do not know
> Why yet I live to say 'This thing's to do';
> Sith I have cause, and will, and strength, and means
> To do't. . . .

He does not know. And if godlike reason cannot tell him why, yet will not let him act in ignorance, what is it but a mockery and a curse? Therefore:

> from this time forth,
> My thoughts be bloody, or be nothing worth!

Upon which negation of all he has been and believed in until now, not envious any longer of "blood and judgment . . . well commingled," but just of brute capacity for deeds of blood, we part from him. A changed and hardened man; yet not so changed. For even while he thinks that at last he is facing facts he is ignoring them, confident that he has not merely "cause and will" but "strength and means" to act—in this very moment of his helplessness and defeat! The idea and not the thing itself, that is what still counts with him.

A Third Movement

This will take us to the end of the play. The King's "counter-action" is the main motive force; Hamlet, till the last scene, an all-but-passive figure.

Three scenes interpose between his departure and return. Before examining them in detail, it may be worth while to note their relation to the action as a whole. Shakespeare, as we have seen, carefully confines this to Elsinore.[1] We do not travel with the

---

[1] See p. 38 *et seq.* One must be wary of imputing dramatic motives to Shakespeare. But I think this "carefully" may be justified. With a continuing need of little "bridge scenes" for the spacing-out of the action, the most convenient, and—for most Elizabethan dramatists, Shakespeare among them—the customary thing would be to transport us to wherever the material for one happened at the moment to be. But several other of the plays of this period—*Twelfth Night, Measure for Measure, Othello*—show a tendency to concentrate the action in some single city or district, at any rate. If the story lends itself to such treatment this does give a certain stability to its framework. And in *Hamlet* this modified "unity of place" is certainly turned to definite dramatic account.

story's travelers; neither to Paris with Laertes nor to Norway
with the Ambassadors, nor even towards England now with
Hamlet. And it will be to the good to be quit of him and the strain
of his troubles for a time—or really we might begin to weary of
them. Yet the distraction should not be complete. For he and they
are the marrow of the play, and the continuity of our interest in
them must not be definitely broken.

In these three scenes the double demand is fulfilled and its
conflict reconciled. Ophelia's lyric madness strikes a new note; but
we are conscious of Hamlet's hand in it, and of something like
pretense with him turned tragic reality for her. Horatio is there
to remind us of him. Laertes' frontal attack and his frank cry for
vengeance, suddenly detonating, contrast sharply with Hamlet's
subtleties; but it is against Hamlet that they are soon deflected.
And even while the plot against him is hatching we are warned
of his return. So the matter of the scenes is not merely incidental,
but rooted in the story, knit together in a certain unity and by a
close continuity of action. And it makes firm passage across that
always difficult interval between a play's mid-crisis and its final
climax and catastrophe.

*The death of her father at the hands of her lover unhinges Ophel-
ia's mind. Laertes, returned from France and believing the
King to blame, raises a rebellion to avenge Polonius. The
King courageously faces it, and calms him and proceeds to tell
him where the guilt really lies.*

> *Enter the Queen, Horatio and a Gentleman . . . .*

—this scene and the three that follow it run to some length, 760
lines and more between them. Except from the last, Hamlet is
absent, and even in that, his cause is not in question. We have,
then, a fresh range, an exempted interplay, of character and incident, and the stagecraft of it repays close analysis.

The Queen's opening lines—

> I will not speak with her. . . . What would she have?

—are keyed to the last we heard of her; she is still nerve-racked
and guilt-ridden, and incapable of facing fresh trouble. Ophelia is
not named. We guess at her from that

> She speaks much of her father . . . .

But there is a sense of grave and uncanny calamity in this very omission of her name.

The Folio thriftily turns over to Horatio the Gentleman's speech describing her. It asks skillful and discreet speaking, certainly, and a minor actor might well not do it full credit. But this is to rob Horatio of the characteristic quiet in which he listens. His considered comment:

> 'Twere good she were spoken with, for she may strew
> Dangerous conjectures in ill-breeding minds.

and the concluding

> Let her come in.

the Folio also gives to the Queen; and modern editors leave her this last, on the ground, presumably, that she should give the order, not he.[2] But I think the Quarto's intention is clear. The Gentleman stands respectfully aloof. Horatio speaks his two lines of prudent counsel in the Queen's ear. She is still too distressed to make more than a gesture of assent, which he translates for her into words. To give the order he leaves her isolated on the outer stage, and her misery finds vent and relief in the plaintive singsong of

> To my sick soul, as sin's true nature is,
> Each toy seems prologue to some great amiss:
> So full of artless jealousy is guilt,
> It spills itself in fearing to be spilt.

Then she pulls herself together to receive Ophelia.

But Ophelia is already there—if we follow the Quarto; and again, I think, the dramatic intention is plain. The editors not only follow the Folio in politely postponing her appearance till the Queen has quite finished speaking, but of their own accord they have the Gentleman go out to fetch her and formally usher her in. That is far too proper and sane. The Folio only has

> *Enter Ophelia distracted.*

The original intention is, surely, that she should dart through the door when it is opened and stand for a moment or so gazing at

---

[2] The Folio only gives it her as an integral part of the gift of the lines taken from Horatio in exchange for the Gentleman's speech.

the Queen, whom she does not in her madness recognize.[8] Hence her

> Where is the beauteous majesty of Denmark?

and its pathetic irony. Where, indeed, in this haggard, fearful woman, is the "beauteous majesty" that has been the cause of all this ill?

We may even here take a hint from Q1 and its

Enter Ofelia playing on a Lute, and her haire downe singing.

Having had her way and been admitted to the presence of this disappointingly unknown lady, she becomes absorbed in her lute and her singing.[4] The three[5] stand hopelessly gazing at her, and listening to the "conceit upon her father," with its

> He is dead and gone, lady,
>   He is dead and gone;
> At his head a grass-green turf;
>   At his heels a stone.

The King comes quietly in. She sings on unheeding:

> White his shroud as the mountain snow . . .
>   Larded with sweet flowers;
> Which bewept to the grave did go
>   With true-love showers.

And from this her poor mind travels to a perverted mirroring of the tragedy of her love for Hamlet:

> To-morrow is Saint Valentine's day,
>   All in the morning betime,
> And I a maid at your window,
>   To be your Valentine.

> Then up he rose, and donn'd his clothes,
>   And dupp'd the chamber door;
> Let in the maid, that out a maid
>   Never departed more.

---

[8] That "she is importunate, indeed distract" is the first thing we have heard of her. Shakespeare and his audience would imagine unseen attendants in some anteroom, barring her way. The King later on implies that his "Switzers" are—or ought to be—there.

[4] The dramatic point of the lute is that you must stand—or, better, sit—still if you are to attempt to play it. Modern Ophelias have an ineffective habit of drifting vaguely about the stage. A lute is at least an admirable anchor.

[5] Or, if the Gentleman has gone, the Queen and Horatio.

Wiseacre warnings against that manner of undoing could not save her from this one. The merry bit of bawdry which follows:

> By Gis and by Saint Charity,
>   Alack, and fie for shame!
> Young men will do't, if they come to't;
>   By cock, they are to blame.
>
> Quoth she, Before you tumbled me,
>   You promised me to wed.
> So would I ha' done, by yonder sun,
>   An thou hadst not come to my bed.

may remind her listeners (and us) that it was with such humor Hamlet so brutally bespattered her as they sat watching the play. Here is its echo now upon her pitiably innocent lips. Then it is as if she tried to reassemble scattered fragments of the thoughts she last controlled:

> I hope all will be well. We must be patient. But I cannot choose but weep, to think they should lay him i' the cold ground. My brother shall know of it . . . .

For the rest, she addresses phantoms—

> Come, my coach! Good-night, ladies; good-night, sweet ladies; good-night, good-night.

—and is gone. The kindly Claudius sends Horatio after:

> Follow her close; give her good watch, I pray you . . . .

and is left alone with the Queen.

Gertrude is silent. She has not spoken since, at his coming, she appealed to him with a

> Alas! look here, my lord.

—for this guiltless suffering confounds her. Claudius can always find words.

His twenty-line speech that follows is technically remarkable. It sets the scene in appropriate time and circumstance. Polonius' death and Hamlet's departure are definitely relegated to the past; the recent past, for

> we have done but greenly
> In hugger-mugger to inter him . . . .

(the implication is of haste as well as secrecy), yet not so recent but that Laertes

> is in secret come from France;
> Feeds on his wonder, keeps himself in clouds,
> And wants not buzzers to infect his ear
> With pestilent speeches of his father's death . . . .

—the "in secret" a subtle stroke of imprecision. It sounds—only sounds—as if the tragic news had brought him from France; but Claudius does not know how long he has been here. Now, had Shakespeare put all this in its more obvious place, linked it directly to Hamlet's parting soliloquy, made it an explanatory prelude to Ophelia's appearance, it would only have been of bare practical use. But by placing it here, the lyric madness is left to be a vibrant sequel to the hard, intellectual drive, the dry sanity, of the soliloquy. It is, moreover, a thing so moving in itself as to banish other things from our mind. Therefore, in this anticlimax which follows, we the more passively accept these incongruous time suggestions. The speech itself is of the very stuff of anticlimax:

> O Gertrude, Gertrude!
> When sorrows come, they come not single spies,
> But in battalions. . . .

Just such unlooked-for, inscrutable, addition to evil it is that will set us brooding, as Gertrude silently broods, or, with Claudius, gloomily summing up errors and chances. And it serves besides to separate Ophelia's pathos from Laertes' anger; they are to be thrown, a little later, into sharp contrast.

Now comes

> *A noise within.*

and the Queen's nerves are at once on edge again.[6] But the King —no coward, it would seem, when his conscience is clear— listens calmly to the scared "messenger's" tale of a Laertes, not merely bent upon amends for his father's death, but head of a rabble that "call him lord" and

---

[6] Here again the Folio knits the action a little closer than does Q2, by giving her the usefully quick, nervous,

> Alack, what noyse is this?

and eliminating the King's "Attend"—his call to someone in the anteroom.

> cry 'Choose we; Laertes shall be king!'
> Caps, hands and tongues, applaud it to the clouds,
> 'Laertes shall be king, Laertes king!'

Not that Laertes proves so very treasonable. Once in the royal presence he seems anxious to be free of his "rabble," who, for their part, too, become biddable enough. The messenger's magniloquent

> Save yourself, my lord;
> The ocean, overpeering of his list,
> Eats not the flats with more impetuous haste
> Than young Laertes . . . .

and the crash proclaiming that

> The doors are broke.

resolve themselves, in fact, into a hubbub in the anteroom and half a dozen fierce speeches from a passionate young man, with whom Claudius very easily deals. The "giant-like" rebellion is stillborn. It is so for a dramatically good reason. Here as elsewhere Shakespeare stops short of enlarging the play's action beyond the bounds of personal conflict. We heard at the outset the tale of Denmark's dangers from abroad, and have seen the formidable Fortinbras and his army march harmlessly by. And here is rebellion—fruit of the rottenness within the state—brought into the very anteroom. But no further. For if once these wider issues took the stage the more intimate ones would lose, by comparison, their intensity and force. It may be owned, however, that this rebellion—shaken in the wings like a thunder-sheet—is not in itself very convincing.[7]

---

[7] The political part of the play's story is told mainly by implication. Claudius, upon his brother's death, and, it would seem, in Hamlet's absence at Wittenberg, has assumed the crown; and his possession of it has been apparently ratified by the Council, over which we first see him presiding. He has been so far "elected" by them that Hamlet can speak of his having

> Popped in between the election and my hopes . . .

And among them he finds the "wisest friends" upon whose support he relies when it comes to sending Hamlet to England.

But Hamlet, we have heard, is

> lov'd of the distracted multitude,
> Who like not in their judgment, but their eyes. . . .

—and he (and Shakespeare) will have had, I fancy, this love in mind when speaking, a scene later, at the very moment of banishment, of having not only the "will" but the "power" to turn the tables on the King. And now the multitude,

Claudius deals with Laertes very skillfully indeed. The quiet
dignity, the cool courage:

> Let him go, Gertrude; do not fear our person:
> There's such divinity doth hedge a king,
> That treason can but peep to what it would . . . .

and the old caressing use of the name, such reproach in its soft
cadence now:

> What is the cause, Laertes,
> That thy rebellion looks so giant-like?
> . . . Tell me, Laertes,
> Why thou art thus incens'd?

the "rabble," have suddenly given their hearts to another handsome, gallant, and
much-wronged young man. This may seem a mere dramatic convenience, and it
is one. But it illustrates also their folly and instability; and, for other strokes to
the picture, we have the King's contempt for them, the Queen's

> false Danish dogs!

(note the implication that she is, by birth, a foreigner to Denmark; such things
slip out at such a moment), Laertes' desire to be quit of their compromising help,
and their own facile conversion from wolves to sheep. Finally they fade away, no
one even troubling to dismiss them. It is certainly not from among them that
Laertes himself is to make choice of the "wisest friends" he will; these, as the
very phrase tells us, are meant to be men akin to the King's own councilors.

Such strokes and hints the Elizabethan actors could be trusted to color in and
elaborate; their implications would be plain to them. A Claudius would instinctively
respond to the outrage of the claim:

> Choose we, Laertes shall be king!

and the messenger as inevitably accentuate the *"we"*—though, indeed, the verse
does it for him. And a Laertes would know just how coldly to temper his

> Sirs, stand you all without. . . . I pray you, give me leave. . . . I thank you;
> keep the door.

Small matters; but, if they stay unadjusted, picture and characters will lack their
exact value.

An Elizabethan audience, moreover, could co-ordinate this and other such fragments; and from their knowledge of kindred actualities fill in the gaps for themselves, and so make a sufficiently definite political background for the play. A
king and his Privy Council, a dispossessed heir sent into banishment, an excitable
populace, a rebellious young noble; they evaluated and related them each to other
without thinking, for it was a familiar scheme of things. To us it is not. The
political story of Hamlet is a sentence left with half the words missing. Shakespeare
purposely left it so that it might not encumber the more intimate theme. But
with no conjecture of the missing words the others must inevitably lack something
of their sense. Dover Wilson, both in his edition and his separate study of the
play, has dealt very illuminatingly with this aspect of it.

—what better defense against windy, overreaching wrath?[8] What better counter to the fierce

> Where is my father?

than the honest, uncompromising

> Dead.

He encourages the young man, not merely to "demand his fill," but to storm his fill also. And to such stuff as

> To hell, allegiance! vows, to the blackest devil!
> Conscience and grace, to the profoundest pit!
> I dare damnation . . . .
>   . . . only I'll be reveng'd
> Most throughly for my father.

responds only with a

> Who shall stay you?

nor even allows the vaunting response:

> My will, not all the world!

to draw from him an ironic smile. And he has reduced his rebel to a readiness, at least, to listen to reason, when the rabble voices are again heard at the door—awed voices now!—and Ophelia reappears.

She stands silent; she does not know him. We shall remember their pretty, familiar parting. This is how they meet again.[9]

There is every difference between this and our recent sight of her, between that phantom of a happy girl singing to her lute and this subdued, silent figure. She has been to the garden to gather herbs and flowers—halfway, so to speak, to the meadow where

---

[8] "The old caressing use of the name": we may not recall it, but the instruction to the actor to repeat the trick of that first

> And now, Laertes, what's the news with you?
>   . . . what is't, Laertes?
>   . . . What would'st thou beg, Laertes . . . ?

is plain.

[9] "This is how they meet again"—in terms of the play, that is to say; and (once more) these are the only effective terms. Shakespeare does not underline this, for that would only raise the question of its likelihood; and we might then recollect that Laertes had "in secret come from France" and ask: how could he not have seen her and already known of her madness? As it is, the effect is made that he sees her thus for the first time.

she is soon to meet her death. And she now begins a solemn sort of mimicry of the funeral her father was denied. She chants:

> They bore him barefac'd on the bier;
> Hey non nonny, nonny hey, nonny;
> And in his grave rain'd many a tear . . . .

and bends over the bier, which only she can see, with a

> Fare you well, my dove!

She reproaches the rest of them for not singing too:

> You must sing, 'a-down a-down,' An you call him a-down-a.[10]

She ceremoniously scatters her rosemary and rue, and distributes it and the flowers to her fellow-mourners. Then the poor brain loses hold for a moment even of its own fantasy, and she carols out a

> For bonny sweet Robin is all my joy.

but recollects, and chants for a second psalm:

> And will he not come again?
> And will he not come again?
> No, no, he is dead,
> Go to thy death-bed,
> He never will come again.
>
> His beard was as white as snow,
> All flaxen was his poll,
> He is gone, he is gone,
> And we cast away moan,
> God ha' mercy on his soul!

adding reverently

> And of all Christian souls, I pray God.

She cannot quite make out, I think, why they are not ready to follow with her to the grave. But if they will not go, she must. So she bids them a solemn

> God be wi' ye!

and departs, head bowed, hands folded, as quietly as she came;

---

[10] Dover Wilson's reading.

and the rough crowd at the door stand silent to let her pass.[11]

To this main melody of the action (so to call it) have been added the grace notes of the imagery of the flowers; rosemary for remembrance, pansies for thoughts, fennel and columbines:

> there's rue for you; and here's some for me; we may call it herb of grace o' Sundays. O! you must wear your rue with a difference. There's a daisy; I would give you some violets, but they withered all when my father died. . . .

And Laertes' part must be noted. His confidence of a moment since turns to bewildered helplessness:

> O rose of May!
> Dear maid, kind sister, sweet Ophelia!

But he can win no answer from her:

> O heavens! is't possible a young maid's wits
> Should be as mortal as an old man's life? . . .

—for indeed he might be speaking to the dead. He has lost her, too, and even more tragically; and, as she goes, he sums all up in the accusing:

> Do you see this, O God?

But his grief has left him malleable, and the King is quick to the advantage. Sympathy itself—

> Go but apart,
> Make choice of whom your wisest friends you will,
> And they shall hear and judge 'twixt you and me:

[11] Whatever the origin and value of Q1 as a text, we may take it, I think, that *Enter Ofelia playing on a Lute, and her haire downe singing* is a genuinely Shakespearian stage direction and that the later *Enter Ofelia as before* merely means "still mad." She will not be encumbered now with her lute; and—though it is a small point—the flowers are pretty certainly real, not imaginary.

The mimicking of a funeral ceremony is, I believe, to be justified by the text. At first Ophelia is spoken of as "importunate and distract." The second entry is, to begin with, a silent one. Its songs—in contrast, at least, to "Saint Valentine's day"—are grave and slow; and it is the first line of the first one—

> They bore him barefac'd on the bier . . .

—that gives, as I take it, the cue for the action intended. And the distribution of the herbs and flowers was an ordinary funeral custom. Carew Hazlitt, in *Popular Antiquities of Great Britain* (1870, Vol. 2, p. 175), quotes Misson: ". . . when the Funeral Procession is ready to set out they nail up the coffin and a Servant presents the Company with sprigs of Rosemary; everyone takes a sprig and carries it in his hand, till the Body is put into the Grave, at which time they all throw in their sprigs after it." There is ample authority besides for the use of other flowers.

> If by direct or by collateral hand
> They find us touch'd, we will our kingdom give,
> Our crown, our life and all that we call ours,
> To you in satisfaction . . . .

—he leads the young man away, and the rest disperse. The rebellion is forgotten.

Horatio receives news of Hamlet's return.

WHILE the King and Laertes are conferring elsewhere, Horatio hears of seafaring men who have letters for him. These prove to be from

> the ambassador that was bound for England . . .

and that is Hamlet, thus anonymously returned. From the reading of one letter, we learn the story—and incidentally that the seafaring men (who may thus look a little apprehensive, perhaps, in these royal and judicatory surroundings) are pirates. They have both attacked and rescued Hamlet:

> They have dealt with me like thieves of mercy; but they knew what they did; I am to do a good turn for them. Let the King have the letters I have sent; and repair thou to me with as much haste as thou wouldst fly death. . . . These good fellows will bring thee where I am. Rosencrantz and Guildenstern hold their course for England: of them I have much to tell thee. . . .

It is a scene of thirty-five lines only; its use to prepare Hamlet's return and save cumbersome explanations when he does appear. But there are signs that Shakespeare means to give it a slight dramatic coloring of its own. Q2 begins it with

> *Enter Horatio and others.*

What others? There is only need for an attendant, to be sent to fetch the sailors. The "others" are then, I fancy, meant to be another Rosencrantz and Guildenstern or the like, keeping a polite watch on the King's behalf upon Horatio, upon Hamlet's friend. It is noticeable that, though they know who he is ("but they knew what they did"), the pirates do not name Hamlet. "The ambassador that was bound for England" would be hint enough to the eavesdroppers; but this could be whispered. Horatio, of course, reads the letter to himself, and, departing with the pirates, only says:

> Come, I will give you way for these your letters;
> And do't the speedier that you may direct me
> To him from whom you brought them.

But (as we hear later) they do not—very wisely—go themselves to the King; the letters are given to one Claudio, and by him again to the "messenger" who does deliver them. A phrase in the letter itself ("These good fellows will bring thee where I am") suggests a hiding-place; and, till he was safely back at Court, Hamlet might well want to keep his whereabouts a secret, lest Claudius should have him privily murdered. It will be quite possible—the watchful courtiers at one side of the stage; Horatio and the pirates, conscious of their attention, at the other—to express enough of this in the scene's acting, to extract it from the dialogue, with no more than legitimate byplay added.[12] And whether or no Horatio is being watched, the pirates certainly make their mission as mysterious as possible.

The King has just proved his own innocence of Polonius' death when the news reaches him that Hamlet has returned. Laertes rejoices at the chance of vengeance thus offered him. The King devises a means for it. The Queen comes to tell them that Ophelia, in her madness, has drowned herself.

THE King and Laertes return, still in talk. The suggestion is—it keeps the action going—that there has been no break in their parley. The revelation of Hamlet's guilt we have not heard; Shakespeare does not want to overmultiply occasions for angry outbreaks by Laertes. And as to the "wisest friends" who were to "hear and judge"—that matter has gone the way of the rebellion —technically, rather in the interests of compression; but Claudius

---

[12] F1 begins the scene

Enter Horatio with an attendant.

(and most modern editors substantially follow). This is of a piece with the rest of its economizing of actors; and it may well be that the Quarto reading and its business—if I am right about it—was not thought important enough to preserve. It is not important. But the play is full of such superfluous touches, which yet enrich its dramatic life and, as in this case, rescue a scene from mere utility.

can do his own persuading, and it is clear that his smooth tongue
has already made good play:

> Now must your conscience my acquittance seal,
> And you must put me in your heart for friend,
> Sith you have heard, and with a knowing ear,
> That he which hath your noble father slain
> Pursu'd my life.

Remaining doubts he flatters away. Why was not Hamlet put
on public trial?

> The Queen his mother
> Lives almost by his looks; and for myself—
> My virtue or my plague, be it either which—
> She's so conjunctive to my life and soul,
> That, as the star moves not but in his sphere,
> I could not but by her. . . .

To have your sovereign so confess himself to you bespeaks intimate friendship indeed! An even likelier reason follows, and a
darker confidence is hinted at:

> you must not think
> That we are made of stuff so flat and dull
> That we can let our beard be shook with danger
> And think it pastime. You shortly shall hear more. . . .

Upon which—shortly indeed!—news comes; but not the expected
happy news of Hamlet's death. He is alive and back in Denmark.

Since we already know it we can the better mark the different
effects of the surprise upon the two of them; the King's perplexity
(and at the queer mockery of the letter, so mysteriously delivered,
the sense of lurking danger stirs in him again); Laertes' joy:

> But let him come;
> It warms the very sickness in my heart
> That I shall live and tell him to his teeth,
> 'Thus didest thou.'

But that prospect does not suit Claudius at all; for what has not
Hamlet to tell in return? We perceive his mind momentarily fum-
bling; it is for the first time:

> If it be so, Laertes,
> As how should it be so? how otherwise? . . .

Then he sees his way clear, and is soon circumspectly leading his tamed young rebel along it.

In the scales against much masterly compression, however, we now find Shakespeare dispensing a hundred lines and more for the winning of Laertes to a murderous plot against Hamlet, and lavishing in the process abundant and very variously relevant talk about Lamord the Norman and his horsemanship, Laertes' own skill in fence and Hamlet's jealousy of it with, besides, some philosophizing by Claudius, which comes, at first blush, a little strangely from him.

Truly the thing could be more thriftily[18] done; but its amplitude can be accounted for. Claudius must advance cautiously, he would feel, towards the very unpleasant proposal he has in mind, and he habitually moves behind a smoke screen of words. Will this exuberant young man consent to forgo an overt, a spectacular revenge? And, say he can be persuaded to agree to the duel in the guise of a fencing match, will he—for he is a gallant fellow—be a party to the "little shuffling" that is to leave him with the "unabated sword," which will be Hamlet's death?

But the management of Laertes here is really masterly; and Claudius, the arch-diplomat, cannot but enjoy—and be ready to linger over—the exercise of his craft. First, we have tonic to vanity in a subtly reinforced dose of praise. The eulogy of the horsemanship of the gentleman of Normandy makes the account of *his* praise of Laertes the swordsman the sweeter hearing:

> He made confession of you,
> And gave you such a masterly report
> For art and exercise in your defence,
> And for your rapier most especially,
> That he cried out, 'twould be a sight indeed
> If one could match you; the scrimers of their nation,
> He swore, had neither motion, guard, nor eye,
> If you oppos'd them. . . .

---

18 Dover Wilson (agreeing with Verity) scents something like topical allusion in the talk of the horsemanship, an indirect reference to Southampton's prowess in this kind. If this be so—and it has something the air of being so—it is another instance (cf. the talk of the "eyrie of children") of Shakespeare's skill at dragging in such things where they will do his play least harm, though we cannot say they do it none. But the passage survives in the Folio. Did its interest, then, prove more than topical, did it justify itself dramatically? Or, a further possibility (privately suggested to me by Dr. R. B. McKerrow); was it never a part of the acted text?

And talk of Hamlet's envy of such skill is a last drop to the mixture, and the sweetest of all.

Youthful complacency is then ruffled by the suddenly distrustful

> Laertes, was your father dear to you?
> Or are you like the painting of a sorrow,
> A face without a heart?

And a dozen sententious lines follow—wide of the mark for Laertes in their talk of the mortality of love and the need to seize the moment as it passes—which have, indeed, for an immediate dramatic excuse only the stoking of his impatience to come to the point. Shakespeare makes them serve also for a rather vague revelation of a Claudius grown conscious that Gertrude's love is lost to him (he knows not why, but, since the scene in her closet, we know), too vague, one must own, to be very effective. Then a touch sets the fume ablaze:

> But to the quick o' the ulcer:
> Hamlet comes back; what would you undertake
> To show yourself your father's son in deed
> More than in words?
>   To cut his throat i' the church.

That is the ripe mood. And the King's bland and (for us) admirably ambiguous response—

> No place, indeed, should murder sanctuarize;
> Revenge should have no bounds.

—should steady him in it. The young man is well in hand. Success indeed betters expectation; for not merely is the trick of the unbated sword embraced, but, says Laertes,

> for that purpose I'll anoint my sword.
> I bought an unction of a mountebank,
> So mortal that but dip a knife in it,
> Where it draws blood no cataplasm so rare,
> Collected from all simples that have virtue
> Under the moon, can save the thing from death
> That is but scratched withal. . . .

Poison! How will Claudius, of all people, respond to that? Interesting to watch him first play with the notion, a little reluctantly; then, with that feline

> Soft! let me see . . . .

yield—once more!—to its fascination. For even so must he have looked when he pictured to himself his brother sleeping in the orchard; even so, perhaps, he may have turned as—at another rumor in his anteroom—he here turns with a tender

> How now, sweet queen!

She comes with the tale of Ophelia's death, its candid beauty in sharp contrast to the secret wickedness brewing. The "fantastic garlands" themselves:

> Of crow-flowers, nettles, daisies and long purples,
> That liberal shepherds give a grosser name,
> But our cold maids do dead men's fingers call them . . .

seem an innocent reproach to the unction which

> no cataplasm so rare,
> Collected from all simples that have virtue
> Under the moon . . .

can counteract.

The speech fulfills divers ends. It gives actuality to Ophelia's unseen death. We have seen her sitting singing to her lute, and back from the garden with flowers in her hands. We now hear how

> There, on the pendant boughs her coronet weeds
> Clambering to hang, an envious sliver broke,
> When down her weedy trophies and herself
> Fell in the weeping brook. Her clothes spread wide,
> And, mermaid-like, awhile they bore her up;
> Which time she chanted snatches of old lauds,
> As one incapable of her own distress,
> Or like a creature native and indu'd
> Unto that element; but long it could not be
> Till that her garments, heavy with their drink,
> Pull'd the poor wretch from her melodious lay
> To muddy death.

—which matches in vividness our last sight of her living. And the beauty and pity of it incidentally help to rescue Gertrude in our eyes from the degradation of Hamlet's painting of her

> In the rank sweat of an enseamed bed,
> Stewed in corruption, honeying and making love
> Over the nasty sty . . .

with the much more to that purpose in the closet-scene. She is to
have no further very prominent part in the play. We shall remember her as well as Ophelia by this.

The effect upon Laertes is interesting too. He has just, for
vengeance' sake, committed himself to an act of callous treachery.
After the first shock he listens quietly, and has no more to say
when the story ends than

<blockquote>Alas, then she is drown'd.</blockquote>

The Queen's speech has been a-brim with tears; and she now—
upon that

<blockquote>Drown'd, drown'd!</blockquote>

—breaks into a passion of weeping. Such grief and the solace of
it are not for him. Still,

<blockquote>It is our trick; nature her custom holds,
Let shame say what it will . . . .</blockquote>

and in spite of him the tears flow. He is not quite so satanic as
he thinks himself.

Hamlet, purged of his "madness," returning with Horatio to
Elsinore, pauses by the way to talk to an old man digging a
grave. It proves to be Ophelia's, and he hears himself cursed
by Laertes as the cause of her death. His love for her surges
up again; he cries his grief aloud. At which seeming mock-
ery, Laertes flies at his throat. They are parted. He is evidently
as mad as ever. He leaves them to think so; for how can he
explain?

To the contrast between the ugliness of the poison-plot and the
innocence of Ophelia's death succeeds another, between the
sophistications of the Court and the simplicity of

<blockquote>*Enter two clowns.*</blockquote>

Is she to be buried in Christian burial that wilfully seeks her
own salvation?

I tell thee she is; and therefore make her grave straight; the
crowner hath sat on her, and finds it Christian burial.[14]

---

[14] Note the slight but sufficient indication of the passing of time, "the crowner
hath sat on her": at least a day has passed. And Hamlet, by his letter in the last
scene, was to reach the Court "to-morrow."

And, while he gets some refreshing fun out of them, Shakespeare turns these two to more than comic use. They are ignorant hinds, with their "argal" and their "*se offendendo*"; but their perversion of an abstruse legal argument—

> Here lies the water; good: here stands the man; good: if the man go to this water and drown himself, it is, will he, nill he, he goes; mark you that; but if the water come to him, and drown him, he drowns not himself: argal, he that is not guilty of his own death shortens not his own life.

—is little more ridiculous than the argument itself[15]; and they pierce through verbiage and pretense to the heart of the present business with

> Will you ha' the truth on't? If this had not been a gentle-woman, she should have been buried out of Christian burial.
> Why, there thou sayest; and the more pity that great folk should have countenance in this world to drown or hang themselves more than their even Christian.

Here, indeed, in this simplicity, is an important element, which has been till now lacking in the play's scheme, and in the various provocations to thought set before Hamlet upon his spiritual journey. But with its addition the gamut will be fairly complete; in its range from the Players and their fiction to these ultimate facts, mirrored in the digging of a grave and in its harvest of Yorick's skull.

While the two bandy their shrewd humor:

> *Enter Hamlet and Horatio afarre off.*

It is the Folio's stage direction, and an unusual one. It brings the two on eight lines before Q2 does and leaves them there, "*afarre off,*" listening. I see dramatic intention in this. From the tenor of the letters to Horatio and the King do we not expect a Hamlet returning primed to prompt vengeance—for his own attempted murder also now? It is one more in the series of such surprises that he should quietly glide back into the action, and stand there so indifferent and detached. He is spiritually far off too. For it is Ophelia's grave that is digging, the Clown's song is a counterpart to hers:

---

15 For which see Furness and Dover Wilson.

> In youth, when I did love, did love,
> Methought it was very sweet,
> To contract, O! the time, for—ah!—my behove,
> O! methought there was nothing meet.

and the allusive pattern is completed by Hamlet's fastidious comment:

> Has this fellow no feeling of his business, that he sings at grave-making?

Had he no feeling either, who could turn his back obliviously upon the havoc he had made? It is he that is digging his grave.[16]

Even as Gertrude was spared by a hairsbreadth the knowledge —though at last she will learn—that her lover and husband is her husband's murderer, so Hamlet is here brought to the very edge of discovering that this grave over which he so serenely chops logic is Ophelia's. Within a little, we feel, he must learn it.

> Whose grave's this, sirrah? . . . What man dost thou dig it for?
> For no man, sir.
> What woman, then?
> For none, neither.
> Who is to be buried in't?

—to which, surely, the shattering answer must be given. But the Clown is his match at a quibble:

> One that was a woman, sir; but, rest her soul, she's dead.

And Hamlet enjoys the joke, and goes on to sentimentalize over Yorick, twenty years and more in his grave, now ousted from it for this newcomer—whoever she may be!—and to spin fancies round Alexander's dust. But so men who have greatly suffered do turn away to wistful sentiment and idle fancy. Hamlet lingers here because, once back at Elsinore, his duty must be done. And, behind this forgetfulness of Ophelia, there is the wish to forget.[17]

[16] Strange in reality that Horatio should not have spoken to Hamlet of Ophelia's madness, but dramatically this passes unnoticed. Of her death, however, Shakespeare takes care to leave him ignorant. He had gone off in haste to meet Hamlet before it occurred.

[17] But we shall not appreciate this irony—of Hamlet's ignorance that it is Ophelia's grave over which he weaves his fancies—unless the Clowns are kept in their place. Even though they speak no more than is set down for them, they can still (and habitually do) set on the more barren spectators to laugh—not at the natural shrewd humor with which Shakespeare has endowed them, but at the mere

A strange little procession now advances; the King and Queen, two or three courtiers, a meager coffin with its bearers, Laertes, a solitary priest.[18] We can interpret its strangeness well enough, and we watch Hamlet as, little by little, the truth dawns on him:

> But soft! but soft! aside: here comes the King,
> The Queen, the courtiers: who is that they follow?
> And with such maimed rites? This doth betoken
> The corse they follow did with desperate hand
> Fordo its own life; 'twas of some estate. . . .

Now, indeed, he cannot but soon guess, as he listens to the recalcitrant priest answering Laertes, who it is that lies here:

> Her obsequies have been as far enlarg'd
> As we have warrantise; her death was doubtful,
> And, but that great command o'ersways the order,
> She should in ground unsanctified have lodg'd
> Till the last trumpet; for charitable prayers,
> Shards, flints and pebbles should be thrown on her;
> Yet here she is allowed her virgin crants,
> Her maiden strewments . . . .

Yet he listens on and makes no sign. For this is the Hamlet who cried "Let me be cruel!"—shards, flints and pebbles themselves no harder than his heart to Ophelia!—and he dreads and resists the breaking of the callous crust that still armors him. Nor does it

clowning they impose on it. The coarseness of this and the guffaws which greet it will fatally break the finer threads of implication and allusion by which the continuity of cause and effect—in this subsidiary story of Hamlet, Ophelia and Laertes—is sustained. Much depends upon continuity of action too; upon the connection—and Shakespeare has woven it all very closely—between his "mad" departure and her madness, the news of his return, the plot against him, her death, the digging of her grave, his arrival; if these things are not kept physically connected, their metaphysical connection will certainly be missed. Here, in a moment, Hamlet is to apostrophize Laertes as "a very noble youth." The irony of that too will be lost, unless Laertes' last appearance, when he was plotting to poison his adversary, is fresh in our memory, its vividness unspoiled by some "act-interval" of distracting talk.

[18] The Folio has *lords attendant*, and there is need of them to pluck Hamlet and Laertes asunder, though at a pinch the bearers of the coffin could do this. But otherwise the rites should be as "maimed" as possible; the text explicitly dictates this; and how the editors, even down to Craig, Dowden and Adams, have allowed a full procession of priests and mourners to intrude it is hard to understand. For a salutary correction read what Dover Wilson has to say on the subject.

break until Laertes—the Church's benison as cruelly denied—
claims Nature's kindlier one:

> Lay her i' the earth;
> And from her fair and unpolluted flesh
> May violets spring! I tell thee, churlish priest,
> A ministering angel shall my sister be,
> When thou liest howling.

This touches his heart, as the soft cry tells us:

> What! the fair Ophelia?

but he listens still. Two more blows fall on him; one from the
lost past, the Queen's

> Sweets to the sweet: farewell!
> I hop'd thou shouldst have been my Hamlet's wife. . . .

the other from Laertes:

> O! treble woe
> Fall ten times treble on that cursed head
> Whose wicked deed thy most ingenious sense
> Depriv'd thee of. . . .

Then the stillness (Hamlet and Horatio motionless in their hiding-place, the rest held so by the presence of the stiller dead) is
suddenly broken by the extravagant emotion of Laertes' leap into
the grave and his cry to them to pile the earth upon him too:

> Till of this flat a mountain you have made
> To o'er-top old Pelion or the skyish head
> Of blue Olympus.

and that brings Hamlet forth. For a moment they will hardly
know him in his rough "sea-gown" and traveling gear. There is
something new to them besides in the measured, potent scorn of

> What is he whose grief
> Bear such an emphasis? whose phrase of sorrow
> Conjures the wandering stars, and makes them stand
> Like wonder-wounded hearers? . . .

and something minatory—to Claudius, at least—in the preroga-
tively royal ending

> This is I,
> Hamlet the Dane.

It is his first assertion in that kind. Laertes, in a flash, is out of the grave and at his throat.[19]

It is a Hamlet now royally master of himself indeed—the Hamlet once resolute to face his father's ghost and his own fate, the Hamlet Fortinbras will mourn and praise—who can sustain the onslaught with the mettled steadiness of

> Thou pray'st not well.
> I prithee take thy fingers from my throat;
> For, though I am not splenitive and rash,
> Yet have I something in me dangerous,
> Which let thy wisdom fear. Hold off thy hand!

But, the next instant, the spiritual schism in him gapes again:

> Why, I will fight with him upon this theme
> Until my eyelids will no longer wag. . . .

~~~~~~~~~~

[19] Neither Q2 nor F1 direct Hamlet to leap into the grave beside Laertes. But Q1 (the text itself being very corrupt at this point) does: *Hamlet leapes in after Laertes.* And Rowe, not copying Q1, which he probably never saw (though, as it happens, his earlier *Laertes leaps into the grave* is Q1 word for word and does not follow F1's *leaps in the grave*), says simply: *Hamlet leaps into the grave.* And editors have—unanimously, as far as I know—followed Rowe. We seem, then, to have here a stage practice, dating from Shakespeare's time, and alive at the Restoration. But even this does not prove, I think, that it represents Shakespeare's intention. It is just the sort of thing that an actor of Hamlet, carried away by his own emotion, his mind anticipating the verbal onslaught, might do; it would prove startlingly effective (why stop to consider the incongruity of two men struggling together upon the top of a coffin?) and editorial sanction would perpetuate it.

Against that what can be cited? The absence of any such stage direction from the two authoritative texts? There are many similar omissions, when the directions are nevertheless plainly implied. The implications of the text itself, therefore, are more important, if Shakespeare's intentions can be discerned in them. And the text here, I think, furnishes two sound arguments against it having been Shakespeare's intention, when he wrote the lines, that Hamlet should leap into the grave.

He can only do so at one point, upon the

> This is I,
>
> Hamlet the Dane.

and the royal dignity of the phrase must be quite ridiculously compromised by such an action. Secondly, it is plain that Laertes is meant to be the aggressor. But if Hamlet leaps into the grave, it can only look as if it was he that attacked Laertes. Therefore Laertes must leap out of the grave to attack him.

I fancy, then, that we may have here a little history of Shakespeare's betrayal by his actors. We need not suppose that he took it very seriously. But the lapse was never justified in the play's official records, Q2 and F1. It is merely thanks to actors and editors that the scene is played to this day in a muddle of excitement which confuses its dramatic intentions, when these are fairly plainly to be read in the text itself.

> I lov'd Ophelia; forty thousand brothers
> Could not, with all their quantity of love,
> Make up my sum. . . .

—he loved Ophelia, and he has killed her. In that terrible paradox is the essence of their tragedy, to which this dullard, glutted with his own grief, is blind. He knows—who better?—the worth of such grieving; and he mocks at it, yet less in Laertes than in his one-time self:

> What wilt thou do for her? . . .
>   Dost thou come here to whine,
> To outface me with leaping in her grave?
> Be buried quick with her, and so will I:
> And, if thou prate of mountains, let them throw
> Millions of acres on us, till our ground,
> Singeing his pate against the burning zone,
> Make Ossa like a wart! Nay, an thou'lt mouth,
> I'll rant as well as thou.

Laertes, kept from strangling him, incapable of other answer, stands silent. Gertrude—the savage irony lost on her—makes the only excuse she can for him:

> This is mere madness . . . .

Then Hamlet, as if in pity for such blindness:

> Hear you, sir;
> What is the reason that you use me thus?
> I lov'd you ever. . . .

—but at that he breaks off. For how make plain to them—when even to himself he cannot—the truth of this tragic discord between will and deed? So he flings them instead, for their satisfaction, a jingling reassurance of his "madness":

> But it is no matter;
> Let Hercules himself do what he may,
> The cat will mew and dog will have his day.

and departs.

   The King, watchfully silent so far, now takes command. There is the old kindly care for the afflicted in his

> I pray you, good Horatio, wait upon him.

The balked Laertes he both soothes and spurs:

Strengthen your patience in our last night's speech;
We'll put the matter to the present push.

—the Queen coming within hearing, he frees himself of her with
another kindly

Good Gertrude, set some watch over your son.

—and departs also; his arm, I think, again linking Laertes', for,
clearly, he must keep an eye on him:

This grave shall have a living monument:
An hour of quiet shortly shall we see;
Till then, in patience our proceeding be.

And to end the scene the curtains of the inner stage would close.[20]

*The story of the embassage to England; the challenge to the fenc-
ing match; the end.*

HAMLET appears again, speaking eagerly to Horatio.[21]

So much for this, sir: now shall you see the other. . . .

The exanimate mood of the talk to the Gravedigger was dis-
pelled by the encounter with Laertes, emotion, it may seem,
finally burnt out of him in that blaze of remorse for Ophelia's
death; and he is purged of his madness. But not of the effects of
it. We feel, in the forced march of his speech and the checks and
divagations of his thought, a still refractory mind, a dangerous
temper. They show too in a trifle, his tone to the faithful Horatio,
in the oddly reiterated "Sir . . . sir . . . sir," and the impatient
requests to that best of listeners to listen. For the first time, moreover, comes a hint that the strain is telling on him physically:

Sir, in my heart there was a kind of fighting
That would not let me sleep; methought I lay
Worse than the mutines in the bilboes. . . .

And what contempt for his own subtle brain and once devious
ways in:

---

[20] That the grave-trap may be closed and the royal "state," etc., prepared for
the fencing match. The intervening scene would allow none too much time for
this, and in this need, it may well be, originated the elaboration of Osric and the
entrance of *A lord*.

[21] What he has been talking about is not clear; but the impression we gain is
of eager businesslike conversation, one subject dismissed for another to be broached.
And this is all that matters.

> Rashly—
> And prais'd be rashness for it—let us know,
> Our indiscretion sometimes serves us well,
> When our deep plots do pall; and that should learn us
> There's a divinity that shapes our ends,
> Rough-hew them how we will.

From this he passes to the tale of his stealing and unsealing the "grand commission," by which Rosencrantz and Guildenstern were to conduct him to his death in England, and forging and sealing another, which is even now conducting them to theirs. He elaborates it beyond need in his grim enjoyment of the business, resavors every detail, the "bugs and goblins" of the King's attainder of him, his skill in the forgery, his parody of his uncle's diplomacy in the

> earnest conjuration from the King,
> As England was his faithful tributary,
> As love between them like the palm should flourish,
> As peace should still her wheaten garland wear,
> And stand a comma 'tween their amities,
> And many such-like 'As'es of great charge. . . .

But Shakespeare makes yet more use of the sixty lines. The gap in the history of his absence is filled, and the Hamlet before us linked to the man of the parting promise:

> O, from this time forth,
> My thoughts be bloody, or be nothing worth!

His task's fulfillment is, in fact, at hand; for we surely need fear no more half measures, nor hysterical self-betrayal, from this expert cracksman, who could sit quietly in his cabin, his one-time friends asleep near him, and forge their death warrant in a fine clerkly hand—and enjoy the work too! Nor have we before heard anything from him quite so cold-blooded as his response to Horatio's

> So Guildenstern and Rosencrantz go to't.

the

> Why, man, they did make love to this employment;
> They are not near my conscience; their defeat
> Does by their own insinuation grow.

'Tis dangerous when the baser nature comes
Between the pass and fell incensed points
Of mighty opposites.

since, base though they may be, the King's stolen letter—which
Horatio has here in his hand and turns to again, exclaiming

Why, what a king is this!

—was sealed, and the two would not have known its contents.[22]
And his tone towards the King has changed. Claudius has now
not only

kill'd my king and whored my mother . . .

but

Popped in between the election and my hopes . . .

It is a sequent thought to that imperious "Hamlet the Dane," a
new weight to his cause. And when Horatio warns him that "It
must be shortly known" what passes in England, the stern

It will be short: the interim is mine;
And a man's life's no more than to say 'One.'

promises imminent and open attack. But *we* know, and have
just been quietly reminded, that attack upon him, by a deadlier
trick than the trick of the play-scene, is imminent also. Which of
the two enemies will strike home first?

For a sudden turn of thought shows him, after all, fatally
guileless:

But I am very sorry, good Horatio,
That to Laertes I forgot myself;
For, by the image of my cause, I see
The portraiture of his: I'll court his favours . . . .

The old sweetness and charm are in that, a little saddened; simplicity besides (he really believes that forgiveness for an injury
should be given for the asking); and in his excuse:

But, sure, the bravery of his grief did put me
Into a towering passion.

---

[22] "There's letters seal'd," says Hamlet, and suspects at once that the two are to
"marshal" him "to knavery" of some sort. But the King has not confided in them;
his last words to them are

Away, for everything is sealed and done . . . .

The implication is plain, I think, that they do not know.

the quizzical self-detachment of the imaginative mind. He and the hot-headed Laertes are not made to understand each other. At which point Osric appears. And if the King fears that Hamlet might suspect something sinister in the fencing match, what better voucher for its mere diversion than this fantastic waterfly?

The verbal fencing match that follows does yet more to dissipate our remembrance of Ophelia in her grave, and to separate the sport from the mourning. Its topical flavor is today at a discount, but the dramatic effect is valid. We know, as we listen, that behind this ridiculous gabble about the wager, about the

> six French rapiers and poniards, with their assigns, as girdle, hangers, and so . . .

the "carriages" that

> are very dear to fancy, very responsive to the hilts, most delicate carriages, and of very liberal conceit.

behind the trippingly sportsmanlike

> The King, sir, hath laid, that in a dozen passes between your-self and him, he shall not exceed you three hits; he hath laid on twelve for nine, and it would come to immediate trial, if your lordship would vouchsafe the answer.

there lurks death.

Hamlet yields, as usual, to the distraction of a little intellectual cat-and-mouse play. And Osric is easy game; as easy as he himself is more practically proving to Claudius. We may note that even at this sort of thing he has grown crueller. The mockery is overt and brutal, with no "madness" for mitigation. We shall note too that, having amused himself with the creature, Hamlet, upon that sudden

> How if I answer no?

comes near to spoiling the whole plan. And he only falls in with it in impatient indifference:

> Sir, I will walk here in the hall; if it please his majesty, 'tis the breathing time of day with me; let the foils be brought, the gentleman willing, and the King hold his purpose, I will win for him if I can; if not, I will gain nothing but my shame and the odd hits.

—with which answer Osric departs; to deliver it to the King, how-ever, with so much "flourish," that a soberer, anonymous Lord has next to be sent to discover what, beyond the fact that he will walk here in the hall, Hamlet did mean.

The Folio omits this Lord. The need for still more matter here while the throne and the furniture for the fencing match were made ready on the inner stage—the origin, possibly, of his existence—may have gone when its text was settled. But Shakespeare, in Q2, had as usual turned the thing forced on him to good dramatic account. Through the mere repetition—

> his majesty . . . sends to know if your pleasure hold to play with Laertes, or that you will take longer time.

—the King's anxiety peeps out. And the impersonal phrases help resolve the scene (to pass from Osric's flummery direct would have been too abrupt a change) into its next and graver key. For there falls about Hamlet now the shadow of death. He is aware of it without knowing it. Through his answer:

> I am constant to my purposes. They follow the King's pleasure. If his fitness speaks, mine is ready, now or whensoever, provided I be so able as now.

sounds a constancy, a fitness, a readiness to meet a weightier challenge than this. And his quiet

> In happy time.

accepts more than the mere fact that

> The King, and Queen, and all are coming down.

It is as if the vanished "madness" had left something like clairvoyance behind.

Horatio warns his friend:

> You will lose this wager, my lord.

—the faithful eye detecting intolerable strain, which Hamlet (after a cool "I do not think so") owns to, with a childlike

> But thou wouldst not think how ill all's here about my heart. . . .

then dismisses:

> It is but foolery; but it is such a kind of gain-giving as would perhaps trouble a woman.

Shakespeare likes to bring his rarer moments home to us by such familiar touches.

But Horatio is just so troubled for him:

> If your mind dislike anything, obey it; I will forestall their repair hither, and say you are not fit.

and the intimate simplicity of it all sets off the simple nobility of the valediction:

> Not a whit; we defy augury; there's a special providence in the fall of a sparrow. If it be now, 'tis not to come; if it be not to come, it will be now; if it be not now, yet it will come: the readiness is all. Since no man has aught of what he leaves, what is't to leave betimes? Let be.

It is to no more than this, at the last, that the subtly questing mind has come.[23]

As the curtains of the inner stage part, the disquieted Horatio is silenced by a gesture; and there once more—it is much the same picture as at the play's beginning—is the sinister brilliance of Claudius and his Court, Hamlet's somber figure outlined against it as before.[24]

~~~~~~~~

[23] I venture to prefer the Folio reading of the last sentence, which I understand (though that may not be the best of reasons), to Q2's, which, despite Dover Wilson's admirable explanation, I do not. But we need not gather from the Folio that Hamlet is merely thinking—with St. Paul and the Burial Service—of the worldly goods a man must leave behind. Surely it is his loss of other things that he has in mind, of things he loved and valued; his father's care, his faith in his mother, the ideal love for Ophelia, hers for him. He could keep nothing of all this. And so, with things such as this, it still would be. What is it, then, to leave betimes, before he has lost more? But let us own that, whatever the meaning may be, it is more than vaguely conveyed.

The final "Let be" has disappeared from the Folio, and in strictness perhaps should not be stolen from Q2 for an addition to its text. But if the Q2 text is corrupt (as, being to me incomprehensible, I cannot but think it) and the Folio's a correction of it, the two small words might well, I suppose, have dropped out in the process. Admit them—as editors commonly do—as an isolated phrase, and their technical dramatic utility is clear. Hamlet's fatidic speech definitely alarms Horatio, who makes a move as if to stop the match after all—in which he is checked by that curt, commanding "Let be." This ends the passage between the two with a sharp touch of suggested action, links it by an arresting moment to the "discovery" of King, Queen and Court, and will hold our attention while that larger spectacle makes good its own hold on us. Therefore, if it is allowable, it will be a strengthening knot here in the dramatic fabric.

[24] The parting of the curtains and the actual discovery behind them of King, Queen and Court is indicated with some probability, I think, by the nature of the stage direction in Q2:

The scene of catastrophe which follows is full of complicated matter, close-packed.[25] Shakespeare will have inherited its holocaust—which may suit him well enough, but he has to harmonize it with his own enrichment of the play's theme. The sudden huddle of violent events is in itself effective after the long delays of plot and counterplot, but character must be eloquent in them still. And this network of action is lucid with character.

We are at the crisis of what we have called the counteraction, the King's war against Hamlet. The first attack—the dispatching him to be murdered in England—has failed. We saw nothing of it, and its mere recounting will not have prejudiced the effect of this, which, doubly provided for, by poisoned sword and cup, can (we are to feel) scarcely fail. Or Hamlet's part there is no more plotting, only cold resolution to do what he has to do; but that, seemingly, is in abeyance for the while. Such is our approach to the scene.

The apology to Laertes is candid:

> Give me your pardon, sir; I've done you wrong;
> But pardon 't, as you are a gentleman.
> This presence knows,

A table prepard, Trumpets, Drums and officers with Cushions, King, Queene, and all the state, Foiles, daggers, and Laertes.

(it is stage direction and property list combined, and entirely businesslike) nor is it even contradicted by the conventional

Enter King, Queene, Laertes . . . .

of the Folio, for "enter" often implies discovery. The drawing of the curtains while Hamlet and Horatio stand there. is certain. The King, Queen and Court *could* then enter in procession. But this would involve a slight delay; and, after the extended preliminaries, Shakespeare would be concerned, I fancy, to close up the action and move steadily towards his climax. In this the discovery is an appreciable help. A likely addition to the stage management would be the simultaneous entry through the doors on the outer stage of extra courtiers or guards, and the table for the foils may have had to be moved down. Hamlet, so I believe, is no longer in mourning (cf. pp. 232 *et seq.*). But he would be in his traveling clothes; and these, against the Court splendor, would look somber. Laertes, and even the King and Queen, it may be said, would be in some sort of mourning for Ophelia, having but just returned from the funeral. I do not think so (though Laertes need not be gaily dressed, and, at the graveside, the King and Queen might have worn some mourning outer garments). Realistic likelihood will always give way to legitimate dramatic effect.

[25] It runs to some 170 lines. Compare it and its complexities—if we are studying Shakespeare's technical progress as a playwright—with the long-drawn-out last scene of *Romeo and Juliet*, which is but 30 lines less than twice the length.

> And you must needs have heard, how I am punish'd
> With a sore distraction. . . .

and the explanation, even in its riddling logic—

> What I have done,
> That might your nature, honour and exception
> Roughly awake, I here proclaim was madness.
> Was 't Hamlet wrong'd Laertes? Never Hamlet:
> If Hamlet from himself be ta'en away,
> And when he's not himself does wrong Laertes,
> Then Hamlet does it not; Hamlet denies it.
> Who does it then? His madness. If 't be so,
> Hamlet is of the faction that is wrong'd;
> His madness is poor Hamlet's enemy.

—is meant to be so. Did his aping of madness send him verily
mad? In the Player who

> But in a fiction, in a dream of passion,
> Could force his soul so to his own conceit . . .

he had discerned that strange confusion between the imagined
and the real (which Shakespeare himself had cause enough to
know). He can look back calmly to the delirium of it now. But
who else will understand? So he ends with a simpler plea:

> Sir, in this audience,
> Let my disclaiming from a purpos'd evil
> Free me so far in your most generous thoughts,
> That I have shot mine arrow o'er the house,
> And hurt my brother.

—and in the sad cadence of that "brother" is the last echo of
Ophelia's story.

Laertes is a still unpracticed scoundrel; and it will not be too
easy for him, with the phial of poison for his sword ready in his
pocket, to respond to the appeal to his "most generous thoughts."
But, with a little quibbling about honor, he manages it. A jury of
gentlemen shall judge his cause against Hamlet later—when he
has murdered him! He can even brave his conscience with an
outspoken

> But till that time
> I do receive your offer'd love like love,
> And will not wrong it.

The two of them thus reconciled, the customary pleasant stir of preparation for such a match begins; the foils are brought, compliments pass and deprecating protests, and Osric adds his expedient touch of frivolity to the affair.

Hamlet is satisfied with the first foil he takes. Laertes demands another, and selects it from among the spare ones on the table. The King is speaking now, with everyone attentive:

> Set me the stoups of wine upon that table.
> If Hamlet give the first or second hit,
> Or quit in answer of the third exchange,
> Let all the battlements their ordnance fire . . . .

and so the "sword unbated" can be secured unnoticed. This screen of oratory, in fact—

> The King shall drink to Hamlet's better breath;
> And in the cup an union shall he throw,
> Richer than that which four successive kings
> In Denmark's crown have worn. Give me the cups;
> And let the kettle to the trumpet speak,
> The trumpet to the cannoneer without,
> The cannons to the heavens, the heaven to earth,
> 'Now the King drinks to Hamlet!' . . .

—permits the "noble youth" privily to "anoint" the sword besides.[26]

[26] These preliminaries to the fight have to be deduced from the text; they should conform to dramatic effect and likelihood combined, but not to one of these at the expense of the other. The King orders Osric to present the foils. If they were modern fencing foils he could carry half a dozen on his arm; of the long Elizabethan sword not more than three or four. But he may well leave two or three upon the table, and it will not do for him to carry them all, or Hamlet (we may think) might select the one that is unbated. This, then, will have been among those left on the table, and Laertes—pretending that his first choice is "too heavy"—can, under cover of the King's speech, secure it later. But does not its merely being left there make Osric an accomplice? If we had time to reason the matter out, there would be grounds for suspicion. But if the foils are discovered on the table when the curtains part, and Osric simply takes the first three or four to his hand, we shall hardly ask ourselves that question. Moreover, when Laertes says "Let me see another" and moves (as I think) towards the table, Osric is answering Hamlet's question:

> These foils have all a length?

and will have his back turned to it. Then, as the King says

> Set me the stoups of wine upon that table.

—*i.e.* upon a table on the opposite side of the stage—we shall see Laertes take the unbated sword, and we shall know by his expression that he has it. It will be even more effective to see him take the phial from his pouch and dip the tip of

The match begun, its conduct becomes for a while the main action of the scene, the dialogue diminishing to an accompaniment. The first bout, indeed, would pass in a tense silence but for the inspiriting

Trumpets the while.[27]

—a silence only broken when Hamlet scores and claims:

One.

~~~~~~

the sword in it; and the King's jovial oratory is, I feel sure, intended—both by Shakespeare and the King—to provide occasion for this; all eyes but ours turned upon Claudius. Even Horatio, that faithful watcher of the play-scene, does not observe Laertes.

Dr. Dover Wilson thinks that Osric is necessarily an accomplice; the chief proof of it that it is to him Laertes says later that he is justly killed with his own treachery. I can only answer that Shakespeare "does not do these things"—does not introduce a ridiculous fribble, and by one *ex post facto* hint in the text convert him to a scoundrel; and, moreover, leave it at that. Nor do I see how the actor of Osric could, merely by facial expression, convey his guilt. Laertes begins his confession—

Why, as a woodcock to mine own springe . . .

—to Osric, because it is he who has gone to his aid, asking him how he does. He continues it to Hamlet a moment after with

Hamlet, thou are slain; . . .
The treacherous instrument is in thy hand,
Unbated and envenom'd . . . .

—all the weight of his remorse in that. And in the interval Hamlet's attention and ours has been turned to the dying Queen; too strong a competition by far for an Osric's guilty grimacings. No, I fancy the poor waterfly can be returned "Not guilty," and allowed to announce "young Fortinbras'" arrival from Poland with a clear countenance and conscience.

Both student and producer, however, should take care to master Dover Wilson's explanations of the wager and the fight (in the new Cambridge Shakespeare and in his preface to the Shakespeare Association facsimile of George Silver's *Paradoxes of Defence*).

The wager, indeed, is a minor matter. If we do not grasp its meaning we can still be amused by the jargon; and I expect that not a few among Shakespeare's audience were in that case. But the proper conduct of the fight is important. I owe much to these elucidations of it.

[27] Q2. The omission of the direction in the Folio may well be accidental, for a little lower down the Q's

Drum, trumpets and shot. Florish, a peece goes off.

is abbreviated to

Trumpets sound, and shot goes off.

though not only does its text still demand the "kettle," but, by stage directions elsewhere, drums are in use.

Laertes (touched too in the self-esteem that Claudius took such pains to foster) protests:

> No!

Hamlet curtly appeals:

> Judgment?

and has it from Osric—who is in his element:

> A hit, a very palpable hit.

Laertes, a peg down, takes fresh breath with

> Well, again!

But the King, for an instant, interposes.

We see now why he thought it well to back the poisoned rapier with the poisoned cup. Hamlet is the better fencer; Laertes may not touch him at all. He is running no risks:

> Stay, give me a drink. Hamlet, this pearl is thine;
> Here's to thy health.   Give him the cup.

A most gracious ceremonial! He drinks from the cup first, then draws the pearl from his finger and drops it in; and we shall guess, if we cannot see, that he has pressed the spring which releases the poison.[28] Then, as the cup is carried to Hamlet:

> *Drum, trumpets and shot. Florish, a peece goes off.*

In truth a splendid pledge! But Hamlet, when the din is over, says quietly and coldly—for he will not drink amity to his uncle:

> I'll play this bout first; set it by awhile.

The second bout proves strenuous, for the bad blood in Laertes is fermenting. Hamlet wins it, and claims it with a gay

> Another hit; what say you?

And Laertes does not wait for the humiliating judgment this time, but confesses wryly:

> A touch, a touch, I do confess.

Then, while the two recover breath, the King's soft voice is heard:

> Our son shall win.

---

[28] Forewarned as they have been, Shakespeare's audience would be fully alive to what the ring and the gesture must imply. Claudius is an expert poisoner; and such subtle methods as this, and the pouring of the poison in his brother's ear, were a recognized part of the equipment of the "Italianate" villain.

It is spoken smilingly to the Queen. There is a taunt in it for
Laertes; let him show his prowess, and quickly, or their enemy
may escape them. Its fatherly affection might well anger Hamlet; but, exhilarated with the sport, he does not heed. For the first
time (the irony of it!) we see him oblivious to all trouble, as sane
in body as in mind, and in the flush of success; the Hamlet of
Ophelia's dreams, of the

> unmatched form and feature of blown youth . . .

—a Hamlet that might have been. And his mother is so happy to
see the change in him—his madness cured, and with this the bitterness which had parted them ended—that she can even banter
him a little:

> He's fat and scant of breath.
> Here, Hamlet, take my napkin, rub thy brows. . . .

She leaves her "state" and trips to where he stands. The page with
the King's cup is still waiting near him. In a merry caprice she
seizes it, and, mischievously parodying the favorite royal phrase
and trumpet-saluted gesture:

> The Queen carouses to thy fortune, Hamlet.

What, upon the instant, is Claudius to do? While Hamlet bows
his thanks, he calls out

> Gertrude, do not drink.

But why should she not? Prettily willful, making him, I think, a
mock reverence:

> I will, my lord; I pray you, pardon me.

she disobeys him and does drink. She has given him, we note,
while she speaks and curtseys, a moment's chance to save her—at
the cost of his own safety. The moment passes; he has let it pass:

> It is the poison'd cup! it is too late.

—retribution outwitting even his quick wit! But she finds, for the
instant, nothing amiss; and her next gesture is to press, in all
innocence and affection, the poisoned cup on her son. If he would
not pledge his uncle and make all well between them, surely he
will not refuse her. Though he does not positively refuse, his
response is cold:

> I dare not drink yet, Madam; by and by.

But she feels so near to winning him again that she bids him, tenderly, as if he were still a child:

> Come, let me wipe thy face.

and, as a child might, he lets her.

While this is passing the thwarted, desperate Laertes is whispering to the King:

> My lord, I'll hit him now.

to get no answer but a grim

> I do not think't.

—for Claudius, his guilty eyes on the doomed Queen, feels himself slipping to confusion and defeat. Is it the sight of mother and son seemingly reunited that prompts Laertes'

> And yet 'tis almost 'gainst my conscience.

Hamlet turns, buoyantly ready for the third bout.

This also passes in silence, and is ended by Osric's

> Nothing, neither way.

But is it ended? Hamlet is half off his guard when Laertes gives himself benefit of the doubt, and with a

> Have at you now!

thrusts and scores his first hit. It is all he will need to score, for he has drawn blood!

Stung by the trickery of the attack, the wound, the treachery of the sharpened sword, Hamlet closes with his man and wrests this from him, forcing on him his own in exchange.[29] The King's

---

[29] For what seems to me the simplest and, more importantly, the most dramatic way of effecting the exchange, see Dover Wilson's note in the new Cambridge *Hamlet*. But he does not make it indubitably clear that Hamlet is "enraged," not merely by the smart of the wound, but by the treachery involved. (He guesses half the truth; the rest is to come.) This is needed, however, to account for the fury of his attack on Laertes, an attack so furious that it stretches him on the ground; and it is illustrated by the King's

> Part them! they are incens'd.

The "traditional" stage business—if I remember it rightly—which involved a fight with modern foils only, was that Hamlet should be wounded in the forearm, should note the blood flowing and surmise the unbuttoned foil (I am not sure that Laertes was not supposed to remove the button from his foil upon the "My lord, I'll hit him now"). Then he had to beat Laertes' foil from his hand, put his foot on it, and offer him his own in exchange—which Laertes would shamefacedly take. The idea involved is the same.

Part them! they are incens'd.

passes unheeded; for eyes are now turned on Gertrude, who, the poison at work in her, stands swaying to and fro. Upon Osric's

Look to the Queen there, ho!

attendants go to her aid. The fight suddenly and finally stops; Horatio's steady voice, heard for the first time, interprets to us what has happened:

They bleed on both sides. . . .

So Hamlet has his death wound. We know it, and he does not. Laertes has his, and knows it; and the pluck goes out of him. Hamlet does not answer his friend's

How is it, my lord?

for, free of the fighting, his eyes are on the Queen. But Osric's

How is it, Laertes?

brings the beginning of confession:

Why, as a woodcock to mine own springe, Osric,
I am justly kill'd with mine own treachery.

It is checked for a moment by Hamlet's peremptory

How does the Queen?

which Claudius answers with a desperate

She swounds to see them bleed.

—for his instinct is to save himself; and Laertes (whose own mouth will soon be shut) has accounted for Hamlet, after all, and the poison might be explained away. But retribution outpaces him again. Gertrude speaks:

No, no, the drink, the drink—O my dear Hamlet!
The drink, the drink! I am poison'd.

—and in the "O my dear Hamlet" what agony of remorse! For at last she understands. "As kill a king . . . a second time I kill my husband dead. . . . he poisons him in the garden for his estate . . . !" And she has seen *this* cup sent on its errand.

At the sound of the one fatal, memorable word Hamlet is transformed. The last shreds of self-conscious weakness fall from him; and he stands there, Hamlet the Dane indeed.

> O villainy! How? Let the door be lock'd:
> Treachery! seek it out.[80]

His command is obeyed without question. Claudius is trapped.

The answer to that "How?" is to come from Laertes. But he must confess his own guilt to Hamlet first. So the King's doom is suspended for a torturing minute or so; and we are aware of him, the glib diplomatist, jovial drinker and dancer, the "very, very peacock," skulking among his bewildered Court. Hamlet hears from Laertes his own doom; but he pays no heed to that; he waits for the end of the story. When he has it—

> thy mother's poisoned—
> I can no more!—the King—the King's to blame.

—he turns, and, no one staying him, takes vengeance.

At the sword thrust the courtiers raise a perfunctory cry of "Treason!" But, though the wounded man cries pitifully

> O, yet defend me, friends; I am but hurt.

they do nothing. Then Hamlet drops the sword, and takes the cup and drags the creature out, and—as one would medicine a dog—chokes his mouth open and pours the poison down; and he consecrates to the consummate moment his last outburst of mockery:

> Here, thou incestuous, murderous, damned Dane,
> Drink of this potion! Is thy union here?
> Follow my mother!

Into the silence which follows, steals Laertes dying

> He is justly served;
> It is a poison tempered by himself.
> Exchange forgiveness with me, noble Hamlet;
> Mine and my father's death come not upon thee,
> Nor thine on me!

He dies, and Hamlet feels death coming upon him too.

His first thought is for his friend:

> I am dead, Horatio . . . .

---

[80] This is (spelling excepted) the Folio's reading. Q2's does not differ except in punctuation. Rowe follows the Folio. Theobald would seem to have been the first to turn the "How?" into a "Ho!" and modern editors, even Dover Wilson, have followed him. Why, I cannot imagine. The "How?" is an obvious question, to which Laertes makes answer; and it knits the sense together and sustains the tension of the moment better than a redundant exclamation can.

only his next for his still-agonizing mother, the source of all this
ill. Speechless, she can yet have heard all; at the end nothing has
been spared her. And from her son comes only a

> Wretched queen, adieu!

He feels men's eyes on him, the assassin of their King:

> You that look pale and tremble at this chance,
> That are but mutes or audience to this act,
> Had I but time—as this fell sergeant, death,
> Is strict in his arrest—O! I could tell you—
> But let it be . . . .

And once more, and for the last time, he seeks help where he has
ever found it:

> Horatio, I am dead;
> Thou liv'st; report me and my cause aright
> To the unsatisfied.

One certain sign of the great writer is that his resourcefulness
does not fail him as he nears the end of book or play. So here. All,
we shall be feeling, is about over; and suddenly the imperturbable
Horatio, the man

> that fortune's buffets and rewards
> Hath ta'en with equal thanks . . .

passionately resolves not to survive his friend:

> Never believe it!
> I'm more an antique Roman than a Dane:
> Here's yet some liquor left.

Hamlet's dying strength cannot wrest the cup from him; but he
knows a better means:

> O God, Horatio, what a wounded name,
> Things standing thus unknown, shall live behind me!
> If thou didst ever hold me in thy heart,
> Absent thee from felicity awhile
> And in this harsh world draw thy breath in pain,
> To tell my story.

New duty laid on him, this friend will be faithful still. And at
once, for reminder of that world without and its claims, we hear

> *A march afarre off.*

an army's drums and fifes, and a shot of salute. It is, says Osric,

> Young Fortinbras, with conquest come from Poland . . .

ambassadors from England too.[31] Hamlet, self-forgetful, calm, orders affairs of state:

> I do prophesy the election lights
> On Fortinbras; he has my dying voice;
> So tell him . . . .

Then, upon

> the rest is silence.

he slips peacefully out of life—to the rhythm of the drumbeats of the triumphant approach of the man whose "divine ambition" put him to such shame.[32] A last quiet stroke of tragic irony.

But the story which Horatio will tell

> to the yet unknowing world . . .

is not that of his weakness and melancholy, his scruples and failings. These are dead with him. Even his blunders, the

> accidental judgments, casual slaughters . . .

will find a less tenebrous place in the picture seen as a whole. For finally he has not failed. The wrong to be righted led him to no such gallant adventure as his father or this hero, whose prowess he

---

[31] Q2 and F. both mark an *Enter Osric* here, having given him no exit. But it looks as if the giving of the speech itself to him had been a matter of theatrical economy on Shakespeare's part—as if this particular actor had been the most competent person available to speak these three important lines; and that implies a shedding of the waterfly—unless we are to suppose an Osric shocked quite out of his fantastic self by what has happened. But such niceties in a minor character would not come into question at such a moment. The lines belong to a "messenger" and they are spoken by Osric (what, however, has become of the anonymous Lord, who reinforced the invitation to the duel? Surely he could have served this turn). His *exit* is of no importance and need not be editorially provided. If he passes for a second or so into the anteroom or is seen to encounter an attendant in the doorway—anything of that sort will be amply sufficient.

[32] He says here besides

> I cannot live to hear the news from England . . . .

into which might—by the so-minded—be read regret that he will never know for certain whether Rosencrantz and Guildenstern have been satisfactorily "hoist with their own petar." But this is certainly not the intention of the line. The ambassadors from England are heralded to him as to Denmark's rightful ruler at the moment, and, so answering, he says he will not live to receive them; that is all.

so envied, would have confidently taken in hand. It was a cancer-
ous wrong—

> carnal, bloody and unnatural . . .

—eating into the sanctities of life and his faith in them. But at
the cost of his life he has righted it at last; and Fortinbras comes
to a heritage purged of evil.

> O, proud death!
> What feast is toward in thine eternal cell,
> That thou so many princes at a shot
> So bloodily hast struck!

—he may well exclaim it! And the whole stately ending reminds
us that this most introspective of plays has also been a tragedy of
great events, which have added their dignity to its own. The note
was early struck; in talk of war, in the ominous

> Something is rotten in the state of Denmark.

and it has echoed through the play. And we are sent from the
theater now with our minds not simply upon the pity of Hamlet's
death, but stirred to some pride in him.

Fortinbras is the fortunate man, the enemy whom happy chance
turns friend, the welcomed stranger with the easier work to do.
The future is his. He the more owes (as he will know when he
has heard Horatio's tale) a tribute to the life here sacrificed. He
pays it as an honorable soldier should:

> Let four captains
> Bear Hamlet, like a soldier, to the stage:
> For he was likely, had he been put on,
> To have proved most royally; and for his passage,
> The soldiers' music and the rites of war
> Speak loudly for him. . . .

> *Exeunt marching: after the which a peal of ordnance are shot off.*

It is not by mere convention that Shakespeare allots him a hero's
end.

A Note on the First Quarto

THE PIRATE AND HIS METHODS

THE *Hamlet* which Shakespeare left us is in the Second Quarto and the Folio. From the First Quarto the positive harvest is a few interesting stage directions and a way of reducing the action to such a "two hours' traffic" (or less) as would be passable on the Elizabethan stage. And a performance of it—the merely verbal corruptions set straight—would be an instructive experiment. We should see what, to the mind of the pirate-compiler, were the qualities which made the play popular.[1]

The theory most commonly accepted at the moment is, I believe, that Q1 does not represent an earlier version by Shakespeare, nor even an earlier alien play partly amended by him; but that it is a "surreptitious" and "assembled" text, a garbling and debasing of the mature *Hamlet* which we have. From a bibliographical standpoint I am incompetent to argue the matter. But it seemed worth while to consider Q1 simply as a piece of playwriting, and, comparing it with Q2, to ask how far, as such, it can or cannot be accommodated to the theory. In the main, no doubt, it can be; but not, I think, altogether.

We have, to begin with, such truncate and clumsy lines as are the likeliest possible result of an attempt to remember the speeches containing them made by someone who had listened to them fairly often (not too intelligently) but had never learned them:

> To be, or not to be, I there's the point,
> To Die, to sleepe, is that all? I all:
> No, to sleepe, to dreame, I mary there it goes . . . .

—the crude sense of the real thing. As to the unrelated lines mixed in with the garbled text:

> And borne before an everlasting Judge . . .
> The happy smile, and the accursed damn'd . . .
> Scorned by the right rich, the rich curssed of the poore?
> The widow being oppressed, the orphan wrong'd,
> The taste of hunger, or a tirant's raigne
> And thousand more calamities besides . . . .

[1] William Poel, among his many other useful services to Elizabethan drama, did, I think, do something like this.

—they are the sort of thing which, recollection failing, anybody familiar with the Elizabethan theater could improvise out of the scraps and ends of plays floating in his memory.

On the other hand, there is Voltimand's speech, which seemingly comes direct from the mouth of an actor who had spoken it in a performance of Q2, or some very similar text (and, if it does, here is a sign that the minor actors in a company were expected to be fairly word-perfect), or from the "part" itself from which he had learned it.

Then there are the twenty-eight lines, peculiar to Q1, which Furnivall declares to be Shakespeare's own.[2] That they might well be is undeniable, and this is a point against a simple acceptance of the "pirated Q2" theory. But they might also have been provided by somebody familiar with Shakespeare's style. In one of them—

> As would have moov'd the stoniest breast alive . . .

—there is a faint echo of *Twelfth Night's*

> Lady, you are the cruellest she alive . . .
> Love make his heart of flint that you shall love. . . .

—the more noticeable, perhaps, because Corambis' lines (which Furnivall does not cite):

> such men often prove
> Great in their wordes, but little in their love.

must surely also derive from Viola's

> for still we prove
> Much in our vows but little in our love.

On the other hand, again, a large proportion of the more memorable phrases—popular tags to this day, likeliest to be so then, and easy quarry for a pirate—come through correctly:

> Frailtie, thy name is Woman.

> He was a man, take him for all in all,
> I shall not looke upon his like againe.

> Angels and Ministers of grace defend us . . . .

> There are more things in heaven and earth *Horatio*,
> Then are Dream't of, in your philosophie.

---

[2] See his introduction to the N.S.S. Grigg's facsimile.

Rest, rest, perturbed spirit.

The time is out of joynt. O, cursed spite
That ever I was borne to set it right.

—and this is but a selection from the first two scenes.

Another very famous tag comes through with the actor trick of repetition attached to it:

O my prophetike soul, my uncle! my uncle!

And Q2's elaborate variations upon

Get thee to a nunnery. . . .

become a mere gabbling, eight times reiterated

to a Nunnery goe.

This is just the sort of thing which an inferior actor, when the substance of a scene has failed to hold the audience (and the emotional structure and the sequences of this one are not easily made clear), is tempted to do; to finish it, that is to say, with a series of effective flourishes. And something of the same sort is to be seen in the triple repetition of Yorick's name, which anticipates—and prejudices—Q2's effective repetition of Alexander's, which is in its turn, when the warrantor of Q1 deals with it, spoiled by being overdone.

These things all point, in the main, to a piracy and a garbling of Q2. Besides which, Q1 gives us a play just as elaborate in plan as the genuine and matured *Hamlet*; as many characters, though they are less fully characterized; and an abundance of incidental material. Fortinbras and Denmark's foreign policy are there; so (his name changed) are Reynaldo and his spying expedition; so, despite compression, is all that is material of the Players and their play, with a reference, even, to "private plays" and "the humour of children"; so are all the circumstances of the journey to England; we have the Gravediggers, we have even an anonymous Osric—not merely, then, the major but most of the minor features of the authentic *Hamlet*. The pirate crams all he can into the smaller space permitted him. And, if slapdash, he is competent after his kind; for the cardinal point of each scene will generally be left us.

Something else suggests the pirate: the fact that it is in the last

third of the play that the text is most contracted and corrupt and
the botching at its worst.[3] The last third of any play will be apt
to suffer so at the hands of a man who fancies himself as no poet,
of course, or "serious" dramatist, but a practical man of the
theater. For there is nothing he so fears as the impatience of his
audience once the excitement of a play's mid-crisis is past. After
that push on quickly to the end, will be his rule. Now Shakespeare, writing generously throughout, is even more generous in
the last third of the play, of incidental matter, and of what a
"practical" pirate might well consider "mere talk." Hamlet is
absent from the action too; that the audience (and possibly the
actor) may not like. And when he does return he has left emotional rhetoric—stuff, says the practical man, much to the taste of
the audience—behind him. Ample reasons here, then, for the
extra contraction we find.

THE CHANGED SCENE-SEQUENCE

But two things at least (apart from the question of Furnivall's
Shakespearean lines) do not fit the theory that Q1 is nothing but
a stolen and garbled version of the mature Q2.

Why should a pirate rename Polonius "Corambis," and Reynaldo "Montano"? I know of no convincing answer.

And why should he displace the "To be or not to be . . ."
soliloquy and Hamlet's scene with Ophelia? If he had gotten the
rest of the action right it would surely be hard to make this mistake.
And why intentionally make such a change? But did he? Must
there not have been some version of the play with this scene-
sequence in it?

There is the trace of one in Q2. In Q1:

> Lets to the King . . . .

says Corambis to Ophelia; and he takes her to the King and
Queen, and the rest follows naturally. In Q2:

> goe we to the King . . . .

---

[3] Compare the pagination of the two Quartos. To the end of the closet-scene
(the mid-crisis); Q1, roughly, 45 pp.; Q2, 64. But from here to the end; Q2, 35
pp.; Q1, 18 only; hardly more than half. It may be worth while remarking that
the more legitimate omissions of the Folio are also mainly to be found in this last
third of the play.

says Polonius; and they set off. But Ophelia never arrives. The thing is not explained; but, of course, in the Q2 scene-sequence she is not wanted. Does this show Shakespeare merely changing his plan of action, or revising an earlier play, either his own or another man's, without troubling to alter the telltale phrase? If it shows a mere currently made change of plan, then the pirate took a hint from Shakespeare, but devised Q1's scene-sequence for himself—which is more than unlikely. If he found his scene-sequence somewhere, was it in an earlier play by Shakespeare, or another man's? One can give a guessing answer to both questions at once. It is as unlikely that he would take so much as he almost provably has done in the shape of character and dialogue from Q2, and go back to a very different play, be it Shakespeare's or another's, simply for this scene-sequence and the change of names.[4] Does it not look, therefore, as if there had existed a version of the play, written by Shakespeare, substantially mature, but which yet contained the Q1 scene-sequence, a Corambis and Montano, and, possibly, the Shakespearean lines (or better versions of them) which Furnivall cites?

There is much to be said, from a more narrowly dramatic point of view, for Q1's scene-sequence. The "To be or not to be . . ." soliloquy comes well from a Hamlet last heard lamenting that the time was out of joint, last pictured to us (in Q1) parting from Ophelia,

> Silent, as in the midtime of the night . . .

And from this picturing of the one encounter to their next, which we ourselves are to see, the thread of their story will be sustained without interruption, save for the few lines given to the introducing of Rosencrantz and Guildenstern and the episode of the returned Ambassadors. And his puzzling talk to her about beauty transforming honesty to a bawd will then follow so much more closely than in Q2 upon his angry grief for his mother's frailty, that the connection between the two should be as much more apparent.

In what, then, is the Q2 scene-sequence an improvement?

---

[4] It is worth noting that Montano-Reynaldo appears only at this point, where the structural difference between Q1 and Q2 is rooted. Also I have ventured to diagnose a reconsideration of the character of Corambis-Polonius at this very juncture also. See p. 205.

It enables Shakespeare (as we have seen) to develop in the long discursive scene with Rosencrantz and Guildenstern, Polonius and the Players, the imaginative, speculative, passive and unpractical side of Hamlet, and to develop it in an appropriately uneventful setting. And from this passivity it is Hamlet who rouses himself, to the self-reproach of

O, what a rogue and peasant slave am I! . . .

and to devising the test of the play-scene. That he should do this of his own accord, self-stimulated, and not (as in Q1) after his nerves have been rewrought upon by the meeting with Ophelia, and he has discovered that the King and Polonius-Corambis have baited their trap with her and are spying on him, adds much moral weight to his character. It is dramatically better too that the hero should keep the initiative; should plot, not merely counter-plot.

The postponing of the scene with Ophelia, and of the shock to the King of the overheard

those that are married already, all but one, shall live. . . .

until the very eve of the play-scene, has advantages of its own besides. The King will not be left sitting still under such a threat, or leaving a leisurely elucidation of it to Rosencrantz and Guildenstern. In Q2 he at once projects Hamlet's dispatch to England. This then becomes—as we have already noted[5]—an important turning point in the play's counteraction, the King's against Hamlet. And, with the train of Hamlet's plot now about to be fired, action and counteraction can, after the discursive delays, be pressed forward together, and the story carried unchecked to its exciting mid-crisis and Hamlet's foiling and departure.

Yet there are signs which could be held to show that the pirate *had* two versions of the play to pick and choose between: one yielding him his Q1 scene-sequence: the other, more lately written dialogue.

For instance; though Corambis does bring Ophelia to the King, she stands there completely ignored while he tells the tale of her love affair with Hamlet and of his own part in it. He tells it, in fact, just as it is more naturally told by Polonius in Q2—of an Ophelia who is really absent.

---

[5] See pp. 41; 76.

Then there is the matter of Hamlet's talk with Corambis-Polonius. In Q1 this follows close upon his discovery that Ophelia has been set in his path as a decoy, and that Corambis and the King have been spying on them. Does not that give much point to the sarcasm of

> y'are a fishmonger.

(a bawd, a pandar), and of

> I would you were so honest a man.

—so much that one is tempted to say: Shakespeare could only have written the lines in this connection?[6] On the other hand, if this beginning best suits Corambis, Hamlet's final and frankly expressive aside, Q1's

> Olde doating foole.

is hardly harsh enough comment upon a so recently detected trap-baiter and spy. And it plainly, one would say, must derive from Q2's

> These tedious old fools!

—which is suitable enough summing-up of the still guiltless Polonius.

What explanation can be offered here? One is, of course, only piling guess upon guess. But is it not possible that the "fish-monger" passage—with, it would be likely, the even more pointed

> if the sun breed maggots in a dead dog. . . Have you a daughter? . . . Let her not walk i' the sun. . . .

which Q1, economizing time, makes no use of—was originally written for the Q1 sequence, to follow close upon the Ophelia-baited trap and Hamlet's discovery of it? But why, then, did Shakespeare not omit the lines when, addressed to a still guiltless Polonius, they had lost their primary point? They are effective lines in themselves; he would be loath to part with them. And he found, besides, I suggest, that the whole passage could as well be interpreted as sardonically oracular praise of the Polonius who has so prudently withdrawn his daughter from the dangers of a corrupt world, in which men—Hamlet not least—are "arrant knaves

---

[6] There is, moreover, the stressed opposition of "honesty" and "bawd" in the scene with Ophelia.

all," and as fishmongerly-minded as he. Moreover, while Corambis, fresh from his spying and trap-setting, could hardly help seeing the point of the sarcasms, with Polonius they will pass, thus fined down, for madness; and with us, in so far as we miss the point of them, as being among those many twilight sayings, whose meaning is rather to be felt than comprehended—a quite legitimate dramatic effect where Hamlet and his "madness" are concerned.[7]

This implies, then, a correction of dialogue just sufficient to suit the change in the action, and our pirate left, for his chief resource, with a play pretty well as mature in plan and characterization as Q2, but still differing in the matter of this scene-sequence. But it looks also as if he must have had some knowledge of Q2 itself and of the changes in its dialogue which followed upon the new scene-sequence, though he did not appreciate their significance.

Not that I have the temerity to offer this as a definite solution of the Q1 problem. There are other difficulties, and other answers, doubtless, to these; and I have a dozen times repented the putting my foot into such a critical quagmire. But Q1's scene-sequence, and "Corambis" and "Montano," are surely not the pirate's invention, and he plainly has a mature play to pilfer from, and Q2's scene-sequence is the more favorable to the exhibiting of Hamlet's character. One is tempted, therefore, to see that change as one of Shakespeare's (probably latest) contributions to the subduing and adapting of the story and the storytelling to this maturer end, and what is left cryptic in the scene between Hamlet and Polonius as an item, then, in the consequent process of subtilizing the character under cover of its madness.[8]

[7] These oracular passages, of course, abound; and the quality of their content ranges from the tragically bitter implication of the "dear mother" farewell to the King, through the cold irony of this one, to the sheer nonsense of the "camel . . . weasel . . . whale" bamboozling of Polonius. It is for the critic and the actor to master their latent significance, where this exists; the audience stands midway between Hamlet and his victim, between the puzzler and the puzzled.

[8] And it is thanks—or otherwise—to Dr. Dover Wilson that I found myself upon the track of this troublesome and, finally, not very important question. He is himself so puzzled by the apparent inapplicability of the "fishmonger" passage that he deduces a now vanished stage direction in Q2, by which Hamlet enters unseen and overhears the plot to "loose" Ophelia to him. It is such a simple solution that one is strongly tempted to accept it. I was tempted, and to the point of

What, finally, of Q1's explicit disclosure of the murder to the Queen and her explicit denial that she was privy to it? Is that the pirate's, or Kyd's; was it ever Shakespeare's? The question is not upon all fours with that of the scene-sequence; for practically only a single line spoken by Gertrude is involved, and this the pirate—who might well prefer his effects cut and dried—could easily have inserted on his own account. But once again, regard for character—this alone—must rule out the disclosure for Shakespeare. Because once the Queen knows of the murder, how is she, throughout the rest of the play, to be shown docile at the King's side, protecting him from Laertes, carelessly gay during the fencing match, and with no more made of the matter? And that she knew and feigned ignorance is not to be supposed; for this would make her a monster.[9]

The Verse and the Prose

VOCABULARY AND IMAGERY

THE Elizabethan dramatist was in thrall to no critical rule. He might do what he would as long as he made what he did effective. He might write as he chose: in prose or verse, and it might be any sort of verse; and he could chop and change from scene to scene, or in the course of a scene, between verse and prose, or one

yielding. But my instincts rebelled. I did not like the spoiling of that entrance *reading on a Booke*, nor the commonplace symmetry of letting Hamlet stand there overhearing a plot by which the plotters were to stand there a little later overhearing him. Besides which—and far more important!—Dover Wilson's argument leads him fatally to having Hamlet regard Ophelia as a decoy the minute he (later on) sets eyes on her, and to knowing from the beginning of their scene together that the King and Polonius are listening. None of this can I admit for a moment. For the result will be to rob Hamlet's part in the scene of all the ebb and flow of tenderness and regret, inexplicable suffering and passion, to reduce it to a dead level of resentment, to make him, indeed, something of a self-righteous scold.

But mere objections are not enough. I felt I must propose, if I could, some alternative solution to the difficulty. For difficulty there is, even though it be—as are many dramatic difficulties—more real than apparent, and, therefore, in effect, the less important. This, then, is what I have found; though it surpasses the needs of an answer; and I had, of course, been puzzling over the question of the scene-sequence on its own account.

[9] For a discussion of the effect that Shakespeare does make—once again, a very subtle one—by bringing Gertrude to the very brink of disclosure but no further, see p. 107, note.

sort of verse and another, just as he would. Shakespeare, in this as in other things, claims every freedom. He develops no cut-and-dried method of his own. He tests and discards. His tendency, from the first, is to be rid of artifice and formula, of all forms which do not prove malleable; they break, indeed, under the stress to which he subjects them, of their molding into seemingly spontaneous expression. For that is what he works towards; but to achieve it without sacrificing the force and distinction of essentially poetic speech. Syntax must be as malleable, since it has to shape not thought only, but the unruliest emotions. And his vocabulary and imagery, however fine, must be but an enhancement of familiar parlance if the effect of it is to come directly home to his audience.

Every language accumulates certain devices for emphasis and display, and the dramatist who bases his dialogue on familiar parlance is bound to employ them. The trouble is that a too casual currency will often have effaced their value, and mere exaggeration will not restore it. A cumulation of two or three epithets, for instance, is a common means of emphasis. Shakespeare, fresh to the theater, finds their accumulation into a very catalogue to be a much-practiced dramatic trick, which he practices himself for a time. Amid the many technical confusions of *Romeo and Juliet* comes that

> Accurst, unhappy, wretched, hateful day! . . .
>
> Beguil'd, divorced, wronged, spited, slain! . . .
>
> Despis'd, distressed, hated, martyr'd, killed! . . .

Yet already he may be sensible that he is skirting the edge of the ridiculous, for he thrusts the Nurse's burlesque of the lamentations into the very midst of them; and we know, besides, that Juliet is not really dead. In *Hamlet* he is still using the trick, but he gives it dramatic validity. Hamlet, lashing himself into fury with his

> Bloody, bawdy villain!
> Remorseless, treacherous, lecherous, kindless villain!

is sensible a second later that he is an ass to unpack his heart with words; and the thing is turned to frankly comic account in Polonius'

The best actors in the world, either for tragedy, comedy, history, pastoral, pastoral-comical, historical-pastoral, tragical-historical, tragical-comical-historical-pastoral. . .

while, for a normal use of it, we have that measured and balanced

How weary, stale, flat and unprofitable. . .[1]

A very common English means of emphasis is what may be called "repetition by complement"; but, again, so common is this, its better-known locutions are so hackneyed, that their value is largely lost. "Flesh and blood," "safe and sound," "hue and cry," "kith and kin," "use and wont"—these are worn currency indeed.[2] Shakespeare, in *Hamlet*, shows an extraordinary fondness for this device, and employs it, one would say, as carelessly as constantly. It may at times betoken the teeming mind—his own or his character's—finding two words as easily as one and too eager to be getting on to choose between them. The use of the conjunction makes smooth going for the verse, the familiar form and the bare addition to the meaning easy listening; and even when this last is negligible, as it is—to take four samples out of Hamlet's mouth alone in a single stretch of a single scene—in "book and volume," "grace and mercy," "strange or odd," "love and friending"—the actor's voice can itself color the second word to a richer implication. But the meaning is often definitely amplified or intensified; amplified in "grunt and sweat"; in "slings and arrows" a sense of piercing is added to a mere blow; and the suggestion in "pitch and moment" carries us upward first and then on.[3] The sense is enlarged in "fit and seasoned" and "mortal and unsure"; its force is modified in "scourge and minister."

The concrete imagery of a noun turned adjective can add weight to the weightiest adjective, as with "ponderous and marble jaws"; or the simple image may be elaborated and made beautiful, as in

[1] Even as we have had in *Julius Cæsar*, but as speech planned to impress the hearers:

> Brutus is noble, wise, valiant and honest;
> Cæsar was mighty, bold, royal and loving. . . .

[2] For an extended list of them, and an interesting discussion of their use, see Logan Pearsall Smith's *Words and Idioms*.

[3] And that this is a complementary image is alone (I suggest) a reason for preferring Q2's "pitch" to the Folio's "pith."

"the morn and liquid dew of youth." There is, on the other hand, little but redundancy in such a huddled couple of samples as

> That monster, custom . . .
> . . . is angel yet in this,
> That to the use of actions *fair* and *good*
> He likewise gives a *frock* or *livery*. . . .

This comes, however, from a fatigued Hamlet in the slack-water of a scene. But surely, we feel, Shakespeare is conscious how tiresome the trick can be if it is overemployed when he gives us Rosencrantz' and Guildenstern's

> Most *holy* and *religious* fear it is
> To keep those *many many* bodies safe
> That *live* and *feed* upon your majesty.
> The *single* and *peculiar* life is bound
> With all the *strength* and *armour* of the mind. . . .

and adds, within a few lines, a "*depends* and *rests*" and a "*mortis'd* and *adjoin'd*."

A yet simpler and commoner device—to be found probably in all languages and literatures, since it reflects what must surely be a universal trick of the mind—is the reiterating of a single significant word, its use as a sort of refrain. As an encouraging watchword; in reiteration to persuade oneself or others that this or that is true; in the pulsing obsessions of temptation or remorse; under a dozen different forms the process is familiar.[4] Again, here is a device that the apprentice Shakespeare found turned to an elaborate dramatic artifice; and as such, to begin with, he adopts it. We have it in its crudity in *Romeo and Juliet*; in *Richard II* for the sake of its musical charm; in *Henry V* the speech on ceremony gives it careful employment; and it is appropriate to the oratory in *Julius Cæsar*. In *Hamlet* it is mere artifice no longer, its psychological rights are restored. We have Hamlet's obsessed iteration—when he is summoned to her closet—of "Mother . . . mother . . . mother . . ," his

> O villain, villain, smiling, damned villain!
> My tables—meet it is I set it down,
> That one may smile and smile and be a villain. . . .

---

[4] Dervishes send themselves into a trance by continually repeating the name of Allah. And there is the Bellman's "What I tell you three times is true," which is the psychological basis of advertising.

his "words, words, words," and "Sir . . . sir . . . sir" to Polonius. And there is the more elaborate flinging-about between Hamlet, Horatio, Marcellus and the Ghost of the "swear . . . sworn . . . sword . . . in faith . . . indeed"; and here the mutual ringing of the changes of emphasis and tone on the reiterated words is like the weaving of a spell. The effect is now legitimately gained, and by no sacrifice of spontaneity; it is kept within the bounds of illusion.

The arresting image is not hard to find, nor one which fits character or occasion. Its employment will be another matter. However sharply it should arrest, it must not retain our attention while the action is moving ahead, and other images accumulate. Its clarity, then, its emotional force, the exact effect of it coming when and where it does; the dramatist must feel sure of all that. A painter uses much the same art in placing some object in a picture. Its independent importance apart, here it will have one value, there another, here help complete the composition, there only disintegrate it, or be itself ignored.

Shakespeare's sense of fitness, both to occasion and character, is very sure. He casts the play's first scene in verse; that lends it impulse and stimulus, dignifies the story's exposition, helps heighten the sense of mystery. But it is at the outset forthright plain stuff; Francisco and Bernardo are just "honest soldiers" both, and their speech fits them. Marcellus strikes a slightly finer note. Only Horatio runs to relative clauses, allusion to Rome and "the mightiest Julius," and, towards the end—as if the supernatural had worked on his imagination—to imagery. We have the differing mental quality of the three men painted in Bernardo's

> It was about to speak when the cock crew.

Marcellus'

> The bird of dawning singeth all night long. . . .

and Horatio's

> But look, the morn in russet mantle clad,
> Walks o'er the dew of yon high eastern hill. . . .

With the action running smoothly, we may often follow by the thread of the imagery the very workings of a character's mind. It is the King's

> How is it that the *clouds* still hang on you?

developed through the Queen's

> Good Hamlet, cast thy *nighted* colour off. . . .

which seems to prompt Hamlet's own

> 'Tis not alone my *inky* cloak, good mother. . . .

And then we see him taking a sour sort of pleasure in elaborating
the idea, which he has, so to speak, snatched from them; first
adding "customary suits" to "solemn black"; next, cutting a layer
inward, so to speak, with his "forc'd breath . . . the fruitful river
in the eye . . . dejected haviour of the visage," as if to warn them
what they may be uncovering; finally, with his "forms, modes,
shows . . . trappings and . . . suits" rounding off the little parable,
his variations upon *their* theme—and they and their courtiers may
make what they will of it!

There are images which recur with the themes that prompted
them. The world, to Hamlet, is

>   an unweeded garden,
> That grows to seed; things rank and gross in nature
> Possess it merely.

Hamlet himself would be, the Ghost tells him,

>   duller . . . than the fat weed
> That rots itself in ease on Lethe wharf . . .

not to revenge his father's murder and his mother's shame.
Gertrude is to find thorns lodged in her bosom to prick and sting
her. And Hamlet pictures Claudius to her

>   like a mildewed ear,
> Blasting his wholesome brother.

and adjures her to keep from him and not to

>   spread the compost on the weeds,
> To make them ranker.

But will the ordinarily attentive listener seize on this connection,
spaced out, as it is, across more than half the play's length? That
is the test of its dramatic validity. It is hard to say positively. But
the image is initially very strongly stressed; and no more notable
place could be given it than it has; in Hamlet's first soliloquy
(when we are all curiosity about him), where too it follows im-

mediately upon the initial emotional outburst (when our attention is well held). Probably there will be at least half-conscious
recognition, with something the same satisfaction in it as one gains
from a half-remembered refrain in music, or the restoring of some
half-forgotten phrase to one's memory.

A similar, if not so clearly connected a sequence, images yet
more strongly the infectious corruption of Claudius, and Gertrude's sin. The Ghost's "lust" that will "prey on garbage"; Hamlet's "maggots in a dead dog" (Polonius has suspected him, he
knows, of lusting after Ophelia); his savage thought of "fatting
the region kites with this slave's offal"; his speech to his mother of
the "flattering unction" which

> will but skin and film the ulcerous place,
> Whiles rank corruption, mining all within,
> Infects unseen.

his elaborate demonstration to Claudius of how that "convocation
of politic worms," to whom Polonius is delivered, will before long
be at him, too, "fat" and triumphant though he now is; the talk
of "pocky corpses," dust and rottenness and the smell of mortality
in the graveyard; Claudius' own

> O, my offence is rank, it smells to heaven . . . .

—the hearer cannot but be affected, consciously or subconsciously,
by such an extended recurrence.

And in contrast to the weeds of Gertrude's sin we have flowers
for Ophelia. Hamlet's garden grown to seed has set against it in
the very next scene Laertes' warning

> The canker galls the infants of the spring
> Too oft before their buttons be disclos'd,
> And in the morn and liquid dew of youth
> Contagious blastments are most imminent . . . .

and her own imaging of such danger is of a "primrose path of
dalliance." Hamlet was for her

> The expectancy and rose of the fair state . . .

and she to Laertes is a "rose of May." In her madness she plays
with flowers; and, as if to clinch the apposition, the pitiful description of her death, garlanded with flowers, is given—to whom
but Gertrude?

The play is, indeed, in one of its aspects a very edifice of related imagery; these three sequences, with their likenesses and contrasts, being but a part, if a salient one, of the whole. It is an edifice no more logically or rigidly constructed than are the schemes of time and place, but as adaptable as these are, a product of the natural economy of the poet's mind, a part of the general lively synthesis of idea which is, for the mature Shakespeare, dramatic form. He submits himself to no other.[5]

The image must never be let pass, leaving us puzzled. A peculiar one in a passage speedy with passion must carry its explanation. To "pigeon-livered" then, is added

> and lack gall
> To make oppression bitter . . .

And if—like the birds in the basket and the famous ape—it needs much explanation, this is perhaps a sign that it had better not have been used.

On the other hand, though exceptionally, a passage crowded with a strange assortment of imagery may make a striking picture of the overwrought mind. But the thing needs to be cunningly done, and the confusion to be more apparent than real. There is Hamlet's speech while he waits for the Ghost to appear, about the "vicious mole of nature" in a man which may corrupt him altogether; with its "pales and forts of reason," "nature's livery," "fortune's star," and "dram of evil."[6] There is the heavily overcharged passage in the scene with Gertrude; when, to his telling her that she is guilty of "such an act" as

> makes marriage vows
> As false as dicers' oaths . . .

he adds:

> O! such a deed
> As from the body of contraction plucks
> The very soul, and sweet religion makes
> A rhapsody of words; heaven's face doth glow,
> Yea, this solidity and compound mass,
> With tristful visage, as against the doom,
> Is thought-sick at the act.

[5] For a thoroughly documented study of Shakespeare's imagery, the student should turn to Dr. Caroline Spurgeon's book on the subject.

[6] For the dramatic purpose and effect of this, see pp. 58 *et seq.*

Spoken as this must be, in all the heat, with all the impulse of passion, the hearer will certainly not grasp its detailed meaning—which leaves, for that matter, editors still disputing. He is not altogether required to. The "body of contraction" is a mere elaboration of the earlier "marriage vows," and "sweet religion" (plainly derivative from "very soul"), with "rhapsody of words," makes a counterpart (therefore easily seized upon) to "false as dicers' oaths"; and all this only leads up to the dominant "heaven's face doth glow. . . ." That having made its clear and vivid effect, the magnificent hyperbole which follows—the "solidity and compound mass . . . tristful visage . . . doom . . . thought-sick . . ."—is meant but to give us a vague sense of the whole world struck pale beneath God's wrath, a thing *not* to be understood but felt, not to be belittled by understanding. This is the *impression* Hamlet means to make on his mother, and Shakespeare on us.

When the elaborating of an image has to be swift and passionate and clear also, cadence and assonance may be put to use:

> Rebellious hell,
> If thou canst mutine in a matron's bones,
> To flaming youth let virtue be as wax,
> And melt in her own fire: proclaim no shame
> When the compulsive ardour gives the charge,
> Since frost itself as actively doth burn,
> And reason panders will.

The sentence is evenly balanced. For a beginning the "Rebellious hell," with its "e's" and doubled "l's," is tellingly arresting. The repeated "m's" ("mutine . . . matron . . . flaming . . . melt") keep the tone of the lines level and clear. "Proclaim no shame" sustains the clarity, while the initial doubled consonants and the half-open vowels (following for contrast upon the "e's" and "i" of "melt in her own fire") add strength and resonance. "Compulsive" gives force to the manifest indignation of the fully open "ardour" and "charge," and the doubled consonants of the final phrase demand and ensure perfect articulation, while its sibilants ("frost itself . . . reason panders") hiss contempt.

THE PROSE

Shakespeare does not try to keep the play at poetic pitch throughout; he has for long seen the dramatic unwisdom of that. But he has also passed beyond any simple mechanical division into poetry and prose; poetry for heroics and sentiment, prose for buffoonery. He has learned how to modulate his verse with ease to the expressing of many moods; his prose too; and to run the gamut, if he will, from the sublime to the commonplace without a break.

Verse prevails, of course. Not only is it by convention the dominant medium for such a play, but he needs, for his subject, its compelling and illusive power. Convention dictates prose for the Gravediggers, and convenience its use for the commentary upon the versified *Murder of Gonzago*. For the rest, Shakespeare will always have, seemingly, a specifically dramatic reason for employing it.

The longest stretch of prose begins when Polonius "boards" Hamlet, continues through the Rosencrantz and Guildenstern examination in lunacy, the reception of the Players (Æneas' tale to Dido relieving it), and is suddenly, violently broken and ended by the outburst of

O, what a rogue and peasant slave am I! . . .

The reason for its use here is obvious enough. The action is at a standstill; the impulse of verse would be wasted on it. Hamlet himself is adrift upon the slack-water of doubt and impotence, no pulsing emotion left in him, nothing for poetry to express. The detached, sceptical mind—

What a piece of work is a man! how noble in reason! . . . And yet, to me, what is this quintessence of dust? . . .

—inevitably speaks in prose.

We have prose for the quiet pessimism of the graveyard. What else is possible? How fatally verse would compromise the gentle gravity, the limpid clarity of

Alas! poor Yorick. I knew him, Horatio; a fellow of infinite jest, of most excellent fancy. . . .

As well try to put the eighteenth chapter of St. Luke into verse!

We have prose for the scene with Osric and the anonymous Lord; a dry prelude to the high-colored drama of the final scene. The encounters with Rosencrantz and Guildenstern and with Claudius after the play-scene are all cast in prose; this, I think, is to throw the harsh mask of Hamlet's eccentricities here into contrast with the soliloquies hereabouts and the scene with Gertrude (all cast in verse), in which we see his true visage. And he is made to break suddenly into prose in the scene with Ophelia, to shatter the delicate melody of her tendering back his gifts, her

> Take these again; for to the noble mind
> Rich gifts wax poor when givers prove unkind.

with the strident

> Ha, ha! are you honest? . . . Are you fair? . . . That if you be honest and fair, your honesty should admit no discourse to your beauty. . . .

—and so, seemingly, to shatter the last of the harmony between them and of the beauty of his love for her. As if for a reversal of the process, the prose of the graveyard-scene shifts, with the arrival of that sorry little procession, to verse, stiff in cadence at first:

> The Queen, the courtiers: who is that they follow?
> And with such maimed rites? This doth betoken
> The corse they follow did with desperate hand
> Fordo its own life. . . .

but kindling to the anguish of

> I lov'd Ophelia; forty thousand brothers
> Could not, with all their quantity of love,
> Make up my sum . . . .

for which prose would never do.

We may say that, in the main, the prose Hamlet is never the innermost man. For the expression of that—of the combination of thought and feeling, instinct and impulse, and of the twilight travail of the spirit which has place there—only poetry will serve.

THE VERSE

Shakespeare's dramatic verse may be said to flow from two fonts: the "lyric" (so to call it) and the rhetorical. His own earliest bent, we are disposed to presume, was towards the delicate discipline of the lyric, and to expanding this, much as Lyly had done, for dramatic use; though—and it at once made a difference—he had men to work for, not children, the virile note must be struck. And if his vein of heroic rhetoric was not quite so happily his own, this

—though only for his theater's and actors' sake—had to be culti- vated too. He was soon doing masterly work enough of the kind. In the earlier plays we can sometimes see the currents running side by side and blending here and there. And he disciplines his rhetoric by learning to put it to more strictly dramatic use, letting his captains and kings and orators find him proper occasion for it. But it is, both for dramatist and actor, a deplorably easy sort of stuff to "unpack." We have a mischievous fling at its extrava- gances embodied in Ancient Pistol. And he is taking at the time ever more extensive refuge in the exactitudes of prose.

There is a sense in which all dramatic speech must have in it something of the enhancement of poetry. It may be given by such a convention as in French classic tragedy forbids the very use of "common" words, by which a spade may be nothing less "noble" than an agricultural implement. This is not a mere piece of literary affectation, but a logical development of the convention employed; nobility of poetic substance being added to the nobility of poetic form to make, with the other conventions of time and place, a flawless unity of impression. Or the enhancement may be cunningly condensed within seemingly commonplace talk. But there it must be. If speech is to be made to "carry" in the theater it must have in it some quality equivalent—for a comparison—to the effective "length" of a well-bowled cricket ball. Nor, in Shake- speare's theater, of all others, can this poetic enhancement be sur- rendered. For there speech has to fulfill a multiple purpose. Not only must it be shaped and colored to the exhibiting of character, but the play's story has to be told far more fully and vividly than the modern dramatist will tell it, the continuous action continu- ously explained and its background suggestively filled in too. For the creating and sustaining on the bare stage of a whole illusionary world the dramatist has little other resource than picturesque and persuasive speech.

All poets, presumably, test their lines by ear as they write them, if not by speech. But with Shakespeare dramatic *writing* was for convenience of record merely; his verse was not only conceived as speech, it was to be so born and only so meant to exist. He provided music for an orchestra of living individual voices that he knew. As nearly as might be, he spoke through his actors. It is the mere notation of this once-living music which remains. Precise notation, moreover, it could not be made. Write for mechanical instruments in a recognized alphabet of crotchets and quavers, tones and semitones, with a metronome marking to rule all, and a large liberty will still be left to the interpreters. And human speech is both more flexible and less biddable than that.[7] Nor does Shakespeare, as he develops dramatically, want to discipline his speakers in measure and cadence. He is not aiming at precision of form, but at an illusion of life. His verse accords even less to measure than to rhythm and stress. Its unity is in an overriding rhythm, its expressiveness in the varying of the stress. Let the actor submit himself to the prevailing rhythm of a passage—he has, presumably, an ear for music and an accordant voice—and he will find that the very cadence of a line gives him its dramatic import, its very melody the due content of emotion. He will note how the shifting of a caesura, the elision or addition of syllables, an assemblage of consonants or profusion of vowels are meant to help produce this or that effect; and he must master the gymnastics of it. But he had then better put such mechanical matters from his mind. For there will be no one correct way of speaking a line or a passage. Within the range of the form Shakespeare invites him to share in the freedom he himself has won—this lifelike freedom. He must first have gained, of course, as intimate a sympathy as may be with Shakespeare's meaning; and the soundness of his sympathy he can test by translating this into his own terms—in just about so much critical detachment from his author may the actor indulge. Then, all study done, let him, as a conscious instrument, simply attune himself to the character he is to play; and he will find it—there is no very rational accounting for the phenomenon—speaking freely through him, and, within the measure of his sympathy, rightly too.

[7] No instrument can be made to compete in variety and significance of expression with the cultured human voice naturally used. Nor, surely, can any system of notation, any conceivable combination of symbols be devised which will represent the scope of its resources. The usual phonetic alphabet very certainly does not. Whatever the uses of this may be (it was a practical means of recording living speech till the gramophone superseded it), a language learned by reliance on it is bound to be inexpressively spoken, if nothing further is done which may set the ear and tongue free from its restraints. A man who has learned a language phonetically speaks it as a deaf man does. A student must hear the music of a language, and the best thing is probably to set him searching for it; for its melodies and cadences in its poetry, and, where English is concerned, in dramatic poetry, since there melody and cadence are at their freest and most characteristic.

There is little pedestrian verse in the play; though Voltimand's account of his mission and a few other such utilitarian passages may be so labeled. But such a one, for instance, as the opening scene's narrative of the Fortinbras quarrel—which might easily be so—is saved by being set in circumstances tensely dramatic in themselves. Horatio, harrowed "with fear and wonder" by one sight of the Ghost, has mind and nerve braced for the next, and puts them to the proof of concentration on his story—whence the close-knit, well-stressed verse, precise in statement, driven rather than flowing along:

> Our last king,
> Whose image even but now appear'd to us,
> Was, as you know, by Fortinbras of Norway,
> Thereto prick'd on by a most emulate pride,
> Dar'd to the combat; in which our valiant Hamlet—
> For so this side of our known world esteem'd him—
> Did slay this Fortinbras, who, by a seal'd compact . . .

—parenthesis preferred to digression, for thus the speech ploughs straight forward; and if this lengthens the line or displaces a caesura, so much the better, for the speaker must then, to keep the rhythm true, speed over the subordinate matter. Melody may be sacrificed to emphasis; ease will not be let prejudice strength.

> Now, sir, young Fortinbras,
> Of unimproved mettle hot and full,
> Hath in the skirts of Norway here and there
> Shark'd up a list of lawless resolutes. . . .

Note in this how the familiar "Now, sir, young Fortinbras . . ." entices our attention for the compressed exactitude of the second line, even as the free flow of the third (its one significant word, "in the *skirts* of . . ." lodged midway; it is not Norway's self that is preparing war) makes easy approach to the richly descriptive

> Shark'd up a list of lawless resolutes . . .

—which asks some assimilation.

It is only after the Ghost has come again and gone and the tension is relaxed that the verse turns melodious and picturesque, with

> The cock, that is the trumpet to the morn,
> Doth with his lofty and shrill-sounding throat
> Awake the god of day; and, at his warning,

Whether in sea or fire, in earth or air,
The extravagant and erring spirit hies
To his confine. . . .

—and so on. Not, that is to say, until Shakespeare has achieved
his dramatic purpose does he indulge in a little scene-painting.
The lonely dark and cold of the beginning have been somehow
blended into the curt exchanges of the two men relieving guard,
made part of the action itself.

The verse will always respond better to a dramatic than a pro-
sodic analysis. In Polonius' injunctions to Ophelia to beware of
Hamlet's courtship:

> I do know,
> When the blood burns, how prodigal the soul
> Lends the tongue vows: these blazes, daughter,
> Giving more light than heat, extinct in both,
> Even in their promise, as it is a-making,
> You must not take for fire. From this time
> Be somewhat scanter of your maiden presence. . . .

The third line and the sixth are prosodically short. Pope sets
things right with a "These blazes, O, my daughter," and various
editors follow him. Capell improves it to "gentle daughter," and
even Coleridge says "A spondee has, I doubt not, dropped out of
the text."[8] The sixth line the Folio itself amends to

> You must not take for fire. From this time, daughter . . .

—and the reading has been authoritatively defended; and, if
condemned, partly so on the grounds that the line, as it stands in
Q2, can be made regular by treating "fire" as a dissyllable.[9]

But approach the question from the dramatic point of view and
there is no difficulty. A midline pause is needed if the sequent
"these blazes, daughter . . ." is to be emphatically attacked; and, as
Polonius' lines are meant in general to ripple on their way unchecked, a pause of this sort must be specifically indicated. In the

---

[8] Quoted from Furness: *Apparatus criticus* and footnote.

[9] Dover Wilson says that the second "daughter" here is simply a careless repetition of the first—by, presumably, the transcriber or compositor. I think it as likely
and likelier that some actor was the original culprit. He had caught the garrulous
flow of the verse, and had ceased to mark the effect Shakespeare makes by these
occasional checks to it.

sixth line there is the pause again, put to the same use. And how can any sensitive speaker miss the increased emphasis, the "No nonsense now!" of the three monosyllables, "From this time . . ," with those two firm "m's" comprised in them? As directions to the actor nothing could be plainer; and that is what Shakespeare is putting on paper.[10]

The Polonius tune is unmistakable, and it connotes him to a nicety. The lines, overfull of weak syllables, run rippling along till they seem to be about to run off the rails of the meter altogether, the flow only arrested now and then, while the old gentleman takes breath and collects his thoughts, by a "Mark you," a "See you now" or a "Perpend." Once, indeed, when he loses the thread of his discourse about Laertes, they do run off the rails into two or three lines of prose; and Reynaldo has, so to speak, to help him on again.

There is with Polonius a stiffening of stricter lines; for though wiseacre, he is no mere babbling fool. The famous "precepts" go to a steady measure, to a melody distinguished enough, if dry. But these belong to a conception of the character afterwards somewhat modified.[11] He can drive his royal master and mistress to distraction with

> That he is mad, 'tis true; 'tis true 'tis pity,
> And pity 'tis 'tis true. . . .
> Mad let us grant him, then; and now remains
> That we find out the cause of this effect,
> Or, rather, say, the cause of this defect,
> For this effect defective comes by cause. . . .

—satire as it is besides, upon much such mental and verbal jugglery in contemporary literature and drama; not a little to be found in Shakespeare's own work! But the adroit politician in him can pass, for a peroration, to the plain, practical

---

[10] This trick (so, not depreciatively, to call it) is something of a favorite with Shakespeare. Take, for an instance, in *Julius Cæsar*, Cassius'

> I, as Æneas our great ancestor
> Did from the flames of Troy upon his shoulder
> The old Anchises bear, so, from the waves of Tiber,
> Did I the tired Cæsar. And this man
> Is now become a god.

[11] See p. 204.

> You know, sometimes he walks four hours together
> Here in the lobby. . . .
> At such a time I'll loose my daughter to him. . . .
> Mark the encounter; if he love her not
> And be not from his reason fall'n thereon,
> Let me be no assistant for a state,
> But keep a farm and carters.

—with its steadying beat, the tense consonants and broad vowels of its conclusion. For all Polonius in a single line take, however, the parenthetic, casual

> As 'twere a thing a little soil'd i' the working. . .

There, in sense as in sound—Laertes' depravity to be lightly accepted; and in the clipped syllables, the pinched consonants, the thin vowels, the tripping acidity of it—the old worldling is epitomized.

The verse at times may not so much express the speaker's own character as reflect either the occasion or the quality of the person spoken to. But this is dramatically justifiable. People do take the moment's color of some vivid experience, or self-forgetfully suppress themselves in their care for others. And no more assurance is needed of Laertes' love for Ophelia than the limpid simplicity of the verse of his farewell to her, which paints her character, not his own. He will be self-expressive enough when he returns to avenge his father. But, even then, at the sight or thought of her, his verse always yields to the tune of her again. And the Queen, as we have noted, quite forgets herself in her description of the girl's death.[12] It is, indeed, only her father and Hamlet who do not yield in this fashion to Ophelia's defenseless innocence. Even Claudius is pitiful to her.

But it is true also that Laertes is—even as Gertrude is—an unstable character. And this Shakespeare paints for us, before we have other proof of it, in the violence and exaggeration of his phrase, and the quick ranging from one extreme to another; from the

> To hell, allegiance! vows, to the blackest devil!
> Conscience and grace, to the profoundest pit!
> I dare damnation . . . .

[12] Cf. p. 133.

through the strained

> O heat, dry up my brains! tears seven times salt
> Burn out the sense of virtue of mine eye! . . .

to—after the more spontaneous

> O rose of May!
> Dear maid, kind sister, sweet Ophelia! . . .

—the conceit of

> Nature is fine in love, and where 'tis fine
> It sends some precious instance of itself
> After the thing it loves.

That image of "the kind life-rendering pelican" is—for him, and at the moment—rather forced and false; and a little later Ophelia is

> A sister driven into desperate terms,
> Whose worth, if praises may go back again,
> Stood challenger on mount of all the age
> For her perfections.

Continually, amid his naturally plainer speech, there come strokes of this sort; till we reach the leaping in the grave, and the

> Now pile your dust upon the quick and dead,
> Till of this flat a mountain you have made
> To o'ertop old Pelion or the skyish head
> Of blue Olympus.

—and Hamlet gibes at his ranting. This is character painting in a poetic medium; and the technique is legitimate.

Save in his soliloquies, the King's verse can hardly be expressive of him, only of the mask he wears, or the occasion he is improving. But this, to a nicety, it is. And such, besides, are the metaphysical resources of the poetry, its powers of suggestion by tone, cadence and rhythm, that enough of what is behind the mask can be implied. The well-balanced sentences of the address to the Council are proper to the occasion; but are they not a thought too well-balanced? The reproof to Hamlet, with each epithet doubling the weight of its noun ("obsequious sorrow . . . obstinate condolement . . . impious stubbornness") and, after a moment, epithet and noun artfully turned about ("heart unfortified

. . . mind impatient . . . understanding simple and unschooled")
is not this a little too calculated; even as the contrasted silky kind
ness to Laertes a minute since has surely been a thought too
smooth?[13] The silky smoothness is still there in the welcome to
"dear Rosencrantz and Guildenstern," the thanks betimes to
"Rosencrantz and gentle Guildenstern." Even the Ambassadors
earn an elaborately considerate

> It likes us well,
> And at our more consider'd time we'll read,
> Answer, and think upon this business.
> Meantime we thank you for your well-took labour:
> Go to your rest; at night we'll feast together:
> Most welcome home!

The revealing soliloquy after the play-scene moves to a very
different measure:

> O, my offence is rank, it smells to heaven;
> It hath the primal eldest curse upon't,
> A brother's murder! . . .

The verse throughout this is dry and unyielding. The sense is
inconsiderate of it. It is hammered out, and the accent never falls
happily upon the illuminating word. It gives us the true temper
of the man; acute, capable, tenacious, but insensible.

With Hamlet a plain danger to him, the smooth mask of
kindliness may be dropped. But through the exhibition of his
judicial severity comes the sound of his fear. We hear it in the
too-sustained stresses of

> How dangerous is it that this man goes loose!
> Yet must not we put the strong law on him:
> He's loved of the distracted multitude. . . .

—the leveled lines and the suppression of the caesura, giving us
the sense of a forced draught of thought; even as in

> To bear all smooth and even,
> This sudden sending him away must seem
> Deliberate pause. Diseases desperate grown
> By desperate appliance are relieved
> Or not at all.

---

[13] One is even tempted to imagine that Shakespeare chose that most unlikely
name because it sounded so smoothly here in the King's mouth.

its displacement and the clumsy midline restarting help to suggest
the speaker checked and harassed by—such secret and unavowable
things as do, nevertheless, find some expression in the mere
dentals and hisses of "This sudden sending . . . deliberate pause
. . . Diseases desperate grown . . . desperate appliance . . ." There
is dread and hate in the very vowels and consonants.

But he shows admirable courage and address in his encounter
with the revolted Laertes; and once again we have the gentle
caressing cadences, in the

> What is the cause, Laertes,
> That thy rebellion looks so giant-like?
>   . . . Tell me, Laertes,
> Why thou art thus incensed.

and, later, in that

> Laertes, was your father dear to you?

in the insinuating

> Not that I think you did not love your father. . . .

and the winning simplicity of the repeated

> But that I know . . .
> And that I see . . .

—phrase after phrase flowing so smoothly one into the other.
Here are the "witchcraft of his wit" and the "traitorous gifts" in
full play. To just such a tune, indeed, was Gertrude wooed and
won. Hence the importance of the scene in the upbuilding of the
character.

Hamlet, the student and thinker, is much alive to the import
of words. His very first utterance is a bitter pun.[14] And the speech
that follows, with its ". . . inky cloak . . . windy suspiration of
forc'd breath . . . fruitful river in the eye," shows him nice in his
choice of them, for sound and sense combined. He is speaking in
public, of course; deliberately and for effect.

Yet words come easily to him, and he takes an artistic pleasure
in them. Imagination finds them for him quicker than thought
will; there is delight in that. And, stirred by passion, he will pile

---

[14] A pun with Shakespeare, needless to say, was not necessarily a comic thing
at all.

them up, phrase upon phrase, until he seems possessed by words
—and he despises the futile satisfaction of it. For words themselves he distrusts; they also are things which "seem," "the trappings and the suits" of reality, tricking the speaker as often as the
hearer; and they are a weak man's weapon. Hamlet, in fact,
despises in himself one of his chief abilities, and this is a part of
the discord which disables him.

There is other witness to this than the notable

> This is most brave,
> That I, the son of a dear father murder'd,
> Prompted to my revenge by heaven and hell,
> Must, like a whore, unpack my heart with words. . . .

The

> Words, words, words!

thrown at the wordy old Polonius is a lightly ironic echo from the
same source. The phrase used to the Queen:

> and sweet religion makes
> A rhapsody of words . . .

cuts deeper, and deeper still the outmatching of the rhetoric of
Laertes' grief, and the bitter comment:

> Nay, an thou'lt mouth,
> I'll rant as well as thou.

But not all the rational means of expression of which he is
master will suffice him for self-explanation. Very naturally they
will not. How should a mode of speech framed for the conveying
of ordered thought, and common to all the world, be adequate
to the elucidating of the mysterious conflict within him—of this
madness, as it seems to all the world: and he himself has no better
name for it? He needs must express himself in poetry, the language of metaphysical things, in which words can be given almost
as mysterious a potency. But even in this he has to search for
strange images, and break all bounds in his effort to bring to
terms those

> thoughts beyond the reaches of our souls . . .

It is by no convention that Shakespeare casts Hamlet into terms
of poetry—and the prose is as poetic as the verse. He could be

expressed by no other means. For he also is essentially and perforce a poet.

Again, the dramatic value of the verse lies, not in its sense only,
but in its melody and rhythm. The first soliloquy:

> O, that this too too solid flesh would melt . . .

is an emotional piece of music. The second:

> O, what a rogue and peasant slave am I! . . .

is a passionate one. Its gestating thought is compressed into the
next seven lines, poured out without pause. But the culminating

> For Hecuba!

is given a line's length to itself. Then comes a section of eight
lines:

> What's Hecuba to him or he to Hecuba,
> That he should weep for her? What would he do
> Had he the motive and the cue for passion
> That I have? He would drown the stage with tears
> And cleave the general ear with horrid speech,
> Make mad the guilty and appal the free,
> Confound the ignorant, and amaze indeed
> The very faculties of eyes and ears. . . .

Here we have a line and a half, the halfline stayed by a query at
the normal point of the caesura. Next comes a sentence accounting for the rest of the line; a full line; and a line hardly begun
before it is broken—by a query again, but this time more abruptly.
The rest is another unchecked rush—and speech and ear alike
deal easily with the simply articulated sentence and the consecutive thought—its ending, however, suspended in midair. Again a
culminating, significant two words are given a line's length's
value:

> Yet I,

And a four-and-a-half line section follows; the first two—to compensate for the preceding hysteria—ballasted and retarded by the
speaker's need to fabricate "dull and muddy-mettled. . . peak like
John-a-dreams, unpregnant . . ."[15]

---

[15] The repeated queries, with their effect of indrawn breath, help to suggest
hysteria. And such a line as

> What's Hecuba to him or he to Hecuba. . . ?

can, by reversing the natural process of the aspirates, actually be spoken so, no

Thereafter the more regular lines, coming two or three together, serve to send the speech forward on an even keel; while a crowded one intervening, a

> Tweaks me by the nose? gives me the lie i' the throat ...

or a

> Remorseless, treacherous, lecherous, kindless villain!

bespeak the choking passion; and a line's length allowed (yet again) to no more than a "Ha!" or an "O, vengeance!" tell now of strength unequal to the strain.[16] Q2 even eloquently prints the petering-out of the storm as

> And fall a-cursing, like a very drab; a stallyon, fie uppon't! foh!

Then follows thought:

> About, my brain! Hum, I have heard
> That guilty creatures, sitting at a play,
> Have, by the very cunning of the scene,
> Been struck so to the soul that presently
> They have proclaim'd their malefactions. . . .

Metrically, the first line here is two beats short. Dramatically it is, of course, nothing of the kind, for the actor will speak it more or less thus:

> About, my brain! Hum-m-m. I've heard ...

This, with the four following regular, smoothly running lines (exceptionally regular; "presently" and "malefactions" given their fullest syllabic value), and the succeeding similar five, give us the brain as smoothly at work. Only one of the nine lines is irregular, the center one of these three:

> For murder, though it have no tongue, will speak
> With most miraculous organ. I'll have these players
> Play something like the murder of my father . . . .

vocal tone being required. That will have been supplied in the immediately preceding "Hecuba."

[16] "O, vengeance!" is, however, the Folio's only; and personally I suspect it to be an actor's interpolation. The next line in the Folio is deplorably weakened by the insertion of an "I sure," which everyone agrees to reject. In Q2 the thought travels from the abuse of Claudius directly to the "Why, what an Asse am I." The Folio's "O, vengeance!" only prejudices by anticipation the entry of the idea upon

> Prompted to my revenge by heaven and hell. . .

But it is the decisive line. Also its caesura coincides with the end of a sentence. This involves a pause; the effect of that being to shorten the final word to "org'n"—as if it died on the speaker's lips as the capital "I'll have these players" came into his mind. The breath taken between the sentences involves also the shortening of the line's last word to "play'rs"; but that, again, prevents it from prejudicing the more important initial "Play . . ." of the next line.

This ten-and-a-half line section of the evolving of his plan, which has followed the exhausting emotional outbreak, ends halfway through a line upon the

> I know my course.

And, again, the caesura becomes also an interval between sentences, and the line's completing must be contracted more or less to

> The sp'rit that I've seen . . .

—not so ugly a contraction in the speaking as in the writing. Except for the one main division between the speech's passion and its thought, every "section" in it does end in midline, but that minimizes the slight pause involved and helps to keep the speech a single whole. The very first line, in fact, to end with a definite full stop is the last; and that has its rhyme—the first and only one —to stress this:

> The play's the thing
> Wherein I'll catch the conscience of the King.

It is a musical full close.

The "To be or not to be . . ." soliloquy is just such dramatic music also. The sentences, each drawn out over four or five lines, the even cadences, suggest the sustained tension of thought; and the iterated

> To die; to sleep!
> No more; and by a sleep . . .
> To die, to sleep!
> To sleep . . .

the pendulum swing of insoluble doubt.

The scansion test for a line—of Hamlet's or any other—will always be the dramatic one. Take such a passage as

> Touching this vision here,
> It is an honest ghost, that let me tell you:
> For your desire to know what is between us,
> O'ermaster't as you may. And now, good friends,
> As you are friends, scholars and soldiers,
> Give me one poor request.

Hamlet is, for the moment, tartly on the defensive against any prying into his secret. Note the admonitory whiplash in the elided end of each line; in the "vis'n here ... tell y' ... between 's." And the "o'ermaster 't"—Q2 actually spells it "Oremastret"—is yet more peremptory. But, to mark his quick apologetic revulsion to friendliness, practically no pause is allowed between this and the

> And now, good friends ...

The four simple but progressively weighty monosyllables are in themselves an appeal, and they prelude the more persuasive

> As you are friends, scholars and soldiers ...

But if this is to be syllabically scanned:

> As/ you/ are/ friends/ scho/ lars/ and/ sol/ di/ ers/

it will not be persuasive at all. Hamlet is standing with Horatio and Marcellus, the scholar and the soldier, at either side of him, and appealing to them together and individually. And what he says is

> As y' are friends// schol'rs// and soldy'rs//

—as far as such symbols can make it clear. The effect lies in the weight and significance given to the three capital words by the slight pause allowed for after each; pauses which, by a skilled speaker, can be made to count in the rhythm without imperiling it in the least.

Lastly, for an example of cadence, color and rhythm turned to dramatic account, dictating the reading, defining the meaning of the lines, take the passage in which Horatio and his two companions reveal to Hamlet that his father's spirit is in arms. For malleable ease and nervous vitality combined there is, moreover, probably no piece of verse-dialogue in all Shakespeare to touch it.

> HORATIO.   Hail to your lordship!
>   I'm glad to see you well:
> HAMLET.   Horatio,—or I do forget myself.

HORATIO.   The same, my lord, and your poor servant ever.
HAMLET.   Sir, my good friend; I'll change that name with
           you.
           And what make you from Wittenberg, Horatio?
           Marcellus!
MARCELLUS. My good lord.
HAMLET.   I'm very glad to see you. (*To Bernardo*) Good
           e'en, sir. . . .

The main rhythm gives us speed without haste, and prevails over
the minor lapses from it. Note the elided endings of "lordship"
and "Horatio." The first is customary. The second has dramatic
point; glad surprise rings out upon the resonant "a," and the
practical suppression of the two last vowels allows for the slightest of pauses in which the gladness can be felt. There is the short
line for the more perfunctory greeting of Marcellus, and a return
to meter for the amending courtesy—which still takes Bernardo in
its stride, for Hamlet's thoughts are on Horatio—of

> I'm very glad to see you. Good e'en, sir.

Then, drawing him apart, he can devote himself to his friend:

           But what, in faith, make you from Wittenberg?
HORATIO.   A truant disposition, good my lord.
HAMLET.   I would not hear your enemy say so;
           Nor shall you do mine ear that violence,
           To make it truster of your own report
           Against yourself; I know you are no truant.
           But what is your affair in Elsinore?
           We'll teach you to drink deep ere you depart.
HORATIO.   My lord, I came to see your father's funeral.
HAMLET.   I pri'thee, do not mock me, fellow-student;
           I think it was to see my mother's wedding.
HORATIO.   Indeed, my lord, it followed hard upon.
HAMLET.   Thrift, thrift, Horatio! the funeral baked meats
           Did coldly furnish forth the marriage tables.
           Would I had met my dearest foe in heaven
           Or ever I had seen that day, Horatio!
           My father! Methinks I see my father!
HORATIO.   O, where, my lord?
HAMLET.   In my mind's eye, Horatio.
HORATIO.   I saw him once; he was a goodly king.

HAMLET. He was a man, take him for all in all,
I shall not look upon his like again.

The rhythm flows easily and evenly; with Horatio, and only with him, is Hamlet continuingly at ease.

Note the effect made by the double echo of the unusual cadence of Horatio's

My lord, I came to see your father's funeral.

There is irony in the very refrain:

I pri'thee, do not mock me, fellow-student;
I think it was to see my mother's wedding.

And, while the words themselves say little, the strict scansion, that firm, five times repeated "d," and the bitten final "n" of

Indeed, my lord, it followed hard upon.

bespeak a Horatio sternly if discreetly of Hamlet's mind about it.

The short space allowed in the line to "Thrift, thrift . . ." tells a Hamlet that, despite their ten consonants to two vowels, he is to speak the words lightly. There is distaste in the very "b . . . k . . . d . . . m . . . ts" of the "funeral baked meats," with which it more levelly ends, and contempt in the repeated "f's" of the "furnish forth." The last line of the speech must be scanned dramatically:

My fath'r!// Methinks I see/ my fath'r!//

—more or less. Allot it its ten written syllables, it will prove practically unspeakable.

Note Hamlet's frequent repetition hereabouts of his friend's name. The word is gentle in itself, and he is always at his gentlest with Horatio; nor ever, till he is dying, gentler than at this moment, for he is no longer lonely in his grief, and the deadlier blow has not yet befallen him.

This section of the scene ends with three simple lines; their rhythm exact; their words—three excepted—of one syllable, fit frame for their simplicity of content. The first line is Horatio's

I saw him once; he was a goodly king.

and, once more, two succeeding lines from Hamlet repeat the cadence; but accordantly, not ironically, this time:

He was a man, take him for all in all,
I shall not look upon his like again.

The three curt final "king . . . all . . . again" give a certain sense of finality too. But we know, with Horatio, that here is rather a beginning than an end.[17] And this repetition with a difference of the three-line duet, the closer drawn accord between the two, the touch of a finality which we know is none, make quietly arresting preparation for the revealing:

> My lord, I think I saw him yesternight.

This fires the train; and from this point the excitement mounts step by step to the scene's crisis, Hamlet's

> I will watch to-night. . . .

The text embodies clear directions to the actors. Hamlet's

> Saw! Who?

is allowed the length of a line. His share of the next line, the echoed

> The King my father!

must—the verse demanding an elided "fath'r"—fade away into breathless wonder. Horatio, with his

> Upon the witness of these gentlemen . . .

brings Marcellus and Bernardo into focus; and the action is at once broadened and strengthened; for, the tale told, Hamlet will have the three to attend to and question. The subsequent dialogue between the four of them falls at first into the regular rhythm of the verse, though the lines are broken:

HORATIO.   I knew your father;
These hands are not more like.
HAMLET.   But where was this?
MARCELLUS. My lord, upon the platform where we watched.
HAMLET. Did you not speak to it?
HORATIO.   My lord, I did;
But answer made it none. . . .
HAMLET. Indeed, indeed, sirs, but this troubles me.
Hold you the watch to-night?

---

[17] Incidentally, this echoed cadence, as a test, condemns the reading, once beloved of actors:

> He was a *man*. Take him for all in all . . .

by which Hamlet was oddly made to imply that kings as kings were not of much account.

MARCELLUS.		We do, my lord.
BERNARDO.	}	
HAMLET.	Armed, say you?	
MARCELLUS.		Armed, my lord.
BERNARDO.	}	
HAMLET.	From top to toe?	
MARCELLUS.		My lord, from head to foot.
BERNARDO.	}	
HAMLET.	Then saw you not his face? ...	

from which point—the rushed "saw'y'not" initiating it—the beat degenerates into a scurry, with the stiffening here and there of a more regular line to prevent the rhythm from disintegrating altogether. The quick unhesitating give-and-take *within* the continuous rhythm gives us Hamlet's mind keen to absorb all that the three can tell him as fast as they can tell it; the *breaking* of the rhythm marks the breaking of this close contact of attention; and his lapse to such *detachment* from it as

> Very like, very like! Stayed it long?

shows us his thought questing beyond their ken.

His mind made up, the verse returns to the consistent strength of

> If it assume my noble father's person,
> I'll speak to it, though hell itself should gape
> And bid me hold my peace. I pray you all,
> If you have hitherto concealed this sight,
> Let it be tenable in your silence still . . . .

which is maintained to the scene's end.[18]

---

[18] Neither Q2 nor Folio displays this dialogue as verse, nor, it may well be, did Shakespeare in his manuscript. The construction would be clear in his mind, and he could tell the actors at rehearsal how to piece their bits together. This could not be done for them in their "parts," which would contain their own lines and cues only. And if he wrote these passages (and the many similar ones) as Q2 vertically displays them, that was probably for the convenience of the prompter, who had not then to cast his eye clear across the line from *Hamlet* to "From top to toe?" or from *Horatio* to "In faith," at a continual risk of error during rehearsals, when prompting is often continuous; and the man who had to copy out the parts would be liable to make similar mistakes. Were Shakespeare not at rehearsals, the prompter and the actors might here and there be hard put to it to reconstruct the verse—even as the editors have sometimes been since. Yet the actors would have highly trained ears; and the rhythm, if they yielded to it, would assert itself. But compare this with the careful setting out of (say) certain scenes in Jonson's *Sejanus*.

The Characters

FRANCISCO AND A FEW FUNCTIONARIES

THE minor characters in Hamlet are not highly developed, nor—
but for two or three—very sharply individualized. There is more
than one reason for this. They may be figures from the old play,
whom Shakespeare has not been at the pains to transform. But
even if he has, or let the character be originally his own, should
it move in Hamlet's orbit—and what in the play does not?—it
will tend to turn satellite, moon to his sun. Opposition of character to character is the very life of drama. Yet even of the King
and Queen, of Polonius, Laertes and Ophelia, it may be said that,
in contact with Hamlet, they put up little more than is needed to
keep them their place. We learn most about them when they are
free of him; yet of some consciousness of him they are never free.

But Shakespeare can by now, if he will, give his actor matter
enough for a vivid sketch of character in fifty words. Francisco,
at the play's opening, speaks just fifty-five. He is on guard. Bernardo approaches; so nervous—we learn why in a moment—that
he does not, as he should, wait to be challenged, but lets out a

> Who's there?
> Nay, answer me; stand, and unfold yourself.
> Long live the King!
> Bernardo?
> He.
> You come most carefully upon your hour.
> 'Tis now struck twelve; get thee to bed, Francisco.
> For this relief much thanks; 'tis bitter cold,
> And I am sick at heart.
> Have you had quiet guard?
> > Not a mouse stirring.

In that short swift exchange between the two, place, time and
season are given us, Bernardo's strung-up nerves, his arrival so
carefully upon his hour lest the Ghost appear to Francisco, who
evidently knows nothing and had better be kept ignorant; and
we have the sharply bitten-in sketch of the "honest soldier," too,
brusque of manner, terse of speech, not insensitive to the haunted
atmosphere, but choosing to account for feeling "sick at heart" by
the plain fact that " 'tis bitter cold."

Nor is this too curious an analysis to be valid. If the ordinary reader does not find it all in the eleven lines—but he can if he will look—well, they were not written for reading. If it be said that the spectator, in the few minutes of their speaking and acting, cannot take in so much, this is not quite the question either. We are not asked to think the matter out, nor given the time to. What we have here, packed into the dialogue, are stage directions to the actors; it is material for the effect they are to make on us, and this effect will be, in the strict meaning of the word, sensational; and if we did, at the moment, analyze the sensation and realize how it was made, the effect of it would be largely lost.[1]

We see no more of Francisco; and such vivid minor characters are apt to disappear from a play when they have served their sensational turn. Barnardine in *Measure for Measure*, sent to his death to remind us of the sinister realities of that so-called comedy; Cinna the poet and the jigging rhymester in Brutus' tent, dashing revolution and war with ridicule of the worth of poetry in such times—to elaborate these lively sketches would give them a distracting importance, to prolong their existence merely would commensurately diminish their value.

To another category of minor parts belong the Ambassadors and the Players. They are units in the machinery of the action, functionaries, little more. Characterless characters of the kind are to be found in every play. The individualities of the actors lend them individuality enough. They furnish something of that indifferent background which life itself provides to all poignant spectacles. Voltimand and Cornelius are appropriately colorless. The message from Norway is a formal one; they are the mere instruments of its delivery. Upon the Players Shakespeare does throw enough reflected life—reflected in Hamlet's kindly greeting to them, in his

> Dost thou hear me, old friend? . . .

and his care for their good treatment—to remind us that players are human beings too.

---

[1] Though it is, of course, possible, without wholly sacrificing the sensation, to gain a consciously critical pleasure in the art of the business too.

HORATIO

Horatio dwells in Hamlet's shadow, yet he is very much himself; and (again) few things are more difficult in drama than to give a character standing of its own, except by setting it in opposition to others, and enkindling it, so to speak, by friction.

But he is established in our knowledge before ever Hamlet appears. He dominates the first scene. Not by any insistence upon himself; that would belie him. It is in his talk of the chances of war with Norway, in his attitude towards the Ghost, that he incidentally discloses himself as a conservatively patriotic and educated gentleman. He takes pride in the dead king's fame and disparages the lawless young Fortinbras; and besides Marcellus' word for it that he is a scholar, we have him citing his Plutarch. He is level-headed and open-minded. The Ghost, when he heard of it, was a "fantasy"; but seeing is believing. Yet he has neither fear of it, for he stays it and speaks to it; nor any superstitious respect for it, since he encourages the frightened Marcellus to strike at it with his partisan. For him it will be what it is proved to be. Yet he is sensitive too. He steadies his nerves for the second sight of it; but he trembled and turned pale when it first appeared. And in his final

> But look, the morn, in russet mantle clad,
> Walks o'er the dew of yon high eastern hill . . . .

a gentle spirit speaks.

MARCELLUS; BERNARDO

Marcellus and Bernardo can best be dealt with in a parenthesis here, for they are what they are as a part of the scheme of this first scene. They strike each his complementary and contrasting note in it. Of the three men Bernardo (though nervous enough at the outset) is the stolidest. Horatio looks to him for some mitigating of Marcellus' fantastic tale. He observes the "thing" when it appears more exactly than do the others, and, a moment later, is bantering the converted sceptic:

> How now, Horatio! you tremble and look pale.
> Is not this something more than fantasy?

For the rest, he says what he has to say as plainly and shortly as possible.

Marcellus is of finer temper, and the whole mysterious business has him the more sharply on edge. What does it portend? He has not dared speak to the Ghost himself. When Horatio, armored in scholarship, does, and it will not answer, he fears it is offended. As timorously as desperately he makes to strike at it with his partisan, and at once repents:

> We do it wrong, being so majestical,
> To offer it the show of violence. . . .

The supernatural is very real to him:

> Some say that ever 'gainst that season comes
> Wherein our Saviour's birth is celebrated,
> The bird of dawning singeth all night long;
> And then, they say, no spirit dare stir abroad;
> The nights are wholesome; then no planets strike,
> No fairy takes, nor witch hath power to charm,
> So hallowed and so gracious is the time.

—to which Horatio answers:

> So I have heard, and do in part believe it.

saving himself, even at this eerie moment, by the "in part" from too much credulity. Marcellus, we notice also, is anxious for Hamlet to be told; it is he who—to turn their minds from the Ghost—sets Horatio recounting the reasons for the "strict and most observant watch" and all the "post-haste and rummage in the land"; he who, in the later scene, at its most poignant moment, breaks out with

> Something is rotten in the state of Denmark.

As we watch the scene, intent on the story it tells, we may not notice—may not positively remark—such points and aspects of character. But (once again) these things are stage directions to the actors, material by which the scene can be convincingly built up. The matter-of-fact Bernardo, who has seen what he has seen; Marcellus, alive to the mystery beyond; Horatio, won from doubt to belief—within that likely combination we find our own transient belief in what we see.

All good dramatic writing has this double content; the overt, with which the immediate effect is made; the covert, in which the actor finds guidance for the modeling of the figure by which that effect is to be made. And the less prominent the character, the less imposing its immediate effects, the greater the need for this modeling to be complete.

HORATIO, *resumed*

Hamlet's affectionate welcome of him adds to Horatio's status; and he adds to it himself by the quiet good sense with which he responds to Hamlet's hysterical treatment of him after the Ghost's vanishing.

Thereafter he disappears from the play for the best part of an hour; until Hamlet—and Shakespeare—need him again, and he is conjured, as if from nowhere, by a simple

What ho, Horatio!

—and the very simplicity of the business somehow suggests that he has been within call all the time. Shakespeare restores him to importance by the as simple means of giving Hamlet, then and there, twenty lines to speak in his praise. The method is nakedly simple but, as it is employed here, dramatically sound. For we have Hamlet's relief and gratitude, as he turns from false friends to this true one,[2] finding spontaneous utterance. And we learn of Horatio what we could hardly—since he has no direct part in the action—learn from him: that he is poor and what the world calls a failure, yet that good and ill fortune alike leave him unmoved (this praise also, save for one gentle protest; he is as little self-regardful as that). For all of which Hamlet loves him and trusts both his judgment and faith. His task now is to stand, silent and apart, keeping, through the acting of *The Murder of Gonzago*, a steadier watch upon the King than Hamlet's can be; and this (seemingly irrelevant) expansion of his character will lend to the still figure, as we watch it, a fresh quality and strength.

But, for self-expression, Shakespeare gives him thrifty measure indeed. Forty-eight words for moral support of Hamlet in this crisis (that is the exact allowance for the play-scene and its sequel); after which he disappears again, to reappear only when Hamlet has gone to England. And though, watching Ophelia and the first to hear of his friend's return, he is then quite an important figure, he speaks, except for the reading of a letter, exactly

---

[2] Cf. p. 83.

twelve lines. Were there no more to say about it, his presenting is a masterpiece of dramatic economy.

From the instant of Hamlet's return, Horatio never leaves his side again, and the faithful watchful presence now becomes as eloquent as any speech. Two perceptive sentences stand out from his encouragement of the anodyne talk with the Clown, and when he has heard of the events on the ship he warns Hamlet that the King must soon learn of them too. He is glad to have him distracted by the ridiculous Osric. He sees how the long strain is telling on him, counsels him to forgo the fencing match; since he will not, can only stand apart again in watchful silence—to exclaim once when the first blood flows. He helps bar the King's escape. Then, death nearing, Hamlet calls to him.

Till now he has responded to princely professions of affection with a "your poor servant" or a "good my lord." Now he asserts himself and his love by a fierce eloquence of deed, in which a man that even Hamlet has not known—and by no means the equable philosopher—stands suddenly revealed.[3] But, the moment past, he lets the poisoned cup be wrested from him, and vows himself, silently and for the last time, to his friend's service. We hear that service begun. And the Horatio who will speak

> to the yet unknowing world
> How these things came about . . .

is a man who has grown in stature under our eyes.

ROSENCRANTZ AND GUILDENSTERN

Rosencrantz and Guildenstern are set and sustained in sharp contrast to Horatio; false friends against true. The difference extends to all they are, the three of them. Horatio; poor and unself-seeking, the student, the philosopher, with his loyal respect for the old king:

> our valiant Hamlet—
> For so this side of our known world esteem'd him . . .

—he had just once seen him living; he journeyed from Wittenberg to stand, a simple looker-on, at his funeral; and after, it was not for him to intrude upon the son's, upon the Prince's, grief. And

---

[3] Though there was a passing hint of him in the Horatio who reproved his Prince for these "wild and whirling words."

Hamlet's greeting to him as "good friend" and "fellow-student" shows him a chosen friend, and of recent days.[4] It is during his absence from the action that "dear Rosencrantz and Guildenstern" come to pervade it. They have been sent for by the King. They, then, are approved of by the new regime; and

> being of so young days brought up with him,
> And since so neighboured to his youth and humour . . .

being, besides (with their supple "gentry") fitter companions for a prince, will they not be taken even nearer to Hamlet's heart?[5] He greets them, with much the same impulsive affection, as "my excellent good friends." But how different—even before suspicion has kindled in him—the smart chop-logic of the talk from the confident refuge he took in Horatio's understanding! The false relation hardens as he screens himself from their prying by oracular evasions and trivial gossip about the Players. He cannot flatly and finally dismiss them; it is a princely penalty to be so "waited upon," and to have to repay treachery with courtesy. But their second intrusion on him provokes, as we noted, his summons to that other friend, and the fervent

> Horatio, thou art e'en as just a man
> As e'er my conversation cop'd withal.

And the contrast here will be heightened by the very look of the three; the smiling, point-device courtiers making their congee on the one side, the grave, sober-suited, simple-mannered student appearing on the other.

From their summoning of Hamlet to the Queen to the departure with him—their own fatal departure—for England, Shakespeare endows the couple with more and with a somewhat more sinister importance. Pretense to good comradeship is over. There is a touch of regret for it in Hamlet's

> why do you go about to recover the wind of me, as if you would drive me into a toil?

but little more than cant, one fears, in Rosencrantz' plaintive

> My lord, you once did love me.

---

[4] Shakespeare, in this part of the play, is still thinking of Hamlet as of student's age.

[5] He speaks of them later on as "schoolfellows," boyhood friends, therefore; and this Horatio specifically is not.

The sprightly schoolfellows, who were "to draw him on to pleasures," are now plainly his enemy's instruments; and he soon finds himself no better than a captive in their hands. Then their tone, quite appropriately, changes:

> What have you done, my lord, with the dead body? . ... Tell us where 'tis, that we may take it thence, and bear it to the chapel. . . . My lord, you must tell us where the body is, and go with us to the King.

That he goes into exile practically their prisoner is clear from the fact that—and for the best of reasons!—it is they who carry, not he, the King's sealed commission; he has to burgle their cabin to secure it. But there is no hint that they knew of its contents.

Horatio (as if to complete the pattern of their relation to him) is allowed a grim comment on their fate:

> So Guildenstern and Rosencrantz go to't.

And Hamlet, hardened to his task by now, callously caps it:

> Why, man, they did make love to this employment;
> They are not near my conscience; their defeat
> Does by their own insination grow.
> 'Tis dangerous when the baser nature comes
> Between the pass and fell incensed points
> Of mighty opposites.

Fit epitaph for them, doubtless; and the fate of the nonentity who yields himself in complacent ignorance to evil employment has its due place in tragedy. And if we feel that they might as well have been let lapse, harmless and unharmed, from the story, it will not be so much in compunction for them as because, dramatically, they seem hardly worth the killing.

As parts to be played, unhappy actors cast for them will protest that they are among the very worst in all Shakespeare. They must not, of course, be judged by what a producer's blue pencil may leave of them; though, as it happens, they are too closely knit into the action for this to be very trenchantly wielded. But do all that legitimately may be done with them, they will yet remain, one fears, superior puppets; for Shakespeare himself has not given them life. That he could have by a touch or so, and without making too much of them, the comparison with Horatio shows. The deficiency is explicable. He did not, I fancy, to begin with, mean them to be more in themselves than supple, superficial nonentities. They are less even than that; a single nonentity split into two. Again we see why. One false friend to balance the one true friend, and to make but one more in the series of decoys, Polonius, Ophelia, Gertrude—the mere pattern would be monotonous. An occasional trio is a welcome relief from successive duets and solos. Nor could Hamlet come off from a single inquisitor of the sort as he does from the pair, lightly playing one against the other, using them as springboard for his antic disposition. So far they suffice. But the stress of the action sequent to the play-scene is too hard on them dramatically. They are not quite of the right stuff for the treacherous embassy to England, for Hamlet's escort to his death. Shakespeare may be feeling so when he imposes on them those two surprisingly solid speeches—which do not fit them, which only leave them, therefore, looking more puppetlike than before.[6] But at that crisis of the play, with everything in rapid movement, he can spare them no more consideration. They remain, then, two rather lifeless strands in its lively fabric.

POLONIUS

As if, again, for contrast, two family groups are presented to us: Claudius, Hamlet, Gertrude, united and divided by evil; Polonius, Laertes, Ophelia, happy together in their ignorance that this same evil is already working to destroy them. The play exists within a framework of these contrasts of character and situation, as must every play more or less, for it is the stress of them which gives it stability. Here is the second dimension—so to call it— which the dramatic form needs and pure narrative does not. Its scheme need not be made very patent. We should probably be left about as conscious of it as we are of the comparable means by which some fine building is kept erect; we feel secure when we stand in it, but do not forget its beauty because of that. But without these means to stability, building or play, for all their beauty, will alike collapse.

We can, I think, see Shakespeare changing his mind a little about Polonius. In his first scene (not to count the single speech at the Council) he is far from being a "tedious old fool." His

---

[6] The point is further discussed on p. 98.

injunctions to Laertes and Ophelia are clear and terse, and contain sound worldly wisdom. The change comes with the charge to Reynaldo; and hence, perhaps, the seemingly undue length allowed to that minor matter; our first impressions of the character must be corrected. After the resolution into the more comic key we have him spontaneously and abundantly himself; though the mere abundance is gradually pruned, for once the garrulity has been demonstrated, the effect of it can be gained without much indulgence in the thing itself.

His adjusted place in the play's character-scheme soon becomes plain. Hamlet doubts and delays, questions and suffers. Claudius, all outward candor, keeps his secret close and moves surely to his ends. Polonius is the complacent wiseacre, infatuate in opinion, precipitate in action—and usually wrong. He is not wholly or obviously a fool, nor externally ridiculous at all. He can occupy his high place with dignity enough—only now and then calling pomposity to his aid—so long as everybody else will keep theirs. He is for order and degree, whether he must be telling his own daughter that

> Lord Hamlet is a prince, out of thy star;
> This must not be. . . .

or simply in using the Players

> according to their desert.

He is loyal to the powers that be:

> Assure you, my good liege,
> I hold my duty as I hold my soul,
> Both to my God and to my gracious king. . . .

—as he will, with like fervency, once have assured him whom Claudius has doubly succeeded (for clearly he has held his old place); nor is he the man to have been pained by his "dear majesty" the Queen's "o'er-hasty marriage."

He is kindly; his manner to his retainer "good Reynaldo" is most affable. As a man of the world he will not idealize his fellow-creatures; and at Ophelia's defense of Hamlet—

> My lord, he hath importuned me with love
> In honourable fashion.

—he scoffs. Yet he is tolerant, as a man of the world must be; and

when it appears that he was wrong—and he ungrudgingly admits
it—his only comment is a perfunctory

> I feared he did but trifle,
> And meant to wreck thee. . . .

Nor do we gather that he will be gravely displeased if Reynaldo
does discover Laertes to have been

> drinking, fencing, swearing, quarrelling,
> Drabbing . . .

as long as no great scandal results. For his last sly injunction—
something of a comedown from the earlier, sententious "to thine
own self be true"—is a

> And let him ply his music.[7]

Of the same pattern as this spying upon Laertes is his "loosing"
of Ophelia, decoylike, to Hamlet, Claudius and he to be the "lawful espials" here. His intentions are excellent. To cure this madness one must first know its cause, and he suspects nothing
sinister in that. He does not stop to consider that it may be somewhat ignoble, a little cruel, to put his daughter to such a use. It is
as like him that, having baited the trap with her and placed a
prayer book in her hands, the sight of her, docile in guile, should
prompt the incongruous platitude:

> We are oft to blame in this—
> 'Tis too much proved!—that with devotion's visage
> And pious action we do sugar o'er
> The devil himself.

and as like him that, when he and Claudius emerge disappointed
from their hiding-place, he ignores her distress.

He is old, of course; and in such shallow natures feelings desic-
cate with age. He looks back whimsically to when

> in my youth I suffered much extremity for love. . . .[8]

He does not—if the very slightest of touches is there to tell us so

---

[7] Which I can hardly believe is meant to disclose a last moment's interest in this
aspect of Laertes' education. It is the equivalent, surely, of "Let him go his own
way and enjoy himself." We have a similar, better known saying in "face the
music."

[8] He is definitely one of Shakespeare's "old" men, no account being taken of
his likelier age as the father of Laertes and, as it concerns the women characters,
Ophelia. See p. 226, note, where the question of this convention is discussed.

—find even the sight of mimic suffering to his taste; for, when the Player pauses in the tale of Hecuba, comes his:

> Look, whether he has not turned his colour and has tears in 's eyes. Prithee, no more.

and whenever he can so turn his busy mind from statecraft:

> he's for a jig or a tale of bawdry, or he sleeps.

Poor Polonius! Were this no other than the world he has so successfully learned to live in, where words are potent and ambassadors correctly come and go, where one so pleasantly "hunts . . . the trail of policy," or may with a "bait of falsehood" take a "carp of truth," and

> of wisdom and of reach,
> With windlasses and with assays of bias,
> By indirections find directions out . . .

where human nature must perforce become

> As 'twere a thing a little soiled i' the working . . .

but to no worse effect than that a prince may seduce your daughter and your son be debauched in Paris—were life, in sum, simply the sort of clever game he thinks it, he then would be the man he so complacently feels himself to be, the tried and wise "assistant for a state," who has never

> positively said ''tis so,'
> When it proved otherwise . . .

whose never-lacking advice has only to be followed for all to be well! But Shakespeare shows us, by a harsher light, a very different picture; of a silly old gentleman pettily maneuvering among passions and forces that are dark to him. No one wishes him ill. But he will meddle. And at last a sword thrust, meant for his master, incontinently ends him. For an elegy:

> Thou find'st to be too busy is some danger.

And as if to mark his pitiful futility his corpse is let lie there, eavesdropping still, while the revealing quarrel rages between mother and son. Then it is lugged away, like so much carrion.

It is a nicely mischievous touch that at the University he "did enact"—of all possible parts!—Julius Cæsar.

LAERTES

In the two earlier scenes before he leaves for Paris, Laertes is a
more or less conventional figure. But even here—in his elder-
brother moralizing, and the import of Ophelia's demure

> But, good my brother,
> Do not, as some ungracious pastors do,
> Show me the steep and thorny way to heaven,
> Whilst, like a puff'd and reckless libertine,
> Himself the primrose path of dalliance treads,
> And recks not his own rede.

and in Polonius' hints to Reynaldo of how he is likely to be found
passing his time, and that suggestion of

> The flash and outbreak of a fiery mind,
> A savageness in unreclaimed blood. . .

—there is preparation for the contrast to be established later between him and Hamlet, between the pensive idealist and full-
blooded confident youth.

When he returns Hamlet, the irresolute bungler, has gone—
presumably to his death—leaving disaster behind him; Polonius
slain, Ophelia "driven into desperate terms." In his place uprises
this gallant fellow, carried into the palace upon a wave of rebellion, but, disdainful of such aid, facing the King alone:

> To hell, allegiance! vows, to the blackest devil!
> Conscience and grace, to the profoundest pit!
> I dare damnation. To this point I stand,
> That both the worlds I give to negligence,
> Let come what comes; only I'll be revenged
> Most throughly for my father.

What—after so much trimming and veering, mining and counter-
mining—could be finer? What more tender too than his grief?

> O rose of May!
> Dear maid, kind sister, sweet Ophelia!

And when—the true culprit known and reported to be again
within his reach—he is ready straightway.

> To cut his throat i' the church.

even that makes pleasant contrast with Hamlet's late refusal to
kill the praying Claudius lest he should spare him hell-fire. Yet

the next moment this "very noble youth" is bettering an already
scoundrelly plan to assure him his revenge with a secretly sharpened sword by proposing to poison it too. Conventional virtue
strangely belied; our edifying young counselor of the earlier scene
with his sister turned the wrong side out indeed!

Shakespeare may not have had the anomaly in mind from the
beginning; it suffices him to have a character here in hand that
is capable of it. His purpose, at its crudest, is to swing our sympathy back to Hamlet, Laertes losing on the balance; but he will
enrich his character-scheme in doing so.[9] It looks very much as
if—lest, misled by his self-depreciation, we misinterpret Hamlet's
failings—he now wished to show us what moral instability may
really be, and to what sort of nature it properly belongs. *Morally*
unstable Hamlet is not. His

> thinking too precisely on the event. . .

may sap his resolution, but it sharpens, not blunts, his sense of
right and wrong. Laertes—swayed by every passion and rash in
action; suspicious, as all unreasoning people are, but the more
blind to flattery—proves wax in the clever fingers of the King. He
is too ignorant of himself to be, by that banal precept, true to
himself, and he can be cajoled and provoked into the ignoblest
crime.

The man of action, with his

> O, thou vile king,
> Give me my father! . . .
> How came he dead? I'll not be juggled with. . . .

is soon maneuvered to an intellectual standstill; and, when grief
for his sister has also worked on him, he becomes the easiest of
dupes. Claudius, finding use for him, first flatters him with confi-
dences and—deadlier than plain praise—by reporting others'
praise of him; then so stings him with doubts of the worth of his
passion and grief that the moment-old honest welcome of the
news of Hamlet's return—

---

[9] In Q1 it is Claudius who proposes to poison the sword; Laertes merely
acquiesces. Whether this shows us Shakespeare's first intention or is (as current
theory about Q1 requires, if it is to be consistently applied; but need it be?) a
part of the pirate's bungling, the improvement in the true text is plain.

> But let him come;
> It warms the very sickness in my heart
> That I shall live and tell him to his teeth,
> 'Thus didest thou.'

—is replaced, not simply by consent to an underhand trick, which would itself normally be abhorrent to him, but—for defiant answer to these taunting doubts—by that

> I will do 't:
> And for that purpose I'll anoint my sword. . . .
>   I'll touch my point
> With this contagion, that, if I gall him slightly,
> It may be death.[10]

Lured into one infamy, from pure bravado he must outpass it with another.

Committed to such partnership, he is in a trap, from which, till it is too late, he will not have the moral courage to escape. Yet he is no murderer at heart; and, when he follows Ophelia to her grave, while Hamlet's

> That is Laertes, a very noble youth. . . .

may echo a little ironically in our ears, since we know what is brewing, the one-time truth of it is mirrored, and is meant to be, in his anguish, in the tender

> Lay her i' the earth,
> And from her fair and unpolluted flesh
> May violets spring!

—even in his flashing attack, with a

> The devil take thy soul!

upon his outrageous rival in mourning, whose "wicked deed" it truly is that has wrought the ill.

He and his enemy pulled apart, he has to stand and listen to strange things; to that

---

[10] Claudius, it is worth noting, has no great confidence either in the young man's self-control—how should he have!—or powers of deception. Laertes is to keep close within his chamber until the moment of the fencing match. And he is warned:

> If this should fail,
> And that our drift look through our bad performance,
> 'Twere better not assayed. . . .

> I lov'd Ophelia; forty thousand brothers
> Could not, with all their quantity of love,
> Make up my sum. . . .

—no vulgar seducer's cry; to the still stranger

> Hear you, sir;
> What is the reason that you use me thus?
> I lov'd you ever. . . .

And he is not the man to unriddle them. But when he is reminded of what his very effective answer is to be by the King's privy

> Strengthen your patience in our last night's speech. . . .

he does not respond to that either; he goes glumly away.

It is again hard listening for him when, all being ready for the treacherous match, Hamlet, before King and Court, craves his pardon for the wrong done:

> Give me your pardon, sir; I've done you wrong;
> But pardon 't, as you are a gentleman. . . .
> Sir, in this audience,
> Let my disclaiming from a purpos'd evil
> Free me so far in your most generous thoughts,
> That I have shot mine arrow o'er the house,
> And hurt my brother.

—and to this he must reply. A glance exchanged with the King will tell us by whose help he has concocted the quibbling

> I am satisfied in nature,
> Whose motive, in this case, should stir me most
> To my revenge: but in my terms of honour. . .

(honor!) which hardens, as before, to the bravado of

> But till that time
> I do receive your offer'd love like love,
> And will not wrong it.

We need not be surprised that he fences ill. He is at odds with himself even as Hamlet was. And since he cannot fairly come near his man with the poisoned blade, his stroke itself must be treacherous—which featherweight addition to his guilt goes, he finds, "almost" against his conscience; a flashlight upon his moral disorder. But, indeed, into such a tangle of wickedness has he got himself that, when the tables are suddenly turned on him, what we hear in his

> Why, as a woodcock to mine own springe, Osric,
> I am justly kill'd with mine own treachery.

is something like thankfulness. He pays his penalty. He sees to it that Claudius does not escape. Hamlet forgives him, and we are meant to, also.

OPHELIA

But while Laertes deserves his fate, and Polonius invites his by his meddling, of what is Ophelia guilty? At worst, of a single lie told to a madman for his good. We may call her docility a fault, when, as she is bid, she shuts herself away from Hamlet; but how not trust to her brother's care for her and her father's wisdom? How even question the part she is made to play later when not her father only but the King and Queen themselves prepare her for it?

She is no fool. Shakespeare shows us that to begin with by the touch of mischievous humor with which she counters Laertes' homily. And beneath the dutifully diffident

> I do not know, my lord, what I should think.

her feeling is clear that Hamlet's love for her is wholly honorable. As to which she is right. But she must obey her father.

"Many a day"—whatever that may mean in the calendar of frustrate love—passes before the two meet again. She has been sending back his letters and refusing to see him; till, one day as she sits sewing in her closet, he suddenly breaks in upon her, dumbly distraught, suffering, mad.

> Mad—for thy love!
>   My lord, I do not know;
> But truly I do fear it.

By parting her from him, then, they have brought this guilt upon her. And next they must needs thrust her in his path again, so that, since her "good beauties" did the harm, her virtues—the kindly Queen hopes—may somehow

> bring him to his wonted way again . . .

When Hamlet discovers and speaks to her she naturally says nothing of their last strange meeting. One does not remind a madman of his madness; though, indeed, he seems sane enough now. She offers—as any girl would—to set the seal on their parting by giving him back the presents he gave her, the verses he wrote her; "ill at these numbers" though he said he was, they were music to her. If he will not take them back things may then begin to mend between them. So simple are her tactics. He does refuse them; but it is with a harsh, unexpected

> No, not I;
> I never gave you aught.

which is like a blow in the face to her, an unkindness far outpassing her obedient repelling of his letters since, and refusals to see him. For it is a denial that he ever did love her—the estranged lover's cruelest revenge.

Why does she not tell him that she only obeyed her father in shutting herself away from him? At the mere thought that he never loved her she would have no heart to. She puts the little packet of his gifts down somewhere; let happen to it what will. He rouses her pride, too, by his sudden sardonic

> Ha, ha! are you honest? . . . Are you fair?

And if there is a certain self-consciousness in the dignity of her

> What means your lordship?

are not those eavesdroppers chiefly to blame? Once more, and perforce, she is obeying her father; but—though surely they all only mean him well—it is to more questionable purpose now.

Hamlet has his secret from her too. Stung by her seeming fickleness he may have been, but that was not the death of his love for her. He cannot tell her of his mother's guilt; nor is there any but this riddling way of telling her what it has meant to him, of his lost faith not simply in womanhood, but in himself where womanhood is concerned:

> I did love you once. . . . You should not have believed me; for
> virtue cannot so inoculate our old stock but we shall relish of it;
> I loved you not.

So her father was right when he scoffed at her tale of her wooing "in honorable fashion." She accepts disillusionment with a miserable

> I was the more deceived.

What with this and with what follows, his bitter

> Get thee to a nunnery; why wouldst thou be a breeder of sinners? ...

she might well by now be forgetting the eavesdroppers and her task here. She is sharply reminded of them by the abrupt, inconsequent, fiercely suspicious

> Where's your father?

What on the instant should she answer? He is "mad," and there is danger in his looks. She tells her loyally defensive lie:

> At home, my lord.

He knows, as he puts the question, that Polonius is hiding there; he does not positively know that she knows it and is lying to him, nor greatly care to know. It is enough that she is a part of the conspiracy of evil around him, and, in her very womanhood, of the "wantonness and ignorance," the lusts of the flesh, in which the evil first took root:

> Go to, I'll no more on 't; it hath made me mad. ...

For her, the well-meant appeasing lie has merely set a match to his madness, which now rages over her meaninglessly. Does *she* paint, jig, amble, lisp? She prays aloud for him. And her thought, when he has left her, is of the "noble mind ... o'erthrown," only later of her "deject and wretched" self. She stays silent and scarce-regarded while the King and her father, emerging from their hiding and having had their use of her, discuss weightier matters. But behind that strained mask of grief her own sanity is already wavering. When they have gone she goes quietly away.[11]

---

11 For a discussion of the contradictory stage directions, see p. 80, note.

One can detect in Hamlet here a slight psychological incongruity, for which the old story or the old play may be responsible, the episode in it which gives us the "fair woman" sent to seduce him and his secret from him. There is nothing in the least wanton about Ophelia; yet (well before, in his mad rage, his obsession about his mother's wantonness shows) his talk to her of beauty transforming honesty to a bawd sounds a little as if he suspected her of such designs on him. There is effective irony, of course, in his speaking thus to an innocent girl, who has been "loosed" to him with a prayer book in her hand; and the subtler thought

Nor will the strain be less when, but a few minutes later, we see her coming with the rest to the performance of the promised play. She has been trained to Court life, and to be merry when merriment is in demand. And here is Hamlet, gaiety itself, no trace of his lunatic passion left on him, joking with the King and her father. And they, seemingly, are as gay as he, and might quite have forgotten their late resolve to send him to banishment or prison. But at least he will have no more to say to her. Far from it; he turns upon her again. She suffers ignorantly, and there is no more pitiful suffering. She is sensible of obscure forces at work around her. She knows now that it is no wrecked love for her insignificant self which has sent him mad. The thing has other roots, and promises—what dreadful harvest? Yet she had to be given by the father she trusts to be scourged by the man she loves; and now she has smilingly to face more unmeet cruelty still. His raging still in her ears, she finds him nearing her again; and, for a sequel to it—sequel besides to that now recanted wooing "in honourable fashion," those "holy vows"!—he sets himself to

—that it is even viler to turn innocence and piety to such uses—is already implicit in Polonius' preparatory

> We are oft to blame in this . . .
>   . . . that with devotion's visage
> And pious action we do sugar o'er
> The devil himself.

Yet it looks as if the genesis of Hamlet's attitude lay in a recollection of the cruder theme. This would fit in, what is more, with the surprisingly indecent treatment of her in the play-scene—since nothing she has said or done gives excuse for that. But again, there is more refined cruelty and more disequilibrium of mind in saying such things to an innocent girl. Have we here then, perhaps, a visible part of the process of Shakespeare's transference of the story from the physical to the psychological plane?

To the generally gentler view of Hamlet—a little out of fashion now—belongs the penetrating remark by Lamb in his essay *On the Tragedies of Shakespeare*: ". . . in all such deep affections as had subsisted between Hamlet and Ophelia there is a stock *supererogatory love* (if I may venture to use the expression) which in any great grief of heart, especially where that which preys upon the mind cannot be communicated, confers a kind of indulgence upon the grieved party to express itself, even to its heart's dearest object, in the language of a temporary alienation. . . ." Lamb was in justified reaction against the ranting bullying Hamlets he too often saw. He touches, needless to say, the heart of the matter, and he must himself have brooded often upon its yet more tragic aspects. But "language of a temporary alienation" is a fairly mild term for what Hamlet does say.

cheapen her before all the Court by squatting familiarly at her feet and launching smutty jokes at her.[12]

She defends herself as best she may, tagging to her distressed interjections a formal "my lord" for some denial of the lewd intimacy—its implications so plain to the smirking courtiers!—thus thrust on her. Later she musters courage to make a little casual conversation herself, even to respond to her Prince, as a Court lady should, with a pretense at his own merry mood. But we shall not have forgotten our recent sight of her desperately praying for him, convulsively weeping for her loss of him; and, for all that she keeps up appearances so bravely, we may wonder, as we look at her now, if the gentle, fragile nature could sustain many more such wrenchings at the root.

She vanishes with the rest when the crisis comes, and we do not see her again. For the mindless wraith that we see is no longer Ophelia. The father she loved and trusted killed by the man she loved; it is the final and fatal wrench. Her madness tragically outmatches his whose work it is.

CLAUDIUS

We have in Claudius the makings of the central figure of a tragedy. Something of him will be found very highly developed in Macbeth. There again is the man who does murder for his crown, cannot repent, and is drawn ever further into ill.[13] But here Hamlet himself is allowed so to sway the action of the play that no other character can be very freely treated if the framework of the accepted story is to be maintained. Claudius in particular, the "incestuous . . . adulterate beast" of its beginning, must remain

---

[12] It is not that a little loose talk at a Renaissance Court would be anything very much out of the way. But this particular passage of equivoque is, to begin with, exceedingly gross; and, as inflicted by Hamlet, the bookish, fine-minded student, upon the strictly schooled, well-guarded, mere girl that Ophelia is, the effect is exceptionally shocking.

[13] And is there not in

> If 'twere done when 'tis done then 'twere well
> It were done quickly. . . .

a distinct echo of Claudius' lines to Laertes:

> That we would do
> We should do when we would; for this 'would' changes,
> And hath abatements and delays as many
> As there are tongues, are hands, are accidents. . . .

the "incestuous, murderous, damned Dane" at the end, whatever may be done with him in between.

It is long before Shakespeare lets us see him as he is. We encounter him first, before the Ghost has spoken, presiding at his Council, the Queen at his side, speaking of his brother's death with dignified sorrow; discreetly implying as to his marriage—in the

> our sometime sister, now our queen,
> The imperial jointress of this warlike state . . .

—that it is chiefly a dynastic business; benevolent to Laertes; gentle but firm with the recalcitrant Hamlet. His kindliness is a little too feline, perhaps, his discourse somewhat overelaborate, his courtesy too uniform to be quite unfeigned; and his protests of fatherly love for the young man, whose succession—with whatever legal warrant—he has forestalled, may slightly smack of hypocrisy. But these are harsh criticisms. He is new to his throne, and naturally anxious, under the particular circumstances, to stand well with everyone around him. And even Hamlet, left alone, his mind only on the marriage, does not hold Claudius so heavily to blame for it. The shame is his mother's.

So far, then, there does not seem to be much against him; and superficially—seeing him with his courtiers' eyes—there is much in his favor. And when, the Ghost's tale told, we see him again, we look in vain for confirmation of it. Everything he does and says is far more consistent with innocence than guilt. The very point, in fact, of that

> O villain, villain, smiling, damned villain!
> My tables—meet it is I set it down,
> That one may smile and smile and be a villain. . . .

has been that, to look at Claudius, the thing *is* incredible. Picture him thus, an urbane, considerate and convivial gentleman, going quietly and confidently about the business of his Court and State, and we understand why Hamlet, in a calmer moment, may feel that it is perhaps "a damned ghost" that he has seen, and that his

> imaginations are as foul
> As Vulcan's stithy.

Claudius is, then, a consummate hypocrite. But everything till now has gone so smoothly for him that he may well think himself secure. Shakespeare, as it happens, has small choice, in the early part of the play, but to present him to us thus, the mask fitting marvelously, unless he is to be given some counterpart to Horatio for a confidant, or indulged, he also, in soliloquy. The technical constraint is turned to advantage. To have a Hamlet and a Claudius matched in method would be to the prejudice of each. Instead—since we for long never see Claudius alone, nor except among those whom it is his business to deceive—there can be most effectively· set against Hamlet's hesitancies, doubts and nervous introspection, this easy, equable assurance. We do see him gradually drawn into ever graver consideration of Hamlet's case, to the point of resolving to dispatch him to England. But even this is no certain evidence of his guilt. While it may at one time be wise to keep a disinherited heir at your Court and under your eye, it may become wiser to send him packing upon some mission abroad. He goes to the entertainment Hamlet has provided apparently in the gayest of moods; and if he lapses into silence—why, even as things are on the surface, he has enough to trouble him. His incontinent flight from its cardinal provocation finally convinces Hamlet of his guilt. But not till even later, till, for the very first time in the play, he is left alone, does he himself definitely confirm it to us, with the

> O, my offence is rank, it smells to heaven;
> It hath the primal eldest curse upon't,
> A brother's murder!

That at least, I am persuaded, is how Shakespeare planned the matter, and I venture to wish he had left it at that. The earlier revealing aside, spoken while Polonius, with his talk of pious action sugaring o'er the devil himself, arms Ophelia with her prayer book for the ambush—that

> Oh, 'tis too true!
> How smart a lash that speech doth give my conscience!
> The harlot's cheek, beautied with plastering art,
> Is not more ugly to the thing that helps it
> Than is my deed to my most painted word.
> O heavy burden!

—has all the look of a subsequently applied patch. It is somewhat flat in itself, and so awkwardly placed, that it can be given no great dramatic force.[14] It is a feeble anticipation of the very effective, long pent outbreak of the soliloquy. What justifies it?

Does Shakespeare want to show us Claudius' conscience at work before risk of discovery rouses it? That may be. Is it that he will not keep us waiting longer for a definite admission of guilt? The dramatic effect so far has not lain, of course, in our doubts of this. We shall have taken the Ghost's word without question. It is Hamlet's own doubting which has been so effectively excused by the sustained appearance of innocence. An audience nowadays not only knows the story of the play, but is insensitive to some of its original significance; and actors have come to suit their reading of the parts to this. The Elizabethan Hamlet had, with his audience, reason enough for doubting whether it was, after all, "an honest ghost" he had seen.[15] His modern successors mostly seem to hold the Ghost's word for gospel and reproach themselves for even momentary disbelief in it. And a modern Claudius, his reputation for all but villainy long lost, plays the villain from the start. If this anticipatory aside is a patch, it may well have been put on to save the Elizabethan Claudius from appearing, on the contrary, too persistently innocent, and for fear the audience should rather come to share Hamlet's doubts than, as they were meant to, detachedly observe them. It must now be accepted, of course, as an integral part of the text; it should equally be a direction to the actor to make—except for this single moment—the "plastering art" of his "most painted word" as convincing as possible.

The "prayer-scene"—but, try as he will, the guilty wretch cannot pray—is a turning point in the presenting of Claudius, as in the action of the whole play. Till now the smiling mask, the mellifluously conventional speech, clouded and frayed but a little even by this alarming business of the play; here, in sharp contrast, the seething mind laid bare. And though the mask goes on again, it will hereafter be transparent to us.

This hard argument about the efficacy of prayer must have been the matter of more than one sermon heard both by Shakespeare

---

[14] Not because it is an aside. Claudius could, indeed, so far isolate himself upon the outer stage as to give it the effect of a soliloquy. But it is irrelevant to the rest of the scene; nothing legitimately leads up to it or away from it.

[15] Cf. (once more) Dover Wilson's convincing argument.

and his audience in those compulsorily theological days—by Claudius from his Court chaplain too. We have, therefore, no simple sinner, with confessor at hand to direct him, if he would, towards penance and absolution, but a man dosed with controversial doctrine, who must struggle with its dilemmas as best he can. From his guilty heart he cannot pray. Yet God's mercy is for the guilty, too, and his fault is past. But its fruits are his still, and

> May one be pardoned and retain the offence?

In this world perhaps; yet

> 'tis not so above . . .
> What then? what rests?
> Try what repentance can: what can it not?
> Yet what can it when one can not repent?

After which, and with some more beating of the breast, argument collapses into

> Help, angels! make assay!
> Bow, stubborn knees, and, heart with strings of steel,
> Be soft as sinews of the new-born babe! . . .

and a weary

> All may be well.

While he is trying what the older submissive routine will do for him Hamlet passes and pauses; and we are shown to what twists of savage theology a finer spirit in its perplexity may be wrought. His sword is out, his enemy helpless. But will it be revenge enough

> To take him in the purging of his soul,
> When he is fit and seasoned for his passage?
> No. . . .

—not death only but damnation must be assured. So Hamlet passes on. And by this perverted scruple he opens the way to all the ills to come; quickly beginning with Polonius' death, Ophelia's to follow, the Queen's, Laertes', and his own little delayed. Had he known the truth—which we learn on his departure, from Claudius' defeated

> My words fly up, my thoughts remain below;
> Words without thoughts never to heaven go.

—that this enemy was *not* purging his soul, but (so we shall gather later on) planning how to save his skin by ridding himself of son as well as father, he might have done straightforward human justice on him. Instead, the adversaries issue from the frustrate encounter—Claudius unaware of Hamlet's presence, Hamlet as blind to what that bowed head hides—these strangely warped religious exercises, the one to worse frustration, the other to dispute for his soul's salvation no more.

This revelation of an inward Claudius does more than rescue the character from conventional villany. Here is a man who can face the truth, not only about his deed and its deserts, but about himself too. His own chaplain could not argue the question better, nor—one may add—to a more orthodox conclusion. But he rises from his knees knowing himself to be as hardened in sin as ever, and so proceeds, with only the more clarity of mind, to give effect to those thoughts which have obstinately remained below. He is in danger, he must act; and it is small wonder that such a weather-cock as Hamlet, veering in spiritual storm, should have, for the time, no chance against him.

Quite naturally, while he is the motive power of the action (as he is from now to near the end of the play), he is more vividly revealed; though the fact may be that only from about now did Shakespeare start developing the borrowed character. But graft and stock are, as usual, made to agree. If the formal, calculated speech belonged to theatrical convention, it also fitted dramatically both the King discoursing and the man of guilty conscience, fearful lest an unguarded word betray him (and the more fearful that, no one suspecting him, he is the likelier to relax his guard). But things, though worse, are now better for him. If Hamlet, by some queer clairvoyance, has happened, as it seems, upon his secret, he has also given him good excuse—and is to make it better by killing Polonius—to deal drastically with such madness. It is the true part of a grieved stepfather and prudent statesman, for the sake of his country's peace, for the culprit's own sake, to get him quickly and quietly out of the way. He subscribes to the madness; for who will believe what a madman may say? Yet once in England the dispossessed heir might turn menacingly sane. There is safety only in his death; so that is duly planned.

And as he cannot—let it cost him his soul—repent the one murder he is the readier to profit by another.[16]

But once that reproachful figure no longer paces his lobbies, he can—being the clear-thinking, practical man he is—banish both the old crime and the new from his mind. And here is the key to the Claudius that we see for a short while, grieving genuinely enough for Polonius' death, over Ophelia's suffering, and facing Laertes with unforced dignity and calm. No merely well-masked villain; but the man that he would be, could his crimes but be left out of account; the man that he likes to be able to feel that he is. And of such is the real and dangerous wickedness of the world! It is this interim picture of him, with its touches of inconsistency, which does most to make Claudius a figure of flesh and blood.

He never relapses after to theatrical convention. And note how by this the writing of the part has changed. For the formal line and sentence we have sensitive, pregnant phrases, which seem to shape themselves spontaneously into verse. We can see his mind at work; and with what agility when, his security shattered by the sudden tidings of the failure of his plot against Hamlet, the awakened devil in him turns on the instant to make Laertes his accomplice in another!

It is masterly diplomacy by which he converts the young man's demand for open justice on his father's murderer into consent to the seemingly friendly fencing match. But if the task were a simple one neither of the two would appear to be such dangerous adversaries to Hamlet as, for this last round of the fight, they must. The biter is bit, however. The fascination of poison—when Laertes so unexpectedly proposes to "anoint" the unbuttoned sword—once more proves too much for him. And he also will be "hoist with his own petar."

Shakespeare finds no occasion to develop him further; he lets him slip back, rather, into the mere machinery of the story. But just so men do, after a period of amnesty, relapse to a routine of guilt. We note his callous silence upon the news of Ophelia's death; his chief care now is to keep Laertes under his eye, under

---

16 Though how it is ever to be explained away, Claudius seemingly does not stop to think. But Shakespeare knows that this chicken will not come home to roost.

his spell. In the last scene the old smiling mask is on again, the speech is as mellifluous as before. But this is dramatically right; Hamlet has returned, and there is fresh guilt to hide. A last blot is added to his swiftly closing account, when he lets the instant pass in which Gertrude could be saved. And, dosed with his own poison, he meets a fittingly ignominious end.

Claudius does not come quite unquestionably to life. The material for the character is there, old and new, and it is all consistent enough. But Shakespeare has left some of it incompletely developed, some indeed to implication only, and the actor must use judgment in assembling it. And though Claudius is the villain of the piece, his guilt undoubted and of the blackest, the evidence for the prosecution must be weighed. But an actor will instinctively make himself Counsel for the Defense of the part he plays, when he can.

There is the question of his love for Gertrude, and hers for him. They never themselves refer to its illicitly passionate days. There are, indeed, no love passages between them. They are only twice, and for the space of a few lines, left alone together, and then trouble is heavy on them. It has, at this time, even begun to separate them; for Gertrude tells him no more than she need of what has passed with Hamlet in her closet. But throughout the play, alone with her, or before the Court, Claudius shows her very much that loving respect which Hamlet says his father showed her. The relation, as it now is, seems not to lack dignity; and the actor may justifiably somewhat discount the "Hyperion to a satyr," and, still more, "the bloat king," and the paddock, bat and gib of the closet-scene as the language of angry grief, the pent-up poison of a sick mind. Even the Ghost qualifies his

> that incestuous, that adulterate beast . . .

and the "shameful lust" by

> With witchcraft of his wit, with traitorous gifts—
> O wicked wit and gifts, that have the power
> So to seduce! . .

—which suggests, surely, good gifts turned to ill account, and a

Gertrude fascinated by them, yet not too easily won.[17] We certainly are not meant to see her enamored of an obvious monster.

How far was it love for her which tempted him to crime? To this we have his own clear-headed answer when he is wrestling with himself alone and speaks of

> those effects for which I did the murder,
> My crown, my own ambition and my queen.

She takes neither pride of place in it, nor comes as an afterthought. But it is in his converse with Laertes (when, as we have noted, Shakespeare brings him most spontaneously to life) that his feelings for her show. Is it odd that he should so confess himself to the young man?

> for myself—
> My virtue or my plague, be it either which—
> She's so conjunctive to my life and soul,
> That, as the star moves not but in his sphere,
> I could not but by her. . . .

It sounds, does it not, as if wrung from him? Later comes the rueful (and equally odd, as part of the provocation to the murdering of Hamlet):

> Not that I think you did not love your father;
> But that I know love is begun by time,
> And that I see, in passages of proof,
> Time qualifies the spark and fire of it.
> There lives within the very flame of love
> A kind of wick or snuff that will abate it . . . .

Of what does that covertly speak—those "passages of proof"—but of Gertrude's mute obedience to Hamlet's behest to deny herself to his bed? He does not know the reason; she could not tell him. To him it only seems the inevitable sad satiety of a passion such as theirs, grown "to a plurisy," dead "in his own too much."[18]

---

[17] It is true that a line or so later, the Ghost refers to him as

> a wretch, whose natural gifts were poor
> To those of mine . . .

and even talks of the difference between a "radiant angel" and "garbage." But of all the evidence for the prosecution this is the most—and the most excusably—biased.

[18] In letting any matter of this kind pass unemphasized into the play, Shakespeare would be unconcerned with what we may call its likelihood in time; he

Not that this can be very clearly brought home to the audience. Had Shakespeare given himself a freer hand with Claudius and Gertrude, nor let the play be so overwhelmingly dominated by Hamlet, he would, we may well suppose, have clinched this and other questions about them more effectively. As it is, the chief dramatic value of the passages is (yet once more) as a direction to the actors. If Gertrude, from the closet-scene onwards, does a little self-consciously hold aloof from him (except when, for a moment, he is in danger from Laertes), and if he shows himself somberly aware of it, the lines, when they come to be spoken, will take color from this. And such an attitude one to the other will in itself be eloquent; especially by contrast to the earlier happiness, shown plainly to the world when at last it may be. But it is a pity that these ends of character are left loose.

Is Claudius a drunkard? We have the promise of the "jocund healths" he means to drink, and Hamlet's scornful

> The king doth wake to-night, and takes his rouse,
> Keeps wassail, and the swaggering upspring reels . . . .

with its sequent

> This heavy-headed revel east and west
> Makes us traduced and taxed of other nations;
> They clepe us drunkards. . . .

But we hear no more of this, except when Hamlet would rather kill his enemy "drunk asleep" than at his prayers—which is still only evidence for the prosecution—and we see nothing of it at all. So Shakespeare does not want to stress it. But it helps picture a Court in which the student-philosopher Hamlet would, at best, feel very out of place; and it gives a significant touch to the picture of the King, no more a drunkard than his neighbor, or than a clever man can afford to be, but the consummate sensualist in this too. And he would find, it might well be, comforting forgetfulness in the nightly wassail, and courage in the "swaggering upspring" and the bravado of those trumpets and drums.[19]

---

would not, that is to say—indeed, he does not otherwise—stop to consider whether the closet-scene had taken place a day or so or a week or so earlier.

[19] But I saw once an Italian actor who had evidently been greatly struck by this aspect of the character, for his nose was reddened and he played the part bibulously throughout. This lightened the play very much. And here, my dear Dover Wilson, is another possible answer to the burning question: Did Claudius see the Dumb

GERTRUDE

However else Shakespeare may have envisaged Gertrude upon his stage, it could not have been as the mature matron, the realistic mother of a man of thirty, to which a later-born tradition has unluckily accustomed us. His boys could play the young Ophelia and the fourteen-year-old Juliet and scarcely call convention into question; and one sees them bringing a certain advantageously sexless distinction to the withered Queen Margaret or the stern Volumnia.[20] But the presenting of ripe womanhood and its charm would obviously be beyond them. As far, then, as appearance went (and setting aside the simply comic) he had to choose between spontaneous youth and conventional "age." Juliet is young. It is against all likelihood that Lady Capulet should be old; but she is made so, for here is an effective contrast which nothing in the story forbids. Ophelia is young; and if likelihood were all, Gertrude, who will certainly never see forty-five again, might better be "old." But that would make her relations with Claudius —and *their* likelihood is vital to the play—quite incredible. There-

Show? My Italian, at that juncture, was far too muzzy and hilarious to have seen any offense—or, indeed, any meaning at all in it.

[20] As to the comic old women, it is likely that they were played by men. Dr. W. J. Lawrence thinks so (and allows me to quote him), pointing out that when, with the Restoration, actresses inherited the Juliets and Rosalinds—though even this change was not suddenly complete—such parts as the Nurse in Otway's *Caius Marius* (his adaptation of *Romeo and Juliet*) were till the end of the century, or near it, acted by men. And this, as he justly says, looks very like a survival of Elizabethan practice.

But that, with Shakespeare at any rate, the men did not trespass into this territory beyond the Mistress Overdones and Dame Quicklys and Angelicas is suggested, I think, by the severe limitation of the number of the women's parts. In no play do we find more than five. And this looks like consideration for the likely number of trained apprentices available, a number limited both by law and custom. In *Richard III*, it is true, there are, besides the women's parts, the young King, the Duke of York and Clarence's son to be cast. But for two of these not much skill is needed, and something may be done by doubling. The doubling would be without regard to sex; in *Romeo and Juliet* Lady Montague's death implies the need for a Balthasar or a page for Paris. Such plays as *A Midsummer Night's Dream* and *The Merry Wives of Windsor* ask, of course, for a number of children. But they were originally intended, it is presumed, for private performance, and any public theater would need outside help for their production. Shakespeare, from first to last, is as sparing as possible of women characters, and particularly of the elderly or middle-aged. A heroine he must have, and she perhaps a companion or an attendant or two. For the rest; while fathers and uncles abound, mothers are fairly scarce. And is there an aunt in the canon?

fore she must still be young, only as much older than Ophelia as dress and conduct can suggest. But Shakespeare, by an adroit twist, converts necessity here to profit. He gives us in Gertrude the woman who does not mature, who clings to her youth and all that belongs to it, whose charm will not change but at last fade and wither; a pretty creature, as we see her, desperately refusing to grow old. And it is actually in this pathetic incongruity that the whole tragedy has struck root.

She is drawn for us with unemphatic strokes, and she has but a passive part in the play's action. She moves throughout in Claudius' shadow; he holds her as he has won her, by the witch-craft of his wit. We first see her sitting in Council at his side, formally presented, too, as "the imperial jointress" of his power. But it is plain that she does little except echo his wishes; some-times—as in the welcome to Rosencrantz and Guildenstern—she repeats his very words, inverting, as with a slight effort, their order. We practically never see her apart from him, except when, at his and Polonius' urging, she has sent for Hamlet to her closet; and then he follows to bid her "translate" what has passed. She does not tell him everything. Polonius' death is news enough; the rest, after all, was madness. But here, we may gather, starts a rift between them; from now on they stay conjugally apart, and he feels he has lost her. Later, during the fencing match, when she has momentarily at least recovered her good spirits, in pretty defi-ance she disobeys him and drinks from the cup he has prepared for her son. That trifling disobedience is her death.

She seems to be fond of Hamlet; though whether she really so much wishes him to stay at Court we can hardly tell, for it is under Claudius' eye and influence that she makes the plea. She is gracious to Ophelia; and if the girl's "good beauties" do turn out to be the "happy cause" of her son's "wildness"—why, their marriage would be just what she feels a marriage should be.

For long she does not admit that Hamlet is positively mad; she never uses the word about him until, in her closet, he sees the thing she cannot see. She knows him well enough to know that her own "o'er-hasty marriage" is at the root of his trouble, but her trivial

> Did you assay him
> To any pastime?

—when Rosencrantz and Guildenstern bring their first report of him—shows her quite insensible to the depth of it.

Yet, watching her, *we* know that this shallow, amiable, lymphatic creature was an adulteress, cunning enough to deceive her husband. Hamlet says that

> she would hang on him,
> As if increase of appetite had grown
> By what it fed on. . . .

It was the obvious way of deceiving him. She wept bitterly when he died. We need not, however, see hypocrisy there. She may well have wept the more bitterly because she had been false to him. And husbands, whose love is of too complacent and Hyperion-like a "dignity," are temptingly easy to deceive. Within a month she has married her lover, and she is still the Queen. She owns that—in the eyes of the world—it was overhasty of them. But of any remorse for the past there is no hint at all. Surely everything —if her morose son would but come to his senses and take a more cheerful view of life—has at last turned out very well.

It is upon such a nature, then, that the cathartic storm of Hamlet's stored resentment—the occasion given him—is to break. He has been expressly warned to

> leave her to heaven,
> And to those thorns that in her bosom lodge
> To prick and sting her.

But her seeming bland immunity from anything of the sort so pricks and stings his own incorrigible moral sense that at last he can restrain himself no more; he must set her up a glass wherein she may see, not the still pretty sight she is used to finding there, the mask of virtue she presents to the world, but the "inmost part" of her, the terrible truth.

He is coming to her, so she supposes, to be rated for his "pranks," which have indeed become "too broad to bear with," when he can, under cover of his play, insult before the whole Court both her and his sovereign and stepfather by gibing at their marriage. And she has primed herself—clearly she does not relish the task; the subject is a ticklish one; it is Claudius, she announces, who is offended—to be "round with him." But his lunatic violence terrifies her, his killing of Polonius breaks her nerve. Within a little he has her cowed. The tables are turned, and he is rating her, scourging her towards repentance for deadly sin.

We have had Claudius a few moments since, facing the evil in him honestly enough; but for a while it seems as if she really did not know what Hamlet meant. Still, bewildered though she may be by the rhetoric and moral fervor, his

> makes marriage vows
> As false as dicers' oaths. . .

(for answer to the bravado of her "What have I done. . . ?") tells her plainly that he knows of her adultery. But it is past and respectably atoned for; and there is genuine perplexity in her

> Ay me! what act,
> That roars so loud and thunders in the index?

What *can* she have done to warrant such tremendous execration?

He sets to work, with a kind of painstaking wrath, to demonstrate to her, as to a reprobate child, her moral obliquity. And now it is, her silence tells us, that she will not understand. Very naturally—this from her own son!—she will not. So he coarsens and coarsens his attack, till finding it intolerable, she pleads guilty. And then he will not spare her. If the carnal sin is all she can recognize, she shall have that painted in its true colors too:

> Nay, but to live
> In the rank sweat of an enseamed bed. . .

She has ample excuse at last for her pitifully reiterated

> O! speak to me no more . . . .
> No more, sweet Hamlet!

When the Ghost appears—and she is spared the yet deadlier blow of a revelation of the murder—she is blind to its presence, deaf to the voice:

> Do you see nothing there?
> Nothing at all; yet all that is I see.
> Nor did you nothing hear?
> No, nothing but ourselves.

and it implies, we feel, a blindness of soul in her besides, a sanity which Hamlet's "madness" puts to shame. He has battered her into admission of her fleshly sin; but spiritual perception—what can give her that? The division between mother and son is here at its deepest, in this picture of mother, father and son, united but divided, together, but in understanding curelessly apart. And here is intrinsic tragedy, the tragedy of what human beings are; and the action is stayed while we absorb the sense of it. Yet in kindliness the two are never nearer to each other. The ghostly presence—itself so softened—is a reproach to his anger, and her very incomprehension makes her tenderer to him.

The mystic moment past, his compassion, truly, is as bitter as his wrath. To him bitterer; for he has no faith, he finds, in her repentance. Let her assume the virtue she has not. Having stripped one mask from her he bids her wear another; the pretense may become reality in time. He turns bitterer still. She will betray her son to her paramour. What else should she do? He ranks her with his traitor schoolfellows, whom he will trust as he would "adders fanged."

But in all this he is wrong. She is repentant and she does not betray him. He is no more just to her than we need expect the one-time chastely romantic adorer of Ophelia, turned misogynist, to be. For truer insight there is the Ghost's

> O, step between her and her fighting soul. . . .

—knowledge, befitting the dead, that even unawares something within her is struggling for salvation. But, with Gertrude as with Claudius, Shakespeare leaves these last threads of their story loose-ended. And Hamlet so dominates the play that we are too apt to see things through his eyes.

A few strokes, however, have still to be added to the character, and in its acting they can be given some significance. The morrow of this ordeal finds her so sick of soul and conscious of guilt, so broken in nerve, that only her ingrain royal sense of duty forces her to receive the "distract" Ophelia. But (in quick and effective contrast) she can gallantly throw herself between the enraged Laertes and her husband. And she can momentarily forget her own trouble in grief for the girl's death; the detached beauty of her tale of it tells us so. Hamlet, when she sees him again at the graveside, is still, it seems, in the grip of his madness, and she pleads for indulgence for him. She is the happier when, at the fencing match, he quietly speaks of it as a thing conquered and left behind; and for a little while—because he is so happily restored to her—her natural gaiety has play again. It is for a very little while. And the terrible knowledge that Hamlet was commanded to spare her, Shakespeare more ruthlessly will not.

The poison does not kill her so quickly but that she must suffer this agony besides. Laertes' last words; the back-rushing memory of much not understood till now, of the mimic murder in the garden, Hamlet's mysterious ". . . as kill a king"; the sight of Claudius here in his grip—she dies companioned by the meaning of all this, conscious even, it may be, of her dying son's implacable farewell. It is the very death her cheated husband died.[21]

HAMLET

As with the play, so—but for one vital difference—with the character. Shakespeare has to reconcile the creature of his imagination with the figure of the borrowed story; the Hamlet we have is the tragic product of his very failure to do so.

The unfitness of the man for his task is at once plain. But Hamlet's continuing effort to be at the same time—so to put it—Kyd's hero and Shakespeare's reveals deeper incongruities. It involves him in a rupture of the entire spiritual treaty between

---

[21] And we have had the effects of such a poison most vigorously painted for us by the Ghost:

> The leperous distilment, whose effect
> Holds such an enmity with blood of man,
> That swift as quicksilver it courses through
> The natural gates and alleys of the body;
> And with a sudden vigour it doth posset
> And curd, like eager droppings into milk,
> The thin and wholesome blood; so did it mine;
> And a most instant tetter barked about,
> Most lazar-like, with vile and loathsome crust,
> All my smooth body. . . .

Shakespeare could have done that at half or a quarter the length (and the modern producer—of opinion, no doubt, that he should have—usually omits the last six lines); but he clearly wants the physical effects of the poison to make a deep impression on us. I do not say that we shall remember the actual lines for so long. But when we see the Queen stricken, the impression made by them should be spontaneously, if only vaguely, renewed. There is nothing in the text to mark the moment of her death; but since she speaks after she has collapsed into the arms of her attendants there is no reason she should not live on, long enough, at least to learn the truth. The King dies swiftly; but by sword as well as poison.

himself and the world in which he must live, and in a conflict between two selves within him, the one that could agree with this world, the other that cannot. There is the fundamental tragedy, exhibited by setting him in contact with a variety of his world's inhabitants; his mother, the girl he has loved, a true friend and two false ones, his secret enemy, the man he unwittingly wrongs, an old Court wiseacre, a shrewd old peasant, those shadows of reality, the Players, and that other shadow, his father's ghost. Each contact has its discord, and sets him playing false to what common sense would expect of him, and to what he once might have expected of himself.

Before the play begins this schism has begun; his mother's remarriage its immediate cause. It is suddenly intensified by the supernatural discovery of his father's murder, shamefully linked to this; so intensified that a salutary intermittent fever of the brain is seemingly all that enables him to discharge its poisons and survive. This fever—called, for want of a better name, his madness—fracturing the surface of his mind, adds yet more facets to our view of him. It adds, too, a fascinating iridescence to the cruder colors of the story, and it gives a fluctuating pulse to the action. Shakespeare found it—this madness—a mechanical trick. He makes it a dramatic symbol of the true tragedy of his Hamlet, which is the tragedy of a spiritual revolution.

HIS LOOKS AND CONDUCT

The exigencies of the action will not let us see a happy Hamlet —if ever there was one. But we have Ophelia's reference to him as he seemed to her to be:

> The expectancy and rose of the fair state,
> The glass of fashion and the mould of form,
> The observed of all observers. . .

And in the forgetful pleasure he finds in the mimic world of the Players is the reflection of a happier man.

We see him directly in three quite distinct guises. There is the black-suited Hamlet, rebelliously singular amid the peacock brilliancy of the Council. Then, in drastic contrast, there will be the Hamlet of the "antic disposition," who must not merely answer, in some degree, to Ophelia's account of him—

with his doublet all unbraced,
No hat upon his head, his stockings fouled,
Ungartered, and down-gyved to his ancle . . .

—but who will (is it not likely?) have "cast his nighted colour off" also. Would he, after promising "in all his best" to obey his mother, have disregarded this command, persisted in his public reproach to her? Would he not, moreover, wish to give Claudius every reason to think that he was no longer brooding on his loss? Tradition is against it; but all Shakespearean tradition is, strictly speaking, truncated at 1660. Most Hamlets, at any rate, in this middle section of the play make too much of their grief (they duplicate, that is to say, the effect of the earlier scenes) and too little of their madness. Except in the scene with Gertrude, the one outspoken reference to the past is not sorrowful at all; it is the bitterly mocking:

look you, how cheerfully my mother looks, and my father died within 's two hours.

When he is alone we have the truth of him, but it is his madness which is on public exhibition. And a very "antic disposition" he will at times display—for he must, if he is to claim the madman's privilege and security—till at last "his pranks" become "too broad to bear with."[22] The description of him and those phrases are specific directions to the actor.

All this will again be changed when he emerges safe from the ambush of his voyage. He should probably appear at the grave-side with his "sea-gown scarfed about" him. By the wistfully humorous detachment of his mood we are to know that the fever in his brain is now burned out. That his one passionately remorseful outburst when he learns of Ophelia's death should be greeted as madness is only a last ironic instance of his spiritual schism with his surroundings. This behind him, what could be more ruthlessly sane than his talk of those exterminated vermin, Rosencrantz and Guildenstern, or shrewder than his sense of his political position? And he takes his intellectual ease with Osric. We see that his strength is worn. He has forebodings of death. Then, to the wronged Laertes, and before King, Queen and Court, he

---

[22] Cf. what Dover Wilson says about the accepted appearance of the stage madman.

makes his apology, purges his offenses, and seemingly would be reconciled to the estranged world. It is a deceptive sunset gleam. The threat of the poisoned sword apart, his heritage of ill and his failure so far to cope with it are taking their own revenge on him. But it is thus that, before the terrible end, Shakespeare shows us the Hamlet that might have been, something the nobler for his ordeal than the romantic figure of Ophelia's adoration, the Hamlet, rather, of whom Fortinbras is to say

> For he was likely, had he been put on,
> To have proved most royally. . . .

HAMLET AND GERTRUDE

The turning point of the play, as we have seen, is when Hamlet postpones his vengeance on the King because it would not be cruel enough to kill him at his prayers, and passes on to wreak as cruel a vengeance as he can upon his mother, hoping only that he may be able to stop short of killing her. For vengeance in large part this is. And while that which is to be fulfilled at last upon the King is a duty laid on him (he has welcomed it truly, and his will and conscience are engaged in it; but the keeping them so is a hard task, and a harder the turning purpose into action), to this impeachment of his mother, which has been expressly forbidden him, he goes with a dreadful zest. Nor does the offense against his father account for the ferocity of his attack. Her sin against herself moves him more. But the springs of his wrath are bared in the climax to the scene's beginning, when she asks him has he "forgot" to whom he speaks thus, and he answers

> No, by the rood, not so:
> You are the Queen, your husband's brother's wife;
> And—would it were not so!—you are my mother.

She has been false to her husband and to herself. But she has also been false to him, to his faith in her.

The relation between any mother and son rests primarily on instinct; and in Hamlet's unbalanced state, at that enkindled moment more particularly, instinct has full play. For all his self-awareness he will not be intellectually aware of the mixture of motives in him; he has not been of the process by which he is brought to this passionate crisis. But we have seen that, with faith in his mother's virtue, his faith in all womanhood has vanished; his own sense of moral health too—for is he not her son, her very flesh and blood? That side of life has been poisoned for him; the taint is betrayed in his treatment of Ophelia. He has been warned to leave his mother's punishment to heaven, but the excitements of the play-scene are too much for him. By what he says when he is summoned to her he means to scourge her to repentance; he will "speak" daggers to her, will wring her heart

> If it be made of penetrable stuff. . .

But beneath this purpose surges—be it known to him or no—an embittered idealist's lust to be avenged upon this traitor to his ideal; and in its sating will be the sense that he is thus ridding himself too of some of the poison in him.

Ophelia is also our witness to Hamlet's unspoiled attitude towards women. His love for her, as we hear of it, was still only in its imaginative phase, finding expression in such pleasant foolishness as

> Doubt thou the stars are fire;
> Doubt that the sun doth move;
> Doubt truth to be a liar . . . .

Thine evermore, most dear lady, whilst this machine is to him. . . .

and given countenance

> With almost all the holy vows of heaven.

But there exist—though they may be rare—these essentially chaste natures, whose manhood's love will be the son's devout love for his mother, rededicate, little changed, to a wife. They are not lacking in passion. Far from it; there are no stronger passions than these pure ones, set on some ideal. And Hamlet's is such a nature, and his love for his mother was just such a passionate love.

He still instinctively feels himself, moreover, so much a partaker of her life that her degradingly hasty marriage to his uncle disgusts him with life itself, brings him to wishing that his own

> too too solid flesh would melt. . .[23]

---

[23] A point which Dover Wilson's reading of "sullied" does most temptingly underline.

Morbidly sensitive in this (the grief for his father's death telling on him too) though he may already be, he has, up to this point, his trouble more or less in hand; he can hold it at arm's length, even, with the wry humor of a

> Thrift, thrift, Horatio! the funeral baked meats
> Did coldly furnish forth the marriage tables. . . .

It is the Ghost's revelation of the murder, and of the baser fact of her adultery with its all too obvious bearing upon the murder, which turns him, as by a sort of balefully miraculous conversion, into a man possessed. Inevitably the shock tells hardest upon the wound already there, a wound which is intellectually so poorly protected too. And thus it is that the grief for her frailty is turned to rage in him, and that the sense of her corruption infects him and all womanly beauty in his eyes. Such moral ignorance and wantonness, he cries, make a man mad. The cleavage between the two of them has significance for Hamlet alone. In his mother's eyes he is, to begin with, simply unreasonable and unkind. His moral indictment, when he launches it, bewilders her. And of the obscure play of thought and feeling within him she has no idea.

But the attack on her, despite its rancor, is his effort to heal the breach between them. Its initial passion—not quelled even by the shock of the calamity to Polonius; it surges up again the moment after—comes in sharp contrast to the cold reasoning that has spared the King. Claudius is damned, and cannot be too deeply damned; but she may still be saved. And he loves her still; it is with a kind of exasperated love that he rages at her. He means to be cruel,

> cruel, only to be kind. . .

and is doubtless crueler than he means to be; for the sensitive nature, set to the harsh task, becomes more cruel than another. By the Ghost's intervention his passionate anger is quelled, and he is kept from inflicting worse cruelty on her. But this link of past love between them proves to be none now. The little cloud of tenderness soon dissolves; and he is left (his pulse as hers temperately keeping time) to see her with a terrible clarity as to his steeled intellect she is, no renewal of virtue in her possible, nor in himself of any faith in such virtue. His anger had hope in it. But its "damned custom" has now sardonically become the "monster," to whom he commits her for as much salvation as she is likely to earn. This is the tepid end to many a moral crusade.

He is remorseful for his overrighteous wrath. His queer

> Forgive me this my virtue. . . .

is not all irony. Forgive me—is the impulse of it—even though the fault be yours, for whatever in me parts me from you. And if it will comfort her he will beg a mother's blessing of her again. But this is playing round realities. And when, about to leave her, he surveys her there, crushed, yet—he is certain—infatuate still, the cold

> One word more, good lady.

unmasks the uncompromising mind.[24] What shall she do? That she can still ask such a question! And in the sarcasm of the

> Not this, by no means, that I bid you do. . .

sounds his despair of her; even as the nausea of

> Let the bloat king tempt you again to bed;
> Pinch wanton on your cheek; call you his mouse;
> And let him, for a pair of reechy kisses. . .

tells us that the poison in himself is by no means purged. Plead as he might, she will relapse, he feels, to this. So she will act, for so at heart she is. And when at last he does leave her it is to the accustomed mockery of

> Mother, good night. . . . Good night, mother!

—a very refrain it has become.

Throughout the play, from that first quiet, ironic

> 'Tis not alone my inky cloak, good mother. . .

what changes of grief and bitterness, love and anger has not Shakespeare set his Hamlet to ring on that one word! Nor are these the last hereabouts. He insinuates a yet bitter farewell to her into the cryptic parting with Claudius:

---

[24] It is not easy to distinguish the significance of Hamlet's varying forms of address to his mother. "Madam" in public would be but a natural term of respect both for mother and Queen; in private there may be some estrangement in it. We have noted the play he makes with Guildenstern's slightly impertinent "your mother's commandment." This present "good lady" is without doubt harshly ironical, if only because it preludes a passage of the very harshest irony.

Farewell, dear mother.
Thy loving father, Hamlet.
My mother. Father and mother is man and wife; man and wife
is one flesh; and so, my mother.

—which is as much as to say that, at last, he surrenders his share
in her to his enemy, to the man who has degraded her in flesh
and soul to what she is.

He troubles no more about her, makes no contact with her
when he returns from his adventurous voyage, his "madness"
shed. He ignores her at the graveside. His one reference to her
is the cursory, brutal

He that hath killed my king and whored my mother. . .

And when, in a breathing-space of the fight, she approaches him
reconcilingly with the pretty, motherly

Here, Hamlet, take my napkin, rub thy brows. . . .

the coquettish

The Queen carouses to thy fortune, Hamlet.

a coldly courteous

Good madam.

is all his response.

In his cry as he kills the King, in the

Follow my mother!

there is a last echo of the old afflicted love. But, stricken himself,
he has no kinder farewell for her than a

Wretched queen, adieu!

as she lies there dying or dead.

The story of Hamlet and his mother is of a second and spiritual
parturition. Every mother is prepared for such a wrench. But this
is a morbid one; and it is the child that suffers and resents.

HAMLET AND OPHELIA

We have, to begin and end with, two explicit indications of
Hamlet's uncorrupted feelings for Ophelia; the first, her account
to her father of his wooing her "in honourable fashion," of his
giving

countenance to his speech . . .
With almost all the holy vows of heaven.

the second, his own cry when he learns that she is dead:

I lov'd Ophelia. . . .

—and, from their very nature, they are meant to be believed. In
the interval the two are at cross-purposes, and people and circumstances and they themselves conspire to make matters worse.
It would be a common tale enough of two lovers, were the circumstances not so terrible and Hamlet other than he is.

We see them alone together only once, and then every element
of mischief is distilled into the situation. They have been parted
for long (but for that single, strange, silent incursion on her which
she describes); he has lost faith in life itself, and she, no more than
obediently faithless to him till now, must now be as obediently
false—for they are not, in fact, even alone together, as she knows.[25]

But from the beginning of the play the whole pernicious process
has been in train. Laertes warns his sister to beware of the
"trifling" of her lover's favor, and of opening her "chaste treasure
. . . to his unmastered importunity," and her father sullies him to
her still more by telling her that his "holy vows" are

> mere implorators of unholy suits,
> Breathing like sanctified and pious bawds,
> The better to beguile.

Plainly this is a slander upon the Hamlet we have just seen; the
young idealist, with his

> Frailty, thy name is woman!

heartbroken by the one betrayal of his ideal. He is to learn within
a little that the betrayal is far worse than he thought it, and
coincidently to find his own love for Ophelia treated as just such
a matter of lust as his uncle's for his mother. What must be the
effect on him?

One index to it is given us, pretty promptly, when Polonius
"boards" him; and out of that picture of natural corruption:

----

[25] "for long." Once again we must remember how arbitrarily Shakespeare turns
time to his account. We are not told, nor allowed to calculate, how long the
separation has been. Ophelia speaks of "this many a day," and of remembrances
which she has "longed long to re-deliver." That is evidence enough.

> For if the sun breed maggots in a dead dog, being a god kissing
> carrion . . .

springs the sudden, irrelevant enquiry:

> Have you a daughter?

(but it *is* a relevant question, surely, since you have been shutting
her away from me for so long) to be followed by:

> Let her not walk i' the sun; conception is a blessing, but not
> as your daughter may conceive:—friend, look to 't.

Ironic tribute to paternal worldly wisdom! It is most prudent of
you, my good sir, to be treating me as a common seducer[26] and
your daughter as a potential harlot. For so, doubtless, all women
are.

Later comes another gibe:

> Oh, Jephthah, judge of Israel, what a treasure hadst thou! . . .
>   *One fair daughter, and no more,*
>   *The which he loved passing well.*

—for he also "sent her away for two months; and she . . . be-
wailed her virginity."[27] But *does* it follow that this is how best to
show you love your daughter "passing well"; or even—hints the
mischievous mockery of

> Why,
>   *As by lot, God wot,*
> And then, you know,
>   *It came to pass, as most like it was* . . .

—that you *will* have kept her so safe after all? What is most like
to come to pass if man and maid should get together? A few
months more may show.

From which opprobrious levity we may gather what Hamlet
thinks of Polonius' part in the matter. And the matter itself,

---

[26] But Hamlet's faith in his own untried virtue has disintegrated too:

> We are arrant knaves all, believe none of us.

[27] Judges 11:38. The coincidence of the two months (in Hamlet's first soliloquy
his father has been dead "but two months . .," and in the now imminent play-
scene Ophelia is to say he has been dead "twice two months"; therefore it is for
two months that he and she have been parted) is more interesting as an indication
of the working of Shakespeare's mind—and Hamlet's—than important as another
solid spot in the fluidity of the play's scheme of time. For even in days when men
knew their Bible far better, not many among his audience will have known it
so well as this.

amidst grimmer troubles, might well be meaning no more to him, supine beneath those as he seems to be. But in another scale is the Hamlet of the strange incursion on Ophelia; a man spiritually stricken, whom we divine too in some reflexive twists to his sarcasms and behind the parade of pessimism, whom we hear railing at his "unpregnant" counterpart, whom we finally see for ourselves—Ophelia now set in his path—with his self-questionings sternly harvested into a questioning of life's very title to be endured; "the pangs of disprized love" but one item in its catalogue of ills. And suddenly he sees her there, a creature from the world of faith he has left behind.

His exclamation; that oddly ruthful

> Nymph, in thy orisons
> Be all my sins remembered.

reflects, I think, in its meaning and music together, as far as a single phrase may, the complex of the effect on him; an emotion at the sight of her which is like the vibrating of a frayed, neglected string; regret for the loss of her, and of his faith in all that the love for her nourished in him—and he half whimsically, a little wistfully, commends his present impiety to her prayers. But there is too a shrinking in the tenor of it (this the keynote of the coming scene) from any risk of a renewed desire for her.[28]

He can never have thought of confiding his secret to her; to her father's daughter, or, his mother's treachery haunting him, to any woman. But for him love and trust go together; and some fear that he might betray it will have been among the other feelings working in him when, as she tells us, after the long perusal of her face

> he lets me go,
> And, with his head over his shoulder turn'd,
> He seem'd to find his way without his eyes;

---

[28] Dowden says, "There is estrangement in the word 'Nymph,' " and other good authorities agree with him. I accept this gladly enough, though I wish I knew more precisely what its emotional significance for Shakespeare's audience was. But when Dover Wilson adds that "The touch of affectation in 'nymph' and 'orisons' (both pretentious words) and of sarcasm in 'all my sins' shows that Hamlet speaks ironically. . . ." I cannot but protest. Hamlet, for one thing, is not apt to be sarcastic about his own sins, and he is, at this moment, in his least sarcastic mood. And how the word "orisons"—in the face of Juliet's earlier and Imogen's later use of it—can be called affected and pretentious I really do not see.

> For out o' doors he went without their help,
> And to the last bended their light on me.

—when he let her go indeed, with that symbolically silent good-
bye. And we see that, in touch with her again, at the first provocation he begins riddling with the truth. And a little later, in his
frenzied excitement, it nearly escapes him.

But, dedicate to his task, what has he to do with love? Nor is he
the man that loved her. Nor is this world of wickedness the world
in which they loved. Her approach to return his gifts stirs his
senses. It is with the violence of self-distrust that he repels her.
Her distress at it touches his pity. Then he will lesson her—all
the kindness he can show her—in the realities of life as he has
learned them. Is she honest as well as fair? Her beauty will corrupt her honesty. He is himself "indifferent honest," yet it were
better his mother had not borne him. In the days of his foolish
innocence he thought that he loved her. He made her believe so.
She should not have believed him. That was not love, and men
are "arrant knaves all." Her father was wise to part them; and
here is sounder counsel still:

> Get thee to a nunnery: why wouldst thou be a breeder of sin-
> ners? . . . Go thy ways to a nunnery. . . .

—and have no share in perpetuating the wickedness of the world.
The menace in his sudden, searching

> Where's your father?

terrifies her into a lie. He cannot be sure, of course, that it is one;
and in that "thou shalt not escape calumny" he is giving her some
benefit of the doubt. But whether, having been kept from him
lest he should debauch her, it is wittingly or unwittingly that she
now lends her purity to his enemies as a bait for him, she is—so
much is certain—a part of their machinery of evil; and his compassion turns to insensate rage. In such a rage the objects of it are
less themselves than typical fuel for its fury. And Ophelia is no
more Ophelia to him, but womankind, the matrix of this evil
which has corrupted the world for him, which has made him mad.
Yet through his wrath we still hear the Hamlet that loved her
pleading with her—in the reiterated

> Get thee to a nunnery. . . . To a nunnery. . . .

⌐—to save herself from the miserable guilt of the giving of life, for such ends as this. It is his second anguished farewell to her. And thus is completed—and dissipated in anguish—the stern reasoning of

> To be, or not to be . . .

Among the gay assemblage for the play he sees her yet more patently—in his tense excitement—as a part of this machinery of evil which surrounds and threatens him. Kept from Court for so long, and now so demurely presented to him; can he doubt, then, that she is but another spy and decoy? His enemies' cue has been to

> drive his purpose on to these delights.

and his is to play the allotted part—to another purpose. Therefore, with a

> No, good mother, here's metal more attractive.

he ostentatiously yields to the pretty magnet. But he can at the same time, as usual, from behind the mask of his madness, take a gratifying toll of verbal revenge on them. They maligned his honorable love for her; he will better the dishonor in which she returns to him, will show his uncle-father and aunt-mother, the old bawd her father, the wretched, compliant girl herself, and all the Court, just what a vile thing it is they are making of her. He will let his mother see, too, how she has taught him to treat women. And even as the gentle nature, given merciless work to do, seeks force for it in cruelty, so is this grossness, with which he now spatters and defames Ophelia, the likely product of a romantically idealist imagination turned the wrong side out. Moreover, his "celestial" Ophelia having failed him, and he having no more use for her, his mind, set only on its task, now needs one that it can, without compunction, reject and forget. And here, in the worthless little trull of his treatment of her, she is.

She is swept out of the way with the rest in the excitement to follow. And he does, it would seem, forget her; until, returning from exile cured of his "madness," and stopping to sentimentalize over that expectant grave, he finds that it is for her they have dug it.

The past echoes back in his agonized

> I lov'd Ophelia; forty thousand brothers
> Could not, with all their quantity of love,
> Make up my sum. . . .

But his mockery of Laertes' ranting is only a bitterer mockery of himself. For, with the quenching of his madness, the Hamlet that felt and imagined and suffered and could love is no more. The passions, whose conflict left him impotent, are burned out of him; he is fitted at last for his task. He can rant about her with the best; but he, at heart, is as dead as she. This is, indeed, the last pang he is to suffer.

THE INTRINSIC HAMLET

His troubles apart, what sort of a man is Hamlet? The course of the action gives us three different views of him: in his disillusioned grief; under the strain of his madness; and returning, hardened, to quit his account with the King. But they are all abnormal views. And, while we discount without much difficulty the antic disposition and even the moments of sore distraction, there would be no measuring the depth of the moral tragedy did not Shakespeare contrive to give us also some refracted glimpses of a more normal man.

The Players are put to this use. The imaginative Hamlet finds forgetfulness in that unreal world, and in the noble music of Æneas' tale to Dido, though his thoughts soon drift back.[29]

Here is the man of fastidious taste, who prefers a play that "pleased not the million" and had "no sallets in the lines to make the matter savoury"—upon which small point alone he will be at odds with his surroundings, with the reveling Claudius, and with that man of the world Polonius, who is

> for a jig or a tale of bawdry, or he sleeps.

Here is a Hamlet, too, as princely in welcoming a common Player as his friend, as (from another standpoint) in his frank mockery of Polonius, and (from yet another) in his curt warning to the favored Player not to follow his example. The famous advice to the Players throws light on the intrinsic Hamlet too. It is like

---

[29] I do not think that he is meant to *choose* the subject of Priam's slaughter with his father in his mind; but it must very soon suggest his father to him.

him, at such a crisis, to trouble with it at all. Upon *what* he has
written for them to act his whole project may depend; but that
they might mouth it, or saw the air with their hands, or o'erstep
the modesty of nature cannot matter in the least. But this is
Hamlet ingrain; delighting in the thing that does not matter, and
delighting in it for its own sake; and only the more because it is
a fictive thing. The imaginative man prefers the unreal to the
real; he can have his will of it.

But the chief use of these glimpses of a sounder Hamlet is for
a counterpoise to the soliloquies—where, at first blush, we might
expect to see him as he most unfeignedly is. But we do not. In
a tragedy of spiritual struggle, discord will be at its worst when
a man is left alone with his thoughts. When we see Hamlet alone
he is either lapsed in self-conscious grief, or savagely self-reproach-
ful, wrought to murderous excitement, or in suicidal despair. And
when, in the calm of defeat, he deliberately questions himself, he
has to admit that he knows nothing of himself at all.

But, this moral turmoil apart, it is not from his self-communings
that we should best learn the simple truth about him. He is too
imaginative a man for that. When he says to his mother:

> you shall not budge;
> You go not till I set you up a glass
> Where you may see the inmost part of you.

it is his own disposition that prompts the image. He is always
looking at himself in the glass of his conscience. He tells the
Players "to hold, as 'twere, the mirror up to nature"; and there is,
indeed, more than a little of the actor in him.[30]

It is not that he is crudely self-conscious.[31] But he is ever trying
to see himself, with his mind's eye, as he is; never, in the nature
of things, succeeding; never satisfied of the truth of what he sees.
Before such a mirror so constantly and provokingly held up, a
man inevitably falls to attitudinizing, and to distorting the truth

---

[30] It is, of course, a very obvious image, and Shakespeare employs it again and
again. But its use comes most naturally to the consciously imaginative man. And
Hamlet's cousin-german Richard II, it will be remembered, at a most poignant
moment actually sends for a looking-glass and moralizes upon it.

[31] Nor, for that matter, will the good actor be. The actor's necessary consciousness of himself, not as himself but as somebody else, is a very different and a far
more complicated thing.

about himself. Till suffering has flogged all self-consciousness out
of him, Hamlet is ever a little apt to be striking spiritual attitudes.
Such morbidly introspective characters are neither truest to
themselves in solitude nor very likely to be happy in the intimacy
of love—when their egoism may be either overfed, if they are the
more loved, or if they are the more loving, starved. But they may
find relief from the obscure and warping tyranny of self in the
generosities of friendship. With their friends they can be confidently and forgetfully and transparently themselves. And while
the play may seem to be but one long opportunity for Hamlet to
express himself, the simple truth about him is rather that which
is reflected from the few moments' self-forgetful praise of his
friend. Here he is free of all antic disposition, assumed or innate.
Such moments are very revealing; they outweigh in their vividness
many wordy apologies, protests and explanations. And the dramatist can, through the undeniable personality of the actor, make
them vivid and convincing indeed.

We learn much about a man when we learn what qualities in
other men or women he unaffectedly admires. Hamlet's is a con-
tinued tale of disillusion about others and about himself. Horatio
is the one human being brought into close touch with him, whom
he does not look on either with contempt or reprobation. So there
is heart of grace in the very music of that

> Horatio, thou art e'en as just a man
> As e'er my conversation coped withal. . . .

and what follows rings out like a true confession of faith:

> Dost thou hear?
> Since my dear soul was mistress of her choice
> And could of men distinguish, her election
> Hath seal'd thee for herself; for thou hast been
> As one, in suffering all, that suffers nothing,
> A man that fortune's buffets and rewards
> Hast ta'en with equal thanks. . . .

This is what he finds best in a man; these are the saving virtues.
There is, then, sounder self-judgment in the wistful

> and bless'd are those
> Whose blood and judgment are so well commingled

> That they are not a pipe for fortune's finger
> To sound what stop she please.

—in that merely implicit confession of his own contrasted weakness—than in all the self-scoldings of the soliloquies. We shall discount these a little in any case. He did not—it was then and there plain—really envy the Player his facile emotion; that was only a stick with which to beat himself. He knows he is no coward. He does not in the least wish that he were Fortinbras; his only interest in the sight of him, "with divine ambition puffed," being that it is an "occasion" which informs against him—and which he can improve. He teems with intellectual pride; and his self-depreciation—the commonest of traits in the sensitively proud —is only a token of it. But when he exclaims to Horatio:

> Give me that man
> That is not passion's slave, and I will wear him
> In my heart's core, ay, in my heart of heart,
> As I do thee. . . .

he is, by the humble title of his love for him, asking the aid and comfort of qualities in his friend which, past the need of protest or excuse, he knows himself to lack.

This spontaneous revelation does not contradict what he says about himself; there is, of course, much actual and more potential truth in that. But it simplifies and clarifies it; helps us winnow the grain of it from the chaff. We see him here with his friend, and the gentle spirit and good mind shine out. But we see too that had his mother lived spotless and his father died of old age, he would still have been the man whose blood and judgment are so ill-commingled that he will always be his "passion's slave." That "vicious mole of nature" in him is rooted deep. Misfortunes do not change a character, they but bring out its weakness or its strength.

THE INNER STRIFE

Hamlet's task would at best be a hard one. He is to kill an anointed king, his uncle and his mother's husband; and, after, he will have to justify his deed to her and to the world—for while he may take the Ghost's word for a thousand pound, will they his mere report of it? Shakespeare does not develop this political and practical aspect of the business. It will have been implicitly clearer to his Renaissance-minded audience than it is to us. The Queen is brought within sight of the vindicative truth. We see the King belatedly protected by his courtiers and Switzers. The protagonist of that potential drama would need all his wits about him.

But Hamlet, from the very outset, is inwardly divided and weakened. The finer the nature, the nicer its balances; his can ill afford such strife. His spirit is in revolt against his natural affections; and the supernatural shock to come makes yet worse work, the unhappy mind alone being poorly armed against it. Thereafter he is triply at odds within himself; affections, faith and reason, warring each with the other; the harvest of it his questioning

> Whether 'tis nobler in the mind to suffer
> The slings and arrows of outrageous fortune,
> Or to take arms against a sea of troubles,
> And by opposing end them? . . .

—end them by killing, not his enemy, but himself? To some such cross-purposes does war within a man fatally lead.

But even were he at one with himself, it will be (he is to find) another sort of self that the task needs. And what we watch in him is the dire process of the conversion. His finer traits must be blunted. Gentleness, simplicity, generosity; of what use are they? In the unexacted courtesy towards Marcellus and Bernardo and the Players is the old Hamlet; in the mockery of Polonius, the overt contempt for Osric, is the new. Of impulsive, trustful affection Rosencrantz and Guildenstern cure him; and they teach him to pay men back in their own coin. He must learn to be callous.

> What a piece of work is a man!

—but after his wanton destruction of a piece of such work, it is

> I'll lug the guts into the neighbour room.

He must learn to be cruel. He has already fleshed his tongue on the helpless Ophelia when, summoned to his mother, he goes, praying only that he may

> speak daggers to her, but use none.

Now a man is always a little ridiculous when he strives to be other than he is; and Hamlet is so, if tragically so. He is conscious of it, for he is conscious of everything concerning him; and the riddling talk and antic disposition, besides being an ambush, are an outward travesty of this ineptitude, behind which the humiliating reality is obscured. It is another source of discord within him. The incongruity between "the soul of Nero" and his own is brought home to him when, for all his arrogated callousness, he suddenly "weeps for what is done."[32] And this effort to be what he is not only increases his self-distrust. He spurs himself from backsliding. Having spoken daggers, and (he hears her cry) cleft his mother's heart in twain, he has relapsed—the Ghost intervening—into pity for her also. That will not do; so he stirs himself to a few more quite superfluously brutal strokes before he leaves her.

His reiterated "Let me be cruel," "I must be cruel. . . ." shows him well aware, in fact, that he is not replacing his weakness and melancholy by confidence and strength, only disguising them as in ill-fitting armor, giving them a weapon—to be so ineptly used that it will prove more dangerous to the innocent than the guilty. By sheer reckless inadvertence he kills Polonius, after he has deliberately spared the guilty King at his prayers, because he must needs catch him

> about some act
> That has no relish of salvation in 't . . .

and trip him so

> that his heels may kick at heaven,
> And that his soul may be as damned and black
> As hell, whereto it goes.

Into such a devil's labyrinth is he led!

And when he departs in custody to England, it is not so much that Claudius has defeated him as that within himself he is still a baffled man; his own primary problem is still unsolved. His

---

[32] Gertrude tells Claudius that he did so; and while she may wish to soften him towards Hamlet, there is nothing to show that she is inventing. The moment is indicated by

> For this same lord,
> I do repent . . . .

But Shakespeare evidently wishes to emphasize this bent in him; for later by the graveside Gertrude assures Laertes that though

> thus awhile the fit will work on him;
> Anon, as patient as the female dove,
> When that her golden couplets are disclosed,
> His silence will sit drooping.

affections are poisoned, his will is self-destructive, and the ever-questing mind, playing so curiously around his purposes, has but betrayed them. Upon which his verdict is:

> from this time forth,
> My thoughts be bloody, or be nothing worth!

And what bitterer contempt could the intellectual Hamlet find to pour upon his "paragon of animals," so "infinite in faculty," and upon "capability and god-like reason," with all that it has done for him so far?

When he returns he is "sane" again; the inner strife is ended. Upon what terms? They show in his placid philosophizings beside the forgotten Ophelia's grave. His power to suffer for his mother's sin has thinned out to the sentiment of "Alas, poor Yorick!" And when we hear of the lethal trick he has played upon his one-time comrades, his enemy's ignorant instruments, and that it comes not near his conscience, plainly he no longer lacks nerve to deal with that enemy himself. The King's doom sounds in his coldly confident answer to Horatio's warning:

> the interim is mine;
> And a man's life's no more than to say 'One.'

So here is a Hamlet fit at last for his task. But in the conversion much that seemed lovely in his nature has perished, failing under the test to which he had to put it. Yet though the physical man issues from the trial sorely strained, and the mind is hardened, the spirit is still not debased. Its nobility shines through the apology to Laertes for the "madness" which has been "poor Hamlet's enemy." Let the terrible task be but fulfilled, there is promise of a Hamlet at peace, and the better a man for his ordeal. But that cannot be. The penalty of things done in that "sore distraction" must be paid.

THE FRUSTRATE MIND

Were Shakespeare not a dramatist but a preacher, or had he confused the two callings, he might well have presented Hamlet to us as a warning of the dangers of thinking for oneself. Beneath the shocks of the action this quiet disintegrant is ever at work. And among the half-dozen passages which outdo, by their poignancy or weight, the rest of the self-revealing, there are two bearing particular witness to it.[33] Midway through his ordeal, and for fruit of his deepest meditation, we have:

> Thus conscience does make cowards of us all,
> And thus the native hue of resolution
> Is sicklied o'er with the pale cast of thought,
> And enterprises of great pitch and moment
> With this regard their currents turn awry
> And lose the name of action. . . .

—and the blunders that follow are proof of it. (This "conscience," needless to say, is not the good or bad conscience of the moralist; it stands for knowledge of himself.[34]) Then, with the consequences of the blunders to be faced, comes the exasperated

> Sure he that made us with such large discourse,
> Looking before and after, gave us not
> That capability and god-like reason
> To fust in us unused. . . .

Yet his use of it has paralyzed his actions, his thought being

> but one part wisdom
> And ever three parts coward. . .

and, what is worse, he remains essentially ignorant still. He breaks off his arguing with the cry:

> I do not know
> Why yet I live to say 'This thing's to do,'
> Sith I have cause and will and strength and means
> To do 't. . . .

For beside that failure his blunders hardly seem to count. His weakness and melancholy and his fits of "madness" are depressions and storms which will pass; the "honesty" of the Ghost, even,

---

[33] Key-passages; those which are given, by one dramatic means or another, an uncommon emphasis. For example:

> O, that this too too solid flesh would melt . . .
> The time is out of joint! O cursed spite,
> That ever I was born to set it right!
>> Give me that man
> That is not passion's slave. . . .

and the two I am about to quote. The interpretative value of such lines is to be measured by their immediately salient effect.

[34] The O.E.D. quotes Swift: "The word Conscience properly signifies, that knowledge which a man hath within himself of his own thoughts and actions."

is a side issue. But here is fundamental frustration. He faces it
with the calm which belongs to the morrow of a defeat. He puts
his case at its best; he has "cause and will and strength and
means." But the keystone of the arch is out. Of what avail a
capability and god-like reason, which offers you all knowledge
except the knowledge of yourself, without which you cannot put
the rest to any certain use? Was ever such mockery? Here, therefore, we have the last of the introspective Hamlet; and the practical man, back from banishment, will mock at reason as reason
once mocked at him:

> Rashly—
> And praised be rashness for it!—let us know,
> Our indiscretion sometimes serves us well
> When our deep plots do pall; and that should learn us
> There's a divinity that shapes our ends,
> Rough-hew them how we will.

A Fortinbras could never find himself so frustrated. But Hamlet, the philosopher forced to action, must needs ask *why* he does
what he does, must pause, "looking before and after," thinking
precisely—much "too precisely on the event."

Disillusion will force from him an ironical good word for "that
monster custom." But in the very first emphatic thing he said, in
that

> Seems, madam? Nay, it is. I know not 'seems.' . . .

we could recognize the discriminating mind, and the contempt
for all

> actions that a man might play . . .

He was for truth in word and deed. The flaw in the position was
that, feeling he had

> that within which passeth show . . .

he assumed that he had there too a paramount judge of what the
truth must be. It is such a mind, set impersonally to work, that
delights to

> trace the noble dust of Alexander till he find it stopping a
> bunghole . . .

and it may happen upon many interesting facts by the way. But its
hairsplitting sensitiveness is only too likely to convert an impulsive

> Haste me to know't, that I, with wings as swift
> As meditation or the thoughts of love,
> May sweep to my revenge.

more swiftly still into a

> The time is out of joint! O cursed spite,
> That ever I was born to set it right!

and, overindulged, as we are let see, it can bring a man, sword poised above his enemy, to the tragi-comic futility of

> Now might I do it pat, now he is praying;
> And now I'll do 't; and so he goes to heaven,
> And so am I revenged. That would be scanned:
> ... and am I then revenged?

Would Fortinbras have paused, and thought so precisely, and looked before and after—and let that consummate moment pass?

Such deadlocked impotence, when it is of the mind only, makes a comic rather than a tragic spectacle; we laugh at mere cleverness self-defeated. It becomes tragic when things beyond the mind's mastery are at stake; and when, affections disabled and spiritual security gone, only "god-like reason" is left a man for guide. Hamlet's is a human soul adrift. And all the wisdom which his rash and lonely mind can teach him is that Denmark is a prison, and the world one, the goodly frame of the earth a sterile promontory, and man—the beauty of the world, the paragon of animals—a quintessence of dust. No better than a beast if he does not use his reason; yet, using it, this is what he finds. Small wonder if a consciousness of such anarchy make him an impotent coward and lead him to the despair which, but for "the dread of something after death," would have him done with it all! Yet to what less barren conclusion is unmitigated reason likely to lead? For is it not by our unreasoning impulses and affections, by our faith in life, that we chiefly live and act? In Hamlet this native faith has been stunned. And he never recovers from the blow.

He never regains a natural spiritual health, nor does he reach self-understanding. His loathing of life only hardens to indifference. The baffled "I do not know. . . ." is his last word on the matter, except for that riddling recognition of a mad Hamlet in him and a sane, the one that did not do the things he willed (so

much for sanity!), the other that did the things he did not will
to do. The dying

> Had I but time—as this fell sergeant, death,
> Is strict in his arrest—O! I could tell you. . .

may hint at belated light breaking in. But Shakespeare leaves the
matter there; and he is, of course, dramatically right to do so. For
if Hamlet understood himself the spiritual tragedy would disappear again in the tragedy of action; and if anyone else explained
him to us he would become a merely interesting "case." While
we know no more of him than he knows himself he holds our
sympathy. And, in a double sense, his trouble is very much our
own.

A SOUL ADRIFT

His heresies, worn by three centuries currency, no longer shock
us. But they are grave enough—and gravest when he faces suicide
—for him to have good cause to wish that his sins may be remembered in Ophelia's prayers.[35] Shakespeare (with his play's licens-
ing to consider) cannot, if he would, meddle with theology. But
he has managed before now to deal with much belonging to it;
and, in this case, the problem of the Ghost brings him as near to
the kernel of the matter as he needs to go.

Hamlet's heart tells him that it is his father's ghost, but his
mind as promptly questions whether it be

> a spirit of health or goblin damned . . .

While he listens he believes; but when, on its vanishing, he in-
vokes the host of heaven, he adds

> And shall I couple hell?

And later, at his calmest, he thinks it well may be

> a damned ghost that we have seen . . .

In this again, then, his native faith is flawed; and the rift but
opens deeper doubts. Insoluble doubts; for if man's mind cannot
master the mortal world, what chance has it against mysteries
beyond? Yet if they can touch him so nearly as this, and since

---

[35] This question of the sin of suicide is amply canvassed; by Hamlet himself
more than once, and from more than one standpoint in Ophelia's case.

death is the common door to them, bring himself to braving them he must. Hamlet, the intellectual hero, very certainly must be allowed to face them. It is the crown to his dignity that he should. Subtract these reckonings from his account, indeterminate though they are, and by how much would not his dramatic stature be diminished?

Little explicit argument emerges; in this, as in the struggle for self-understanding, no more than the play's action can be brought to engender. But that central soliloquy questions eternity itself:

> To be or not to be . . .

not simply here—a dagger thrust will settle that—but hereafter. And the

> consummation
> Devoutly to be wished . . .

is not merely the body's death, but the soul's. The proud faith that could still brave the Ghost with

> And for my soul, what can it do to that,
> Being a thing immortal as itself?

is gone, and doubt and dread replace it. The infection, which his mother's treachery to his faith in her sowed in his heart, has spread and deepened. The disillusioned mind now asks: may not this seeming spirit of my father be even as treacherous, be abusing me to damn me? And out of such doubt he builds a dreadfully imagined limbo around him, where evil is still potent and the departed soul as helpless as in a dream.

The Ghost is proved to be an honest ghost, but this does not give Hamlet back the old confident possession of his soul. He has let himself be made an instrument of these supernatural powers. No blind instrument; the enfranchised mind rebels against the indignity of that, against working for mere "bait and salary." He is lending his mind to their work to better the occasion offered him when he spares for a worse fate the kneeling, guilty King. A minute later he has involuntarily killed Polonius. These powers he serves—who have tricked him into that—are truly not nice in their dealings:

> but heaven hath pleased it so,
> To punish me with this and this with me,
> That I must be their scourge and minister. . . .

To punish him with this indeed; a lonely soul seeking its right and wrong amidst such anarchy!

The strange little scene of the Ghost's return opens sadder uncertainties. The armored figure of the battlements is now:

> My father, in his habit as he liv'd!

—here in a fleeting happiness with wife and son. Commands to vengeance have become "this piteous action"; the majestic, memorable farewell turns to a stealing-away out at the portal; and his mother is blind and deaf to what he must still believe he sees. Evil which no vengeance can expiate; the helpless suffering of the dead, the irremediable estrangement of these three that once were one. Matter, indeed, far more for tears than blood.

Hamlet, after this, talks no more of the Ghost, nor of the soul.[36] As to the hereafter:

> To what base uses we may return, Horatio! . . . Alexander died, Alexander was buried, Alexander returneth into dust; the dust is earth, of earth we make loam; and why of that loam, whereto he was converted, might they not stop a beer barrel?

And when he comes to die, his hope is simply that the rest will be silence.

SHAKESPEARE'S PROPHETIC SOUL

To the more perceptive of Shakespeare's audience the most interesting thing about *Hamlet* must have been that in the old story retold an old issue was dealt with afresh. There must always be interest in this. To every age the same problems recur, differently decked out; and men have to decide whether to attack them as their fathers did, obey habit and authority, or seek and take their own conscientious way. And in that age of the breaking-up of creeds which was Shakespeare's, this, under one guise or another, was a dilemma with which many men were faced.

Hamlet is a man adrift from old faiths and not yet anchored in new; a man of his time in that, more particularly. The theologians had been busy, patching and repatching. But formulas, which the mind may accept, are one thing; and the lively faith, by which we live in unconscious harmony with our surroundings, is

---

[36] Such statistics are not necessarily significant; but the word is in very ample use up to this point in the play, and by Hamlet himself is not once used after.

very much another. This faith extends to secular everyday things. Let it be flawed here and there, it will be weakened everywhere. Put it then to some extraordinary test, and we at once find that its integrity is broken. Reason, brought to the rescue, cannot help, for it works by other means; it cannot even tell us what is wrong. Act we must, if action is what is asked of us, for the world will not stand still. But with crippled faith and enfranchised reason at odds in us we do self-defeating things, and may lapse into impotence and despair. That is Hamlet's case. And while none of those first spectators may have stood, as he did, with

> a father killed, a mother stained . . .

and under ghostly command to avenge the crime, not a few of them must have seen in his spiritual troubles only a more vivid shadowing-forth of their own.

He is of an intellectual generation to whom the word has been let penetrate: Prove all things; for only so can one learn to hold fast that which is good. Could he simply have been set to prove the theory of a carefully selected few—he and his fellow-student Horatio—in the shelter of that Protestant Wittenberg to which he so longed to return, all might have been well. But he has to face an urgent, practical problem, which is colored for him, moreover, by his own most intimate concern with it. How can a man treat such a matter dispassionately and trust to his own isolated judgment of the right and the wrong of it? And if it is a question, as this is, of life and death, and even worse, of salvation or damnation—let him go arguing such issues as these forth and back and back and forth again in terms of his own doubts and griefs and fears, into what dark and vertiginous places may not the lonely mind be lured?

> What if it tempt you toward the flood, my lord,
> Or to the dreadful summit of the cliff
> That beetles o'er his base into the sea,
> And there assume some other horrible form,
> Which might deprive your sovereignty of reason
> And draw you into madness?

Such is Horatio's poetic picture of what does, in fact, occur.

Some men manage, seemingly, to reduce these high issues to their own measure, and will emerge from such an ordeal with their God in their pocket, as it were, justifying whatever they may now choose to do. Some will stay lost in the moral anarchy, which is all they have found. Many retreat baffled from the adventure, and the readier to act thereafter as habit or authority or the formulas of their dead faith dictate. Many a man, then, can find touches of himself in the later Hamlet at least, who returns weary of questioning, hardened (by a sea-fight and some ruthless practice upon his jailers) to his deadly task, and looking back to the old self-torture as "madness."

Yet his soul's adventure, which seemed but to lead him to defeat, was heroic too. For if men shirk such perils, how are these high matters to be brought home to spiritual freedmen? Nor will mere intellectual venturing suffice, if lively faith, in its health and strength, is to be found and enjoyed again. Hamlet, being called upon, flings his whole being—mind and affections both, the best and the worst of him, weakness no less than strength—into the trial. And he widens the issue till he sees eternal life and death, his own and his enemy's, at stake. He will reconcile himself, as he is and in all he is, with these now unveiled verities of this world and the next, if that may be. In which Promethean struggle towards the light he is beaten—as who has not been?—with havoc wrought, not in him only, but by him, even to his own despite. It is none the less a heroic struggle.

Here, for me, is the master-clue to Hamlet's "mystery." The "sane" world around him has naturally no sense of it, nor the too sane spectator of the play. He does not pluck out the heart of it himself. Neither are we meant to. For his trouble is rooted in the fact that it is a mystery. Shakespeare, for his part, must order his play in terms of action (even as Hamlet is called on to act); the tragedy of thwarted thought and tortured spirit is the rich soil in which he replants his borrowings. Yet while the action keeps us interested, it is this tragedy and the mystery of it, which is enthralling.

If we are at one with Polonius in thinking that

> to expostulate
> What majesty should be, what duty is,
> Why day is day, night night, and time is time,
> Were nothing but to waste night, day and time . . .

and that, as to Hamlet,

> to define true madness,
> What is't but to be nothing else but mad?

why, Shakespeare will not, so to say, have spoiled our Kyd for us.
The play is attractively alive on the surface; the riches of its
underworkings of emotion and thought fall to those whose own
are a touchstone for them. And it fulfills, in this, the double
demand of drama, which is not for action alone nor the revelation
of character only, but for character in action. Pertinently so; since
the character-revealing problems of life present themselves as
problems of action, which men attack even as Hamlet does, imaginatively, thoughtfully, passionately too. And the play's progress,
like a stream in flood, here flowing deeply and evenly, here eddy-
ing and spreading, there rushing down some steep channel—it is
thus, and not to any clocklike measure, that human affairs do
move.

In England, for the best part of a century before *Hamlet* was
written, and for sixty years after, the finer issues of the spiritual
revolution which the Renaissance had begun were obscured by
secular discord, persecution and civil war; and the ensuing peace
left them hardened into formula. To the popular mind thus distressed and coarsened the finer issues implicit either in play or
character might well make small appeal. Nor would they be
likelier to touch the conscience of the positive eighteenth century.[37]
Not till it was waning, and many men had come to find their set
creeds unsatisfying, till they began to ask the old essential questions once again, to have a better answer if they might, did the
Hamlet of spiritual tragedy come by his own; then to become,
indeed, the typical hero of a new "age of doubt." It was as if
Shakespeare, so alive to the spirit of his own time, had been in this
mysteriously attuned besides to some

> prophetic soul
> Of the wide world dreaming on things to come.

While our age of doubt endures, and men still cry despairingly,

---

[37] See Johnson's note to the play. He praises the conduct and, in particular, the
"variety" of the action. But "of the feigned madness of Hamlet there appears no
adequate cause, for he does nothing which he might not have done with the
reputation of sanity."

"I do not know. . . ," and must go on uncomforted, the play will keep, I should suppose, its hold on us. If a new age of faith or reason should succeed, or one for a while too crushed by brute reality to value either, Hamlet may then be seen again simply as the good Polonius saw him.

King Lear

"Lear is essentially impossible to be represented on a stage"—and later critics have been mostly of Charles Lamb's opinion. My chief business in this Preface will be to justify, if I can, its title there.

Shakespeare meant it to be acted, and he was a very practical playwright. So that should count for something. Acted it was, and with success enough for it to be presented before the king at Whitehall. (Whatever his faults, James I seems to have had a liking for good drama.) And Burbage's performance of King Lear remained a vivid memory. At the Restoration it was one of the nine plays selected by Davenant for his theater. He had in mind, doubtless, its "reforming and making fit"—all of them except *Hamlet* and *Othello* were to suffer heavily from that. But Downes, his prompter, tells us that it was ". . . *Acted* exactly as Mr *Shakespear* wrote it. . . . "—several times apparently—before Nahum Tate produced his version in 1681. This hotchpotch held the stage for the next hundred and fifty years and more, though from Garrick's time onwards it would generally be somewhat re-Shakespeareanized.[1] One cannot prove Shakespearean stage-worthiness by citing Tate, but how far is it not Tate rather than Shakespeare that Lamb condemns? He has Shakespeare's play in mind, but he had never seen it acted. Part of his complaint is that ". . . Tate has put his hook in the nostrils of this Leviathan, for Garrick and his followers, the showmen of the scene, to draw the mighty beast about more easily." And he never considers Shakespeare's play in relation to Shakespeare's stage. He came near to doing so; for, later in the essay, with *The Tempest* for

---

[1] Elliston and Kean, after a little hesitation, went so far as to restore the tragic ending. Then, in 1838, Macready acted Shakespeare's play again. But even he tampered with its structure, and—by much omission—with its text.

theme, he speaks of ". . . the elaborate and anxious provision of scenery, which the luxury of the age demands . . ." which ". . . works a quite contrary effect to what is intended. That which in comedy, or plays of familiar life, adds so much to the life of the imitation, in plays which appeal to the higher faculties positively destroys the illusion which it is introduced to aid." Had he followed out this argument with *King Lear* for an example, giving credit to Shakespeare the playwright as well as to Shakespeare the poet—I do not say that he would have reached a different conclusion, for there is still the plea to be met that here, for once, Shakespeare the playwright did overreach himself, but he must at least have recognized another side to the question. Lamb's essay should be read, of course, as a whole. He loved the drama; the theater alternately delighted and exasperated him. The orotund acting of his day, its conventional tricks, can have been but a continual offense to his sensitive ear and nicety of taste. He here takes his revenge—and it is an ample one—for many evenings of such suffering. He never stopped to consider whether there might not be more even to the actor's despised art than that.

A profounder and a more searching indictment of the play's stage-worthiness comes from A. C. Bradley in the (for me) most remarkable of those remarkable lectures on Shakespearean Tragedy. To him it seems ". . . Shakespeare's greatest achievement, but . . . *not* his best play." The entire argument should be read; but this, I think, sums it up not unfairly. He says that "The stage is the test of strictly dramatic quality, and *King Lear* is too huge for the stage. . . . It has scenes immensely effective in the theatre; three of them—the two between Lear and Goneril and between Lear, Goneril and Regan, and the ineffably beautiful scene in the Fourth Act between Lear and Cordelia—lose in the theatre very little of the spell they have for imagination; and the gradual interweaving of the two plots is almost as masterly as in *Much Ado*. But (not to speak of defects due to mere carelessness) that which makes the *peculiar* greatness of *King Lear*,—the immense scope of the work; the mass and variety of intense experience which it contains; the interpenetration of sublime imagination, piercing pathos, and humour almost as moving as the pathos; the vastness of the convulsion both of nature and of human passion; the vagueness of the scene where the action takes place, and of the movements of the figures which cross this scene; the strange atmosphere, cold and dark, which strikes on us as we enter this scene, enfolding those figures and magnifying their dim outlines like a winter mist; the half-realised suggestions of vast universal powers working in the world of individual fears and passions, all this interferes with dramatic clearness even when the play is read, and in the theatre not only refuses to reveal itself fully through the sense but seems to be almost in contradiction with their reports." And later: "The temptation of Othello and the scene of Duncan's murder may lose upon the stage, but they do not lose their *essence*, and they gain as well as lose. The Storm-scenes in *King Lear* gain nothing, and their very *essence* is destroyed." For this essence is poetry, and, he concludes, ". . . such poetry as cannot be transferred to the space behind the foot-lights, but has its being only in imagination. Here then is Shakespeare at his very greatest, but not the mere dramatist Shakespeare."

Notice, first of all, how widely Bradley's standpoint is removed from that—we may venture to surmise it—of "the mere dramatist Shakespeare" and his fellows the actors. To say of certain scenes that they were "immensely effective in the theatre" and add that they *lost* there "very little of the spell they have for imagination," to argue that "the temptation of Othello and the scene of Duncan's murder may lose upon the stage, but they do not lose their *essence*, and they gain as well as lose"—it would have sounded to them queer commendation. For in whatever Shakespeare wrote was the implied promise that in the theater it would *gain*. Bradley passes easily to: "The Storm-scenes in *King Lear* gain nothing, and their very *essence* is destroyed." But the dramatist, on his defense, would rightly refuse to follow him; for the premises to the argument are not the same.

Bradley and Lamb may be right in their conclusions. It is possible that this most practical and loyal of dramatists did for once —despite himself, driven to it by his unpremeditating genius— break his promise and betray his trust by presenting to his fellows a play, the capital parts of which they simply could not act. Happily for them, they and their audiences never found him out. But if Bradley is right, not the most perfect performance can be a fulfillment, can be aught but a betrayal of *King Lear*. There is the issue. The thing is, of course, incapable of proof. The best that imperfect human actors can give must come short of perfection, and the critic can always retort to their best that his imagination betters it. Bradley's argument is weighty. Yet—with all deference to a great critic—I protest that, as it stands, it is not valid. He is contending that a practical and practiced dramatist has here written a largely impracticable play. Before condemning these "Storm-scenes" he should surely consider their stagecraft—their mere stagecraft. For may not "the mere dramatist" have his answer hidden there? But this—starting from his standpoint of imaginative reader—he quite neglects to do.

Ought we, moreover, to assume—as Bradley seems to—that a play must necessarily make all its points and its full effect, point by point, clearly and completely, scene by scene, as the performance goes along? Not every play, I think. For the appreciation of such a work as *King Lear* one might even demand the second or third hearing of the whole, which the alertest critic would need to give to (say) a piece of music of like caliber. But leave that aside. No condoning of an ultimate obscurity is involved. And comedy, it can be admitted, demands an immediate clarity. Nor is the dramatist ever to be dispensed from making his story currently clear and at least provisionally significant. But he has so much more than that to do. He must produce a constant illusion of life. To do this he must, among other things, win us to something of a fellow-feeling with his characters; and even, at the play's critical moments, to identifying their emotions with our own.

Now the *significance* of their emotions may well not be clear to the characters themselves for the moment, their only certainty be of the intensity of the emotions themselves. There are devices enough by which, if the dramatist wishes, this significance can be kept currently clear to the audience. There is the Greek chorus; the earlier Elizabethans turned Prologue and Presenters to account; the *raisonneur* of nineteenth century comedy has a respectable ancestry. Shakespeare uses the *raisonneur* in varying guises. In this very play we detect him in the Fool, and in Edgar turned Poor Tom. But note that both they and their "reasoning" are blended not only into the action but into the moral scheme, and are never allowed to lower its emotional temperature by didactics —indeed they stimulate it. For here will be the difficulty in preserving that "dramatic clearness" which Bradley demands; it would cost—and repeatedly be costing—dramatist and actors their emotional, their illusionary, hold upon their audience. Lear's progress—dramatic and spiritual—lies through a dissipation of egoism; submission to the cruelty of an indifferent Nature, less cruel to him than are his own kin; to ultimate loss of himself in madness. Consider the effect of this—of the battling of storm without and storm within, of the final breaking of that Titan spirit—if Shakespeare merely let us look on, critically observant. From such a standpoint, Lear is an intolerable tyrant, and Regan and Goneril have a case against him. We should not side with them; but our onlooker's sympathy might hardly be warmer than, say, the kindly Albany's.[2] And Shakespeare needs to give us more than sympathy with Lear, and something deeper than understanding. If the verity of his ordeal is really to be brought home to us, we must, in as full a sense as may be, pass through it with him, must make the experience and its overwhelming emotions momentarily our own.

Shakespeare may (it can be argued) have set himself an impossible task; but if he is to succeed it will only be by these means. In this mid-crisis of the play he must never relax his emotional hold on us. And all these things of which Bradley complains, the confusion of pathos, humor and sublime imagination, the vastness of the convulsion, the vagueness of the scene and the movements of the characters, the strange atmosphere and the half-realized suggestions—all this he needs as material for Lear's experience, and ours. Personally, I do not find quite so much vagueness and confusion. To whatever metaphysical heights Lear himself may rise, some character (Kent and Gloucester through the storm and in the hovel, Edgar for the meeting with the blinded Gloucester), some circumstance, or a few salient and explicit phrases will always be found pointing the action on its way. And if we become so at one with Lear in his agony that for the time its full significance escapes us, may not memory still make this clear? For that is very often true of our own emotional experiences. We are in confusion of suffering or joy at the time; only later do we realize, as we say, "what it all meant to us." It is, I suggest, this natural

---

[2] Whom Shakespeare carefully keeps out of the angry scenes which lead to Lear's self-banishment to the wild and the storm.

bent which Shakespeare turns to his account in these larger passages of *King Lear*. In the acting they move us profoundly. The
impression they make remains. And when the play is over they,
with the rest of it, should cohere in the memory, and clarify; and
the meaning of the whole should be plain. Shakespeare, I protest,
has not failed; he has—to the degree of his endeavor—triumphantly succeeded. But to appreciate the success and give effect
to it in the play's performance we must master and conform to
the stagecraft on which it depends.

In this hardest of tasks—the showing of Lear's agony, his spiritual death and resurrection—we find Shakespeare relying very
naturally upon his strongest weapon, which by experiment and
practice he has now, indeed, forged to an extraordinary strength,
and to a suppleness besides: the weapon of dramatic poetry. He
has, truly, few others of any account. In the storm-scenes the
shaking of a thunder-sheet will not greatly stir us. A modern
playwright might seek help in music—but the music of Shakespeare's day is not of that sort; in impressive scenery—he has
none. He has, in compensation, the fluidity of movement which
the negative background of his stage allows him. For the rest,
he has his actors, their acting and the power of their speech. It is
not a mere rhetorical power, nor are the characters lifted from the
commonplace simply by being given verse to speak instead of
conversational prose. All method of expression apart, they are
poetically conceived; they exist in those dimensions, in that freedom, and are endowed with that peculiar power. They are dramatic poetry incarnate.

Thus it is that Shakespeare can make such calls upon them as
here he must. In the storm-scenes they not only carry forward the
story, revealing and developing themselves as they do so, they
must—in default of other means—create the storm besides. Not
by detachedly describing it; if they "lose themselves" in its description, they will for that while lose something of their own
hold on us. The storm is not in itself, moreover, dramatically
important, only in its effect upon Lear. How, then, to give it
enough magnificence to impress him, yet keep it from rivaling
him? Why, by identifying the storm with him, setting the actor
to impersonate both Lear and—reflected in Lear—the storm. That,
approximately, is the effect made when—the Fool cowering,

drenched and pitiful, at his side—he launches into the tremendous:

> Blow, winds, and crack your cheeks! rage! blow!
> You cataracts and hurricanoes, spout
> Till you have drench'd our steeples, drown'd the cocks!
> You sulphurous and thought-executing fires,
> Vaunt-couriers of oak-cleaving thunder-bolts,
> Singe my white head! And thou, all-shaking thunder,
> Strike flat the thick rotundity of the world!
> Crack nature's moulds, all germens spill at once
> That make ungrateful man.

This is no mere description of a storm, but in music and imaginative suggestion a dramatic creating of the storm itself; and there is Lear—and here are we, if we yield ourselves—in the midst of it, almost a part of it. Yet Lear himself, in his Promethean defiance, still dominates the scene.

But clearly the effect cannot be made by Lamb's "old man tottering about the stage with a walking-stick"; and by any such competitive machinery for thunder and lightning as Bradley quite needlessly assumes to be an inevitable part of the play's staging it will be largely spoiled. What actor in his senses, however, would attempt to act the scene "realistically"? (I much doubt if any one of Lamb's detested barnstormers ever did.) And as to the thunder and lightning, Shakespeare uses the modicum to his hand; but it is of no dramatic consequence, and his stagecraft takes no account of it.[8] Yet if the human Lear seems lost for a moment in the symbolic figure, here is the Fool to remind us of him:

> O nuncle, court holy water in a dry house is better than this rain-water out o' door. Good nuncle, in, ask thy daughters' blessing; here's a night pities neither wise men nor fools.

—and to keep the scene in touch with reality. Yet note that the fantasy of the Fool only *mitigates* the contrast, and the spell is held unbroken. It is not till later—when Lear's defiant rage, hav-

---

[8] Bradley argues in a footnote that *because* Shakespeare's "means of imitating a storm were so greatly inferior to ours" he could not have "had the stage-performance only or chiefly in view in composing these scenes." But this is, surely, to view Shakespeare's theater and its craft with modern eyes. The contemporary critic would have found it easier to agree that just *because* your imitation storm was such a poor affair you must somehow make your stage effect *without* relying on it.

ing painted us the raging of the storm, has subsided—that Kent's sound, most "realistic" common sense, persuading him to the shelter of the hovel, is admitted.

But Shakespeare has other means of keeping the human and the apocalyptic Lear at one. Though the storm is being painted for us still—

> Rumble thy bellyful! spit, fire! spout, rain!
> Nor rain, wind, thunder, fire are my daughters:
> I tax not you, you elements, with unkindness;
> I never gave you kingdom, call'd you children,
> You owe me no subscription: then let fall
> Your horrible pleasure; here I stand, your slave;
> A poor, infirm, weak and despis'd old man.

—both in the sense of the words and the easier cadence of the verse the human Lear is emerging, and emerges fully upon the sudden simplicity of

> here I stand, your slave;
> A poor, infirm, weak and despis'd old man.

But the actor is not meant, therefore, suddenly to drop from trenchant speech to commonplace, present us a pathological likeness of poverty, infirmity and the rest, divest himself of all poetic power, become, in fact, the old man with a walking-stick. For if he does he will incontinently and quite fatally cease to be the Lear that Shakespeare has, as we said, conceived and embodied in poetry. In poetry; not, one must again insist, necessarily or simply in verse. And it is no more, now or later, a mere question of a method of speaking than of form in the writing. Verse, prose, and doggerel rhyme, in those strenuous scenes, each has its use, each asks an appropriate beauty of treatment, and the three in harmony are, by dramatic title, poetry.

The actor has then, not simply or chiefly to speak poetically, but, for the while, somehow to incarnate this poetry in himself. He can do so—paradoxically—by virtue of an exceptional self-sacrifice. Physically, Shakespeare's Lear must surrender to *him*; he makes himself in return an intellectual and emotional instrument for its expression. That is the way of all honest acting. If the actor's personality is the richer, a character will be absorbed in it. In a play of familiar human commerce actor and character may collaborate, so to say, upon equal terms. But give the character the transcendent quality of poetry, the actor can no longer bring it within the realistic limits of his personality. He may—obtusely—try to decompose it into a realism of impersonation, decorated by "poetic" speech. It is such a treatment of Lear which produces Lamb's old man with a walking-stick, and, for Bradley, dissipates the poetic atmosphere. But what Shakespeare asks of his actor is to surrender as much of himself as he can—much must remain; all that is physical—to this metaphysical power.

The thing is easier to do than to analyze. Children, set to act Shakespeare, will fling themselves innocently at the greatest of the plays; and, just because they do not comprehend and so cannot subdue the characters to their own likeness, they let us see them—though diminished and feeble—as through a clear glass. For the matured actor it is not quite so easy. He must comprehend the character, identify himself with it, and then—forget himself in it. Yet in this play and these very scenes he will find the example of Lear's own relation to the storm; in the reflection of its grandeur upon him, and the force lent by his fellowship with it to the storm devouring his mind. One must not push the comparison too far, nor is the psychology of acting a subject to be compassed in a sentence or two. But very much as the storm's strength is added to Lear's when he abandons himself to its apprehension, so may the Lear of Shakespeare's poetic and dramatic art be embodied in the actor if he will but do the same. And *there* should be the Lear of Lamb's demand, great "not in corporal dimension but in intellectual." Upon a "realistic" stage the thing cannot well be done. With Shakespeare made to delegate half his privileges to scene-painter and property-man a like dissociation will be forced upon the actor. And it is not only that the apparently real heath and hovel and the all but real thunder and lightning will reduce the characters which move among them to mere matter of fact also, but that by the dissociation itself, the appeal to our imagination—upon which all depends—is compromised. For the strength of this lies in its unity and concentration. It is the unity of the appeal that allows Shakespeare to bring so much within its scope. And, with time, place and circumstance, night, storm and desolation, and man's capacity to match them in despair all caught into a few lines of poetry, it should not be so hard to absorb besides—he willing—the ego of the actor who speaks them.

Then he will stand before us not physically ridiculous by comparison with them, but invested with their dynamic quality.

Shakespeare contrives within this harmony the full range of the effects he needs. There are not two Lears—the Titan integrating the storm and the old man breaking under it. In the accommodating realm of dramatic poetry they can remain one. Those contrasted aspects of them are shown in the swift descent we noted from magniloquence to simplicity, from rivalry with the elements to the confession of

> here I stand, your slave;
> A poor, infirm, weak and despis'd old man.

Or, we may say, there are the two Lears in one: the old man pathetic by contrast with the elements, yet terribly great in our immediate sense of his identity with them.

At best, of course, the actor can be but a token of the ideal Lear; and (thanking him) some of us may still feel that in the rarefied spaces of our imagination without his aid we come nearer to Shakespeare's imaginings—though what have we after all but a token of words upon paper to measure these by? But does the actor only remove us a stage farther from our source? I think not. He gives the words objectivity and life. Shakespeare has provided for his intervention. He can at least be a true token.

The Main Lines of Construction

King Lear, alone among the great tragedies, adds to its plot a subplot fully developed. And it suffers somewhat under the burden. After a few preliminary lines—Shakespeare had come to prefer this to the grand opening, and in this instance they are made introductory to plot and subplot too—we have a full and almost formal statement of the play's main theme and a show of the characters that are to develop it, followed by a scene which sets out the subplot as fully. The two scenes together form a sort of double dramatic prologue; and they might, by modern custom, count as a first act, for after them falls the only clearly indicated time-division in the play. The Folio, however, adds the quarrel with Goneril before an act-pause is allowed: then—whatever its

authority, but according to its usual plan—sets out four more
acts, the second allotted to the parallel quarrel with Regan, the
third to the climax of the main theme; the fourth we may call
a picture of the wreck of both Lear and Gloucester, and in it subplot and main plot are blended, and the fifth act is given to the
final and rather complex catastrophe. This division, then, has
thus much dramatic validity, and a producer may legitimately
choose to abide by it. On the other hand, one may contend, the
play's action flows unchecked throughout (but for the one check
which does not coincide with the act-division of the Folio). Still
it is not to be supposed that a Jacobean audience did, or a modern
audience would, sit through a performance without pause. Yet
again, it does not follow that the Folio's act-divisions were observed as intervals in which the audience dispersed and by which
the continuity of dramatic effect was altogether broken. A producer must, I think, exercise his own judgment. There may be
something to be said for more "breathing-spaces," but I should
myself incline to one definite interval only, to fall after Act III.
To this point the play is carried by one great impetus of inspiration, and there will be great gain in its acting being as unchecked.
If the strain on actors or audience seems to be too great, I should
choose a breathing-space after Act I, Scene ii, for all the Folio's
authority to the contrary. But the strain should not be excessive
upon either audience or actors. Shakespeare's stagecraft—his interweaving of contrasted characters and scenes—provides against
this, as does the unity of impression and rapidity of action, which
his unlocalized staging makes possible.[4]

The scene in which Lear divides his kingdom is a magnificent
statement of a magnificent theme. It has a proper formality, and
there is a certain megalithic grandeur about it, Lear dominating
it, that we associate with Greek tragedy. Its probabilities are
neither here nor there. A dramatist may postulate any situation

[4] Modern scenic productions, even at their simplest, not only destroy this unity
of impression, but lengthen the performance of the plays considerably, and the
acting habits they have engendered lengthen them still more. Mr. Nugent Monck
has produced *King Lear* at the Maddermarket Theatre, Norwich, upon an unlocalized stage. He cut approximately 750 of the 3340 lines of text (the Folio will give
authority for the cutting of some 200), allowed a ten minutes' interval, did not
play overrapidly, and the whole performance only lasted two hours and a half.

he has the means to interpret, if he will abide by the logic of it after. The producer should observe and even see stressed the scene's characteristics; Lear's two or three passages of such an eloquence as we rather expect at a play's climax than its opening, the strength of such single lines as

> The bow is bent and drawn, make from the shaft.

with its hammering monosyllables; and the hard-bitten

> Nothing: I have sworn; I am firm.

together with the loosening of the tension in changes to rhymed couplets, and the final drop into prose by that businesslike couple, Goneril and Regan. Then follows, with a lift into lively verse for a start, as a contrast and as the right medium for Edmund's sanguine conceit, the development of the Gloucester theme. Shakespeare does this at his ease, allows himself diversion and time. He has now both the plot of the ungrateful daughters and the subplot of the treacherous son under way.

But the phenomenon for which Shakespeareans learn to look has not yet occurred, that inexplicable "springing to life"—a springing, it almost seems, into a life of its own—of character or theme. Very soon it does occur; Lear's entrance, disburdened from the care of state, is its natural signal. On his throne, rightly enough, he showed formal and self-contained. Now he springs away; and now the whole play in its relation to him takes on a liveliness and variety; nor will the energy be checked or weakened, or, if checked, only that the next stroke may be intenser, till the climax is past, till his riven and exhausted nature is granted the oblivion of sleep. This is the master-movement of the play, which enshrines the very soul of the play—and in the acting, as I have suggested, there should be no break allowed. To read and give full imaginative value to those fifteen hundred lines at a stretch is certainly exhausting; if they were written at one stretch of inspiration the marvel is that Shakespeare, with his Lear, did not collapse under the strain, yet the exactions of his performance he tempers with all his skill. Lear is surrounded by characters, which each in a different way take a share of the burden from him. Kent, the Fool, and Edgar as Poor Tom are a complement of dramatic strength; and the interweaving of the scenes concerning Oswald, Edmund and Gloucester saves the actor's energy for the scenes of the rejection and the storm.[5]

As the Lear theme expanded under his hand Shakespeare had begun, and perforce, to economize his treatment of the Gloucester-Edgar-Edmund story. Edgar himself is indeed dismissed from the second scene upon no more allowance of speech than

> I'm sure on't, not a word.

—with which the best of actors may find it hard to make his presence felt; and at our one view of him before he had been left negative enough. Edmund is then brought rapidly into relation with the main plot, and the blending of main plot and subplot begins.[6] Edgar also is drawn into Lear's orbit; and, for the time,

---

[5] Therefore the producer who will for the sake of his scenery (as has been the pleasant picture-stage custom) run two or three of the storm-scenes into one, presents himself and his Lear with failure.

[6] We find, too, at this point, some signs that the emphasis of the play's whole scheme was altered.

> Have you heard of no likely wars toward,
> 'Twixt the Dukes of Cornwall and Albany?

Curan asks Edmund, who answers "Not a word." Edmund, with admirable promptitude, turns the notion to the further confusing of the so easily confused Edgar, but the wars themselves come to nothing. Kent, in an involved speech in Act III (for him most uncharacteristically involved), suggests that it is the threat of them which is bringing the French army to England. But the vagueness is suspicious. It looks a little as if Shakespeare had thought of making the hypocrite inheritors of Cordelia's portion fall out over it (an obvious nemesis) and had changed his mind. There are slight signs indeed that greed of possessions was to have been the axis for the whole play to turn upon. It begins with the parting of the realm; and

> Legitimate Edgar, I must have your land. . . .

is the coping point of Edmund's first soliloquy. Did the discovery of deeper spiritual issues in Lear's own character and fate give us the present play? Another and a later change in the plot can be divined. The King of France comes armed with Cordelia to Lear's rescue, as is natural. Then, by virtue of the clumsiest few lines in the play, he is sent back again. Did Shakespeare originally mean Cordelia to restore her father to his throne as in the old play; but would a French victory in England not have done? It may be; though I cannot think he ever intended Lear to survive. On the other hand, Cordelia herself is not a figure predoomed to death. This catastrophe, though the moral violence of the play may aesthetically justify it, and though it is needed dramatically, as a final blow to Lear (see p. 299 for the fuller argument of this), always seems to me a wrench from his first plan. This decided on, though, he would certainly have to get rid of France. The point for the producer is that the Folio cuts the clumsy explanation, as if on the principle—and it is an excellent one in the theater—of: "Never explain, never apologize." In fact it cuts the whole scene, which later contains as dramatically feeble an excuse to the complete sacrifice of his own interests in the play. "Poor Tom" is in effect an embodiment of Lear's frenzy, the disguise no part of Edgar's own development.

As we have seen, while Act III is at the height of its argument, Shakespeare is careful to keep alive the lower-pitched theme of Edmund's treachery, his new turn to the betrayal of his father He affords it two scenes, of twenty-five lines each, wedged between the three dominant scenes of the storm and Lear's refuge from it. They are sufficient and no more for their own purpose; in their sordidness they stand as valuable contrast to the spiritual exaltation of the others. The supreme moment for Lear himself, the turning point, therefore, of the play's main theme, is reached in the second of the three storm-scenes, when the proud old king kneels humbly and alone in his wretchedness to pray. This is the argument's absolute height; and from now on we may feel (as far as Lear is concerned) the tension relax, through the first grim passage of his madness, slackening still through the fantastic scene of the arraignment of the joint-stools before that queer bench of justices, to the moment of his falling asleep and his conveyance away—his conveyance, we find it to be, out of the main stream of the play's action. Shakespeare then deals the dreadful blow to Gloucester. The very violence and horror of this finds its dramatic justification in the need to match in another sort—since he could not hope to match it in spiritual intensity—the catastrophe to Lear. And now we may imagine him, if we please, stopping to consider where he was. Anticlimax, after this, is all but inevitable. Let the producer take careful note how Shakespeare sets out to avoid the worst dangers of it.[7]

for the delay in handing Lear over to his daughter's care, though it gives none for the devoted Kent letting the distracted old man out of his sight to roam the fields crowned with wild flowers. I think on the whole that the Folio gives a producer a good lead. Yet another slight change of plan may be guessed at; it would effect some economy in the working-out of the subplot. Edmund says to Gloucester about Edgar:

> If your honour judge it meet, I will place you where you shall hear us confer of this . . . and that without any further delay than this very evening.

But he never does. Shakespeare may have remembered, besides, that he had lately used this none too fresh device in *Othello*.

[7] It is worth remarking here upon the fact that of Edgar's two soliloquies—the one which ends Act III, Scene vi, and the one which begins Act IV—the Folio omits the first. They are somewhat redundant in mood if not in matter. The interesting thing is that the Folio omission is of a speech ending a scene and

Had the play been written upon the single subject of Lear and his daughters, we should now be in sight of its end. But the wealth of material Shakespeare has posited asks for use, and his own imagination, we may suppose, is still teeming. But by the very nature of the material (save Cordelia) left for development the rest of the play must be pitched in a lower key. Shakespeare marshals the action by which the wheel of Gloucester's weakness and Edmund's treachery is brought full circle with extraordinary skill and even more extraordinary economy. Yet for all this, except in a fine flash or two, the thing stays by comparison pedestrian. He is only on the wing again when Lear and Cordelia are his concern; in the scenes of their reconciliation and of the detached tragedy of Lear's death with the dead Cordelia in his arms, as in the still more detached and—as far as the mere march of the action is concerned—wholly unjustifiable scene of Lear mad and fantastically crowned with wild flowers. We must add, though, to the inspired passages the immediately preceding fantasy of Gloucester's imaginary suicide, an apt offset to the realistic horror of his blinding, and occasion for some inimitable verse. The chief fact to face, then, is that for the rest of the play, the best will be incidental and not a necessary part of the story.[8] The producer therefore must give his own best attention to Albany, Goneril and Regan and their close-packed contests, and to the nice means by which Edgar is shaped into a hero; and in general must see that this purposeful disciplined necessary stuff is given fullness and, as far as may be, spontaneity of life in its interpretation. If he will take care of this the marvelous moments will tend to take care of him.

Shakespeare strengthens the action at once with the fresh interest of the Edmund-Goneril-Regan intrigue, daring as it is to launch into this with the short time left him for its development and resolving. He is, indeed, driven to heroic compressions, to impli-

moralizing upon the event; it forms a "considering point." Without it the catastrophe to Gloucester is linked more closely to Lear's misfortunes, and the long due development of Edgar's character then begins—and importantly—the fourth act. For further argument upon this point, see pp. 319, 331.

[8] The meeting of mad Lear and blind Gloucester (I give the scene more attention on p. 295) is, of course, most germane to the play's *idea*—a more important thing to Shakespeare than the mere story—but it does check the march of the story.

cations, effects by "business," action "off," almost to "love-making
by reference only." Goneril's first approach to Edmund (or his to
her; but we may credit the lady, I think, with the throwing of
the handkerchief) is only clearly marked out for the actors by
Regan's reference to it five scenes later, when she tells us that
at Goneril's

> late being here
> She gave strange œilliads and most speaking looks
> To noble Edmund.

(Regan credits her with what, if we prefer our Shakespeare mod-
ernized, we might literally translate into "giving the glad eye.")
But this silent business of the earlier scene is important and must
be duly marked if the arrival of the two together and Edmund's
turning back to avoid meeting Albany, the "mild husband," is to
have its full effect. For the first and last of their spoken love-
making, excellently characteristic as it is, consists of Goneril's

> Our wishes on the way
> May prove effects. . . .
> This trusty servant
> Shall pass between us: ere long you are like to hear,
> If you dare venture in your own behalf,
> A mistress's command. Wear this; spare speech;
> Decline your head: this kiss, if it durst speak,
> Would stretch thy spirits up into the air.
> Conceive, and fare thee well.

and Edmund's ("Spare speech," indeed!)

> Yours in the ranks of death!

—all spoken in Oswald's presence too. It is, of course, not only
excellent but sufficient. The regal impudency of the woman, the
falsely chivalrous flourish of the man's response—pages of dialogue
might not tell us more of their relations; and, of these relations, is
there much more that is dramatically worth knowing? The point
for the producer is that no jot of such a constricted dramatic
opportunity must be missed.

For the whole working-out of this lower issue of the play the
same warning stands true; an exact and unblurred value must be
given to each significant thing. The interaction of circumstance
and character is close-knit and complex, but it is clear. Keep it

clear and it can be made effective to any audience that will listen, and is not distracted from listening. Let us underline this last phrase and now make the warning twofold. In working out a theme so full of incident and of contending characters Shakespeare allows for no distraction of attention at all, certainly not for the breaking of continuity which the constant shifting of realistically localized scenery must involve. The action, moreover, of these later scenes is exceptionally dependent upon to-ings and fro-ings. Given continuity of performance and no more insistence upon whereabouts than the action itself will indicate, the impression produced by the constant busy movement into our sight and out again of purposeful, passionate or distracted figures, is in itself of great dramatic value, and most congruous to the plot and counterplot of the play's ending. The order for Lear's and Cordelia's murder, the quarrel over Edmund's precedence, Albany's sudden self-assertion, Regan's sickness, Edgar's appearance, the fight, his discovery of himself, Goneril's discomfiture, the telling of Kent's secret, Regan's and Goneril's death, the alarm to save Lear and Cordelia—Shakespeare, by the Folio text, gets all this into less than two hundred lines, with a fair amount of rhetoric and incidental narrative besides. He needs no more, though bareness does nearly turn to banality sometimes. But unless we can be held in an unrelaxed grip we may not submit to the spell.

He has kept a technical master-stroke for his ending:

Enter Lear with Cordelia in his arms.

There should be a long, still pause, while Lear passes slowly in with his burden, while they all stand respectful as of old to his majesty. We may have wondered a little that Shakespeare should be content to let Cordelia pass from the play as casually as she seems to in the earlier scene. But this is the last of her, not that. Dumb and dead, she that was never apt of speech—what fitter finish for her could there be? What fitter ending to the history of the two of them, which began for us with Lear on his throne, conscious of all eyes on him, while she shamed and angered him by her silence? The same company are here, or all but the same, and they await his pleasure.[9] Even Regan and Goneril are here to

---

[9] And this must not be counted as chance, for the bodies of Goneril and Regan have been brought on—why else?

pay him a ghastly homage. But he knows none of them—save for a blurred moment Kent whom he banished—none but Cordelia. And again he reproaches her silence; for

> Her voice was ever soft,
> Gentle and low, an excellent thing in woman.

Then his heart breaks.

The Method of the Dialogue

THE dialogue of *King Lear* is remarkable for its combination of freedom and power. Of the plays that neighbor it, the sustained melodies of *Othello* may give greater dignity. In *Macbeth* there are passages that seem to wield a sort of secret sway. *Antony and Cleopatra* has ease and breadth for its normal virtues as *Coriolanus* has strength; and, thereafter, Shakespeare passes to his last period of varied and delightful ease. But the exact combination of qualities that distinguishes the writing of *King Lear* we do not find again; nor indeed should we look to, since it is the product of the matter and the nature of the play. Shakespeare was in nothing a truer artist than in this, that, having mastered his means of expression, journeyed from the rhymed couplets and fantastic prose of *Love's Labour's Lost* to the perfected verse and balanced prose of *Henry V* and the mature Comedies, he yet fettered himself in no fixed style. He may write carelessly; here and there amid the poetic splendors we find what seem to be claptrap couplets and lines flatter than a pancake. But, his imagination once fired, the idea seldom fails of the living vesture it needs. This, it may be said, it is any writer's business to discover. But Shakespeare's art lies in the resource, which can give individual expression to a thought or emotion within the bounds, for instance, of a stretch of formal verse if his first need is for the solid strength of this; or, more often, in the molding of verse and prose into such variety of expressive form that it is a wonder any unity of effect is kept at all—yet it is. It lies in the daring by which, for a scene or two, he may dispense with all unity of form whatever, if his dramatic purpose will so profit. Witness such a seemingly haphazard mixture of verse, prose and snatches of song as we find in the scenes between Lear, Kent, Gloucester, the Fool and Poor Tom. Yet the dramatic vitality of these scenes lies largely in this variety and balance of orchestration; their emotional strain might be intolerable without it. But the root of the matter, of course, is in the imaginative vitality with which he dowers the characters themselves. It is always instructive to watch Shakespeare getting his play with its crew under way, to see him stating his subjects, setting his characters in opposition. Some lead off, fully themselves from the start, some seem to hang on his hands, saying what they have to say in sound conventional phrase, some he may leave all but mute, uncertain yet, it would seem, of his own use for them. Not till the whole organism has gathered strength and abounds in a life of its own is the true mastery to be seen. Even so, in *King Lear* there is more to be accounted for. In no other of the plays, I think, unless it be *Macbeth*, are we so conscious of the force of an emotion overriding, often, a character's self-expression, and of a vision of things to which the action itself is but a foreground. And how this and the rest of the play's individuality is made manifest by the form as well as the substance of the dialogue, by the shaping and color of its verse and prose, it is, of course, of primary importance for producer and actors to observe. There is no one correct way of speaking Shakespeare's verse and prose, for he had no one way of writing it. One way grew out of another with him. Little of the method of *Romeo and Juliet* will be left in *King Lear*, much of the method of *Hamlet* still may be. But the fresh matter of a play will provoke a fresh manner, and its interpretation must be as freshly approached.

For more reasons and in more directions than one, Shakespeare seeks strength in simplicity in the writing of *King Lear*. The noble conventional speech of its beginning will not serve him long, for this is the language of such an authority as Lear discards. There is needed an expression of those fiercer, cruder strengths which come into play when a reign of order ends and a moral code is broken. Edmund begins glibly, but is indulged neither with subtle thought nor fine phrases. Goneril becomes like a woman with a fever in her: "I'll not endure it . . . I will not speak with him . . . the fault of it I'll answer . . . I'd have it come to question . . . I would breed from hence occasions, and I shall. . . ." Mark how broken is the eloquence of Lear's appeal to Regan; mark the distraction of his

> No, you unnatural hags,
> I will have such revenges on you both
> That all the world shall—I will do such things,
> What they are yet I know not, but they shall be
> The terrors of the earth. You think I'll weep;
> No, I'll not weep:
> I have full cause of weeping, but this heart
> Shall break into a hundred thousand flaws
> Or ere I'll weep.

Here, one would say, is verse reduced to its very elements.

Shakespeare has, besides, to carry us into strange regions of thought and passion, so he must, at the same time, hold us by familiar things. Lear, betrayed and helpless, at an end of his command of self or circumstance, is dramatically set above the tyranny and logic of both by being made one with the storm, and by his harmonizing with the homely fantasies of the Fool and the mad talk of Poor Tom, till his own "noble anger" breaks the bounds of reason too. Without some anchorage in simplicity, this action and these characters would range so wide that human interpretation could hardly compass them. Kent does something to keep the play's feet firm on the ground; Gloucester a little; the Fool was to Shakespeare's audience a familiar and sympathetic figure. But Lear himself might escape our closer sympathy were it not for his recurrent coming down from the heights to such moments as

> No, I will be the pattern of all patience;
> I will say nothing.

as

> My wits begin to turn.
> Come on, my boy. How dost, my boy? Art cold?
> I am cold myself. Where is this straw, my fellow?

as

> No, I will weep no more. In such a night
> To shut me out! Pour on, I will endure.
> In such a night as this!

or as

> Make no noise, make no noise; draw the curtains; so, so, so.
> We'll go to supper i' the morning; so, so, so.

This final stroke, moreover, brings us to the simplest physical actualities; Lear's defiance of the elements has flickered down to a mock pulling of the curtains round his bed. Later, when he wanders witless and alone, his speech is broken into oracular fragments of rhapsody; but the play of thought is upon actuality and his hands are at play all the time with actual things; with the flower (is it?) he takes for a coin, with whatever serves for a bit of cheese, for his gauntlet, his hat, for the challenge thrust under Gloucester's blind eyes. Let us note, too, how one of the finest passages of poetry in the play, Edgar's imaginary tale of Dover cliff, consists of the clearest-cut actualities of description. And when Lear wakes to his right senses again, simplicity is added to simplicity in his feeling the pin's prick, in his remembering not his garments. The tragic beauty of his end is made more beautiful by his call for a looking-glass, his catching at the feather to put on Cordelia's lips, the undoing of the button. These things are the necessary balance to the magniloquence of the play's beginning and to the tragic splendor of the storm.

Amid the sustained magnificence of the first scene we find the first use of an even more simple device, recurrent throughout the play.

> what can you say to draw
> A third more opulent than your sisters? Speak.
> Nothing, my lord.
> Nothing?
> Nothing.
> Nothing will come of nothing; speak again.

Again and again with varying purpose and effect Shakespeare uses this device of reiteration. Note Edmund's

> Why brand they us
> With base? with baseness? bastardy? base, base?
> . . . Well, then,
> Legitimate Edgar, I must have your land.
> Our father's love is to the bastard, Edmund,
> As to the legitimate: Fine word,—legitimate!
> Well, my legitimate, if this letter speed,
> And my invention thrive, Edmund the base
> Shall top the legitimate.

The repetition itself does much to drive in on us the insistent malice of the man.

Lear summons Oswald with

> O! you sir, you sir, come you hither, sir.
> Who am I, sir?

and the tragic counterpart of this is

> Hear, Nature, hear! dear goddess, hear.

Gloucester's grieved refrain falls casually enough:

> O, madam, my old heart is crack'd, is crack'd. . . .
> O, lady, lady, shame would have it hid. . . .
> I know not, madam; 'tis too bad, too bad.

And for a rounded elaboration of the effect, we have Lear's

> O! reason not the need; our basest beggars
> Are in the poorest thing superfluous:
> Allow not nature more than nature needs,
> Man's life is cheap as beast's. Thou art a lady;
> If only to go warm were gorgeous,
> Why, nature needs not what thou gorgeous wear'st,
> Which scarcely keeps thee warm. But, for true need—
> You heavens, give me that patience, patience I need!

Half a dozen other such instances, more or less elaborate, of major and minor importance, can be found; till we come to the effect at its crudest in

> Howl, howl, howl, howl! O, you are men of stones . . . .

and to the daring and magic of

> Thou'lt come no more.
> Never, never, never, never, never!

It is a simple device indeed, but all mature artists tend to seek strength in simplicity of expression. It is, at its simplest, a very old device, and older than drama. Iteration casts, of itself, a spell upon the listener, and the very sound of that echoing "Never" can make us sharers in Lear's helplessness and despair.[10] Bradley says of this

---

[10] It is, moreover, an old device with Shakespeare. Set beside Lear's

> O! reason not the need . . .

Juliet's

> Hath Romeo slain himself? Say thou but 'I'
> And that bare vowel 'I' shall poison more

last speech that it leaves us "on the topmost peaks of poetry"; and so, surely, it does. Rend it from its context, the claim sounds absurd; but dramatic poetry is never to be judged apart from the action it implies.

King Lear—are we still to think?—cannot be acted. The whole scheme and method of its writing is a contrivance for its effective acting. This contrast and reconciliation of grandeur and simplicity, this setting of vision in terms of actuality, this inarticulate passion which breaks now and again into memorable phrases—does not even the seeming failure of expression give us a sense of the helplessness of humanity pitted against higher powers? All the magnificent art of this is directed to one end; the play's acting in a theater.

The Characters and Their Interplay

LEAR

LEAR himself is so dominant a figure that the exhaustion of his impetus to action with the play's end barely in sight leaves Shakespeare a heavy task in the rallying of its forces for what is still to do. The argument has been raised by then, moreover, to such imaginative heights that any descent from them—even Lear's own —must be precarious. They are heights that Shakespeare himself, perhaps, did not clearly envisage till the soaring had begun. Not that there is anything tentative in the presentation of Lear. Never was character in play, one exclaims, so fully and immediately, so imminently and overwhelmingly set forth! But in this lies the actor's first difficulty.

> Than the death-dealing eye of cockatrice.
> I am not I, if there be such an 'I,'
> Or those eyes shut that make thee answer 'I.'
> If he be slain say 'I,' or if not, no;
> Brief sounds determine of my weal or woe.

The puns may destroy its emotional value for us, though they did not for the Elizabethans. But the effect aimed at is about the same. The difference in the means to it may be made one measure of Shakespeare's development of his art. Not but that he could pun dramatically to the end. He came, however, to prefer single shots to fusillades.

With the dividing of the kingdom and Cordelia's rejection the trend of the action is clearly foreshadowed:

> So be my grave my peace, as here I give
> Her father's heart from her!

By all the rules of drama we know within a little what the retribution for that must amount to; and Shakespeare will not disappoint us. But equally it would seem that for this massive fortress of pride which calls itself Lear, for any old man indeed of eighty and upwards, there could be no dramatic course but declension. Who would ever think of developing, of expanding, a character from such overwhelming beginnings? Yet this is what Shakespeare does, and finds a transcendent way to do it. So the actor's difficulty is that he must start upon a top note, at what must be pretty well the full physical stretch of his powers, yet have in reserve the means to a greater climax of another sort altogether. It is here, however, that the almost ritual formality of the first scene will help him. The occasion itself, the general subservience to Lear's tyranny (Kent's protest and Cordelia's resolution only emphasize this), Lear's own assertion of kingship as something not far from godhead, all combine to set him so above and apart from the rest that the very isolation will seem strength if the actor takes care to sustain it. There need be, there must be, no descent to petulance. Lear marking the map with his finger might be marking the land itself, so Olympian should he appear. The oath by the sacred radiance of the sun is one that only he may swear. That Kent should call him an "old man" is in itself a blasphemous outrage.

> Come not between the dragon and his wrath. . . .
>
> The bow is bent and drawn, make from the shaft. . . .
>
> Nothing: I have sworn; I am firm.

Lines like these mark the level of Lear, though their fatality may be a trifle mitigated by the human surliness of

> Better thou
> Had'st not been born than not to have pleased me better.

by the grim humor which lies in

> Nothing will come of nothing: speak again.

in the ironic last fling at Kent of

> Away! By Jupiter,
> *This* shall not be revoked.

and in the bitter gibe to Burgundy:

> When she was dear to us we did hold her so,
> But now her price is fall'n . . . .

even, one would like to suspect, in the reason given for his fast intent to shake all cares of state from him, that he may

> Unburden'd crawl toward death.

—for our next sight of his Majesty will show him back from hunting with a most impatient appetite for dinner! Note, too, the hint of another Lear, given us in the music of three short words— the first touch in the play of that peculiar verbal magic Shakespeare could command—when, sated with Goneril's and Regan's flattery, he turns to his Cordelia with

> Now, our joy . . .

But Lear must leave this first scene as he entered it, more a magnificent portent than a man.

He has doffed his kingship; free from its trappings, how the native genius of the man begins to show! It flashes on us as might the last outbursts of some near-extinct volcano. He is old and uncertain; but a mighty man, never a mere tyrant divested of power. He has genius, warped and random genius though it may be, and to madness, as will appear, very near allied. And Shakespeare's art lies in showing us this in nothing he does—for what he does now is foolish—but in every trivial thing that he is. All the action of the scene of the return from hunting, all his surroundings are staged to this end. The swift exchanges with the disguised Kent and their culmination:

> Dost thou know me, fellow?
> No, sir, but you have that in your countenance which I would fain call master.
> What's that?
> Authority.

—his encounter with the pernickity jack-in-office Oswald, and with the frail, whimsical Fool who mockingly echoes his own

passionate whimsies; all this helps set in motion and sets off a new
and livelier, a heartier Lear. Not that Shakespeare bates us one
jot of the old man's stiff-necked perversities. He no more asks our
sympathy on easy terms for him than will Lear yield an inch to
Goneril's reasonable requests. A hundred useless knights about
the house—even though, from their master's point of view, they
were men of choice and rarest parts—must have been a burden.
Lear's striking Oswald really was an outrage; after due complaint
Goneril would doubtless have reproved his impertinence—for all
that she had prompted it! Even with the petted Fool, and in the
very midst of the petting, out there snaps

> Take heed, sirrah, the whip!

We need look for no tractable virtues in him.

The play's adopted story has its appointed way to go, but here
begins the way of Lear's soul's agony and salvation as Shakespeare
is to blaze it. The change in him shows first in the dialogue with
the attendant knight and the delicate strokes which inform it.
The knight, dispatched to bid that mongrel Oswald come back,
returns only to report the fellow's round answer that he would
not. "He would not!" flashes Lear at the unbelievable phrase. But
when, picking his words—as, if you were not a Kent (and there
had been room at best for but one Kent at Court), no doubt you
learned to do with Lear—the knight hints hesitatingly at trouble,
the quiet response comes:

> Thou but remember'st me of mine own conception: I have per-
> ceived a most faint neglect of late; which I have rather blamed as
> mine own jealous curiosity, than as a very pretence and purpose
> of unkindness: I will look further into't. But where's my fool? I
> have not seen him this two days.
> Since my young lady's going into France, sir, the fool hath much
> pined away.
> No more of that; I have noted it well. Go you, and tell my
> daughter I would speak with her. Go you, call hither my fool. O!
> you sir, you sir, come you hither, sir!

—this last to the mongrel Oswald who has appeared again. But
Lear—can this be the Lear of the play's first scene?—to be turning
his knight's "great abatement of kindness" to "a most faint neglect," and blaming, even so, his own jealous curiosity for noting

it! But the Fool's grief for Cordelia he has noted well. Lest it echo too loudly in his proud unhappy heart, with a quick turn he brings the old Lear to his rescue, rasps an order here, an order there, and—takes it out of Oswald.

From now on the picturing of him is lifelike, in that it has all the varied, unexpected, indirect and latent eloquence of life. Shakespeare is at his deftest, his medium at its freest and most supple. Let the interpreter be alert too. This Lear is as quick on the uptake as it is his Fool's business to be. An unnatural quickness in an old man, is it, and some sign of a toppling brain? His silences are as pregnant. He listens and finds cheer in the Fool's chatter and song, throws him an answer or so to keep it alive, snarls now and then like an old lion if a sting goes too deep. Yet his thoughts, we can tell, are away. We must visualize this scene fully and accurately; the Fool caroling, his poor heart being heavy with Cordelia's loss he carols the more; the old king brooding; and Kent ever watchful, with a dog's eyes. Mark the effect of Goneril's appearance before her father, in purposed, sullen muteness; the Fool's speech points it for us, should we be unobservant; then her break into the prepared formality of verse, as this verse will seem, capping the loose prose of the scene and the Fool's rhyming. Mark, too, the cold kingliness of Lear's four words, all his response to her careful address:

Are you our daughter?

He resorts to irony, the fine mind's weapon, which blunts itself upon the stupid—for Goneril is stupid, and she has stupidity's stubborn strength. But when the storm of Lear's wrath does break, I think she inwardly shakes a little.

You strike my people, and your disordered rabble
Make servants of their betters.

sounds like scared bravado. She can wait, though, for the storm to pass; and, for the moment, it does pass in senile self-reproaches. A few more such futile outbursts, she is confident, and the extravagant old tyrant will be spent and tame enough. But, suddenly, the servants are dismissed and she is alone with husband and father. And her father, rigid, transformed, and with slow, calm, dreadful strength, is calling down the gods' worst curse upon her.

Hear, Nature, hear! dear goddess, hear!
Suspend thy purpose if thou didst intend
To make this creature fruitful! . . .

The actor who will rail and rant this famous passage may know
his own barnstorming business, but he is no interpreter of Shakespeare. The merely superficial effect of its deadlier quiet, lodged
between two whirlwinds of Lear's fury, should be obvious. But its
dramatic purpose far outpasses that. Not indifferently did Shakespeare make this a pagan play, and deprive its argument of comfortable faith in virtue rewarded, here or hereafter. And it is upon
this deliberate invocation of ill that we pass into spiritual darkness. The terror of it moves Albany rather than Goneril, whom,
indeed, nothing is ever to move. But as he rouses himself to plead
against it Lear is gone.[11]

Now havoc begins in him. We have his raging, distracted return, tears of helpless despair punctuating hysterical threats; later
the stamping, muttering impatience of his wait for his horses. We
know that he sets out on a long hard ride, dinnerless after his
hunting. Later we learn that the journey was wasted; he had to
post on to Gloucester's. Did he ride through the night without rest
or pause? Shakespeare is hunting both Lear and the play's action
hard and using every device to do it.

Yet the next day when he reaches Gloucester's house—this old
man past eighty, and physically we should suppose near exhaustion
—he is master of himself, is his most regal self again.[12] We are given
the scene with Kent awaked in the stocks to show it.

Ha!
Makest thou this shame thy pastime?

All the old dignity in this; there follows the brusque familiar
give-and-take which true authority never fears to practice with
its dependents; then again the majestic

[11] The "Away, away," is thus spoken to the propitiatory Albany, and has no
reference to the servants, who have already been sent off, nor, I think, to Lear's
own departure. The point is disputable, no doubt, and I would not go to the stake
for my reading of it. The Quartos have "Go, go, my people" repeated, as if his
first order had not been obeyed. I must leave it to better judges of their origin
and value to say whether this is mere muddlement of text. But, even if it is not,
the Folio's change of phrase might cover a change of meaning too.
[12] But the outward signs of exhaustion must begin to be upon him.

> Resolve me, with all modest haste, which way
> Thou might'st deserve, or they impose, this usage
> Coming from us.

and the iron self-control in which the shameful tale is heard. When the tale is ended he still stands silent, while the Fool pipes for us an artless mockery (the art of this!) of his bitter and ominous thoughts. Regan too, Regan too! The grief of disillusion has now become physical pain to him,

> O, how this mother swells up toward my heart;
> *Hysterica passio!* down, thou climbing sorrow!

But he masters it.

> Where is this daughter? . . .
> Follow me not; stay here.

And, solitary in his pride, he goes to face and prove the worst.

If the play, with the invocation of the curse upon Goneril, entered an arena of anarchy and darkness, Lear himself is to pass now from personal grievance to the taking upon him, as great natures may, the imagined burden of the whole world's sorrow—and if his nature breaks under it, what wonder! And Shakespeare brings about this transition from malediction to martyrdom with great art, by contrivance direct and indirect, by strokes broad and subtle; nor ever—his art in this at its greatest—does he turn his Lear from a man into an ethical proposition. The thing is achieved—as the whole play is achieved—in terms of humanity, and according to the rubric of drama.

Lear comes back with Gloucester; the well-meaning Gloucester, whose timid tact is the one thing least likely to placate him. He is struggling with himself, with the old tyrannic temper, with his newfound knowledge of himself, with his body's growing weakness. He is like a great oak tree, torn at the roots, blown this way and that. When the half-veiled insolence of Regan's and Cornwall's greeting must, one would think, affront him, a pathetic craving for affection peeps through. When he once more finds refuge in irony, it is to turn the edge of it against himself. But with four quick shocks—his sudden recall of the outrage upon his servant, the sound of a trumpet, the sight of Oswald, the sight of Goneril—he is brought to a stand and to face the realities arrayed against him. This must be made very plain to us. On the one side stand Goneril and Regan and Cornwall in all authority. The perplexed Gloucester hovers a little apart. On the other side is Lear, the Fool at his feet, and his one servant, disarmed, freed but a minute since behind him. Things are at their issue. His worst errors, after all, have partaken of nobility; he has scorned policy. He has given himself, helpless, into these carnal hands. He will abide, then, as nobly the fate he has courted. Note the single touch of utter scorn for the cur Cornwall, who, the moment looking likely, takes credit for those stocks.

> I set him there, sir; but his own disorders
> Deserved much less advancement.
>   You! Did you!

But all consequences he'll abide, even welcome, he'll abjure his curses, run from one ingrate daughter to the other, implore and bargain, till the depth is sounded and he stands at last surrendered, and level in his helplessness and deprivation with the least of his fellow-men.

> GONERIL.   Hear me, my lord,
> What need you five-and-twenty, ten, or five,
> To follow in a house where twice so many
> Have a command to tend you?
> REGAN.   What need one?
> LEAR. O! reason not the need; our basest beggars
> Are in the poorest thing superfluous:
> Allow not nature more than nature needs,
> Man's life is cheap as beast's. . . .
>   But, for true need—
> You heavens, give me that patience, patience I need!
> You see me here, you gods, a poor old man
> As full of grief as age, wretched in both!

"O! reason not the need . . ."! This abandoning of the struggle and embracing of misfortune is a turning point of the play, a salient moment in the development of Lear's character, and its significance must be marked. He is now at the nadir of his fortunes; the tragic heights are at hand.

It may be thought that by emphasizing so many minor points of stagecraft the great outlines of play and character will be obscured. But while Shakespeare projects greatly, asking from his interpreters a simplicity of response, lending them greatness by virtue of this convention that passes the play's material through the sole crucible of their speech and action, he yet saves them alive, so to speak—not stultified in an attempt to overpass their own powers nor turned to mere mouthpieces of mighty lines—by constant references to the commonplace (we noted more of them in discussing the methods of the dialogue). He invigorates his play's action by keeping its realities upon a battleground where any and every sort of stroke may tell.

Thus there now follows the tense passage in which Goneril, Regan and Cornwall snuff the impending storm and find good reason for ill-doing. What moralists! Regan with her

> O! sir, to wilful men,
> The injuries that they themselves procure
> Must be their schoolmasters.

Cornwall, with his

> Shut up your doors, my lord; 'tis a wild night:
> My Regan counsels well; come out of the storm.

This is surely the very voice—though the tones may be harsh—of respectability and common sense? And what a prelude to the "high engender'd battles" now imminent! Before battle is joined, however, the note of Kent is interposed to keep the play's story going its more pedestrian way and to steady us against the imaginative turmoil pending. This use of Kent is masterly; and, in the storm-scenes themselves, the contrasting use of the Fool, feeble, fantastic, pathetic, a foil to Lear, a foil to the storm—what more incongruous sight conceivable than such a piece of Court tinsel so drenched and buffeted!—is more than masterly.

But it is upon Lear's own progress that all now centers, upon his passing from that royal defiance of the storm to the welcomed shelter of the hovel. He passes by the road of patience:

> No, I will be the pattern of all patience;
> I will say nothing.

of—be it noted—a thankfulness that he is at last simply

> a man
> More sinn'd against than sinning . . .

to the humility of

> My wits begin to turn.
> Come on, my boy. How dost, my boy? Art cold?
> I am cold myself. Where is this straw, my fellow?
> The art of our necessities is strange
> That can make vile things precious. Come, your hovel. . . .

and, a little later yet, mind and body still further strained towards breaking point, to the gentle dignity, when Kent would make way for him—to the more than kingly dignity of

> Prithee, go in thyself: seek thine own ease.
> This tempest will not give me leave to ponder
> On things would hurt me more. But I'll go in:
> In, boy; go first.[13]

Now comes the crowning touch of all:

> I'll pray, and then I'll sleep.

In the night's bleak exposure he kneels down, like a child at bedtime, to pray.

> Poor naked wretches, wheresoe'er you are,
> That bide the pelting of this pitiless storm,
> How shall your houseless heads and unfed sides,
> Your loop'd and window'd raggedness, defend you
> From seasons such as these? O, I have ta'en
> Too little care of this! Take physic, pomp;
> Expose thyself to feel what wretches feel,
> That thou mayst shake the superflux to them,
> And show the heavens more just.

To this haven of the spirit has he come, the Lear of unbridled power and pride. And how many dramatists, could they have achieved so much, would have been content to leave him here! Those who like their drama rounded and trim might approve of such a finish, which would leave us a play more compassable in performance no doubt. But the wind of a harsher doctrine is

---

[13] There are practical reasons for postponing the entering of the hovel by a scene. For Kent to lead Lear elsewhere fits both with the agitated movement of the action and the freedom of Elizabethan stage method. It enables Shakespeare both to relieve the high tension of the storm-scenes and to provide for the continuity of the Gloucester-Edmund story. And he takes advantage of all this to show us some further battering at Lear's sanity. Note in particular the ominously broken thoughts and sentences of the end of the speech to Kent just before the hovel is reached; and these, as ominously, are set between connected, reasoned passages.

blowing through Shakespeare. Criticism, as we have seen, is apt to fix upon the episode of the storm as the height of his attempt and the point of his dramatic defeat; but it is this storm of the mind here beginning upon which he expends skill and imagination most recklessly till inspiration has had its will of him; and the drama of desperate vision ensuing it is hard indeed for actors to reduce to the positive medium of their art—without reducing it to ridicule. The three coming scenes of Lear's madness show us Shakespeare's art at its boldest. They pass beyond the needs of the plot, they belong to a larger synthesis.[14] Yet the means they employ are simple enough; of a kind of absolute simplicity, indeed.

The boldest and simplest is the provision of Poor Tom, that living instance of all rejection. Here, under our eyes, is Lear's new vision of himself.

> What! have his daughters brought him to this pass?
> Could'st thou save nothing? Did'st thou give them all?

Side by side stand the noble old man, and the naked, scarce human wretch.

> Is man no more than this? Consider him well. Thou owest the worm no silk, the beast no hide, the sheep no wool, the cat no perfume. Ha! here's three on's are sophisticated; thou art the thing itself; unaccommodated man is no more but such a poor, bare, forked animal as thou art. Off, off, you lendings! Come; unbutton here.

Here is a volume of argument epitomized as only drama can epitomize it, flashed on us by word and action combined. And into this, one might add, has Shakespeare metamorphosed the didactics of those old Moralities which were the infancy of his art.

> What! hath your grace no better company?

gasps poor Gloucester, bewailing at once the King's wrongs and his own, as he offers shelter from the storm. But Lear, calmness itself now, will only pace up and down, arm in arm with this refuse of humanity:

---

[14] It is worth noting that the Folio cuts out the lunatic trial of Regan and Goneril. This episode proves so admirable on the stage that it is hard to suppose Shakespeare's actor failed to make it effective. But if it was a question of time and a choice between two scenes, doubtless his audience would be supposed to prefer the rhetoric of the storm.

Noble philosopher, your company.

—nor will he seek shelter without him. So they reach the outhouse, all of his own castle that Gloucester dare offer. What a
group! Kent, sturdy and thrifty of words; Gloucester, tremulous;
the bedraggled and exhausted Fool; and Lear, magnificently
courteous and deliberate, keeping close company with his gibbering fellow-man.[15]

They are in shelter. Lear is silent; till the Fool—himself never
overfitted, we may suppose, in body or mind for the rough and
tumble of the world—rallies, as if to celebrate their safety, to a
semblance of his old task. Edgar, for his own safety's sake, must
play Poor Tom to the life now. Kent has his eyes on his master,
watching him—at what new fantastic trick? The old king is setting two joint-stools side by side; they are Regan and Goneril,
and the Fool and the beggar are to pass judgment upon them.

The lunatic mummery of the trial comes near to something we
might call pure drama—as one speaks of pure mathematics or
pure music—since it cannot be rendered into other terms than its
own. Its effect depends upon the combination of the sound and
meaning of the words and the sight of it being brought to bear
as a whole directly upon our sensibility. The sound of the dialogue
matters almost more than its meaning. Poor Tom and the Fool
chant antiphonally; Kent's deep and kindly tones tell against the
higher, agonized, weakening voice of Lear. But the chief significance is in the show. Where Lear, such a short while since, sat in
his majesty, there sit the Fool and the outcast, with Kent whom
he banished beside them; and he, witless, musters his failing
strength to beg justice upon a joint-stool. Was better justice done,
the picture ironically asks, when he presided in majesty and
sanity and power?

But what, as far as Lear is concerned, is to follow? You cannot
continue the development of a character in terms of lunacy—in
darkness, illuminated by whatever brilliant flashes of lightning.
Nor can a madman well dominate a play's action. From this
moment Lear no longer is a motive force; and the needs of the
story—the absolute needs of the character—would be fulfilled if,
from this exhausted sleep upon the poor bed in the outhouse, he

---

[15] And Kent is unknown to Lear and Edgar to his father, as we shall sufficiently
remember.

only woke to find Cordelia at his side. But Shakespeare contrives
another scene of madness for him, and one which lifts the play's
argument to a yet rarer height. It is delayed; and the sense of
redundancy is avoided partly by keeping Lear from the stage
altogether for a while, a short scene interposed sufficiently reminding us of him.[16]

His reappearance is preluded—with what consonance!—by the
fantastically imaginative episode of Gloucester's fall from the cliff.
There also is Edgar, the aura of Poor Tom about him still. Suddenly Lear breaks in upon them.[17] The larger dramatic value of
the ensuing scene can hardly be overrated. For in it, in this
encounter between mad Lear and blind Gloucester, the sensual
man robbed of his eyes, and the despot, the light of his mind put
out, Shakespeare's sublimation of the two old stories is consummated. No moral is preached to us. It is presented as it was when
king and beggar fraternized in the storm and beggar and Fool
were set on the bench of justice, and we are primarily to *feel* the
significance. Yet this does not lack interpretation; less explicit than
when Lear, still sane, could read the lesson of the storm, clearer
than was the commentary on the mock trial. It is Edgar here that
sets us an example of sympathetic listening. His asides enforce it,
and the last one:

> O! matter and impertinency mixed,
> Reason in madness!

will reproach us if we have not understood. The train of fancies
fired by the first sight of Gloucester, with its tragically comic

---

[16] In the Quarto another preceding scene is also concerned with him.

[17] *Mad*, says the stage direction, and no more; the usual *fantastically dressed
with wild flowers* is Capel's addition. But something of the sort is justified by
Cordelia's speech in the earlier scene. And the dramatic purpose of them is plain:
to emphasize the contrast between this and our last sight of him amid the barren
wildness of the heath and the storm.

There are signs, it may be noted, that this Gloucester-Lear encounter is a
second thought on Shakespeare's part. Apart from its redundance to the action, the
Gloucester-Edgar scene is complete without it; and originally, one would guess,
Gloucester's

> Henceforth I'll bear
> Affliction till it do cry out itself
> 'Enough, enough!' and die.

was followed directly by Edgar's

> Well pray you, father!

Ha! Goneril with a white beard!

(Goneril, disguised, pursuing him still!) asks little gloss.

> They flattered me like a dog. .... To say 'Ay' and 'No' to every-
> thing I said! ... When the rain came to wet me once and the
> wind to make me chatter, when the thunder would not peace at
> my bidding, there I found 'em, there I smelt 'em out. Go to, they
> are not men o' their words; they told me I was everything; 'tis a
> lie, I am not ague-proof.

Gloucester's dutiful

> Is't not the king?

begins to transform him in those mad eyes. And madness sees a
Gloucester there that sanity had known and ignored.

> I pardon that man's life: What was thy cause?
> Adultery?
> Thou shalt not die: die for adultery! No:
> The wren goes to't, and the small gilded fly
> Does lecher in my sight.
> Let copulation thrive; for Gloucester's bastard son
> Was kinder to his father than my daughters
> Got 'tween the lawful sheets.

Gloucester knows better; but how protest so to the mere erratic
voice? Besides which there is only the kindly stranger-peasant
near. A slight unconscious turn of the sightless eyes toward him, a
simple gesture—unseen—in response from Edgar, patiently biding
his time, will illuminate the irony and the pathos.

Does the mad mind pass logically from this to some uncanny
prevision of the ripening of new evil in Regan and Goneril? Had
it in its sanity secretly surmised what lay beneath the moral surface of their lives, so ready to emerge?

> Behold yon simpering dame
> Whose face between her forks presageth snow;
> That minces virtue and does shake the head
> To hear of pleasure's name;
> The fitchew, nor the soiled horse, goes to't
> With a more riotous appetite.[18]

---

[18] The (superficial) inappositeness of this passage is quoted nowadays as evidence of Shakespeare's morbid occupation, about now, with the uncleaner aspects
of sex. But it is by no means inapposite to the larger moral scheme of the play.
Goneril's lust has become an important factor in the action. Shakespeare cannot

But a man—so lunatic logic runs—must free himself from the
tyrannies of the flesh if he is to see the world clearly:

> Give me an ounce of civet, good apothecary, to sweeten my
> imagination.

And then a blind man may see the truth of it, so he tells the
ruined Gloucester:

> Look with thine ears: see how yond justice rails upon yond
> simple thief. Hark in thine ear: change places, and, handy-dandy,
> which is the justice, which is the thief? Thou hast seen a farmer's
> dog bark at a beggar? . . . And the creature run from the cur?
> There thou might'st behold the great image of authority; a dog's
> obeyed in office.

It is the picture of the mock trial given words. But with a difference! There is no cry now for vengeance on the wicked. For
what are we that we should smite them?

> Thou rascal beadle, hold thy bloody hand!
> Why dost thou lash that whore? Strip thine own back;
> That hotly lust'st to use her in that kind
> For which thou whip'st her. The usurer hangs the cozener.
> Through tattered clothes small vices do appear;
> Robes and furr'd gowns hide all. Plate sin with gold,
> And the strong lance of justice hurtless breaks;
> Arm it in rags, a pigmy's straw doth pierce it.

Shakespeare has led Lear to compassion for sin as well as suffering, has led him mad to where he could not hope to lead him sane
—to where sound common sense will hardly let us follow him:

> None does offend, none, I say, none.

To a deep compassion for mankind itself.

> I know thee well enough; thy name is Gloucester;
> Thou must be patient; we came crying hither:
> Thou know'st the first time that we smell the air
> We wawl and cry. I will preach to thee: mark. . . .
> When we are born, we cry that we are come
> To this great stage of fools.

---

give much space to its developments, nor does he care to set the boys acting
women to deal directly and elaborately with such matters. So he uses, I think, this
queer intuition of the mad mind as a mirror in which the vileness is reflected
and dilated.

This afterpart of Lear's madness may be redundant, then, to the strict action of the play, but to its larger issues it is most germane. It is perhaps no part of the play that Shakespeare set out to write. The play that he found himself writing would be how much the poorer without it!

The simple perfection of the scene that restores Lear to Cordelia one can leave unsullied by comment. What need of any? Let the producer only note that there is reason in the Folio's stage direction:

> *Enter Lear in a chair carried by servants.*

For when he comes to himself it is to find that he is royally attired and as if seated on his throne again. It is from this throne that he totters to kneel at Cordelia's feet.[19] Note, too, the pain of his response to Kent's

> In your own kingdom, sir.
> Do not abuse me.

Finally, Lear must pass from the scene with all the ceremony due to royalty: not mothered—please!—by Cordelia.

Cordelia found again and again lost, what is left for Lear but to die? But for her loss, however, his own death might seem to us an arbitrary stroke; since the old Lear, we may say, is already dead. Shakespeare, moreover, has transported him beyond all worldly issues. This is, perhaps, why the action of the battle which will seemingly defeat his fortunes is minimized. What does defeat matter to him—or even victory? It is certainly the key to the meaning of the scene which follows. Cordelia, who would "out-frown false fortune's frown," is ready to face her sisters and to shame them—were there a chance of it!—with the sight of her father's wrongs. But Lear himself has no interest in anything of the sort.

> No, no, no, no! Come, let's away to prison.
> We two alone will sing like birds i' the cage:
> When thou dost ask me blessing, I'll kneel down,
> And ask of thee forgiveness[20]: so we'll live,
> And pray, and sing, and tell old tales, and laugh
> At gilded butterflies, and hear poor rogues
> Talk of court news. . . .

[19] Shakespeare kept—and transformed—this piece of business from the old play; for Cordelia kneels, too, of course. It should be given its full value.

[20] That scene in the old play haunted Shakespeare.

He has passed beyond care for revenge or success, beyond even the questioning of rights and wrongs. Better indeed to be oppressed, if so you can be safe from contention. Prison will bring him freedom.

> Upon such sacrifices, my Cordelia,
> The gods themselves throw incense. Have I caught thee?
> He that parts us shall bring a brand from heaven
> And fire us hence like foxes. Wipe thine eyes;
> The good years shall devour them, flesh and fell,
> Ere they shall make us weep: we'll see 'em starve first.

Lear's death, upon one ground or another, is artistically inevitable. Try to imagine his survival; no further argument will be needed. The death of Cordelia has been condemned as a wanton outrage upon our feelings and so as an aesthetic blot upon the play. But the dramatic mind that was working to the tune of

> As flies to wanton boys are we to the gods;
> They kill us for their sport.

was not likely to be swayed by sentiment. The tragic truth about life, to the Shakespeare that wrote *King Lear*, included its capricious cruelty. And what meeter sacrifice to this than Cordelia? Besides, as we have seen, he must provide this new Lear with a tragic determinant, since "the great rage . . . is kill'd in him," which precipitated catastrophe for the old Lear. And what but Cordelia's loss would suffice?

We have already set Lear's last scene in comparison with his first; it will be worth while to note a little more particularly the likeness and the difference. The same commanding figure; he bears the body of Cordelia as lightly as ever he carried robe, crown and scepter before. All he has undergone has not so bated his colossal strength but that he could kill her murderer with his bare hands.

> I kill'd the slave that was a-hanging thee.
> Tis true, my lords, he did.

says the officer in answer to their amazed looks. Albany, Edgar, Kent and the rest stand silent and intent around him; Regan and Goneril are there, silent too. He stands, with the limp body close clasped, glaring blankly at them for a moment. When speech is torn from him, in place of the old kingly rhetoric we have only the horrible, half human

Howl, howl, howl, howl!

Who these are, for all their dignity and martial splendor, for all
the respect they show him, he neither knows nor cares. They are
men of stone and murderous traitors; though, after a little,
through the mist of his suffering, comes a word for Kent. All his
world, of power and passion and will, and the wider world of
thought over which his mind in its ecstasy had ranged, is nar-
rowed now to Cordelia; and she is dead in his arms.

Here is the clue to the scene; this terrible concentration upon
the dead, and upon the unconquerable fact of death. This thing
was Cordelia; she was alive, she is dead. Here is human tragedy
brought to its simplest terms, fit ending to a tragic play that has
seemed to outleap human experience. From power of intellect
and will, from the imaginative sweep of madness, Shakespeare
brings Lear to this; to no moralizing nor high thoughts, but just to

> She's gone for ever.
> I know when one is dead and when one lives;
> She's dead as earth. Lend me a looking-glass;
> If that her breath will mist or stain the stone,
> Why, then she lives.

Lacking a glass, he catches at a floating feather. That stirs on her
lips; a last mockery. Kent kneels by him to share his grief. Then
to the bystanders comes the news of Edmund's death; the business
of life goes forward, as it will, and draws attention from him for
a moment. But what does he heed? When they turn back to him
he has her broken body in his arms again.

> And my poor fool is hang'd. No, no, no life!
> Why should a dog, a horse, a rat, have life,
> And thou no breath at all? Thou'lt come no more,
> Never, never, never, never, never!
> Pray you, undo this button; thank you, sir.
> Do you see this? Look on her, look, her lips,
> Look there, look there![21]

[21] Bradley has an admirable note upon this passage, just such a fine piece of
perception as we expect from him. Lear, he says, at the very last, thinks that
Cordelia lives, and dies of the joy of it.

GONERIL, REGAN AND CORDELIA

Shakespeare's point of departure for all three is that of the crude old story. Moreover, with regard to Goneril and Regan he is quite content to assume—we shrink from the assumption nowadays—that there are really wicked people in the world. That admitted, these two exemplars of the fact are lifelike enough. Their aspect may be determined by the story's needs, but their significance does not end here; and, within the limits afforded them, they develop freely and naturally, each in her own way.

Likeness and difference are marked from the beginning. They are both realists. Their father wants smooth speech of them and they give it, echoing his very phrases and tones. They ignore Cordelia's reproaches; she is exiled and in disgrace, so they safely may. Left alone together (and the drop here from verse to prose seems to bring us with something of a bump to the plain truth about them), they are under no illusions at all, we find, about their own good fortune.

> he always loved our sister most; and with what poor judgment he hath now cast her off appears too grossly.

There are few things more unlovely than the passionless appraisement of evil and our profit in it. They are as wide-awake to the chances of trouble ahead; but while Regan would wait and see, Goneril means to go to meet it.

If the quarrel between King Lear and his two daughters had been brought into the law courts, counsels' speeches for Regan and Goneril would have been interesting. But what a good case Goneril makes for herself unaided! The setting-on of Oswald to provoke Lear might, one supposes, have been kept out of the evidence. True, the reservation of a hundred knights was a definite condition of his abdication. But their behavior was impeachable; it may well have been if Lear's own treatment of Oswald set them an example. He was almost in his dotage; unbalanced certainly. His outbursts of ironic rage, the cursing of Goneril, his subsequent ravings—his whole conduct shows him unfit to look after himself. For his own sake, then, how much better for his daughters' servants to wait on him! And Regan, though she needs Goneril's prompting, makes an even better case of it; the weaker nature is the more plausible. A jury of men and women of common sense might well give their verdict against Lear; and we can hear the judge ruling upon the one point of law in his favor with grave misgiving that he is doing him no good. How then can we call Regan and Goneril double-dyed fiends? They played the hypocrite for a kingdom; but which of us might not? Having got what they wanted and more than they expected they found good excuse for not paying the price for it. Like failings have been known in the most reputable people. Their conduct so far, it could be argued, has been eminently respectable, level-headed and worldly-wise. They do seem somewhat hard-hearted, but that is all. Says the broken, mad old king:

> let them anatomize Regan, see what breeds about her heart.
> Is there any cause in nature that makes these hard hearts?

But from now on the truth about them grows patent. Does prosperity turn their heads? It releases hidden devils. When Gloucester's defection is discovered they waste no words.

> Hang him instantly.
> Pluck out his eyes.

And the weaker Regan grows the more violent of the two; she turns crueler even than that bloody wolf, Cornwall, her husband. For amid the scuffling a little later she can think to tell Gloucester that his own son has betrayed him; and even as he faces her, blinded and bleeding, she can jeer at him.

The devil of lust comes now to match with the devil of cruelty. Goneril has hardly seen Edmund but she marks him down with those

> strange œilliads and most speaking looks . . .

—which rouse Regan to jealousy as quickly. In their plot upon their father they were clever enough, self-controlled, subtle. But, the beast let loose in them, they turn reckless, shameless, foolish. Regan, with a little law on her side, presumes on it; so Goneril poisons her as she might a rat. And the last note of Goneril is one of devilish pride.

> Say, if I do, the laws are mine, not thine:
> Who can arraign me for it?

Flinging this at her husband when he confronts her with the proof that she meant to have his life, she departs to take her own.

We may see, then, in Goneril and Regan, evil triumphant, self-degrading and self-destructive. It may also be that, from beginning to end, Shakespeare, for his part, sees little to choose between hot lust and murdering hand and the hard heart, in which all is rooted.

It will be a fatal error to present Cordelia as a meek saint. She has more than a touch of her father in her. She is as proud as he is, and as obstinate, for all her sweetness and her youth. And, being young, she answers uncalculatingly with pride to his pride even as later she answers with pity to his misery. To miss this likeness between the two is to miss Shakespeare's first important dramatic effect; the mighty old man and the frail child, confronted, and each unyielding.

> So young and so untender?
> So young, my lord, and true.

And they both have the right of it, after all. If age owes some tolerance to youth, it may be thought too that youth owes to age and fatherhood something more—and less—than the truth. But she has courage, has Cordelia, amazing courage. Princess though she be, it is no small matter to stand her ground before Lear, throned in the plenitude of his power, to stand up to him without effort, explanation or excuse. Nor does she wince at the penalty, nor to the end utter one pleading word. Nor, be it noted, does Kent, who is of her temper, ask pity for her. His chief concern is to warn Lear against his own folly and its consequences.[22] It is her strength of mind he emphasizes and praises.

> The gods to their dear shelter take thee, maid,
> That justly think'st and hast most rightly said!

Nor would she, apparently, open her mouth again to her father but that she means her character shall be cleared. And even this approach to him is formal and uncompromising:

> I yet beseech your majesty . . .

She does (Shakespeare keeps her human) slip in, as if it hardly mattered, a dozen words of vindication:

---

[22] And certain small alterations from Quarto to Folio emphasize this.

> . . . since what I well intend,
> I'll do't before I speak.

Yet, lest even that should seem weakness, she nullifies its effect for a finish. Nor does Lear respond, nor exonerate her except by a noncommittal growl. Still, she is not hard.

> The jewels of our father, with wash'd eyes
> Cordelia leaves you. . . .

Shakespeare has provided in this encounter between Cordelia and Lear that prime necessity of drama, clash of character; that sharpest clash, moreover, of like in opposition to like. He has added wonder and beauty by setting these twin spirits in noble and contrasted habitations. Pride unchecked in Lear has grown monstrous and diseased with his years. In her youth it shows unspoiled, it is in flower. But it is the same pride.

The technical achievement in Shakespeare's staging of Cordelia is his gain of a maximum effect by a minimum of means. It is a triumph of what may be called "placing." The character itself has, to begin with, that vitality which positive virtues give. Cordelia is never in doubt about herself; she has no vagaries, she is what she is all circumstances apart, what she says seems to come new-minted from her mind, and our impression of her is as clean cut. Add to this her calm and steadfast isolation among the contending or subservient figures of that first scene—and the fact, of course, that from this very thrift of herself the broadcast violence of the play's whole action springs—then we see how, with but a reminder of her here and there, Shakespeare could trust to her reappearance after long delay, no jot of her importance nor of our interest in her bated. Indeed, if the Folio text gives us in the main his own reconsiderations, he found his first care to reinstate her in our sympathy a scene before she reappears to be needless.[23] But at this point the play itself is beginning to have need of her return. Somehow its intolerable agonies must be eased; and amid the dreadful flux our memory of her certainty abides.

There is not, at any time, much to explain in Cordelia. Nor does she now herself protest her love and expand her forgiveness. She has not changed; elaboration would only falsify her. Not that she

---

[23] Act IV, Scene iii.

is by nature taciturn; she can resolve the harmonies of her mind,
and Shakespeare gives a flowing music to them.

> Was this a face
> To be opposed against the warring winds?
> To stand against the deep dread-bolted thunder?
> In the most terrible and nimble stroke
> Of quick cross lightning? to watch—poor perdu!
> With this thin helm? Mine enemy's dog,
> Though he had bit me, should have stood that night
> Against my fire.

But even this is not spoken to Lear. To him she still says little. It
is as if speech itself were not a simple or genuine enough thing
for the expressing of her deep heart. And her

> No cause, no cause!

when he would welcome her reproaches, is not at all the kindly,
conventional, superior "Let's forget it" of the morally offended. It
is but the complement of that "Nothing" which cost her a kingdom, and as true of her in its tenderness as the other was true. For
the simple secret of Cordelia's nature is that she does not see
things from the standpoint of her own gain or loss. She did not
beg, she does not bargain. She can give as she could lose, keeping
a quiet mind. It is no effort to her to love her father better than
herself. Yet this supremest virtue, as we count it, is no gain to him;
we must note this too. Her wisdom of heart showed her Regan
and Goneril as they were; yet it was an inarticulate wisdom and
provoked evil in Lear, and could but hold her bound in patience
till the evil was purged. Is there, then, an impotence in such goodness, lovely as we find it? And is this why Shakespeare lets her
slip out of the play a few scenes later to her death, as if, for all
her beauty of spirit, she were not of so much account? Neither
good fortune nor ill can touch Cordelia herself; this is her strength
and her weakness both.

> For thee, oppressed king, am I cast down;
> Myself could else outfrown false fortune's frown. . . .

she says; and so she could, we are sure. Then she falls into dumbness—into such a dumbness as was her first undoing—and passes,
silent, from our sight.

KENT

Here is another positive, absolute being; he, Lear and Cordelia
make a trinity of them. He has not Lear's perilous intellect nor
Cordelia's peace of soul. His dominant quality is his unquestioning courage; akin to this the selflessness which makes it as easy
for him to be silent as to speak. And he springs from Shakespeare's imagination all complete; full-flavored and consistent
from the first. Surer sign yet of his author's certainty about him is
the natural inconsistency of the man as we see him. Through the
first three acts there is never a stroke in the drawing of Kent
which is merely conventional, nor yet an uncertain one. But
neither is there one which, however unexpected, need perplex us.
And for a small sign of Shakespeare's confidence in the sufficiency
of his creature, see the shrewd critical thrust which he lets Cornwall have at him:

> This is some fellow,
> Who, having been praised for bluntness, doth affect
> A saucy roughness. . . .

Even though it be a Cornwall disparaging a Kent, the thrust is
shrewd enough for Shakespeare not to risk it unless he is confident that Kent's credit with the audience is firm.

This variety and apparent inconsistency give great vitality.
From the Kent of the first scene, quick of eye, frank at a question:

> Is not this your son, my lord?

impatient at half answers:

> I cannot conceive you.

yet tolerant, discreetly courteous, dry, self-contained:

> I cannot wish the fault undone, the issue of it being so
> proper.

but gentle and kindly too:

> I must love you and sue to know you better.

—from this we pass without warning to the impetuous outburst
against Lear; and unmannerly though this may be, it is still dignified, collected and cool. From this to the Kent of the borrowed
accents—but never more himself than in his disguise, to the man of

What would'st thou?
Service.
Who would'st thou serve?
You.
Dost thou know me, fellow?
No, sir; but you have that in your countenance which I would
fain call master.
What's that?
Authority.

to the Kent of the tripping of Oswald; and, at their next meeting,
with Oswald so unwary as to ask him

What dost thou know me for?

to the Kent of

A knave, a rascal, an eater of broken meats; a base, proud,
shallow, beggarly, three-suited, hundred-pound, filthy, worsted-
stocking knave; a lily-livered, action-taking knave; a whoreson,
glass-gazing, super-serviceable, finical rogue; a one-trunk inherit-
ing slave; one that wouldst be a bawd in way of good service, and
art nothing but the composition of a knave, beggar, coward,
pandar, and the son and heir of a mongrel bitch; one whom I
will beat into clamorous whining if thou deniest the least syllable
of thy addition.

to the resourceful, humorous disputant of the scene with Cornwall
and Regan, and to the philosopher in the stocks, with his

Fortune, good-night; smile once more; turn thy wheel!

Having so opulently endowed him with life, Shakespeare, we
may say, can now afford to be thriftier of attention to him for a
while; he had better be, we might add, or the balance of the
play's interest will go awry. But it is of a piece with the character
that, when misfortune overwhelms Lear, Kent should sink himself in it, that his colorfulness should fade, his humor wane, and
the rest of the play find him tuned to this one key of vigilant
unquestioning service; till he comes to the final simplicity of

I have a journey, sir, shortly to go.
My master calls me, I must not say no.

Nevertheless Shakespeare does seem in Act IV to lose interest in
him, thus straitened, and he keeps him a place in the action care-

lessly enough. Throughout the storm-scenes, of course, his sober, single-minded concern for the King does but reinforce his dramatic credit; it is, besides, a necessary check to their delirium. He could have even less to say here, and his very presence would be a strength. It is like Kent not to fuss as poor Gloucester fusses, not to talk when he need not, to think of the morrow and do the best he can meanwhile. Shakespeare allows him—a just economy —two flashes of emotion; the first when Lear turns to him with

> Wilt break my heart?
> I'd rather break my own . . . .

he says. And once—

> O pity!

No more than that.

It is after he has taken Lear to Dover that, as a character, he begins to live upon the credit of his past. Shakespeare seems not quite sure what more he may want of him; he only does not want him to complicate with his vigorous personality the crowded later action of the play. What his purpose may be in sustaining his disguise—

> Pardon, dear madam;
> Yet to be known shortens my made intent:
> My boon I make it that you know me not
> Till time and I think meet.

—is never very clear. But Shakespeare's own purpose here is clear enough; not to spoil Lear's reconciliation with Cordelia, by adding to it a recognition of Kent. The couplet with which Kent ends the scene:

> My point and period will be throughly wrought,
> Or well or ill, as this day's battle's fought.

has in the event neither much significance nor consequence. It is a safe remark and sounds well. We might suppose (we may do so, if we like; but in fact an audience will not stop to consider a commentator's point) that Kent is counting, if Lear is defeated, on serving him still in disguise, when known he could not. But he does not appear in the battle or the defeat; and this we might think (if, again, we stopped to think; but while the play is acting

we shall not) as strange as his neglect which had let Lear escape
to wander

> As mad as the vex'd sea; singing aloud ...

But the simple explanation probably is that Shakespeare finds he
has no more dramatic use for Kent till he can bring him on, the
play all but done, with

> I am come
> To bid my king and master aye good-night.

So he must just keep him in being meanwhile.

That Kent should survive so effectively to the play's end is at
once a tribute to the vitality of his first projection and to the tact
with which Shakespeare can navigate the shallows of his art. And
the actor who can express himself and impress himself upon us
as well by silence as by speech will find no difficulties in the part.[24]

THE FOOL

The Fool can never, of course, be to us what he was to the
play's first audience. For them, Shakespeare's achievement lay in
the double conversion of a stock stage character and a traditional
Court figure to transcendent dramatic use. There are few greater
pleasures in art than to find the familiar made new; but to us
stage Fool and Court Fool alike are strange to start with. Court
Fool has, to be sure, a likely claim to a place in the play, and can
claim a place too in our historical consciousness. Grant the old
King such a favorite: it is good character scheming to contrast
his royal caprices with such spaniel affection; dramatic craft at its
best to leave Lear in adversity this one fantastic remnant of
royalty. This, and much more of intrinsic value, we cannot lose.
But what, from the transcended stage Fool, did Shakespeare gain
besides?

---

[24] If it be said that there is nothing in the Kent of Act IV which, upon analysis,
belies his character, yet this Preface is concerned also with his presentment, and
that is ineffective and even halting. But what of his sudden outburst in Act IV,
Sc. iii:

> It is the stars;
> The stars above us, govern our conditions . . . .

—is this the authentic Kent? And even if Shakespeare were here starting to develop a new phase of the man, he never goes on.

For a masterly analysis of the whole character we should turn to A. C.
Bradley's lecture on *King Lear*.

Elizabethan acting did not inhabit the removed footlight-defended stage of the theater of today, and all its technique and conventions and the illusion it created differ appropriately in consequence; this is the constant theme of these Prefaces, and must be of any study of the staging of Shakespeare plays. But certain effects, however gained, are common to all drama, certain problems recur. A problem in the writing and acting of tragedy is the alternate creating and relaxing of emotional strain; the tenser the strain, the less long can an audience appreciatively endure it. "Comic relief" has a crude sound; but, to some degree and in some form or other, the thing it suggests is a necessity. Greek tragedy had "choric relief"; emotion in the Greek theater was magnified and rarefied at once, and sharp transitions were neither wanted nor workable. Shakespeare had the constant shift of scene and subject, usual in his theater, to help him; and his most strenuous scenes, we may remark, tend to be short ones.[25] We may suppose him ever mindful of the difficulty of keeping the attention of a motley audience fixed, but still alert; and in the body of a scene, if it needs must be a long one, we shall always find what may be called "points of rest and recovery."

But the problem can be stated in other terms. Tragedy, it may be said, takes us out of ourselves; how else can it be enjoyed? A dash of comedy will, by contrast, restore us to ourselves; yet, for the tragedy's sake, the less conscious of the process we are the better. Here lay for Shakespeare, in this play, the histrionic value of the Fool. He wanted no comic relief in the crude sense; but this familiar stage figure, even though turned to tragic purpose, kept for that audience, if insensibly, its traditional hail-fellow quality. Only the dramatic and human value of the character is preserved us for today to the full. Of the effect of the snatches of song and rhyme, the lyric lightening of the epic strength of these scenes, we keep only the most manifest part. The things themselves are queer to us, and this is just what they should not be. And of the friendly feeling, the sense of being at ease with our-

---

[25] This play apart, they are noticeably so in *Macbeth* and in *Antony and Cleopatra*. In *Hamlet* and in *Othello* it may be said they are not. But in *Hamlet* the action is—and characteristically—not consistently strenuous; and the sustaining of the anguish in *Othello* is typical of the tragedy, helps give us the heroic measure of Othello himself.

selves, which the stage Fool, a-straddle between play and audience, could create for the Elizabethans, we save nothing at all. We have felt something of the sort as children perhaps, when, at the Pantomime, after the removed mysteries of the transformation scene, came the harlequinade and the clown, cuddling us up to him with his "Here we are again." It may seem a far cry from red-hot poker and sausages to *King Lear*. But these indigenous attributes of the Fool are the underlying strength of the part once its acting is in question; and it is Shakespeare's use and restraint and disguise of them at once that is so masterly. Out went the character, as we know, from the eighteenth century versions of the play; nor actors nor audience, it was thought, could countenance such an aberration. Macready restored it with many misgivings and gave it to a girl to act. The producer today faces another difficulty. He finds a Fool all etherealized by the higher criticism. His first care, in the part's embodying, must be to see restored as much as may be of its lost aboriginal strength. Its actor must sing like a lark, juggle his words so that the mere skill delights us, and tumble around with all the grace in the world. Satisfy these simpler demands, and the subtleties will have their effect; neglect them, and you might as well try to play tunes on a punctured organ stop.

About the Fool's character in the personal sense there is really not much to be said, though it is a subject upon which the romantic commentator has rejoiced to embroider his own fancies. He is, not a half-wit, but—the old word fits—a "natural"; he does not, that is to say, draw all our practical distinction between sense and nonsense, the wise thing to do, and the unwise. But he lives in a logical world of his own. Lear has petted him as one pets a dog; he shows a dog's fidelity. It is foolish of him, no doubt, to follow his master into such a storm—but, then, he *is* a fool. Shakespeare, having had his dramatic use of him, drops him incontinently; this alone should label the part of merely incidental importance to the scheme of the play. But even this he makes a measure of the human pathos of the creature. We are told by the attendant knight before ever we see him:

> Since my young lady's going into France, sir, the fool
> hath much pined away.
> No more of that; I have noted it well . . . .

Lear answers (lest we should not note it well enough). But not a word more; above all never a hint from this professional jester himself that he has, or has a right to, any feelings of his own. His jests have grown bitterer lately perhaps, to suit with Lear's changing fortunes; yet, for compensation, he is more full of song than ever. And come weal, come woe, he sticks to his job, sticks to it and to his master till the storm batters him into silence. With a ha'porth of warmth and comfort in him, he flickers bravely into jest again. But his task is done now, and he himself pretty well done for. He tells us so in a very short and bitter jest indeed:

> And I'll go to bed at noon.

And this is the last we hear or see of him; and what happens to him thereafter, who knows or cares? Which is quite according to the jesters'—and players'—code of professional honor, and to the common reward of its observance, as Shakespeare, of all men, would know well. To pursue the Fool beyond the play's bounds, to steep him in extraneous sentiment, is to miss the most characteristically dramatic thing about him.

One minor point about the part is yet an important one. The soliloquy with which Act III, Scene ii, is made to end is certainly spurious.[26] Its own incongruity can be left out of the question; its offense against the dramatic situation disallows it. The very heart of this is Lear's new-found care for the shivering drenched creature at his side.

> Come on, my boy. How dost, my boy? Art cold? . . .
> Poor fool and knave, I have one part in my heart
> That's sorry yet for thee.

Shakespeare is incapable—so would any other dramatist in his senses be—of stultifying himself by dispatching Lear from the scene immediately after, and letting him leave the Fool behind him.

GLOUCESTER, EDGAR AND EDMUND

Gloucester and his sons are opposite numbers, as the phrase now goes, to Lear and his daughters. Gloucester himself is the

---

[26] And surely it is time that all editions of Shakespeare put certain passages, whose fraud can be agreed upon, in expurgatorial brackets. We are ready for another—and another sort of—Bowdler.

play's nearest approach to the average sensual man. The civilized world is full of Gloucesters. In half a dozen short speeches Shakespeare sets him fully before us: turning elderly but probably still handsome; nice of speech if a little pompous; the accomplished courtier (he seems to be Lear's master of ceremonies); vain, as his mock modesty shows, but the joking shamelessness that succeeds it is mainly swagger; an egotist, and blind, knowing least of what he should know most, of his own two sons.

> He hath been out nine years, and away he shall again.

That carelessly jovial sentence of banishment for Edmund proves his own death-sentence. Still, who could suspect the modest young newcomer, making his bow with

> **Sir, I shall study deserving.**

of having such unpleasant thoughts in mind?

Gloucester, like so many sensual men, is good nature itself, as long as things go their easy, natural way; but when they fail to he is upset, rattled. Kent's banishment, the quarrel with Cordelia and France, and the King's utter recklessness set his mind off at one tangent and another and make him an easier victim to very simple deceit. We must not, however, appraise either his simplicity or Edgar's, at this moment, with detachment—for by that light, no human being, it would seem, between infancy and dotage, could be so gullible. Shakespeare asks us to allow him the fact of the deception, even as we have allowed him Lear's partition of the kingdom. It is his starting point, the dramatist's "let's pretend," which is as essential to the beginning of a play as a "let it be granted" to a proposition of Euclid. And, within bounds, the degree of pretense makes surprisingly little difference. It is what the assumption will commit him to that counts; once a play's action is under way it must develop as logically as Euclid, and far more logically than life. The art of the thing is to reward the spectator for his concession by never presuming on it; one should rather dress up the unlikely in the likelier. Thus Shakespeare makes Gloucester, with his pother about "these late eclipses of the sun and moon," the sort of man who might at any moment be taken in by any sort of tale; the more improbable, indeed, the better. He makes Edmund plausible even if the

incriminating letter is not. And what better way to confirm a
nervous, puzzled, opinionated man in an error than to reason
calmly with him against it? Your victim will instinctively take
the opposite point of view and forget that this was yours to begin
with.[27] Does not the credulous nature crave to be deceived? Moreover, Shakespeare's first concern is to develop character, to put us
on terms with these people; not till that is done, he knows, will
their doings and sufferings really affect us. So it suits him, in any
case, to subordinate, for a little, what they do to what they are.
And we part from Gloucester in this scene knowing him for a
start pretty well.

The sensual man does not stand up very resolutely against
blows dealt to his complacent affections. Disillusion leaves Gloucester not only wax in Edmund's hands but more helpless than it
belongs to him to be—fair-weather sailor though he has ever
been!—in the alien troubles that now center round him. Shakespeare's maneuvering of him through these scenes—from the
welcome to the "noble arch and patron" to the moment when his
guest's honored fingers are plucking at his eyes—is a good example of the fruitful economy with which, once a character has
"come alive," its simplest gesture, its very muteness is made significant. And Gloucester has been alive from the beginning; no
illustration for a thesis, but unself-consciously himself. This very
unself-consciousness is turned later to tragic account. Fate's worst
revenge on him is that, blinded, he comes to see himself so clearly
as he is, and to find the world, which once went so comfortably
with him, a moral chaos. We might wonder at the amount of
agonized reflection in this kind allotted to him. But mark its
culmination:

[27] But it follows that upon these lines we cannot be brought to a very close
knowledge of Edgar too. Give him the same scope, and he must either get on the
track of the truth or prove himself as great a fool as his father. So Shakespeare,
now and at his next appearance, does as little with him as possible. This delays
—and dangerously—our gaining interest in him. But a play survives sins of
omission when the smallest sin of commission may damn it. Besides, time is
valuable; and a subplot cannot, for the moment, be spared much more. The likelihood of the detail of this traffic between father and sons, the sending of letters, the
"retire with me to my lodging . . . there's my key" and the rest, depends somewhat upon the large, loose organization of a great nobleman's household of that
day, of which Shakespeare's audience would know well enough.

> The king is mad: how stiff is my vile sense
> That I stand up, and have ingenious feeling
> Of my huge sorrows! Better I were distract:
> So should my thoughts be sever'd from my griefs,
> And woes by wrong imaginations lose
> The knowledge of themselves.

The one thing, it seems, that the average sensual man cannot endure is knowledge of the truth. Better death or madness than that!

Yet which of us must not feelingly protest that the Gloucester, who threads and fumbles his way so well-meaningly about the family battlefield his house is turned into (much against his will), is very harshly used indeed? Is this poetic justice? He does all that one who respects his superiors may do to save Kent from the ignominy of the stocks. He does his best to pacify Lear.

> I would have all well betwixt you.

How familiar is that heartfelt cry of the man who sees no sense in a quarrel! When he does take sides his reasons and his method are not heroic, it is true.

> These injuries the king now bears will be revenged home; there is part of a power already footed; we must incline to the king. I will look to him and privily relieve him, go you and maintain talk with the duke, that my charity be not of him perceived. If he asks for me, I am ill and gone to bed.

No, truly, it is not heroic, when battle is joined, to be ill and go to bed. But caution is a sort of a virtue; and the keeping of a family foot in each camp has good sanction. Yet who can be altogether wise? In his next breath comes

> If I die for it, as no less is threatened me, the king, my old master, must be relieved.

And this his best impulse is his undoing. Unwittingly he is telling Edmund how best to betray him. He points the way; Edmund has but to follow it—just a little further. Irony deepens when later he calls upon Cornwall to spare him in the sacred name of that hospitality which, towards his king, he himself has so spinelessly betrayed. Yet, "tied to the stake," he can "stand the course" courageously enough; and he recovers self-respect in hopeless defiance of his tyrants. With just a little luck he need never have lost it. Now he is blinded and turned helpless from his own doors. Is this poetic justice upon a gentleman, whose worst fault has been to play for safety, his worst blunder to think ill of a man without question and to believe a liar? Disquieting to think that it may be![28]

Edmund is, in wickedness, half-brother to Iago. Having no such great nature as Othello's to work on, Shakespeare has no need of such transcendent villainy; and he lessens and vulgarizes his man by giving him one of those excuses for foul play against the world which a knave likes to find as a point of departure. His first soliloquy is a complete enough disclosure. The fine flourish of

> Thou, Nature, art my goddess . . . .

(finer by its surprise for us in the mouth of the modest young man of the earlier scene), and the magnificent rejection of conventional morality narrow to their objective in

> Well, then,
> Legitimate Edgar, I must have your land.

And from this firm businesslike basis Edmund, except for pure pose, never soars again. The later

> This is the excellent foppery of the world . . . .

is enjoyable argument doubtless, and doubtless he chuckles over it. There is a sporting and imaginative touch, perhaps, in the trick that finally gets rid of Edgar; the stabbing his own arm, we feel, is to his credit. But for the rest, a strict attention to business, and a quick eye to one main chance after the other, suffice him. And this, really, is almost the loathliest thing about the man. He not only betrays his father to Cornwall, but he cants about loyalty the while. He accepts the attentions of Regan and Goneril without surprise or embarrassment (he is a handsome young fellow and he knows it), calculates which will be the more desirable connection, but will leave Goneril to get rid of her husband alone

---

[28] For an earlier stroke of irony—only to be fully appreciated perhaps by the shade of Lady Gloucester—consider the exclamation wrung from the distracted old man at the climax of his wrath against Edgar:

> O strong and fasten'd villain!
> Would he deny his letter? *I never got him.*

And this to Edmund his bastard!

if that risky task has to be undertaken. It even passes through his mind that she herself—if not Regan—may in her turn have to be "put away." His tardy repentance does not touch us; and he puts it into practice too tardily.[29] The queer snobbery which prompts him to say to the still visored Edgar

> If thou'rt noble,
> I do forgive thee.

and the still queerer vanity (at such a moment!) of

> Yet Edmund was beloved.
> The one the other poison'd for my sake,
> And after slew herself.

may strike upon some ears as all but ridiculous. He is an ignoble scoundrel and he makes an ignoble end.

Still, his methods have been interesting. The first attack upon his father's credulity was, as we saw, both bold and apt; and what could be safer support to the fiction of Edgar's plot than the counterfeit truth of

> When I dissuaded him from his intent . . .
> > he replied,
> Thou unpossessing bastard! dost thou think,
> If I would stand against thee, would the reposal
> Of any trust, virtue, or worth in thee
> Make thy words faith'd? No: what I should deny,—
> As this I would; ay, though thou didst produce
> My very character, I'd turn it all
> To thy suggestion, plot, and damned practice.

For masterly confounding of counsel this should rouse the admiration of the most practiced liar. Whether, later, there is need for him to be so snivelingly hypocritical with Cornwall we may question. But he is still on promotion; and that shrewd, forthright brute, if not deceived, will be the more flattered by this tribute of vice to his virtue.

But once he is in the saddle, and when not one royal lady, but two, have lost their heads over him, what a change!

> Know of the duke if his last purpose hold,
> Or whether since he is advised by aught

---

[29] His "Ask me not what I know," in which he takes example from Goneril—and Iago!—is given by one Quarto and some editors to Goneril herself, with (I fancy) good enough reason.

To change his course; he's full of alteration
And self-reproving; bring his constant pleasure.

This he says publicly of no less a man than Albany, whom later
he salutes with an ironically patronizing

Sir, you speak nobly.

He is losing his head, one fears, in the flush of his fire-new fortune.
Albany, however, waits his time and prepares for it; this mild
gentleman should have been better reckoned with. For, of a
sudden, Edmund finds that he has climbed, even as his blinded
father set out in misery to climb, to the edge of a steep. And it is
an apposite phrase indeed which flashes the depths on him:

Half-blooded fellow, yes!

—from an Albany not so mild. The wheel is coming circle.

This individual catastrophe and its contriving are a good
example of Shakespeare's adapting of end to means (that constant
obligation of the dramatist), and of his turning disability to
advantage. His very need to compress close these latter incidents
of Edmund's rise to fortune helps him make it the more egregious.
The fact that but a dozen speeches seem to lift the fellow towards
the grasping of the very power of which Lear divested himself
at the play's beginning should make our recollection of that modest young man in the background of its first scene the more
amazing to us. It is, at this juncture, a breathless business for all
concerned. Then at the climax comes the sudden isolation of the
upstart, brave in his armor, flushed with his triumph. And Shakespeare releases the tension—and rewards himself for his economy
—in the sounding of trumpets, the fine flow and color of some
heroic verse quite in his old style, and all the exciting ceremony
of the duel.[30] Late in the play as this comes, and of secondary
concern to the greater tragedy as it may be, not a point of its
thriftily developed drama must be missed.

Edgar is a "slow starter" and shows no promise at all as a hero.
Not here, however, but in Shakespeare's use of him as Poor Tom
will be the actor's greater handicap. For by the time he is free from

[30] Compare the "defiances" of this scene with the passage between Mowbray
and Norfolk in the beginning of *Richard II*.

this arbitrary bondage the play has put our attention and emotions
to some strain and we are no longer so well disposed to the
development of a fresh serious interest. Otherwise there is every
dramatic fitness in his tardy coming to his own. Edmund flashes
upon us in pinchbeck brilliance; the worth of Edgar waits discovery, and trial and misfortune must help discover it—to himself
above all.

> a brother noble,
> Whose nature is so far from doing harms
> That he suspects none; on whose foolish honesty
> My practices ride easy!

says Edmund of him in proper contempt. "What are you?" asks
his unknowing father, when his fortunes are still at their worst.
And he answers:

> A most poor man, made tame to fortune's blows;
> Who, by the art of known and feeling sorrows,
> Am pregnant to good pity.

But, by the play's end, it is to him as well as to Kent that Albany
turns with

> Friends of my soul, you twain
> Rule in this realm, and the gor'd state sustain.

What are the steps by which he passes from nobody to somebody?
His very reserve at the beginning can give him a stamp of
distinction, and should be made to do so. And the notion of that
strange disguise would not come, we may say, to a commonplace
man. Through the ravings of Poor Tom we can detect something
of the mind of Edgar with its misprision of the sensual life—of
his father's life, is it? We can certainly see his pitiful heart; this
Shakespeare stresses. But only in the soliloquies that end Act III,
Scene vi, and begin Act IV do we discover the full mind of the
man[31]:

> When we our betters see bearing our woes,
> We scarcely think our miseries our foes.
> Who alone suffers, suffers most i' the mind,
> Leaving free things and happy shows behind;

---

[31] The Folio rejects the first of those two and (see p. 274, note) the producer may be wise to.

> But then the mind much sufferance doth o'erskip,
> When grief hath mates, and bearing fellowship. . . .

and

> Yet better thus, and known to be contemn'd,
> Than still contemn'd and flatter'd. To be worst,
> The lowest and most dejected thing of fortune,
> Stands still in esperance, lives not in fear;
> The lamentable change is from the best;
> The worst returns to laughter. . . .

We seem to have found the play's philosopher. And the sententiousness of the earlier soliloquy, differing both in form and tone from anything that has preceded it in the play, is surely a deliberate contrivance to lower the tension of the action and to prepare us for the calmer atmosphere—by comparison—of the play's ending. Shakespeare may afterwards have repented of it as sounding too sententious and as coming uselessly for its wider purpose immediately before the blinding of Gloucester. But Edgar's philosophy of indifference to fortune, of patience with life itself, of the good comfort of fellowship, is now, certainly, to dominate the play. It is summed up for us more than once.

> Bear free and patient thoughts.

he tells his father, when, by his queer stratagem—again, it was not the notion of a commonplace mind—he has saved him from despair. His playing the peasant with the insufferable Oswald is, yet again, not commonplace; and, having killed him:

> He is dead. I am only sorry
> He had no other deathsman.[32]

To him is given the answer to Gloucester's deadly

> As flies to wanton boys, are we to the gods;
> They kill us for their sport.

in

> therefore, thou happy father,
> Think that the clearest gods, who make them honours
> Of men's impossibilities, have preserved thee.

---

[32] "Chill pick your teeth, sir," suggests that he stabs him, either with a knife he wears, or, possibly, with Oswald's own dagger, wrested after a tussle.

To him is given

> The gods are just, and of our pleasant vices
> Make instruments to plague us.

But before this, his good name and his father's death justly
avenged, what is the first thing he says as he discloses himself to
the doubly damned scoundrel lying at his feet?

> Let's exchange charity.

Edgar, in fact, has become a man of character indeed, modest, of
a discerning mind, and, in this pagan play, a very Christian
gentleman.[33]

BURGUNDY, FRANCE, ALBANY, CORNWALL

Burgundy and France hardly outpass convention, though the
one gains enough character from his laconic indifference, while
the spirit and quality of France's speeches should keep him a
pleasant memory to the play's end.[34]

Cornwall has "character" in abundance. He and Albany stand
all but mute at their first appearance.[35] But from our next sight of
him to our last he justifies in action and speech Gloucester's
description:

> My dear lord,
> You know the fiery quality of the duke;
> How unremoveable and fix'd he is
> To his own course.

---

[33] He is, I think, as true a gentleman as the plays give us. And he is kept himself and no mere moralizer to the last. When Lear sinks dying, it is Edgar who
starts forward to recover him, till Kent checks him with the immortal

> Vex not his ghost: O! let him pass; he hates him
> That would upon the rack of this tough world
> Stretch him out longer.

For Edgar is still very young.

[34] Here is one of the difficulties incidental to the production of such a play as
King Lear with a company gathered in for the occasion. The quality of the actors
available tends to diminish with the importance of the parts. Pay apart, an actor
of authority and distinction will not attach himself to a theater for the sole purpose of playing France. Hence the need of an established company with all its
compensating opportunities. France is a powerful king and Cordelia's husband;
and if he does not impress us as he should, and lodge himself in our memories, not
only is the play immediately the poorer, but Cordelia, returning, is robbed of a
background of great importance to her.

[35] By the text of the Quarto absolutely mute.

He is a man, we may suppose, in the prime of life; old enough, at least, to say to Edmund

> thou shalt find a dearer father in my love.

He is by no means a stupid man: the cynical humor with which he appraises Kent shows that. He asserts himself against his wife as Albany does not. He can speak up to Lear when need be, but he is not too swift to do it. In his vindictiveness he still keeps his head.

> Go seek the traitor Gloucester,
> Pinion him like a thief, bring him before us.
> Though well we may not pass upon his life
> Without the form of justice, yet our power
> Shall do a courtesy to our wrath, which men
> May blame but not control.

But this hardly makes him the more likable. And though we might allow him some credit for at least doing his own dirty work, it is evident that he enjoys Gloucester's blinding, for he sets about it with a savage jest. The taste of blood seems to let loose all the wild beast in him; and, like a wild beast, Shakespeare has him dispatched. Yet Cornwall is a forceful character; and there are those who—having no more concern with them than to profit by their forcefulness—can find, strangely enough, something to admire in such men. So he may be allowed a certain dog-toothed attractiveness in performance.

Albany is at the opposite pole. He prefers a quiet life with Goneril while he can contrive to lead it, even at the cost of some self-respect.

> Striving to better, oft we mar what's well.

seems to stand as his motto; and it sounds the more sententious by its setting in a rhymed couplet. His "milky gentleness," his "harmful mildness" ring true enough as accusations: does he think to tame a tigress with a platitude? His wife, quite naturally, departs to seek Regan's help without him.

Much has happened, though, by the time we see him again, when Goneril is on the full tide of reckless triumphant wickedness. She takes no heed of Oswald's

> never man so changed . . .

still presumes on

> the cowish terror of his spirit . . .

and even, when she meets him changed indeed, is blind and deaf to the change. That Albany had loved his wife is made plain. We hear him speak in his quiet way of "the great love" he bore her. He has been slow to think ill of her. But he is of those who let their wrath gather beneath a placid surface till, on a sudden, it boils over, and if the cause of it lies deep they are never the same again. Shakespeare, who cannot spare much space for his development, gives us this impression of the man by allowing us chiefly these contrasted sights of him, the long interval between. And the first stern clash with Goneril has a double purpose and nets a double dramatic gain. It wins Albany the authoritative standing that he now needs in the play, and it shows us a Goneril so possessed by self-will that our own surprise at the change in him turns to surprise that she can be so oblivious of it. We may count her a doomed creature from this moment.

Henceforth he is pitted against Edmund; the aristocrat against the upstart; the man with nothing to gain for himself against the man who must win and still win or perish; the man who, to the taunt of "moral fool," can answer

> Where I could not be honest,
> I never yet was valiant.

against the man who can tell his follower as he sends him to commit an atrocious murder:

> know thou this, that men
> Are as the time is; to be tender-minded
> Does not become a sword; thy great employment
> Will not bear question; either say thou'lt do 't,
> Or thrive by other means.

The world's allegiance is ever swaying between such leaderships.

Albany, once in action, is as distinguished a figure as any in the play. Shakespeare endows him with a fine sense of irony. The slight sting in the tail of his compliment to Edmund after the battle:

> Sir, you have showed to-day your valiant strain,
> And fortune led you well . . . .

the cutting courtesy of

> Sir, by your patience,
> I hold you but a subject of this war,
> Not as a brother.

his cool preparation of his stroke; the stroke itself:

> Stay yet, hear reason. Edmund, I arrest thee
> On capital treason; and, in thy arrest,
> This gilded serpent. For your claim, fair sister,
> I bar it in the interest of my wife;
> 'Tis she is sub-contracted to this lord,
> And I, her husband, contradict your banns.
> If you will marry, make your loves to me,
> My lady is bespoke.

—are not bad for a moral fool.

Nor does he trust to the appearance of the unknown champion for Edmund's undoing. He throws his own gauntlet down. A touch of gallantry, though Shakespeare does not—does not need to—compromise his dignity by setting him to fight. And he is left from now to the play's end in command of its action.[36]

OSWALD AND THE MINOR PARTS

A modern audience must lose almost as much of the flavor of Oswald as of the Fool; and more still must be lost if he is stripped of his doublet and hose, forbidden his swagger and his curtseys and thrust back into the dark ages. We cannot be expected to cheer—as I doubt not Shakespeare's audience did—when Kent breaks out with

> That such a slave as this should wear a sword,
> Who wears no honesty!

nor to take the precise point of Lear's

> How now, where's that mongrel?

that newfangled fellow, neither gentleman nor plain servant, mimicking the manners of the one, doing dirtier work than the other. Kent sizes him up when he dresses him down, with enjoyable completeness; so does Lear, later, in a dozen words:

---

[36] Though the last speech should possibly, in accordance with the Folio, be Edgar's.

> This is a slave, whose easy-borrowed pride
> Dwells in the fickle grace of her he follows.

So does Edgar, having rid the world of him, as

> a serviceable villain;
> As duteous to the vices of thy mistress
> As badness would desire.

Oswalds have existed in every age and been good game for abuse, but the London of Shakespeare's day had evidently produced an unusually fine crop of them. His own sayings are colorless compared with what is said of him. It follows, then, that his "Ay, madams" and "No, madams," his "I'll not be strucken, my lord," his "Prithee, if thou lovest me, tell me," and his "Out, dunghill," when the peasant's cudgel threatens to knock his dishonorable sword out of his hand, must answer exactly in accent and attitude, as he himself in look and manner, to the very sort of being Shakespeare had in mind. In himself he is nothing; a "whoreson zed," an "unnecessary letter," and he should seem no more. But, as a tailor made him, he must be tailored right.

It remains to notice one or two of Shakespeare's minuter touches. When Gloucester has been blinded, branded a traitor and turned from his own house to smell his way to Dover, he finds one fearless friend; the old peasant who has been his tenant and his father's tenant "these fourscore years." The savagery of the blinding itself had stirred one common fellow to risk and lose his life stopping the worst of it. Two other common fellows have the charity to bind up the wounds; but they'll risk no more than that. The old peasant, too old himself to go far with his lord, shakes a sad head at leaving him in such company as Poor Tom, and will risk his fortunes to do Gloucester, in his ruin and disgrace, a last simple service. Close following the transcendent scenes of Lear's madness and the extreme brutality of the blinding comes this interlude of servant and peasant, of common humanity in its bravery and charity with its simple stumbling talk. The whole effect is made in a dozen lines or so, but gains importance by its homespun contrast and by its placing across the main dividing line of the play's action.

And for a happy instance of Shakespeare's power to suggest a

man in a dozen words, take the reply of the Captain to whom
Edmund confides the murder of Lear and Cordelia:

> I cannot draw a cart nor eat dried oats;
> If it be man's work, I'll do it.

Staging and Costume

No more need be urged, I hope, against a realistic staging of the
play or anything approaching one. But whether the single alternative to this is the actuality of Shakespeare's own theater is
another question, which the producer must answer for himself. If
he protests that his audience will never sit so unconsciously before
a reproduction of the Globe stage as did Shakespeare's before the
thing itself one cannot contradict him. But he cuts from the
anchorage at his peril. And the doubt is as to whether when he
has found some, presumably, atmospheric sort of background,
which does not positively conflict with the play's stagecraft, the
result—for all its visual beauty—will be worth the risk and the
trouble.

Abide by Shakespeare's own stage, and no questions of importance arise upon the use of it. But for Edgar's moment "above,"
some need for the masking of Lear's "state," and again for the
discovery of the joint-stools and bench in the scene of the mock
trial, the play could indeed be acted upon a barer stage than was
the Globe's.[37] The great chair with the unconscious Lear in it
may be more conveniently carried from an inner stage, and Poor
Tom will emerge more effectively from one than from a sidedoor.
But this is all; and it may even be that Shakespeare minimized
such localization as his theater did afford him to give the play
spaciousness of action, and to magnify his characters the more in
isolating them from needless detail of circumstance. Let the
producer, at any rate—and at all costs—provide for the action's
swift unencumbered movement and for our concentration upon
the characters themselves, in whom everything is concentrated.

As for costume, this is one of the few plays in which Shakespeare took some trouble to do more than its subject itself would

---

[37] There are one or two signs that the stage to which the Folio version was
fitted differed a little from that of the Quarto.

do to dissociate it from his own time; though even so he will not
have relied overmuch upon costume to help him. But only here
and there is his own seventeenth century patent, and that in
character or incident of minor importance. The prevailing atmosphere and accent is barbaric and remote. Edmund's relationship
to Iago may seem to us to give him a certain Italianate flavor, and
Edgar's beginning suggests bookishness and the Renaissance. But
clothe these two as we please, their substance will defy disguise.
Oswald, as we have argued, is a topical picture; in the Ancient
Briton he will be all but obliterated. That must be faced. Of the
Fool, by shifting him back a dozen centuries, we lose little, because, as we have argued, we are bound already to lose so much.
And if a Fool in a barbarous king's retinue seems to us an
anachronism (though it may be doubted if—for all the preciseness
that would take offense at a Henry V in doublet and hose—it
will), the fantasy of the part marks it out as the fittest note of
relief from consistency. To consistency in such matters no dated
play of Shakespeare can be submitted. Here our main losses by
desertion of seventeenth century habit and manners will end. And
such anachronism as may lie in Cordelia's chance of being Duch-
ess of Burgundy, in "base foot-ball player" and "unfee'd lawyer,"
in the stocks, in some of Poor Tom's talk and Lear's ravings, and
in the procedure of the challenge and the duel, will be inconsid-
erable however the characters are clothed.

So a producer is free to balance these items against an imagined
Britain, whose king swears

> by the mysteries of Hecate and the night . . .

(not to mention Apollo), and where a Duke of Cornwall turns
public executioner. There is no doubt, I think, in which scale
advantage lies. The play should be costumed according to the
temper that Shakespeare has given it, a splendid barbaric temper.
It is equally clear that archaeological accuracy profits nothing.
Nor should the producer lose more than he need of such sophistication as Shakespeare himself retained.

The Music

ABOUT the music there is little to be said. I do not imagine much improvement possible upon "the consort of viols," to the quiet harmonies of which Lear was meant, one presumes, to be waked. The sennet that announces his first regal appearance should be noted, as well as the flourish to herald France and Burgundy, and the ceremonial difference between the two. The *Horns within,* which prelude Lear's return from hunting, ask no comment. A trumpet is used with dramatic effect before Cornwall's entrance in Act II, Scene i; it reinforces Gloucester's excitement. The same sound stirs Lear a little later and strings him up for the encounter with Goneril. And, towards the play's end, the triple sounding by the herald, to be answered, when our suspense is keenest, by Edgar's trumpet without, is a most carefully calculated dramatic effect.[38] We have noticed earlier how the battle in which Cordelia's forces are defeated is dramatically minimized; its musical symbolism consists only of an alarum and an alarum and retreat. But the *Drum afar off,* to the ominous sound of which the longest and most varied scene of the fourth act closes, has very definite value. So has the dead march with which the play itself ends.

The Fool is allotted no formal and completed song, but, needless to say, his snatches of melody should be melodious indeed. This musical and lyrical relief to the strain of Lear's passion is, as we have argued elsewhere, an essential part of the play's stagecraft. The technique of the singing should not be artificial; rather that of an accomplished folk-song singer. And where no authentically traditional tunes exist, folk music will prove a sufficient quarry.

The Text

THE complications of the text are troublesome. Corruptions, obvious and suspected, apart, the producer is confronted by the problem of the three hundred lines, or nearly, that the Quartos give and the Folio omits, and of the hundred given by the Folio and omitted from the Quartos. Editors, considering only, it would seem, that the more Shakespeare we get the better, bring practi-

---

[38] Beethoven found a similar one useful in *Fidelio.*

cally the whole lot into the play we read. But a producer must ask himself whether these two versions do not come from different prompt books, and whether the Folio does not, both in cuts and additions, sometimes represent Shakespeare's own second thoughts. In general, surely, the Folio is of better authority; it is at least more carefully transcribed. Some of its cuts are of passages which seem to have been found constructionally unnecessary. Some only "ease" the dialogue; they are of varying importance and aptness. Where Quarto and Folio offer alternatives, to adopt both versions may make for redundancy or confusion.[39]

To deal with the major differences. In the scene of the dividing of the kingdom the Folio's stressed identification of Albany and Cornwall, France and Burgundy, seems deliberate and is certainly valuable. Of the additions to the Gloucester-Edmund-Edgar scene the same may be said. Gloucester can hardly be shown too distracted, and the hiding-away of Edgar from his father is a good point made. But, in compensation, the Folio cuts the mockery of Gloucester's foibles with which Edmund preludes his attempt on Edgar's confidence—and one sees why.

In Goneril's first scene with Oswald the Folio's omissions save some repetition and show her to us terser and less familiar with her servant. A Folio cut in the Fool's part a little later—his rhyming upon the "sweet and bitter fool," and the joke about monopolizing—may seem at a first glance a little clumsy. But we shall hardly appreciate the gibe at monopolies unless we rewrite it "trusts"; probably the Quarto's audiences had appreciated it too well. The whole cut is a useful tightening of the dialogue. Yet a little later the Folio gives us (as the Quarto does not) a passage in which Goneril justifies herself to Albany; undoubtedly useful.

When Lear finds Kent in the stocks and has listened in silence to the story of his being set there, by the Quarto

O, how this mother swells up toward my heart . . . .

follows immediately upon Kent's story. The Folio gives the Fool a little piping song, while Lear still stands speechless, his agony upon him. The dramatic effect will be appreciably different.

---

[39] I speak from now on of "the Quarto" because for the purposes of this argument the "Pied Bull" and "Butter" Quartos might be one.

Later the Folio alone gives us a passage in which Regan justifies Goneril.

In Act III, Scene i, the Folio cuts some important lines out of the Gentleman's second speech. In particular

> Strives in his little world of man to outscorn
> The to-and-fro-conflicting wind and rain.

has vanished. An inefficient actor might have been the cause of this. A few lines later Folio and Quarto offer us alternative cuts. That of the Folio is perhaps the clumsier of the two. It stresses the call for Cordelia's help but barely hints at her army's landing, which the Quarto emphasizes. We may or may not have here the cutting of a common original (of which still more may have existed; for of the

> servants, who seem no less,
> Which are to France the spies and speculations
> Intelligent of our state . . .

we do not hear again). The object of the cut in both cases—and possibly the cutting of the Gentleman's speech also—is evidently to shorten this prelude to Lear's great entrance. What should a producer do here? Shakespeare leaves us to the end a little unconvinced by the machinery of Cordelia's return. There is no dramatic profit in the confusion. Neither text may be as Shakespeare left it. But in this instance I prefer the Quarto's to an amalgam of the two.

Of Merlin's prophecy I have spoken elsewhere.[40]

Let us in passing note the Folio's most important addition of two lines' preparation for the critical

> Poor naked wretches, wheresoe'er you are . . .

In them the kindness to the half-drowned Fool is emphasized; and he is (I think) sent off the stage so that there may be no danger whatever of discord or incongruity. The actor of the Fool, possibly, was never quite to be relied on; and even if he could be, there was always the chance that some buffoon in the audience would vent an incongruous guffaw at the mere sight of him sitting there. But, above all, by these two lines the meaning and intention of what is to come are emphasized:

----

[40] P. 312.

In, boy; go first. You houseless poverty—
Nay, get thee in. *I'll pray, and then I'll sleep.*

I italicize the vitally important phrase. It is dangerous to dogmatize; but this addition has to me all the air of being a second thought of Shakespeare's own.

We come to the Folio's omission of the mock trial. Time may, as we said, have demanded some omissions, and this scene may have been chosen rather than something better liked by the actors or (seemingly) audience. It can hardly have proved ineffective, technically "daring" though it is. It certainly does not today; and very certainly one cannot imagine Shakespeare regretting he had written it.

The cut at the end of this scene, however, asks more consideration; for a purely dramatic reason can be found for the omission of Edgar's soliloquy. It must lower the tension of the action. This may damage the scene of Gloucester's blinding, which follows immediately; and if an act-pause is to follow, the tension will, of course, be lowered then. The chief purpose of the soliloquy, moreover, is to give Edgar a fresh start in his dramatic career. It is a quiet start, the effect of which the violent scene that follows must do much to obliterate. When the Folio, then, postpones it to the beginning of Act IV, it does Edgar a double service, as the Quarto doubles the disservice by making the second soliloquy, when it comes, seem dramatically redundant. Without hesitation, I should here follow the Folio text. The further cutting of Kent's lines, however,

Oppressed nature sleeps . . .

is probably due to a quick closing of the inner stage, which may have obviated the lifting of the sleeping Lear, and it has not the same validity.

The Folio also cuts the significant piece of dialogue between the two servants with which the third act ends. I cannot pretend to say why, if it was not that when this text was settled, the actors to speak the lines were lacking. No one need abide by this cut.

The disappearance of Edgar's "Obidicut, Hobbididance" and the rest from the first scene with his father is, I think, to the good. A few lines before he says:

I cannot daub it further.

And in any case the effect of the mad lingo will have been exhausted in the scenes with Lear.

We next come to some ruthless cutting of Albany by the Folio. Shakespeare may have yielded here to the exigencies of bad acting or to a wish to knit the action more closely. But he is taking some pains at this juncture to develop Albany, and we shall be on the safe side in keeping to the fuller text.

Now, however, the Folio omits one entire scene. It is a carpentered scene if ever there was one. It begins with a lame explanation of the nonappearance of the King of France; it goes on to a preparation for the reappearance of Cordelia and it ends with some unconvincing talk about Lear's "burning shame" and Kent's disguise. I could better believe that Shakespeare cut it than wrote it. There is, certainly, a little life in the description of Cordelia, and a case can be made for so heralding her return to the play. The rest is explanation of what is better left unexplained; and whoever, between the making of the Quarto and the Folio, discovered this—Shakespeare or another—did the play a good service, which we shall wisely profit by.

The remaining differences between the two versions show, in the Folio, a further cutting of explanatory stuff, by which we may well abide; a certain slicing into Albany and Edmund that neither hurts them much now, nor, it is true, does much to spur the action; the loss of one or two lines (Cordelia's in particular) that we shall not want to lose, and the gain of a few that seem good second thoughts. There are, besides, one or two changes that seem merely to reflect change in stage practice as between Quarto and Folio.

On the whole, then—and if he show a courageous discretion—I recommend a producer to found himself on the Folio. For that it does show some at least of Shakespeare's own reshapings I feel sure.

Among other slightly vexed questions, the following are particularly worth attention (the lineal references are to the [English] Arden Shakespeare).

Act I, Scene i, 35. There is no authority for Edmund's exit, and the producer is quite at liberty to let him stay and listen to the momentous proceedings.

Scene v, 1. I give a guess that "Gloucester" in this line is a slip
for "Cornwall." There is no other evidence that Lear writes
to the Earl of Gloucester, nor any reason he should, nor any
evidence at all that Cornwall lived near the town.

52-3. This couplet has the sanction (as Merlin's prophecy has not)
of both Quarto and Folio. But I find its authenticity hard to
credit. Shakespeare could write bawdry, and sometimes at
what seem to us the unlikeliest moments. This does not
smack of the Fool, though, or of what Shakespeare wants
of him.

Act II, Scene i, 20. *Enter Edgar.* This stage direction is wrongly placed
—and typically—in modern editions. The Quarto places it
four lines, the Folio a line, earlier. Even the Folio, then,
shows that he enters on the upper stage and is visible to the
audience before Edmund sees him. It may seem a small matter, but the difference between an independent entrance and
being called on like a dog is appreciable, and can affect a
character's importance. Edgar does descend, of course.

Scene ii, 168-73. "Nothing almost sees miracles, But misery . . .
and shall find time From this enormous state, seeking to give
Losses their remedies." Cut this much, and an actor can make
sense of a passage otherwise as obscure as it is evidently
corrupt.

Scene iii. I think, on the whole, that there is no scene-division
here; there is not, that is to say, a cleared stage. Curtains
might be drawn before Kent in the stocks, but he may as
well sit there asleep while Edgar soliloquizes. On an *unlocalized* stage I doubt its puzzling even a modern audience if
he does; it certainly would not have troubled Shakespeare's.

Act III, Scene iii. The Quarto stage-direction *Enter . . . with lights*
shows, I think, if nothing else does, the use of the inner stage
for this scene.

Scene vii, 23. Neither Quarto nor Folio specifies Oswald's exit,
and they get Edmund's and Goneril's wrong. But it is plain
that Oswald should be gone immediately on the command to
get horses for his mistress. Edmund's and Goneril's leave-
taking then stands out the plainer, and the "strange œilliads
and most speaking looks" that pass between them as they
go may be made noticeable to Regan—and to us.

Act IV, Scene iv, 6. "Centurie" says the Quarto and "centery" the
Folio; and this surely will be understood even now (and
whatever the anachronism) to mean a hundred men. Why

, send one sentry to look for Lear? And why a sentry, any how?

Act V, Scene iii, 161. "Ask me not what I know." The Quarto gives this to Goneril and marks her exit accordingly. It is at least a question whether the Folio's change is not erroneous. For Edmund's so sudden change of front is not easily explicable.

284. This is the first and only indication that Kent's name in disguise has been "Caius." I cannot discover that any editor has commented upon the strangeness of Kent—Kent of all people, and at this moment of all others—asking Lear, apparently, a kind of conundrum. The Pied Bull Quarto at least gives no note of interrogation. If the line can be spoken as if it meant

> Your servant Kent, who was your servant Caius . . .

it will at least not be confusing. Can it not, perhaps, be so read? Kent in his next line plainly appropriates the question to himself.

324. The Quarto gives the last speech to Albany, the Folio to Edgar. Convention would allot it to Albany as the man of rank. "We that are young" sounds more like Edgar. But remembering how much Albany's part is cut in the Folio, it is likely, I think, that this change to Edgar was deliberately made, and therefore it should stand.

1927; PARTLY REVISED in 1935

The Merchant of Venice

THE MERCHANT OF VENICE is a fairy tale. There is no more reality
in Shylock's bond and the Lord of Belmont's will than in Jack
and the Beanstalk.

Shakespeare, it is true, did not leave the fables as he found them.
This would not have done; things that pass muster on the printed
page may become quite incredible when acted by human beings,
and the unlikelier the story, the likelier must the mechanism of
its acting be made. Besides, when his own creative impulse was
quickened, he could not help giving life to a character; he could
no more help it than the sun can help shining. So Shylock is real,
while his story remains fabulous; and Portia and Bassanio become
human, though, truly, they never quite emerge from the enchanted thicket of fancy into the common light of day. Aesthetic
logic may demand that a story and its characters should move
consistently upon one plane or another, be it fantastic or real. But
Shakespeare's practical business, once he had chosen these two
stories for his play, was simply so to charge them with humanity
that they did not betray belief in the human beings presenting
them, yet not so uncompromisingly that the stories themselves
became ridiculous.

What the producer of the play must first set himself to ascertain
is the way in which he did this, the nice course that—by reason or
instinct—he steered. Find it and follow it, and there need be no
running on the rocks. But logic may land us anywhere. It can turn
Bassanio into a heartless adventurer. Test the clock of the action
by Greenwich time, it will either be going too fast or too slow.
And as to Portia's disguise and Bellario's law, would the village
policeman be taken in by either? But the actor will find that he

simply cannot play Bassanio as a humbug, for Shakespeare does
not mean him to. Portias and Nerissas have been eclipsed by wigs
and spectacles. This is senseless tomfoolery; but how make a
wiseacre producer see that if he does not already know? And if,
while Shylock stands with his knife ready and Antonio with his
bared breast, the wise young judge lifting a magical finger between them, we sit questioning Bellario's law—why, no one
concerned, actors or audience, is for this fairyland, that is clear.

The Merchant of Venice is the simplest of plays, so long as we
do not bedevil it with sophistries. Further, it is—for what it is!—as
smoothly and completely successful, its means being as well fitted
to its end, as anything Shakespeare wrote. He was happy in his
choice of the Portia story; his verse, which has lost glitter to gain
a mellower beauty and an easier flow, is now well attuned to such
romance. The story of Shylock's bond is good contrast and complement both; and he can now project character upon the stage,
uncompromising and complete. Yet this Shylock does not over-
whelm the play, as at a later birth he might well have done—it is
a near thing, though! Lastly, Shakespeare is now enough of the
skilled playwright to be able to adjust and blend the two themes
with fruitful economy.

The Construction of the Play

THE PROBLEM OF "DOUBLE-TIME"

THIS blending of the themes would, to a modern playwright,
have been the main difficulty. The two stories do not naturally
march together. The forfeiture of the bond must be a matter of
months; with time not only of the essence of the contract, but of
the dramatic effect. But the tale of the caskets cannot be enlarged,
its substance is too fragile; and a very moderate charge of emotion
would explode its pretty hollowness altogether. Critics have cred-
ited Shakespeare with nice calculation and amazing subtlety in his
compassing of the time-difficulty. Daniel gives us one analysis,
Halpin another, Eccles a third, and Furness finds the play as good
a peg for the famous Double Time theory as Wilson, its inventor,
found Othello. All very ingenious; but is the ingenuity Shake-

speare's or their own?[1] For him dramatic time was a naturally
elastic affair. (It still is, though less so, for the modern playwright,
whose half-hour act may commonly suggest the passing of an hour
or two; this also is Double Time.) Shakespeare seems to think of
it quite simply in terms of effect, as he thought of dramatic space,
moving his characters hither and thither without considering the
compassing of yards or miles. The one freedom will imply and
enhance the other. The dramatist working for the "realistic" stage
must settle definitely where his characters are to be and keep
them there till he chooses to change the scenery. Shakespeare need
not; and, in fact, he never insists upon place at all, unless it suits
him to; and then only to the extent that suits him.[2] In this play,
for instance, where we find Shylock and Antonio will be
Venice, but whereabouts in Venice is usually no matter; when it
is—at Shylock's door or in court before the Duke—it will be
made clear enough to us. And where Portia is, is Belmont. He
treats time—and the more easily—with a like freedom, and a like
aim. Three months suits for the bond; but once he has pouched
the money Bassanio must be off to Belmont, and his calendar,
attuned to his mood, at once starts to run by hours only. The wind
serves, and he sails that very night, and there is no delay at Belmont. Portia would detain him some month or two before he
ventures; and what could be more convenient for a Shakespeare
bent on synchronizing the two stories? For that matter, he could
have placed Belmont a few hundred miles off, and let the coming
and going eke out the time. Did the problem as a whole ever even
occur to him? If it did, he dismissed it as of no consequence. What
he does is to set each story going according to its nature; then he
punctuates them, so to speak, for effect. By the clock they are not
even consistent in themselves, far less with each other. But we

---

[1] If the effect is one and the same, one might think the question unimportant.
But Daniel, making out his three months, is generous of "intervals," not only
between acts, but between scenes; and even Furness, on his subtler scent, can say,
"One is always conscious that between the acts of a play a certain space of time
elapses. To convey this impression is one of the purposes for which a drama is
divided into acts." Therefore an important and a much-disputed question is
involved—and begged. And, in practice, the pernicious hanging-up of performances by these pauses is encouraged, to which scenery and its shifting is already
a sufficient temptation.

[2] See also Preface to *Antony and Cleopatra*.

should pay just the sort of attention to these months, days or hours that we do, in another connection, to the commas and semicolons elucidating a sentence. They give us, and are meant to, simply a *sense* of time and its exactions. It is the more easily done because our own sense of time in daily life is far from consistent. Time flies when we are happy, and drags in anxiety, as poets never tire of reminding us. Shakespeare's own reflections on the phenomenon run to half a column of the concordance, and he turns it quite naturally to dramatic account.

THE TRUE PROBLEM

How to blend two such disparate themes into a dramatically organic whole; that was his real problem. The stories, linked in the first scene, will, of themselves, soon part company. Shakespeare has to run them neck and neck till he is ready to join them again in the scene of the trial. But the difficulty is less that they will not match each other by the clock than that their whole gait so differs, their very nature. How is the flimsy theme of the caskets to be kept in countenance beside its grimly powerful rival? You cannot, as we said, elaborate the story, or charge it with emotion; that would invite disaster. Imagine a Portia seriously alarmed by the prospect of an Aragon or a Morocco for husband. What sort of barrier, on the other hand, would the caskets be to a flesh-and-blood hero and heroine fallen in love? Would a Romeo or Rosalind give a snap of the finger for them? As it is, the very sight of Bassanio prompts Portia to rebellion; and Shakespeare can only allow his lovers a few lines of talk together, and that in company, dare only color the fairy tale with a rhetorically passionate phrase or so before the choice is made and the caskets can be forgotten—as they are!—altogether. Nor does anything in the play show the artist's supreme tact in knowing what *not* to do better than this?

But you cannot neglect the Portia story either, or our interest in her may cool. Besides, this antiphony of high romance and rasping hate enhances the effect of both. A contrasting of subjects, scene by scene, is a trick (in no depreciatory sense) of Shakespeare's earliest stagecraft, and he never lost his liking for it.[3]

---

[3] It is, one may say, a commonplace of stagecraft, Elizabethan or other; but none the less worthy for that.

Then if the casket-theme cannot be neglected, but cannot be elaborated, it must somehow be drawn out, its peculiar character sustained, its interest husbanded while its consummation is delayed.

Shakespeare goes straightforwardly enough to work. He puts just as little as may be into Portia's first scene; but for the one sounding of Bassanio's name there would be only the inevitable tale of the caskets told in tripping prose and the conventional joking upon the suitors. Portia and Nerissa, however, seen for the first time in the flesh, give it sufficient life, and that "Bassanio" one vivid spark more. Later, in due course, come Morocco's choice of the gold casket and Aragon's of the silver. We remark that Morocco is allotted two scenes instead of one. The reason is, probably, that Shakespeare has now enriched himself with the Lorenzo-Jessica story (not to mention the episode of the Gobbos, father and son), and, with this extra weight in the Venetian scale of the action, is put to it to maintain the balance. He could, of course, finish with both Morocco and Aragon earlier and give Bassanio two scenes instead of one.[4] And if a romantic hero could not well wait till after dinner to make his choice, as Morocco does, Solanio's arrival with the ill news of Antonio could easily have been kept for the later scene. But this will not do either—most characteristically will not do for Shakespeare. He has held his lovers apart, since the air of the Belmont of the caskets is too rarefied for flesh and blood to breathe. And Portia herself has been spellbound; we have only had jaunty little Nerissa to prophesy that love (by the pious prevision of the late lord) would somehow find out the way.[5] But once he brings them together

---

[4] And such interest as there is in Aragon's scene is now lessened, perhaps, by our knowledge that Bassanio is on his way; even more, by the talk in the scene before of Antonio's misfortune. But Shakespeare, as his wont is, plucks some little advantage from the poverty of the business by capping Aragon's vapidity with the excitement of the news of Bassanio's arrival.

[5] Though there are commentators who maintain that Nerissa—even Portia, perhaps—gives Bassanio the hint to choose lead, or has it sung to him:

Tell me, where is fancy *bred*,
In the heart, or in the *head*?
How begot, how nouri*shed*?

And if he'll only listen carefully he will note that they all rhyme with *lead*.

Shakespeare was surely of a simpler mind than this—his audiences too. And he had some slight sense of the fitness of things. Would he—how *could* he?—wind

Bassanio must break the spell. It is the story of the sleeping beauty and the prince in another kind; a legitimate and traditional outcome. And once Shakespeare himself has broken free of the fairy tale and brought these two to life (for Bassanio as well has been till now a little bloodless) it is not in him to let them lapse from the scene unproved, and to the full. The long restraint has left him impatient, and he must, here and now, have his dramatic fling. We need not credit—or discredit him, if you like—with much calculation of the problem. It was common prudence both to keep Belmont as constantly in our view as Venice, and the emancipating Bassanio clear of it for as long as possible. And he is now in the middle of his play, rather past it, ready to link his two stories together again. He worked forthrightly; that is written plain over most of his work. Though he might now find that he had here material for two scenes, he would not return in his tracks, telescope Aragon and Morocco—and take, in fact, all the sort of trouble we, who are his critics, must take to explain what a much more compact job he could have made of it! Besides, here is his chance to uplift the two as hero and heroine, and he will not dissipate its effectiveness.

For Bassanio, as we said, has been till now only little less bound than Portia in the fetters of a fairy tale; and later, Shylock and the bond will condemn him to protesting helplessness, and the affair of the rings to be merrily befooled.[6] The wonder indeed is, considering the rather poor figure—painfully poor by the gospel according to Samuel Smiles—the coercion of the story makes him cut, that throughout he measures up so well to the stature of sympathetic hero. Shakespeare contrives it in two ways. He en-

---

up this innocent fairy tale with such a slim trick? Besides, how was it to be worked; how is an audience to be let into the secret? Are they likely to tag extra rhymes to the words of a song as they listen to it? Or is Nerissa—not Portia, surely!—at some point to tip Bassanio "the wink" while he smiles knowingly back to assure her that he has "cottoned on"? Where, oh, where indeed, are such dramatic fancies bred? Not in any head that will think out the effect of their realization.

[6] Little to be found in him, upon analysis, to refute the frigid verdict lately passed upon him by that distinguished and enlightened—but in this instance, surely, most mistakenly whimsical—critic, Sir Arthur Quiller-Couch, of fortune-hunter, hypocrite and worse. Is anything more certain than that Shakespeare did not *mean* to present us with such a hero? If Sir Arthur were producing the play, one pities the actor asked to give effect to his verdict.

dows him with very noble verse; and, whenever he can, throws into strong relief the Bassanio of his own uncovenanted imagination. He does this here. The fantasy of the caskets brought to its due crisis, charged with an emotion which blows it for a finish into thin air, he shows us Bassanio, his heart's desire won, agonized with grief and remorse at the news of Antonio's danger. Such moments do test a man and show him for what he is; and this one, set in bright light and made the scene's turning point, counts for more in the effect the character makes on us than all the gentlemanly graces of his conventional equipment. Unless the actor is much at fault, we shall hear the keynote to the true Bassanio struck in the quiet simplicity—such contrast to his rhetoric over the caskets, even though this was less mere rhetoric than Morocco's and Aragon's—of the speech which begins

> O sweet Portia,
> Here are a few of the unpleasant'st words
> That ever blotted paper! . . .
> Rating myself at nothing, you shall see
> How much I was a braggart. When I told you
> My state was nothing, I should then have told you
> That I was worse than nothing; for indeed
> I have engaged myself to a dear friend,
> Engaged my friend to his mere enemy,
> To feed my means. . . .

Here speaks Shakespeare's Bassanio; and it is by this, and all that will belong to it, that he is meant to live in our minds.

Producer and actors must look carefully into the way by which in this scene the method that has served for the casket story is resolved into something better fitted to the theme of the bond (dominant from the beginning of the play, and now to absorb and transform the dedicated Portia and her fortunes). It is a change—though we must not insist on the contrast more than Shakespeare does—from dramatic convention to dramatic life. From the beginning the pulse of the scene beats more strongly; and Portia's

> I pray you, tarry: pause a day or two
> Before you hazard; for in choosing wrong,
> I lose your company; therefore forbear awhile. . . .

is not only deeper in feeling (there has been little or nothing to rouse her till now; she has had to be the picture of a Portia, hardly more, with a spice of wit to help her through), but how much simpler in expression! When Bassanio turns to those obsessing caskets she must lapse again for a space into fancies of his swan-like end, her eye the watery deathbed for him, into talk about Hercules and Alcides (borrowed, one fears, from Morocco), about Dardanian wives and the like—even as he will be conventionally sententious over his choice. But note how, within the convention, preparing an escape from it, emotion is roused and sustained. With the rhetoric of Portia's

> Go, Hercules!
> Live thou, I live: with much, much more dismay
> I view the fight, than thou that mak'st the fray.

for a springboard, the song and its music are to stir us,

> *whilst Bassanio comments on the caskets to himself.*

So (let the actor remember) when he does at last speak, the emotional ascent will have been half climbed for him already. And while he pays his tribute of trope and maxim, Portia, Nerissa and the rest watch him in silence, at full strain of attention, and help to keep us, too, intent. The speech itself sweeps unhindered to its height, and the pause while the casket is unlocked is filled and enriched by the intensity of Portia's

> How all the other passions fleet to air . . .

most cunningly contrived in meaning and melody, with its emphasis on "despair" and "ecstasy" and "excess," to hold us upwrought. The fairy tale is finally incarnate in the fantastic word-painting of the portrait and the reading of the scroll. Then, with a most delicate declension to reality, Bassanio comes to face her as in a more actual world, and the curtains can be drawn upon the caskets for the last time. Observe that not for a moment has Shakespeare played his fabulous story false. He takes his theater too seriously to go spoiling an illusion he has created. He consummates it, and turns the figures of it to fresh purpose, and they seem to suffer no change.

Throughout the scene—throughout the play, and the larger part of all Elizabethan drama for that matter—effects must be valued very much in terms of music. And, with the far adventuring of his playwriting hardly begun, Shakespeare's verse is already fairly flawless, and its maneuvering from mood to mood masterly, if still simple. We have the royal humility of the speech in which Portia yields herself (Bassanio slips back to his metaphors for a moment after this); then, for contrast, the little interlude of Gratiano and Nerissa, with the tripping monosyllables of Gratiano's

> I wish you all the joy that you can wish;
> For I am sure you can wish none from me . . . .

to mark the pace and the tone of it. Then follows the arrival of Antonio's messenger with Lorenzo and Jessica; done in plain, easy-moving verse that will not discount the distressed silence in which he reads the letter, nor the quiet candor of his confession to Portia. Now comes another crescendo—two voices added to strengthen it—leading up to her generous, wide-eyed

> What sum owes he the Jew?
> BASSANIO. For me, three thousand ducats.
> PORTIA. What, no more!
> Pay him six thousand, and deface the bond;
> Double six thousand, and then treble that. . . .

which itself drops to the gentleness of

> Since you are dear bought I will love you dear.

Then, to strengthen the scene's ending, we have the austere prose of Antonio's letter, chilling us to misgiving. And since—in stage practice, and with the prevailing key of the play's writing to consider—this will not do for an actual finish, there is a last modulation into the brisk coda of

> Since I have your good leave to go away,
> I will make haste: but till I come again,
> No bed shall e'er be guilty of my stay,
> Nor rest be interposer 'twixt us twain.

Lorenzo and Jessica make another link (though their relation to Belmont is pretty arbitrary) between the two stories. This, however, is but the secondary use of them. There must be a sense of time passing in Venice while the bond matures, yet we must have continuous action there, too, while the ritual at Belmont goes its measured way; so, as there can be little for Shylock and Antonio to do but wait, this third, minor theme is interposed. It brings fresh impetus to the action as well as new matter; and it shows us—very usefully—another and more human side of Shylock. Shakespeare does not scheme it out overcarefully. The masking and the elopement and the coming and going they involve are rather inconveniently crowded together (the pleasant episode of the Gobbos may have stolen a little necessary space); and one chapter of the story—for were we perhaps to have seen Shylock at supper with Bassanio, Lorenzo and the rest while the disguised Jessica waited on them?—was possibly crowded out altogether.

Once the fugitives, with some disregard of likelihood, have been brought to Belmont, Gobbo in attendance, Shakespeare turns them to account quite shamelessly. They play a mighty poor scene to give Portia and Nerissa time to disguise themselves as doctor and clerk.[7] They will have to play another while doctor and clerk change to Portia and Nerissa again; but for that, as if in compensation, they are to be dowered with the loveliest lines in the play.[8] With the junction of the themes in the trial-scene the constructive problem is, of course, solved. Shylock disappearing, the rest is simple.

Shakespeare's Venice

IF Lorenzo and Jessica and a little poetry and the consort of music, which no well-regulated great household of his time would be without, are Shakespeare's resources (he had no other; and what better should we ask?) for the painting of the starlit garden of Belmont at the play's end, for its beginning he must show us Venice. He troubles with no verbal scene-painting here; throughout the first scene the very word is but spoken twice, and quite casually. We might be anywhere in the city, or out of it, even. Thereafter we hear of the Rialto, of a gondola, of the common ferry and suchlike incidentals; but of the picturesque environment to which modern staging has accustomed us there is no

---

[7] Possible extra time was needed for the shifting of the caskets and their furniture and the setting of the chairs of state for the Duke and the Magnificoes. But in that case these last must have been very elaborate.

[8] For the bearing of this upon the question of act-division, see p. 364.

suggestion at all. Yet he does present a Venice that lived in the Elizabethan mind, and it is the Venice of his dramatic needs; a city of royal merchants trading to the gorgeous East, of Jews in their gaberdines (as rare a sight, remember, as to us a Chinese mandarin is, walking the London streets today), and of splendid gentlemen rustling in silks. To the lucky young Englishman who could hope to travel there Venice stood for culture and manners and the luxury of civilization; and this—without one word of description—is how Shakespeare pictures it.

We are used nowadays to see the play begun by the entry of a depressed, sober-suited, middle-aged man and two skipping youths, who make their way with a sort of desperate merriment through such lines as the producer's blue pencil has left them, vanish shamefacedly, reappear at intervals to speak the remnant of another speech or two, and slip at last unregarded into oblivion. These are Solanio and Salarino, cursed by actors as the two worst bores in the whole Shakespearean canon; not excepting, even, those other twin brethren in nonentity, Rosencrantz and Guildenstern.[9] As characters, Shakespeare has certainly not been at much pains with them; they could exchange speeches and no one would be the wiser, and they move about at everybody's convenience but their own. But they have their use, and it is an important one; realize it, and there may be some credit in fulfilling it. They are there to paint Venice for us, the Venice of the magnificent young man. Bassanio embodies it also; but there are other calls on him, and he will be off to Belmont soon. So do Gratiano and Lorenzo; but they will be gone too. Solanio and Salarino will not fail us; they hoist this flag at the play's beginning and keep it bravely flying for as long as need be. When Salarino, for a beginning, addresses Antonio with

> There, where your argosies with portly sail,
> Like signiors and rich burghers on the flood,
> Or, as it were, the pageants of the sea,
> Do overpeer the petty traffickers,
> That curt'sy to them, do them reverence
> As they fly by them with their woven wings.

—there should be no skipping merriment in this.

[9] But Rosencrantz and Guildenstern, as Shakespeare wrote them, are not the mere puppets that the usual mangling of the text leaves them.

They are argosies themselves, these magnificent young men, of high-flowing speech; pageants to overpeer the callow English ruffians, to whom they are here displayed. The talk passes from spices and silks into fine classical phrases; and with what elaborate, dignified dandyism it ends!

Enter Bassanio, Lorenzo and Gratiano.

SOLANIO. Here comes Bassanio, your most noble kinsman,
Gratiano, and Lorenzo. Fare you well;
We leave you now with better company.

SALARINO. I would have stayed till I had made you merry,
If worthier friends had not prevented me.

ANTONIO. Your worth is very dear in my regard.
I take it, your own business calls on you,
And you embrace the occasion to depart.

SALARINO. Good-morrow, my good lords.

BASSANIO. Good signiors both, when shall we laugh? Say,
when?
You grow exceeding strange: Must it be so?

SALARINO. We'll make our leisures to attend on yours.

No apologetic gabbling here: but such a polish, polish as might have satisfied Mr. Turveydrop. Solanio—if one could distinguish between them—might cut the finer figure of the two. When the Masque is in question:

'Tis vile [he says], unless it may be quaintly ordered,
And better, in my mind, not undertook.

Salarino has a cultured young gentleman's turn for classical allusion. He ranges happily from two-headed Janus and Nestor to Venus' pigeons.

But it is, as we said, when Bassanio and Gratiano and Lorenzo with his Jessica have departed, that the use these two are to the play becomes plainest. They give us the first news of Antonio's losses, and hearsay, filtering through them, keeps the disaster conveniently vague. If we saw the blow fall on Antonio, the far more dramatic scene in which Shylock is thrown from depth to heights and from heights to depth as ill news and this good news strike upon him would be left at a discount. In this scene they are most useful (if they are not made mere targets for a star actor to shoot at). For here again is Venice, in the contrast between sordid Shylock and Tubal and our magnificent young gentlemen, superfine still of speech and manner, but not above a little Jew-baiting. They sustain that theme—and it must be sustained—till it can be fully and finally orchestrated in the trial-scene. It is a simple stagecraft which thus employs them, and their vacuity as characters inclines us to forget this, their very real utility. Forgetting it, Shakespeare's histrionic Venice is too often forgotten also.

The Characters, and the Crisis of the Action

NONE of the minor characters does much more than illustrate the story; at best, they illuminate with a little lively detail their own passage through it. Not the Duke, nor Morocco, Aragon, Tubal, Lorenzo, Jessica, nor the Gobbos, nor Nerissa, had much being in Shakespeare's mind, we feel, apart from the scenes they played, and the use they were to him. It is as futile, that is to say, to discuss Jessica's excuses for gilding herself with ducats when she elopes as it is to work out her itinerary via Genoa to Belmont; we might as well start writing the life-story of Mistress Margery Gobbo.

PORTIA

Shakespeare can do little enough with Portia while she is still the slave of the caskets; incidentally, the actress must resist the temptation to try and do more. She has this picture of an enchanted princess to present, verse and prose to speak perfectly, and she had better be content with that. But we feel, nevertheless (and in this, very discreetly, she may at once encourage us), that here, pent up and primed for escape, is one of that eminent succession of candid and fearless souls: Rosaline, Helena, Beatrice, Rosalind —they embodied an ideal lodged for long in Shakespeare's imagination; he gave it expression whenever he could. Once he can set his Portia free to be herself, he quickly makes up for lost time. He has need to; for from the moment of that revealing

You see me, Lord Bassanio, where I stand. . . .

not half the play's life is left her, and during a good part of this she must pose as the young doctor of Rome whose name is

Balthasar. He does not very deliberately develop her character; he seems by now to know too much about her to need to do that. He reveals it to us mainly in little things, and lets us feel its whole happy virtue in the melody of her speech. This it is that casts its spell upon the strict court of Venice. The

> Shed thou no blood. . . .

is an effective trick. But

> The quality of mercy is not strained;
> It droppeth as the gentle rain from heaven
> Upon the place beneath. . . .

with its continuing beauty, gives the true Portia. To the very end she expands in her fine freedom, growing in authority and dignity, fresh touches of humor enlightening her, new traits of graciousness showing. She is a great lady in her perfect simplicity, in her ready tact (see how she keeps her guest Antonio free from the mock quarrel about the rings), and in her quite unconscious self-sufficiency (she jokes without embarrassment about taking the mythical Balthasar to her bed, but she snubs Gratiano the next minute for talking of cuckoldry, even as she snubbed Nerissa for a very mild indelicacy—she is fond of Nerissa, but no forward waiting-women for her!). Yet she is no more than a girl.

Here is an effect that we are always apt to miss in the acting of Shakespeare today. It is not the actress's fault that she cannot be what her predecessor, the boy-Portia, was; and she brings us compensation for losses which should leave us—if she will mitigate the losses as far as she can—gainers on the whole. But the constant play made in the Comedies upon the contrast between womanly passion or wisdom and its very virginal enshrining gives a delicacy and humor to these figures of romance which the limited resources of the boy left vivid, which the ampler endowment of the woman too often obscures. This is no paradox, but the obvious result of a practical artistry making the most of its materials. Portia does not abide in this dichotomy as fully as, for instance, Rosalind and Viola do; but Shakespeare turns it to account with her in half a hundred little ways, and to blur the effect of them is to rob her of much distinction.

The very first line she speaks, the

> By my troth, Nerissa, my little body is aweary of this great
> world.

is likely to come from the mature actress robbed of half its point.
This will not matter so much. But couple that "little body" with
her self-surrender to Bassanio as

> an unlessoned girl, unschooled, unpractised;
> Happy in this, she is not yet so old
> But she may learn . . . .

and with the mischief that hides behind the formal courtesies of
the welcome to Aragon and Morocco, with the innocence of the
amazed

> What no more!
> Pay him six thousand and deface the bond . . . .

with the pretty sententiousness of her talk of herself, her

> I never did repent of doing good,
> Nor shall not now. . . .

followed by the artless

> This comes too near the praising of myself . . . .

and the figure built up for us of the heiress and great lady of
Belmont is seen to be a mere child, too, who lives remote in her
enchanted world. Set beside this the Portia of resource and command, who sends Bassanio posthaste to his friend, and beside that
the schoolgirl laughing with Nerissa over the trick they are to
play their new lords and masters. Know them all for one Portia,
a wise and gallant spirit so virginally enshrined; and we see to
what profit Shakespeare turned his disabilities. There is, in this
play, a twofold artistry in the achievement. Unlikelihood of plot
is redeemed by veracity of character; while the artifice of the
medium, the verse and its convention, and the stylized acting of
boy as woman, re-reconciles us to the fantasy of the plot.

But a boy-Portia's advantage was chiefly manifest, of course, in
the scene of the trial; and here in particular the actress of today
must see that she lessens it no more than she need. The curious
process of what we may call the "double negative," by which an
Elizabethan audience first admitted a boy as a girl and then

enjoyed the pretense that the girl was a boy, is obsolete for us; make-believe being the game, there was probably some pleasure just in this complication of it. This beside, there was the direct dramatic effect, which the boy made supremely well in his own person, of the wise young judge, the Daniel come to judgment. Shylock (and Shakespeare) plucks the allusion from the popular story of Susanna; but there may be some happy confusion, perhaps, with that other Daniel who was among ". . . the children of Israel, of the king's seede and of the Prince's: Springaldes without any blemish, but well-favoured, studious in all wisdome, skillful for knowledge, able to utter knowledge, and such as have livelinesse in them, that they might stand in the king's palace. . . ." For this is the very figure we should see. Here is the strict court of Venice, like enough to any law court, from East to West, from Shakespeare's time to now, in that it will seem to the stranger there very dry and discouraging, airless, lifeless. Age and incredulity preside; and if passion and life do enter, they must play upon muted strings. The fiercely passionate Shylock is anomaly enough in such surroundings. Then comes this youth, as brisk and businesslike as you please, and stands before the judges' bench, alert, athletic, modest, confident. He is life incarnate and destined to victory; and such a victory is the fitting climax to a fairy tale. So the Portia that will—as most Portias do—lapse into feminine softness and pitch the whole scene in the key of the speech on mercy, and that in a key of sentiment, damns the scene and herself and the speech, all three. This amazing youth has the ear of the court at once; but he'll only hold it by strict attention to business. Then, suddenly, out of this, comes the famous appeal, and catches us and the court unaware, catches us by the throat, enkindles us. In this lies the effect. Prepare for it, or make the beauty of it overbeautiful (all the more now, because it is famous and hackneyed) and it becomes a dose of soothing syrup.

This, be it further remembered, is not the scene's top note; conflict and crisis are to come. They are brought about simply and directly; the mechanical trick of the "No jot of blood" that is to resolve them asks nothing else. Shakespeare keeps the medium of the verse as simple; it flows on with hardly a broken line. The conflict is between Portia and Shylock. Bassanio's agony, Antonio's stoic resignation cannot be given great play; the artifice of the story will not even now sustain crosscurrents of human passion. But the constraint of the business of a court accounts well enough for their quiescence (the actors need do nothing to discount it) and the few notes that are struck from them suffice. The action must sweep ahead and no chance be given us to question its likelihood. Even when all is over the Duke departs with not much more comment upon this amazing case than an invitation to the learned young doctor to come to dinner, and Antonio and his friends are as casual about it and almost as calm. There is tactful skill in this. Shylock has gone, that fairy tale is done with; the less we look back upon it, the sooner we come to fresh comedy again the better.

Throughout the scene a Portia must, of course, by no smallest sign betray to us—as well betray it to Bassanio—that she is other than she now seems. No difficulty here, as we said, for Shakespeare's Portia, or his audience either. There was no wondering as he faced the judges why they never saw this was a woman (since very obviously he now wasn't) nor why Bassanio did not know his wife a yard off. The liquid sentences of the Mercy speech were no betrayal, nor did the brusque aside of a young lawyer, intent upon his brief—

> Your wife would give you little thanks for that,
> If she were by to hear you make the offer.

—lose its quite casual humor. All this straightforwardness the modern actress must, as far as she can, restore.

ANTONIO, GRATIANO AND OTHERS

In these early plays character does not as a rule outrun the requirements of the plot. Shakespeare is content enough with the decorative, the sententious, the rhetorical, in his casual Venetians, in Aragon and Morocco; with the conventional in Launcelot, who is the stage clown—the juggler with words, neat, agile, resourceful and occasionally familiar with the audience, as a clown and a juggler should be—under a thin disguise of character; with old Gobbo for a minute or two's incidental fun; with the pure utility of Tubal.

Antonio is flesh and blood. He is the passive figure of the story's demand; but Shakespeare refines this in the selflessness that can send Bassanio to Belmont and be happy in a friend's happiness, in the indifference to life that lets him oppose patience to his enemy's fury; and he makes him more convincingly this sort of man by making him just a little self-conscious too.

> In sooth, I know not why I am so sad . . . .

If he does not, it is not for want of thinking about it. He takes a sad pleasure in saying that he is

> a tainted wether of the flock,
> Meetest for death . . .

But there is a redeeming ironic humor in

> You cannot better be employed, Bassanio,
> Then to live still and write mine epitaph.

He is sufficiently set forth, and there is conveyed in him a better dignity than mere words give.[10]

Nerissa is echoing merriment; not much more.

Shakespeare may have had half a mind to make something a little out of the way of Gratiano. He starts him with a temperament and a witty speech; but by the play's end we have not had much more from him than the "infinite deal of nothing" of Bassanio's gibe, rattling stuff, bouncing the play along, but revealing no latent Gratiano. It all makes a good enough pattern of this sort of man, who will be a useful foil to Bassanio, and can be paired off for symmetry with Portia's foil, Nerissa; and the play needed no more. But there is enough of him, and enough talk about him, for one to feel that he missed by only a little the touch of magic that would have made something more of him and added him to the list of those that survive the lowering of the lights and the theater's emptying. There is a moment while he waits to take his share in Jessica's abduction, and sits reflecting:

> All things that are,
> Are with more spirit chased than enjoyed.
> How like a yonker or a prodigal,
> The scarfed bark puts from her native bay,
> Hugg'd and embraced by the strumpet wind!
> How like a prodigal doth she return;

---

[10] It is worth remarking that the word "sad," as Shakespeare uses it, may mean rather solemn and serious than definitely miserable.

With over-weather'd ribs, and ragged sails,
Torn, rent and beggared by the strumpet wind!

Harsh enough similes for such an occasion! Is this another side
to the agreeable rattle? Does the man who exclaims

Let me play the fool!
With mirth and laughter let old wrinkles come . . . .

find life in fact rather bitter to his taste? But one must beware of
reading subtleties into Shakespeare. If such a Gratiano was ever
shadowed in his mind, he made no solid substance of him.

Bassanio we have spoken of; play the part straightforwardly
and it will come right.

SHYLOCK

There remains Shylock. He steps into the play, actual and individual from his first word on, and well might in his strength (we
come to feel) have broken the pinchbeck of his origin to bits, had
a later Shakespeare had the handling of him. As it is, his actuality
is not weakened by the fantasy of the bond, as is Portia's by her
caskets. For one thing, our credulity is not strained till the time
comes for its maturing, and by then—if ever—the play and its
acting will have captured us. For another, the law and its ways
are normally so uncanny to a layman that the strict court of an
exotic Venice might give even stranger judgments than this and
only confirm us in our belief that once litigation begins almost
anything may happen. Despite the borrowed story, this Shylock
is essentially Shakespeare's own. But if he is not a puppet, neither
is he a stalking-horse; he is no more a mere means to exemplify-
ing the Semitic problem than is Othello to the raising of the
color question. "I am a Jew." "Haply, for I am black. . . ." Here
we have—and in Shylock's case far more acutely and completely
—the *circumstances* of the dramatic conflict; but at the heart of
it are men; and we may surmise, indeed, that from a maturer
Shakespeare we should have had, as with Othello, much more of
the man, and so rather less of the alien and his griefs. However
that may be, he steps now into the play, individual and imaginatively full-grown, and the scene of his talk with Bassanio and
Antonio is masterly exposition.

The dry taciturnity of his

> Three thousand ducats; well?

(the lure of that thrice-echoed "Well"!) and the cold dissecting of
the business in hand are made colder, drier yet by contrast with
the happy sound of Portia's laughter dying in our ears as he
begins to speak. And for what a helpless innocent Bassanio shows
beside him; overanxious, touchy, overcivil! Shylock takes his
time; and suddenly we see him peering, myopic, beneath his brows.
Who can the newcomer be? And the quick brain answers beneath
the question's cover: They must need the money badly if Antonio
himself comes seeking me. Off goes Bassanio to greet his friend;
and Shylock in a long aside can discharge his obligations to the
plot.[11] These eleven lines are worth comment. In them is all the
motive power for drama that the story, as Shakespeare found it,
provides; and he throws this, with careless opulence, into a single
aside. Then he returns to the upbuilding of *his* Shylock.

Note the next turn the scene takes. From the snuffling depre-
ciation of his present store, for his own wonted fawning on
these Christian clients, Shylock unexpectedly rises to the digni-
ties of

> When Jacob grazed his uncle Laban's sheep. . .

And with this the larger issue opens out between Gentile and
Jew, united and divided by the scripture they revere, and held
from their business by this tale from it—of flocks and herds and
the ancient East. Here is another Shylock; and Antonio may well
stare, and answer back with some respect—though he recovers
contempt for the alien creature quickly enough. But with what
added force the accusation comes:

> Signior Antonio, many a time and oft
> In the Rialto you have rated me. . . .
> You called me misbeliever, cut-throat dog,
> And spit upon my Jewish gaberdine. . . .

---

[11] This is one of the ever-recurring small strokes of stagecraft that are hardly
appreciable apart from an Elizabethan stage. Shylock and Bassanio are to the
front of the platform. Antonio, near the door, is by convention any convenient
distance off; by impression, too, with no realistic scenery to destroy the impression. Shylock is left isolated, so isolated that the long aside has all the importance
and the force of a soliloquy.

The two Venetians see the Ghetto denizen again, and only hear the bondman's whine. But to us there is now all Jewry couched and threatening there, an ageless force behind it. They may make light of the money bond, but we shall not.

Shakespeare keeps character within the bounds of story with great tact; but such a character as this that has surged in his imagination asks more than such a story to feed on. Hence, partly at least, the new theme of Jessica and her flight, which will give Shylock another and more instant grudge to satisfy. It is developed with strict economy. Twenty-one lines are allowed to Jessica and Launcelot, another twenty or so to her lover and their plans; then, in a scene not sixty long, Shylock and his household are enshrined. As an example of dramatic thrift alone this is worth remark. The parting with Launcelot: he has a niggard liking for the fellow, is even hurt a little by his leaving, touched in pride, too, and shows it childishly.

> Thou shalt not gormandize
> As thou hast done with me. . . .

But he can at least pretend that he parts with him willingly and makes some profit by it. The parting with Jessica, which we of the audience know to be a parting indeed; that constant calling her by name, which tells us of the lonely man! He has looked to her for everything, has tasked her hard, no doubt; he is her jailer, yet he trusts her, and loves her in his extortionate way. Uneasy stranger that he is within these Venetian gates; the puritan, who, in a wastrel world, will abide by law and prophets! So full a picture of the man does the short scene give that it seems hardly possible we see no more of him than this between the making of the bond and the climacteric outbreak of passion upon Jessica's loss and the news of Antonio's ruin.[12]

References to him abound; Shylock can never be long out of

---

[12] And so strange has this seemed to many a producer of the play and actor of Shylock, that we have been given scenes of pantomime in which Shylock comes back from Bassanio's supper to find Jessica flown. The solitary figure with a lantern, the unanswered rapping at the door, has become all but traditional. Irving did it, Coghlan had already done something of the sort, and—I fancy— Booth. An ingenious variation upon a theme by Shakespeare, that yet merely enfeebles the theme. The lengthier elaboration of a Shylock seen distracted at the discovery of his loss is, of course, even more inadmissible, since Shakespeare has deliberately avoided the situation.

our minds. But how deliberate is the thrift of opportunity we
may judge by our being shown the first effect of the loss on him
only through the ever-useful eyes of Salarino and Solanio. This is
politic, however, from other points of view. Look where the scene
in question falls, between Morocco's choice of his casket and Aragon's. Here or hereabouts some such scene must come, for the
progress of the Antonio and Shylock story cannot be neglected.
But conceive the effect of such a tragic outcry as Shylock's own,

> So strange, outrageous, and so variable. . .

—of such strong dramatic meat sandwiched between pleasant
conventional rhetoric. How much of the credibility of the casket
story would survive the association, with how much patience
should we return to it? But Salarino and Solanio tone down tragedy to a good piece of gossip, as it becomes young men of the
world to do. We avoid an emotional danger zone; and, for the
moment at least, that other danger of an inconvenient sympathy
with "the dog Jew." When Shylock's outbreak of anguish does
come, the play is nearer to its climax, Bassanio's choice is about to
free Portia's story from its unreality, and his savage certainty of
revenge upon Antonio will now depress the sympathetic balance
against him.

But, considering the story's bounds, what a full-statured figure
we already have! Compare the conventional aside, the statement
of the theme, in the earlier scene, the bald

> I hate him for he is a Christian. . . .

with the deluge of molten passion which descends upon the devoted Solanio and Salarino, obliterating their tart humor; compare
the theme, that is to say, with its development, mere story with
character, and measure in the comparison Shakespeare's growing
dramatic power.

In tone and temper and method as well this scene breaks away
from all that has gone before. The very start in prose, the brisk

> Now, what news on the Rialto?

even, perhaps, Solanio's apology for former

> slips of prolixity or crossing the plain highway of talk . . .

seem to tell us that Shakespeare is now asserting the rights of his own imagination, means, at any rate, to let this chief creature of it, his Shylock, off the leash. And verily he does.

The scene's method repays study. No whirling storm of fury is asked for; this is not the play's crisis, but preparation for it still. Shylock is wrapped in resentful sorrow, telling over his wrong for the thousandth time. Note the repetition of thought and phrase. And how much more sinister this sight of him with the wound festering than if we had seen the blow's instant fall! His mind turns to Antonio, and the thrice told

> let him look to his bond.

is a rope of salvation for him; it knots up the speech in a dreadful strength. Then, on a sudden, upon the good young Salarino's reasonable supposition that what a moneylender wants is his money back; who on earth would take flesh instead?—

> What's that good for?

—there flashes out the savagery stripped naked of

> To bait fish withal: if it will feed nothing else, it will feed my revenge.

Now we have it; and one salutes such purity of hatred. There follows the famous speech—no need to quote it—mounting in passionate logic, from its

> He hath disgraced me . . . and what's his reason? I am a Jew.

to the height of

> If a Jew wrong a Christian, what is his humility? Revenge. If a Christian wrong a Jew, what should his sufferance be by Christian example? Why, revenge. The villainy you teach me I will execute, and it shall go hard but I will better the instruction.

This is a Shylock born of the old story, but transformed, and here a theme of high tragedy, of the one seemingly never-ending tragedy of the world. It is the theme for a greater play than Shakespeare was yet to write. But if this one cannot be sustained on such a height, he has at least for the moment raised it there.

Solanio and Salarino are quite oblivious to the great moral issue opened out to them; though they depart a little sobered—this Jew seems a dangerous fellow. There follows the remarkable passage with Tubal; of gruesome comedy, the apocalyptic Shylock shrunk already to the man telling his ill-luck against his enemy's, weighing each in scales (love for his daughter, a memory of his dead wife thrown in!) as he is used to weigh the coin which is all these Christians have left him for his pride. It is technically a notable passage, in that it is without conflict or contrast, things generally necessary to dramatic dialogue; but the breaking of a rule will be an improvement, now and then, upon obedience to it. So Shakespeare, for a finish, lowers the scene from its crisis, from that confronting of Christian and Jew, of hate with hate, to this raucous assonance of these two of a kind and mind, standing cheek to cheek in common cause, the excellent Tubal fueling up revenge.

Such a finish, ousting all nobility, both shows us another facet of Shylock himself (solid figure enough now to be turned any way his maker will) and is, as we saw, a shadow against which the high romance of Bassanio's wooing will in a moment shine the more brightly. Sharp upon the heels of this, he comes again; but once more apocalyptic, law incarnate now.

> SHYLOCK. Gaoler, look to him; tell me not of mercy;
>   This is the fool that lent out money gratis:
>   Gaoler, look to him.
> ANTONIO.   Hear me yet, good Shylock.
> SHYLOCK. I'll have my bond; speak not against my bond:
>   I have sworn an oath that I will have my bond.

Verse and its dignity are needed for this scene; and note the recurring knell of the phrases:

> I'll have my bond; I will not hear thee speak:
> I'll have my bond, and therefore speak no more.
> I'll not be made a soft and dull-eyed fool,
> To shake the head, relent, and sigh, and yield
> To Christian intercessors. Follow not;
> I'll have no speaking: I will have my bond.

Here is a Shylock primed for the play's great scene; and Shakespeare's Shylock wrought ready for a catastrophe, which is a deeper one by far than that the story yields. For not in the missing of his vengeance on Antonio will be this Shylock's tragedy, but in the betrayal of the faith on which he builds.

> I've sworn an oath that I will have my bond . . . .

How many times has the synagogue not heard it sworn?

> An oath, an oath. I have an oath in Heaven . . . .

He has made his covenant with an unshakable God:

> What judgment shall I dread, doing no wrong?

—and he is to find himself betrayed.

It is the apocalyptic Shylock that comes slowly into court, solitary and silent, to face and to outface the Duke and all the moral power of Venice.[13] When he does speak he answers the Duke as an equal, setting a sterner sanction against easy magnanimity—at other people's expense! One could complain that this first appeal for mercy discounts Portia's. To some extent it does; but the more famous speech escapes comparison by coming when the spell of the young doctor is freshly cast on us, and by its finer content and larger scope. Structurally, the Duke's speech is the more important, for it sets the lists, defines the issue and provokes that

> I have possessed your grace of what I purpose;
> And by our holy Sabbath have I sworn
> To have the due and forfeit of my bond . . . .

So confident is he that he is tempted to shift ground a little and let yet another Shylock peep—the least likable of all. He goes on

> You'll ask me, why I rather choose to have
> A weight of carrion flesh, than to receive
> Three thousand ducats: I'll not answer that,
> But say it is my humour . . . .

Legality gives license to the hard heart. Mark the progression. While the sufferer cried

> The villainy you teach me I will execute, and it shall go hard but I will better the instruction.

with the law on his side it is

> What judgment shall I dread, doing no wrong?

from which he passes, by an easy turn, to the mere moral anarchy of

---

[13] Upon the modern stage he usually has Tubal for a companion; one has even seen him seconded by a small crowd of sympathetic Jews. How any producer can bring himself so to discount the poignant sight of that drab, heroic figure, lonely amid the magnificence around, passes understanding!

> The pound of flesh, which I demand of him,
> Is dearly bought; 'tis mine, and I will have it. . . .

and in satanic heroism stands defiant:

> If you deny me, fie upon your law!
> There is no force in the decrees of Venice.
> I stand for judgment. Answer: shall I have it?

There is a dreadful silence. For who, dwelling unquestioningly under covenant of law, shall gainsay him?

It says much for the mental hypnosis which the make-believe of the theater can induce that this scene of the trial holds us so spellbound. Its poetry adds to the enchantment—let anyone try rewriting it in prose—and the exotic atmosphere helps. But how much more is due to the embroidering of character upon story so richly that the quality of the fabric comes to matter little! Shakespeare, at any rate, has us now upon the elemental heights of drama. He cannot keep us there. Portia must perform her conjuring trick; perhaps this is why he gives Shylock full scope before she arrives. But he brings us down with great skill, maneuvering character to the needs of the story, and turning story to character's account.

The coming of the young judge's clerk does not impress Shylock. How should it? Little Nerissa! He has won, what doubt of it? He can indulge then—why not?—the lodged hate and loathing he bears Antonio. The Duke is busy with Bellario's letter and the eyes of the court are off him. From avenger he degenerates to butcher. To be caught, lickerish-lipped, by Bassanio; and Gratiano's rough tongue serves him as but another whetstone for savagery! He turns surly at first sight of the wise young judge— what need of such a fine fellow and more fine talk?—and surlier still when it is talk of mercy. He stands there, he tells them yet again, asking no favors, giving none.

> My deeds upon my head! I crave the law,
> The penalty and forfeit of my bond.

Why does Shakespeare now delay the catastrophe by a hundred lines, and let Portia play cat-and-mouse with her victim? From the story's standpoint, of course, to keep up the excitement a while longer. We guess there is a way out. We wonder what it can be; and yet, with that knife shining, Antonio's doom seems to come nearer and nearer. This is dramatic child's play, and excellent of its sort. But into it much finer stuff is woven. We are to have more than a trick brought off; there must be a better victory; this faith in which Shylock abides must be broken. So first she leads him on. Infatuate, finding her all on his side, he finally and formally refuses the money—walks into the trap. Next she plays upon his fanatical trust in his bond, sets him searching in mean mockery for a charitable comma in it—had one escaped his cold eye—even as the Pharisees searched their code to convict Christ. Fold by fold, the prophetic dignity falls from him. While Antonio takes his selfless farewell of his friend, Shylock must stand clutching his bond and his knife, only contemptible in his triumph. She leads him on to a last slaveringly exultant cry: then the blow falls.

Note that the tables are very precisely turned on him.

> if thou tak'st more,
> Or less, than just a pound, be it so much
> As makes it light or heavy in the substance,
> Or the division of the twentieth part
> Of one poor scruple, nay, if the scale do turn
> But in the estimation of a hair. . .

is exact retaliation for Shylock's insistence upon the letter of his bond. Gratiano is there to mock him with his own words, and to sound, besides, a harsher note of retribution than Portia can; for the pendulum of sympathy now swings back a little—more than a little, we are apt to feel. But the true catastrophe is clear. Shylock stood for law and the letter of the law; and it seemed, in its kind, a noble thing to stand for, ennobling him. It betrays him, and in the man himself there is no virtue left.

> Is *that* the law?

he gasps helplessly. It is his only thought. The pride and power in which legality had wrapped him, by which he had outfaced them all, and held Venice herself to ransom, are gone. He stands stripped, once more the sordid Jew that they may spit upon, greedy for money, and hurriedly keen to profit by his shame.

> I take this offer then; pay the bond thrice,
> And let the Christian go.

Here is Shakespeare's Shylock's fall, and not in the trick the law plays him.

He is given just a chance—would the story let him take it!—to regain tragic dignity. What is passing in his mind that prompts Portia's

> Why doth the Jew pause? Take thy forfeiture.[14]

No, nothing, it would seem, but the thought that he will be well out of the mess with his three thousand ducats safe.

Shakespeare has still to bring his theme full circle. He does it with doubled regard to character and story.

> Why, then the devil give him good of it!
> I'll stay no longer question.

If he were not made to stay, by every canon of theatrical justice Shylock would be let off too lightly; wherefore we find that the law has another hold on him. It is but a logical extending of retribution, which Gratiano is quick to reduce to its brutal absurdity. Here is Shylock with no more right to a cord with which to hang himself than had Antonio to a bandage for his wound. These quibbling ironies are for the layman among the few delights of law. Something of the villainy the Jew taught them the Christians will now execute; and Shylock, as helpless as Antonio was, takes on a victim's dignity in turn. He stays silent while his fate, and the varieties of official and unofficial mercy to be shown him, are canvassed.[15] He is allowed no comment upon his impoverishing for the benefit of "his son Lorenzo" or upon his forced apostasy. But could eloquence serve better than such a silence?

> PORTIA.   Art thou contented, Jew? What dost thou say?
> SHYLOCK.   I am content.

With the three words of submission the swung pendulum of the drama comes to rest. And for the last of him we have only

---

[14] See Furness for an elaborate, illuminating and witty comment upon the situation.

[15] It is hard to see why Antonio's taking the money to pass on to "the gentleman that lately stole his daughter" and providing that, for his half-pardon "he presently become a Christian," should be so reprobated by some critics. If we have less confidence today than had Antonio in the efficacy of baptism, have we none left in the rightfulness of reparation? Not much in its efficacy, perhaps. Antonio, one must insist, does not mean to keep any of the money for himself. One hopes he never lapsed into self-righteousness in recalling this. Nothing is said, however, about the original three thousand ducats!

> I pray you give me leave to go from hence;
> I am not well. Send the deed after me,
> And I will sign it.

Here is the unapproachable Shakespeare. "I am not well." It nears banality and achieves perfection in its simplicity. And what a completing of the picture of Shylock! His deep offense has been against human kindness; he had scorned compassion and prayed God himself in aid of his vengeance. So Shakespeare dismisses him upon an all but ridiculous appeal to our pity, such as an ailing child might make that had been naughty; and we should put the naughtiness aside. He passes out silently, leaving the gibing Gratiano the last word, and the play's action sweeps on without pause. There can be no greater error than to gerrymander Shylock a strenuously "effective exit"—and most Shylocks commit it. From the character's point of view the significant simplicity of that

> I am not well.

is spoiled; and from the point of view of the play the technical skill with which Shakespeare abstracts from his comedy this tragic and dominating figure and avoids anticlimax after is nullified.

The Return to Comedy

THE tragic interest is posted to oblivion cavalierly indeed. Seven lines suffice, and the Duke's processional departure. The business of the rings is then briskly dispatched, and made the brisker by the businesslike matter of the signing of the deed being tacked to it. Thence to Belmont; and while Lorenzo and Jessica paint its moonlit beauty for us, Balthasar and his clerk have time to change costume and tire their heads again for Portia and Nerissa. They have evidently, as we saw, none too much time; for Launcelot is allowed a last—and an incongruously superfluous—piece of clowning. But the musicians can play ahead for an extra minute or two if hooks and eyes refuse to fasten, and no one will notice the delay. The last stretch of dialogue is lively; a comic quartet coming after the consort of viols, and it asks for a like virtuosity. The play ends, pleasantly and with formality, as a fairy tale should.

One may wonder that the last speech is left (against tradition) to Gratiano; but one practical reason is plain. Portia and Bassanio, Antonio, Lorenzo and Jessica must pace off the stage in their stately Venetian way, while Gratiano's harmless ribaldry is tossed to the audience as an epilogue. Then he and Nerissa, now with less dignity than ever to lose, skip quickly after.

Act-Division and Staging

However well the First Folio's five-act rule may fit other plays, and whatever, in Elizabethan stage practice, division into five acts implied, there is ample evidence that *The Merchant of Venice* was meant to be played without an effective break. The scenes, and the padding in them, that give time for Portia and Nerissa to change clothes, are one sign of it. The first of these is padding unalloyed, and very poor padding at that. For the second, Shakespeare finds better and pleasanter excuse; but in part, at least, we owe that charming duet between Lorenzo and Jessica to this practical need.[16]

A case of a sort can be made out for the division in the Folio. Granted five acts, this fourth and fifth are manifest; the beginnings and finishings of the first three make useful milestones in the story, but others every bit as useful could be set up. It is worth noting that this act-division does nothing to elucidate the complex time-scheme of our anxious editors; but the Folio's expert play-divider would be no more bothered by that problem than Shakespeare had been. Nor was he concerned to end his acts memorably; the second leaves Aragon in our minds and the third ends with Jessica and Lorenzo's and the play's worst scene.[17] There might, however, be good enough reason in the Elizabethan theater for making an act's first scene arresting and for letting its last tail away; for they had, of course, no curtain to lower upon a climax, and after an interval interest would need quick re-

16 The two scenes are, to a line, of the same length. Add to the one the opening of the trial-scene, and to the other, for safety's sake, twenty bars or so of music, and we have the time allotted for the change of costume.

17 Furness sees dramatic point in the second act ending with Bassanio on the doorstep. I suggest that Nerissa's tag is meant to keep Belmont a little in our minds during the strenuous scene between Shylock and Tubal which follows; but that, if anything, it tells against an act-pause falling here, rather than for it.

kindling. No producer today, one hopes, will want to lower a picture-stage curtain at such points. Nor, if he is wise, while his stories are working to their joint crisis will he give us pause to think by what strange leaps in time and space they travel.

But surely there are many signs that—however, for convenience sake, it is to be acted, with or without pause—Shakespeare has conceived and constructed the play indivisibly. There is the alter nating between Venice and Belmont, and the spinning-out of the Portia story to fit with the other; neither device gains by or coun· tenances act-division. There is the unhesitating sweep of the action up to the trial-scene, and indeed beyond it. One can parcel it up in various ways—the Folio's and half a dozen others—and on various pleas; but will any one of them make the story clearer; will it not, on the contrary, do something to disclose its confusions? Prose and blank verse, rhymed couplets and a quatrain are used indifferently for tags; so these form no consistent punctuation. There is no scene, not even the trial-scene, that ends with a full close, until the play ends. There is, in fact, no inherent, no dramatic pause in the action at all; nor can any be made which will not be rather hindrance than help to a performance.

Well-paced acting will take the play straight through in the traditional, vague two hours. But if, for the weakness of the flesh, there must be pauses, division into three parts will be a little less awkward than into two. If you do not stop before the trial-scene you cannot, of course, stop at all; the play will be virtually over. You may reasonably pause at the end of the Folio's Act III. This alone, though, will make very unequal division. For an earlier pause, the moment of Bassanio's departure from Venice will serve.[18] This splits the first three acts of the Folio all but exactly in two. Delay the pause another scene and we shall have done with Morocco. The second part would then begin with the tale of how Shylock took his loss and our first news of Antonio's losses, and would develop this interest till the eve of the trial. Incidentally it would hold all the inordinate time-telescoping; a helpful quickening, this, to its pulse. But these divisions and the choice

_____
[18] There is, as we have seen, a possible contracting of the action here that gives a summariness to the last few lines and suggests (to the modern ear, truly) a "curtain."

of them have no other validity than convenience; the play must be thought of as an integral whole.

Needless to say that the confusion of scene-divisions in most modern editions (a very riot of it when Jessica is eloping) is not Shakespeare's; nor is the expert of the Folio responsible, nor even Rowe, who contents himself with marking the moves from Venice to Belmont and back.[19] For a century editors disputed as to when *Venice, a street*, shifted to *A room in Shylock's house*, or to *Another street*, or to *Before Shylock's house*, and chopped up the action and checked its impetus, when one glance at Shakespeare's stage, its doors and balcony and traverses, shows with what swift unity the play and its playing flow on. And whatever picturing of Venice and Belmont a producer may design, this swift-flowing unity he must on no account obstruct. Let that be clear.

But there is little difficulty in the play's production, once its form is recognized, its temper felt, the tune of its verse and the rhythm of its prose rightly caught. The text is very free from errors, there are no puzzles in the actual stagecraft. The music may come from Elizabethan stock, and the costuming is obvious. Nothing is needed but perception and good taste, and from the actors, acting.

---

[19] Lord Lansdowne's Jew held the stage in Rowe's time; and for this reason, it may just possibly be, he does not trouble to bring the play into closer relation with his own theater.

Antony and Cleopatra

HERE is the most spacious of the plays. It may lack the spiritual intimacy of *Hamlet*, the mysterious power of *Macbeth*, the nobilities of *Othello*, may reach neither to the heights nor depths of *King Lear*; but it has a magnificence and a magic all its own, and Shakespeare's eyes swept no wider horizon.

Eight years or so earlier he had written *Julius Cæsar*. There already are these rivals Antony and Octavius, comrades then; and the main clash of fortune and character is between Antony and Brutus, between the man of action and the idealist. Antony comes from it victorious; the tragedy is the soul's tragedy of Brutus. Thereafter Shakespeare gives us play after play upon this theme of the self-torturing soul. Hamlet (its chief exemplar), Othello, Macbeth, Lear are all concerned with the world within themselves. Now he returns to the world of great affairs, and, almost as if for emphasis, to the very pair that he left standing over the dead body of the idealist in defeat.[1]

We have a play of action, then, not of spiritual insight; that is the first thing to mark. Of a large field of action too. For if with *Julius Cæsar* the insularity of the earlier Histories was left behind, we are shown now not Rome in her might only, but the whole range of the Empire, eastward to Athens, Egypt and the Parthian bounds. Antony, the once-triumphant man of action, is hero; we are to watch his defeat by his subtler sometime pupil. Truly it is his passion for Cleopatra that is his ruin, and the action pulses to this; but the wider issue dictates form, method and the bulk of the play's content.

---

[1] And a little later he took Coriolanus, another Roman, another man of action, for tragic hero.

A tragedy of disillusion, we might call it. As to the lovers, from the beginning they have little to learn about each other.

> She is cunning past man's thought.

says Antony; and Cleopatra is very soon lashing at him with

> O most false love!
> Where be the sacred vials thou shouldst fill
> With sorrowful water? Now I see, I see,
> In Fulvia's death, how mine received shall be.

(though the event belies her). But the whole picture is shaded to this sere hue. "My son," said Oxenstierne, "you will be amazed to discover with how little wisdom the world is governed." We may sit through this play and add, "With how little honor or honesty or decency either!" Shakespeare had not idealized the earlier Antony, nor—though the sketch of him is so slight— underrated Octavius.[2] But the dead Cæsar's champion was at least a gallant fellow, able and alert. In his stead we now see

> The triple pillar of the world transformed
> Into a strumpet's fool.

And that industrious apprentice Octavius, as he nears his reward, grows under our eyes ever colder of heart, more meanly calculating, more deliberately false. We meet Lepidus again, the "barren-spirited fellow," as barren still of everything but efforts to keep the peace somehow, since only so can he hope to keep his own weak head above water; and we see Octavius belatedly following Antony's politic advice to

> turn him off,
> Like to the empty ass, to shake his ears
> And graze in commons.

We meet Pompey, the foolish optimist, the lucky fighter cajoled to an unstable peace, standing on his honor, but as willing to profit by the vilest treachery. Ventidius is the one Roman to be found fighting Rome's enemies instead of his fellow Romans; and he dare not push victory home for fear of Antony's jealousy. We have Enobarbus; a man (the bitter paradox!) corrupted most by fidelity to his friend, then turning traitor—too late! Towards the

---

[2] And we may even read into passages of *Julius Cæsar* a foreshadowing of the breach between the two.

play's end comes a very procession of generals, soldiers and dutiful servants, their fidelity abused, their valor wasted. Some desert while they can and some are caught in their leader's insensate ruin. While as to the Roman people themselves, the republic for which Brutus and Cassius died, the Friends, Romans, Countrymen who were Antony's "good friends, sweet friends," what have their saviors and masters to say of them now? For Antony they are

> our slippery people,
> Whose love is never linked to the deserver
> Till his deserts are past . . .

and Cæsar, a scene or so later (it cannot be fortuitously), is made to speak of

> The ebb'd man, ne'er loved till ne'er worth love . . .

and, with what contempt, of how

> This common body,
> Like to a vagabond flag upon the stream,
> Goes to and fro, lackeying the varying tide,
> To rot itself with motion.

Not, on the whole then, a hopeful picture of the Roman world. And it is, in the main, Shakespeare's own picture; if he pillages Plutarch for facts, even for phrases, their interpretation and emphasis—all that makes a picture—are his.

Bradley will not place the play with the four great tragedies, because, he says, Antony and Cleopatra themselves do not kindle pity and admiration to the full. He admits, though, that their passion and its ending is by no means the whole of the story. Certainly it is not. What are we shown to begin with? Far less a pair of tragic lovers in the making than—through the indignant Roman eyes of Philo and Demetrius—a doting general, effeminate in Egyptian finery,[8] ignoring Cæsar's messengers, capable of a

> Let Rome in Tiber melt, and the wide arch
> Of the ranged empire fall! . . .

(whoever will may hear it!), and a debauched Eastern queen, mocking at things Roman, battening on his apostasy. Here at once

---

[8] The "strumpet's fool" is some warrant for this; Cæsar's reference to Cleopatra not being "more womanly than he" is more.

is the larger theme emphasized, the discord which is to be resolved at last to a full close in the elaborate confusions of their defeat and death. The love-tragedy, we might almost say, is not made the main question till no other question is left, till the ruin wreaked by Triumvir and Queen is accomplished. And the action of the play is schemed throughout for the picturing of this wider ruin. Hence its diffuseness; and hence, if this is not understood, much misunderstanding of its artistry.

"*Feliciter audax*," says Coleridge of the style, and the label has stuck. Dr. Johnson, however, is stern. "The events, of which the principal are described according to history, are produced without any art of connection or care of disposition." It never does to neglect Johnson. His plain-sailing sanity will cut a clear way for us through many a metaphysical fog of nineteenth century criticism. Even if at last we must disagree with him, he takes answering. But he owns besides that "this play keeps curiosity always busy and the passions always interested" and that "the continual hurry of the action, the variety of incidents, and the quick succession of one personage to another call the mind forward without intermission from the first Act to the last." So in the end—Johnson exhibiting, perhaps, less consistency than usual—he and Coleridge are found not so far apart.

Feliciter audax! Shakespeare does seem to be amazingly at his ease. He brings in characters lavishly, flings Plutarch into dialogue; his verse is at its supplest, we are hardly conscious of the convention, and he shifts it to prose and back again without a jar. The action moves forthright and unchecked. Yet little or nothing in it shows superfluous; and, though endowed with but a line or two, the characters never fail to come to life. And if all this comes about "without any art of connection or care of disposition," if it all seems haphazard, is it not just possible Shakespeare may mean it to, may at least be content that it should? There is little luck in these matters, as the inexpert playwright who tries his along these lines will find. Do we perhaps pay a tribute to this art in so condemning it? Critics have found themselves performing this feat before now. But, in fact, the play's scheme is plain and ordered enough once we grasp its purpose, and—the essential thing—once we relate it to the theater of its nativity.

The Play's Construction

THE MAIN PROBLEM AND SOME
MINOR ONES

WE should never, probably, think of Shakespeare as sitting down to construct a play as an architect must design a house, in the three dimensions of its building. His theater did not call for this, as the more rigorous economics of modern staging may be said to do. He was liker to a musician, master of an instrument, who takes a theme and, by generally recognized rules, improvises on it; or even to an orator, so accomplished that he can carry a complex subject through a two-hour speech, split it up, run it by divers channels, digress, but never for too long, and at last bring the streams abreast again to blend them in his peroration. Clarity of statement, a sense of proportion, of the value of contrast, justness of emphasis—in these lie the technique involved; and these, it will be found, are the dominant qualities of Shakespeare's stagecraft—of the craft merely, be it understood.

He is apt to lay the main lines of his story very firmly and simply, and to let us see where we are going from the start, to cut the complexities from borrowed plots, and if any side issue later promises distraction, to make (literally) short work of it. Here he reduces the actual story to simplicity itself. Antony breaks from Cleopatra to patch up an insincere peace with Cæsar, since Pompey threatens them both; he marries Octavia, and deserts her to return to Cleopatra; war breaks out, Cæear defeats them and they kill themselves. That is the plot; every character is concerned with it, hardly a line is spoken that does not relate to it; and much strength lies in this concentration of interest. There is no underplot, nor any such obvious relief (which must, however, bring dissipation of interest too) as Falstaff, Nym, Bardolph, Pistol and Fluellen give to the heroics of the Henriad.

But, for a broad picturesque contrast, Roman and Egyptian are set against each other; and this opposition braces the whole body of the play, even as conflict between character and character will sustain each scene. He asserts the contrast at once; for we assemble expectant in a theater, therefore first impressions cut deep and a first stretch of action will be of prime importance. We have the two indignant, hard-bitten Roman campaigners, who must stand aside while the procession passes—

> *Cleopatra, her ladies, the train, with Eunuchs fanning her.*

—and see Antony in the toils. Their bitter comments follow it. Next, we have a taste of the chattering, shiftless, sensual, credulous Court, with its trulls and wizards and effeminates.[4] Then we see Antony, with Rome, the "garboils" of his wife's making and the threats of Pompey calling him, breaking his toils for a time; and the statement of the theme is complete.

Do events now proceed (we ask Dr. Johnson) "without any art of connection or care of disposition"? We are shown Cæsar, the passionate Antony's passionless rival, correct and charmless, in conference with Lepidus—that third and very feeble pillar of the world!—upon their poor prospects, while Antony's "lascivious wassails" hold him in Egypt. The action then swings back to a Cleopatra sighing after an Antony, who is already travelling Romeward; then to Pompey, questionably confident in his rising star.

> If the great gods be just, they shall assist
> The deeds of justest men.

Much virtue—and some risk—in such an if! And we pass at once to the knitting-up of the alliance that is to eclipse him.

Cæsar and Antony (when he is in his senses) are realists both, and there is neat wary work all round before their bargain is made, with the marriage to Octavia for a seal to it. A long passage, comparatively; but how artfully it is proportioned and modulated! First comes the straight dispute between the rivals. This must, of course, be given full importance, for here is the play's main clash. But it is salted by the ironies of Enobarbus, lightened by Lepidus and his fussiness, eased by Mæcenas and Agricola and their tact. Now, the dispute over and the alliance made, the worth of it will be shown us. The great men depart to the sound of

---

[4] There was possibly more matter in the scene at one time. Lamprius, Rannius and Lucillius, whose entrance survives, will hardly have been brought on, this first and last time, for nothing. Was there chaffing between Romans and Egyptians? Nothing is left of it, if so, but Enobarbus'

> Mine, and most of our fortunes to-night shall be—drunk to bed.

Or did Shakespeare, having written the stage directions, discover he could make enough effect without them?

trumpets; the three pillars of the world, mutual in its support again. And while Antony, absent from our sight, does his brisk wooing, Enobarbus talks to the gloating Agrippa, and the somewhat shocked Mæcenas—of Cleopatra! Note that the famous panegyric comes from a coarse-mouthed cynic; he, too, can feel her witchery.

> MÆCENAS.　Now Antony must leave her utterly.
> ENOBARBUS.　Never! He will not.
> 　　　　　　Age cannot wither her, nor custom stale
> 　　　　　　Her infinite variety. Other women cloy
> 　　　　　　The appetites they feed: but she makes hungry
> 　　　　　　Where most she satisfies; for vilest things
> 　　　　　　Become themselves in her, that the holy priests
> 　　　　　　Bless her when she is riggish.

With this in our ears,

> *Enter Antony, Cæsar, Octavia between them.*

and we hear Octavia (the difference!) with her gentle gravity, saying

> 　　　　　　Before the gods my knee shall bow my prayers
> 　　　　　　To them for you.

So Shakespeare weaves his pattern—for another simile—as he goes along, setting color against color, coarse thread by fine. And certainly the thing is done with such seeming ease and natural subtlety that we hardly note the artistry involved. We should feel the flat poverty of its absence soon enough.

Now another thread is woven in. The Soothsayer, symbol of the East, comes shadowing Antony, warping and weakening his will.[5] Then follows (contrast again) a touch of Roman energy; Ventidius is dispatched to Parthia. Then we are flung back to Egypt and to Cleopatra; and in redoubled contrast—for Shakespeare has now begun to bite upon the ironies of his theme—to a Cleopatra most unlike the golden vision of Cydnus, a spitting

---

[5] The Romans had their soothsayers too; but this one, by costume and association, would recall us to Cleopatra's Court. What modern playwright would so opulently employ him—bring him from Egypt, too, even by Plutarch's permission —to such seemingly small purpose? Here we see the extravagant ease of Shakespeare's maturest stagecraft. But the episode yields the exact effect needed, not an iota more.

fury that hales the messenger of Antony's faithlessness up and down by the hair of his head. Truly

> Age cannot wither her, nor custom stale
> Her infinite variety.

Now we return to Cæsar and his policies, to the successful maneuvering of Pompey to a peace, thanks to Antony and his prestige. What the worth of this also will be we learn as before when the great men have done and their followers talk things over (harsh truths are heard in anterooms). Or we might judge it for ourselves by its crowning in a drinking bout. The wretched Lepidus cannot last this out; and that first bitter outbreak at the sight of the "strumpet's fool" has its derisive echo in Enobarbus'

> There's a strong fellow, Menas . . . . 'A bears the third part of the world, man: see'st not?

And the chivalrous Pompey, we find, would be glad to have his guests' throats cut—by someone less chivalrous than he! Cæsar alone keeps his head; but we hardly like him the better for that. Then, sharp upon the crapulous business, Shakespeare shows us

> *Ventidius, as it were in triumph, . . the dead body of Pacorus borne before him.*

He has beaten back the Parthians. But now he dare not, for his own safety's sake, do Rome better service still, with such masters —hers and his—jealously watching him.

> Oh Silius, Silius,
> I have done enough; a lower place, note well,
> May make too great an act: for learn this, Silius;
> Better to leave undone, than by our deed
> Acquire too high a fame when him we serve's away.

Here is so notable and typical a piece of stagecraft that it is worth while to try and see the full effect of it. There is, of course, the aspect, which any alert reader discovers: the contrasting of the soldiers at their duty with the rulers at their drinking bout.[6] But we must keep Shakespeare's stage well in mind if we are to realize the dramatic value to the spectator of the quick shift from

---

[6] The Folio page displays the relation between the two scenes. But Rowe made an act-division between them, and later editors have copied him (of which more on p. 378), so that even this much of the effect may pass unnoticed.

singing and dancing and the confusion of tipsy embracings to the strict military march that brings Ventidius *as in triumph* upon the stage. There was no pause at all; Enobarbus and Menas would hardly have vanished, their drunken halloos would still be echoing when Ventidius and his procession appeared. This set the contrast at its sharpest; yet, since change of scene did not mean change of scenery, there was no distracting of mind or eye, a unity of effect was kept, and the action flowed on unchecked.

With one more interweaving of themes we shall be halfway through the play. Enobarbus' and Agrippa's mockeries give an acrid aftertaste to feast, treaty and marriage, all three; and we are to guess that poor Lepidus—so spendthrift of good nature!—will be made bankrupt soon. Antony and Octavia take their loving farewell of Cæsar and lovingly depart. An instant after we see Cleopatra, recovered from her fury, having Octavia's attractions picked to pieces for her comfort by the much repentant messenger.

> Dull of tongue and dwarfish! . . .
> Widow! Charmian, hark! . . .
>   Why, methinks by him
> This creature's no such thing. . . .
> The man hath seen some majesty, and should know. . . .
> All may be well enough.

And, watching her smile, we need have little doubt but that it will be. Very little; for as she leaves the stage (yet again only upon an Elizabethan stage will the effect fully count),

Enter Antony and Octavia.

with the rift that is to part them already showing.

Thus (if Johnson still needs answering, we can turn his own words against him now) curiosity has been kept busy and the passions interested, and the continual hurry of the action, the variety of incidents and the quick succession of one personage to another have called the mind forward without intermission . . . which is what Shakespeare has set out to do. He has told his story, woven his pattern, kept conflict alive and balance true, character prompting action, and action elucidating character, neither made to halt for the other. This really is the be-all and end-all of his stagecraft—and might well be said to be of any stagecraft; it is only the application of the method that will differ from stage to stage.

We may note in passing how he turns one small technical difficulty that he stumbles on to his profit (he has always had the faculty of doing this), and thereafter how he cuts his way out of another. Throughout this first part of the play he has more Roman than Egyptian material to deal with. Somehow he must keep the balance true and Cleopatra pretty constantly in our minds; but all the story asks is that she should be left by Antony and then sit waiting, patiently or impatiently, for his return. A more mechanical minded playwright would have begun, then, with Cæsar and Pompey, and so have accounted for some of the overplus at once; would have made, consequently, a mild beginning, and given a minor interest precedence. With Shakespeare what most matters will have pride of place, nor will he, when he has it, abate a chance; and, as we see, he lets the impulse of his opening carry him to the point of Antony's departure, over a stretch of 365 lines, abundant in life and color (it is actually a tenth of the entire play), till he has his story's master-motive made fertile in our minds. But now he must eke out the rest of the Egyptian material very carefully. The glimpse of Cleopatra pursuing her Antony before he is well away from her with "twenty several messengers" could (if the need were rather for compression) be dispensed with; but it is true and significant Cleopatra, so this may fill up a space. What next? When the news of her lover's treachery has been brought her the material will have run out; so this episode is split up and spread over two scenes. And at once Shakespeare sees and seizes the chance to show us, first the savage and suffering Cleopatra; next, on the rebound, the colder, baser-natured woman, feeding on flattery and deceit—and well aware of their worth. The story is molded to the development of character. Each scene of Cleopatra's, throughout this first part of the play, adds something to our knowledge of her; they accumulate to inform the tragedy of her end.

But now, though the two themes are abreast (Antony's concord with Cæsar seen on the wane, while Cleopatra, spiderlike, sits spinning a new web for him), it is clear, both that the Roman political material still outmeasures the Egyptian and that it may lengthen this part of the play into dangerous monotony. The Antony-Octavia theme might be elaborated for a variation. Shakespeare decides against this; it would still leave Cleopatra in the air. There is no more for her to do, that's evident, till Antony returns to her. Roman politics, then, must in turn suffer heroic compression. The wars upon Pompey and his murder, Cæsar's new quarrel with Antony, the extinction of Lepidus, are reported in a scene or so.

But neither are we shown Antony's return to Cleopatra; Cæsar recounts it to Octavia and his friends. There were other reasons against this. Shakespeare is not, as we have argued, writing a mere love-story, he is transplanting history to the stage; the causes and circumstances of the quarrel and the war that is to end at Actium are, at this juncture, the more important matter to him, and they must be given the widest significance words can give them, a wider if vaguer significance than concrete action will give. He could have shown us effectively enough how

> In Alexandria . . .
> I' the market-place, on a tribunal silvered,
> Cleopatra and himself [Antony] in chairs of gold
> Were publicly enthroned . . . .

But in Cæsar's

> No, my most wronged sister, Cleopatra
> Hath nodded him to her. He hath given his Empire
> Up to a whore; who now are levying
> The kings o' the earth for war. He hath assembled
> Bocchus, the king of Libya; Archelaus,
> Of Cappadocia; Philadelphos, king
> Of Paphlagonia; the Thracian king, Adallas;
> King Manchus of Arabia; King of Pont;
> Herod of Jewry; Mithridates, king
> Of Comagene; Polemon and Amyntas,
> The kings of Mede and Lycaonia,
> With a more larger list of sceptres.

a threat to the whole Roman world seems sounded.

Besides, the play's crisis is to come. These scenes are preparation for it, no more; they must be kept tense, but low in tone. The rivals are still only strengthening themselves for the struggle, with indignation as with arms.

Incidentally, Shakespeare will be glad to avoid a scene of reconciliation if it is to involve his boy-actress in any sort of "amorous transports." The play is dominated by sexual passion, no bones are made about the carnality of it either; yet how carefully he avoids writing any scene which a boy could not act without unpleasantness or in fear of ridicule![7] The fatal reunion is far more significantly marked by Cleopatra's spitfire quarrel with Enobarbus.

> CLEOPATRA. I will be even with thee, doubt it not . . . .
> Thou hast forspoke my being in these wars,
> And sayst it is not fit.
> ENOBARBUS. Well, is it, is it? . . .
> Your presence needs must puzzle Antony,
> Take from his heart, take from his brain, from 's time,
> What should not then be spared. He is already
> Traduced for levity, and 'tis said in Rome,
> That Photinus an Eunuch, and your maids
> Manage this war.

For from this it is that disaster springs; this is the beginning of the end.

Yet we are but halfway through the play; and here is another sign that a larger theme than the love-story is being worked out. Would Shakespeare otherwise be giving, against all precedent, half his play's length to its catastrophe? Now, it is the craft and the art of this long ending that have been most distorted by editors, its intention most grievously misunderstood by critics. A producer must not only start afresh from the untouched text, he must read it in the light of a clear understanding of the stage of its origin.[8]

The Question of Act–Division

To begin with he must free the play from act and scene divisions. The Folio gives none. The first five-act division was Rowe's. Johnson thought the first scene of his second act might better be

---

[7] For the further, and important, implication of this, see p. 435 *et seq.*

[8] The Folio text itself may have been edited, I know; but not to the measure of another stage than Shakespeare's.

the last scene of his first, but added ". . . it is of small importance, where these unconnected and desultory scenes are interrupted." Pope made the first scene of Rowe's fifth act into the last scene of Act IV, and after this all the later editors seem to have fallen unquestioningly into line. A five-act division for any play has, of course, its sanctions. The editors of the Folio indulge in it when they think they will. They (they or their printer for them) start out each time with an *Actus Primus, Scæna Prima*; a schoolboy's heading for his copybook. Sometimes they keep this up, once or twice they get halfway through the play and give it up; sometimes, as with *Antony and Cleopatra*, they just leave it at that. Now, whatever other dramatists may have done, whatever Shakespeare may have done in other plays, whatever may have been the custom of the public and private theaters for which he wrote—and it was probably a differing and a changing one—in the matter of making pauses during a performance, and whether those pauses were formal or prolonged, in this play there is no *dramatically* indicated act-division at all. There is, that is to say, (as far as I can discover) no juncture where the play's acting will be made more effective by a pause. On the contrary, each scene has an effective relation to the next, which a pause between them will weaken or destroy. There may have been four pauses in the original performing, or three, two or one; there may have been none at all, though that is hardly likely. But it would always (again, as far as I can discern) be a question of custom or convenience, not of dramatic effect.

Granted five acts, a case can be made for Rowe's choice of them, or Johnson's, or Pope's, or for half a dozen others, doubtless; and as good a one perhaps for a four-act division or a three. And if, pleading weakness of the flesh in actors or audience, a producer thinks it well to split the play into two, he can call a convenient halt, he'll find, at the turn of the action when Antony's drift back to Cleopatra is plainly to be seen. He may pause with some effect after that

All may be well enough.

or pass on a little further before he pauses and begins again (perhaps with better) with the news that

Cæsar and Lepidus have made wars upon Pompey.

or with Cæsar's own outburst of indignation and the return of
Octavia; or, more forcibly still, with the squabble between Cleopatra and Enobarbus and the launching of the war. But let him
plead convenience merely; for any halt hereabouts must mean
rather the loss of an effect than the making one. And this will be
as true of any other pauses in any other places; and the lengthier
they are the worse it will be.

For the fact is that Shakespeare's work never parcels up very
well. He was not among those writers who industriously gather
material, sort and arrange and rearrange it before they fit it
together. When his mood is operative he creates out of an abundance of vitality, and it is no good service to him to start obstructing the flow of it. He keeps, however, for all his fervor, a keen
sense of form; it is largely in this marriage of impulse and control
that his genius as pure playwright lies. And when inspiration
flags, he must come to contriving. He is businesslike at that, quite
callously businesslike sometimes. But even to the most workaday
stuff he gives a certain force. And should carelessness—for he can
be wickedly careless—land him in a tight place, there is, to the
practiced observer, a sort of sporting interest in seeing him so
nimbly and recklessly get out of it.

He does not (*pace* Dr. Johnson) write haphazardly; it is not
that. He plans—and more spaciously than those that have need to
plan. He is seldom to be found following a formula, even a proved
one of his own. Incidental devices he'll use again and again, as
we all repeat words and phrases—and the deeper (one notices) the
feelings beneath them the simpler these are apt to be. He is the
last man we should look to find submitting himself to an arbitrary
scheme, whatever its sanction, a five-act scheme or any other. Custom might even be imposing this on a play's performance and
impose it no further on him. And by now he has brought much
to the theater, broken much new ground, has the medium very
plastic in his hands. With such a task as this before him, and his
imagination fired, he will be out to do it as effectively as he can.
There will be no other question. He will have to muster all his
resources, and he will need full freedom for the use of them.

A Digression, Mainly upon the Meaning
of the Word "Scene"

BUT it is hard for us to meet him with a mind as free. The medium that he worked in so spontaneously is alien to us. Even the nomenclature under which we discuss it betrays us to error. Setting disputable act-division aside, what do we mean by scene-division and by "scene"? There are no reliable scene-divisions in the Quartos.[9] The editors of the Folio sometimes run to them, and they customarily draw their dividing lines at each clearance of the stage. But this does not commit them to an imagined change of place, nor connote any check to the action.[10] By Rowe's time, however, "scene" had taken on, though still uncertainly, a new meaning. Painted scenery, of a more or less conventional sort, was in current use. This defined locality; and a change of scene meant a change of place, was a diversion and a check to the action in every sense. The old fluidity of the Elizabethan stage, which really could "call the mind forward without intermission," was gone.

If Rowe finds act-division in the Folio he leaves it, and he cuts the plays with none to a similar pattern. His chief editorial task is to give them geography; but as he leaves scene-division too when he finds it he cannot do this very consistently; his "scene" being no longer the "scene" of the Folio editors. In *As You Like It,* for instance, he must leave some of the old scene-divisions unexplained; there are far too many for him. In *Othello* there are too few; the action will not abide throughout some of these where he has placed it. In *A Midsummer Night's Dream* he announces, to begin with, *Athens, and a wood not far from it,* and troubles no more. He looks at the plays when he can in the light of his own theater, for he is presenting them to readers accustomed to it. He disregards the many signs that they do not really belong there;

---

[9] I insert "reliable," because Q1 of *Romeo and Juliet* does happen to show some uncertain recognition of scenes.

[10] They make their slips, however (see the Preface to *Cymbeline,* p. 483). They followed classic practice, even as today the French, going further, generally begin a fresh scene whenever a fresh character enters or when a character leaves the stage. Scene does not connote place at all, and the "scene" of the play, in the pictorial sense of the word, stays unchanged throughout.

the matter, for one thing, is of no great importance, for another, some memory of the old theater still survives.

Antony and Cleopatra, however, offers Rowe a clean sheet, and he takes trouble. At first he does no more scene-dividing than the sense of place in his own stagecraft compels him to. He is content with a generalized *Alexandria*; *Rome*; *Sicily*; *The coast of Italy near Misenum*; *Athens*. He particularizes the very obvious *Pompey's Galley*, and later rises to the enthusiasm of *A Magnificent Monument*. But the comings and goings of the three days' battle defeat him. *Cæsar's camp* is a clear enough locality. *Cleopatra's Palace* and *Before the walls of Alexandria* will do. But the maneuverings of the armies, and, above all, that tiresome *noise of a sea-fight*, cannot be given exact place; and he is still free enough from realism to let them, with a few more such confusions, take their chance. Nevertheless he has now turned the long, unchecked stretch of action which was Shakespeare's into an Act III and IV of eight localized scenes each.[11] Later editors are to better him. As the theater of their day moves ever further from Elizabethan freedom and is the more committed to integrity of place they, for their part, dissect and define ever more closely; till modern editions give us a third act of thirteen scenes and a fourth of fifteen, with *A Plain near Actium*; *Another part of the Plain*; *Another part of the Plain*, following each other breathlessly. Only that tiresome *noise of a sea-fight* still refuses its pigeonhole.

What of Shakespeare's stagecraft is left? What dramatic purpose of any kind is conveyed by this?

Act III. *Scene viii. A Plain near Actium.*

Enter Cæsar and Taurus with his army, marching.

CÆSAR.   Taurus!
TAURUS. My lord?
CÆSAR.   Strike not by land; keep whole: provoke not battle
           Till we have done at sea. Do not exceed
           The prescript of this scroll: our fortune lies
           Upon this jump.

Exeunt.

Scene ix. Another part of the Plain.
Enter Antony and Enobarbus.

11 Strictly speaking, Rowe begins his three days' fighting with Act III, Scene vi, *Actium*.

ANTONY. Set we our squadrons on yond' side o' the hill,
In eye of Cæsar's battle; from which place
We may the number of the ships behold,
And so proceed accordingly.

Exeunt.

Scene x. Another part of the Plain.
Canidius marcheth with his land army one way over
the stage; and Taurus, the lieutenant of Cæsar, the
other way. After their going in is heard the noise
of a sea-fight.
Alarum. Enter Enobarbus.

ENOBARBUS. Naught, naught, all naught! I can behold no longer:
Th' Antoniad, the Egyptian admiral,
With all their sixty, fly and turn the rudder. . . .

This last so-called "scene" does run on for thirty-five lines more.

The layman must remember that he is reading a play, and should be imaginatively translating it into performance as he reads. Into what sort of performance do the editors help him to translate this, and the whole stretch of action from the eve of the first battle with Cæsar to the carrying of Antony dying to the Monument? They parcel it into twenty-two scenes, two of four lines each, one of six, one of nine, one of ten, three of sixteen lines and two of twenty-two; the rest are of more normal length. Scenes, as the editors of the Folio understood the word, they may be; as localized scenes they make dramatic nonsense.

Do the modern editors mean us to envisage the play in performance with painted scenery shifting every minute or so, transporting us round Actium, from one camp to another, to Alexandria and back again? Apparently. They know that Shakespeare's theater provided for nothing of the sort; do they never stop to think what the effect of this cinematographic patchwork of their devising must be?[12] But strike out their place-headings, and still think in terms of "scenes," and even then where are we? For Sir Edmund Chambers, who carries the Elizabethan stage pretty vividly in his eye, can tell us that in these passages "Shakespeare is in some danger of outrunning the apprehensions of his auditory." Is it so? Sir Edmund will be using the word "auditory" with

---

[12] Modern producers, never looking back past them, have, of course, solved the problem with a liberal blue-pencil.

intention; but is he thinking of its members, not as listening merely, and looking at the actors, but imaginatively staring beyond them, making efforts to conjure up backgrounds that are never described, barely indicated, and being kept on the jump, asking themselves—while Cæsar and his men leave the stage empty for Antony and his men to fill it, only to leave it in a moment to Cæsar again—"Where on earth are we now?"

If the play's first audiences sat trying to do anything of the sort, Shakespeare certainly did outrun their apprehensions; and if Sir Edmund supposes that Shakespeare meant them to, no wonder he is dubious about its stagecraft; and no wonder that critics with not a tithe of his knowledge, vaguely agreeing, will cry it down. But (with respect) Shakespeare's intentions were utterly different, and his audiences were not puzzled at all.

Convention in art is hard to discount, and we accept the accustomed conventions of the theater more unquestioningly than most. The visual side of our modern "realistic" drama is itself conventional; but it has come, by slow degrees, so fully to its own that we are apt to apply the laws of it, quite unconsciously, to every sort of theater and play, as if they were natural laws.[18] The "visual law" of drama was, to the Elizabethans, a very different, and an arbitrary and inconstant thing besides. It had existed, crudely, in the miracle plays, and it became elaborately, decoratively dominant in the Masques. But on the public stages it was, for various reasons, unprofitably hard to develop, and only in the candle-lit "private" theaters were its claims finally made good. By "visual law" must be understood, of course, not the sight of the actors and their acting, unescapable in any play, but their environment, the background, against which they show, and which can be as histrionic in its kind as they. We are now so used to seeing this pictured, be it as *A drawing room in Mayfair*, or as *Piccadilly Circus*, or *The Forest of Arden*, or *A street in Venice*, or *Verona*, or *Rome*, that if it is not set before us we set ourselves to imagine it there; and we assume that the Elizabethans did the same—for, after all, the characters in a play must be somewhere. Yes, they must be, if we push the enquiry. But the Elizabethan dramatist seldom encour-

---

[18] This is less true certainly than it would have been twenty years ago, before so many experiments in newfangled (which is really oldfangled) staging had been made. But the normal stage of today is still the realistic stage.

ages us to push it; and his first audiences assuredly, as a rule, did not do so in despite of him. For them the actors were very plainly on the stage, but the characters might, half the time, be nowhere in particular. It was, for the dramatist of that day, a privilege akin to the novelist's, who may, if he chooses, detach characters, through page after page, from fixed surroundings. It was a freedom which the promise of the scenic stage gradually sapped; but Shakespeare, at least, never surrendered it, and we here find him in the maturity of his craftsmanship, enjoying and exploiting it to the full.

He will always have, of course, as the novelist has, the whereabouts of his characters in mind, and casual allusion to it will crop out. There may also be the demands of the action for a house door, a balcony, a tree or a cavern to be satisfied; but these things will have rather the utility of furniture than the value of scenery. And—this is the point—he need never give more attention to his play's background than he feels will be dramatically profitable. Moreover, he can give it—yet again as does the novelist—the *sort* of attention he chooses. Look at *Richard II*. Poetry is lavished on the characters and the theme in general. But it is never put to use for the verbal painting of a background.

> Believe me, noble lord,
> I am a stranger here in Gloucestershire:
> These high wild hills and rough uneven ways
> Draw out our miles and make them wearisome.

is the extremest instance of it. We are left, as a rule, to judge by the tenor of the action where the actors are; and in many cases it would be impossible for the listener to say. If we need to know with any precision, the simple label of such a line as

> Barkloughly Castle call they this at hand?

will suffice to tell us.

Take two of the Comedies.

> Well, this is the Forest of Arden.

sets us (in *As You Like It*) accurately enough where Shakespeare wishes us to be.[14] Scene after scene, so called, once this impression

---

[14] This, however (to be accurate oneself), is not our first introduction there. But we only know *where* the Banished Duke should be when we first meet him by a reference to him in the scene before.

is given us, may be taking place anywhere thereabouts; and, as it is a comedy of character, not much time is spent upon picturing the forest itself. Such description of it as we do get is fantastic and reflects the artifice of the story. But *A Midsummer Night's Dream* is one long lyrical painting of the wood near Athens, with its English banks of primroses and thyme, the oxlip and the nodding violet; for this is what the play's theme demands.

From such direct simplicity as this turn to *Macbeth*, to such passages as

> This castle hath a pleasant seat; the air
> Nimbly and sweetly recommends itself
> Unto our gentle senses. . . .

as

> The west yet glimmers with some streaks of day;
> Now spurs the lated traveller apace
> To gain the timely inn. . . .

to the recurring chorus of the witches—the play's writing is full of pictorial suggestion. It is suggestion rather than description, an elaborate creating of atmosphere:

> Light thickens; and the crow
> Makes wing to the rooky wood. . . .

Description in this play is, indeed, as nothing compared with suggestion. Whereabouts in the castle at Inverness we are throughout the comings and goings of Duncan's tragic sojourn we should never know if the editors did not tell us, nor what the rooms or courtyards look like. But what scene-painter will create such darkness for us as that in which a magic of words wraps the night of the murder?

But all through, and in every phase of Shakespeare's development, it is a question of dramatic profit and the particular need of the play. In *Antony and Cleopatra* we find, except for the one episode of the sentries on guard listening to the mysterious music, no verbal scene-painting of any sort, direct or implicit, nor, as we have noted, more than the very minimum of reference to the locality of the scenes. The reason is plain. It is a play of action and of multiplied incident. The story is simple, but the tributary threads of it are manifold, and the interweaving conflicts of purpose complex enough. Its theme (once again) is not merely Antony's love for Cleopatra, but his ruin as general and statesman, the final ascension of Octavius, and the true end of

> that work the ides of March begun.

Therefore the dead Fulvia's doings, Pompey's grievances, Cæsar's policy, Lepidus and his timeserving, Ventidius balked of a bigger victory—these things and their like are of first importance, and we must be kept alive to them. But an audience has only a certain amount of attention to bestow, and it must be economized. It does not matter much where Cæsar and Lepidus, Pompey and Menecrates and Menas have their talks, nor whether the bargaining with Antony takes place indoors or out; so Shakespeare spends hardly a thought or a line upon it. Nor upon the beauties of the prospect —nor the weather! Antony and Cæsar, we feel, would certainly take a prosaic view of such things; and, for our part, we shall know them no better for viewing them against a picturesque background. But that each turn in the battle of their quick, ruthless Roman minds should be made clear to us—this matters a great deal, and to this all else, if need be, is sacrificed. Emotion, and at full pitch, is in store; but it will not be freed till the issues of the action are narrowing to the point of solution. Meanwhile, we have clarity, the clarity of a desert landscape, the theme in its stark integrity. *Antony and Cleopatra* is, among other things, the most businesslike of plays.

And if, for a beginning, this has been Shakespeare's aim, how much more, when we come to the confusions of the three days' battle, with its blunders and false hopes, its chances and changes, must not perfect clarity be achieved? Nor in the writing only, and by suppressing picturesque inessentials. Could he do what he sets out to do if he did not now exploit to the full the freedom from circumstance which the convention of his stage allows him? For this in itself gives clarity; it lets the dramatist concentrate upon the single subject. Complicate these twenty-two "scenes" as they flash past us by thinking of their whereabouts, and our limited power of attention will certainly not suffice.[15] But listen without further conjecture to the mere tale as the dialogue unfolds it, and watch just what we are asked to watch, the characters as they

---

[15] And if our eyes are distracted by changing scenery the strain will, of course, be worse still.

come and go and the symbolic marching of the armies, and there is no confusion whatever—only such, at any rate, as Shakespeare is at positive pains to be painting for us, in the hectic uncertainties through which Antony moves to his end.

An audience need do no more than listen and look at what there is to see and ask no questions. And audiences, as a fact, do no more than they are asked to do. Would that they always did that! Nothing will be heard of Actium, nor of a plain near it, nor anything of the sort. There is talk of the obviously distant Toryne and Peloponnesos. But from the beginning of this long stretch of action to the end, till Antony is carried dying to the Monument, there is hardly a hint to let us know where, at any moment, we may imaginatively be. Shakespeare does not set out to inform us, and he might sometimes be hard put to it to say himself.

> Cæsar sits down in Alexandria ....

we are told. The next day he is to be beaten to his camp, and Antony will give the order:

> Through Alexandria make a jolly march.

But that same night, with Cæsar still in occupation, Antony's sentries are on guard "about the streets." What streets? What does it matter? Just nothing at all. We not only do not want to know; it would be worse than useless to trouble us with the information.

If Shakespeare knows these things himself (perhaps he does) and wants to tell us, there are half a dozen ways open. He never seems to have rejected simplicities of the

> Barkloughly Castle call they this at hand?

sort merely because they were simple. He can range from this to the subtle expounding of geography and history, too, by which Ventidius lets us know where he is in the first few lines spoken upon his entrance *as in triumph*. But, simply done or subtly, this sort of thing would overlengthen the action here, check its flow and distract our attention—as badly, almost, as our own perverse efforts to imagine a whereabouts for each "scene" distract it.

To give anything of the spaciousness of a true scene to the four or five terse lines, by which now Cæsar, now Antony, show us the quality of their generalship, they would need to be multiplied by four; and this would weaken the present effect even in magnifying it. The larger episodes could easily be localized; but the others would then lose substance by comparison; what is more, the unity of the whole complex event would be destroyed. And it is in this unity that its dramatic strength lies. It is by the welding of the mixed mass of incident and character into a consistent whole, freed from all irrelevant circumstance, that its value is isolated and made clear. Obliterate scenic locality, we have still the stage itself left, with its formal furnishings, certainly. But make-believe makes short work of those familiar features; and, once we are enthralled and they vanish, there is nothing left to stand between us and the essential drama; we are at one with its realities. Here, surely, is a technical achievement of some account.

Why show us this long panorama of detail? Why not (as a Greek and probably a modern dramatist would) plan a few full-charged organic, significant scenes, and shape and compress the story to fit them? Again (if we could imagine Shakespeare putting himself the question) the answer is plain. Antony's is a great captain's downfall, the end of a man who has ruled half the Roman world, and we are to see both why he ends and how; and to see, as near as may be, the very process of it. The poor strategy, the weak will, the useless bargaining, set against Cæsar's steady mind; these are as significant every whit as the passion that wreaks vengeance on the wretched Thidias[16] and storms at Cleopatra. And the strung-out sequence of events, that are tense often and feverish while they matter little, slackened to triteness though they matter much, now catching up, now shedding their actors as they pass, time and place apt to seem the most fortuitous things about them—does not this both show us the true process of the matter, and give us, besides, just the impression that in life will belong to our share in such a crisis? Bouts of noisy fighting with heart-rent love-scenes in between would doubtless make a good show. But here, if Plutarch tells true, is a picture of the business of war as these Roman realists waged it, with luck and cunning, passion and judgment and interest all at odds in leaders and followers too. It is history directly dramatized.

―――――――

16 So the Folio calls him, with a variation to "Thidius." Theobald, apparently, first made him into Plutarch's "Thyreus" again, and other editors have followed. But the change is surely too marked for Shakespeare not to have made it purposely.

Shakespeare neither takes nor uses his material haphazardly. If, with one dramatic aim, he frees himself from ties of place, with another he creates for himself ties of time. He telescopes Plutarch's vague weeks into a strict three days. They mark the ebb and flow and ebb of Antony's fortunes. First, there is the night's carouse after defeat, while the sentries keep their strange watch; then the next night's after victory, while Cæsar's sentries mark Enobarbus creeping out to die; then the third day's ebb to disaster. This gives him rhythm and form, and increases tension; it makes the story clearer, and our interest easier to hold. It is deliberate stagecraft.

The Play's Construction, *Continued*

THE THREE DAYS' BATTLE

WE are plunged, for a beginning to the business, amid the squabbling distractions of Antony's counsels. Enobarbus, level-headed, caustic of tongue, does what he can to stem the tide of folly. Antony stands, weakly obstinate, under Cleopatra's eye. Against all reason, he will meet the enemy at sea—

> For that he dares us to't.

The news accumulates of Cæsar's swift, unchecked advance. We have the veteran legionary breaking all bounds of discipline in a last desperate protest.

> O noble emperor, do not fight by sea;
> Trust not to rotten planks: do you misdoubt
> This sword, and these my wounds?

Then, as they disappear,

> *Enter Cæsar, with his army, marching.*

The first day's fighting is compressed into the symbolism (it is little more) of a dozen lines of dialogue and business. This is a sort of variation upon the old dumb show, to an Elizabethan audience a familiar and pregnant convention. But note the niceties of effect. Cæsar enters *with his army, marching*; a formal processional entrance, capping the news of his approach that has threaded the preceding scene. In two sentences he shows us his strategy and his quality in command. Next, Antony and Enobarbus appear alone on the emptied stage. Antony speaks four hur-

Antony and Cleopatra 391

ried and half-purposed lines, Enobarbus never a word, but his glum looks will be eloquent; and they vanish. Then comes the marching and countermarching of the armies that are not to fight (pure symbolism!), each with its subordinate general in command. The stage empties again, and its emptiness holds us expectant. Then, of a sudden, comes the climax, the significant event; *the noise of a sea-fight* is heard.[17] Then, actual drama reasserting itself, Enobarbus, with alarums to reinforce his fury, bursts upon us, tongue-tied no more, to interpret disaster with

> Naught, naught, all naught! I can behold no longer:
> Th' Antoniad, the Egyptian admiral,
> With all their sixty, fly and turn the rudder. . . .

He is reinforced by Scarus, younger and fierier still[18]:

> Gods and goddesses,
> All the whole synod of them! . . .
> The greater cantle of the world is lost
> With very ignorance; we have kissed away
> Kingdoms and provinces.

This symbolism of war is not in itself dramatic, one sees. Shakespeare could hardly make it so, but he hardly needs it to be. He gives us, however, very little of it. His drama lies in the consequences of the fighting, as these are reflected in the conduct of his characters. We are shown, it is to be remarked, no actual fighting at all, come no nearer to it than the sight of young Scarus and his fresh wounds. He is marked out for us as the gallant warrior, and Antony gives him generous praise. Antony's own valor we may take for granted. But his challenge to Cæsar to fight him single-handed is stressed, and as a ridiculous thing. Says Enobarbus:

---

[17] I cannot pretend to say how "the noise of a sea-fight" was made. Professor Stuart-Jones (who spoke with authority upon one aspect of the matter) suggested to me that what one heard was the breaking of the sweeps of the galleys. But is that—would it have been to Shakespeare's audience—a recognizable sound? I fancy that a hurly-burly flavored with "Avasts," "Belays" and other such sea-phrases from the landman's vocabulary would be a likelier refuge in a difficulty for the prompter and his staff. But there may have been some recognized symbolism of a sea-fight.

[18] There is no authority (that I know of) for Scarus' age. But the dramatic value of the contrast between his keen youth and Antony's waning powers is indubitable.

> Cæsar, thou hast subdued
His judgment too.

This is stressed because in it and all it implies lie his failure and his tragedy.

The sequel to the first battle is shown us at length. Scarus' boyish wrath spends itself; Enobarbus, shame rankling deeper in him, relapses to his gibing; Canidius coolly plans to make his peace with Cæsar, and departs, no man hindering him; Antony appears. The gradation from the convention of the battle to the actuality of the scene to come between the broken Antony and Cleopatra, all repentance, is nicely adjusted. First we have had the angry agony of defeat, which needs human expression; next, the few lines Canidius speaks give us an abstract of many happenings; then Antony, in the exhaustion of despair, sums up against himself and tells to the end the chapter of disaster. Here is Plutarch's ". . . and so Antonius . . . went and sat down alone in the prowe of his ship, and said never a word, clapping his head between both his hands . . . and so lived three days alone without speaking to any man. But when he arrived at the head of Tænarus there Cleopatra's women first brought Antonius and Cleopatra to speak together, and afterwards to sup and lie together. . . . Now for himself he determined to crosse over into Africk and toke one of his carects or hulks loden with gold and silver and other rich cariage, and gave it unto his friends, commanding them to depart, and to seeke to save themselves. They answered him weeping, that they would nether doe it nor yet forsake him. Then Antonius very curteously and lovingly did comfort them. . . ." And it is interesting to see how Shakespeare, contracting the circumstances, can yet keep the sense and temper of the events, can even, by the tune and rhythm of a dozen lines of verse, by a suggestive phrase or so, and by the indicated business of the scene, give us the slack sense of days of breathing-space following on the blow.

The encounter with Cleopatra brings us back to matter more his own, and of more immediacy, closer therefore in tension. It is to be the first of three in which Antony will face perforce the truth of what is between them, mounting the scale of suffering to madness at the last. This one, then, must be in a low key (Shakespeare even skirts the edge of the comic at its start, with the lead-

ing of Cleopatra, spectacularly pitiful, up to the weeping hero),
and it holds no contest; he is but too ready with his

> Fall not a tear, I say; one of them rates
> All that is won and lost . . . .

We pass to Cæsar's diplomatic exploiting of his victory, his
curt rejection of Antony's overtures, the sending of Thidias to
wean Cleopatra from him. Antony rises to nobility again, with his
"Let her know't" for sole comment upon the offer of peace to
Cleopatra if she will yield him up. But with his next breath he
falls to the fatuity of the challenge to Cæsar.

There follows Cleopatra's ignoble reception of Thidias. Enobarbus can have at least one taste of revenge upon her, and
Antony is fetched to see her smiling on Cæsar's messenger.

> 'Tis better playing with a lion's whelp
> Than with an old one dying.

The savage outburst, which sends the glib fellow back, dumb and
bleeding from his stripes, is, for all its passion, as futile—and is
meant to seem so—as were the heroics of the challenge; so is the
moral stripping and lashing of Cleopatra. For, his rage glutted
and appeased by the sight of the wretch half-slaughtered at his
feet, he can turn back to her, open-eyed to the truth about her,
and, listening to the easy lies, can end them with an easier—and a
hopeless—

> I am satisfied.

After this we may be sure that he is doomed. Enobarbus is sure
of it, and Cæsar's comment is contemptuous and brief. Shakespeare adds, for the ending of the day, the strange little hysterical
passage in which, by

> one of those odd tricks which sorrow shoots
> Out of the mind. . .

we find him melting his followers to tears as he pathetically paints
the prospects of his defeat and death—to show us yet again, one
supposes, how helplessly off the rails the man has run.[19]

Now comes, to mark the passing of the night, the episode of the
sentries on their watch. It is, as we have noted, the one piece of

---

[19] Shakespeare elaborates this from a couple of sentences in Plutarch; and the
suggestion (from Enobarbus) that Antony almost deliberately "makes a scene,"
is all his own.

scene-painting in the play; a developing of atmosphere, rather—
for the single line,

> Heard you of nothing strange about the streets?

is the only hint of locality—of the ominous atmosphere of a night
of reprieve between battles. The means to it are merely a few
whispering voices and the

> *Music of the hoboyes ... under the stage.*

It is after the couples have met, gossiped a moment and parted
with "good-night," that they hear this.

4TH SOLDIER.   Peace! what noise?
1ST SOLDIER.   List, list!
2ND SOLDIER.   Hark!
1ST SOLDIER.   Music i' the air!
3RD SOLDIER.   Under the earth.
4TH SOLDIER.   It signs well, does it not?
3RD SOLDIER.   No.
1ST SOLDIER.   Peace, I say.
               What should this mean?
2ND SOLDIER.   'Tis the god Hercules, whom Antony loved,
               Now leaves him.

They feel their way towards each other and whisper confusedly
in the darkness, their nerves a little ragged.

2ND SOLDIER.   How now, masters!
ALL TOGETHER.   How now?
               How now? do you hear this?
1ST SOLDIER.   Ay: is't not strange?
3RD SOLDIER.   Do you hear, masters? do you hear?
1ST SOLDIER.   Follow the noise so far as we have quarter.
               Let's see how it will give off.
         ALL.   Content! 'Tis strange.

And, holding all together as the music dies into distance, they
vanish. The entire effect, simple in itself, is made with masterly
economy. The scene has two uses: it preserves the continuity of
the action, and is gloom before the bright beginning of the second day.

Antony has not slept. He comes jovial and confident from
night-long revelry, calling for his squire. Cleopatra, seeming a
lissom girl again, beneath the spell of this still magnificent spend-

thrift of fortune, plays at buckling on his armor; and with shouts and the flourish of trumpets and the clangor of the gathering of armed men Shakespeare rings up the dawn. Trumpets sound again; it is as if they set out to sure victory. Two notes of doubt are struck: by a shrewder Cleopatra with her

> That he and Cæsar might
> Determine this great war in single fight!
> Then, Antony—! But now—?

—before she retires to her chamber to recover what she may of her lost night's rest; and by the news, greeting Antony as he marches forth, that Enobarbus—Enobarbus!—has deserted. He puts the treason behind him with a gentle magnanimity which comes strangely—does it?—from a man who could have his enemy's ambassador half flayed alive. But this is Antony.

Next we see Cæsar. But this—upon a mere half-victory won—is an overconfident Cæsar, not the cautious general of the earlier battle. Between the brilliant opening and the brilliant end of Antony's day we have, for contrast, Enobarbus repentant. There is, of course, no strict measuring out of time; and we return to some degree of symbolism when, after alarum, drums and trumpets, Agrippa enters with

> Retire, we have engaged ourselves too far:
> Cæsar himself has work, and our oppression
> Exceeds what we expected.[20]

He and his staff pass, unflurried, across the stage. They have been quickly cured of their confidence. Antony and Scarus pursue them, the youthful elation of Scarus a foil to Antony's self-posses-sion. He is the potent general still, one might believe—set him free from Cleopatra! Drums and alarums subsiding in the dis-tance give us the battle's ending. The emptied stage here is the equivalent of a line of asterisks on a printed page. Then with

Enter Antony again in a march.

comes the brilliant consummation of this last day of good fortune that he is to see. It ends as it began, with trumpets sounding; and

---

[20] The Folio's stage direction brings Agrippa on alone, but this, his speech pretty clearly shows, must be an error. He may have Dolabella or Mæcenas with him. It will hardly, however, be a symbolic army in full retreat. All the disorder of battle Shakespeare is giving us by sound, its thrills through individuals; and his massed entries are processional. The stage directions hereabouts are all rather cursory.

it has shown us Antony at his best, generous, gallant, a born leader of men.

Cæsar's sentries on their watch mark the second night's passing; and our sight of Enobarbus, sick of his ague, broken in spirit, crawling out into the misty moonlight to die, gives it a dreary coloring. The dawn breaks dully.

Drums afar off.

> Hark, the drums
> Demurely wake the sleepers. . . .

The armies parade again. First Antony leads his across. He is smiling grimly, yet there is a desperate edge to his

> I would they'd fight i' the fire, or i' the air;
> We'd fight there too . . . .

Then we see Cæsar, sober caution itself this time. He passes, heading his men, and the stage stays empty a moment.

Antony and Scarus appear alone. No tokens of fighting so far, and Antony is in suspense. With

> Yet they are not joined: where yond pine does stand
> I shall discover all: I'll bring thee word
> Straight, how 'tis like to go.

he vanishes, leaving Scarus to turn suspense to misgiving with

> Swallows have built
> In Cleopatra's sails their nests: the augurers
> Say they know not, they cannot tell; look grimly,
> And dare not speak their knowledge. Antony
> Is valiant and dejected, and, by starts,
> His fretted fortunes give him hope and fear
> Of what he has and has not.

Through this comes sounding an

Alarum afar off, as at a sea-fight.

—to our remembrance, a most ominous sound. And hard upon it, transformed, wrought to a grand climacteric of fury, Antony reappears.

> All is lost!
> This foul Egyptian hath betrayed me:
> My fleet hath yielded to the foe; and yonder
> They cast their caps up and carouse together

Like friends long lost. Triple-turned whore! 'tis thou
Hast sold me to this novice; and my heart
Makes only wars on thee. Bid them all fly!
For when I am revenged upon my charm,
I have done all. Bid them all fly: begone.[21]

From now till he is carried exhausted and dying to the Monument Antony's passion dominates the action. Eros, Mardian, the Guard, Dercetas, Diomedes are caught distractedly in the wind of it; we see nothing of Cæsar; panic quickly obliterates Cleopatra. It is a long passage and highly charged; but Shakespeare can find all the change and variety he needs in its own turbulent ebb and flow. Nor, when the medium is rhetoric raised to such a pitch and given such coloring, could any competition be admitted; the audience must be caught and rapt by the mood. The shock of the first outburst should capture us. Then, the brilliant Scarus, Enobarbus' successor, Antony's new right hand, having been sent packing like a lackey (and as ready to go: or do we wrong him?) we are held by the simple magnificence of

Oh, sun, thy uprise shall I see no more:
Fortune and Antony part here; even here
Do we shake hands. All come to this? The hearts
That spanieled me at heels, to whom I gave
Their wishes, do discandy, melt their sweets
On blossoming Cæsar; and this pine is barked
That over-topped them all.

---

[21] The Folio gives the stage direction

Alarum farre off, as at a sea fight.

in the interval between Cæsar's exit with his army and Antony's entrance with Scarus. This is almost certainly wrong. Antony would not enter upon an alarum with a "Yet they are not joined." But it does not as certainly follow that the editors (from 1778 onwards, according to Furness) are right in transferring it to the instant before his re-entrance with "All is lost." They may be. But it is an "alarum afar off," and might come more effectively before, or even during, Scarus' speech. The point is not a very important one. It is hard to tell what sheer dramatic value there was for the Elizabethans in these symbolic alarums and the like, and what variety of effect could be given them. Some without doubt; they speak a language, if a simple one. The effect of that, first *noise of a sea-fight* which precipitated Enobarbus' outburst of "Naught, naught, all naught" is evidently not precisely the same—nor meant to be—as this *alarum afar off* which brings Antony on to the greater crisis of "All is lost." We may note that, besides the "symbolism," Shakespeare gives about a dozen illustrative lines of dialogue to each of the first two battles, to the third about twenty.

His fury soon begins to work again; it is like yeast in him; and when he turns, expectant of Eros coming to his call, to find Cleopatra herself, he chokes for a moment, long enough for her smooth incongruity,

> Why is my lord enraged against his love?

to give a fresh twist to his torture. In this babyish line, and in her flabbergasted, tongue-tied, sudden, very unqueenlike bolting, in his frenzied pursuit of her, Shakespeare again skirts the ridiculous; and closely enough this time to provoke in us a sort of half-hysteria which will attune us to his next shift of key—into the delirium which brings Antony, exhausted, to a pause. We must picture the actor, transfigured to the terms of

> The shirt of Nessus is upon me: teach me,
> Alcides, thou mine ancestor, thy rage:
> Let me lodge Lichas on the horns o' the moon. . . .

and storming from the stage. While we still hear him we see Cleopatra with her scared women and her sapless eunuch scurrying across like rabbits. And as they vanish he follows, vertiginous, insensate! It is a wild, roundabout chase, hazardously raised to poetic power.

If we were not first thrown off our emotional balance we might find the fantasy that follows—for all its beauty—too much an intellectual conceit, and too long-drawn-out.

> ANT. Eros, thou yet behold'st me?
> EROS.   Ay, noble lord.
> ANT. Sometime we see a cloud that's dragonish,
>   A vapour sometime like a bear or lion,
>   A tower'd citadel, a pendent rock,
>   A forked mountain, or blue promontory
>   With trees upon't, that nod unto the world
>   And mock our eyes with air: thou hast seen these signs;
>   They are black vesper's pageants.
> EROS.   Ay, my lord.
> ANT. That which is now a horse, even with a thought
>   The rack dislimns and makes it indistinct,
>   As water is in water,
> EROS.   It does, my lord.
> ANT. My good knave Eros, now thy captain is
>   Even such a body. . . .

We should feel with Antony the relief this strange sense of dissolution brings from the antics of passion, and how, as he does, one would prolong the respite, playing with these fancies that the half-freed spirit conceives!

From this he sinks to quiet grief. The sight of the "saucy eunuch," on tiptoe with his glib tale, sets fury glowing for a moment again. Then comes the news, worded as piteously as ever Cleopatra, safe now in her Monument, could desire—the news that she is dead. He greets them as Antony must.[22] The fact that they are false is of a piece with the other futilities of these three days that have gone to his undoing. Yet another is to follow when he stands waiting for the merciful sword-stroke which Eros turns on himself; yet another when he bungles his own, and has to lie there, begging the guard to dispatch him—and, instead, off they go and let him lie![23]

With his carrying to the Monument the long phase of more particularly "unlocalized" action, germane to the three days of fighting, ends. We have been "ideal" spectators, we know what happened, and why; and just such an impression has been made on us as the reality itself would leave behind. It is a great technical achievement, and one of great artistry too.

Cleopatra Against Caesar

Antony dead, the domination of the play passes at once to Cleopatra. She asserts it in the lament over him; a contrast to his stoic greeting of the news of her death. And from now to the end, the action (but for one short scene) is definitely localized in the Monument. As suited, this, to the intensity and cunning of Cleopatra's battle with Cæsar as was diversity of place to the chances and changes of the other; and by contrast made more telling.

---

[22] If we remember his

On:
Things that are past are done with me.

[23] Eros is dispatched from the stage for a moment or so by an apparently motiveless "From me awhile." The practical need is probably to dispose of Antony's armor; for soon there will be both Antony and the body of Eros himself to be carried off by *four or five of the guard*, Diomed and (more doubtfully) Dercetas. But Shakespeare, by merely leaving it unexplained, lets it seem part of the general slack confusion.

But Antony's death leaves Shakespeare to face one obvious problem: how to prevent Cleopatra's coming as an anticlimax. Plutarch is still lavish of material, but it will need some choosing and molding.

Cæsar is surprised by the news—here is one risk of slackening tension avoided—and shocked into more feeling than we expect of him. Then at once the last round of the play's contest is opened, and we see what the struggle is to be. A humble anonymous messenger comes from Cleopatra, his message as humble. Cæsar sends him back with fair words; and promptly thereafter:

> Come hither, Proculeius; go and say
> We purpose her no shame: give her what comforts
> The quality of her passion shall require,
> Lest in her greatness by some mortal stroke
> She do defeat us; for her life in Rome
> Would be eternal in our triumph. . . .

It is to be Cæsar's wits against Cleopatra's pride and despair. He fought Antony to the death; it may take more generalship to secure Cleopatra alive. Proculeius, we notice, is sent; the one man about Cæsar, said Antony, that Cleopatra was to trust. Is it in some distrust of him (for his own part) that Cæsar sends Gallus too; and, on yet further thought, Dolabella to watch them both, lest Cleopatra wheedle her way round them? It turns out to be Dolabella that needs watching. But here, unfortunately, the text, as we have it, plays us false. There has been cutting and botching, and the niceties of the business we can now only guess at.[24] The main trend of it is clear, though. In their Roman fashion, Gallus and Proculeius add force to diplomacy and manage to capture Cleopatra in her Monument. Proculeius finds a few moments with this tiger in a trap quite enough for him, and gladly gives place to Dolabella.

The passage that follows is a notable one. He fancies himself, does Dolabella; he is a ladies' man, and quite the jailer, surely, for this most wonderful of wantons.

> Most noble Empress, you have heard of me?

is his ingratiating beginning. From a Roman there is flattery in the very title; it owns her Antony's widow and ignores Octavia.

---

[24] This is discussed in more detail on p. 405.

She is far from responsive. She sulks and snarls, gives him half a glance, and forthwith breaks into invidious praise of her dead hero. But she knows she can twist the conceited fellow round her finger. She has only to turn to him with a smile, with an "I thank you, sir," and a "Nay, pray you, sir," and he promptly betrays his master to her, blurts out that, for all these comforting messages, Cæsar does mean to lead her chained in his Triumph. At which point Cæsar himself appears.

He comes in full state and circumstance, his staff surrounding him, guards clearing the way. And if Cleopatra thinks to impress him in turn, his opening sally might well damp her somewhat. For he faces this marvel among women as she stands there with her mere maids beside her, and coolly asks which of them is the Queen of Egypt. Which? And once it was

> Remember
> If e'er thou look'st on majesty.

The duel of lies that follows—a pretty piece of fighting!—epitomizes this second and subtler struggle. We have Egyptian against Roman now, neither with much simplicity left to shed; but Cleopatra, passionate and unstable, shows a very child beside Cæsar. She kneels, and he raises her. He repeats his smooth promises, and she smiles her gratitude, alive to the worth of them—had she ever doubted it!—thanks to coxcomb Dolabella. But, surely, for a man so very indifferent to her, he is a little anxious to be gone. Has she any hope of winning him, and does he suspect this? It is second nature in her to be wily with men—and to lie. Seleucus and the false inventory of "money, plate and jewels" make illuminating matter of dispute. Are not these barbarians to be bribed, and tricked too? Cæsar is neither to be tricked—nor shocked by the attempt made on him. And as for her raging and her nobly pathetic attitudes, he counters them, her lies and her flatteries, too, with the same cold smile. She is beaten. Even Seleucus can withstand her scoldings now; it is Cæsar, contemptuously considerate, who orders the man off. She is helpless in his clutches, but for the one sure escape. And he thinks, does he, to lure her from that with his lies? She fawns on him as he leaves her; let him think he has!

> He words me, girls, he words me, that I should not
> Be noble to myself! . . .

If any doubt were left, any chance of yet another of her accustomed conquests, Dolabella—the paltry proof that she still can conquer—comes back to disperse it.

> DOLABELLA.   Madam, as thereto sworn by your command,
>   Which my love makes religion to obey,
>   I tell you this: Cæsar through Syria
>   Intends his journey, and within three days
>   You with your children will he send before:
>   Make your best use of this: I have performed
>   Your pleasure and my promise.
> CLEOPATRA.   Dolabella,
>   I shall remain your debtor.[25]

She again makes his name sound beautiful in his ears (it is a name that can be lingered on), perhaps gives him her hand to kiss (he does not pay Thidias' price for the honor) and he goes. Her way is clear now to death.

But she has still to rise to that final, secure nobility, with which the sight of the dead Antony inspired her.

> and then, what's brave, what's noble,
> Let's do it after the high Roman fashion,
> And make death proud to take us . . . .

She climbs there by no straight path. The longing to die never leaves her. But we all long to die at times; and there is much protesting, a stealthy look or so for chances of escape, some backsliding into the old twisted passions; and she must at last lash herself—with, for company, poor frail Iras—through agony and beyond it before she can repose upon

> My resolution's placed, and I have nothing
> Of woman in me: now from head to foot
> I am marble-constant. . . .

Then, for one more mitigation before the play's last tragic height is reached, Shakespeare gives us the countryman and his figs. By

---

[25] He made no promise. At most he is so enthralled by her that he would have—feels, perhaps, he must have done. Here is an interesting instance of the way in which Shakespeare makes an *ex post facto* effect, which he knows will pass muster.

now (here is the art of it) Cleopatra is past bitterness or fear, and can smile and take the simple pleasure in his simplicity that we do. She jokes with him. This must have been, if one comes to think of it, not the least of her charms. When she would royally

> Hop forty paces through the public street . . .

how the people—the common people, so despised by Cæsar and the politicians—how evidently they would adore her! It is very right that one of them should bring her the comfort of death in a basket slung on his arm, and that she should trust him, and joke with him, a great lady at her ease.

From this she turns to a queenliness unapproached before.

> Give me my robe, put on my crown; I have
> Immortal longings in me . . . .

Long ago, we learn, a dead king's servants would be slaughtered around him. This is a still more royal death; for Iras' heart breaks silently at the sight of it, and Charmian only lags behind to set a crooked crown straight once again, and to send triumphant mockery echoing to Cæsar's ears.

He accepts his defeat like a gentleman, let us own. The ceremony of his coming matches the ceremony of her dying; and the end of the play, we should note, is sensibly delayed while they stand gazing—tough soldiers that they are—at a queen so strangely throned:

> she looks like sleep,
> As she would catch another Antony
> In her strong toil of grace.

The Staging

THE action makes no extraordinary calls upon an Elizabethan stage as we now think we know it to have been. Two things are noticeable, however. There are, for five-sixths of the play, few definite indications of the use of the inner stage. This keys with the scant localization of the scenes; the inner and upper stages are always likelier to be "places" than the main stage will be. But the full stage, *i.e.* the main stage with the inner stage curtains open and the inner stage itself accessible, would probably be used from the general entrance of Charmian, Iras, Mardian, Alexas, the

Soothsayer and the rest to Antony's departure for Rome; for all
Cleopatra's scenes while she sits waiting news of him—and receiving it; for the long scene of reconciliation between Antony and
Cæsar; and for the scene in Pompey's galley.[26] The intermediate
scenes will be played on the main stage, with the inner stage
curtains closed. When the battles begin it looks as if Cleopatra's
scenes again employed the inner stage (as hinterland at least to
the outer); she and Antony retiring to it or through it at such
points as

> Some wine within there, and our viands! . . .

> > > Let's to supper, come,
> And drown consideration.

—the curtains then closing on them. She may come from the
inner stage when she welcomes him from his victory; and

> > Through Alexandria make a jolly march . . .

may imply that they all pass back, as if into the city in triumph.
Cæsar's scenes, the marching and countermarching and the swifter
coming and going, take place on the main stage, that is clear.[27]
    Now comes disputable matter.

> *Enter Cleopatra and her Maides aloft, with Charmian and Iras.*

They are in the Monument, to which, in a moment, the dying
Antony has to be hoisted. There are two slight difficulties. The
hoisting of a full-grown man ten or twelve feet in the air asks
some strength. However, this could be provided ostensibly by the
"and her Maides," actually by stagehands helping from behind
the curtains; and Shakespeare makes dramatic capital out of the
apparent difficulty. But the upper stage of the public theater must
have had a balustrade at least three feet high. Swinging a dying
man over it and lowering him again asks some care. Granted this

---

[26] This, it may be said, was the normal way of employing the inner stage; the
action would seldom be wholly confined there. But furniture, and the localization
this implies, would tend to focus the action within its bounds. See also the Preface
to *Cymbeline*, p. 471 *et seq.*

[27] But the stage direction

> *Canidius marcheth with his land army one way over the stage,
> and Taurus, the lieutenant of Cæsar, the other way: After their
> going in . . .*

could be more slickly obeyed if there were an inner as well as an outer stage to
march over. With two doors only available, it will be a long-drawn-out affair.

done with skill and grace, what of the effect of the rest of the scene, of Antony's death and Cleopatra's lament over him, played behind the balustrade as behind bars? Clearly it would be a poor one. The balustrade must, one presumes, have been removed for the occasion or made to swing open, if the ordinary upper stage was used.[28]

When we next see Cleopatra she is obviously still in the Monument; as obviously she is not still upon such an upper stage as we believe the Globe's to have been. Nor is there any sign that—as with Romeo's farewell to Juliet and her encounter with her mother —the acting of the scene began above and finished below. The stage directions, however, are incomplete, and the text may have been altered. In the previous scene Proculeius and Gallus have been sent to parley with Cleopatra and keep her, if they can, from doing herself a mischief. By the Folio's stage direction only Proculeius arrives. A simple supposition is that he finds her on the inner stage behind a barred gate and speaks to her through it.[29] This at any rate reproduces Plutarch's "For Proculeius came to the gates that were very thick and strong, and surely barred; but yet there were some craneries through the which her voyce might be heard. . . ." When she has protested her submission he evidently makes as if to go, with

> This I'll report, dear lady.
> Have comfort, for I know your plight is pitied
> Of him that caused it.

But now, with no other speech nor stage direction intervening, the Folio has

> Pro. You see how easily she may be surpriz'd;
> Guard her till Cæsar come.

Modern editors (following Theobald in the main) give the speech to Gallus, whom they have brought on with Proculeius, and add:

> *Here Proculeius and two of the Guard ascend the*
> *monument by a ladder placed against a window,*

---

[28] There seems commonly to have been a trap in the floor of the upper stage. But the use of this and the need to place Antony directly under it would rob the dialogue—would rob the all-important "I am dying, Egypt, dying"—of much of its effect.

[29] Just such a barred gate as shuts in Juliet's tomb.

and, having descended, come behind Cleopatra.
Some of the Guard unbar and open the gates.[30]

A minor objection to this is that Gallus in the Folio is *persona muta*; the full speaking strength of the company is, we may well suppose, already employed, and here is a super. A more serious one must be that so much climbing up and climbing down again would take time. There is no concurrent dialogue, and a long pause at such a moment is dramatically unthinkable.[31]

No great difficulty arises if we see Gallus and the guard left at the door while Proculeius advances to the gate that bars the inner stage. Cleopatra would not see them. Let him give them the order quietly as he returns to the door, and, with no climbing involved, they can be upon the inner stage by the back way in a couple of seconds, seize Cleopatra and unbar the gates; and Gallus may well go off to report to Cæsar; his exit as his entrance, if he stays *persona muta*, being a likely omission from stage directions, which would need to be unwontedly elaborate if all this were to be made clear.[32]

The discussion is fairly barren from a modern producer's point of view; he can provide for all these exigencies without violating the text or distorting the action.

But if for this and all the rest of the action the recognized Elizabethan stage does not content him, then he must devise one which will not violate its fundamental liberties and laws—its liberties, above all. He will probably find in the end that he has devised something not so very different. If he is for painted scenes of *Cleopatra's palace, Cæsar's house, Antony's camp, The plain near Actium* and a variety of "other parts of the same"—well, the

---

[30] Thus, at least, the (English) Arden edition. But it also presumes (in a footnote) and the Oxford edition definitely states that Cleopatra has so far been upon the upper stage. How and when she gets down is left a mystery.

[31] Johnson proposed to insert part of the speech earlier so that the guards could come quietly behind and seize Cleopatra at the cue. But the three previous speeches allow of no such interruption. If Cleopatra had to be *brought* down to the lower stage, it would be ten times worse.

[32] There remains the unnatural hiatus between Proculeius' two speeches, if they are both his. Suppose that the upper stage to which Antony is hoisted were not the usual balcony, but something a little more accessible, to which the guards might climb without delay, and from which Cleopatra might be as easily brought down. The hiatus *may* point to some change in staging, or in the stage itself, or to the shifting of the play from one theater to another of different resources.

reading of this Preface will only have wasted his time. He must somehow provide a staging free from actuality of place; that is his main problem. He may decorate it; but if the decoration distracts us from the hearing of Shakespeare's lines—and they ask, as we have noted, pretty close attention—it will be a positive nuisance. It is a hard problem to solve; for one thing, because self-effacement is the rarest of artistic virtues. And let the decorator set out, however discreetly, to interpret the play in his own terms, if he find himself—and it is an ever-present danger—competing with the actors, the sole interpreters Shakespeare has licensed, then it is he that is the intruder, and he must retire. Even if his picturesque effects are but an anodyne to our vigilance—and much modern stage decoration is of this sort—they will do the play negative harm. We need to have our minds kept clear and alert. Still, if we cannot take the Elizabethan stage for granted as the Elizabethans did, producer and decorator must certainly face the problem of providing something that we can.

Costume

ONCE we are freed from pictures of Rome and Alexandria, brought (so to speak) archaeologically up to date, the difficulty of costume is not acute.

Cut my lace, Charmian.

summarizes it, and, upon a narrow view, may be said almost to exhaust it. Shakespeare's Cleopatra wore a stomacher of some sort, that is evident. But it is an error to suppose that Shakespeare dressed all his plays in the ordinary costume of his time. It is also an error, for that matter, to suppose that nowadays we all carry accurate pictures of the past in our minds. Dress Cleopatra as a Queen of the Tenth Dynasty instead of as an Alexandrian Greek, and how many of us would be the wiser? Careful research might find us an Alexandrian fashion plate of the right period with laces to cut (Sir Arthur Evans has brought us corsets from Knossos), but our conscientiously Egyptian Cleopatras have so far been left laceless and waistless, and the line without meaning.

In all this, as in everything else of the sort, the Elizabethans thought first and last—whether by choice or necessity—of dramatic profit. It is not likely that Shakespeare troubled to give a specifically French touch to *Love's Labour's Lost* and an Italian to *Much Ado About Nothing*; nor, had his knowledge run to it, would he probably have seen much gain in dressing Romeo and Juliet by "the paintings of Giotto and his pupils."[33] But when some dramatic end was to be served it is clear that he did not lack means of a kind, and he used them. In *Macbeth* the Scots and the English can be told apart, British and Romans in *Cymbeline*; and in this play, quite evidently, Roman and Egyptian stood in picturesque contrast. There would be little archaeology about the business and less consistency. We can guess at the sort of figures they made by turning to extant designs for the Court Masques. The theaters could not run, perhaps, to such splendor as that; but they were prosperous, finery was popular, and they probably did pretty well. Rome meant the romantic past, Egypt the exotic East; and Shakespeare would do what he could to capitalize both. The dialogue of the play is colored with every sort of allusion to the wonders of that far world, from the description of Cleopatra at Cydnus, to the talk of Syria and the Parthians, from the story of Antony in the Alps, from his call to Alcides his ancestor, to tales of "pyramises" and crocodiles.

We know better about all these things than did Shakespeare; but it is too late now to put him right. We have to interpret, not to correct him; we are committed even to his errors. Our concern is with the Egypt and Rome of his imagination, not of our own. The difference is manifest less in this detail or the other than in the whole texture of the play. Cut the knot of the "Cut my lace, Charmian" difficulty, and there is still the larger problem. In the National Gallery hangs Paolo Veronese's "Alexander and the Wife and Daughter of Darius." This will be very much how Shakespeare saw his Roman figures habited. Antony would wear Alexander's mixture of doublet, breastplate, sandals and hose. Here too is something very like Octavia's costume; and though Cleopatra might be given some Egyptian stigmata, there would

---

[33] This is how Charles Knight tells us they should be dressed (I quote from the quotation in Furness). "But," he adds, "for the younger and lighter characters ... some very different habit would be expected by the million, and indeed, desired by the artist." He is writing in the mid-nineteenth century. The quest for accuracy in these matters is a new thing.

still be laces to cut. It is all grievously incorrect; but we do not like
the picture less for that, nor are students set to copy it and told to
redraw the costume in the light of the latest information available.
Its good painting apart, we even gain by its being a Renaissance
view of a Classic subject, for the spirit of the picture is in that.
Now, no one will contend that by clothing Antony and Cleopatra
and Cæsar and ordering their Court and their armies according
to our modern imagination we shall crush the dramatic life out of
them, for this is rooted far deeper. But we shall at every moment,
both on the main issue and in countless little ways, be falsifying
Shakespeare, and doing him far more damage than the simple
logic of the case implies. We do him, of all dramatists, great damage. For he has an extraordinary faculty of making the great
things vivid to us by means of the little things, by just such
strokes, in fact, as that

> Cut my lace, Charmian.

This play is exceptionally full of them, very homely things; and
it is bare chance that one of the finest, Charmian's

> Your crown's awry:
> I'll mend it, and then play.

does not get us into more sartorial trouble. He has absorbed Rome
and Egypt into his own consciousness; but it is a consciousness
opening upon his own world, not the historical Antony's, and
naturally not upon our vision of that.

Shakespeare in modern dress is as inappropriate as archaeological Shakespeare, and for the same good reason. And the very
argument that great drama is not dependent upon its trimmings
should surely help us to accept the trimmings that we find. Cleopatra in a farthingale! The orthodox playgoer may turn pale at
the thought. But surrender to the idea that this is Shakespeare's
Cleopatra we are looking at, not the product of our schoolbooks
(is that more difficult than to look up from our program and
admit that the well-known Miss Blank, lately seen as Nora in
A Doll's House, is the real thing?), and by the end of the first
scene the oddity will be forgotten; and thenceforward we shall be
anachronism-proof. There will be one further gain. An historical
play of any sort has a double victory to win; the play's own and

a victory over our preconceptions of its history. The less familiar its figures the better the chance of the play with us—as a play.

The Music

TRUMPETS and cornets and drums are needed; and the flourishes, the sounding of a sennet, the beating of the drums have each their import. Enobarbus is borne away dying to the sound of *Drummes afarre offe*. A consort of woodwind is also used. The "hoboyes" play under the stage, and their pungent vibrations should make excellent assault on the nerves.

The music for the revels on Pompey's galley is given to woodwind (the accompaniment of the song included), trumpets and drums reinforcing it occasionally. The clamor is insisted on.

> Make battery to our ears with the loud music. . . .
> These drums! these trumpets, flutes, what!
> Let Neptune hear we bid a loud farewell
> To these great fellows: sound and be hanged, sound out!

It is a soldiers' revel. But it never slips from the distinction of poetry; and the song itself—the boy's voice singing it—is like light beside the darkness of Menas' whisper to Pompey:

> These three world-sharers, these competitors,
> Are in thy vessel: let me cut the cable;
> And, when we are put off, fall to their throats. . . .

The scene falls midway through the play. It is a rest point in the action. Shakespeare has taken care to give it solidity, variety and color.

Cleopatra calls once for music, but countermands it with her next breath. She would have needed a consort of viols; and it is possible that strings and woodwind both were more than could be always reasonably demanded at one performance.

The Verse and Its Speaking

ROME and its Empire are ever a clarion call to Shakespeare's imagination; and the strength of his answer to it lies in his power to make the alien characters his own. For he leaves them in no classic immunity, casting his care upon their impressive reputations. They must be sifted through his dramatist's conscience; he brings them to terms on the ground of common humanity. What is Cleopatra's passport to tragic heights?

> No more but e'en a woman, and commanded
> By such poor passion as the maid that milks
> And does the meanest chares. . . .

With this, of course, they risk the loss of their conventionally heroic stature. But it is preserved for them by the magic of poetry.

This is literally a sort of magic, by which the vibrations of emotion that the sound of the poetry sets up seem to enlarge its sense, and break the bounds of the theater to carry us into the lost world of romantic history. Conceive such a story and such characters so familiarly, and then tie their expression to plain prose—Dido will be in danger of becoming a dowdy indeed, and Cleopatra a gypsy. But Shakespeare has traveled far since Mercutio could thus mock Romeo's poetic prowess, and is now himself by no means "for the numbers that Petrarch flowed in." He has come to the writing of a verse which combines actuality and power, and is malleable to every diversity of character and mood. Here and there we may begin to feel a strain. Sometimes emotion will not quite vivify thought, which stays constricted or confused; or a too constant repetition of effect or an oversimplifying of simplicity may show fatigue. But Shakespeare has always had the tact to seize on the subject that will best fit his artist's mood, or to adapt mood and method to subject—which, it is not our business to inquire. And in its qualities and defects alike his present method and ability, resourceful, audacious, spontaneous, ripe if to over-ripeness, fit this subject most consummately well.

Big though the task will be, he feels no need to economize his strength. He begins at what a pitch!

> Nay, but this dotage of our general's
> O'erflows the measure; those his goodly eyes,
> That o'er the files and musters of the war
> Have glow'd like plated Mars, now bend, now turn,
> The office and devotion of their view
> Upon a tawny front: his captain's heart,
> Which in the scuffles of great fights hath burst
> The buckles on his breast, reneges all temper,

> And is become the bellows and the fan
> To cool a gipsy's lust.

Ample and virile in substance, consonant in its music. One tremendous sentence, the ends of the lines not answering to pauses either; these, such as they are, fall midway (a bare four of them in nine lines and more, though), so that fresh impulse may overleap the formal division, and the force be the force of the whole. Note, too, the placing of the dominant "o'erflows the measure" and its complement "reneges all temper" with the doubled parenthesis between them, and how the "now bend, now turn" saves this from slackness; how "files and musters" and "office and devotion" strengthen the beat of the verse, with "plated Mars" coming like the sudden blare of a trumpet, and "burst the buckles on his breast" to sound the exploding indignation which culminates in the deadly

> And is become the bellows and the fan
> To cool a gipsy's lust.

A fairly opulent dramatic allowance for this Philo, of whom we know nothing, are never to see again. But throughout the play we shall find the least considered characters, and on no special occasion, with as meaty stuff—is there a better term for it?—in their mouths. Mæcenas greets Octavia, upon her disillusioned return, with

> Welcome, dear Madam.
> Each heart in Rome does love and pity you:
> Only the adulterous Antony, most large
> In his abominations, turns you off;
> And gives his potent regiment to a trull,
> That noises it against us.

The anonymous legionary, even, has no less vivid and stirring a moment to his share than

> O noble emperor, do not fight by sea;
> Trust not to rotten planks: do you misdoubt
> This sword and these my wounds? Let the Egyptians
> And the Phœnicians go a-ducking: we
> Have used to conquer, standing on the earth,
> And fighting foot to foot.

And from Pompey in his first scene (Shakespeare himself well into his stride by this!) comes the full enrichment of

But all the charms of love,
Salt Cleopatra, soften thy waned lip!
Let witchcraft join with beauty, lust with both!
Tie up the libertine in a field of feasts,
Keep his brain fuming; Epicurean cooks
Sharpen with cloyless sauce his appetite;
That sleep and feeding may prorogue his honour
Even till a Lethe'd dullness.

Too much rich writing of this sort would be like Cleopatra's feasts, and clog the march of the action. But when mere argument is in hand we fall back to nothing less pedestrian than Antony's

Sir,
He fell upon me ere admitted: then
Three kings I had newly feasted, and did want
Of what I was i' the morning: but, next day,
I told him of myself; which was as much
As to have asked him pardon. Let this fellow
Be nothing of our strife: if we contend
Out of our question wipe him.

This, and such a passage as Cæsar's somewhat smug

Let's grant it is not
Amiss to tumble in the bed of Ptolemy;
To give a kingdom for a mirth; to sit
And keep the turn of tippling with a slave;
To reel the streets at noon, and stand the buffet
With knaves that smell of sweat; say this becomes him—
As his composure must be rare indeed
Whom these things cannot blemish—yet must Antony
No way excuse his foils, when we do bear
So great weight in his lightness.

or as Pompey's

To you all three,
The senators alone of this great world,
Chief factors for the gods,—I do not know
Wherefore my father should revengers want,
Having a son and friends, since Julius Cæsar,
Who at Philippi the good Brutus ghosted,
There saw you labouring for him.

may be taken as the norm of the play's poetic method, upon

which its potencies are built up. And it is upon this norm, of course, that the actors must model their own style.

The elemental oratory of this verse needs for its speaking a sense of rhythm that asks no help of strict rule. Shakespeare is so secure by now in the spirit of its laws that the letter may go. He does not commonly stray far. A cæsura may fall oddly or there may be none distinguishable, a syllable or so may splash over at the end. Dramatic emphasis is the thing, first and last; to get that right he will sacrifice strict meter—yet never music—grammar now and then, and at a pinch, if need be, exact sense too.

These freedoms gain in effect as the play's temper heightens. Cæsar's calculated indignation is sounded in the two swelling catalogues:

> I'the common show place where they exercise.
> His sons he there proclaimed the kings of kings:
> Great Media, Parthia and Armenia
> He gave to Alexander; to Ptolemy he assign'd
> Syria, Cilicia and Phœnicia. . . .
>
> > He hath assembled
> Bocchus, the king of Libya; Archelaus
> Of Cappadocia. . . .

The latter passage has been quoted already; the scansion is highly individual.

But no Cleopatra, with an ear, can miss the shrill arrogance of

> Sink Rome, and their tongues rot
> That speak against us! A charge we bear i' the war,
> And, as the president of my kingdom, will
> Appear there for a man. Speak not against it;
> I will not stay behind.

The upward run of semiquavers in "A charge we bear i' the war" is as plain as any musical stave could make it; and the pauses seem to mark so many snaps of the jaw. The lines are not, of course, here or elsewhere to be reckoned by syllables, but by beat.

Listen, on the other hand, to the weary descent to depression's depths in Antony's

> Fall not a tear, I say; one of them rates
> All that is won and lost: give me a kiss;
> Even this repays me. We sent our schoolmaster;
> Is 'a come back? Love, I am full of lead.

—given us by a regular caesura, followed by an irregular one, followed by a mid-line full stop; the line then finished with an effort by the banal "We sent our schoolmaster" (who could get anything but exhaustion out of that "schoolmaster"?); the next line with its dead monosyllables dragging after, the pause in the middle made the longer because of them. Then comes a sudden rally in the rhymed couplet:

> Some wine, within there, and our viands! Fortune knows
> We scorn her most when most she offers blows.

—its irregular first line just saving it from sounding mechanical.

The violence of Antony's anger when he finds Thidias kissing Cleopatra's hand has its own notation and tune.

> Approach there! Ah, you kite! Now, gods and devils!
> Authority melts from me. Of late, when I cried 'Ho!',
> Like boys unto a muss, kings would start forth
> And cry 'Your will?' Have you no ears?
> I am Antony yet. Take hence this jack and whip him.

Long lines, giving a sense of great strength. Exclamatory phrases, prefacing and setting off the powerful center-phrase, with its ringing "kings" for a top note. The caesura-pause of two beats that the short line allows is followed by the repeated crack of two more short phrases, the first with its upward lift, the second with its nasal snarl and the sharp click of its ending; the last line lengthens out, and the business finishes with the bitten *staccato* of

> Take hence this jack and whip him.

Note the deadly flick of the last two words!

The sense apart, what an almost willful pathos we feel in the smoothly sustained, one- and two-syllable worded, predominantly thin-vowelled speech of Antony's to the weeping servants!

> Tend me to-night;
> May be it is the period of your duty:
> Haply you shall not see me more; or if,
> A mangled shadow: perchance to-morrow
> You'll serve another master. I look on you
> As one that takes his leave. Mine honest friends,
> I turn you not away; but, like a master
> Married to your good service, stay till death.
> Tend me to-night two hours. I ask no more;
> And the gods yield you for 't.

Note in particular the importance given to "A mangled shadow" by the sustaining tripled consonant, and the two-beat pause that follows ("to-morrow," with its weak ending, ranking for a dissyllable), and how the repeated, "Tend me to-night" rounds in the speech a trifle artificially.

Throughout these scenes, throughout the play indeed, one can so analyze the verse, find its rhythm and music, often transcending rule, but always close fitted to mood and meaning. The best moments need no analysis, and seem to defy it. One must not appear to be praising.

> I am dying, Egypt, dying; only
> I here importune death awhile, until
> Of many thousand kisses the poor last
> I lay upon thy lips.
>   I dare not, dear—,
> Dear, my lord, pardon,—I dare not,
> Lest I be taken:

merely for the way in which a short first line allows for the two silent breaths that will show Antony's flagging strength, nor for the infallible accenting of Cleopatra's fear, first upon the "dare," and then, with repetition, upon the "not." But actors have to concern themselves with such impertinences.

The passionate hysteria of her

>   Where art thou, death?
> Come hither, come! come, come, and take a queen
> Worth many babes and beggars!

PROCULEIUS.   O, temperance, lady!
CLEOPATRA.   Sir, I will eat no meat, I'll not drink, sir—
                  If idle talk will once be necessary—
                  I'll not sleep neither: this mortal house I'll
                  ruin . . . .

asks neither comment nor analysis. Why waste time trying to scan the last line? It is right, and not the extremest perversity could speak it wrongly, one would suppose. Nor will much more be gained by trying to extract meaning from the last line but one. If it has any in particular (which seems doubtful) no audience could be made to grasp it. But as a setting of hysterical gibbering to verbal music, it is perfect.

But one technical excellence among many it is hard to pass by. As Shakespeare nears the last great moment, that of Cleopatra's death, he wants to give his verse solid strength and dignity; and the pulse of it now throbs with a steady intensity, goes processionally forward, as it were.

> Give me my robe, put on my crown; I have
> Immortal longings in me: now no more
> The juice of Egypt's grape shall moist this lip.
> Yare, yare, good Iras: quick! Methinks I hear
> Antony call; I see him rouse himself
> To praise my noble act; I hear him mock
> The luck of Cæsar, which the gods give men
> To excuse their after wrath. . . .

Regular meter, saved from formality by the subtle variety of the mid-line stopping; the whole welded into unity by the constant carrying-on of the sentences from line to line. But, lest the effect grow all too set, Charmian is let interpose, a little later, not a single line but one and a half. Then, lest life die out of it, we have—after the added emphasis of an irregular line, in which Cleopatra lays hands on the asp with a heavily accentuated "Come . . ."—the words clipped, the pace quickened. Twice more Charmian interrupts, but now with phrases that sustain rather than break the rhythm.

> CLEOPATRA.   Come, thou mortal wretch,
> With thy sharp teeth this knot intrinsicate
> Of life at once untie; poor venomous fool,
> Be angry, and despatch. O, could'st thou speak,
> That I might hear thee call great Cæsar ass
> Unpolicied!
> CHARMIAN.   O eastern star!
> CLEOPATRA.   Peace, peace!
> Dost thou not see my baby at my breast,
> That sucks the nurse asleep?
> CHARMIAN.   O break! O break!
> CLEOPATRA. As sweet as balm, as soft as air, as gentle!
> O, Antony!—Nay, I will take thee too:
> What should I stay—?

Not one beat has been missed till her dying breaks the last line; yet we have been no more conscious of the form than when the verse was at its loosest, only of the added power.

Shakespeare no longer divides his characters into speakers of verse and speakers of prose, nor makes this distinction regularly between scenes. The freedom and variety of his verse writing allow him to pass almost imperceptibly from poetry to prose and back again. Thus he ranges an unbroken scale, from a pedestrian exactitude in stating plain fact at one end of it to the conventional flourish of the rhymed couplet at the other. But he can still make the sharp contrast of a change effective between scene and scene; or in the midst of a scene he can bring passion or pretentiousness down to earth—and prose, or as suddenly restore force and dignity with rhythm and tone. And he can go to work more subtly than that. As in stagecraft, so in his play's actual writing, exploiting freedom to the full, he has forged a weapon of extraordinary suppleness and resource.

For instance, in the ostensibly prose scene that follows the play's more formal opening, we have the Soothsayer countering Charmian's impudent chatter with single lines of verse. Their recurrence lends him peculiarity and a slight portentousness; but the surrounding prose is so subtly adjusted that the device itself passes unnoticed.[34] Later, upon Cleopatra's entrance, the scene is suddenly braced to forcefulness by half a dozen consecutive lines of (not too regular, lest the effect be too noticeable) verse. Later still, with a strong dose of prose, Enobarbus turns Antony's philosophic realism very much the seamy side out.

Enobarbus (he in particular) speaks now verse, now prose, either as the scene requires it of him for harmony or contrast, or as his humors dictate; his character being just such a compound of contrasts. Antony only occasionally relapses to prose, and his verse is regular on the whole. Cleopatra hardly touches prose at all; her verse is apt to be a little freer. Cæsar speaks only verse; it is fairly formal, and expressive of his calculated dignity.

But the supreme virtue of the writing lies in its peculiar combination of delicacy and strength, of richness with simplicity. For simple strength take the quick passage in which Menas tempts Pompey to put to sea and then cut the throats of his guests.

MENAS.   Wilt thou be lord of all the world?
POMPEY.   What say'st thou?

---

[34] We also find Enobarbus entering with a blank verse line. The scene, it is true (see p. 372), shows some signs of rewriting.

MENAS.   Wilt thou be lord of the whole world? That's twice.
POMPEY.   How should that be?
MENAS.   But entertain it,
And though thou think me poor, I am the man
Will give thee all the world.

For simplicity, Cleopatra's

O well-divided disposition! Note him,
Note him, good Charmian, 'tis the man; but note him.
He was not sad, for he would shine on those
That make their looks by his; he was not merry;
Which seemed to tell them his remembrance lay
In Egypt with his joy; but between both:
O heavenly mingle!

For delicacy, her

But bid farewell and go: when you sued staying,
Then was the time for words: no going then;
Eternity was in our lips and eyes,
Bliss in our brows' bent; none our parts so poor,
But was a race of heaven. . . .

or Antony's

Come, let's all take hands;
Till that the conquering wine hath steeped our sense
In soft and delicate Lethe.

or his picture of Octavia:

Her tongue will not obey her heart, nor can
Her heart inform her tongue—the swan's down-feather,
That stands upon the swell at the full of tide,
And neither way inclines.

For strength, his malediction of Cleopatra:

You were half-blasted ere I knew you; ha!
Have I my pillow left unpressed in Rome,
Forborne the getting of a lawful race,
And by a gem of women, to be abused
By one that looks on feeders?

or his dismissal of the half-flayed Thidias.

Get thee back to Cæsar;
Tell him thy entertainment: look thou say
He makes me angry with him; for he seems

> Proud and disdainful, harping on what I am,
> Not what he knew I was. He makes me angry;
> And at this time most easy 'tis to do't,
> When my good stars, that were my former guides,
> Have empty left their orbs, and shot their fires
> Into the abysm of hell.

We constantly have that favorite device, the enrichment of a simple effect by an echoing phrase; as when Cleopatra turns to Antony in pathetic dignity with

> Sir, you and I must part, but that's not it:
> Sir, you and I have loved, but there's not it. . . .

—as in the Soothsayer's response to Antony's command to him to speak no more:

> To none but thee; no more, but when to thee.

The thought also is echoed in Cleopatra's

> That time—O, times!—
> I laughed him out of patience; and that night
> I laughed him into patience: and next morn
> Ere the ninth hour, I drunk him to his bed. . . .

and in Enobarbus' remorseful

> This blows my heart:
> If swift thought break it not, a swifter mean
> Shall outstrike thought: but thought will do't, I feel.

Such devices easily degenerate into trick; as this comes near to doing with Cleopatra's

> These hands do lack nobility, that they strike
> A meaner than myself; since I myself
> Have given myself the cause.

—even as the power of concentration which can pack three clear thoughts into those seven words of hers:

> Therefore be deaf to my unpitied folly . . . .

has overreached itself a moment earlier in

> O, my oblivion is a very Antony,
> And I am all forgotten.

The most delicate and precise accenting of the "oblivion" and the "all" may fail to make the meaning of this last clear upon the instant.

But we have concentration, clarity, strength, simplicity all combined in the swift exchange between Alexas and Cleopatra when he brings her the first news of the absent Antony with

> His speech sticks in my heart.
> Mine ear must pluck it thence.

she answers; and in her dark misgiving as the unlucky second messenger faces her:

> But, sirrah, mark, we use
> To say the dead are well: bring it to that,
> The gold I give thee I will melt and pour
> Down thy ill-uttering throat.

and in the primitive

> Call the slave again:
> Though I am mad, I will not bite him: call!

Such things seem easy only when they are done—and well done.

Again, there is artistry of the subtlest in the freedom and apparent ease of this (the same wretched messenger is now atoning for his fault by disparaging Octavia, Charmian abetting him):

MESSENGER.   She creeps:
> Her motion and her station are as one;
> She shows a body rather than a life,
> A statue than a breather.
CLEOPATRA.   Is this certain?
MESSENGER.   Or I have no observance.
CHARMIAN.   Three in Egypt
> Cannot make better note.
CLEOPATRA.   He's very knowing;
> I do perceive 't: there's nothing in her yet;
> The fellow has good judgment.
CHARMIAN.   Excellent.
CLEOPATRA.   Guess at her years, I prithee.
MESSENGER.   Madam,
> She was a widow.—
CLEOPATRA.   Widow! Charmian, hark!

—in the way the continuing swing of the verse keeps the dialogue swift while the dividing of the lines gives spontaneity.

Note how actual incoherence—kept within bounds by the strict rhythm of the verse—leads up to, and trebles the nobility of a

culminating phrase. (She and her women surround the dead
Antony.)

> How do you, women?
> What, what, good cheer? Why, how now, Charmian!
> My noble girls! Ah women, women, look!
> Our lamp is spent, it's out. Good sirs, take heart:
> We'll bury him; and then, what's brave, what's noble,
> Let's do it after the high Roman fashion,
> And make death proud to take us. . . .

The compelled swiftness of the beginning, the change without
check when she turns to the soldiers, the accordant discipline of
the line which follows, so that the last two lines can come out
clarion-clear; here, again, is dramatic music exactly scored. In like
fashion Antony's mixed metaphors (when he has been told she
is dead), which include something very like a pun, lead up to and
enhance a luminous close.

> I will o'ertake thee, Cleopatra, and
> Weep for my pardon. So it must be, for now
> All length is torture: since the torch is out,
> Lie down and stray no farther: now all labour
> Mars what it does: yea, very force entangles
> Itself with strength: seal then, and all is done.
> Eros!—I come, my queen: Eros!—Stay for me:
> Where souls do couch on flowers, we'll hand in hand,
> And with our sprightly port make the ghosts gaze:
> Dido and her Æneas shall want troops,
> And all the haunt be ours.

While, for a glorious and famous passage that is music itself—but
what more?—take:

> O see, my women,
> The crown o' the earth doth melt. My lord!
> O, withered is the garland of the war,
> The soldier's pole is fall'n: young boys and girls
> Are level now with men; the odds is gone,
> And there is nothing left remarkable
> Beneath the visiting moon.

This, in analysis, is little better than ecstatic nonsense; and it is
meant to sound so. It has just enough meaning in it for us to feel
as we hear it that it may have a little more. Art must by so much
at least improve on nature; in nature it would have less or none.

But it gives us to perfection the reeling agony of Cleopatra's mind; therefore, in its dramatic setting, it ranks as supreme poetry.

Utterly sure of himself, Shakespeare has, in fine, reached in the writing as in the shaping of this play limits of freedom and daring that he will not, but for the worse, overpass.

The Characters

ANTONY

IN the two early episodes of his breaking from Egypt and of his welcome to Rome Antony is painted for us in breadth and detail; they give us the man complete, and thereafter the drama of his actions needs no alloy of analysis or explanation.

Shakespeare's first strokes seldom fail to be significant. The four words to the messenger, who crosses Antony's uncharted path as he and Cleopatra saunter by, with

> News, my good lord, from Rome.
> Grates me! The sum?

(the harsh, impatient, yet slightly conscience-stricken sound of it!); the next three to Cleopatra:

> How, my love?

(the softened vowels!), then the full diapason of the heroic, yet fustian-flavored

> Let Rome in Tiber melt, and the wide arch
> Of the ranged empire fall! . . .

—here, in a few phrases, we have the gallant grown old and the confident conqueror in decline. He passes on; the keynote has been struck. But Philo's sad, scrupulous

> Sir, sometimes when he is not Antony,
> He comes too short of that great property
> Which still should go with Antony.

promises, and Cleopatra's descent upon her giggling maids preludes another tune in him with

CLEOPATRA. Saw you my lord?
ENOBARBUS. No, lady.
CLEOPATRA. Was he not here?

CHARMIAN. No, madam.
CLEOPATRA. He was disposed to mirth; but on the sudden
           A Roman thought hath struck him. . . .

She sees him coming and will have him see her go, her offended
nose in the air. But if he does he ignores her.[35]

The so-lately snubbed messenger is with him, talking, and
encouraged to, as man to man. (These messengers, by the bye,
are not errand boys, but men of responsibility.) This is the Antony—or little less than he—that could coolly outface and out-
scheme the mob of Cæsar's murderers, outgeneral the ideologue
Brutus and Cassius the fanatic; it is Antony the realist, and never
a starker one than when he needs to see himself coldly and clearly
as he is. And he is enough a master of men to dare to let them see
him so!

           Who tells me true, though in his tale lie death,
           I hear him as he flattered.

This encounter with the messengers sets him very relentlessly
before us. Shakespeare has never had more illusions about Antony
than he about himself. In *Julius Cæsar* how swiftly the heroics of
the Capitol and the flattering eloquence of the Forum were followed by the calm proposal to Lepidus and Octavius to cheat the
citizens, whose hearts he had just won, of part of their legacies;
and, Lepidus being sent on this errand, to jockey *him* next out of
his share of the spoils. But, whatever he was at, there was a sportsmanlike gaiety about him then. He has grown colder with the
years, cynically philosophical. It is a quality of greatness in a man,
no doubt, that seeks the truth and sees it even in himself, boldly
lets others see it. But such truth, seen and shown with such indifference! Colder; and callous, one adds.

The second messenger's appearance is heralded by ominous
hesitations. (The play abounds in these delicacies of craftsmanship.) And, when he does appear, Antony, by that unusual

---

[35] The Folio gives us Antony's entrance before Cleopatra's line

           We will not look upon him; go with us.

Modern editions are too apt to place it after, and after her departure, quite
obliterating the intended effect. There is even the shadow of a further one. If
Enobarbus has already gone to look for Antony, it is with a little train of Egyptians
that Cleopatra sails off, leaving the barbarian Romans to their business.

What are you?

reads trouble in the sight of him. The answer comes straight:

Fulvia thy wife is dead.

The response, the curt question,

Where died she?

makes no sentimental pretenses; and, the messenger dismissed, he is as honest with himself.

> There's a great spirit gone! Thus did I desire it.
> What our contempts doth often hurl from us,
> We wish it ours again: the present pleasure
> By revolution lowering, does become
> The opposite of itself.—She's good, being gone . . . .

And Enobarbus, summoned to make ready for departure, is in talk with him a minute or more before, casually abrupt, he says

> Fulvia is dead.
> Sir?
> Fulvia is dead.
> Fulvia!
> Dead.

We recall Brutus and Cassius and Portia's death.[36] This also, then, would seem to be in "the high Roman fashion." But how truly English, too, the avoidance of the subject, the curt exchange to hide emotion—which, it may be, is not there to hide!

Enobarbus' frank brutalities lend by contrast dignity to his chief, as, lost now in "Roman thoughts," he passes on to take his leave of Cleopatra. He knows her

cunning past man's thought. . .

He is free of her forever if he would be; and it is hardly, one would say, a very fatal passion that shows in his farewell. He looks for tantrums.

I am sorry to give breathing to my purpose . . . .

An uncomfortably polite opening; it is an awkward business.

---

[36] *Brutus.*   No man bears sorrow better. Portia is dead.
    Cassius.   Ha! Portia!
    Brutus.   Dead.

She plays her every pretty trick on him; but she can tell that the Roman thought has, for the moment, conquered.[37] His protests come easily; she makes short work of them. She stirs him to candor by twitting him with "Liar"; but she unmasks more reality than she bargained for.

> Hear me, queen.
> The strong necessity of time commands
> Our services awhile. . . .

—and when Antony bites thus on his words, it is as well to be silent and listen. We are at the pivot of the scene, its revealing moment. He unfolds for her, with all the force of his mind, his tangled task ahead. She listens indifferently: what are politics and Sextus Pompeius to her? Then he adds—as if it were an item forgotten in the sum—

> My more particular,
> And that which most with you should safe my going,
> Is Fulvia's death.

Spoiled wanton of a woman she may be, but she has a sensitiveness he lacks and a humanity he has lost. On the instant there possesses her such a sense of the pitiful transient littleness of life:

> Though age from folly could not give me freedom
> It does from childishness. Can Fulvia 'die'?

—of her own life too, and of their love:

> Now I see, I see,
> In Fulvia's death, how mine received shall be.

Yet the next instant she is trifling it away and at her tricks again.

The duel goes on, he obstinately asserting that it is all to her queenly advantage he should go, she pricking and stinging him with her woman's grievances. She cannot change his purpose, but she knows how to conquer in retreat.

> But, sir, forgive me,
> Since my becomings kill me when they do not
> Eye well to you! Your honour calls you hence:
> Therefore be deaf to my unpitied folly,
> And all the gods go with you. Upon your sword

---

[37] Note a technicality. Cleopatra has not to be told that he is going; she guesses or has already heard; she saw him, indeed, confabulating with that fatal messenger. This starts the scene at the needed pitch; no time is wasted working up to it.

> Sit laurel victory! and smooth success
> Be strewed before your feet!

That, she sees to it, shall be his remembrance of her.

He is found next in Rome, confronting Cæsar and outtopping him; and by how much more the lesser men around, Lepidus, Agrippa, Mæcenas and the rest. In this scene and those deriving from it we have Antony at his ablest, the seasoned statesman. That prefatory hint at his soldiership, peaceably though he now comes,

> 'Tis spoken well,
> Were we before our armies and to fight,
> I should do thus.

the quick opening of the argument, when courtesies with Cæsar have been exchanged,

> I learn, you take things ill that are not so,
> Or, being, concern you not.

give him vantage of position. He has, it would appear, a poor enough case to plead. He makes neither useless defense nor impulsive apology, but with clever dialectic shapes the issue, as far as may be, to his liking. Cæsar is pettish, but Antony—diplomatist that he is—remains proof against pin-pricks. He even jokes about the dead Fulvia and her "garboils."

> As for my wife,
> I would you had her spirit in such another.
> The third o' the world is yours, which with a snaffle
> You may pace easy, but not such a wife.

He makes shrugging confession of his own failings; and in all so takes the wind out of Cæsar's sails that that self-conscious respectability is stung at last into taxing this elderly scapegrace point blank with perjury—very much to Lepidus' alarm. Antony still stays unruffled. But, with his adversary trapped into such rashness, we can feel his wrist harden and see the steely eye above the easy smile.

> No,
> Lepidus, let him speak:
> The honour is sacred which he talks on now,
> Supposing that I lacked it. But, on, Cæsar;
> The article of my oath.

Cæsar does not shirk; but he speaks now by the card. Antony (in his own phrase) paces them all with a snaffle. Let them take no liberties, though. He may jest about Egypt; they had better not.

Then Mæcenas and Agrippa take up their allotted part in the peacemaking. The marriage with Octavia is broached.

> great Mark Antony
> Is now a widower.

The outmatched Cæsar cannot resist a malicious gibe.

> Say not so, Agrippa:
> If Cleopatra heard you, your reproof
> Were well deserved of rashness.

He earns the snub direct.

> I am not married, Cæsar: let me hear
> Agrippa further speak.

But business is business, and a peace is patched up between the two, "according to plan."

From now to the consummating of the treaty with Pompey, and thereafter to the brotherly parting with Cæsar, Antony stands in the sun. These men know his worth to them and he knows it. Secure in reputation, he can be generous to Pompey, who girds at him too; he is even civil to Lepidus. And he brings to Octavia such a boyish penitence—

> My Octavia,
> Read not my blemishes in the world's report:
> I have not kept my square; but that to come
> Shall all be done by the rule.

—that how should we not, with the good Mæcenas, trust to her beauty, wisdom and modesty to settle his chastened heart? But Enobarbus has warned us betimes; and we see him, on the instant, turn from her to the Soothsayer, that sinister shadow of his bewitchment; and the very next we hear is

> I will to Egypt:
> And though I make this marriage for my peace,
> I' the East my pleasure lies.

He is lost. And the significant thing is that he sinks without an effort from sanity to folly. He has won back his lost ground. We have seen him, with easy authority, outmatching Cæsar, and

Cæsar, for all his jealousy, shrewdly content to be outmatched. Yet here he is flinging everything away. This is not the Antony of Philippi, of the Capitol and the Forum. His spirit all afraid to govern him near Cæsar! Is it, indeed!? Cæsar has all the luck at dicing and cockfighting. No doubt! But the naked truth is that the sensual man in him must find excuse for the

> I will to Egypt. . . .
> I' the East my pleasure lies.

and any is better than none.

This is the nemesis of the sensual man. Till now Antony's appetites have not fatally played him false. Such gifts and vitality as his can for long enough make the best of both worlds, the sensual and the world of judgment too; for life is bred in passion, and has continuing need of it. But the time comes when Nature finds no more profit in a man, and her saving graces fail him. Antony has never learned to bargain with life; his abundant strength could take politics and love-affairs, interest and inclination in its stride. And now that judgment does pull one way and appetite another there is neither struggle nor dispute, no overt choice made, even. Appetite wins, while judgment winks and ignores defeat. He knows what going back to Cleopatra means.

> These strong Egyptian fetters I must break,
> Or lose myself in dotage.

Yet in the very knitting-up of the new ties that are to save him from her he can say, "I'll go," nor seem to count the cost. He speaks his own doom in a careless phrase—and forgets it. He will have his chance to make a brave show still and a nobler end; but shameful, secret moments such as this are the true counterpart to that earlier conscienceless success. No agony, nor darkening of the spirit before defeat, nor a Promethean defiance of the partial gods. This hero's fate is sealed quite casually, in a talk with a soothsayer about dice and fighting cocks.

Shakespeare adds yet one more touch to his disintegrating. Antony, we shall remember, came with Ventidius to the conference, saying

> If we compose well here, to Parthia.

—to avenge his Egypt-bred defeats there. But now it is

> O, come, Ventidius,
> *You* must to Parthia.

while he will wait the chance to step back to his sty.

This phase of the study of him, in sober businesslike relation to Cæsar and his fellow-Romans, gives great ballast to the play. Cleopatra's hectic scenes stand in current contrast to it, and it is steadying preparation for the violence of the end. It is prose in its temper, but the pitch and swing of the actual verse lend it a more heroic life. There come no exciting clashes; but these close-woven contrasts of character that are its substance are the very stuff of drama.

Shakespeare is never the vindictive moralist, scourging a man with his sins, blind to all else about him. Antony's ending, when we reach it, is of a piece with his life. It is the garment of his good fortune turned inside out; and if some virtues have more luster, some vices are more tolerable in failure than success. Once again, here is no spiritual tragedy of ideals betrayed. The man has had what he wanted from the world; with luck, daring and judgment to bring it him. A debauched judgment, no luck left to draw upon, mere daring become folly, and he loses it; that is the whole story. But he loses like a man, and there is some spiritual tragedy in it too; for if no ideals betray him, yet at every turn he is conscious that he betrays himself. He knows—who better?—that he should not fight Cæsar by sea. He has no reasons to give but

> For that he dares us to't.

All his answer to argument, as he stands supine under Cleopatra's eye, is a weakly obstinate

> By sea, by sea!

though he adds, for excuse, a futile

> But if we fail,
> We then can do't at land.

His mind seems a blank. He has no plan of battle; and with one defeat his nerve and self-respect are gone.

This is his lowest fall, and there in helpless ignominy we might have to leave him

> unqualitied with very shame . . .

to humble himself before his conqueror, to

dodge
And palter in the shifts of lowness . . .

—but for Cæsar! Thanks to his enemy, the old courage and a new
nobility are made to stir in him. There is a cold unloveliness about
Cæsar. With Antony at his mercy—well, he might accord it or
refuse it; but surely he need not so promptly send an envoy to
win Cleopatra from him who has lost everything for her sake, to
tempt her at any price to drive from Egypt

>   her all-disgraced friend,
>   Or take his life there . . .

Conquerors, it would seem, cannot even learn the common sense
of magnanimity. The clever trick comes near, though, to costing
Cæsar all he has won and more.

Antony has been no great precisian in such matters himself; but
he is thinking now, we may suppose, less of his own shortcomings
than of old days of comradeship with Cæsar when the diffident
schoolmaster-ambassador returns.

>   Is *that* his answer?
>   Ay, my lord.
>   The queen shall then have courtesy, so she
>   Will yield us up.
>   He says so.
>   Let her know't.

He recovers some at least of his stature as hero with that.

But if this is not spiritual tragedy, still less is it a moral tale, with
the scales of vice and virtue neatly tipped for our edifying; Shakespeare has left all that behind with artifice of plot and characters
cut to suit it. The light is shining for us here upon things as they
were and men as they are. So the heroic gesture can be followed
by the folly of the challenge to Cæsar and the savagery of the
whipping of Thidias; by the bitter purging of the illusion that
was Cleopatra, and at her beck, the prompt re-embracing of it
with a narcotic

>   I am satisfied.

Yet if Cleopatra is all that in his fury he says she is, and even
readier, it may be, to betray him than he thinks, she is not cold-
hearted toward him, strange though that may seem.[38] And while

---

[38] Enobarbus believes the very worst of her. But, of course, *he* would!

(by every rule of ready-made morality) his open-eyed return to
bondage and debauch should bring him swiftly to defeat,—and
fact-facing Enobarbus makes sure it will—on the contrary, it
preludes temporary victory, and it is the overconfident Cæsar
that must learn a lesson.

But Cæsar is quick to learn, and Enobarbus will prove right in
the end (though remorse and malaria end him before he finds it
out), and Shakespeare forthwith shows us very plainly the flaws
in the prospect. There is the omen of the strange music that the
soldiers hear, the sign that

> the god Hercules, whom Antony loved,
> Now leaves him.[39]

and the strange mood in Antony himself that sets him, on the
eve of battle, to making his followers weep his likely death.

> The gods make this a happy day to Antony!

is the old legionary's greeting to him as he marches out in the
morning; and the response is generous:

> Would thou and those thy scars had once prevailed
> To make me fight at land!

The gods do grant him one more happy day, and we see him at his
best in it. Shakespeare shows it as the briefest of the three; a ray
shooting through sunset clouds.

He begins it with what may be called the single touch of
romantic sentiment in the play. Antony and Cleopatra come out
in the early dawn—come from a night of revel, moreover!—like
a young bride and bridegroom, laughing together at her pretty
fumblings as she helps him put his armor on. A spoiled child's
useless fingers; Octavia would have made a neater job of it, one
fears! He flatters and pets her:

> Well, well:
> We shall thrive now!

Her glee when she has slipped a strap into place!

> Is not this buckled well?
> Rarely, rarely! . . .

[39] Shakespeare finds this in Plutarch, of course; but there it occurs before the
last defeat. He adds an ironic value to it by setting it before the intermediate day
of victory.

> Thou fumblest, Eros, and my queen's a squire
> More tight at this than thou.

Seen among his soldiers he is still the Antony of her worship:

> The demi-Atlas of this earth, the arm
> And burgonet of men.

But there are qualities in him that a little pass her understanding, perhaps. For, even as he sets forth, he learns that Enobarbus has deserted; and, very quietly, with no touch of anger, and but one most human shade of bitterness, comes

> What say'st thou?
>
> SOLDIER.   Sir,
> He is with Cæsar.
>
> EROS.   Sir, his chests and treasure
> He has not with him.
>
> ANTONY.   Is he gone?
>
> SOLDIER.   Most certain.
>
> ANTONY.   Go, Eros, send his treasure after; do it;
> Detain no jot, I charge thee: write to him—
> I will subscribe—gentle adieus and greetings;
> Say that I wish he never find more cause
> To change a master. O, my fortunes have
> Corrupted honest men! Despatch. Enobarbus!

He goes to fight, not confident of the issue (not stained with such overconfidence as Cæsar's, certainly), nor braggart of his cause. And when he beats his enemy and returns in triumph, his first thought is to thank his soldiers and to praise before them all the young and wounded Scarus, the hero of the day, who, for his reward, shall kiss Cleopatra's hand. Does she remember Thidias at this juncture, and *his* wounds?

Not much is made of the third day's fighting; nor does Shakespeare trouble with the question which Plutarch leaves unanswered, whether Cleopatra did "pack cards" with Cæsar or no. It is enough that fortune crashes upon Antony in final ruin. There is little noble about him now, in his beastlike rage and thirst for her blood; much though that is pitiful in the wreck of such a man.

> The soul and body rive not more in parting
> Than greatness going off.

For, if but in his folly, he has been great. He has held nothing back, has flung away for her sake honor and power, never weighing their worth against her worthlessness; there is a sort of selfless greatness in that. The lust to kill her before he kills himself is the due backwash of such spendthrift love. He sees her and cannot; folly is folly and weakness is weakness still, he can only damn her to a shamefuller end. Fury racks him again; and then the merciful riving of spirit from body begins. Shakespeare turns, as we have seen, to pure poetry to express it:

ANTONY. Eros, thou yet beholdest me?
EROS.   Ay, noble lord.
ANTONY. Sometimes we see a cloud that's dragonish . . . .

He is coming to the end of his strength—even his!—and the body's passions begin to seem unreal, and he to be slipping free of them. Yet another wrench or so of anger, suffering and shame; and the news comes that, in despite of him, she it is that has slipped free.

It is a lie; and he will be a laughingstock in death. What more fitly tragic end for the brilliant general and statesman, the great realist and paragon of worldly wisdom, than to be tricked into emulating the heroism of a Cleopatra, who is, we know, even now safe in her Monument; than to be outdone in quiet courage by his servant; than to bungle his own death-stroke and have to lie begging, in vain, to be put out of his misery? And, as he lies there, he learns the ridiculous truth.

Shakespeare spares him no ignominy; yet out of it rises, not, to be sure, an Antony turned angel, but a man set free of debt to fate, still abiding in his faith, justified of it, then, at the last. When the news of Cleopatra's death comes, he reproaches her no more, says not a word of any loss but this, has no thought but to follow her. What purpose is left him?

Unarm, Eros; the long day's task is done,
And we must sleep.

He is nothing without her; the world is empty and time has no meaning.

Since Cleopatra died,
I have lived in such dishonour, that the gods
Detest my baseness . . . .

Since she died, the single minute's passing has been to him as years. And when, dying, he learns that she lives he makes no comment upon that; what do Fate's pettinesses matter now? He asks only to be carried to her that he may die in her arms. Even of this he comes near to being cheated. She will not risk her safety for his sake. But she has them draw him up to her; and his thoughts are for her safety and peace of mind.

> The miserable change now at my end
> Lament nor sorrow at; but please your thoughts
> In feeding them with those my former fortunes,
> Wherein I lived the greatest prince o' the world,
> The noblest; and do now not basely die,
> Not cowardly put off my helmet to
> My countryman—a Roman by a Roman
> Valiantly vanquished. Now my spirit is going;
> I can no more.

He has loved her, the worst and the best of her; and given her the best and the worst of him. He won much from the world, so he had much to lose. Losers ought not to whine. Antony stays a soldier and a sportsman—and a gentleman, by his lights—to the end.

CLEOPATRA

Shakespeare's Cleopatra had to be acted by a boy, and this did everything to determine, not his view of the character, but his presenting of it. Think how a modern dramatist, a practical man of the theater, with an actress for his Cleopatra, would set about the business. He might give us the tragedy of the play's end much as Shakespeare does, no doubt—if he could; but can we conceive him leaving Cleopatra without one single scene in which to show the sensual charm which drew Antony to her, and back to her, which is the tragedy's very fount? Yet this is what Shakespeare does, and with excellent reason: a boy could not show it, except objectionably or ridiculously. He does not shirk her sensuality, he stresses it time and again; but he has to find other ways than the one impracticable way of bringing it home to us. What is the best evidence we have (so to speak) of Cleopatra's physical charms? A description of them by Enobarbus—by the misogynist Enobarbus—given us, moreover, when she has been out of our sight for a quarter of an hour or so. Near her or away from her, Antony himself never speaks of them. He may make such a casual joke as

> The beds i' the East are soft.

or reflect in a fateful phrase,

> I will to Egypt . . . .
> I' the East my pleasure lies.

but Shakespeare will not run even so much risk of having a lover's ecstasies discounted. Enobarbus may grumble out gross remarks about her; but Antony's response, as he plans his escape, is

> She is cunning past man's thought.

The lovers are never once alone together; and the only approach to a "love-scene" comes with our first sight of them, walking in formal procession and reciting antiphonally:

CLEOPATRA.   If it be love indeed, tell me how much.
ANTONY.   There's beggary in the love that can be reckoned.
CLEOPATRA.   I'll set a bourn how far to be beloved.
ANTONY.   Then must thou needs find out new heaven, new
              earth.

This is convention itself. Antony's

> Here is my space.
> Kingdoms are clay: our dungy earth alike
> Feeds beast as man: the nobleness of life
> Is to do thus; when such a mutual pair
> And such a twain can do't. . . .

is pure rhetoric.[40] And the poetry of

> Now, for the love of Love and her soft hours,
> Let's not confound the time with conference
> harsh.
> There's not a minute of our lives should stretch
> Without some pleasure now. What sport to-
> night?

CLEOPATRA.   Hear the ambassadors.
ANTONY.   Fie, wrangling queen!
              Whom everything becomes, to chide, to laugh,
              To weep; whose every passion fully strives
              To make itself in thee, fair and admired! . . .

is sensuality sublimated indeed.

----

[40] The "*embracing*" which Pope and editors after him tagged on to "thus," is not Shakespeare's direction. Whether he means the two to embrace here may be a moot point; but this sort of thing was *not* what he meant by suiting the action to the word and the word to the action.

Not till their passion deepens as tragedy nears does Shakespeare give it physical expression. Antony leaves her for battle with "a soldier's kiss" (it is the first the action definitely shows) and, returning triumphant, hails her with

> O thou day o' the world,
> Chain mine armed neck: leap thou, attire and all,
> Through proof of harness to my heart, and there
> Ride on the pants triumphing.

A very open and aboveboard embrace. And not till death is parting them do we reach

> I am dying, Egypt, dying; only
> I here importune death awhile, until
> Of many thousand kisses the poor last
> I lay upon thy lips.

with, for its matching and outdoing, her

> welcome, welcome! die where thou hast lived:
> Quicken with kissing: had my lips that power,
> Thus would I wear them out.

By which time, if dramatist and actors between them have not freed the imaginations of their audience from the theater's bonds, all three will have been wasting it. Throughout the play Cleopatra herself gives us glimpses enough of her sensual side.

> Thou, eunuch Mardian!
>   What's your highness' pleasure?
> Not now to hear thee sing. I take no pleasure
> In aught an eunuch has: 'tis well for thee
> That, being unseminared, thy freer thoughts
> May not fly forth of Egypt.

But Shakespeare never has her turn it towards a flesh-and-blood Antony, inviting response.

His only choice, then, is to endow her with other charms for conquest: wit, coquetry, perception, subtlety, imagination, inconsequence—and this he does to the full. And had he a veritable Cleopatra to play the part, what other and what better could he do? How does a Cleopatra differ from the common run of wantons but in just such gifts as these? It would take a commonplace dramatist to insist upon the obvious, upon all that age does wither, while custom even sooner stales its infinite monotony!

It is, of course, with his magic of words that Shakespeare weaves Cleopatra's charm. To begin with, we may find ourselves somewhat conscious of the process. Though that first duet between the lovers is with good reason conventional, they seem slightly self-conscious besides; less themselves, at the moment, than advocates for themselves. Not till Cleopatra reappears has this cloud about her vanished; but nothing of the sort ever masks her again.

CLEOPATRA. Saw you my lord?
ENOBARBUS.   No, lady.
CLEOPATRA.   Was he not here?
CHARMIAN. No, madam.
CLEOPATRA. He was disposed to mirth; but on the sudden
           A Roman thought hath struck him. Enobarbus!
ENOBARBUS. Madam.
CLEOPATRA. Seek him and bring him hither. Where's Alexas?
ALEXAS.   Here, at your service. My lord approaches.
CLEOPATRA. We will not look upon him; go with us.

And when she returns:

See where he is, who's with him, what he does:
I did not send you: if you find him sad,
Say I am dancing: if in mirth, report
That I am sudden sick: quick, and return.

Here is actuality; and forged in words of one syllable, mainly. This is the woman herself, quick, jealous, imperious, mischievous, malicious, flagrant, subtle; but a delicate creature, too, and the light, glib verse seems to set her on tiptoe.

For the scene with Antony, Shakespeare rallies his resources. We have the pouting

I am sick and sullen.

the plaintive

Help me away, dear Charmian; I shall fall:
It cannot be thus long, the sides of nature
Will not sustain it.

the darting ironic malice of

I know, by that same eye, there's some good news.
What says the married woman? You may go. . . .

and pretty pettishness suddenly throbbing into

> Why should I think you can be mine and true,
> Though you in swearing shake the throned gods,
> Who have been false to Fulvia? . . .

Then the vivid simplicities melt into a sheer magic of the music of words.

> But bid farewell and go: when you sued staying,
> Then was the time for words: no going then;
> Eternity was in our lips and eyes,
> Bliss in our brows' bent; none our parts so poor
> But was a race of heaven. . . .

And so, up the scale and down, she enchants the scene to its end.

For a moment in the middle of it we see another Cleopatra, and hear a note struck from nearer the heart of her. She is shocked by his callously calculated gloss upon Fulvia's death. Vagaries of passion she can understand, and tricks and lies to favor them. But this hard-set indifference! She takes it to herself, of course, and is not too shocked to make capital of it for her quarrel. But here, amid the lively wrangling, which is stimulus to their passion, shows a dead spot of incomprehension, the true division between them. They stare for an instant; then cover it, as lovers will. Fulvia's wrongs make the best of capital; there are poisoned pin-pricks in them, and the second round of the fight leaves him helpless—but to turn and throttle her. The rules of the ring are not for Cleopatra. She takes woman's leave to play the child, and the great lady's to outdo any wench in skittishness; she matches vulgar gibing with dignity and pathos, now loses herself in inarticulate imaginings, now is simple and humble and nobly forgiving. He must leave her; she lets him go. But to the unguessed riddle that she still is he will return.

Let the actress of today note carefully how the brilliant effect of this first parade of Cleopatra is gained. There is no more action in it than the dignity of a procession provides, and the swifter coming and going and returning which ends in this duel of words danced at arm's length with her lover. There is no plot to be worked out; Antony is departing, and he departs, that is all. What we have is the transposing of a temperament into words; and it is in the changing rhythm and dissolving color of them, quite as much as in the sense, that the woman is to be found. Neither place nor time is left for the embroidery of "business," nor for the overpainting of the picture by such emotional suggestion as the author of today legitimately asks of an actress. Anything of that sort will cloud the scene quite fatally. If the shortcomings of a boy Cleopatra were plain, we can imagine his peculiar virtuosity. To the adopted graces of the great lady he would bring a delicate aloofness, which would hover, sometimes very happily, upon the edge of the absurd. With the art of acting still dominantly the art of speech—to be able to listen undistracted an audience's chief need—he would not make his mere presence disturbingly felt; above all, he could afford to lose himself unreservedly—since his native personality must be lost—in the music of the verse, and to let that speak. So in this scene must the Cleopatra of today, if *we* are not to lose far more than we gain by her. There will be the larger demands on her later, those that Shakespeare's indwelling demon made on him; he had to risk their fulfillment then, as now.

But her presenting continues for awhile to be very much of a parade. She is never, we notice, now or later, left to a soliloquy.[41] Parade fits her character (or if Shakespeare fits her character to parade the effect is the same). She is childishly extravagant, ingenuously shameless; nothing exists for her but her desires. She makes slaves of her servants, but she jokes and sports with them, too, and opens her heart to them in anger or in joy; so they adore her. It is not perhaps an exemplary Court, in which the Queen encourages chaff about her paramours, and turns on her lady-in-waiting with

> By Isis, I will give thee bloody teeth,
> If thou with Cæsar paragon again
> My man of men.

but it is at least a lively one, and its expansiveness would be a boon to any dramatist.

She is indeed no sluggardly sensualist; double doses of mandragora would not keep her quiet. What she cannot herself she

---

[41] Nor is anyone else in the play for more than a few lines; another token of it as drama of action rather than of spiritual conflict. We see in this too how far Shakespeare's stagecraft had outgrown the older, conventional, plot-forwarding use of soliloquies. In his earlier plays of action they abound.

must do by proxy; she cannot follow Antony, but her messengers gallop after him every post. Her senses stir her to potent imagery:

> O happy horse, to bear the weight of Antony!
> Do bravely, horse! for wot'st thou whom thou movest. . . .

—if perverted a little:

> now I feed myself
> With most delicious poison.

And in that

> Think on me,
> That am with Phœbus' amorous pinches black,
> And wrinkled deep in time.

there is elemental power. And if her praise of Antony for his "well-divided disposition" seems incongruous; why, a nature so sure of itself can admire the qualities it lacks.

Shakespeare shirks nothing about her. What will be left for us of her womanly charm when we have seen her haling the bringer of the news of Antony's treachery up and down by the hair of his head, and running after him, knife in hand, screaming like a fish-fag? But this also is Cleopatra. He allows her here no moment of dignity, nor of fortitude in grief; only the pathos of

> CLEOPATRA. In praising Antony, I have dispraised Cæsar?
> CHARMIAN. Many times, madam.
> CLEOPATRA.   I am paid for't now.

—which is the pathos of the whipped child, rancorous against its gods, resigned to evil. There is the moment's thought, as she calls the scared messenger back again:

> These hands do lack nobility, that they strike
> A meaner than myself; since I myself
> Have given myself the cause.

And this is a notable touch. It forecasts the Cleopatra of the play's end, who will seek her death after the "high Roman fashion"; it reveals, not inconsistency, but that antithesis in disposition which must be the making of every human equation. It is the second touch of its sort that Shakespeare gives to his picturing of her; and both, in the acting, must be stamped on our memories.[42]

---

[42] The first, her stinging reproach to him for his callousness at Fulvia's death.

The end of the scene sees her, with her maids fluttering round her, lapsed into pitifulness, into childish ineptitude. But again, something of spiritual continence sounds in its last note of all, in the

> Pity me, Charmian;
> But do not speak to me.

The complementary scene, in which the unlucky messenger is re-examined, would be more telling if it followed a little closer; but, as we have seen, Shakespeare has hereabouts an overplus of Roman material to deal with. It is pure comedy, and of the best. She is calm again, very collected, making light of her fury; but an echo of it can be heard in that sudden nasty little snarl which ends in a sigh. Charmian and Iras and Alexas have evidently had a trying time with her. They conspire to flatter her back to confidence—and she lets them. The messenger has been well coached too. But the best of the comedy is in Cleopatra's cryptic simplicity. She likes flattery for its own sake. There is a sensuality of the mind that flattery feeds. What does it matter if they lie to her; of what use is the truth? Anger is crippling; but in the glow of their adulation she uncurls and feels her lithe strength return, and this is her only need.

> All may be well enough.

Yet the words savor faintly of weariness too.

Now comes the war and her undoing. Her disillusion first; for Antony, won back, is no longer the all-conquering captain, from whom she may command Herod of Jewry's head—or Cæsar's!—nor does her own reckless generalship prove much help. We do not, as we have noted, see the reuniting of the lovers; we find her at a nagging match with Enobarbus, and turned, with her Antony, to something very like a shrew. And if to the very end she stays for him an unguessed riddle, "cunning past man's thought," there is much in which Shakespeare is content to leave her so for us—thereby to manifest her the more consummately. By what twists of impulse or of calculation is she moved through the three fateful days of swaying fortune? How ready was she to "pack cards" with Cæsar? What the final betrayal amounted to, that sent Antony raging after her, Shakespeare, it may be said, could not tell us, because he did not know; and her inarticulate terror at this

point may therefore show us his stagecraft at its canniest. But in
retrospect all this matters dramatically very little; what does matter is that as we watch her she should defy calculation.

It is futile, we know, to apply the usual moral tests to her, of
loyalty, candor, courage. Yet because she shamelessly overacts her
repentance for her share in that first defeat it by no means follows
that she feels none. She lends an ear to Thidias, and the message
to Cæsar sounds flat treason; this is the blackest count against her.
But soft speech costs nothing, and perhaps it was Cæsar who was
to be tricked. Can we detect, though, a new contempt for Antony
as she watches him, his fury glutted by the torment of the wretched
envoy? She might respect him more had he flogged her instead!
Is there in the sadly smiling

> Not know me yet?

with which she counters his spent reproach, and in her wealth of
protest, something of the glib falsity of sated ardors? Next morning she buckles on his armor and bids him good-bye like a happy
child; but, his back turned:

> He goes forth gallantly. That he and Cæsar might
> Determine this great war in single fight!
> Then, Antony—! But now—?

It is a chilling postscript.

She is like Antony in this at least—and it erects them both to
figures of heroic size—that she has never learned to compromise
with life, nor had to reconcile her own nature's extremes. To call
her false to this or to that is to set up a standard that could have
no value for her. She is true enough to the self of the moment;
and, in the end, tragically true to a self left sublimated by great
loss. The passionate woman has a child's desires and a child's fears,
an animal's wary distrust; balance of judgment none, one would
say. But often, as at this moment, she shows the shrewd scepticism
of a child.

From now till we see her in the Monument and Antony is
brought to die in her arms, Shakespeare sinks the figure into the
main fabric of the play. He makes a moment's clear picture of the
welcome to Antony returned from victory. The

> *Enter Cleopatra, attended.*

might be radiance enough; but, for surplus, we have her ecstatic

> Lord of lords!
> O infinite virtue, comest thou smiling from
> The world's great snare uncaught!

When defeat follows quickly, her collapse to terror is left, as we saw, the anatomy of a collapse and no more. Then, from being but a part of the general swift distraction, she emerges in fresh strength to positive significance again; and—this is important—as a tragic figure for the first time.

From wantonness, trickery and folly, Shakespeare means to lift her to a noble end. But, even in doing it, he shirks no jot of the truth about her. She loses none of her pristine quality. If she victimizes the complacent Dolabella with a glance or two, who shall blame her? But how far she would go in wheedling Cæsar— were there a joint to be found in that armor of cold false courtesy —who shall say? She cheats and lies to him as a matter of course, and Seleucus would fare worse with her than did that once un- lucky messenger. Misfortune hardly lends her dignity, the correct Cæsar may well think as he leaves her there. He will think other- wise when he sees her again. But it is not till the supreme moment approaches that she can pretend to any calm of courage. She must sting herself to ever fresh desperation by conjured visions of the shame from which only death will set her free; we hear that "Be noble to myself," "my noble act," repeated like a charm. Yet she is herself to the end. It is the old willful childishness, tuned to a tragic key, that sounds for us in

> O Charmian, I will never go from hence.
> CHARMIAN. Be comforted, dear madam.
> CLEOPATRA.   No, I will not:
> All strange and terrible events are welcome,
> But comforts we despise. . . .

and in the extravagant magnificence of her grief she is the Eastern queen, who could stir even an Enobarbus to rhapsody, and beggar all description. She has no tears for Antony.[43] The shock of his death strikes her senseless, but her spirit is unquelled. Defiant over his body:

---

[43] Throughout the play Cleopatra never weeps. Antony does.

> It were for me
> To throw my sceptre at the injurious gods;
> To tell them that this world did equal theirs
> Till they had stolen our jewel. . . .

The rest may find relief in grieving; not she!

Shakespeare allows her one touch of his favorite philosophy. She reappears, confirmed in her loss.

> My desolation does begin to make
> A better life. 'Tis paltry to be Cæsar;
> Not being Fortune, he's but Fortune's knave,
> A minister of her will. . . .

This is the note, once struck by Brutus, sustained by Hamlet, of failure's contempt for success. We hear it in life, more commonly, from quite successful men, who also seem to find some needed comfort in the thought. It is a recurring note in all Shakespearean tragedy, this exalting of the solitary dignity of the soul; and he will not end even this most unspiritual of plays without sounding it. He passes soon to a somewhat truer Cleopatra—here is the same thought pursued, though—when she counters Dolabella's bland assurance with

> You laugh when boys or women tell their dreams.
> Is't not your trick? . . .
> I dreamt there was an Emperor Antony.
> O, such another sleep, that I might see
> But such another man!

and utterly bewilders him with the hyperbole that follows, strange contrast to Cæsar's recent decorous regret. But it is on such ridiculous heights that genius—even for wantonness—will lodge its happiness. And the next instant he appears, the manikin Cæsar, who has triumphed over her "man of men"! She stares, as if incredulous, till Dolabella has to say

> It is the emperor, madam.

Then she mocks their conqueror with her humilities. But the scene is, besides, a ghastly mockery of the Cleopatra that was. Compare it with the one in which she laughed and pouted and turned Antony round her finger. She is a trapped animal now, cringing and whining and cajoling lest the one chink of escape be stopped. There is no cajoling Cæsar. He betters her at that with his

> Feed and sleep:
> Our care and pity is so much upon you,
> That we remain your friend.

Even so might a cannibal ensure the tenderness of his coming meal. She knows; and when he is gone:

> He words me, girls, he words me, that I should not
> Be noble to myself!

One last lashing of her courage; then a flash of glorious, of transcendent vanity—

> Show me, my women, like a queen: go fetch
> My best attires: I am again for Cydnus,
> To meet Mark Antony.

—a last touch of the old frolicsomeness as she jokes with the clown, peeping the while between the fig-leaves in which the aspics lie; and she is ready.

> Give me my robe, put on my crown; I have
> Immortal longings in me: now no more
> The juice of Egypt's grape shall moist this lip.
> Yare, yare, good Iras: quick! Methinks I hear
> Antony call; I see him rouse himself
> To praise my noble act; I hear him mock
> The luck of Cæsar, which the gods give men
> To excuse their after wrath. Husband, I come:
> Now to that name my courage prove my title! . . .

The dull Octavia, with her "still conclusions," defeated and divorced!

> I am fire and air; my other elements
> I give to baser life. So; have you done?
> Come then, and take the last warmth of my lips.
> Farewell, kind Charmian, Iras, long farewell. . . .

Iras so worships her that she dies of the very grief of the leave-taking.

> Have I the aspic in my lips? Dost fall?
> If thou and nature can so gently part,
> The stroke of death is as a lover's pinch,
> Which hurts and is desired. Dost thou lie still?

> If thus thou vanishest, thou tell'st the world
> It is not worth leave-taking.

Sensuous still, still jealous; her mischievous, magnificent mockery surpassing death itself.

> This proves me base.
> If she first meet the curled Antony,
> He'll make demand of her, and spend that kiss
> Which is my heaven to have. Come, thou mortal wretch,
> With thy sharp teeth this knot intrinsicate
> Of life at once untie; poor venomous fool,
> Be angry and despatch. O, couldst thou speak,
> That I might hear thee call great Cæsar ass
> Unpolicied!

Charmian sees her uplifted, shining:

> O eastern star!

Then follows the consummate

> Peace, peace!
> Dost thou not see my baby at my breast,
> That sucks the nurse asleep?

and in another moment she is dead.

Very well, then, it is not high spiritual tragedy; but is there not something still more fundamental in the pity and terror of it? Round up a beast of prey, and see him die with a natural majesty which shames our civilized contriving. So Cleopatra dies; defiant, noble in her kind, shaming convenient righteousness, a miracle of nature that—here is the tragedy—will not be reconciled to any gospel but its own. She is herself to the very end. Her last breath fails upon the impatient

> What should I stay—?

Her last sensation is the luxury of

> As sweet as balm, as soft as air, as gentle!

And what more luminous summary could there be of such sensual womanhood than the dignity and perverse humor blended in this picture of her yielded to her death—suckling an asp? It defies praise. So, for that matter, does Charmian's

> Now boast thee, death, in thy possession lies
> A lass unparalleled.

—the one word "lass" restoring to her, even as death restores, some share of innocence and youth.

This scene shows us Shakespeare's artistry in perfection, and all gloss upon it will doubtless seem tiresome. But though the reader be teased a little, it cannot hurt him to realize that this close analysis of every turn in the showing of a character and composing of a scene—and much besides—must go to giving a play the simple due of its acting. As reader he cannot lose by knowing what demands the play's art makes on the actor's. The greater the play, the more manifold the demands! When he sees them fulfilled in the theater his enjoyment will be doubled. If they are not, he will a little know why, and so much the worse for the actor; but, at long last, so much the better.

OCTAVIA

Octavia speaks a bare thirty lines, and they are distributed, at that, through four scenes. She is meant to be a negative character, set in contrast to Cleopatra; but if only as an instance of what Shakespeare can do by significant "placing," by help of a descriptive phrase or so, and above all by individualizing her in the music of her verse, she ranks among the play's achievements. She first appears hard upon the famous picturing of Cleopatra in her barge on Cydnus, with this for preface:

> If beauty, wisdom, modesty can settle
> The heart of Antony, Octavia is
> A blessed lottery to him.

—turned, though, to irony by the comment of Enobarbus' grimmest smile and shrug. We then have but a passing sight of her, and only hear her innocently answer Antony's most ambiguous

> The world and my great office will sometimes
> Divide me from your bosom.

with

> All which time
> Before the gods my knee shall bow my prayers
> To them for you.

She departs with her brother; but before the scene ends the ambiguity is resolved. Antony, we learn, will take his first chance to go back to Cleopatra, and Octavia is already befooled. An unpromising beginning for her.

Next we see her parting from her brother, setting out with an already faithless husband, pledge of an amity between the two as hollow to the sound as mocking comment and bland protest can show it; she helpless to make the false thing true. She weeps at the parting. Antony is kindly in deceit—

> The April's in her eyes: it is love's spring.
> And these the showers to bring it on. Be cheerful.

—and, as she turns back to whisper some woman's misgivings to Cæsar, he sums up their usage of her, and paints her quite inimitably in the sense and very music of

> Her tongue will not obey her heart, nor can
> Her heart inform her tongue—the swan's down-feather,
> That stands upon the swell at the full of tide,
> And neither way inclines.

A gentler victim of great policies one could not find. Another scene shows her shaken off by Antony with the same kindly deceit, grown colder now; another, her return to Cæsar, to a welcome humiliating in its sympathy; and so, impotent in goodness, she vanishes from the play. But we should remember her, if only by such melodies as

> A more unhappy lady
> If this division chance, ne'er stood between,
> Praying for both parts.

as

> The Jove of power make me most weak, most weak,
> Your reconciler! . . .

The gentle and sustained purity of the cadence is all her own. To Cleopatra, of course, she is "dull Octavia," and Antony, in the fury of defeat, can credit her with revengefully "prepared nails"; their obvious tribute to a woman they have wronged.

OCTAVIUS CÆSAR

Cæsar is the predestinate successful man. Beside his passionate rival, he is passionless; no puritan though. If, as he says, Antony merely

> filled
> His vacancy with his voluptuousness. . .

it would be his own affair. But how not lose patience with a part-
ner, and such a man as Antony, when he behaves even as boys will,

> who being mature in knowledge,
> Pawn their experience to their present pleasure,
> And so rebel to judgment.

Still, it is his business as politician, to see things as they are, and he
knows well enough that his prosaic virtues will never fire the
enthusiasms of the Roman mob. He must have the gallant Antony
to counter the danger that the gallant Pompey has now become.
Not that he undervalues himself—far from it! Much as he needs
Antony, he makes no concessions to him; insists rather on his own
correct conduct:

> You have broken
> The article of your oath; which you shall never
> Have tongue to charge me with.

He must not only be in the right, but keep proving that he is.
This alone labels him second-rate.

But is not this the sort of man that Rome now needs to bring
the pendulum of conflict to a stand? Such genius as Julius
Cæsar's was not to be endured. There was small profit in the
zealotries of a Cassius and a Brutus; and to what Antony will
bring the Empire we see. Octavius Cæsar may seem no great
general. Doubtless at Philippi he "dealt in lieutenantry"; but at
least he does not now send a Ventidius to Parthia to do his work
for him, while he is yet so jealous that the work stays half done.
And is not the best general the one who does deal in lieutenantry
—when he has chosen his lieutenants well? Here is, at any rate,
the industrious, unflagging, cautious man, who wins through in
the end, and can say and mean, most luckily for Rome, that

> The time of universal peace is near.
> Prove this a prosperous day, the three-nook'd world
> Shall bear the olive freely.

though, as we saw, the moment's overconfidence in which he
says it is followed by a day's defeat. Not even the best-regulated
characters can wholly discipline fortune!

Personally he is in many ways, no doubt, an estimable man. If
he sells his sister to Antony— and we should not, of course, take
a sentimental view of such a marriage—he still holds her dear,

and is jealous of her honor. His grief for Antony's death, for
his one-time

> mate in empire,
> Friend and companion in the front of war. . .

is not hypocrisy, even though he has, in his own interest, just
passed from trying to bribe Cleopatra to have "the old ruffian's"
throat cut to orders that he be "took alive," to be brought to Rome
to walk (as Antony well knows) chained in his conqueror's
Triumph. And if he lies to Cleopatra he does but pay her in her
own coin. Nor when she outwits him is he angry; he respects
her rather.

> Bravest at the last;
> She levelled at our purposes, and, being royal,
> Took her own way. . . . .

Not a lovable man, but a very able one; and we see him growing
in ability—such ungenerous natures do—as opportunity matures.
If he were not rather humorless, we might suspect him of irony
in giving as his excuse for getting rid of Lepidus—having had his
use of him—that this meekest of incompetent parasites "was
grown too cruel." And there is a savor of cant, perhaps, in the
assurance to poor wronged Octavia that

> the high gods
> To do you justice, make their ministers
> Of us and those that love you.

But one may poke fun at a Lepidus with safety; and righteousness
—even self-righteousness—is an asset in public life. In sum, he
knows the purblind world for what it is, and that it will be safer
in his hands than in a greater man's. And while this is so, does it
become us, who compose that world, to criticize him very harshly?

ENOBARBUS[44]

When at last this good friend turns traitor Antony says re-
morsefully:

> O, my fortunes have
> Corrupted honest men! . . .

[44] Enobarbus, it is worth remarking, is wholly Shakespeare's own, with nothing
owed to Plutarch but the incident of the restored treasure and the (altered) name.

And Enobarbus himself very early shows a sense of some small part of the corruption:

> Mine and most of our fortunes to-night shall be—drunk to bed.

His is the tragedy of cynic mind coupled with soft heart, a tragedy of loyalty to something other than the best one knows.

He is a misogynist confessed, and his talk about women is brutal. Misogyny is recognized armor for a soft-hearted man. But he is as plain-spoken about men, and to their faces besides; nor sparing of himself. Nor is this mere bombast. He sees these chaffering traders in the event as they truly are, and sees further into consequences than do any of them. Antony is his master, and when things go ill he does his best to save him; but good sense and plain speaking will not serve. So far he is a simple variant of the outspoken, honest, disillusioned fellow, a type very useful to the dramatist lacking a chorus; Shakespeare has found it so often enough.

But Enobarbus is not all prose and fault-finding. The rhapsody upon Cleopatra stands out significantly; and when, later, the disintegrating rays of his mind turn inward, they discover him to himself a part and a victim of this timeserving world that he so scorns. It is in the process of his lapse from loyalty, in his sudden collapse from cynicism to pitifulness, that we find Shakespeare's maturer mind and art.[45] We see the moral self-destruction of the man upon whom no man's weakness has imposed, and the completing of a figure of far subtler purport than the conventional, plain blunt image which, at a too careless glance, he may seem to be.

The competent soldier rages against Antony's blundering. But when, with the rest, he could save himself from its consequences, he will not. He chooses the losing side, though his reason "sits in the wind" against him.

---

[45] This minor tragedy is worked out in a few asides. It is done, as it seems, very casually, but it shows what can be done with thrifty skill in the freedom of the Elizabethan stage; divorced from this, it will be ineffective, probably. It is worth remarking that the asides might well, most of them, be joined up into a long soliloquy; and by Shakespeare's earlier method they probably would be. But by parceling the matter out he preserves the unity and prominence of the main action, and keeps it flowing on. And the whole episode, in its detached quietness, helps to throw Antony's vociferation into high relief.

> The loyalty well held to fools does make
> Our faith mere folly. Yet he that can endure
> To follow with allegiance a fall'n lord,
> Does conquer him that did his master conquer,
> And earns a place i' the story.

This is strange doctrine for an admitted cynic. Then he argues back and forth as things go from bad to worse; at last cold reason conquers, and he rats. It is too late now; and he is but half-hearted in treason. We next see him standing silent, aloof, ignored by the sufficient Cæsar—and not sorry to be. Then Antony, by one simple, generous gesture of forgiveness, breaks his heart.

There is excellent irony in his end. That the rough-tongued, thick-skinned Enobarbus, of all men, should expire sentimentally, by moonlight, of a broken heart! But the superficial effect is not all. Thus ends another unbalanced man; and whether the inequity lies between passion and judgment as with Antony, or, more covertly, as with Enobarbus, between the armored and the secret self, here was tragedy prepared. And we have seen the waste of a man. For this it is to bring sound sense and loyalty into the service of the Antonys of the world. With blind folly to serve, loyalty and good sense must come to odds; then one will oust the other, and master and man and cause go down in disruption.

POMPEY, LEPIDUS AND THE REST

If in a scheme of things so warped by passion, jealousy and self-seeking, the robust Enobarbus is broken, how shall such weaklings as Pompey and Lepidus survive? "Fool Lepidus" is doomed from the start. He must be everybody's friend; and, while the patching-up of quarrels is in train, who more useful than this mild-mannered little man, with his never-failing, deprecating tact, his perfect politeness?[46] Cæsar condescends to him with scarcely veiled contempt.

> 'tis time we twain
> Did show ourselves i' the field. . . .

But the "twain" are Antony and Cæsar; Lepidus, the "poor third" (as Eros calls him later), counts for nothing. The colleagues "Sir" each other in this scene, we notice, with suspicious

---

[46] One sees him, for the play's purposes, physically also, as a little man.

courtesy. There is a touch of mockery in Cæsar's. Later, the
generous Antony pays him compensation for one quite unde-
served snub. The little man has started off the critical debate with
Cæsar by a reconciling speech, his only eloquent effort:

> then, noble partners,
> The rather for I earnestly beseech,
> Touch you the sourest points with sweetest terms,
> Nor curstness grow to the matter.

and thereafter is so ready—yet never too ready—with cooing interjections, all ignored. Difficulties resolved, he does mildly assert
himself; but Cæsar still ignores him, and is departing. Whereupon Antony:

> Let us, Lepidus,
> Not lack your company.
>   Noble Antony,
> Not sickness should detain me.

The little man is grateful.

He cannot carry his liquor, and they laugh at him for that.
And all but the last we hear of him is in the mocking duet between Agrippa and Enobarbus.[47]

AGRIPPA.   'Tis a noble Lepidus.
ENOBARBUS.   A very fine one: O, how he loves Cæsar!
AGRIPPA.   Nay, but how dearly he adores Mark Antony!
ENOBARBUS.   Cæsar? Why he's the Jupiter of men!
AGRIPPA.   What's Antony? The god of Jupiter.
ENOBARBUS.   Spake you of Cæsar? How! the nonpareil!
AGRIPPA.   O Antony! O thou Arabian bird!
ENOBARBUS.   Would you praise Cæsar, say 'Cæsar'; go no
                         further.
AGRIPPA.   Indeed, he plied them both with excellent
                         praises.
ENOBARBUS.   But he loves Cæsar best: yet he loves Antony:
                         Hoo! hearts, tongues, figures, scribes, bards,
                              poets, cannot
                         Think, speak, cast, write, sing, number—hoo!—
                         His love to Antony. But as for Cæsar;
                         Kneel down, kneel down and wonder.

---

[47] Shakespeare also throws him into contact with Enobarbus for a brief exchange
before the reconciling of Cæsar and Antony begins, and the smoothness and rough-
ness make an illuminating contrast.

He comes to no heroic end. Cæsar stows him away somewhere, as one puts a pair of old boots in a cupboard.

> the poor third is up, till death enlarge his confine.

It is a sketch of a mere sketch of a man; but done with what skill and economy, and how effectively placed as relief among the positive forces of the action! Shakespeare (as dramatist) had some slight affection for the creature too. For a last speech, when Octavia is tearfully taking leave as she sets forth with her Antony, he gives him the charming

> Let all the number of the stars give light
> To thy fair way.

Should one call Pompey a weakling? He makes a gallant show; but we suspect from the first that facile optimism:

> I shall do well:
> The people love me, and the sea is mine;
> My powers are crescent, and my auguring hope
> Says it will come to the full . . . .

And in a moment we are finding him out. Bad news must be denied; and when it persists, and there is no doubt that the Triumvirs, all three, are to be in the field against him, why,

> let us rear
> The higher our opinion, that our stirring
> Can from the lap of Egypt's widow pluck
> The ne'er lust-wearied Antony.

The scene ends with an empty flourish:

> Be't as our gods will have't! It only stands
> Our lives upon to use our strongest hands.

Pompey is full of flourishes; for he seems to be conscious of a certain intellectual hollowness within him, he whistles to keep his followers' courage up, and his own.

He is a great man's son. He must not forget it, for no one else will, and there is a certain debility in this. He makes peace discreetly, is magniloquent, scores a verbal point or so; no one may say he is overawed. Then comes Menas' offer to cut the throats of his new allies and make him lord of the world; and he answers

> Ah, this thou shouldst have done
> And not have spoke on't. In me 'tis villainy;

> In thee't had been good service. Thou must know
> 'Tis not my profit that does lead mine honour;
> Mine honour, it.

These gallant gentlemen who look to their honor to profit them, and will profit by other men's dishonor! When the Cæsars of the world override them, the world loses little, one must confess. Pompey fades out of the play. To fit him with an appropriate metaphor, he carries too much sail for his keel.

Relays of minor characters, each with a life of its own, help keep the play alive. Shakespeare's fertility in this kind is here at its full; but so forthright is the work that the action is never checked, each character answers its purpose and no more. Nothing very startling about any of them, nothing very memorable as we look back; but this is as it should be, they are accompaniment to the theme, and, at their liveliest, should never distract us from it. Demetrius and Philo, soldiers ingrain, move for a moment in contrast, make their indignant protest against epicene Egypt and Antony in its toils; they have served their purpose, and we see them no more. The Soothsayer does his mumbo-jumbo, a peculiar figure; and Egypt and what it stands for will flash back to us when we see him, in Roman surroundings, again. The messengers are conventional figures merely; but Shakespeare gives to the person of each one the weight that belongs to his errand, and so augments the strength of the scene. Menecrates and Menas come out of Plutarch as famous pirates. Menas sustains the character most colorfully (and his admittance to distinguished company may throw a little light upon the Elizabethan conscience in this matter), but Menecrates is needed to offer a sententious check to Pompey's soaring confidence.

> We, ignorant of ourselves,
> Beg often our own harms, which the wise powers
> Deny us for our good; so find we profit
> By losing of our prayers.

A philosophic pirate, indeed; and we may see, if we will, the more pragmatic Menas, chafing, but scornfully silent in the background.

Agrippa and Mæcenas hover after Cæsar to the end, putting in the tactful word—which ripens to flattery, we notice, the minute he is secure in power. Such men, of such a measure, are always forthcoming. Shakespeare once spices their utility with the humor of their hanging back to hear the latest Egyptian scandal from Enobarbus; they are gleefully shocked by the eight wild boars at a breakfast and the goings-on of that royal wench Cleopatra. Their names apart, there is no history in them, of course. Ventidius, with good dramatic reason, dominates a single scene; and Eros, Thidias, Scarus, Dolabella and the others give vigor and variety to incident upon incident. They and the rest of the incidental characters provide, one might say, a fluid medium of action with which the stronger colors of the play may be mixed.

Of Charmian and Iras there is rather more to be said. They attend upon Cleopatra and she puts them in the shade; but Shakespeare has touched them in with distinct and delicate care. To give them betimes a little importance of their own we have the scene with the Soothsayer with the irony of its prophecy.

> find me to marry with Octavius Cæsar, and companion me
> with my mistress.

laughs Charmian. And he answers her:

> You shall outlive the lady whom you serve.

So she does, by one minute!

Thereafter the two of them decorate the Egyptian scenes; deft and apt, poised for their mistress' call. Iras is the more fragile, the more placid; Charmian, the "wild bedfellow," will be the quicker of her tongue, when a word may be slipped in. It is an impudent tongue too; she has no awe of her betters. Worthless little trulls, no doubt! But when disaster comes, and Antony's men, all save one, make their peace with the conqueror, for these two there is no question. They also see what lies behind Cæsar's courtesy; and the timid, silent Iras suddenly breaks silence with

> Finish, good lady; the bright day is done,
> And we are for the dark.

—revealing herself in a dignity of spirit of her own. Another moment and she is trembling again; one would think she could hardly carry her share of the heavy robe and crown. Her service consummated by her mistress' kiss, she dies, as the people of the

East can, so they say, by pure denial of life. Charmian, we know, is of fiercer breed. Quick, desperate, agonized, sticking to her task to the end—when all is over she is at it still, fighting her Queen's battles still, mocking the enemy. She laughs in triumph as she too dies.

Cymbeline

CYMBELINE is said to have been a product, probably the first, of Shakespeare's leisured retirement to Stratford. Professor Ashley Thorndike thinks it was written in emulation of Beaumont and Fletcher's successful *Philaster*. There are signs that it was intended for the "private" theater of the Blackfriars. More than one editor has scented a collaborator; the late Dr. Furness, in particular, put many of the play's weaknesses to this account.

The Folio labels it tragedy, but it is not; it is tragi-comedy rather, or romance. Through treachery and mischance we move to a providentially happy ending. Repentance for wrong done, and then

Pardon's the word to all.

is the moral outcome, two of the least pardonable characters having conveniently been dispatched beyond human pardon's reach. In which digest of charitable wisdom—and the easing of the occasion for it—we may see if we will a certain leisured weariness of mind. The signs of association with the Blackfriars must be looked into carefully when we come to consider the play's staging, if for no other reason than that here was a theater far liker to our own than the open-air Globe. As for collaboration; we shall not deny Imogen to Shakespeare, nor Iachimo, the one done with such delight, the other, while he sways the plot, with exceeding skill. Here is not the master merely, but the past-master working at his ease. Much besides seems to bear his stamp, from Cloten to that admirable Gaoler. Was he as content, in his leisure, to set his stamp on such a counterfeit as the dissembling tyrant Queen? There is a slick professional competence about the writing of her, one may own. And how far is he guilty of the inepter lapses, with which the play is undeniably stained?

It is pretty poor criticism (Dr. Furness owns it) to fasten all the faults upon some unknown collaborator and allow one's adored Shakespeare all the praise. Lackeying of that sort leads us first to the minor, then, if we are not careful, into the larger lunacies. Better take shelter behind Johnson, who, like a schoolmaster with cane in hand, sums up his indignation in one tremendous sentence and lets his author—this author, when need be, as well as another —know that he, at any rate, will not "waste criticism upon unresisting imbecility, upon faults too evident for detection, and too gross for aggravation." Johnson was spared the dilemmas of modern research. He would not have taken kindly to our armament of the hair sieve. Nor would he ever have subscribed, one feels sure, to the convenience of a whipping-boy, whatever other tribute he might pay to Shakespeare's majesty. Still, even he approves Pope's opinion—for he quotes it—that the apparitions of the Leonatus family and the jingle they speak were "plainly foisted in afterwards for meer show, and apparently [are] not of Shakespear."

How much further must we go? The apparitions and their rubbish—

> When once he was mature for man,
> In Britain where was he
> That could stand up his parallel,
> Or fruitful object be
> In eye of Imogen, that best
> Could deem his dignity?

—are not only, one swears, not Shakespeare's, but could hardly have been perpetrated even by the perpetrator of the worst of the rest of the play. One searches for a whipping-boy to the whipping-boy; the prompter, possibly, kept in between rehearsal and performance, thumping the stuff out and thumbing it down between bites and sips of his bread and cheese and ale.

But Furness quotes a round dozen of passages besides, which he declares Shakespeare never, never could have written; and they all, or nearly all, have certainly a very tinny ring. Did the author of *King Lear* and *Antony and Cleopatra* descend to

> Triumphs for nothing and lamenting toys
> Is jollity for apes and grief for boys.

or to

> Th' imperious seas breed monsters; for the dish,
> Poor tributary rivers as sweet fish?

But he also, we notice, will have nothing to do—on Shakespeare's behalf—with

> Golden lads and girls all must,
> As chimney-sweepers, come to dust.

and he rejects Belarius altogether on the grounds, mainly, that the old gentleman's demand to be paid twenty years' board and lodging for the children he had abducted touches turpitude's lowest depths. But this surely is to deny even the whipping-boy a sense of pleasantly whimsical humor. It is hard to follow Furness all the way. There are, however, other directions in which we can look for this collaborator or interpolator; and we may possibly find, besides, a Shakespeare, who, for the moment, is somewhat at odds with himself.

The Nature of the Play

IF the play's construction is his unfettered work he is at odds with himself indeed. From the beginning he has been a good craftsman, and particularly skillful in the maneuvering of any two stories into a symmetrical whole. But here the attempt results in a very lopsided affair. The first scene sees both themes stated: Imogen's marriage to Posthumus, and the strange loss, years before, of her brothers. Then Iachimo's intrigue against her is pursued and completed, most expeditiously; the entire business is done in less than twelve hundred lines, with Cloten and his wooing thrown in. But meanwhile we see nothing, and hear only once, of the young princes. Certainly Imogen cannot set out on her wanderings and encounter them any sooner than she does; and, once she does, this part of the story—it is the phase of the blending of the two stories, and customarily would be the penultimate phase of the plot as a whole—makes due progress. But what of Posthumus? He is now banished from the scene for the space of another fourteen hundred lines or so. That is bad enough. But when he does return to it, the only contrivances for his development are a soliloquy, a mute duel with Iachimo, a quite undramatic encounter with an anonymous "Lord," a talk with a gaoler,

and a pointless pageant that he sleeps through. This is far worse.
He was never much of a hero, but here he becomes a bore. The
difficulties are plain. Once his faith in Imogen is destroyed and he
has commanded her murder (and we do not need both to see him
sending the command and Pisanio receiving it), there is nothing
left for him to do till he returns repentant; and once he returns he
cannot openly encounter any of the more important characters, or
the dramatic effect of his sudden appearance in the last scene (and
to that, in its elaboration, every thread, obviously, is to be drawn)
will be discounted. But it is just such difficulties as these that the
playwright learns to surmount. Can we see Shakespeare, past-
master in his craft, making such a mess of a job? If nothing else
showed a strange finger in the pie, this letting Posthumus slip
from the current of the story, and the clumsiness of the attempt
to restore him to prominence in it, should suffice to. Nevertheless,
Shakespeare's stamp, or an excellent imitation of it, is on much of
the actual writing hereabouts. One would not even swear him
entire exemption from the apparitions.

> Poor shadows of elysium, hence, and rest
> Upon your never-withering banks of flowers:
> Be not with mortal accidents opprest;
> No care of yours it is; you know 'tis ours.
> Whom best I love I cross; to make my gift
> The more delay'd, delighted. . . .

That, though pedestrian, is, for the occasion, good enough.

These structural clumsinesses concern the last two-thirds of the
play. The passages that Furness gibbets—the most and the worst
of them—fall there too; and there we may find, besides, minor
banalities of stagecraft, set as a rule in a poverty of writing, the
stagecraft and writing both showing a startling change from the
opulently thrifty methods that went to the making of *Coriolanus,
Antony and Cleopatra, King Lear, Othello*, this play's predecessors.

Are we to debit the mature Shakespeare with the dramatic
impotence of Pisanio's soliloquy:

> I heard no letter from my master since
> I wrote him Imogen was slain: 'tis strange:
> Nor hear I from my mistress, who did promise

To yield me often tidings; neither know I
What is betid to Cloten, but remain
Perplex'd in all. The heavens still must work.
Wherein I am false I am honest; not true, to be true.
These present wars shall find I love my country,
Even to the note o' the king, or I'll fall in them.
All other doubts, by time let them be clear'd:
Fortune brings in some boats that are not steer'd.

It is poor stuff; the information in it is hardly needed; it does not seem even meant to provide time for a change of scene or costume. Nor does Shakespeare now use to let his minor characters soliloquize to help his plots along.[1] There are two other such soliloquies: the Queen's rejoicing over Imogen's disappearance, rising to its forcible-feeble climax with

                    gone she is
To death or to dishonour; and my end
Can make good use of either: she being down,
I have the placing of the British crown.

This is nearly as redundant in matter; but villainy has its rights, and premature exultation over the misfortunes of the virtuous is one of them. Though it be Shakespeare at his worst, it may still be Shakespeare. So, more certainly, is the Second Lord's soliloquy, with which Cloten's second scene ends. This probably owes its existence to Imogen's need of a little extra time for getting into bed. But it adds information, and, more importantly, reiterates the sympathy of the Court for her in her trouble. It falls earlier in the play, in the stretch of the action that few will deny to be wholly Shakespeare's.

But, quality of writing and the unimportance of the speakers apart, is there not a curious artlessness about nearly all the soliloquies in the play? They are so frankly informative. Shakespeare's

---

[1] The writing of the rest of this scene is poverty itself (in fact, from Lucius' rescue of Imogen, just before, to the beginning of the long last scene of revelation, there is—except for the character of the Gaoler—marked deterioration of writing). The First Lord's

                So please your majesty
The Roman legions, all from Gallia drawn,
Are landed on your coast, with a supply
Of Roman gentlemen by the senate sent.

about touches bottom. Sheridan's burlesquing in *The Critic* has more life in it.

use of the soliloquy is no more subject to rule than are any other
of his methods; but his tendency, as his art matures, is both to
make it mainly a vehicle for the intimate thought and emotion of
his chief characters only, and to let its plot-forwarding seem quite
incidental to this. *Antony and Cleopatra*, a play of action, contains
few soliloquies, and they are not of dominant importance; Coriolanus, the man of action, is given hardly one; Hamlet, the reflec-
tive hero, abounds in them, but they are germane to idea rather
than story. Iago's soliloquies, it may be said, frankly develop the
plot. It will be truer to say they forecast it; the dramatic justification for this being that it is a plot, in both senses, hatched in his
own brain.[2] And we notice that once it is well under way he soliloquizes little more.

But in *Cymbeline*, what a disintegrating change! Posthumus'
soliloquies are reflectively emotional enough. The first is an outburst of rage; it would not, one supposes, have been any differently framed for Othello or Antony. The others contain such
simply informative passages as

> I am brought hither
> Among the Italian gentry, and to fight
> Against my lady's kingdom. . . .
> I'll disrobe me
> Of these Italian weeds, and suit myself
> As does a Briton peasant. . . .

as the seemingly needless

> I have resumed again
> The part I came in. . . .

And one asks, without being quite sure of the answer, how far is
that

> You married ones,
> If each of you should take this course, how many
> Must murder wives much better than themselves,
> For wrying but a little! . . .

meant to be addressed plump to his audience? But the flow of
emotion is generally strong enough to sweep any such obstacles
along.

[2] Edmund's soliloquies in *King Lear* come into the same category.

Iachimo passes from the dramatic perfection of the soliloquy in the bedchamber to the feebleness of his repentant

> Knighthoods and honours, borne
> As I wear mine, are titles but of scorn.
> If that thy gentry, Britain, go before
> This lout as he exceeds our lords, the odds
> Is that we scarce are men and you are gods.

—with which we hesitate to discredit Shakespeare in any case.

But what of that not merely ingenuously informative, but so *ex post facto* confidence from Belarius:

> O Cymbeline! heaven and my conscience knows
> Thou didst unjustly banish me: whereon,
> At three and two years old I stole these babes,
> Thinking to bar thee of succession as
> Thou reft'st me of my lands. Euriphile,
> Thou wast their nurse, they took thee for their mother,
> And every day do honour to her grave.
> Myself, Belarius, that am Morgan called,
> They take for natural father.

We shall have to search far back in Shakespeare's work for anything quite so apparently artless, and may be doubtful of finding it even there. Furness would make the collaborator responsible for Belarius. But what about the long aside—a soliloquy, in effect—by which Cornelius lets us know that the Queen is not to be trusted, and that the poison he has given her is not poison at all? This is embedded in the admittedly Shakespearean part of the play.

The soliloquies apart, when we find Imogen-Fidele, welcomed by Arviragus-Cadwal with

> I'll make 't my comfort
> He is a man: I'll love him as my brother. . . .

then glancing at him and Guiderius-Polydore and exclaiming

> Would it had been so, that they
> Had been my father's sons. . . .

and when the trick by which Cloten must be dressed in Posthumus' garments (so that Imogen waking by his corpse may mistake it) is not glossed over but emphasized and advertised, here, we feel, is artlessness indeed. But it is obviously a sophisticated,

not a native artlessness, the art that rather displays art than con-
ceals it.[3]

A fair amount of the play—both of its design and execution—is
pretty certainly not Shakespeare's.[4] Just how much, it is hard to say
(though the impossible negative seems always the easier to prove
in these matters), for the suspect stuff is often so closely woven
into the fabric. It may have come to him planned as a whole and
partly written. In which case he worked very thoroughly over
what are now the Folio's first two acts. Thereafter he gave attention to what pleased him most, saw Imogen and her brothers and
Cloten through to the end, took a fancy to Lucius and gave him
reality, did what more he could for Posthumus under the circumstances, generously threw in the First Gaoler, and rescued
Iachimo from final futility. This relieves him of responsibility for
the poor planning of the whole; he had been able to refashion the
first part to his liking. But why, then, should he leave so many of
the last part's ineptitudes in place? Or did the unknown cling
affectionately to them, or even put them back again after Shakespeare had washed his hands of the business? We are dabbling
now, of course, in pure "whipping-boy" doctrine, and flaws enough
can be found in it. Of the moments of "unresisting imbecility"
Shakespeare must be relieved; careless or conscienceless as he
might sometimes be, critical common sense forbids us to saddle
him with them. But, trying his hand at a new sort of thing (emulating Beaumont and Fletcher and their *Philaster*—why not?—he
had never been above taking a hint), and if, moreover, he was
trying it "by request" in hard-won leisure at Stratford, his grip
might easily be looser than usual. We find him with a firmer one,
that is certain, in *A Winter's Tale* and *The Tempest*. Allowing,
then, for some collaboration, and some incertitude besides, at what,
are we to suppose, is he aiming, what sort of play is he setting out
to write? And if the sophisticated artlessness is his, what end is
this meant to serve? These are the practical questions to be
answered here.

He has an unlikely story to tell, and in its unlikelihood lies not

---

[3] For a similar artlessness of method, compare the Prospero-Miranda, Prospero-
Caliban scenes in *The Tempest,* by which the story is told. But *The Tempest* is
a Masque rather than a play, and may properly be artificial.

[4] Both more and less, I myself feel, than Furness allows to be.

only its charm, but largely its very being; reduce it to reason, you would wreck it altogether. Now in the theater there are two ways of dealing with the inexplicable. If the audience are to take it seriously, leave it unexplained. They will be anxious—pathetically anxious—to believe you; with faith in the dose, they will swallow a lot. The other plan is to show one's hand, saying in effect: "Ladies and gentlemen, this is an exhibition of tricks, and what I want you to enjoy among other things is the skill with which I hope to perform them." This art, which deliberately displays its art, is very suited to a tragi-comedy, to the telling of a serious story that must yet not be taken too seriously, lest its comedy be swamped by its tragedy and a happy ending become too incongruous. Illusion must by no means be given the go-by; if this does not have its due in the theater, our emotions will not be stirred. Nor should the audience be overwhelmed by the cleverness of the display; arrogance in an artist antagonizes us. This is where the seeming artlessness comes in; it puts us at our ease, it is the equivalent of "You see there is no deception." But very nice steering will be needed between the make-believe in earnest and in jest.

Shakespeare sets his course (as his habit is, and here we may safely assume that it is he) in his very first scene. We have the immediately necessary tale of Posthumus and Imogen, and the more extraordinary one of the abducting of the princes is added. And when the First Gentleman brings the Second Gentleman's raised eyebrows down with

> Howsoe'er 'tis strange. . . .
> Yet is it true, sir.

we of the audience are asked to concur in the acquiescent

> I do well believe you.

For "this," Shakespeare and the First Gentleman are telling us, "is the play you are about to hear; and not only these facts, but their rather leisurely amplifying, and that supererogatory tale of Posthumus' birth, should show you the sort of play it is. There is trouble in the air, but you are not to be too strung up about it. Moreover, the way you are being told it all, the easy fall of this verse, with its light endings and spun-out sentences, should be wooing you into the right mood. And this talk about Cassibelan is to help send you back into a fabulous past in which these

romantic things may legitimately happen. So now submit yourselves, please, to the illusion of them."

The beginning, then—quite properly—inclines to make-believe
in earnest, rendering to the theater its normal due. And the play's
story will follow its course, nor may any doubt of its likelihood
be hinted; that is a point of dramatic honor. But in half a hundred
ways, without actually destroying the illusion, Shakespeare can
contrive to prevent us taking it too seriously.

Cornelius lets us know at once that the poison is not poison;
for, monster though the Queen is, we must not fear tragedy of
that stark sort to be impending. We must be interested in watching for the working-out of the trick played upon her, and amused
the while that

She is fool'd
With a most false effect . . . .

There is a subtler aim in the artlessness of Belarius' soliloquy.
By accepting its frank familiarity we become, in a sense, Shakespeare's accomplices. In telling us the story so simply he is at the
same time saying, "You see what an amusing business this playwriting is; take it, please, no more seriously than I do." The
stressing of the coincidence of the meeting of the sister and her
lost brothers has a like effect. We feel, and we are meant to feel,
"What a pretty fairy tale!" The emphasizing of the artifice, the
"folly of the fiction," by which Cloten's corpse comes to be mistaken for Posthumus' does much to mitigate the crude horror of
the business, to bring it into the right tragi-comic key. Keep us
intrigued by the preparations for the trick, and we shall gain
from its accomplishment a half-professional pleasure; we shall be
masters of the illusion, not its victims. And throughout the whole
elaborate scene of revelation with which the play ends we are
most artfully steered between illusion and enjoyment of the ingenuity of the thing. *We* hold all the clues; the surprises are for
Cymbeline, Imogen, Posthumus and the rest, not for us. We soon
foresee the end, and our wits are free to fasten on the skill of the
approach to it. But there is an unexpected turn or so, to provide
excitement; and the situation is kept so fully charged with emotion that our sympathy is securely held.

This art that displays art is a thing very likely to be to the taste of the mature and rather wearied artist. When you are exhausted with hammering great tragic themes into shape it is a relief to find a subject you can play with, and to be safely able to take more interest in the doing than the thing done. For once you can exercise your skill for its own sake. The pretty subject itself seems to invite a certain artlessness of treatment. But the product will have a sophisticated air about it, probably.

The Blackfriars and Its Influence

WHETHER the style of the play—out of whatever combination of circumstances this was compacted—owes anything (and, if so, what) to its probable connection with the Blackfriars, is not much easier to determine; for our knowledge of the stage there, and the degree of its difference from the Globe's, is still much in the realm of guesswork.

Cymbeline must be dated about 1610. It was in 1609 that the King's Men first went to act in these quieter, candle-lit surroundings. They did not desert the Globe, which remained their summer quarters; a successful play would be seen there also. The open-air theaters stayed in use for another thirty years, and the old audiences had still to be catered for. But critical opinion would now come to center, taste to be dictated, at the Blackfriars; and the dramatists attached there would have to consider what sort of work made most effect in these changed conditions. Beaumont and Fletcher may have scored an early hit with *Philaster*[5] and so (if theater managers of yesterday were as managers of today, and possibly they were) set a fashion which would be hastily followed. But sooner or later, a specifically indoor drama must have developed. The change would come slowly, and not very certainly. There would be reaction again it. The elder dramatists might no more take kindly to it than would the old audience when they saw its new effects show up a little pallidly, perhaps, in the sunlight at the Globe. But the shifting from outdoors in made all the difference, finally. Our drama of today, with its scenic illusion, its quiet acting, its gains in subtlety and loss in power,

---

[5] They had already written a play or two for the Paul's children and their indoor theater.

was born, not upon the platforms of the inn-yards, but of the patronage and prosperity that produced the private theater.

Not that indoor performances were a novelty. The children had always played indoors. Such a man as Lyly had written exclusively for them, and other dramatists gave them plays that might differ little, or not at all, from those provided for their elders. But a boy Tamburlaine could "holla" his loudest and yet break no windows; though the plays did not differ, the performances would. The adult companies had played indoors too. *A Midsummer Night's Dream* has a delicacy of fiber and the early *Love's Labour's Lost* a preciosity which may show that Shakespeare devised them for select audiences. When James's Scottish extravagance replaced Elizabeth's English thrift, Court performances were frequent. But the Globe had been the breeding-ground of the greater work. *Hamlet, Othello, Lear* and *Macbeth* had come to birth there; and there force and simplicity were cardinal virtues. This was not because a slice of the audience would be uncultured (so it would be at Court), but because the theater's every condition enhanced such virtues; the daylight, and the actors on their platform, making point-blank unvarnished appeal. Subtleties could be achieved, but they must be lodged in simple and accustomed forms; they were, as we find, thought safest and surest of effect in the comparative intimacy of the soliloquy. Scraps of scenery might come into use; but in daylight there could be nothing like scenic illusion.

What would the confined quiet of the "private" theater bring? The style of the acting of the old plays would change; bad actors would not shout so much, and good actors could develop new delicacies of expression. The plots of new plays might well grow more elaborate and their writing more diffuse, for it would be easier to keep an audience attentive and see that no points were missed. If violence is still the thing, noise will not be. The old clattering battles may gradually go out of favor; but processions will look finer than ever, and apparitions and the like will be twice as effective. Rhetoric will lose hold a little (to regain it when the theaters grow larger and the groundlings come to their own again) and sentiment will become as telling as passion. This would bring softer and slacker versifying, and the impetus to carry through the old powerful speeches will no longer be needed.

Humor may be less brisk; the pace of the acting in general will tend to slow down. Mere tendencies, all these, with little consistency to be seen in them for a long while, and recurrent reaction against them.

One speculates upon what might have happened had Shakespeare reached London as a young man, not when he did, but a generation later, to serve his apprenticeship at the Blackfriars instead of at the Theatre, the Rose and the Curtain. As it is he is an old hand when the change comes, and will live out the rest of his life retired, more or less, from the stage. But while he still wrote for it he would remain a most practical playwright. We might look to find in his latest plays signs that he was as sensitive as the youngest to this shift of direction. If *Cymbeline* was written for the Blackfriars it may well owe a few of its idiosyncrasies to that mere fact.

The Play's First Staging

THOUGH we do not know how the stage there differed from the Globe's (and there is much about the staging at the Globe which still keeps us guessing), that the two did differ somewhat we may be sure. "The hall," Sir Edmund Chambers tells us, "was 66 ft. from north to south and 46 ft. from east to west. . . . The stage was at one end of the hall." Not much more than 20 ft. of the whole length, then, would be spared to it. Of this, 8 or 10 ft. would be needed for back stage and passage. That would leave a main stage 10 or 12 ft. in depth, by, perhaps, the full 46 ft. in width. An awkward shape; but about 10 ft. each side would be taken up by the rows of stage stools. The practicable main stage would be, say, 12 ft. by 26. Cramped acting-space, after the Globe, even if we deepen it by a foot or so. We do not know the height of the hall; but it could hardly match the Globe's three stories, which gave an upper stage, and room above that for the working of machines, and probably room above that again. On the other hand, if it were ceiled and not too lofty, the descent of deities enthroned would be an effective and fairly easy business, and the present apostrophe to Jupiter, with its

> The marble pavement closes, he is entered
> His radiant roof.

could be exactly illustrated.

While plays had to serve for both theaters, the principles (so to call them) of the Globe staging would be likely to endure, but its practice would need to be adapted to the Blackfriars material conditions; and these—doors, openings, balconies—would have been dictated by the restricted space there and its different disposition. With more breadth than depth available, the inner stage opening might well be widened, both to improve the inner stage itself and to give better access from the main stage. The action upon the inner stage would in any case be more prominent with the main or front stage reduced in size. That was turning already into the "apron" of its final metamorphosis. But if it has now been brought to a 10 or 12 ft. depth it is to suffer no further in size, nor very much in importance, for another two hundred years to come. The inner stage will be widened still more, and deepened and again deepened as opportunity serves. This, however, will be for the accommodation of the coming scenery, and to give lighting its effect; and for long the actors will confine themselves there as little as may be.

The action of *Cymbeline* evidently makes no demands that the stage at the Globe could not quite well fulfill. But one scene, at least, would be doubly effective at the Blackfriars. It would be played at either house wholly on the inner stage. Imogen is asleep, the taper has been left burning near her. Iachimo comes softly from the trunk, steals about the room, noting all its features on his tablets, stands over her gloating. The dramatic value of all this will depend upon his expression being well seen; and the verse is written for subtle and gentle speaking. How much would not be lost on the removed inner stage of the Globe, and gained in the intimacy of the Blackfriars, where the candlelight too—the effect of it is twice emphasized—would be something more than a symbol!

One other thing about the scene should be noted. Iachimo says:

> I will write all down:
> Such and such pictures; there the window; such
> The adornment of the bed; the arras, figures,
> Why, such and such. . . .

and leaves it at that. Not till two scenes later are we—and Post-humus—given the description of the room, with its tapestry of silk and silver, its chimney

> south the chamber; and the chimney-piece
> Chaste Dian bathing. . .
> The roof o' the chamber
> With golden cherubims is fretted: her andirons—
> I had forgot them—were two winking Cupids
> Of silver, each on one foot standing, nicely
> Depending on their brands.

The inference is plain. Whatever changes had been made at the Blackfriars, this scene was not thought to need an individual background; and Shakespeare carefully refrains from calling our attention to—something that is not there![6]

Belarius' cave, however, is a piece of scenery of some sort. The text makes this clear.

> A goodly day not to keep house, with such
> Whose roof's as low as ours! Stoop, boys: this gate
> Instructs you how to adore the heavens. . . .

A few lines later comes a casual "We house i' the rock," but there is no definite reference to "this our pinching cave" for thirty-eight lines. It would be a conventional, decorative piece of scenery, probably, but very obviously a cave; the audience could not be left, for a large part of the scene, to wonder what it was had provoked that "Stoop, boys . . ." and the sequent moralizing.

Of Jupiter we have spoken already; if he could descend through an actual marble pavement of a ceiling, so much the better. Post-humus' prison seems to call for the inner stage. He would lie down to sleep not too far back from the line of its opening. Sicilius and the rest, entering *as in an apparition*, would probably come through curtains (very probably through slits in them) behind him. *They circle Posthumus round as he lies sleeping* means, I think, that they stand, not march, round him.[7] When Jupiter

[6] Dramatically, as usual, he is the gainer. The Cupids and Chaste Dian and Cleopatra staring us in the face would only have distracted our attention from Iachimo. But it is excellent material for the "madding" of Posthumus, and the better for being freshly used.

[7] *With music before them*, read in conjunction with *after other music*, becomes a careless phrase for music played before they enter. It cannot imply attendant apparitions performing upon recorders. Cf. p. 483.

descends, he can hardly come all the way down. As a god he must hold the center of the stage; and if he did come all the way he would then obliterate the sleeping Posthumus, who, for decorative reasons (important when apparitions are in hand), would almost certainly be in the center, too. Besides, godhead is less impressive on the ground; nor does any one want to lower those machines further than need be—they are tricky things. He might stay suspended in mid-air; but he would be terribly likely to swing about. His best resting-place would be the upper stage. It is just possible that, at the Blackfriars, this may not have been the inconvertible, railed, low-roofed balcony which we commonly imagine for the public theaters. A deep gallery above the inner stage, not more than 8 or 10 ft. up, with its center open, or able to open, to the ceiling, would answer this particular purpose very well. No other use, we notice, is made of the upper stage throughout the play[8]; Cloten even serenades Imogen at her door, instead of beneath her window.

The comprehensive last scene asks for the full extent of main and inner stage together, especially if Posthumous' listening *behind* is to be made effective. The First Gaoler's soliloquy—if he is to speak it on the main stage with the inner stage curtains closing behind him—may have been put in to make time for the shifting of the pallet upon which Posthumus had been lying.[9] For the rest of the action, inner stage, outer stage and the two doors we know of function normally enough.

The Style of the Play

WITH furnishing and costume comes the problem—if we choose to make it one—of the play's anachronisms. But why make it one? No such difficulty exists as in *Antony and Cleopatra*, over the Rome and Egypt that we have learned to see, that Shakespeare

---

[8] Nor is any use made of it in *A Winter's Tale*; nor, apparently, in *The Tempest*, except upon one occasion, when the stage direction reads, instead of the usual *above: Prospero on the top (invisible).* One must not base too much upon carelessly written stage directions; one must remember, too, that stage terminology is not exact. But a systematic study of them in the plays that can be safely held to have been written for the Blackfriars will do much to tell us what the stage there was like; and the knowledge is needed.

[9] But here the question of act-division is involved. This is discussed on p. 487.

had not; nor as in *King Lear*, over a Court Fool and a topical Oswald, no longer topical to us, set unconcernedly in a barbarous scene. There one can at least contend—though it is a poor plea— for tragedy and its integrity or history and its verities; but why cultivate an archaeological conscience towards *Cymbeline's* Britain and such a story as this? Shakespeare knew as well as we know that war chariots and the god Jupiter did not fit with a Posthumus made Gentleman of the King's Bedchamber, who waves his farewells with hat and glove and handkerchief, with a Cloten who fights duels and plays at bowls, a Belarius who talks of rustling at Court in unpaid-for silks, a Guiderius joking about a tailor, an Imogen disguised in doublet and hose; and—if he had stopped to think about it—that in a Rome over which Augustus Cæsar ruled, Frenchmen, Dutchmen and Spaniards would not be found discussing their country mistresses, or an Iachimo making a bet of ten thousand ducats. We commonly say he was careless about these things; it is a very fertile carelessness that shows here. For from this collection of inconsistencies emerges a quite definite picture all illuminative of the fantasy of the story. In a work of art, for what other consistency should we ask?

The style of the play; this is what, above all, its staging must elucidate, for, far more than with most plays, this is its life. Its contents may be mongrel, but it has a specific style. Set Imogen in her doublet and hose beside Rosalind or Viola and—all difference of character and circumstance allowed for—note the complete change of method; the verse with its varied pace and stress, complex, parenthetical, a vehicle for a strange mixing of artifice and simplicity, of naked feeling and sententious fancy—the old forthright brilliance has given place to this.

It is style (nor of writing only; for writing is but half, or less, of the dramatic battle) that gives their due complexion to all the actualities of the play. Critics have exclaimed against the blinding of Gloucester in *King Lear*. Upon the face of it, Imogen's discovery of Cloten's headless corpse should be as horrible a business; more so, indeed, for much more is made of it. But, thanks to the style of its contriving, this passes unremarked.[10] The artless artifice of the preparations for the episode, this we have noted

---

[10] I have not pursued comment much beyond the pages of Furness. The outcry against the blinding of Gloucester is misguided, as I have tried to show elsewhere.

already. But much more is done in mitigation. We do not see
Cloten killed; no moment of poignancy is allowed him; he vanishes bombasting and making a ridiculous fight of it. The next
we see of him is his ridiculous head; and the boyish unconcern
of the young savage who has slaughtered him puts us in the
mood to make as little of the matter.

> This Cloten was a fool, an empty purse;
> There was no money in't: not Hercules
> Could have knock'd out his brains, for he had none. . . .

Then, before the body is brought on, comes the long, tender
passage of the mourning over the unconscious Fidele; and our
attention is so fixed upon her, Cloten already a memory, that
when she wakes beside the dummy corpse it is really not much
more to us than a dummy and a pretext for her aria of agony. The
setting of the scene, too, must have helped to rob the business of
poignancy. There is one sort of realism to be gained on a bare
stage and another in scenic illusion; but before a decoratively
conventional cave we shall not take things too literally. The right
interpretation of all this will depend upon a style of production
and acting fitted to the style of the play.

Not too much emphasis, naturally, is to be placed upon so very
parliamentary a war; and we notice that the stage directions for
the battle are unusual.

> *Enter Lucius, Iachimo and the Romane army at one doore: and
> the Britaine army at another: Leonatus Posthumus following like
> a poore souldier. They march over and goe out. Then enter
> againe in skirmish Iachimo and Posthumus: he vanquisheth and
> disarmeth Iachimo, and then leaves him. . . . The Battaile con-
> tinues, the Britaines fly, Cymbeline is taken. Then enter to his
> rescue, Belarius, Guiderius, and Arviragus. . . . Enter Posthumus
> and seconds the Britaines. They rescue Cymbeline and exeunt.
> . . . Enter Cymbeline, Belarius, Guiderius, Arviragus, Pisanio
> and Romane captives. The Captaines present Posthumus to Cym-
> beline, who delivers him over to a Gaoler.*

Here is action enough, certainly. But why are there none of the
accustomed directions for alarums, drums and trumpets? And
why is there such a strangely small allowance of intermediate
dialogue to so much and such elaborate business? Belarius and

Guiderius color their thrusting-in with a line or so, Iachimo soliloquizes shortly between whiles, and Posthumus, the battle being
over, is given a speech which might be modeled upon a messenger's in Greek tragedy. But while fighting heroically as a peasant,
and when he is brought a prisoner to Cymbeline he utters not a
word; and Cymbeline himself stays mute as a fish, nor seems
(incidentally) to recognize his son-in-law. Stage directions make
a perilous basis for argument; and we ought, it may be, to lay
these to the account of some editor preparing the text for printing—for the rest, there are few enough signs of the prompt book
about it. But, as it stands, the elaborate pantomime really looks
not unlike an attempt to turn old-fashioned dumb show to fresh
and quaint account. It is certainly not a battle by either of the
very different patterns of *Antony and Cleopatra* or *Coriolanus*,
nor is it at all like the simplified affair we find in *King Lear*. It
has, one would say, a style of its own.

Then there are Jupiter and the apparitions; and upon them
hangs that highly fictitious soothsayer with his

> The piece of tender air, thy virtuous daughter,
> Which we call 'mollis aer'; and 'mollis aer'
> We term it 'mulier.' . . .

There are, as we noted, the (for Shakespeare) archaic soliloquies,
and such strokes of still more deliberate artifice in this kind as
that by which, in his scene with Imogen, Iachimo is made to
speak an eight-line aside, which he intends her to overhear.
There is Belarius' "ingenuous instrument" sounding "solemn
music" in that salutary cave.

Make all the allowance we may for the vagaries of collaboration, the result still shows strange divergence from Shakespeare's
precedent work. In our art-jargon of today (or is it yesterday
already?) the thing is very "amusing." At the core of the best of
it the strong dramatic pulse beats still, and the craftsman still
delights in the ease of his cunning. But it is Shakespeare with a
difference.

If the garment of the play's writing is artifice, the costuming
of the characters must take account of it. The Masque and its
fancies were in vogue at the moment. We should not ascribe
too much to that; but look at those drawings by Inigo Jones,

then read some of the more decorative passages—Iachimo's, for instance—of this verse and prose; there is a common fancy in both. These figures, though, must stand solidly and upon firm ground in their amorphous world. Shakespeare may play tricks with historic time, but to his own chronology—slips apart—he will be true; to his own natural history, so to speak, as well. He knows, for instance, how to etherealize nature without fantasticating the plain facts of it. When the two brothers find Fidele dead:

> Why, he but sleeps.
> If he be gone he'll make his grave a bed;
> With female fairies will his tomb he haunted,
> And worms will not come to thee.
>   With fairest flowers,
> While summer lasts, and I live here, Fidele,
> I'll sweeten thy sad grave. Thou shalt not lack
> The flower that's like thy face, pale primrose, nor
> The azured harebell, like thy veins; no, nor
> The leaf of eglantine, whom not to slander,
> Out-sweetened not thy breath. . . .

No mannerism of costume, or of speech or behavior, must be let obscure the perfect clarity and simplicity of that.

And cheek by jowl with the jingling twaddle of the apparitions (with which no one is ready to discredit Shakespeare) we find the Gaoler and his stark prose (which no one will deny him). The contrast alone makes an effect. In the morning, we must suppose, Posthumus is roused[11]:

> GAOLER. Come, sir, are you ready for death?
> POSTHUMUS. Over-roasted rather; ready long ago.
> GAOLER. Hanging is the word, sir; if you be ready for that, you are well cooked.

---

[11] We only suppose so because the vision should naturally occupy a night, and a criminal goes to his death at dawn. But, on the face of it, Posthumus is taken to prison, has his nap, sees his vision and is roused for execution, all within the time it takes Cymbeline to tidy himself up after the battle and return to his tent (as the editors have it), or wherever else the last scene may be supposed to take place. Yet another instance of the clumsiness of the penultimate section of the play's action. As to the contrast between the Gaoler's plain prose and the decorative mystery of the apparitions, though Shakespeare did not write the jingle, some of the other verse may well be his; and he was, one supposes, a consenting party to the main scheme of the scene.

POSTHUMUS. So, if I prove a good repast to the spectators, the dish pays the shot.

GAOLER. A heavy reckoning for you, sir. But the comfort is, you shall be called to no more payments, fear no more tavern-bills, which are often the sadness of parting, as the procuring of mirth: you come in faint for want of meat, depart reeling with too much drink; sorry that you have paid too much, and sorry that you are paid too much: purse and brain both empty—the brain the heavier for being too light, the purse too light, being drawn of heaviness: of this contradiction you shall now be quit. O, the charity of a penny cord! It sums up thousands in a trice: you have no true debitor and creditor but it; of what's past, is, and to come, the discharge: your neck, sir, is pen, book and counters; so the acquittance follows.

The elaborate pattern of this, the play upon thought and words, the sententious irony, is as sheer artifice as is the vision itself, the "ingenuous instrument," or Iachimo's overheard asides. Compare this gaoler with his cousin-german Abhorson, in *Measure for Measure*. But he is a figure of crass reality, nevertheless. And further fantastication than Shakespeare has already allowed for the fitting of him into the general scheme will be his ruin. That flash of a phrase which gives him life,

> O, the charity of a penny cord!

is actuality supercharged; there is solid man summed up in it.

The problem is, then, to devise a setting and costuming which will neither eccentrically betray the humanity which is at the heart of the play nor, on the other hand, wall it round with ill-fitting exactitudes. Rome, Britain, the cave near the Severn, Cornelius and his drugs, Cassibelan and his tribute, these are decorative material to be turned to account; but to the play's peculiar account. Lucius must be a figure capable of

> A Roman with a Roman's heart can suffer . . . .

neighbored though he is by Iachimo, described as an Italian always, from whom comes naturally enough such talk of Post-humus as

> I never saw him sad.
> There is a Frenchman his companion, one,
> An eminent monsieur, that, it seems, much loves
> A Gallian girl at home. . . .

Cloten and Cymbeline and the Queen must be as at home in serenading and talk of knighthood and the distilling of perfumes as in argument over Mulmutius. There is no great difficulty about it once we realize that it is a problem of fancy, not of research; and how and why it was that Shakespeare saw his Princess Imogen, first with

> All of her that is out of door most rich! ...

then in

> A riding-suit, no costlier than would fit
> A franklin's housewife.

then dressed in

> doublet, hat, hose, all
> That answer to them ...

(a figure quite intimately familiar to his audience, that's to say), and yet gave her for her bedtime prayer:

> To your protection I commend me, gods!
> From fairies and the tempters of the night
> Guard me, beseech ye!

—why he wished both to bring her as close to us as he could, at the same time transporting her, not to a distant world of historic fact, but into a timeless picture-book. He has, when he needs it, his measure of accuracy for depicting the past, though it is not ours. The Rome of *Julius Cæsar, Antony and Cleopatra* and *Coriolanus* is integrated by a very definite purpose; and it is quite other than the one which dictates these allusions to Sinon and Æneas, Gallia and the Pannonians, scattered as if from a pepper-pot, with (three several times) fairies thrown in besides.[12]

We can divine, though dimly, one or two details of the play's first costuming. Posthumus, when he returns with the Roman army, wears distinctive "Italian weeds," over which he can slip (apparently) the disguise of a "poor" British soldier. In this he fights Iachimo, who does not recognize him. He then slips it off again (he is allowed but a few seconds for either change) for the

---

[12] It is needless to point out, surely, that by dressing the play in present-day clothes we shall *not* be reproducing the effect of the first performances. Cloten is no more to be seen in Piccadilly today than he was in the streets of Lud's-town. We only add another anachronism, which the text does not provide for.

encounter with the British Lord, who for his part does not recognize him as an enemy. Were the Italian weeds, then, not so very distinctive? But neither does Cymbeline recognize him when he is "presented" as a prisoner.[13] Possibly he is meant to wear some sort of visored helmet. Everything hereabouts is pretty slipshod, be the blame Shakespeare's or another's, and the audience must borrow a blind eye from Cymbeline and Iachimo.

And if "Italian weeds," had not those mute guests of Philario's, the Dutchman and the Spaniard, also some such distinguishing marks about them? Either they had or, with the Frenchman, an explanatory line or two, now lost, must have been allotted to each. Who was to know, otherwise, what they were? It would be a slight, amusing touch or so; an unusual hat or ruff, a peculiar doublet, a strange pair of breeches, possibly. It is no great matter; another sign, though, of the decorative bias of the play.[14]

If the scenic embryo of the cave is to be made the excuse for a full-fledged family of pictures of Britain and Rome, the designer of them must go warily to work. Just because he will not be flying so fully in the face of this play's stagecraft, he will be insidiously led into one temptation after another. He can fairly safely make, for Cymbeline's Court and Philario's house, the battlefield, Posthumus' prison, a tent, for the royal headquarters, a similar provision to that the cave makes for Imogen's adventures; a decorative background, that is to say, which will be in purpose no more than furniture for the action. If he goes further towards

---

[13] The stage direction is precise: *The Captaines present Posthumus to Cymbeline, who delivers him over to a Gaoler.* If he were recognizable the situation is too obvious not to have been enlarged upon—even by the here suspected whipping-boy!

[14] Cf. *The Parlement of Pratlers*, 1593, reissued by the Fanfrolico Press, 1928.
JOHN.   God speed, Taylor.
TAYLOR.   Welcome, sir.
JOHN.   How many elles of sattin must I buy to make me a doublet?
TAYLOR.   Four elles and a quarter, sir.
JOHN.   And how much velvet for my breeches?
TAYLOR.   If you will have them made after the Spanish fashion you must have three elles and a halfe.
JOHN.   How much broad cloath must I have to make me a cloake after the Romane fashion, or a riding cloake after the Dutch maner?
TAYLOR.   You must have little lesse than five elles and a halfe, to make one large enough for you with a coxcombado of the same cloth.
Philario, perhaps, wore a "cloake after the Romane fashion."

realism or illusion he will soon find himself at odds with his theme. We may now have no such elaborate painting by words and their music of this forest and its cave as forbids us to transpose the moonlit wood of *A Midsummer Night's Dream* into any other medium, nor such magic invoked as will make the best paint-and-canvas versions of *King Lear's* heath or *Macbeth's* Inverness redundant and commonplace; but realism and illusion will as surely damnify the artifice in which the idiosyncrasy of this action lies. Conventional decoration may do; yet against too much of that, even, the figures of the actors will be blurred. Actors are human; they cannot conform to arbitrary design. Artifice of scene must be measured to the artifice of the play; it should remain, simply and modestly, in the shadow of it, moreover.

Nor, as we have seen, must a designer discount the description of Imogen's bedchamber, with which Iachimo whips his victim into a frenzy, by having painted us a plain picture of it in another medium first. Nor had he better bring Jupiter into a very practicable prison. Nor should he too positively define any whereabouts which the play's text leaves vague. Nor, of course, must he, whatever else he does, let any need for the shifting of his scenery obstruct the easy march of the action.

The Music

CLOTEN's aubade will be sung by a man or boy, and most probably to the accompaniment of a consort of viols.[15] But before its "wonderful sweet aire" we have "First a verye excellent good conceyted thing," some piece for the consort alone. A glance at the Folio text shows us why; Imogen otherwise will have but a column and a half of it in which to change from her night attire back to her princess' robes (she had had just a column

---

[15] It might well have been sung by the actor of Arviragus. He, we find later, is ready enough to sing the dirge over Fidele, while Guiderius' excuse for not joining him in singing it is so palpable and overcharged that we may well set it down to domestic difficulties supervening—and the whipping-boy.

> For notes of sorrow, out of tune, are worse
> Than priests and fanes that lie.

This (it sticks fast in Furness' throat) is indeed just such a pretentious piece of nonsense as a fourth-rate writer would proudly devise for the disguising of a little difficulty—making it, in the event, ten times more noticeable.

of dialogue—though possibly an act-pause besides—in which to prepare for bed; but undressing is a quicker business). The consort will be employed again for the *Solemn musick* that comes from Belarius' "ingenuous instrument," and again to accompany the apparitions.

No cornets, we notice, are sounded when Cymbeline receives the Roman ambassador in state; we have already discussed the absence of drums, trumpets or alarums from the battle. This may in each case be editorial omission—or it may not.

The Play's Construction

THE scene-dividing in the Folio has not been consistently done. The editor apparently set out to mark a fresh scene at every clearance of the stage. But upon the very first page he tripped; for the two Gentlemen, seeing the Queen, Imogen and Posthumus approach, will only disappear as they appear.[16] He trips again (in the other direction) when Philario and Iachimo *Exeunt* and Posthumus returns for his soliloquy,

> Is there no way for men to be, but women
> Must be half-workers? . . .

and again when Guiderius and Cloten *Fight and exeunt*. Here, in both cases, is a cleared stage, and he gives us no scene-division. Can one follow the process of his mind? If the staging was as we have been imagining, he has the cave before him, and he comes to think of "scene" in this other sense. But he is far from fixed in the notion; for a while back, when Imogen entered the cave, leaving just such a cleared stage with just such an entrance to follow, he had marked a fresh scene. In the other case he may have had the furniture of Philario's house in his mind's eye.

There are signs in the text itself that the opening or shutting of the inner stage, the drawing of its curtains, is meant to mark change of place, and, what is more important, that it is only done

---

[16] But it is, of course, possible that this effect, a commonplace upon the stage at the Globe, could not be so well contrived in the smaller space at the Blackfriars, and that therefore, to give the three important characters the full sweep of their "entrance," the two Gentlemen had to disappear first.

to that end. The scheme—if it is a scheme—does not work out with absolute consistency, but it is worth attention.[17] From the first scene till after Pisanio's account to Imogen of Posthumus' sailing, when she is sent for by the Queen, there is no change of place implied (nor lapse of time[18]). Now we have both; for we are taken to Rome with Posthumus already arrived there, and this scene can best be played (though of course it need not be) with the inner stage revealed; the Dutchman and Spaniard, at any rate, will better serve such purpose as they do serve seated and in the background. We then come back to Cymbeline's Court, and, once there, neither change of place nor lapse of time is implied (nor is any furniture required; so the action can go forward on the front stage) till after Cloten's second scene and the Lord's soliloquy. By "place," of course, we need never understand anything more definite than a particular scene's action indicates.

The bedchamber-scene now occupies the inner stage; of this there is no doubt at all. The next scene contains the aubade, and would, as certainly, be played on the outer stage. It gives ample time for the removal of the bed and Iachimo's chest, and for the resetting of Philario's furniture, if the inner stage is to be used again for his house at Rome. There is not quite the same need for this; but certainly Philario and Posthumus *sound* like men sitting waiting (from the play's point of view) for Iachimo. There is also an interval of time to account for.

If the inner stage has been used again (furniture and all) for Philario's house, there might now supposedly be some difficulty, for the next scene's first stage direction begins: *Enter in state, Cymbeline, . .* and we at once envisage the conventional throne set on the inner stage. But the direction continues:

> *. . . Cymbeline, Queene, Cloten and Lords at one*
> *doore, and at another, Caius Lucius and attendants.*

---

[17] The so-called "alternation theory," hard pressed by Brodmeier and Allbright as a comprehensive rule of Elizabethan stagecraft, and (as that) pretty thoroughly exploded, has been applied, much modified, by Professor Thorndike to this very play and to *Antony and Cleopatra* (*Shakespeare's Theatre*, pp. 121-25). But his arrangement, and his explanation of it, differ in some significant ways from that which follows.

[18] The half-hour allowed Pisanio in which to see Posthumus aboard is filled up by Cloten's first scene.

So that apparent difficulty is surmounted, whether purposely or by chance.[19]

There is now no change of place nor use for anything but the front stage till the introducing of Belarius, Guiderius and Arviragus discloses the cave—and the inner stage, of course. And if this "place" that the sight of the cave suggests is a little more generalized as forest than the "place" we have called Cymbeline's Court, which, in turn, was as much more generalized than Philario's house and Imogen's bedchamber, then a hypothetical plan of shifting from outer to inner stage or back only to mark change of place (and secondarily, it may be, lapse of time) works out well enough. For, Belarius and his boys departed, Pisanio and Imogen arrive.[20] They ignore the existence of the cave, as they have no use for it, but it remains in our eye as a symbol of the forest. Incidentally, the reminder that Imogen in her trouble is near her lost brothers will both sharpen and sweeten that dramatic effect.

We then return to the Court and the front stage; then again to the forest and the cave for a long stretch of action, which is broken only by that seemingly futile fifteen-line Roman irruption of two Senators and the two Tribunes. We may observe that Imogen, after two nights' wandering, is still in front of the cave. So we should put it, sitting in an "illusionary" theater; and then, perhaps, start to argue that she might have wandered round and round. But it was long enough before audiences granted scenery such autonomy. She was in the forest before, and here she still is; that is all the sight of the cave would testify at the Blackfriars— or the Globe.

But why are we presented (upon the front stage; and the cave will be hidden) with the paltry little episode of the Senators

---

[19] It could equally have been surmounted by Posthumus re-entering for his

> Is there no way for men to be, but women
> Must be half-workers? . . .

soliloquy upon the outer stage; this, indeed, he may be meant to do in any case. Moreover, the act-division, if this implied a pause, would have surmounted it. We come to that question later.

[20] Rowe, re-editing the play eighty years later, quite disregards the Folio's *Scena Quarta* and brings them on in this same scene, which he, the first, has labeled "A Forest with a Cave." He sees scenes broadly in terms of scenery; just about as broadly, rather more logically, than this editor of the Folio sees them.

and Tribunes? One reason is that it will not do to let the Roman invasion lapse for too long from the story; the arrival of Lucius and his legions must be prepared for. Another is that an impression of the passing of time must be given us, between Imogen's welcome to the cave and the setting-out for the morning's hunt. There is Cloten's soliloquy to serve the purpose; but if this is to be spoken with the cave in sight—as it probably should be, to "place" him in the forest—it may not be sufficient. Here, then, would seem to be change of place employed to mark lapse of time.[21]

We probably see no more of the cave once Lucius has led the weeping Imogen away. Belarius and the young princes could play their next scene before it. The question is, have they not been too identified with it for us not to remark, then, *their* never remarking that Cloten's body and Fidele's have vanished? With scenery still embryonic, it is upon nice points of this sort that good stagecraft would depend.

The panoramic process of the battle will pass upon the main stage (would pass more slickly if the two doors faced each other or even were askew instead of being flat in the wall). This will give ample time for the making of the inner stage into Posthumus' prison; and, after, there will be just enough, as we have seen, to clear it, so that the elaborate finale, with every character involved, can have all the space and freedom which main stage and inner stage together will afford.

There is, as we said, nothing very logical in this stagecraft. Its aim would seem to be to create impressions, definitely of a change of place, more vaguely sometimes of a lapse of time, without prompting the audience to ask how they have been created; but (if we divine it rightly) it may show us roughly what the use and wont was at the Blackfriars (and possibly for the Jacobean stage generally) in these matters, and how the old Elizabethan freedom very slowly, almost imperceptibly, contracted. For some time to come it shrinks no further. Rowe, editing the play little

---

21 Would not the act-division, which falls after the Senators' scene, serve? One would suppose so. Then, if this is an authentic part of the play, the little scene is upon that count redundant, and it certainly has no merits of its own. But an editor might well place an act-division here to reinforce the effect of a passage of time. For the whole question see p. 487.

less than a century later, and interpreting it, as his wont was, in terms of his own theater, does not find such stagecraft at all strange to him. He accepts the Folio's act-division; and his localizing of scenes involves very little change. He gives us *A Palace, Rome, A forest with a cave, A* (convenient) *field between the British and Roman camps*, deduces for the finale a *Cymbeline's tent*, has a fancy for *A magnificent bedchamber*; and all this, in effect, coincides with the main stage, inner stage alternation which we have been working out.[22] Later editors, blindly turning the Folio's "scenes" into scenery, with their *A garden of Cymbeline's Palace, A public place, A room in Cymbeline's Palace, Another room, Before Cymbeline's Palace, An ante-chamber adjoining Imogen's apartments*, and so on and so forth, make, of course, a hash of the whole matter. The producer today is naturally not to be exempt from direct study of the text, and he may well prefer a closer adherence to the ways of the stage of the play's origin, when he can divine them. But if he is for something more of scenery, Rowe marks for him the limits to which he may safely go.

THE QUESTION OF ACT-DIVISION

As to act-division; have we the Folio editor working by rule of thumb without warrant of what had been done in performance (that is one question), did he reproduce what had been done (that is another), did he work with a careful eye to the play's dramatic structure (that is a third), or was its very being incarnate from the beginning in these five acts? It is dangerous to dogmatize. Let us put down the pros and cons as they occur.

For what, dramatically, do the five acts of the Folio stand? The first is preparatory, and its end leaves us expectant of Iachimo's trick; in the second the trick is consummated, and for a climax and a finish we are shown its effect upon Posthumus; the third act prepares the Roman invasion, shows us Imogen falsely accused and brings her to an encounter with her unknown brothers, but it actually ends upon the anticlimax of the Senators' talk with the Tribunes; the fourth act is short and has little in it but the episode

---

[22] I should add, perhaps, that it was worked out with no reference at all to Rowe.

of Cloten's death and Imogen's mistaking of his body (it, also, ends expectantly with the battle beginning); in the fifth act we have the rather clumsy unfolding of the battle to its issue, the spectacle in the prison, the very lengthy (it is by eighty lines the longest scene in the play) and skillful elucidation of the end. This is a fairly well proportioned arrangement; each act has its own chief interest (the last an adventitious spectacle thrown in) and bears a just relation to the whole. There is nothing inevitable about it; one could probably contrive as significant an arrangement in three acts or in four, and quite certainly shift the lines of division a little without greatly prejudicing the general effect. But this would naturally be so in a play fitted to a stage which still encourages fluidity of action; granted division, if there is a best way, there can hardly fail to be several second-best.

As to principles involved, if there were any; it is plain that act-division is not used to mark lapse of time nor change of place (is not in this play, certainly, when it so easily might be, and when scene-division, in the sense of a shifting from inner stage to center, quite possibly is), and that while one may prefer to begin a fresh act upon a note of revived interest, the effectiveness of its end matters little. An act seems to exist in virtue of its content and of its relation to the play's scheme as a whole. But, with a twofold story to be told, the content must be mixed (one part of it may be dominant, of course) and the relation to the whole can hardly be exact. The Folio's authority apart, then, it will not be very easy to know an act—so to speak—when one sees it.

As to the benefit of this act-division in performance; there is no check in the interest or march of the action between first act and second, though a pause here, as we noted, might conveniently give Imogen more time to get into bed; the third act does definitely and emphatically begin a new interest, but a pause after it robs the poor little scene between the Senators and the Tribunes of one reason for its existence. The fifth act's beginning brings Posthumus back; except for this, it could be as well begun a scene or even two scenes earlier. There is no check to the march of the story here, and its themes by now are blended.

The producer of today must marshal these considerations and any others that occur to him, and come to his own conclusions. The play is not passionate and precipitate in mood like *Romeo and Juliet,* nor such a simple and neatly woven affair as *The Merchant of Venice;* it will not suffer from interruption as these must do. There are, on the other hand, no dramatically effective pauses provided (nor, if we do provide them, can the audience employ them very profitably in thinking over the likelihood of the play's story); and as the tension of the action is on the slack side already, it certainly does not need more relaxing. Four prolonged intervals will be too many. Division by subject will provide two. Iachimo's plot is worked out by the end of the Folio's Act II; Imogen's flight and her adventures by the cave have a unity of their own[23]; the Folio's fifth act, with the repentant Posthumus to set it going, makes a substantial final section.

THE LAST SCENE

The finer phases of the play's construction are to be seen in the swift forwarding of the first part of the story, in the subtle composition of Iachimo's three scenes (best studied in relation to him) and in the elaboration of the finale.

This last has not lacked praise. Steevens summed up its merits in one of those excellently comprehensive eighteenth century phrases, calling it "a catastrophe which is intricate without confusion, and not more rich in ornament than in nature"; and Barrett Wendell tells us that "into four hundred and eighty-five lines Shakespeare has crowded some two dozen situations, any one of which would probably have been strong enough to carry a whole act."[24] It is at any rate so important a piece of the play's economy that the producer must analyze it with care and see that its every twist and turn is given value.

A final, and often a fairly elaborate, unraveling of confusions is, of course, a commonplace of Elizabethan stagecraft. Compare this one to the endings of *Measure for Measure, Romeo and Juliet* and *Othello.* It is far more elaborate in workmanship, but it hardly differs in kind. *Romeo and Juliet* ends upon anticlimax,

[23] And possibly its *Scena Tertia* and *Scena Quarta* are better tagged to this than prefixed to the last division.

[24] I quote from the footnotes of the Furness Variorum. Thorndike, on the other hand, seeing in it Shakespeare's effort to beat the young Beaumont and Fletcher at their own game, is critical and calls it "a dénouement . . . so ingeniously intricate that it is ineffective on the stage. . . ." But was it—and will it be—upon Shakespeare's stage?

no more is to be done and we have nothing left to learn; in *Othello*, the disclosures feed Othello's agony, which dominates everything; in *Measure for Measure* we share the plot's secret with the Duke, but we are kept uncertain what the end will be. But here we surmise a happy ending. Our interest must be kept alive, therefore, by the strategy of its bringing-about, and—the dramatic decencies observed—the more frankly we are shown how the thing is done, the better. That aspect of the scene is of a piece with the general artifice of the play's method; but something much better than mechanical skill is now put to use. Not only is the tangle of the story straightened; the characters are brought into harmony, and we, too, are reconciled to faith in their happiness.

For the scene to be effective one rule must be observed in its acting; it is a fundamental rule in all acting, strangely liable to neglect. Each actor must resolutely sustain his part through his long intervals of listening. The action is kept alive by a series of surprises—there are eighteen of them; each character in turn provides one, or is made its particular victim—and it must be *kept* alive, not saved from extinction in a series of jerks. We, who are not surprised, find our interest in watching for each turn to come, and the producer must see that each figure in the group has its point of vantage. As it is the last scene of the play each character is well known to us, and can be effective, therefore, even in silence.

The main action is preluded by the knighting of Belarius and the two boys, by the doctor bringing the news of the Queen's death, and the disclosure of her villainies. Cymbeline certainly takes this very calmly, with his "How ended she?"; "Prithee, say"; and his "Proceed."[25] But the plain fact is that this Goneril-like lady has never been in place in the play, and her dismissal from it is as awkward. He seems to relapse with thankfulness upon

> Mine eyes
> Were not in fault, for she was beautiful,
> Mine ears that heard her flattery, nor my heart

[25] Nor can we acquit him of tactlessness in his prompt remark to Cornelius that
death
Will seize the doctor too.

That thought her like her seeming; it had been vicious
To have mistrusted her.

There is the authentic note again; we are back among golden
unrealities.

The scheme of the scene begins to work with the entrance of
Lucius, Iachimo and the other Roman prisoners; Posthumus and
Imogen are among them, disguised, unknown to each other and
to the rest.[26] The first chord struck comes from a certain calm
savagery in Cymbeline, an answering stoicism in Lucius; this
gives a firm foundation to build on. Sentiment and emotion must
not come too soon; if the pendulum is to swing to harmony and
peace it must be held back for a start at the other extreme. The
more effective, too, in quick contrast, will be Lucius' bringing
forward of the fragile Fidele and his plea for the lad to be spared,
the gentle Fidele who can in an instant "look himself" into
Cymbeline's graces. The transparent

> I have surely seen him;
> His favour is familiar to me. . . .

is in the true key of the play's artifice. Yet Fidele can—it is
another quick contrast—the next instant coldly turn his back on
his benefactor, to that noble Roman's indignation and surprise.
But we know that Imogene knows she has time enough in which
to save him; and Cymbeline, plainly, is looking for an excuse
to spare him. These grace notes enrich the theme and soften its
present asperity.

Then comes the puzzle of her picking upon Iachimo, and the
little mystification of her walk aside with Cymbeline—which is
indeed mere excuse for the dramatist to let Belarius and the
brothers, on the one hand, recognize their Fidele, Pisanio, on the
other, learn that Imogen is safe; artifice unashamed, but they are
thus made livelier lookers-on. Then the truth—or enough of it—
is wormed from Iachimo.[27] The spider must unweave his web;

---

[26] *Leonatus behind*, says the Folio's stage direction. His chief disguise now is
the "Italian weeds," and these would hardly conceal him from Imogen. He may
have some helmet or headdress he can throw off. But guards keep the prisoners
from mingling; and, generally speaking, there is much goodwill in these disguises.

[27] Critics dispute as to whether, and why, Iachimo is purposely embroidering
his story. It is the sort of dispute that the nineteenth century idolaters of Shakespeare particularly rejoiced in, demonstrating the master's super-subtlety by their

and the Italian brain, operating so tortuously, sets British Cymbeline stamping with impatience: will this damned foreigner never come to the point?

But it is not, of course, upon Cymbeline chiefly that we are meant to mark the cumulative effect of the long-drawn-out confession; upon Posthumus rather, there in the background, ready for death, roused to the hearing of these horrors, mocked by this scoundrel's iterated praise of him, only so slowly seizing on the full truth; when he does, though, breaking all bounds in his agony of remorse.[28] And Imogen? The long ordeal of the telling of the story sets her before us in sharp contrast to anxious father and agonized husband both. She stands listening stonily, almost indifferently, one would say. True, her good name will be cleared; but Posthumus is dead. When she heard that her life would be spared (Fidele's life, truly; Imogen's would be safe enough, but it is the surface effect which counts here) and that any boon should be hers for the asking, she had only dully responded with

> I humbly thank your highness.

When she sees the ring, it is, she says,

> a thing
> Bitter to me as death. . .

She stands gazing dumbly at this enigmatically evil Iachimo, till Cymbeline has to urge her with

> On, speak to him.

Very clearly, coldly and quietly the few words come:

> My boon is that this gentleman may render
> Of whom he had this ring.

And thereafter she stays silent. These two figures make the center of the dramatic picture. The floridly gesticulating Italian, wounded and weak, his gesture wounded, too, pitiful, a little

---

own (doubtless today we err as far in other directions). But will any audience now remember the play's early scenes in such inessential detail as to be able to check his equivocations? Surely it simply is that Iachimo is "making a story of it," the "Italian brain" operating as tortuously as ever, and to no purpose now. That, at any rate, is the obvious effect made; and it is a very good one.

[28] Iachimo does not know he is there (*Enter . . . Leonatus behind*), though in reality there was no reason he should not. This, again, is artifice.

ridiculous. And Imogen, dead at heart, white and still, gazing wide-eyed, and wondering that such wickedness can be.

Even when Posthumus is raised from the dead before her eyes she cannot of a sudden turn joyful, the ice will not break so easily. The torrent of his ecstatic self-reproach would indeed take some stemming. He is still the manly egotist. But she, when she can swear she is in her senses, thinks only of him, of calming and comforting him, forgets her disguise, but finds so inarticulate a tongue with her

> Peace, my lord! Hear, hear—

that, his rage unspent, he turns and strikes little Fidele to the ground. To avoid anticlimax, Pisanio is ready (and his earlier aside has brought him under our eye) with his

> O, gentlemen, help!
> Mine and your mistress! O, my lord Posthumus!
> You ne'er killed Imogen till now. Help, help!
> Mine honoured lady!

And so, recovered after a few tense moments from her swoon, Imogen also stands revealed.

Consider the dramatic achievement. The double disclosure itself is the simplest part of it, and could well be done in half a dozen different ways. But it is given emotional value by the slow crescendo which leads up—till the strain becomes intolerable —to Posthumus' outburst. This, when it comes, violently reverses the situation's appeal; the shock is not mere shock, it contains fresh stimulus both to interest and emotion. Our eyes have been chiefly on Imogen; she thinks Posthumus is dead, and, though we suffer with her, we know better. Now, of a sudden, our eyes are on Posthumus; he thinks Imogen is dead, and we know better. What matters far more, though, is that his outburst restores him a little to our sympathy. His moralizing soliloquies will have left us cold. When a man has behaved like a wicked fool he had better not be too philosophic in repentance. Posthumus, stamping and bellowing in his despair and calling for the street dogs to be set on him, is a far more attractive figure than Posthumus reasoning out retribution with the gods.

This is the scene's dramatic pinnacle. Surmounted, and the anticlimax saved, now, by an admirable little device, the theme is resolved into its key of semicomedy again. Imogen, waking from her swoon, finds "old-dog" Pisanio fussing over her; and in a flash we have

> O, get thee from my sight.
> Thou gavest me poison: dangerous fellow, hence!
> Breathe not where princes are.
> > The tune of Imogen!

cries Cymbeline. It is indeed. Doublet and hose despite, the timid Fidele has vanished in the princess, very much her royal self again.

Now twenty lines are given to quite subsidiary talk about the poison. Why? So that Posthumus may be left standing apart, silent and shamed.[29] He will not face her in his unworthiness. She is watching; she understands. And in a minute, dropping her royalty, she goes to him and puts her arms around his neck. It is a fragile embrace; but the man, it seems, would fall if she did not hold him. They stand there as it might be two wrestlers with the fortune of their love. And what she says is one of those odd humorous things which make reconciliation easy, and with which Shakespeare knew so well how to temper feelings too secret and too sacred for fine words. She is half-laughing, half-crying in her joy!

> Why did you throw your wedded lady from you?
> Think that you are upon a lock, and now
> Throw me again.

This is her forgiveness; he is man enough to take it, and his amending is pledged with

> Hang there like fruit, my soul,
> Till the tree die![30]

Now the second theme, the discovery of the two princes, must be worked out; and we are brought to it by another twenty thrifty

---

[29] Or to speak by the card, the poison-story is needed for the symmetry of the plot; the dramatist turns this to account for the more vital business of illuminating character.

[30] Dowden is the first to give us "lock" in place of the Folio's "rock," and no one, envisaging the business of the scene, can doubt that he is right. This single minute or so, felt and acted as it should be, makes the play's production worth while. And one likes to think of the dying Tennyson, the play in his hand opened at this very passage, one among those he loved best.

lines, which are chiefly given to Pisanio for his account of the crapulous Cloten's vanishing into the forest, and are capped by the little calmly loosed thunderclap of Guiderius'

> Let me end the story:
> I slew him there.

—young prince and young savage in a sentence!

From now to the end the scene runs a stabler course. Guiderius has again tuned it to dramatic pitch and holds it there in his terse defiance of his unknown father; the due dash of humor added too:

> I have spoke it, and I did it.

CYMBELINE. He was a prince.
GUIDERIUS. A most uncivil one. The wrongs he did me
Were nothing prince-like; for he did provoke me
With language that would make me spurn the
sea,
If it could so roar to me. I cut off's head;
And am right glad he is not standing here
To tell this tale of mine.

Then Belarius brings his weight into the contest, speaking, so to say, bass to the young man's tenor; Arviragus, when the chance comes, adding his alto, now tremulously, now bravely, he the only one of the three to be abashed by these regalities. The simile is permissible, for the verse takes on a regular rhythm and full-toned harmonies. The sententious contrast between

> the art of the Court,
> As hard to leave as keep, whose top to climb
> Is certain falling, or so slippery that
> The fear's as bad as falling. . .

and the life of honest freedom in the pinching cave is here brought to visible issue. They confront each other, the noble mountaineers and the none too noble Cymbeline. Needless to say, Belarius' simple eloquence—not untinged, however, with very courtly respect—carries all before it.

The princes restored to their true father, it only remains to have Posthumus recognized as

> The forlorn soldier, that so nobly fought. . .

This rounds in the story; and the moral scheme is completed
by his forgiveness of Iachimo, which prompts Cymbeline in turn
to spare his prisoners:

> Pardon's the word to all.[31]

One may own perhaps to a little impatience with the post-
scriptal soothsayer, and the rereading (surely once is enough!) of
Jupiter's missive. We can call the whipping-boy to account if we
will. These fifty lines are, in a strict view, dramatically redundant,
and, at such a moment, dangerously so; this cannot be denied.
Even so, there is a quaintness about the business which makes it
a not unfitting finish to a charmingly incongruous play. It does
not help to hold us spellbound in excitement to the end. But must
we always insist on excitement in the theater? Let the producer
consider whether something—not too much—cannot be done to
give the rococo symbolism of

> The lofty cedar, royal Cymbeline. . .

and of

> the Roman eagle
> From south to west on wing soaring aloft. . .

a significant setting.

> Laud we the gods;
> And let our crooked smokes climb to their nostrils
> From our blest altars. Publish we this peace
> To all our subjects. Set we forward: let
> A Roman and a British ensign wave
> Friendly together: so through Lud's town march,
> And in the temple of great Jupiter
> Our peace we'll ratify. . . .

There need be no stage directions here, at any rate, to show us
Cymbeline and Lucius, Posthumus, Imogen and her brothers,
Belarius, Iachimo and the rest setting out in elaborate procession;
the play dissolving into pageantry.

---

[31] As Ruggles notes (I quote from the Furness Variorum), if Posthumus had
not spared Iachimo when he had him down, there could have been no disclosure
of his villainy. But this is perhaps to consider things a little too closely.

The Verse and Its Speaking

THE verse flows with amazing ease, and often seems the very natural rhythm of speech; yet it is set to music, in its kind, as certainly as if it were staved and barred—time, tone and all are dictated to a sensitive ear. The first scene sees it in full swing; the first lengthy speech is the story of Posthumus:

> I cannot delve him to the root: his father
> Was called Sicilius, who did join his honour
> Against the Romans with Cassibelan,
> But had his titles by Tenantius, whom
> He served with glory and admired success,—
> So gained the sur-addition Leonatus:
> And had, beside this gentleman in question,
> Two other sons, who in the wars o' the time
> Died with their swords in hand; for which their father,
> Then old and fond of issue, took such sorrow
> That he quit being; and his gentle lady,
> Big of this gentleman, our theme, deceased
> As he was born. . . .

Straightforward narrative; not so mellifluous that the sound can slip in at the ear and leave the sense outside; masculine, with a few firmly finished lines, but a proportion of feminine endings to save the whole thing from sounding too clarion; the carried-over sentences give it speed; one rich unusual phrase at the beginning—

> I cannot delve him to the root:

—arrests attention; while the limpidity of

> for which their father,
> Then old and fond of issue, took such sorrow
> That he quit being. . .

(with the need to linger ever so slightly over the doubled consonants and sibilants) runs a fine little thread of sentiment all unobtrusively into the speech and out again.[32]

For a still more straightforward passage, take Belarius' soliloquy:

---

[32] From a speaker's point of view, it makes, of course, little difference whether a doubled consonant falls in one word or connects two. Needless to say, the symbol "th" as in "the" and "that" is not included in the term.

> How hard it is to hide the sparks of nature!
> These boys know little they are sons to the king;
> Nor Cymbeline dreams that they are alive.
> They think they are mine: and though trained up thus
>   meanly,
> I' the cave wherein they bow, their thoughts do hit
> The roofs of palaces, and nature prompts them
> In simple and low things to prince it much
> Beyond the trick of others. . . .

The first three lines, each a completed phrase, gain our attention, the feminine ending of the first and (for variety) the similar "little" coming before the caesura of the second make easy speaking, while the dominating "dreams" in the third gives force—just enough; and after this, carried-over sentences and half-elided syllables send the speech familiarly on its way.

The verse throughout is very rich in texture; and if sometimes it seems overrich, this suits it to the frank artifice of the play, and the actors may allow themselves a certain slight sophistication of style for its delivery. Shakespeare in fact—the wheel come full circle—seems almost to be cultivating a new Euphuism. It has no close likeness to the old; by the difference, indeed, we may measure something of the distance he has traveled in twenty years of playwriting.[33] It is a Euphuism of imagination rather than expression. This will often be simple enough; it is the thought or emotion behind that may be too far-fetched for the occasion or the speaker. What she means is made plain, but would Imogen, we ask, even if it took her so long to break the seals of Posthumus' letter, excogitate meanwhile to such effect as this?

---

[33] But the degree of likeness will depend upon how much of Cymbeline we allow to be Shakespeare's. Biron's

> Light seeking light doth light of light beguile:
> So, ere you find where light in darkness lies,
> Your light grows dark by losing of your eyes.

has, for instance, a more than distant likeness to Arviragus'

> Nobly he yokes
> A smiling with a sigh, as if the sigh
> Was that it was, for not being such a smile;
> The smile mocking the sigh. . . .

But then Furness—and others of his opinion, supposedly—will allow Shakespeare none of this.

> Good wax, thy leave. Blest be
> You bees that make these locks of counsel! Lovers
> And men in dangerous bonds pray not alike:
> Though forfeitors you cast in prison, yet
> You clasp young Cupid's tables.

Would Posthumous, still full of faith in Imogen, regreeting Iachimo, cap his tribute to her as one of the fairest ladies he had looked upon with

> And therewithal the best, or let her beauty
> Look through a casement to allure false hearts,
> And be false with them.

And would Cloten at any time be found reflecting

> I know her women are about her: what
> If I do line one of their hands? 'Tis gold
> Which buys admittance; oft it doth; yea, and makes
> Diana's rangers false themselves, yield up
> Their deer to the stand o' the stealer; and 'tis gold
> Which makes the true man kill'd and saves the thief;
> Nay, sometimes hangs both thief and true man; what
> Can it not do and undo?

Cloten's sentiments, no doubt; but "Diana's rangers" are hardly within his intellectual range.[34] Is Pisanio so confirmed a moralizer that, even though Imogen be stupent with horror at the accusation of adultery, he (and his author) must keep her standing there while he informs us that

> 'tis slander,
> Whose edge is sharper than the sword, whose tongue
> Outvenoms all the worms of Nile, whose breath
> Rides on the posting winds and doth belie—
> All corners of the world—kings, queens and states,
> Maids, matrons; nay, the secrets of the grave
> This viperous slander enters.

And if he does stop to think of the peril it will be to her complexion to wander disguised through the forest, is this how he will warn her of it?

---

[34] Furness refuses Shakespeare's responsibility for the lines, and argues that Cloten is too much of an ass to have such ideas. Cloten is by no means pure ass; a diseased vanity is his trouble; with Caius Lucius he puts up a by no means despicable show of the bluff, blunt Englishman.

> nay, you must
> Forget that rarest treasure of your cheek,
> Exposing it—but, oh, the harder heart!
> Alack, no remedy!—to the greedy touch
> Of common-kissing Titan. . . .

These are, indeed, sheer lapses from dramatic integrity. They are not the worst to be found in the play; but we cannot, as with the worst, simply deny them all to Shakespeare. They are the failures, the spoiled specimens of a method which is half-successful in such effects of antithesis and conceit of thought as Posthumus' later

> so I'll die
> For thee, O Imogen, even for whom my life
> Is, every breath, a death . . . .

as Imogen's rather schoolma'amish (but Iachimo at the moment is certainly making her feel most uncomfortable)

> pray you,
> Since doubting things go ill often hurts more
> Than to be sure they do—for certainties
> Either are past remedies, or, timely knowing,
> The remedy then born—discover to me
> What both you spur and stop.

It is, however, only the parenthesis that overloads this and robs it of spontaneity.

For complete success in making the formal antithetical phrase do dramatic service take the Queen's description of Imogen:

> she's a lady
> So tender of rebukes that words are strokes
> And strokes death to her.

For a clever woman's bitter-sweet summing-up of her foe, what could be better? Take Pisanio's reproachful

> O, my master!
> Thy mind to her is now as low as were
> Thy fortunes. . . .

Brooding indignation does gather itself into just such epitome. We shall not even find his description of the departing Posthumus, standing on deck,

> Still waving, as the fits and stirs of 's mind
> Could best express how slow his soul sail'd on,
> How swift his ship.

out of keeping. It is in the key of the scene; and Imogen, we feel, thrilled through with love and faith, might move a stone to eloquence.

And coming to Iachimo, how else should the subtle, tricky Italian express himself but in paradox and overwrought metaphor? The device of the asides, that are meant to be overheard while Imogen rereads the letter he has brought her, is pure artifice. But it seems no more the dramatist's than Iachimo's, touches, on that stage, the limits of convention, but by no means exceeds them; and the high-colored, harlequin phrases are all Iachimo's own.

> What, are men mad? Hath nature given them
>   eyes
> To see this vaulted arch and the rich crop
> Of sea and land, which can distinguish 'twixt
> The fiery orbs above and the twinned stones
> Upon the numbered beach, and can we not
> Partition make with spectacles so precious
> 'Twixt fair and foul?

IMOGEN.   What makes your admiration?

IACHIMO. It cannot be i' the eye; for apes and monkeys,
> 'Twixt two such shes, would chatter this way and
> Contemn with mows the other: nor i' the judg-
>   ment;
> For idiots, in this case of favour, would
> Be wisely definite; nor i' the appetite;
> Sluttery, to such neat excellence opposed,
> Should make desire vomit emptiness,
> Not so allured to feed.

IMOGEN. What is the matter, trow?

IACHIMO.   The cloyed will—
> That satiate yet unsatisfied desire, that tub
> Both filled and running—ravening first the lamb,
> Longs after for the garbage.

IMOGEN.   What, dear sir,
> Thus raps you? Are you well?

IACHIMO.   Thanks, madam, well.

This is the new Euphuism *in excelsis*. For yet another taste of it, here is his outburst to her some fifty lines later.

> O dearest soul, your cause doth strike my heart
> With pity that doth make me sick! A lady
> So fair, and fastened to an empery,
> Would make the great'st king double, to be partner'd
> With tomboys hired with that self-exhibition,
> Which your own coffers yield! with diseased ventures,
> That play with all infirmities for gold,
> Which rottenness can lend nature! such boil'd stuff
> As well might poison poison!

But the mature dramatist has turned decorative flourishes to strict dramatic account. Belarius and his cave and his bluff talk stand for rustic honesty; here, at the other end of the scale, is this degenerate Italian, come to Cymbeline's Court

> to mart
> As in a Romish stew, and to expound
> His beastly mind. . .

and he presents us, in his arrogance, with an approach to a travesty of himself, which is also a travesty of the very medium in which he exists. A subtle and a daring piece of craftsmanship, germane to this hybrid tragi-comedy. Instead of opposing the heroic and the comic, Shakespeare blends the two. But the integrity of the character must be preserved; it would not do for Iachimo to become even half-conscious of what a figure he cuts in the eyes of the gods—and in ours. And it is this that is achieved by the modulating of the medium itself. Artifice is its norm throughout the play; but the range is wide. Iachimo's mean of expression lies at the florid end, and itself ranges from the polished prose by which he asserts himself among his fellows in Rome (made here and there a little plainer to suit the blunt Englishman's understanding), from the argute, sensuous verse of the soliloquy over the sleeping Imogen (the man himself, this), from the elaborate, parenthetical repentance at the last, even to the high-colored complexity of these speeches, in which, as we said, he is meant to seem to us not only pretentious and false, but—all unconsciously, and that he may not rank as too tragic a villain—just a trifle ridiculous.

For simpler and subtler examples of this molding of verse and its conventions to the expression of character, we can turn to Imogen, and notably to the scene in which she learns from Pisanio what is Posthumus' doom for her. The verse is full of metaphor;

but it is all (or nearly all; we have noted a peccant passage or so) directly dramatic, prompted by the occasion, by the very properties of the scene.

> Come, here's my heart,
> (Something's afore't—soft, soft! we'll no defence)
> Obedient as the scabbard! What is here?
> The scriptures of the loyal Leonatus,
> All turn'd to heresy? Away, away,
> Corrupters of my faith! You shall no more
> Be stomachers to my heart. Thus may poor fools
> Believe false teachers: though those that are betrayed
> Do feel the treason sharply, yet the traitor
> Stands in worse case of woe. . . .

We are conscious neither of the metaphor nor of the structure of the verse, only of its music. The fusion of substance into form is complete.

Even when the prompting is not immediate, it is but at one remove.

> False to his bed! What is it to be false?
> To lie in watch there, and to think on him?
> To weep 'twixt clock and clock? If sleep charge nature,
> To break it with a fearful dream of him,
> And cry myself awake? That's false to 's bed, is it?

We have seen her lying so, glad to have tired herself by hours of reading to the point of sleep.

She has dressed for her journey in the

> riding-suit, no costlier than would fit
> A franklin's housewife.

There will, then, be sufficient strangeness in the now unroyal look of her to sharpen for us, to strengthen by its touch of incongruity (though we shall not guess why) the image of

> Poor I am stale, a garment out of fashion;
> And, for I am richer than to hang by the walls,
> I must be ripp'd . . . .

That it is a princess speaking who has stooped to her subject, to a marriage at once made desolate and homeless, is vividly implicit in

> When thou sees't him,
> A little witness my obedience. Look!
> I draw the sword myself: take it, and hit
> The innocent mansion of my love, my heart;
> Fear not; 'tis empty of all things but grief;
> Thy master is not there, who was indeed
> The riches of it. . . .

These are the subtler strokes. But the simplest actualities are given a place. They talk of the tired horses, of the doublet, hat and hose she is to wear; and the talk is matched with action. The language is ordinary, and the brief sentences would often disintegrate the verse if the rhythm were not kept regular. But this triple combination, of simple speech, short sentence and regular rhythm, gives an effect of familiar strength. Imogen is speaking:

> Thou toldst me, when we came from horse, the place
> Was near at hand: ne'er long'd my mother so
> To see me first, as I have now. Pisanio! man!
> Where is Posthumus? What is in thy mind
> That makes thee stare thus? Wherefore breaks that sigh
> From the inward of thee? One but painted thus
> Would be interpreted a thing perplexed
> Beyond self-explication: put thyself
> Into a 'haviour of less fear, ere wildness
> Vanquish my staider senses. What's the matter? . . .

Two lines that can be strictly scanned; the third has "Pisanio! man!" for its two last beats, each word being one; five more regular lines, only the sense and the sentences breaking their regularity; two lines with feminine endings to ease the rhythm and a long sentence running through them to give them, for the finish, continuity and strength.

The technique of the scene's writing can so be analyzed through speech after speech. But the art of it is not calculated; it shows us a Shakespeare so at one with his medium that he manipulates it as easily, as instinctively as he expects his actors, in their turn, to move and speak. Too easily, if anything; tension will slacken, ideas tangle, and with emotional pressure lacking, the verse will hang loose. But it is still a very far cry from this easy freedom that has succeeded the decorative contrivings of the earlier plays, the ordered march of the rhetoric of the Histories, and the tragic pas-

sion in which he fired verse as in a furnace—it is still a far cry
from this to the flaccidities of a Massinger or Shirley, or of Fletcher
at his worst. Dryden, in the end, had good reason to bring some
discipline to bear. Whatever Shakespeare's metrical willfulness, his
verse will be pregnant with drama; and in this, this only, will be
found the significance of its vagaries. Verse was his supreme
dramatic resource. We may well expect to find it, in its full
development of craftsmanship, alive with purpose, a very inventory for the acting of the play; and to find it so in this play more
than another, for romantic substance is malleable into many
delicate effects.

Its dictation can be minute. Can anyone miss the indrawn gasp-
ing sob with which

> To break it with a fearful dream of him,
> And cry myself awake? That's false to 's bed, is it?

finishes? Or not hear how the expanding vowels and doubled
consonants conspire to give Pisanio's long-bottled up

> Hence, vile instrument!
> Thou shalt not damn my hand.

just the explosiveness it should have? Or not find the Imogen
that, once disillusioned about Posthumus, has little faith left for
anyone or anything, that will suspect Pisanio of murdering him
and poisoning her, in the quick exchange of

> IMOGEN. But speak.
> PISANIO. Then, madam,
> I thought you would not back again.
> IMOGEN. Most like,
> Bringing me here to kill me!

and in that contemptuous, bitter, Iachimo-poisoned

> Some Roman courtezan!

The play abounds in such matter for her. In the first scene her
attitude to her father (and her private opinion of his weakly
tyrant's temper), the quality of her love for her husband, the dead
blow that his banishment is to her, the uncompromising dignity
with which she suffers it, are all summed up for us in five lines.

> IMOGEN. I beseech you, sir,
> Harm not yourself with your vexation;

> I am senseless of your wrath; a touch more rare
> Subdues all pangs, all fears.

CYMBELINE.   Past grace? obedience?

IMOGEN.   Past hope and in despair; that way, past grace.

And when, twenty lines later, news comes as she stands there with the Queen, of Cloten's flourishing attack on the departing Posthumus:

> Your son's my father's friend; he takes his part.
> To draw upon an exile! O, brave sir!
> I would they were in Afric both together,
> Myself by with a needle, that I might prick
> The goer-back. Why came you from your master?

That is another view of her: the scornful girl, flashing artless indignation at her stepmother. Note the daintily vixenish "Afric ... needle ... prick," with slick syllables joining them; then the sudden imperious turn upon Pisanio. Tune, time, attitude, movement, what amount of stage direction could make them plainer?

Effect after effect will be found lodged in the simple cadence of the verse. Take these few more lines from Cymbeline's rating of his daughter,

>   That mightst have had the sole son of my
>   queen!

IMOGEN.   O blessed, that I might not! I chose an eagle,
>   And did avoid a puttock.

CYMBELINE.   Thou took'st a beggar; wouldst have made my
>   throne
>   A seat for baseness.

IMOGEN.   No, I rather added
>   A lustre to it.

CYMBELINE.   O, thou vile one!

IMOGEN.   Sir. . . .

Shrill puerile scolding in the monosyllables of the first line; the blend in Imogen of pugnacity and respect shown by one overflowing line, the next truncated; Cymbeline's anger then gathering and deepening in weightier words, the last three regular lines giving strength, the shortening sentences adding violence to the quarrel—till, after the full stop of that "Sir!", Imogen resolves it into a calmer, but still very positive

It is your fault that I have loved Posthumus;
You bred him as my playfellow. . . .

Half the effect of Cloten's first scene lies in the peculiar pattern given to the action of it by the Second Lord's strange succession of asides. Cloten is crossing the stage, returning to his apartments from the frustrated duel, the First Lord fawning on him. The Second Lord follows, five paces or so behind, commenting on the conversation he can just overhear. There will be a very slight mid‑way pause; then the walk continues. Within reach of the door Cloten turns and sees the Second Lord for the first time, catches him, probably, in the midst of his final mocking aside, suspects nothing though—for who would dare to laugh at him? Then follows

CLOTEN.	You'll go with us?
FIRST LORD.	I'll attend your lordship.
CLOTEN.	Nay, come, let's go together.
SECOND LORD.	Well, my lord.

and the three depart; the Second Lord constrained to congee too. A scene of no great importance; it serves to introduce Cloten, and to fill up the "half-hour" needed for Posthumus' embarking. But its odd perambulation gives it comic distinction; the passing across the stage hints at the passing of time; the slipping-in of the asides keeps it moving and denies it solid emphasis.

There is, naturally, less flexibility in the writing of the prose scenes. Iachimo's provoking of the wager is remarkable rather for the way in which the close-knit, unrelaxing sentences are made to suggest a certain intellectual power in the man. Posthumus is no fool; he can to a point play up to him. But early in the scene, and in the midst of the prose, has come his heartfelt tribute to his Imogen:

She holds her virtue still and I my mind.

—and, of itself, the sudden melody of the single line of verse pro‑claims the honest romantic fellow, tempting prey to a sensualist cynic. We seem to see Iachimo stalking him in the stealthy prose line that follows pat:

You must not so far prefer her 'fore ours of Italy.

In the verse scenes, on the other hand, a sudden line of free rhythm may be used to ease the strain of a situation; as when Imogen accepts Iachimo's apology for his experimental libeling of Posthumus with a

> All's well, sir: take my power i' the court for yours.

The limpid flow of the line does, indeed, far more than this; it speaks—its sense apart—of the nobly innocent nature, ready to be twice deceived. We hear the selfsame tune when Arviragus welcomes her to the cave:

> The night to the owl and morn to the lark less welcome.

In the very tune there is generous frank affection, flowing from a nature like her own.

The free rhythm of long, simply worded lines makes its best effect in the pastoral scenes. It fits with pathos and gentle humor, not with wit; wit asks for the discipline of stricter scanning or of prose. When Imogen, disguised as Fidele, has been discovered in the cave:

> Good masters, harm me not.
> Before I entered here I called; and thought
> To have begged or bought what I have took; good troth,
> I have stolen nought; nor would not, though I had found
> Gold strewed i' the floor. Here's money for my meat:
> I would have left it on the board so soon
> As I had made my meal, and parted,
> With prayers for the provider.

the form and color of the lines redouble their meaning; the timid half-line for a beginning, the appeal of the long, evenly stressed, all but monosyllabled sentence, the apologetic hiatus that ends the last line but one—it is all a painting in sound of helpless indomitable Imogen.[35]

More regular verse, thriftily worded, simply phrased, and of a fine virile swing, is to be found when it is wanted; as it is for Imogen's flashing response to Iachimo's first crude attempt upon her.

> What ho, Pisanio!
> The king my father shall be made acquainted
> Of thy assault: if he shall think it fit

---

[35] Early editors merely surmised a word missing from the penultimate line, and filled in the gap with a "thence" or "hence." A banal solution.

> A saucy stranger in his court to mart
> As in a Romish stew, and to expound
> His beastly mind to us, he hath a court
> He little cares for, and a daughter who
> He not respects at all.

And it is instructive to compare Imogen's outbreaking horror and grief, when she wakes to find the headless body beside her, with Juliet's when the Nurse brings her, as she thinks, the news of Romeo's death. Between that

> I am not I, if there be such an 'I,'
> Or those eyes shut that make thee answer 'I' . . . .

and

>   Damn'd Pisanio
> Hath with his forged letters—damn'd Pisanio—
> From this most bravest vessel of the world
> Struck the main-top! O Posthumus! alas,
> Where is thy head? where's that? Ah me, where's that?
> Pisanio might have kill'd thee at the heart,
> And left this head on. How should this be? Pisanio!
> 'Tis he and Cloten: malice and lucre in them
> Have laid this woe here. O, 'tis pregnant, pregnant!
> The drug he gave me, which he said was precious
> And cordial to me, have I not found it
> Murderous to the senses? . . .

what a gulf! From purely verbal effect, a dervish-whirling feat of elocution, we have passed to a subtly elaborate use of parenthesis and reiteration, which gives us, as nearly naturally as need be, her anguish and the reeling agonies of her mind, yet never destroys the integrity of the verse nor breaks from the mood of the play.

There are, as always, those pregnant phrases and passages, in which all that is most significant in a character or the turn of an event will seem to be packed, or by which a whole scene may suddenly be keyed to a strange nobility.

We have Iachimo's self-portrait reflected from his very painting of Posthumus, unfaithful, slavering,

> with lips as common as the stairs
> That mount the Capitol. . .
>   . . . by-peeping in an eye

> Base and illustrous as the smoky light
> That's fed with stinking tallow. . .

There is the painting of the candle-lit silence of Imogen's bed-room, of the night and its passing. It ranks among Shakespeare's masterpieces of mere writing; from that

> The crickets sing, and man's o'er-laboured sense
> Repairs itself by rest. . . .

to the

> Swift, swift, you dragons of the night, that dawning
> May bare the raven's eye! I lodge in fear;
> Though this a heavenly angel, hell is here.
> One, two, three! Time! Time!

There is the description of the dead Fidele:

GUIDERIUS. How found you him?

ARVIRAGUS.   Stark, as you see:
Thus smiling, as some fly had tickled slumber,
Not as death's dart, being laugh'd at; his right cheek
Reposing on a cushion.

GUIDERIUS.   Where?

ARVIRAGUS.   O' the floor;
His arms thus leagued: I thought he slept, and put
My clouted brogues from off my feet, whose rudeness
Answer'd my steps too loud.

There are a dozen other such luminous passages, and more.

Finally it is worth noting how full of concrete imagery the verse is. This would be so. The mood of the play is not introspective, but romantic, concerned with things as they seem, and with emotion little purged by thought. The expression of it will rightly be picturesque.[36]

---

[36] The actual text of the play is unusually troublesome, but I do not propose to discuss all the minor difficulties here. They are complicated, and, in some cases, so much matter for bibliographers that it would not be for me to venture an opinion.

The Characters

IN the best of these, and in these (one must qualify it) at their best, we find the unfailing Shakespeare. Imogen is the life of the play; it would be a pedestrian affair without her. Posthumus, in execution as in quality, is only half a hero, a torso of the study of a man, but he is justly viewed. Iachimo is excellently done. If the last part of the story had more use for him, and if he did not suffer such a dull wordy declension from his brilliant beginning, he might rank as a masterpiece in his kind. Cloten has blood and bones, is by no means a mere stage figure of fun. He is, indeed, an uncommon if not unique item in the Shakespearean catalogue, a comic character drawn with a savagely serious pen. Nor are Guiderius and Arviragus mere romantic fictions, for all their provenance from that pasteboard cave. Guiderius, in particular, exists in his own right, stands firmly on his feet. He is, in a double sense, set against Cloten, true heir against usurper, noble barbarian beside degenerate debauchee. And as the bestial truth beneath the comic mask turns convention into character with the one, so it is with Guiderius once he is set in motion; copybook maxims will by no means contain him. Caius Lucius, little as we see of him, stands clear cut as a soldier and a gentleman; and as an instance of temperance in character made interesting—nothing is harder to do. There is vigor enough in Belarius and enough stability in Pisanio to beget belief in them while they are on the scene. But, apart from their use to the story, they have little life in them, and Cymbeline and his Queen have less.

The Queen is indeed worth some study as a failure. She is given fairly prominent place. She has to dominate husband and son, be double-faced to Imogen, cajole Pisanio, she is even allowed a most masculinely impressive address to the Roman envoy. She soliloquizes; no advantage is denied her. But never is she co-ordinate into a human being. How account for it? For one thing, her wickedness proves of singularly little effect. Imogen is not taken in by her, nor are Pisanio and Cornelius. Pisanio does metaphorically swallow the "poison-cordial" as Imogen does actually; but the episode is so obviously—and very clumsily—contrived for the sake of the sensational waking beside the headless corpse that it can hardly reflect much dramatic credit upon the poor lady. It really looks as if Shakespeare, committed to the story and not interested enough to remodel this part of it, had said to her, as he sat down to write scene after scene: "Well, come alive if you can." And when with her fifth scene it becomes clear that—very excusably under such treatment—she cannot, he finishes her off, the quality of her last couplet telling us pretty plainly what he thinks of her and her wicked-stepmother banalities:

> and my end
> Can make good use of either: she being down,
> I have the placing of the British crown.[87]

Most unfair treatment; but dramatists do sometimes behave so to their unsatisfactory offspring.

IACHIMO

It is cursory criticism that will see in Iachimo a shadow of the master-villain with the "Italian brain." He is made of quite other stuff than Iago, and it is very solid stuff too. He is most objectively viewed (a corollary of the picturesque figurative method of the play's writing, a corrective, for Shakespeare, to its romantic spirit, would seem to be a colder detachment from the characters— Imogen excepted—than usual), and he and his villainy are nicely suited to the story and its ending; for from the first there is something fantastic about the fellow, and no tragically-potent scoundrel, we should be sure, will ever come out of a trunk. He is wicked for the pure pleasure of it, for the sake of the sport; there could hardly be a more hazardous speculation than the adventure in seduction into which he incontinently plunges. At the bottom of the business is his vanity. The very first note struck from him—and Shakespeare, we know, will mean it to be a leading note—is of that grudging envy which vanity can breed. He is speaking of Posthumus:

> Believe it, sir, I have seen him in Britain: He was then of a crescent note; expected to prove so worthy as since he hath been allowed the name of: but I could then have looked on him without the help of admiration, though the catalogue of his endowments had been tabled by his side and I to peruse him by items.

---

[87] She has, to be quite accurate, still another, a broken one.

No woman, he is confident, can resist him (though his opinion of women is so low that the compliment he pays himself is a poor one), and when Imogen does, he has his trick in store; he will do anything but own himself beaten. He is a sensualist and something of an aesthete. He has a quick and sensitive mind. He can size up another man's weaknesses, and play on them with artistic skill.

Posthumus proves fairly easy quarry. For there will be, one fears —though he may mask it with good manners—just such a slight complacency about Posthumus as a life-diet of praise and nothing but praise is likely to produce; it does not, at any rate, give one overmuch interest in other people's points of view. Even this banishment, his first misfortune, is a kind of tribute to his conquering charm. His lessons are all to learn. He is a little patronizing, too; the more British, and the blinder for that.

In some such terms, while he leaves him to change greetings with the Frenchman, and the two of them fight their old battles over, Iachimo will be summing up the stranger. Then he goes delicately to work. His first approach:

> Can we with manners ask what was the difference?

the Frenchman must respond to. Posthumus does not like the look of this fellow, insinuating himself into the conversation, hinting, is he? ("with manners" indeed!), that they are ill-mannered to leave him out of it. Forced to speak to him, he can give him, at any rate, a straight snub.

> Iachimo. That lady [Posthumus' so vaunted mistress] is
> not now living, or this gentleman's opinion by this worn out.
> Posthumus. She holds her virtue still and I my mind.

But it takes more than a line of blank verse, however conclusive its cadence, to defeat Iachimo. Adroitly:

> You must not so far prefer her 'fore ours of Italy.

And as Posthumus, after all, is a guest here, the ironic appeal to his courtesy cannot be ignored. With his response to it (which is a little crude, perhaps, but he has small turn for irony),

> Being so far provoked as I was in France...

Iachimo has him in hand, and he begins to play him.

It is an amusing, if unequal, contest. On the one side, delicate dialectic, ironic humor, the salty cynical mind. On the other, Posthumus does his blunt, blundering best, encounters at every point; but with only his plain British common sense and simple pride in his Imogen for weapons, he has much ado even to keep his touchy British temper.

Iachimo's tactics are to lead his man on to challenge *him* to make good his boast that with "five times so much conversation" he'll "get ground" even of this paragon among ladies and "make her go back even to the yielding." Patently, that will be the better position to be in; and we mark him feeling for the steps to it, every faculty alert. In this finesse lies the interest of the scene. It is Posthumus' moral sense that he plays upon (better sometimes to attack a man at what he thinks his strongest point than at one he knows to be weak); and how artfully he moves from the disarming tribute of

> I make my wager rather against your confidence than her reputation. . . .

—which is a seeming retreat from the cynical

> You may wear her in title yours; but, you know, strange fowl light upon neighbouring ponds. . . .

—through the designedly preposterous

> commend me to the court where your lady is, with no more advantage than the opportunity of a second conference, and I will bring from thence that honour of hers which you imagine so reserved.

to the provocative, brutal

> If you buy ladies' flesh at a million a dram, you cannot preserve it from tainting. . . .

Posthumus is duly shocked by this last:

> This is but a custom of your tongue; you bear a graver purpose, I hope.

is his comment. Yet somehow or other—he would be infinitely at a loss to say how—within a minute more, for all Philario can do, the outrageous wager is laid. What notion he has of what he is after, poor muddlehead, must lie in

My mistress exceeds in goodness the hugeness of your unworthy thinking: I dare you to this match: here's my ring.

Imogen shall show the world, so she shall, and this contemptible foreigner in particular, what an English lady is.

It is, we may say, if we take a detached view of the business, a thing that no man in his senses could ever be brought to do. Better not be too sure of that; is there any conceivable folly that some man has not at some time committed? But Shakespeare, it must be remembered, is not approaching his dramatic problem by that way. He has chosen a story; his task is to make the events of it look likely. He need not even make them seem so in calm retrospect; the best of audiences will be content to be convinced at the time. The facts he must take for granted (if he does, so shall we); and it is in the characters themselves, in the why and wherefore of the things they do, nor in that only, but in the processes by which men's minds, shot with vanity or passion, work and can be made to work, oftenest to their own confusion, that we are to be interested. Too fine a study for the theater, it will sometimes prove to be; and much preoccupation with it goes with dangerously dwindling regard—or capacity!—for the enlivening of plain-as-a-pikestaff issues. But Shakespeare's art has been consistently developed towards this end, the popular borrowed story and his own businesslike sense of the stage serving to keep the balance roughly true. He had always the soliloquy to turn from a confidential talk about the plot into a mirror of a mind's working; and once the whole action of a play and every means he could command were bent to show us how the acid of Iago's guile eats into Othello's heart. Iachimo's is a prettier game, and there is but a scene or so in which to play it. It can be the more subtly, and must be the more cleverly, played for that. One might even suspect that Shakespeare was attracted by its very difficulties. Put the problem thus: here were a hundred and eighty lines (he could not allow himself much more) with which to introduce Iachimo and let him persuade Posthumus to this preposterous wager, and persuade us that he *had* persuaded him. The thing asked some doing. But, absorbed by that curious combat of disparate minds, we shall admit when the scene ends that it has been done.

But what possesses Iachimo, we ask, who can turn Posthumus

round his finger, to make such a crassly blundering approach to
Imogen that he comes within an ace of being thrown neck and
crop from the Court? The answer is an index to the man, and
shows no more inconsistency in him than goes to make him a
living character, not, as he might have been—as the Queen is—a
mere joint in the mechanism of the plot. It is an illuminating
inconsistency. He has a keen eye for a man's weaknesses; they are
food for his cynicism and a sop to his vanity. But the ways of such
honest innocence as Imogen's are without the range of his understanding. For, even if we must acknowledge it, we cannot understand what we do not believe in.

At a first sight of her he guesses she will be no good game for
a seducer. Still, he has his trick of the trunk in reserve, so why not
try? He makes the classic opening moves; marvels at her beauty,
cryptically deplores the lucky husband's gross unworthiness—
overdoes this somewhat, to her puzzled amusement.

We must, by the way, make liberal allowance in this scene for
the exigencies of dramatic time; its effects, in fact, may be said to
disregard time altogether. We shall not question Iachimo's rising
to these deliberate ecstasies within a minute of his arrival (though
note the touch of the comic in them that discounts any incongruity
there may seem to be); nor will it trouble our sense of likelihood
that within ten more he should have played out his first game and
lost it. Mere haste is not meant to be his error. The scene is framed
to another pattern, as a conspectus of the assault upon Imogen; the
effect would be poorer strung out in terms of time. But, while the
verse and its modulations provide color and excitement, the business of the scene and the shifting of the subjects of its talk give
the checks and suspensions and slackenings that the use of time
would give.

Iachimo's next move is to rid himself of the watchful Pisanio,
who leaves them most unwillingly, not liking the look of the
stranger at all. Then, alone with her, he stands deliberately mute,
as oddly so as he was oddly eloquent a moment since, till she
must break the silence with

> Continues well my lord? His health, beseech you?
> Well, madam!

he answers, putting a chapter of considerate mystery into the two words! She tries again:

> Is he disposed to mirth? I hope he is.

He sees the opening and swiftly takes it:

> Exceeding pleasant; none a stranger there
> So merry and so gamesome; he is call'd
> The Briton reveller.

This is not quite what she expects, nor, even in her generous love, can be too glad of.

> When he was here,
> He did incline to sadness, and oft-times
> Not knowing why.
> I never saw him sad. . . .

Deftly now he gets to work, picking at the fabric of her faith with a fascinatingly evil skill. Imogen is, after all, not a woman of the world. Rome, seen from the shelter of her British Court, is Babylon. The picture of the Frenchman, mocked at for faithfulness to his "Gallian girl at home" by a Posthumus

> who knows
> By history, report, or his own proof,
> What woman is, yea, what she cannot choose
> But must be. . .

—by Posthumus, who thought far otherwise of women here, and of her (here is not there, though), a little sears her mind.

Note that they are his own convictions which Iachimo lends to Posthumus; thus they sound the more credible as he vents them; this is the accepted technique of slander. But though he does excellently for a while, with his obvious wish to be quite just to Posthumus, with his flair for that unusual mingling in Imogen of humility and pride (two strengths that love and sacrifice have turned into a weakness he can play upon), with his pity of her that shames and angers her at once (he is bringing her, he must feel sure, into a very likely mood), the one warped factor in his combination—is himself. In slandering Posthumus he paints himself to her, all unaware. For who but he is now

> by-peeping in an eye
> Base and illustrous as the smoky light
> That's fed with stinking tallow. . .

—at Imogen!—oblivious of him yet, her grieved mind far away. It
is he, who thinks he knows

> What woman is, yea, what she cannot choose
> But must be. . .

that can mirror himself—to Imogen—in the significance of those

> diseased ventures,
> That play with all infirmities for gold,
> Which rottenness can lend nature! such boil'd stuff
> As well might poison poison!

can, when at last she does turn to him, make confident attempt—
upon Imogen!—with

> Should he make me
> Live like Diana's priest, betwixt cold sheets,
> While he is vaulting variable ramps,
> In your despite, upon your purse? Revenge it.
> I dedicate myself to your sweet pleasure,
> More noble than that runagate to your bed,
> And will contrive fast to your affection
> Still close as sure. . . . .
> Let me my service tender on your lips.

Where indeed is the Iachimo, subtle, dexterous, shrewd, that could
turn Posthumus round his finger? Vanished in this slavering, lascivious fool!

Chastity—and married chastity, that larger virtue—is the chief
theme of the play. Imogen is its exemplar. Iachimo and Cloten, the
clever fellow and the blockhead, are alike blind in lust. In the story
Shakespeare borrowed the villain relies only on his trick, makes
no attempt at all on the wife's virtue.[88] But Iachimo's insensate
blunder (Cloten's bestiality too) is most germane to the play he
evolves from it.

He makes, does Iachimo, a most brilliant recovery, nevertheless;
winning her forgiveness out of hand with his ingenious

> O happy Leonatus! I may say
> The credit that thy lady hath of thee
> Deserves thy trust, and thy most perfect goodness
> Her assured credit. . . .

---

[88] This is true also of *Westward for Smelts*, the other possible source.

and the rest of the dithyramb. If we feel that she now is a bit of
a fool to be taken in by him—well, he is a foreigner, it must be
remembered, and all foreigners are eccentric; he had shown himself so upon the moment, in those strange extollings of her beauty.
Besides, to hear Posthumus praised, when no one here dares praise
him any longer! Even that

> He sits 'mongst men like a descended god:
> He hath a kind of honour sets him off,
> More than a mortal seeming. . . .

will not sound overextravagant to her. Iachimo, once he can rein
in that satyr-demon of his, knows how to win her good opinion.

His sensuality is dominant again in the soliloquy in her bedchamber. But the night's lonely silence brings it to an aesthetic
fineness. Here is Iachimo, his stallion vanity quiescent, the artist
in life. Yet from

> Cytherea,
> How bravely thou becom'st thy bed! fresh lily!
> And whiter than the sheets! . . .

he must still pass to

> That I might touch!
> But kiss; one kiss! . . .

and risk his whole enterprise on the chance that she will wake as
he kisses her:

> Rubies unparagon'd
> How dearly they do't! . . .[39]

But, his lickerishness appeased, he can refine it again to

> 'Tis her breathing that
> Perfumes the chamber thus: the flame o' the taper
> Bows toward her, and would under-peep her lids
> To see the enclosed lights, now canopied

---

[39] The text, surely, leaves us in no doubt that he kisses her. Most editors will not
have this at any price, their sensibilities being offended by the notion of it, and
they find ingenious reasons why he should not—he would never risk waking her—
and still more ingenious (mis)interpretations, since they must then have them,
of the manifest "How dearly they do't." But a kiss is no more likely to wake her
than is the stealing of the bracelet, even if Shakespeare were one to trouble about
such trifles. And our sensibilities are meant to be offended. The sight of the fellow
smacking his own lips that have just polluted hers should veritably make us
squirm.

> Under these windows, white and azure-laced
> With blue of heaven's own tinct.

—which are arguably the most purely beautiful lines in the play.

By now we have the figure fully drawn in, and colored too. Iachimo, then, is the sensual aesthete, the amoral man. And this scene is, among other things, an exercise in the perversion of the sense of beauty. As we watch him weaving his evil web around her, making his damning inventory, even to the mole upon her breast,

> cinque-spotted, like the crimson drops
> I' the bottom of a cowslip. . .

we should be made to feel him only the wickeder for his seeing the while how beautiful in her purity she is. But Shakespeare, we may note, does not weaken the character by cant.

> Though this a heavenly angel, hell is here.

A modern villain would hardly be so simple-minded.

Back in Rome, with men to encounter, Iachimo is his masterful self again. A bracelet, after all, is not irrefragable evidence; he will need to have his wits well about him. Shakespeare sees that he has; the "madding" of the victim into belief in his betrayal is as skillfully contrived as was his bringing to the point of the wager (and it presents the dramatist with no easier a problem).

Posthumus, chafed by his exile, wears, while he waits, that positively confident front which may so often mask, not a doubt, but the fear of one. He greets Iachimo with stiffly tolerant good nature, even rallies him, rather frostily, upon his failure. Behind that too there may be lurking the shadow of the shadow of a doubt. Iachimo, as before, watches his man, keeps a cryptic countenance, lets Posthumus make what he will of

> Your lady
> Is one of the fairest that I have looked upon.

and waits to be questioned. Posthumus cannot question him; that would be to admit a doubt. He holds to his raillery:

> Sparkles this stone as it was wont? or is't not
> Too dull for your good wearing?

Iachimo counters it by assuring him coolly and categorically that

the ring is won.
POSTHUMUS. The stone's too hard to come by.
IACHIMO.   Not a whit,
Your lady being so easy.
POSTHUMUS.   Make not, sir
Your loss your sport: I hope you know that we
Must not continue friends.

So far, so good. Here is the quarry lured from behind his humorous defense, pricked to the beginnings of anger. Then, with a yet more categorical

but I now
Profess myself the winner of her honour,
Together with your ring, and not the wronger
Of her or you, having proceeded but
By both your wills.

Iachimo brings him to the direct grim challenge of

If you can mak't apparent
That you have tasted her in bed, my hand
And ring is yours: if not, the foul opinion
You had of her pure honour gains or loses
Your sword or mine, or masterless leaves both
To who shall find them.

—and to make it, we note, Posthumus must needs bring from the far back of his consciousness the brutal image of that "tasted her in bed." It will stay staring at him now, and Iachimo knows better than to disturb it by a word. For his part, he will avoid all mention of Imogen for awhile. Distrust shall be left to work. So he launches into his elaborate, choice description of the bedchamber, which the exile knows so well, making the lost joy of it yet more vivid to him, quickening his senses to render them the more vulnerable, smirching the picture with just one lewd parenthesis, one drop of irritant poison to the compound; yet for all his hardihood making so reticent a case of it that Posthumus, though puzzled, is reassured. But to feel reassured is to feel that you have needed assurance. And, having brought him to this state of sensitive, unbalanced discomfort, he produces the bracelet.

The bracelet is good evidence, and far better than Iachimo has till this moment known, for he did not know Posthumus had given it her. But how quick he is to seize the advantage, and to better it!

POSTHUMUS.   is it that
      Which I left with her?
IACHIMO.   Sir—I thank her—that.
      She stripped it from her arm; I see her yet;
      Her pretty action did outsell her gift
      And yet enrich'd it too. . . .

(Posthumus sees her yet; and writhes)

                  she gave it me
      And said she prized it once.

Even so, a bracelet—this bracelet, even!—ranged with things of its own kind, inanimate things, put plump down on a table, might be matter for reason, for argument. Iachimo makes better use of it than that.

          I beg but leave to air this jewel; see!
      And now 'tis up again . . . .

Held for a horrid moment in the husband's face, and then returned so caressingly to his bosom, it seems a living thing. Posthumus makes one clutch at reason:

            May be she plucked it off
      To send it me.

But Iachimo is ready for this, has led him, indeed, into the trap of it.

           She writes so to you, doth she?

Whereupon, without more warning, this hero and his brittle faith collapse.

He is but half a hero; and while things went so smoothly with him, while he was Cymbeline's favorite,

            most praised, most loved,
      A sample to the youngest, to the more mature
      A glass that feated them . . .

what chance had he to store up resistant virtues? And exile has been hard on him. Still, it is a pretty ignominious collapse. Soothed by Philario, he makes yet one more clutch at common sense. The bracelet was stolen. Iachimo has his oath in reserve:

          By Jupiter, I had it from her arm.

nor is he perjured swearing it; and with this the wretched Posthumus is utterly undone.

> Hark you, he swears; by Jupiter, he swears.
> 'Tis true:—nay, keep the ring—'tis true: I am sure
> She would not lose it: her attendants are
> All sworn and honourable:—they induced to steal it!
> And by a stranger!

They, who are nothing to him, may be trusted; she, who is all the
world, no! An admirable stroke! Iachimo has won. He contem-
plates in quiet detachment this moral fool demoralized. Such a
short step is it from the boast of "her pure honour" to

> Never talk on't;
> She hath been colted by him.

Partly to seal his victory, partly, one supposes, for the simple
pleasure of seeing the human animal suffer, he goes on:

> If you seek
> For further satisfying, under her breast—
> Worthy the pressing—lies a mole, right proud
> Of that most delicate lodging: by my life,
> I kiss'd it, and it gave me present hunger
> To feed again, though full.

—to discover (interesting phenomenon!) that the victim now asks
to be tortured:

> No swearing.
> If you will swear you have not done 't you lie,
> And I will kill thee if thou dost deny
> Thou'st made me cuckold.

—with which, and a little more raging, he breaks from them in
impotent fury. The shocked Philario gazes after him:

> Quite besides
> The government of patience! you have won:
> Let's follow him and pervert the present wrath
> He hath against himself.
> With all my heart!

The artist in Iachimo must be conscious of a fine piece of work
done; and he feels, for the moment, quite good-natured.

It has been worth while, perhaps, to subject these three scenes to such close analysis, for this is how their actors must work at them, and their artistry ranks high even among Shakespeare's mature achievements of the kind.

CLOTEN

Cloten (pronounced "Clotten" to rhyme—most appropriately —with "rotten," by warrant of the pun "I have sent Cloten's clot-pole down the stream," which is reinforced by several spellings in the Folio) is far from being a merely comic character. His aspect is amusing; without that much mitigation, the truth about him (and Shakespeare does not shirk it) would be intolerable in such a play—in any play! He stands in the character-scheme contrasted with Iachimo; scoundrels both, the coarse numskull beside the clever hedonist, but each, as we saw, the other's complement in lechery—with Imogen, but for providence, their victim. He is a booby; even so, less booby than brute, and debased brute at that.

The first we hear of him is as

a thing
Too bad for bad report. . .

We see him with one sycophant companion, and another mock·ing him, all but to his face. It is harsh, unsavored mirth, though; and we shall hardly laugh at him, unless as harshly. For to laugh at a man is to be at least in the way of forgiving him; and Cloten, gibbeted for vermin from the start, is turned round and round till all the foulness under his folly can be seen, to be slaughtered like vermin at last. Shakespeare was to evolve a little later a more picturesque and far more pardonable monster. But this civilized Caliban!

He is not pure poltroon. He challenges Posthumus (pretty confident, no doubt, that the "gentlemen at hand" will part them) and fights the hefty young Guiderius (who is only armed, it would seem, with hunting knife and club[40]). He has as much courage, that's to say, as will go to make a bully.

Would there had been some hurt done!

—but not, of course, to him. He is lit up for us in that line; and

---

[40] "With his own sword," says Guiderius, ". . . I have ta'en his head from him."

shortly by two more. Never was there a more patient man in loss, his ironic flatterer tells him. He is

> the most coldest that ever turned up ace.
>
> CLOTEN. It would make any man cold to lose.
>
> FIRST LORD. But not every man patient after the noble temper of your lordship. You are most hot and furious when you win.
>
> CLOTEN. Winning will put any man into courage.

It will never enter his thick head that he is being laughed at. Cockered and coached by his mother, and thanks to his tailor, he makes some sort of figure at Court, woos Imogen, assails her with "musics" in the morning, being told this will "penetrate," orders the musicians about, we notice, as if they were dogs. The music not penetrating sufficiently, he must bribe her ladies, he thinks; his own idea, this. He goes about it with true delicacy:

> There's gold for you;
> Sell me your good report.

When she does at last give him a word he manages to start with

> Good morrow, fairest sister: your sweet hand.

But soon he is hectoring her too. He is not in love with her, needless to say. She is "this foolish Imogen"; when he has got her he will "have gold enough," that is all. He makes not a little noise at the reception of the Roman envoy. Critics have objected that Cymbeline would never admit such a blockhead to his counsels. Bless their innocence! At such Courts as Cymbeline's any loud-voiced bully who is in royal favor, given chance to say

> Come, there's no more tribute to be paid. . . .

and damn the consequences, will have his cheering backers. What's Rome to them? But when the fighting comes it will be one of them that Posthumus finds

> Still going? This a lord! . . .
> To-day how many would have given their honours
> To have saved their carcasses! took heel to do't,
> And yet died too. . . .

Yet Cloten rises to a sort of dignity when he bids farewell to
Lucius with

> Your hand, my lord.
> Receive it friendly; but from this time forth
> I wear it as your enemy.

Even Cloten, we are tempted to say, can show himself at his
country's call to be a soldier and a gentleman.

One of Shakespeare's touches of grim mischief, this; for he has
not done with him. Imogen fled and in disgrace, the gallant
gentleman scents the opportunity for another sort of wooing of
her. He will pursue her, dressed (the story demands it) in the
very garments Posthumus wore at their leave-taking, those that
she said she held, the meanest of them—that insult particularly
rankles!—in more respect than his "noble and natural person";
and

> With that suit upon my back, will I ravish her; first kill him,
> and in her eyes; there shall she see my valour, which will then be a
> torment to her contempt. He on the ground . . . and when my
> lust hath dined . . . to the Court I'll knock her back, foot her
> home again . . . .

"When my lust hath dined. . ."! Shakespeare can, on occasion,
lodge a fair amount of meaning within four words, give us the
marrow of a man in them too. This is Cloten with the comic
mask lifted, the soldier and gentleman shed, the beast showing. A
Cloten hardly in his right mind, one would suppose—even *his*
right mind. He does, a little later, when he recapitulates the program, seem to realize that her father

> may haply be a little angry for my so rough usage; but my
> mother, having power of his testiness, shall turn all into my
> commendations. . . .

A Cloten merely weaving these Alnaschar fancies for his private
delight, is he? By no means. War is beginning; his fine defiance
of the Romans and the Court's applause of it have swollen his
vanity yet higher; he and his kind, surely, are to have things their
own way now; his appetites are whetted. The Clotens of the
world, in Shakespeare's age, or Cymbeline's, or any other, ask no
more than opportunity. Scarcely a comic character!

POSTHUMUS

Iachimo's victim we have already studied; is there more to be said for Imogen's husband? It will be hard for any dramatic hero to stand up, first to such praise as is lavished upon Posthumus before we see him (though when we do he is not given much time or chance to disillusion us), next against the discredit of two scenes of befoolment, then against banishment from the action for something like a dozen scenes more. Nor in his absence are we let catch any lustrous reflections of him. Were he coming back, Othello-like, to do his murdering for himself, we might thrill to him a little. He is a victim both to the story and to the plan of its telling. Even when he reappears there is no weaving him into the inner thread of the action. He cannot, as we saw, openly encounter any of its prime movers without prejudicing the elaborate revelations saved up for the last scene. He can only soliloquize, have a dumb-show fight with Iachimo, a didactic talk with an anonymous "Lord" who has nothing to say in return, a bout of wit with a gaoler who has much the best of it; worst of all, he becomes the unconscious center of that jingling pageant of his deceased relatives—a most misguided attempt to restore interest in him, for we nourish a grudge against him for it. One can detect, nevertheless, unworked veins of interest in the man. He is among those who live (the benefits of their natural happy egoism apart), rather by credulity than faith, and not at all by judgment, whose moral balance, then, is easily upset, hard to recover, no solid base being there to rest it on. No wisdom in him, nor ever likely to be much; but, in its place, some humility of heart.

> And sweetest, fairest,
> As I my poor self did exchange for you
> To your so infinite loss. . .

That is not spoken to Imogen the princess, but to the woman; he knows himself, for all men's praise of him, coarse clay beside her. We like him too for his boyish boastfulness of her perfections—it is its very innocence that sets the cynic Iachimo compassing his downfall—and can find something pitiful in the as boyishly passionate disillusionment of

> Could I find out
> The woman's part in me! For there's no motion

That tends to vice in man but I affirm
It is the woman's part: be it lying, note it,
The woman's; flattering, hers; deceiving, hers;
Lust and rank thoughts, hers, hers; revenges, hers.
Ambitions, covetings, change of prides, disdain,
Nice longing, slanders, mutability,
All faults that may be named, nay, that hell knows,
Why, hers in part or all, but rather, all;
For even to vice
They are not constant, but are changing still
One vice but of a minute old for one
Not half so old as that. . . .

Whoever has not at some time felt the better for such an outburst (no inconvenient plot of a play pending to translate it into action), let him laugh at poor Posthumus.

But there is matter of more interest in his remorse. It overwhelms him before ever he has learned that Imogen is guiltless, and here is the drift of it:

You married ones,
If each of you should take this course, how many
Must murder wives much better than themselves,
For wrying but a little! . . .
                              Gods! if you
Should have ta'en vengeance on my faults, I never
Had lived to put on this; so had you saved
The noble Imogen to repent, and struck
Me, wretch, more worth your vengeance.

Neither Othello nor Leontes, those other exemplars of the jealous husband repentant, reach this point of view. It belongs to the humility of heart which, we may like to think, was what Imogen found to love in him. And it is the same humility and generosity —for the accepting of forgiveness makes as much call on generosity as offering it, and more—that takes him back to her with no wordy repentance, no closer promise of amendment than his

Hang there like fruit, my soul,
Till the tree die!

He finds his new faith in her, and in himself, in her forgiveness of him. She understands; and so should we.

GUIDERIUS AND ARVIRAGUS

They are dowered with some of the best poetry in the play; but there is more to them than this.[41] They stand, of course, for products, the very choicest, of the simple life. What would they have come to be at Court; with Imogen for a sister, it is true, but with Cloten for a stepbrother besides? As it is, they skip ruddy and skin-clad from their cave, exhorted by the good Belarius:

> Stoop, boys: this gate
> Instructs you how to adore the heavens, and bows you
> To a morning's holy office: the gates of monarchs
> Are arch'd so high that giants may jet through
> And keep their impious turbans on, without
> Good morrow to the sun. Hail, thou fair heaven!
> We house i' the rock, yet use thee not so hardly
> As prouder livers do.

GUIDERIUS.   Hail, heaven!

ARVIRAGUS.   Hail, heaven!

Nor does he let any other occasion, great or small, pass unimproved. Luckily for their characters (dramatically speaking, at any rate) they are at once set in opposition to this sort of thing: it is the simplest dramatic recipe for giving a scene life. But it is not till Guiderius, in particular, comes into action on his own account (this shows the authentic dramatist too) that he effectively reveals himself. Himself, and another aspect of the simple life at once. Cloten, we shall agree, gets no more than his deserts. But when Guiderius appears, swinging his head as a gardener might a turnip:

> This Cloten was a fool, an empty purse;
> There was no money in 't: not Hercules
> Could have knock'd out his brains, for he had none:
> Yet I not doing this, the fool had borne
> My head as I do his.

—departing a moment later with

> I'll throw 't into the creek
> Behind our rock, and let it to the sea,
> And tell the fishes he's the queen's son, Cloten:
> That's all I reck.

---

[41] Burdened with some few vapidities besides—of the worst of which, though, we have argued, Shakespeare can hardly have been guilty.

—here is simplicity with a vengeance, we feel. And young Arviragus' only comment is

> Would I had done 't—
> So the revenge alone pursued me! Polydore,
> I love thee brotherly—but envy much
> Thou hast robb'd me of this deed.

The slaughterhouse side of the business is mitigated as much as
may be, by more sententious talk from Belarius, by the contrasting
fancy of the dirge over Fidele, by the palpable artifice of the whole
affair. But Shakespeare keeps the values of his picture true. Beside the tailored brute the noble savage is as sharply drawn; and,
at the salient moment, made no merely flattering figure. There
is another side to the simple life.

IMOGEN

When Shakespeare imagined Imogen (for she is to be counted
his, if anything in the play can be) he had but lately achieved
Cleopatra. And whether meant to be or no, they make companion
pictures of wantonness and chastity; and, of women, are the
fullest and maturest that he drew. Chastity, faith, fidelity, strike the
ideal chord in *Cymbeline*; and Imogen is their exemplar.

But a pleasantly human paragon! She has married without
her father's consent (a grave matter that in Shakespeare's time),
has been a clandestine wife for some while, what is more, under
Cymbeline's very nose—which shows, for a start, some ability in
deception.[42] Doubtless her stepmother is a tyrant and worse, and
the prospect of Cloten as a husband would justify much; but her
father has excuse for his anger. And she does not—before his
courtiers too!—yield him very great respect, granted that he

---

[42] Furness falls into the (for him) amazing error of supposing that the marriage
had not been consummated, that it is in the nature of a "troth-plight." But, apart
from repeated "husbands," this is to ignore Posthumus' specific

> Me of my lawful pleasure she restrained
> And pray'd me oft forbearance; did it with
> A pudency so rosy. . . .

And as to the still threatened marriage with Cloten (another difficulty he makes)
the Second Lord speaks definitely enough of

> that horrid act
> Of the divorce he 'ld make. . .

Relationship and situation are made amply clear.

inspires very little. We find her answering him, indeed, with something uncomfortably near to condescending irony, an invidious weapon to be wielded by the young against the old.

> I beseech you, Sir,
> Harm not yourself with your vexation:
> I am senseless of your wrath. . . .

She has retorts, calm and conclusive, for his every splutter; she is not, from the parent's point of view, an easy young lady to manage.

It is, of course, her innate truthfulness and, even more, her inextinguishable sense of realities which are to blame; couple these with as inextinguishable a courage, and we have the first flush of the effect she is meant to make upon us. Her first words are to tell us that she is not for a moment taken in by her stepmother's ready smiles. She has nothing save her courage with which to meet her father's powerful wrath; but that is enough, and somehow, somewhere Posthumus will be restored to her. And, princess to the marrow though she be, her

> Would I were
> A neat-herd's daughter, and my Leonatus
> Our neighbour shepherd's son!

is no mere flourish of a phrase. She has not condescended to Posthumus.

> he is
> A man worth any woman . . . .

she says. What more is there to say? She is princess most in her utter unself-consciousness. Pisanio is her servant, and she orders him about sharply enough.[48] But, as she trusts him, why should she not show him how fathom-deep she is in love? When he comes back to tell her of the ship's sailing:

---

[48] More properly he is Posthumus' servant left with her for a faithful watchdog. The Queen's repeated reference to him as hers—in particular the

> This hath been
> Your faithful servant . . . .

has something of irony in it. For he has obviously helped the two of them to conceal the marriage and hoodwink the Court.

> Thou should'st have made him
> As little as a crow, or less, ere left
> To after-eye him.

> Madam, so I did.

(stolid, honest, categorical Pisanio!)

> I would have broke mine eye-strings, crack'd them, but
> To look upon him, till the diminution
> Of space had pointed him sharp as my needle:
> Nay, followed him, till he had melted from
> The smallness of a gnat to air; and then
> Have turned mine eye and wept. But, good Pisanio,
> When shall we hear from him?

> Be assured, Madam,
> With his next vantage.

(Much solid heartening comfort in Pisanio! And how, by the way, Shakespeare does love that word "air"!) Imogen speaks half to herself now; her thoughts aboard the ship.

> I did not take my leave of him, but had
> Most pretty things to say: ere I could tell him
> How I would think on him, at certain hours,
> Such thoughts or such; or I could make him swear
> The shes of Italy should not betray
> Mine interest and his honour; or have charged him,
> At the sixth hour of morn, at noon, at midnight,
> To encounter me with orisons, for then
> I am in heaven for him; or ere I could
> Give him that parting kiss which I had set
> Betwixt two charming words, comes in my father,
> And like the tyrannous breathing of the north,
> Shakes all our buds from growing.

The long-drawn-out sentence, fading to an end, paints the flagging of her spirit from that intense

> I would have broke my eye-strings, crack'd them. . . .

to the loneliness of the prospect she faces. The fresh simplicity of it all; the little joke about the "shes of Italy" (which is to come back upon her in poisoned earnest, as such jokes will); the wifely sanctity of the

> for then
> I am in heaven for him . . .

—such strokes complete the statement of her; gallant, generous, royal, innocent, unguarded. To round it in:

Enter a lady.
                    The queen, Madam,
    Desires your highness' company.

—and the girl-wife stiffens to princess again.

Would she for one moment tolerate Iachimo, credit his excuse for his outrage upon her, or accept his apology? There are the claims of the borrowed story; and once again Shakespeare—artfully, tactfully, and by what he leaves out or suggests far more than by what he puts in—brings them to tally with the character he is creating.

This queer foreigner comes from Posthumus. That in itself will frank him past much eccentricity of behavior. But though she makes remorseful amends for her harsh misjudgment of him her courtesy turns cool, even to wariness. And it is her pathetically pretty fancy to have the plate and jewels near her for a while, only because

    My lord hath interest in them. . . .

—to do even so much for him!—that serves to bring the fatal necessary trunk into her bedchamber.

Her attitude throughout the scene is quietly eloquent of her miseries. And when Iachimo, spreading his net, baits her with a little pity, her quick proud resentment speaks of other pitying eyes, which follow her now about the Court, to which she'll turn as proud a front; even as the wistful

            My lord, I fear,
    Has forgot Britain.

with its unspoken, questioning echo "is forgetting me?" tells of happy humilities of love left starving, comfortless, to wear down to secret self-distrust.

We see her braving the worst of her afflictions, her wooing by the wretched Cloten; the high-mettled courage that she showed her father is edged here with a sharper scorn—the object of it so contemptible! But the strain of the misery is telling on her; that final, gratuitously defiant fling at the Queen, for answer to Cloten's

> I will inform your father.
>
>   Your mother too!
> She's my good lady, and will conceive, I hope,
> But the worst of me. . . .

savors of desperation.

The godsend, then, of the news that Posthumus has returned, is at Milford Haven, expects her there!

> O, for a horse with wings! Hear'st thou, Pisanio?
> He is at Milford Haven: read and tell me
> How far 'tis thither. If one of mean affairs
> May plod it in a week, why may not I
> Glide thither in a day? Then, true Pisanio—
> Who long'st like me to see thy lord; who long'st—
> O, let me 'bate—but not like me—yet long'st,
> But in a fainter kind. O, not like me;
> For mine's beyond beyond: say, and speak thick,—
> Love's counsellor should fill the bores of hearing,
> To the smothering of the sense—how far it is
> To this same blessed Milford.

In a moment all the stored suffering and doubt convert into oblivious joy, and she is at the height, again, of her old confident vitality. The lines are yet another example of the raising of simple, seemingly natural speech to poetic power, and of Shakespeare's maturest craft in this kind.[44] The whole scene is finely contrived. For Imogen clouds have vanished; but the glum, taciturn figure of Pisanio to remind us that they are gathering more blackly than she can imagine. She appeals to him:

>   Prithee, speak;
> How many score of miles may we well ride
> 'Twixt hour and hour?
>
> PISANIO.   One score 'twixt sun and sun,
> Madam, 's enough for you and too much too.
> IMOGEN.   Why, one that rode to 's execution, man,
> Could never go so slow. . . .

As it is to hers, he knows—and we know—that she is going, the joke is a grimly good one. She enjoys it!

---

[44] And some of us—nineteenth century playgoers—can remember Ellen Terry speaking and acting them, and seeming, for those few moments, to fill the Lyceum Theatre with dancing sunbeams. There was the fine achievement, too, of Irving's Iachimo—with its angular grace and intellectual art.

> But this is foolery.
> Go, bid my woman feign a sickness, say
> She'll home to her father; and provide me, presently,
> A riding-suit no costlier than would fit
> A franklin's housewife.

Reluctantly he·departs to obey her; and off she flies to make herself ready. This is the last we are to see of the princess, of the imperious Imogen.

The sight of her in the drab riding-suit will speak of changing and diminishing fortune; she is adventuring into a strange un-privileged world, made the stranger, the more ominous, by Pisanio's silence as the two of them go on their way. At last she wins the truth from him; and rather, we note, by pleading than command—she is conscious already of her declension. He hands her the fatal letter.

But she is very Imogen in her meeting of the blow. She risked all when she loved Posthumus and married him. Her trust has brought her to this. It never occurs to her to try to escape the reaping of what she has sown. That she is innocent is beside the point. When she gave herself she made no reservation that it should be for as long as he loved her, or treated her well, or as it might suit with her self-respect. So, "When thou sees't him," she tells Pisanio,

> A little witness my obedience. Look!
> I draw the sword myself: take it, and hit
> The innocent mansion of my love, my heart.
> Fear not; 'tis empty of all things but grief;
> Thy master is not there, who was indeed
> The riches of it. . . .

We have had just a flash, though, of her shrewd, unilluded temper:

> Iachimo,
> Thou didst accuse him of incontinency;
> Thou then look'dst like a villain; now, methinks,
> Thy favour's good enough. Some jay of Italy,
> Whose mother was her painting, hath betray'd him.

She knows (she thinks) the fate of such a handsome hero, finding another Court to flatter him. *She* fell a victim to him. She is wrong; it is the mud of Iachimo's flinging that has stuck, as mud will; shrewdness, wounded, does thus go astray. We hear the transcendent Imogen again in

> And thou, Posthumus, thou that didst set up
> My disobedience 'gainst the king, my father,
> And make me put into contempt the suits
> Of princely fellows, shalt hereafter find
> It is no act of common passage, but
> A strain of rareness: and I grieve myself
> To think, when thou shalt be disedged by her
> That now thou tirest on, how thy memory
> Will then be pang'd by me. . . .

—for in such perception and detachment lies greatness of soul. Her grief it is that is stressed; grief that such faith as hers, such love as theirs, should be thus brought to ruin.

> All good seeming,
> By thy revolt, O husband, shall be thought
> Put on for villainy. . . .

It is love and faith itself—all that she knew of good in an evil world—which stand betrayed.[45]

But while she may grieve nobly, meek mournfulness is no part of her nature, nor has she much patience with Pisanio's remorse.

> The lamb entreats the butcher; where's thy knife?
> Thou art too slow to do thy master's bidding,
> When I desire it too.
>
> PISANIO.   O gracious lady,
> Since I received command to do this business
> I have not slept one wink.
>
> IMOGEN.   Do 't, and to bed then.

He means to spare her and save her, has some hope of the future. She hardly believes him (what should she believe in now!) or cares to be saved. But her native pride (at least she will never return to the father she has defied), her courage and the instinctive hope that dwells in her youth (though she admits none of Posthumus, nor indeed any, yet she will act as if she did), all conspire to set her on the path he opens to her. Stoically:

---

[45] A touch of this nobility was left to Posthumus too. He speaks, his letter to Pisanio says, "not out of weak surmises, but from proof as strong as my grief." The word can, of course, be used in the mere sense of injury. But Imogen certainly does not so use it, and we may read the deeper meaning into it here as well.

> this attempt
> I am soldier to, and will abide it with
> A prince's courage.

—with the old dignity that her drab garmenting cannot disguise; with a new quietude. When they part, her answer to his

> may the gods
> Direct you to the best!
> Amen: I thank thee.

—in the four words (if an actress can speak them) is an Imogen white from the fire.

We shall hardly know her as Fidele; the tiny fragile figure, once so commanding in her Court brocades and lately buckramed in her riding-gown. Nor is this all the change. Her utter helplessness, as she wanders lost in the forest, breeds a new humor in her; a sense, half comic, half pathetic, of what is ridiculous in her plight, of fellowship with the wretched, in their follies, even in their sins, a whelming sense of the pitifulness of things and of poor humanity astray.

> I see a man's life is a tedious one:
> I have tired myself, and for two nights together
> Have made the ground my bed. . . .

It needs no more than that and an empty stomach to make one very tolerant. Even Posthumus' wronging of her rouses no bitterness in her now:

> My dear lord!
> Thou art one o' the false ones. . . .

—only a wistful, still loving, regret.

The conventional disguise, the sententious tone of the play (doubly sententious in these scenes around the cave), are turned to good account for this latter phase of the picturing of Imogen. They help her steer the nice course between comedy and tragedy that the story demands. As she enters the cave:

> Best draw my sword; and if mine enemy
> But fear the sword like me, he'll scarcely look on 't.
> Such a foe, good heavens!

That ever-useful joke at once blunts the tragic edge of the business.

The marvel of her meeting with her brothers is dramatically subdued by the matching of such frank artifice as Arviragus'

> I'll love him as my brother,
> And such a welcome as I'ld give to him
> After long absence—such is yours; most welcome!

with her

> Would it had been so, that they
> Had been my father's sons! . . .

It must be kept subdued, not only for the sake of the elaborate finale of revelations, but because a fresh emotional interest here, which involved Imogen, would discount the intensity of the climactic moment of her waking beside Posthumus' supposed corpse. This itself we find very subtly prepared for; producer and actors must carefully note how.

She is wooed from the worst of her sorrow by such brotherly love. Once again—far more effectively here indeed—the sense of indeterminate time gives atmosphere to the picture. For "two nights together" she has made the ground her bed; that is long enough to leave her starving, and there is no more point in the exactitude. But we are not to calculate that she reaches the cave one afternoon and is found seemingly dead in it the morning after. We are simply to see her gratefully happy with these good companions, the cruelties of the Court fading to oblivion, while she busies herself with homely duties:

> BELARIUS.   Pray, be not sick,
> For you must be our housewife.
> IMOGEN.   Well or ill,
> I am bound to you.
> BELARIUS.   And shalt be ever.
>   (*She goes into the cave.*)
> This youth, howe'er distressed, appears he hath
>   had
> Good ancestors.
> ARVIRAGUS.   How angel-like he sings!
> GUIDERIUS. But his neat cookery! he cut our roots in char-
>   acters,
> And sauced our broths, as Juno had been sick,
> And he her dieter.

An idyllic interlude, with its idyllic sequel in the speaking of
the dirge over the dead boy. For if Imogen is to survive to happiness, Fidele is dead. The three good companions are to meet
again, but never in this wondrous world—which will fade for
them (as imaginings of it do for us) into the commonplace;
even as

> Golden lads and girls all must,
> As chimney-sweepers, come to dust.

With the dirge and the departure of Belarius and the boys their
idyllic life ends too—they pass to war and its realities. And
Imogen returns to consciousness to fancy herself upon her lonely
desperate journey again—

> Yes, sir, to Milford Haven; which is the way?—
> I thank you.—By yond bush? Pray, how far thither?
> 'Ods pittikins! can it be six mile yet?—
> I have gone all night. . . .

—with the friendly comfort of the cave become a dream. Her
last waking words had been the smiling

> Well or ill,
> I am bound to you.

and by the contrast the horror of the waking is redoubled.

But now that we have reached this most effective situation, we
must own it, and the whole business of it, to be, from one point
of view at least, dramatically inexcusable. It is a fraud on Imogen;
and we are accomplices in it. We have watched the playwright's
plotting, been amused by his ingenuity. We shall even be a little
conscious as we watch, in this sophisticated play, of the big
bravura chance to be given to the actress. But Imogen herself is
put, quite needlessly, quite heartlessly, on exhibition. How shall
we sympathize with such futile suffering? And surely it is a
faulty art that can so make sport of its creatures.[46]

[46] Hermione's reported death in *A Winter's Tale* is a somewhat similar fraud;
but to this we are not made party. We should not sympathize overmuch with
Leontes, in any case. But if we knew that he was suffering needlessly would not
the retributive balance of the scene be truer, its dramatic value greater, therefore?
This (if so) is sacrificed to the surprise of the living statue at the end. Would it
not be better if we were in the secret and our interest set upon the effect of the
revelation on Leontes? Once we know the story the practical test is hard to make.
But there are more signs than one that Shakespeare never fully "found himself" in

All this is true. But tragi-comedy—in this phase of its development, at least—is a bastard form of art; better not judge it by too strict aesthetic law. Tact can intervene; that reconciling grace which sometimes makes stern principle so pleasant to forswear. And Shakespeare palliates his trick with great dramatic tact; he veils its crudity in beauty (a resource that seldom fails him) and even manages to make it serve for some enriching of his character.

The atmosphere of artifice in which the whole play moves—in these scenes in the forest it is at its densest—helps soften, as we saw, the crudity of the butchered corpse. The long, confused waking (dream, to Imogen's drugged senses, only emerging into dream) tempers the crassness of the horror too. Such a touch of sheer beauty as

> Good faith,
> I tremble still with fear; but if there be
> Yet left in heaven as small a drop of pity
> As a wren's eye, fear'd gods, a part of it! . . .

will sweeten it. And from the positive

> A headless man! The garments of Posthumus!
> I know the shape o's leg: this is his hand;
> His foot Mercurial. . . .

we are carried very quickly to the agonized climax and as quickly on. There is no shirking. Shakespeare, once committed, will have every ounce of his effect.

> O Posthumus! alas,
> Where is thy head? where's that? Ah me, where's that?
> Pisanio might have kill'd thee at the heart,
> And left this head on. . . .

is material for as blood-curdling an exhibition as any actress need wish to give. But—here is the master-stroke—even while she is thus racked, and beyond endurance, Imogen's heart is purging of a deeper pain. There is no remotest reason for her jumping to

this new form of play. For how seldom, in earlier plays, have we ever had to ask, when he was in the vein and going full swing, whether there could be a more effective way of doing what he wants to do!

> Pisanio,
> All curses madded Hecuba gave the Greeks,
> And mine to boot, be darted on thee! Thou,
> Conspired with that irregulous devil, Cloten,
> Hast here cut off my lord. . . .

She does not even know of Cloten's attempt to suborn him. But her suffering—and her sex, if we like—is excuse enough for anything of the sort. And to find that Posthumus, even though she finds him dead, was not after all her reviler and would-be murderer, cleanses and exalts her grief. Shakespeare does not insist on this. Imogen, for one thing, is not in a very analytical or explanatory mood. It is as clear as he needs it to be. He leaves it to become effective in the acting:

> That confirms it home:
> This is Pisanio's deed and Cloten's: O!
> Give colour to my pale cheek with thy blood,
> That we the horrider may seem to those
> Which chance to find us: O, my lord, my lord!

She rallies from delirium; the pictorial phrase is a resolution into the play's proper key; and in the simple "O, my lord, my lord!"— spoken as it can be spoken—we are to hear, as she faints away, her reconciliation with her dead.

Nevertheless, contrive as he may, it is a pretty damnable practical joke; and Shakespeare, the creator of Imogen, must now pay the price of Shakespeare the showman's escapade.[47] He does; to whatever else he may yield we shall not find him at this time of day finally playing false to character. A happy ending may be the play's due, but Imogen can make no full recovery from what has been pure poignant tragedy for her. When the kind hands of Roman enemies recover her from her "bloody pillow" she stands tongue-tied at first. Lucius has to question and question before she answers his "What art thou?" with

> I am nothing: or if not,
> Nothing to be were better.

She is stunned and dazed; what wonder! She will follow whither she is bid:

---

[47] Or we may, of course, make the whipping-boy the original culprit, if we prefer.

> But first, an 't please the gods,
> I'll hide my master from the flies, as deep
> As these poor pickaxes can dig. . . .

The royal Imogen, to whom Posthumus kneeled with his

> My queen! my mistress!

who could gallantly defy her father and his Queen, and laugh at the brute Cloten and his wooing, has traveled far. "Happy ending" looks little congruous with the sight of her now.

So Shakespeare finds. He frees her from the action for four full scenes, gives her time, as it were, for recovery; but restored to it, restored to husband and father, united to her brothers, her path fair before her, she is a wounded woman still. Her ring on Iachimo's finger; that only means she may learn how all the evil came to pass, the tale cannot bring her dead back to life; she listens to its verbiage in numb silence. When it does, when by miracle Posthumus stands there before her, the very joy leaves her speechless; she can only cling to him and stammer helplessly. Just for one moment, when she turns upon Pisanio, she rallies to "the tune of Imogen," and they know her by it. The "happy ending" is duly brought about. But Shakespeare gives her little more to say; that little quiet and colorless, almost. He could not in conscience set her—or set any of them—merrymaking.

Lady Martin, who wrote pleasant reminiscences of Miss Helen Faucit's applauded performances of Shakespeare's heroines, ends the study of Imogen with a sentimental picture of a slow decline (the play being over), of her dying—". . . fading out like an exhalation of the dawn"—surrounded by the rest of the cast in appropriate attitudes of grief and remorse. This is certainly not criticism; and one is apt to smile at such "Victorian" stuff, and to add "and nonsense" as one puts the book down. But there is something to be said for acting a part if you want to discover those last few secrets about it that the author knew but did not see fit to disclose. And Lady Martin is essentially right here. The figure of Imogen is lifelike, of a verity that transcends the play's need; and the blows that Shakespeare had to deal her were death-blows. It is something of a simulacrum that survives. But there is a truth to life in this too.

No one will rank *Cymbeline* with the greater plays. It is not conceived greatly, it is full of imperfections. But it has merits all its own; and one turns to it from *Othello*, or *King Lear*, or *Antony and Cleopatra*, as one turns from a masterly painting to, say, a fine piece of tapestry, from commanding beauty to more recondite charm.

THE HEADBAND USED ON THE TITLE PAGE
AND AT VARIOUS OTHER PLACES IN THIS BOOK
WAS TAKEN FROM THE FIRST FOLIO
OF SHAKESPEARE
PRINTED IN LONDON BY ISAAC JAGGARD
AND ED. BLOUNT, IN 1623

THIS EDITION OF GRANVILLE-BARKER'S
PREFACES TO SHAKESPEARE
HAS BEEN COMPOSED IN 11 PT. GRANJON TYPE

TYPOGRAPHY BY P. J. CONKWRIGHT

Prefaces to Shakespeare: I

This first volume in the American edition of Granville-Barker's famous critical essays on the plays of Shakespeare is published in the hope of introducing more Americans to one of the most distinguished Shakespeare scholars of all time. It includes the book-length *Hamlet* and four shorter Prefaces. The author has rearranged the order in which they appeared in England, and some changes of importance have been made in the Preface to *King Lear*.

Modern Shakespeare scholarship to which Granville-Barker contributed so enormously sees Shakespeare in the theater for which he wrote, and by this means strips away the accumulation of centuries of progressive misconceptions and distortions of his playwright's art. In these Prefaces, Granville-Barker examines the plays in the light of the interpretation Shakespeare designed for them, so far as this can be deduced, to discover the production he would have desired.

"Stagecraft" is a key word in his criticism. To his watchful working-out of the main lines of dramatic construction, the plays yield many of their riddling secrets. The interplay of characters, the quality of the verse, the vagaries of the texts, the possibilities of the Elizabethan stage—these are the lines he explores, with a wit and penetration that make his work as stimulating as a fine production in the theater.